Genealogical & Local History Books in Print

5th Edition

U.S. Sources & Resources Volume

A – N

GENEALOGICAL & LOCAL HISTORY BOOKS IN PRINT

5th Edition

U.S. Sources & Resources Volume

Alabama – New York

Compiled and Edited by
Marian Hoffman

Published by Genealogical Publishing Co., Inc.
1001 N. Calvert St., Baltimore, MD 21202
Library of Congress Catalogue Card Number 97-70714
International Standard Book Number, Volume A–N: 0-8063-1536-9
Set Number: 0-8063-1535-0
Made in the United States of America

Contents

Introduction vii
List of Vendors (organized numerically) ix
List of Vendors (organized alphabetically) xxvii

New England 1
Mid-Atlantic 7
South 11
Mid-West 16
West 17

Alabama 19
Alaska 26
Arizona 27
Arkansas 27
California 51
Colorado 62
Connecticut 63
Delaware 79
District of Columbia 82
Florida 84
Georgia 87
Hawaii 108
Idaho 109
Illinois 109
Indiana 135
Iowa 167

Kansas 176
Kentucky 183
Louisiana 209
Maine 214
Maryland 229
Massachusetts 255
Michigan 300
Minnesota 306
Mississippi 315
Missouri 319
Montana 341
Nebraska 342
Nevada 346
New Hampshire 347
New Jersey 359
New Mexico 374
New York 375

Author Index 439
Title Index 459
Index to Advertisers 539

Introduction

The *U.S. Sources and Resources Volumes* of the 5th edition of *Genealogical & Local History Books in Print* are devoted specifically to genealogical books that deal with U.S. regions, states, counties, towns, and smaller municipalities. This, the first of two volumes, begins with coverage of the five major regions of the U.S.—New England, Mid-Atlantic, the South, the Mid-West, and the West—and proceeds alphabetically through the states from Alabama through New York. The second volume covers the remaining states. Each of these two volumes lists thousands of books that were available and in print at the time of the volume's publication.

Books are listed alphabetically by authors' names or the names of sponsoring institutions and, within each state, are arranged under a statewide and regional heading or by county. Typically, each entry gives the full title of the work, the author or sponsoring institution, date of publication, whether indexed or illustrated, in cloth or paper, number of pages, selling price, and vendor number (publisher, bookseller, etc.). Any inconsistencies and/or omissions in the listed information reflect what was provided to us by the vendor. In a number of cases, where a book has been produced or reprinted by two or more vendors, the reader has a choice of formats and prices to choose from. Vendors are listed separately in the front of the book, both numerically and alphabetically, with addresses and special ordering information given to enable you to place orders. In addition, for maximum convenience in your research, both volumes contain separate author and title indexes.

To order any of the listed publications, locate the vendor number at the bottom right of each listing. The names and addresses of these vendors are listed in the front of the book. Send your order directly to the vendor and include the proper fee. Be sure to mention that you saw their work listed in *Genealogical & Local History Books in Print*. Unless otherwise stated next to the price or in the special ordering information included in the List of Vendors on page ix, the prices given in this volume include shipping and handling costs. They do not, however, include sales tax. *You must pay the state sales tax required by the government of the state in which you reside if you order books from vendors operating in your state.*

The aim of these volumes is to include as many books containing reference literature and source material of a localized nature as possible. Some books that are printed on demand or do not remain in print for any length of time have not been included. Compilation of the next edition of the *U.S. Sources & Resources Volumes* will begin almost as soon as these volumes are published; all authors or publishers are invited to list their publications. Write for information to Genealogical & Local History Books in Print, 1001 N. Calvert Street, Baltimore, MD 21202. Authors and publishers are also encouraged to send in listings for the *Family History Volume* and the *General Reference & World Resources Volume* of *Genealogical & Local History Books in Print*.

List of Vendors
(organized numerically)

G0004 William S. Farley, 6592 E. Jackson Court, Highlands Ranch, CO 80126

G0007 Randall C. Maydew, 6908 Brandywine Loop NE, Albuquerque, NM 87111; tel. 505-821-0102

G0009 Virginia Carlisle d'Armand, 3636 Taliluna Ave. Apt. #235, Knoxville, TN 37919

G0010 Genealogical Publishing Co., Inc., 1001 N. Calvert Street, Baltimore, MD 21202-3879; tel. 410-837-8271; Fax: 410-752-8492
Shipping & handling: On orders over $10.00: one book $3.50, each additional book $1.25; on orders totaling $10.00 or less: $1.50. When ordering sets: First volume $3.50, each additional volume, $1.25. MD residents add 5% sales tax; MI residents add 6% sales tax.

G0011 Clearfield Company, 1001 N. Calvert Street, Baltimore, MD 21202; tel. 410-625-9004; Fax: 410-752-8492
Shipping and handling: One item $3.50, each additional item $1.25. MD residents add 5% sales tax, MI residents add 6% sales tax.

G0015 Helen R. Long, 2536 Brockman Street, Manhattan, KS 66502

G0016 Barbara Wisnewski, Coastal Bend Genealogical Society, 2 Bobwhite Trail, Robstown, TX 78380; tel. 512-387-6462

G0019 Carol Cox Bouknecht, 2420 Castletowers Lane, Tallahassee, FL 32301; tel. 904-878-5762

G0021 SFK Genealogy, Mrs. Shirley F. Kinney, 12 Dell Place, Rome, GA 30161-7006; tel. 706-295-2228

G0024 Hilde Shuptrine Farley, 10325 Russell Street, Shawnee Mission, KS 66212-1736

G0028 Susan R. Alexander, PO Box 460614, Houston, TX 77056-8614

G0032 Linda Berg Stafford, PO Box 5261, Bloomington, IN 47407

G0035 James W. Lowry, 13531 Maugansville Road, Hagerstown, MD 21740

G0036 Tallahassee Genealogical Society, Inc., PO Box 4371, Tallahassee, FL 32315

G0039 Mount Holly Cemetery Association, PO Box 250118, Little Rock, AR 72225

G0040 Frances H. Wynne, 104 Gordon Street, Clayton, NC 27520-1746

G0042 Historical & Genealogical Society of Indiana Co., PA, 200 S. Sixth Street, Indiana, PA 15701-2999

G0055 Lorain County Chapter—OGS, PO Box 865, Elyria, OH 44036-0865

G0056 Herman W. Ferguson, 600 Chad Drive, Rocky Mount, NC 27803; tel. 919-443-2258

G0057 S. Worrel, PO Box 6016, Falls Church, VA 22040-6016

G0058 Poestenkill Historical Society, PO Box 140, Poestenkill, NY 12140-0140

G0059 Broken Arrow Genealogical Society, PO Box 1244, Broken Arrow, OK 74013-1244

G0061 Family Publications—Rose Caudle Terry, 5628 60th Drive NE, Marysville, WA 98270-9509; e-mail: cxwp57a@prodigy.com

G0064 Arkansas Research, PO Box 303, Conway, AR 72033; Fax: 501-470-1120

G0067 Arnold Kepple, PO Box 77, Callensburg, PA 16213

G0068 Susan L. Mitchell, 34233 Shawnee Trail, Westland, MI 48185

G0069 Gloucester County Historical Society, 17 Hunter Street, Woodbury, NJ 08096-4605

G0070 Remsen-Steuben Historical Society, PO Box 284, Remsen, NY 13438

G0074 Joan W. Peters, PO Box 144, Broad Run, VA 22014

G0075 Prince George's County Genealogical Society, PO Box 819, Bowie, MD 20718-0819

G0076 Pauline Williams Wright, PO Box 1976, Glenwood, AR 71943

G0077 Roy F. Olson, Jr., 360 Watson Road, Paducah, KY 42003-8978

G0079 Henrietta C. Evans, 638 First Avenue, Gallipolis, OH 45631-1215; tel. 614-446-1775

G0080 Champaign County Genealogical Society, PO Box 680, Urbana, OH 43078

G0081 Genealogical Books in Print, 6818 Lois Drive, Springfield, VA 22150
Shipping and handling: Add $1.75 for first $10.00, $.35 for each additional $10.00.

G0082 Picton Press, PO Box 250, Rockport, ME 04856; tel. 207-236-6565; (sales) 800-742-8667; Fax: 207-236-6713; e-mail: Picton@midcoast.com
Shipping and handling: Add $4.00 for the first book, $2.00 for each additional book.

G0083 Riley County Genealogical Society, 2005 Claflin Road, Manhattan, KS 66502; tel. 913-537-2205

G0084 Dolores Rench, 2508 Airway Road, Muncie, IN 47304

G0085 Buffalo & Erie County Historical Society, 25 Nottingham Court, Buffalo, NY 14216; tel. 716-873-9644

G0087 Don Mills, Inc., PO Box 34, Waynesville, NC 28786; tel. 704-452-7600

G0088 Carter County History Book Committee, c/o Juanita Wilson, Route 7, Box 2085, Elizabethton, TN 37643

G0089 Holston Territory Genealogical Society, PO Box 433, Bristol, VA 24203; tel. 615-787-2228

G0093 Heart of the Lakes Publishing, PO Box 299, Interlaken, NY 14847-0299; tel. 800-782-9687; Fax: 607-532-4684; e-mail: HLP Books@AOL.com
Visa & MasterCard accepted. Shipping additional: $4.00 for the first book, $1.00 for each additional book; most shipping via UPS—provide appropriate delivery address.

G0094 Glyndwr Resources, 43779 Valley Rd, Decatur, MI 49045

G0095 Delaware County Historical Alliance, PO Box 1266, Muncie, IN 47308

G0096 Ronald R. Templin, 2256 River Oak Lane SE, Fort Myers, FL 33905; tel. 813-694-8347

G0103 Elaine Obbink Zimmerman, PO Box 276, Woodstock, MD 21163-0276

G0108 Jane E. Darlington, C.G.R.S., 793 Woodview S Drive, Carmel, IN 46032; tel. 317-848-9002

G0109 Indiana Historical Society, 315 W. Ohio Street, Indianapolis, IN 46202; tel. 317-232-1882
  Shipping and handling: Add $2.75 for first book, $1.00 for the second and other books ordered.

G0110 St. Clair County (IL) Genealogical Society, PO Box 431, Belleville, IL 62222-0431

G0112 W. E. Morrison & Co., Ovid, NY 14521; tel. 607-869-2561

G0113 Nickell Genealogical Books, PO Box 67, West Liberty, KY 41472

G0115 Mrs. Barbara Knott Horsman, 14704 Jefferson Avenue, Chester, VA 23831

G0116 Goodenow Family Association, Route 2, Box 718, Shepherdstown, WV 25443; tel. 304-876-2008

G0117 John T. Humphrey, PO Box 15190, Washington, DC 20003; tel. 202-544-4142

G0118 Scholarly Resources, 104 Greenhill Avenue, Wilmington, DE 19805-1897; tel. 800-772-8937

G0121 Donald Lewis Osborn, 322 SE Willow Way, Lee's Summit, MO 64063-2928; tel. 816-524-5785

G0122 Joan Kusek, 9640 Walmer, Overland Park, KS 66212-1554

G0123 Minnesota Veterinary Historical Museum, 2469 University Avenue, St. Paul, MN 55114

G0126 Catoctin Press, PO Box 505, New Market, MD 21774-0505; tel. 301-620-0157; Fax: 301-620-1817; e-mail: ghmj48b@prodigy.com

G0130 South Carolina Department of Archives and History, PO Box 11669, Columbia, SC 29211; tel. 803-734-8590
  Make checks payable to "Archives and History."

G0131 Jo White Linn, PO Box 1948, Salisbury, NC 28145-1948

G0135 Ohio Genealogy Center, c/o Kenneth Luttner, PO Box 395, St. Peter, MN 56082; tel. 507-388-7158

G0139 Yakima Valley Genealogical Society, PO Box 445, Yakima, WA 98907-0445; tel. 509-248-1328

G0140 Family Line Publications, Rear 63 E Main Street, Westminster, MD 21157; tel. 800-876-6103
  Shipping and handling: First item $2.00, each additional item $.50.

G0145 Mildred S. Wright, 140 Briggs, Beaumont, TX 77707-2329; tel. 409-832-2308

G0148 Archive Publishing/Microform Books, 4 Mayfair Circle, Oxford, MA 01540-2722; tel. 508-987-0881

G0149 Howard County Genealogical Society, PO Box 274, Columbia, MD 21045-0274

G0151 Indian River Genealogical Society, PO Box 1850, Vero Beach, FL 32961

G0154 Pau Hana Press, 1116 Kealaolu Avenue, Honolulu, HI 96816-5419

G0156 Newton County Historical Commission, PO Box 1383, Newton, TX 75966; tel. 409-379-2109

G0157 Diane K. McClure, 105 4th Avenue NE, St. Petersburg, FL 33701

G0160 Hope Farm Press & Bookshop (publishers & distributors), 1708 Route 212, Saugerties, NY 12477; tel. 914-679-6809 (inquiries; 1-6 p.m. eastern time); 800-883-5778 (orders); e-mail: hopefarm@hopefarm.com; website: http://www.hopefarm.com
  Shipping and handling: Add $3.95 for the first book, $1.00 for each additional book. NY residents must pay sales tax.

G0163 Jeffrey L. Haines, 6345 Armindale Avenue, Rural Hall, NC 27045-9753

G0167 Patricia Morrow, PO Box 116, Maplecrest, NY 12454-0116

G0170 Mrs. William H. Counts, 3801 Glenmere Road, North Little Rock, AR 72116

G0172 Nancy Justus Morebeck, 409 Dennis Drive, Vacaville, CA 95688

G0174 Colorado Genealogical Society Inc., Pub. Dir., PO Box 9218, Denver, CO 80209

G0175 Ozarks Genealogical Society, Inc., PO Box 3494, Springfield, MO 65808

G0176 Margaret M. Cowart, 7801 Tea Garden Road SE, Huntsville, AL 35802

G0177 Patricia D. Smith, PO Box 1, Garden City, KS 67846-0001; tel. 316-275-4554

G0180 Hunterdon County Historical Society, 114 Main St, Flemington, NJ 08822; tel. 908- 782-1981

G0181 Frank J. Doherty, 181 Freedom Road, Pleasant Valley, NY 12569

G0182 New York Genealogical and Biographical Society, 122 East 58th Street, New York, NY 10022; tel. 212-755-8532

G0183 Tennessee Valley Publishing, PO Box 52527, Knoxville, TN 37950-2527; tel. 800-762-7079; Fax: 423-584-0113; e-mail: tvp1@ix.netcom.com

G0184 Solano County Genealogical Society, Inc., PO Box 2494, Fairfield, CA 94533

G0187 McCraken County Genealogical & Historical Society, c/o Paducah Public Library, 555 Washington St., Paducah, KY 42003-1735

G0188 Greene County Historical & Genealogical Society, 120 N 12th Street, Paragould, AR 72450

G0190 Worthy-Brandenburg Index, 365 Lake Forrest Lane, Atlanta, GA 30342-3213; tel. 404-255-1471

G0191 The Ancestor Shoppe, 5501 Duncan Road #315, Fort Smith, AR 72903

G0195 Origins, 4327 Milton Avenue, Janesville, WI 53546 608-757-2777

G0197 Ernest Thode, RR 7, Box 306GB, Kern Road, Marietta, OH 45750-9437

G0199 -ana Publishing, Norma R. Lantz, 66543 26th Street, Lawton, MI 49065-9678; tel. 616-624-7324

G0202 The Genealogical Society of Pennsylvania, 1305 Locust Street, Philadelphia, PA 19107-5661; tel. 215-545-0391; Fax: 215-545-0936.
Pennsylvania residents must pay 6% sales tax.

G0238 Family History & Genealogy Center, 1300 E. 109th Street, Kansas City, MO 64131-3585; Fax: 816-943-0477

G0245 Rosamond Houghton Van Noy, 4700 Hwy. K East, Conover, WI 54519; tel. 715-479-5044

G0256 Arthur Louis Finnell Books, 9033 Lyndale Avenue S., Suite 108, Bloomington, MN 55420-3535

G0259 Higginson Book Co., publishers and reprinters of genealogy and local history, 148-BP Washington Street, PO Box 778, Salem, MA 01970 508-745-7170; Fax: 508-745-8025
Complete catalogs are available free with your order, or $4.00 separately. To order: We accept checks or money order, or MC/VISA. Please add $3.50 for the first book and $1.00 for each additional book. We bind our books to order; please allow six to eight weeks for delivery, plus two additional weeks for hardcover books.

G0261 Betty R. Darnell, 204 Hartford Drive, Mount Washington, KY 40047; tel. 502-538-8743; Fax: 502-538-8743

G0274 Clark County Historical Association, PO Box 516, Arkadelphia, AR 71923; tel. 501-245-5332

G0278 Bartlesville Genealogical Society, c/o Public Library, 600 South Johnstone, Bartlesville, OK 74003

G0305 Irish Genealogical Society, Intl., PO Box 16585, St. Paul, MN 55116-0585; Fax: 612-574-0316

G0307 Margaret B. Kinsey, PO Box 459, Lamesa, TX 79331; tel. 806-872-3603

G0312 Michal Martin Farmer, PO Box 140880, Dallas, TX 75214-0880

G0313 Cobb County GA Genealogical Society, Inc., PO Box 1413, Marietta, GA 30061-1413

G0314 William E. Wise, 411 Elm Street, Ravenna, Ky 40472; tel. 606-723-7279

G0319 John H. Stoddard, PO Box 434, Elmhurst, IL 60126; tel. 630-617-4906

G0332 Virginia B. Fletcher, 721 NW 73 Avenue, Ft. Lauderdale, FL 33317-1140; e-mail: VBFletcher@aol.com

G0333 Oscar H. Stroh, Ph.D., 1531 Fishing Creek Valley Road, Harrisburg, PA 17112-9240; tel. 717-599-5117
Add $3.00 for packing and mailing regardless of number of books ordered.

G0335 Warren Co. (OH) Genealogical Society, 300 East Silver Street, Lebanon, OH 45036; tel. 513-933-1144

G0337 Nancie Todd Weber, 22309 Canyon Lake Drive South, Canyon Lake, CA 92587; e-mail: nanciet@inland.net

G0372 Robert Haydon, 12 Fenchley Court, Little Rock, AR 72212 501-224-1313; Fax: 501-224-7081

G0387 Bland Books, Route 5, Box 412 "Dreamwood," Fairfield, IL 62837-8903

G0399 Nathan Mathews, PO Box 1975, Fayetteville, GA 30214; e-mail: Prodigy KNHK84A

G0406 New England Historic Genealogical Society Sales Dept., 160 N. Washington Street, 4th floor, Boston, MA 02114-2120; tel. 617-536-5740; Fax: 617-624-0325; e-mail: nehgs@nehgs.org

G0430 Barbara Stacy Mathews, 1420 D Street, Marysville, CA 95901; tel. 916-741-2967

G0440 Infopreneur Publishing Co., PO Box 4241, Harrisburg, PA 17111-0241

G0450 Kinship, 60 Cedar Heights Road, Rhinebeck, NY 12572; tel. 914-876-4592; e-mail: 71045.1516@compuserve.com
Shipping and handling: Add $1.50 per book. NY residents must add sales tax; 10% discount if 4 or more books ordered.

G0456 Janet Nixon Baccus, 5817 144th Street East, Puyallup, WA 98373-5221; tel. 206-537-8288

G0458 AKB Publications—Annette K. Burgert, 691 Weavertown Road, Myerstown, PA 17067-2642

G0459 Tabernacle Cemetery Trust Fund, 1421 North Fork Road, Black Mountain, NC 28711

G0460 Janice L. Jones, 4839 Towne Centre Drive, St. Louis, MO 63128-2816

G0461 Luxemberg Publications, PO Box 1359, Sutter Creek, CA 95685; Fax: 209-267-5101; e-mail: lensales@cdepot.net

G0462 Grant County Historical Society, 12 Charlotte Heights, Williamstown, KY 41097

G0463 Patricia M. Steele, 10 Cherry Street, Brookville, PA 15825

G0464 M. P. Dolph, 134 E. Goodwin Place, Mundelein, IL 60060

G0465 Jaussi Publications, 284 East 400 South, Orem, Utah 84058-6312; tel. 801-225-7384

G0466 Joyce Martin Murray, 2921 Daniel, Dallas, TX 75205; e-mail: Jmurray785@aol.com
 Shipping & handling: Add $3.50 plus $.50 for each additional book/$1.00 each title fiche.

G0467 Judy A. Deeter, 4 Altezza Drive, Mission Viejo, CA 92692-5107

G0468 Mechling Associates, Inc., 203 Pine Tract Road, Butler, PA 16001-8412; tel. 800-941-3735; Fax: 412-285-9231

G0469 Eunice J. Filler, PO Box 251, Burkburnett, TX 76354

G0470 Connie L. Young, 3001 Hillcrest Drive, Irving, TX 75062

G0471 Poplar Grove Press, PO Box 445, Arkadelphia, AR 71923-0445; tel. 501-246-7461; e-mail: swright@iocc.com

G0472 David N. Walters, 1630 N. Buchanan Street, Arlington, VA 22207-2048; tel. 703-525-2551

G0474 Rose Family Association, 1474 Montelegre Drive, San Jose, CA 95120; tel. 408-268-2137

G0476 Old Jail Museum, 326 Thomaston Street, Barnesville, GA 30204; tel. 770-358-0150

G0477 Lincoln-Lancaster County Genealogical Society, PO Box 30055, Lincoln, NE 68503-0055
 Please write for price information.

G0478 Ancestor Publishers, 6166 Janice Way, Dept. GBIP96, Arvada, CO 80004-5160; tel. 800-373-0816; Fax: 303-425-9709; e-mail: ancestor@net1comm.com

G0479 Westchester County Historical Society, 2199 Saw Mill River Road, Elmsford, NY 10523; tel. 914-592-4323; Fax: 914-592-4323

G0480 Ms. Connie Jean Casilear, PO Box 611, Winchester, VA 22604-0611

G0482 Bonnie Peters, 3212 Curtis Lane, Knoxville, TN 37918-4003; tel. 423-687-3842

G0483 GenLaw Resources, c/o Patricia Andersen, 9346 Bremerton Way, Gaithersburg, MD 20879-1427; tel. 301-977-8062; Fax: 301-977-8062

G0484 Skipwith Historical & Genealogical Society, PO Box 1382, Oxford, MS 38655

G0486 William B. Bogardus, 1121 Linhof Road, Wilmington, OH 45177-2917

G0487 Woolkoch Publishing, 459 Ross Road, Columbus, OH 43213-1953

G0488 Illinois State Genealogical Society, PO Box 10195, Springfield, IL 62791-0195; tel. 217-789-1968

G0489 Jim W. Faulkinbury, CGRS, PO Box 60727, Sacramento, CA 95860-0727

G0491 Westland Publications, PO Box 117, McNeal, AZ 85617; e-mail: worldrt@primenet.com

G0492 Marietta Publishing Company, 2115 North Denair Avenue, Turlock, CA 95382; tel. 209-634-9473
 California residents add 7.375% sales tax.

G0493 Centre County Historical Society, 1001 E. College Avenue, State College, PA 16801; tel. 814-234-4779

G0494 Muskingum County Footprints, 2740 Adamsville Road, Zanesville, OH 43701

G0495 Bedford Historical Society, PO Box 46282, Bedford, OH 44146; tel. 216-232-0796

G0496 TCI Genealogical Resources, PO Box 15839, San Luis Obispo, CA 93406; tel. 805-739-1145

G0497 Camp County Genealogical Society, PO Box 1083, Pittsburg, TX 75686

G0498 Linda Mearse, 2841 Paso del Robles, San Marcos, TX 78666; e-mail: lm@itouch.net

G0499 Connellsville Area Historical Society, 275 South Pittsburgh Street, Connellsville, PA 15425; tel. 412-628-5640

G0500 Maryland Acadian Studies, 11725 Kingtree Street, Wheaton, MD 20902; tel. 301-933-5491

G0501 Illinois State Historical Society, 1 Old State Capitol Plaza, Springfield, IL 62701-1507; tel. 217-782-4286; Fax: 217-524-8042

G0503 Whatcom Genealogical Society, PO Box 1493, Bellingham, WA 98227-1493

G0504 Family History World®, PO Box 22045, Salt Lake City, UT 84122-1045, Publication Division, The Genealogical Institute; tel. 800-377-6058

G0505 Cottage Grove Genealogical Society, PO Box 388, Cottage Grove, OR 97424

G0506 Family Tree, PO Box 4311, Boise, ID 83711

G0507 Betty J. Masley/IDL Research, PO Box 20654, Indianapolis, IN 46220-0654

G0508 James E. Williams, Route 1, Box 864, Milano, TX 76556-9759

G0509 Genealogical Society of North Brevard, Inc., PO Box 897, Titusville, FL 32781-0897

G0510 Library Council of Metropolitan Milwaukee, Inc., 814 W. Wisconsin Avenue, Milwaukee, WI 53233; tel. 414-271-8470; Fax: 414-286-2794

G0511 Rev. Albert H. Ledoux, 11007 Montgomery Road, Beltsville, MD 20705. After June 1998, address is c/o Registrar M.S.M. Seminary, Emmitsburg, MD 21727.

G0512 The Ohio Genealogical Society, PO Box 2625, Mansfield, OH 44406; tel. 419-522-4077; Fax: 419-522-0224; e-mail: OGS@freenet.richland.oh.us

G0514 Fair Printing Company, 10417 Long Meadow Road, Oklahoma City, OK 73162

G0517 InfoServ, Louise K. Pollard, 1497 Cheever Lane, Farmington, UT 84025

G0519 Darlene F. Weaver, 386 Shadwell Drive, Circleville, OH 43113

G0520 Historical Research Associates, PO Box 242, Marshfield Hills, MA 02051; tel. 617-834-7329

G0521 Jean S. Morris, PO Box 8530, Pittsburgh, PA 15220-0530

G0522 The Book Shelf, William R. Snell, 3765 Hillsdale Drive, NE, Cleveland, TN 37312-5133; tel. 423-472-8408

G0524 NCOHA, Inc., PO Box 2811, Dept. GPC, Ponca City, OK 74602; tel. 405-765-7169; website: http://www.brigadoon.com/~nipperb

G0525 Richard H. Taylor, 1211 Seneca Road, Benton Harbor, MI 49022; tel. 616-925-9813

G0526 Mrs. Joyce Ray Lea, 1099 Clay Street, Apt. 1110, Winter Park, FL 32789-5478

G0527 Coiny Publishing Co., PO Box 585, Greenfield, IN 46140; tel. 317-462-7758

G0528 Shirlene Salter, McKinney Memorial Public Library, 220 N. Kentucky Street, McKinney, TX 75069

G0529 GSNOCC, PO Box 706, Yorba Linda, CA 92885-0706; Fax: 801-359-7391

G0530 Audrey Gilbert, 604 State Rt. 503 South, West Alexandria, OH 45381

G0531 The Bookmark, PO Box 90, Knightstown, IN 46148; tel. 800-876-5133, ext. 170; Fax: 1-800-695-8153
    Indiana residents must add 5% sales tax.

G0532 Tad Evans, 1506 Stillwood Drive, Savannah, GA 31419; tel. 912-925-1478

G0533 Margaret H. Gentges, 9251 Wood Glade Drive, Great Falls, VA 22066-2209; tel. 703-759-2218; e-mail: mgentges@mindspring.com

G0534 ALDean Enterprises, PO Box 1942, Richmond, IN 47375

G0535 Tom C. Martinet, 82 Hummingbird Lane, Cabot, AR 72023-8883; tel. 501-843-4856; Fax: 501-982-0054

G0536 Closson Press, 1935 Sampson Drive, Apollo, PA 15613-9209; Fax: 412-337-9484; e-mail: rclosson@nauticom.net
    Shipping and handling in the Continental U.S.A. is $4.00 for any size order except for special order books where additional shipping/handling is requested.

G0537 Grand Prairie Research, Marilyn Hambrick Sickel, Route 1, PO Box 125A, DeValls Bluff, AR 72041-9753

G0538 Christ Church Parish Preservation Society, Inc., c/o Mary-Julia Royall, 349 Bay View Drive, Mount Pleasant, SC 29464; tel. 803-884-4265

G0539 Minnie Pitts Champ, PO Box 801515, Dallas, TX 75380-1515; tel. 972-562-6543

G0540 Washington County Historical Assoc., PO Box 205, Jonesborough, TN 37659

G0541 Mrs. Thelma S. McManus, C.G.R.S., 507 Vine Street, Doniphan, MO 63935-1466; tel. 573-996-2596
    Send SASE to inquire about the availability of any books listed or out of print.

G0542 Altamonte Springs City Library, 281 N. Maitland Avenue, Altamonte Springs, FL 32701; tel. 407-830-3904; Fax: 407-263-3716; e-mail: rmiller@merlin.cflc.lib.fl.us

G0543 Fairfax Genealogical Society, PO Box 2290, Dept. L, Merrifield, VA 22116-2290

G0544 Cemeteries, PO Box 451206, Grove, OK 74345-1206
    Shipping and handling: Add $2.50 for the first book, $1.50 for each additional book.

G0545 Donna J. Robertson, 9380 90th Street, North, Largo, FL 34647-2415

G0547 Alma A. Smith, 554 Anna May Drive, Cincinnati, OH 45244; tel. 513-528-1840

G0549 Mountain Press, PO Box 400, Signal Mountain, TN 37377-0400; tel. 423-886-6369; Fax: 423-886-5312

G0551 The Reprint Company, Publishers, PO Box 5401, 601 Hillcrest Offices, Spartanburg, SC 29304; tel. 864-582-0732
    Shipping and handling: Add $3.50 for the first book, $1.25 for each additional book. When ordering a multi-volume set, count each volume as one book. South Carolina residents must add 5% sales tax.

G0552 AGLL, PO Box 329, Bountiful, UT 84011-0329; tel. 801-298-5446
    Contact vendor for shipping and handling rates.

G0553 The Library Shop, The Library of Virginia, 800 E. Broad Street, Richmond, VA 23219-1905; tel. 804-692-3524; Fax: 804-692-3528
Shipping and handling: Add $4.50 for the first book, $.50 for each additional book. VA residents must add 4.5% sales tax.

G0554 Pennsylvania Historical & Museum Commission, Publications Sales Program, PO Box 11466, Harrisburg, PA 17108-1466; tel. 717-783-2618; Fax: 717-787-8312

G0559 Avotaynu, Inc., PO Box 900, Teaneck, NJ 07666; tel. 201-387-7200; Fax: 201-387-2855; e-mail: infor@avotaynu.com; website: www.avotaynu.com
Shipping and handling in U.S.: Up to $25, $2.50; $25.01 to $35, $3.50; $35.01 to $75, $4.50; $75.01 to $130, $6.50; $130 and above, $8.50. NJ residents add 6% sales tax.

G0561 Hunterdon House, 38 Swan Street, Lambertville, NJ 08530; tel. 609-397-2523

G0567 Florida State Genealogical Society, Inc., John H. Baxley, 1909 W. Hanna Avenue, Tampa, FL 33604

G0569 Dr. George K. Schweitzer, 407 Ascot Court, Knoxville, TN 37923-5807

G0570 Ancestry, Inc., PO Box 476, Salt Lake City, UT 84110-0476; Fax: 801-531-1798
Call for shipping and handling costs. Utah residents add 6.13% sales tax.

G0571 Kansas Statistical Publishing Co., 7609 West 64th Street, Overland Park, KS 66202

G0572 Lancaster County Historical Society, 230 North President Avenue, Lancaster, PA 17603; tel. 717-392-4633; e-mail: jasper@LanClio.org

G0573 Los Banos Genealogical Society, Inc., PO Box 2525, Los Banos, CA 93635

G0574 Ye Olde Genealogie Shoppe, 9605 Vandergriff Road, PO Box 39128, Indianapolis, IN 46239; tel. 317-862-3330; Fax: 317-862-2599
Shipping and handling: Add $4.00 per order. IL, IN, MI, MN, OH, & WI residents add sales tax.

G0577 Byron Sistler & Associates, 1712 Natchez Trace, PO Box 120934, Nashville, TN 37212; Fax: 615-298-2807
Shipping & handling: Add $3.50 per order. Tennessee residents add 8.25% sales tax.

G0578 Connecticut Society of Genealogists, Inc., PO Box 435, Glastonbury, CT 06033

G0581 Henry Z Jones, Jr., F.A.S.G., PO Box 261388, San Diego, CA 92196-1388
California residents pay 6% sales tax.

G0582 Virginia Genealogical Society, 5001 W. Broad Street #115, Richmond, VA 23230-3023
Shipping and handling: Add $3.00 for the first book, $1.00 for each additional book. VA residents add 4.5% tax.

G0583 Park Genealogical Books, PO Box 130968, Roseville, MN 55113-0968; tel. 612-488-4416; Fax: 612-488-2653; e-mail: mbakeman@parkbooks.com

G0585 New Jersey State Archives, 185 W. State Street, CN 307, Trenton, NJ 08625-0307

G0586 North Carolina Division of Archives and History, Historical Publications Section Department of Cultural Resources, 109 East Jones Street, Raleigh, NC 27601-2807; tel. 919-733-7442; Fax: 919-733-1439
Shipping and handling: Add $2.00 for orders of $1.00-$5.00; $3.00 for orders of $6.00-$12.00; $3.00 for orders over $12.00. NC residents add 6% sales tax.

G0587 New York State Archives and Records Administration, 10D45 Cultural Education Center, Albany, NY 12230
Make check payable to New York State Archives.

G0590 Broadfoot Publishing Company, 1907 Buena Vista Circle, Wilmington, NC 28405; tel. 910-686-4816; Fax: 910-686-4379
Shipping & handling: Add $4.00 for the first volume, $1.75 for each additional volume. NC residents add 6% sales tax (before adding shipping).

G0593 Maryland State Archives Publications, 350 Rowe Boulevard, Annapolis, MD 21401

G0594 Martha W. Jackson, 509 Pea Ridge Road, Scottsville, KY 42164

G0595 Cass County Genealogical Society, PO Box 880, Atlanta, TX 75551-0880
Shipping and handling: Add $2.00 for the first book, $.50 for each additional book.

G0596 State Historical Society of Missouri, 1020 Lowry, Columbia, MO 65201-7298

G0597 Delaware Public Archives, Hall of Records, Dover, DE 19901; Fax: 302-739-2578; e-mail: archives@state.de.us

G0598 New Hampshire Society of Genealogists, PO Box 2316, Concord, NH 03302-2316
Shipping and handling: Add $3.00 for each book.

G0599 Mrs. Margaret R. Jenks, 24 Mettowee Street, Granville, NY 12832-1037; tel. 518-642-1894

G0600 Peabody Essex Museum, Museum Shop, East India Square, Salem, MA 01970; Fax: 508-744-6776
Shipping and handling: Orders up to $15.00, $3.50; $15.01-$35.00, $4.50; $35.01-$50.00, $5.50; $50.01-$75.00, $6.95; over $75.00, $7.95.

G0601 Texas State Archives, Texas State Library, PO Box 12927, Austin, TX 78711-1276
Texas residents add 8% sales tax. Add $1.00 to total amount for postage and handling on all orders. Make checks or money orders payable to the Texas State Library.

G0602 Brent H. Holcomb, PO Box 21766, Columbia, South Carolina 29221
Mailing charges: Add $3.00 for the first book, $1.00 for each additional book to the same address.

G0603 John A. Haid, Haid History, 157 E. Fairway Dr., Hamilton, OH 45013; tel. 513-868-1488; Fax: 513-868-1488

G0605 Sonoma County Genealogical Society, Inc. (GP), PO Box 2273, Santa Rosa, CA 95405; website: http://web.wco.com/~hwmiller/genealogy/scgs/htw
Please add $2.00 per item for postage and handling (except postpaid microfiche).

G0606 DuPage County (IL) Genealogical Society, PO Box 133, Lombard, IL 60148

G0607 North Hills Genealogists, c/o E. S. Powell, 720 Highpoint Drive, Wexford, PA 15090-7571; e-mail: Powell@nauticom.net

G0609 T.L.C. Genealogy, PO Box 403369, Miami Beach, FL 33140-1369; tel. 800-858-8558; e-mail: staff@tlc-gen.com; website: http://www.tlc-gen.com/
All prices are postpaid. Florida residents add 6.5% sales tax.

G0610 Southern Historical Press, Inc., PO Box 1267, 275 West Broad Street, Greenville, SC 29602-1267; tel. 864-233-2346
Shipping and handling: Add $3.50 for the first book, $1.50 for each additional book. SC residents add 5% sales tax.

G0611 Frontier Press, PO Box 3715, Suite 3, Galveston, TX 77552; tel. (order line) 800-772-7559; Fax: 409-740-7988; e-mail: kgfrontier@aol.com
Shipping and handling: Add $3.50 for the first book, $1.00 for each additional book. Phone for shipping rates to international and Canadian addresses.

G0612 Hartmann Heritage Productions of Texas, RR 2, Box 148A, 932 East Main Street, Yorktown, TX 78164-9538; tel. 512-564-9200; Fax: 512-564-9200

G0613 Gene L. Williams, Route 2, Box 72, Stephenville, TX 76401; tel. 817-968-5727

G0615 Western Pennsylvania Genealogical Society, 4400 Forbes Avenue, Pittsburgh, PA 15213-4080
Shipping and handling: Add $2.50 for the first item, then $1.00 for each additional item. PA residents must pay sales tax on items & handling.

G0617 Maryland Historical Society, 201 West Monument Street, Baltimore, MD 21201 Non-member and book trade orders to: Alan C. Hood and Co., Inc., PO Box 775, Chambersburg, PA 17201.
Add $3.50 shipping and handling. MD residents add 5% sales tax; PA residents add 6%.

G0618 The Everton Publishers, Inc., PO Box 368, Logan, UT 84323-0368; tel. 800-443-6325; Fax: 801-752-0425
Shipping and handling: Add $1.50 for the first book, $.50 for each additional book.

G0620 General Society of Mayflower Descendants, Mayflower Families, PO Box 3297, Plymouth, MA 02361
Shipping and handling: Add $3.00 for orders under $12.00, $4.00 for orders over $13.00. MA residents add 5% sales tax.

G0622 Hoenstine Rental Library, 414 Montgomery Street, PO Box 208, Hollidaysburg, PA 16648; tel. 814-695-0632

G0623 North Carolina Genealogical Society, PO Box 1492, Raleigh, NC 27502
Shipping and handling: Add $2.00 for the first book, $1.00 for each additional book. NC residents must pay 6% sales tax.

G0624 Laine Sutherland, 2695 North Pebble Beach Drive, Flagstaff, AZ 86004-7419; e-mail: PTPM52A@Prodigy.com

G0625 Tennessee Valley Genealogical Society, PO Box 1568, Huntsville, AL 35807

G0626 Baxter County, Arkansas Historical and Genealogical Society, c/o Mr. Gene Garr, 1505 Mistletoe, Mountain Home, AR 72653

G0627 National Genealogical Society, 4517 17th Street N., Arlington, VA 22207-2399; e-mail: 76702.2417@compuserve.com
Discount given to members.

G0628 California Genealogical Society, 300 Brannon Street, Suite 409, PO Box 77105, San Francisco, CA 94107-0105; tel. 415-777-9936
Shipping and handling: Add $2.00 for each book. CA residents add 8.5% sales tax.

G0629 Family History Library, Salt Lake City Distribution Center, 1999 West 1700 South, Salt Lake City, UT 84104-4233; Fax: 801-240-3685

G0630 Rebecca DeArmond, 1054 Ozment Bluff, Wilmar, AR 71675-9007; tel. 501-367-8712; e-mail: rdea@seark.net

G0631 Lloyd R. Bailey, 4122 Deep Wood Circle, Durham, NC 27707

G0632 Iberian Publishing Company (publishers and distributors), 548 Cedar Creek Drive, Athens, GA 30605-3408; tel. (orders) 800-394-8634

G0633 Genealogical Forum of Oregon, Attn: Publisher, 2130 S.W. Fifth Avenue, Suite 220, Portland, OR 97201-4394; tel. 503-227-2398
  Shipping and handling: $2.00 for orders up to $10.00; add $1.00 for each additional $10.00.

G0634 Oregon Genealogical Society, PO Box 10306, Eugene, OR 97440-2306; tel. 503-746-7924

G0635 Lycoming County Genealogical Society, PO Box 3625, Williamsport, PA 17701; e-mail: LCGSgen@aol.com
  PA residents add 6% sales tax.

G0636 The Georgia Historical Society, 501 Whitaker Street, Savannah, GA 31499; Fax: 912-651-2831

G0645 Connecticut Historical Society, 1 Elizabeth Street, Hartford, CT 06105; tel. 860-236-5621; Fax: 860-236-2664; website: http://www.hartnet.org/chs/

G0646 Ohio Historical Society, c/o The Museum Store, 1982 Velma Avenue, Columbus, OH 43211; 800-797-2357
  Free catalogues are available upon request; we have over 1,000 publications available. Call or write for shipping information.

G0648 Peter Smith Publisher, Inc., 5 Lexington Avneue, Magnolia, MA 01930; Fax: 508-525-3674

G0649 Tazewell County Historical Society, PO Box 916, Tazewell, VA 24651

G0650 Maine State Archives, Station #84, Augusta, ME 04333-0084

G0651 Kentucky Department for Libraries and Archives, Public Records Division, Archives Research Room, PO Box 537, Frankfort, KY 40602-0537
  KY residents must add 6% sales tax. Shipping and handling: $2-$15, add $3; $16-$25, add $4; $26-$55, add $8; $56-$100, add $7; $101 and up, add $10. Make check or money order payable to: Kentucky State Treasurer.

G0653 Delaware Genealogical Society, 505 Market Street Mall, Wilmington, DE 19801-3091

G0654 Smoky Mountain Historical Society, PO Box 5078, Sevierville, TN 37864

G0655 Margie Garr, 1505 Mistletoe, Mountain Home, AR 72653

G0656 Southern California Genealogical Society (SCGS), PO Box 4377, Burbank, CA 91503-4377; tel. 818-843-7247
  Add $2.50 for postage and handling.

G0659 Institute of Science and Public Affairs, 361 Bellamy Building, Tallahassee, FL 32305-4016

G0660 McClain Printing Company, PO Box 403, 212 Main Street, Parson, West Virginia 26287; Fax: 304-478-4658

G0661 Southwest Oklahoma Genealogical Society, PO Box 148, Lawton, OK 73502-0148
  Shipping and handling: Add $2.50 for the first book, $.50 for each additional book.

G0662 Allegheny Regional Family History Society, PO Box 1804, Elkins, West Virginia 26241
  WV residents should add 6% sales tax.

G0663 Diane Snyder Ptak, 12 Tice Road, Albany, NY 12203
  Shipping and handling: Add $2.00 for the first book, $1.00 for each additional book.

G0664 Barrington Public Library Trustees, Attn: Traditions and Transitions, 39 Province Lane, Barrington, NH 03825
Make check payable to Barrington Public Library.

G0665 Brazos Genealogical Association, PO Box 5493, Bryan, TX 77805

G0666 Joyce Hardy Cates, 4900 Pleasant Avenue, Fairfield, OH 45014

G0667 Rudena Kramer Mallory, 6920 Pennsylvania, Kansas City, MO 64113
MO residents add 6.475% sales tax.

G0668 Idaho Genealogical Society, 4620 Overland Road #204, Boise, ID 83705

G0669 Willow Bend Books, Route 1, Box 15A, Lovettsville, VA 22080-9703

G0670 G. P. Hammond Publishing, Box 546, Strasburg, VA 22657

G0672 Partin Publications, 230 Wedgewood, Nacogdoches, TX 75961-1849

G0673 William T. and Patricia Thomas Martin, 4501 SW 62 Court, Miami, FL 33155-5936

G0674 Genealogical Society of Yuma, Arizona, PO Box 2905, Yuma, AZ 85366

G0675 Arkansas Ancestors, 222 McMahan Drive, Hot Springs, AR 71913-6243

G0676 Hempstead County Genealogical Society, PO Box 1158, Hope, AR 71801

G0677 C. L. Boyd, PO Box 222, Dover, AR 72837

G0678 Laurie Nicklas, 1320 Standiford #4-300, Modesto, CA 95350

G0679 Marin County Genealogical Society, PO Box 1511, Novato, CA 94948
Shipping and handling: Add $2.50 for the first book, $1.00 for each additional book.

G0680 Namaqua Chapter NSDAR, PO Box 697, Loveland, CO 80539-0697

G0681 Mrs. Pauline Martin, 455 Martin Road, Carnesville, GA 30521

G0682 Marion Lavender Reynolds, PO Box 352, Harrisburg, IL 62946-0352

G0683 Joan A. Griffis, 105 Poland Road, Danville, IL 61832
IL residents add sales tax.

G0684 Larry and Cynthia Scheuer Publications, 722 E. Center Street, Warsaw, IN 46580
IN residents add 5% sales tax.

G0685 Elkhart County Genealogical Society, PO Box 1031, Elkhart, IN 46515-1031
IN residents add 5% sales tax.

G0686 Brenda Joyce Jerome, PO Box 325, Newburgh, IN 47629-0325
IN residents add 5% sales tax.

G0687 Simmons Historical Publications, PO Box 66, Melber, KY 42069-0066
Shipping and handling: Add $2.00 per order.

G0688 Laurel County Historical Society, PO Box 816, London, KY 40743
KY residents add 6% sales tax.

G0689 Faye Sea Sanders, 311 Sage Road, Louisville, KY 40207

G0690 Michael R. Olson, 10153 Piney Mountain Road, Frostburg, MD 21532
Make checks payable to Percy Cemetery Commission. MD residents add $1.00 sales tax per book.

G0691 Aceto Bookman, Charles Delmar Townsend, 5721 Antietam Drive, Sarasota, FL 34231

G0692 Northeast Michigan Genealogical and Historical Society, c/o Jesse Besser Museum, 491 Johnson Street, Alpena, MI 49707

G0693 Ben Strickland, PO Box 5147, Moss Point, MS 39563-1147
   MS residents add 7% sales tax.

G0694 Janice Soutee Looney, PO Box 231, Walnut Grove, MO 65770

G0695 Nodaway County Genealogical Society, Box 214, Maryville, MO 64468

G0696 The Detroit Society for Genealogical Research, Inc., c/o Burton Historical
   Collection, Detroit Public Library, 5201 Woodward Avenue, Detroit, MI 48202-
   4093
   MI residents add 6% sales tax.

G0697 Libra Pipecreek Publications, 5179 Perry Road, Mt. Airy, MD 21771

G0698 Historical Data Service, 14 Clark Street, Glens Falls, NY 12804

G0699 Northwest Missouri Genealogical Society, PO Box 382, St. Joseph, MO 64502

G0700 Hyde County Historical and Genealogical Society, Route 1, Box 74, Fairfield,
   NC 27826

G0701 Joyce M. Gibson, 14921 McFarland Road, Laurel Hill, NC 28351

G0702 Greene County Chapter, OGS, PO Box 706, Xenia, OH 45385
   OH residents must add sales tax.

G0703 Lucas County Chapter, OGS, c/o Beverly Todd Reed, 1302 Corry Avenue,
   Toledo, OH 43624
   OH residents must add sales tax.

G0704 Paulding County Chapter, OGS, 205 South Main Street, Paulding, OH 45879
   OH residents must add sales tax.

G0705 Williams County Genealogical Society, PO Box 293, Bryan, OH 43506

G0706 Wood County Chapter, OGS, PO Box 722, Bowling Green, OH 43402
   OH residents add 6% sales tax.

G0707 Mrs. Helen Tice, 4239 Carolyn Drive, Memphis, TN 38111-8143

G0708 Warrine Hathaway, PO Box 8063, Dothan, AL 36304

G0709 Mahoning County Chapter, OGS, c/o Lois Glasgo, PO Box 9333, Boardman,
   OH 44513-9333
   OH residents add 6% sales tax.

G0710 Bryan County Heritage Association, PO Box 153, Calera, OK 74730-0153
   *Shipping and handling: Add $2.50 for the first book, $1.00 for each additional
   book.*

G0711 Sandra Tedford, 400 Sherry Lane, Farmersville, TX 75442-1538
   TX residents must add sales tax.

G0712 Eldorado Historical Society, Box 234, Eldorado, OK 73537

G0713 Deschutes County Historical Society, PO Box 5252, Bend, OR 97709

G0715 Juanita Davis Cawthon, 944 Acklen Street, Shreveport, LA 71104-3904

G0716 Lewis & Clark County Genealogical Society, PO Box 5313, Helena, MT
   59604

G0717 Clark County Genealogical Society, Attn: Rose Marie Harshman, PO Box
   2728, Vancouver, WA 98668
   WA residents add 7.6% sales tax.

G0718 Irene Martin, PO Box 83, Skamokawa, WA 98647
   WA residents must add sales tax.

G0719 Janice Cale Sisler, PO Box 113, Bruceton Mills, WV 26525-0013
   WV residents add sales tax.

G0720 West Central Wisconsin Genealogy, W10254 Gaylord Road, Merrilan, WI 54754-7933
   Shipping and handling: Add $3.00 for the first book, $1.00 for each additional book.

G0721 Waukesha County Genealogical Society, PO Box 1541, Waukesha, WI 53187-1541

G0722 LaCrosse Public Library Archives, 800 Main Street, LaCrosse, WI 54601-4122

G0723 Illiana Genealogical & Historical Society, Box 207, Danville, IL 61834-0207

G0724 VESCO, Inc., PO Box 1044, Vidalia, GA 30475

G0727 Venango County Historical Society, PO Box 101, Franklin, PA 16323
   Shipping and handling: Add $2.00 for the first book, $1.00 for each additional book. PA residents must add sales tax.

G0728 Richland County Genealogical Society, PO Box 3823, Mansfield, OH 44907-0823
   OH residents must add sales tax.

G0729 Oklahoma Genealogical Society, Special Publications Chairman, PO Box 12986, Oklahoma City, OK 73157
   Shipping and handling: Add $2.50 for the first book, $.50 for each additional book. OK residents add 8.375% sales tax.

G0730 Guilford County Genealogical Society, PO Box 9693 Plaza Station, Greensboro, NC 27429-0093

G0733 Eastern Washington Genealogical Society, PO Box 1826, Spokane, WA 99210-1826
   Make check payable to EWGS.

G0734 Dwight Shubert, 8703 Oakhaven Drive, Sherwood, AR 72120

G0736 Paradise Genealogical Society, Inc., PO Box 460, Paradise, CA 95967-0460
   Shipping and handling: Add $2.00 for the first book, $.50 for each additional book.

G0737 San Mateo County Genealogical Society, PO Box 5083, San Mateo, CA 94402
   Shipping and handling: Add $2.00 for 1 book, $2.50 for 2 books.

G0738 Cemeteries of Oglethorpe County, PO Box 1793, Lexington, GA 30648

G0739 Lake County Genealogical Society, c/o M. P. Dolph, 134 E. Goodwin Place, Mundelein, IL 60060-1896
   Make checks payable to Lake County Genealogical Society.

G0740 Macoupin County Illinois Genealogical Society, PO Box 95, Staunton, IL 62088

G0741 Genealogy Society of Southern Illinois, c/o Mrs. Tullyne Oliver, 303 Timothy Lane, Carterville, IL 62918-5021
   Make checks payable to Genealogy Society of Southern Illinois.

G0742 Chicago Genealogical Society, PO Box 1160, Chicago, IL 60690
   Shipping and handling: Add $2.50 for the first book, $.50 for each additional book.

G0743 South Bend Area Genealogical Society, PO Box 1222, South Bend, IN 46624
   IN residents must pay sales tax.

G0744 The Confederate Research Center, Hill College Press, PO Box 619, Hillsboro, TX 76645
   TX residents must add sales tax.

G0745 John and Enid Ostertag, 3005 Charles, St. Joseph, MO 64501
  MO residents must add sales tax.

G0746 Edna Montgomery Burgin, 4533 Lake Dreamland Road, Louisville, KY 40216

G0747 Loretta E. Burns 1804 Zapp Lane, Pasadena, TX 77502-3123

G0748 Starke County Genealogical Society, c/o Henry F. Schricker Public Library, 152 West Culver Road, Knox, IN 46534
  IN residents add 5% sales tax.

G0749 Jeanne Hallgren, 1111 Blue Star Highway, South Haven, MI 49090

G0750 Mrs. Melvin J. Bates, 410 - 20 Mile Road, Cedar Springs, MI 49319-9629

G0751 Shiawassee County Historical Society, 224 Curwood Castle Drive, Owosso, MI 48867

G0752 Fort William Bent Chapter NSDAR, c/o Marcella Swanson, 38724 Co. Rd. T, Walsh, CO 81090-9761

G0753 Mrs. Dean Gransee, RR 2, Box 47, Sanborn, MN 56083-9312

G0754 North Antelope County Genealogical Society, PO Box 56, Orchard, NE 68764
  NE residents add 5% sales tax.

G0755 City of Keene Police Department, Attn: PA c/o Capt. Hal G. Brown, 11 Washington Street, Keene, NH 03431

G0756 Catherine Machan Martin, 7195 South Geeck Road, Durand, MI 48429-9102

G0757 Dr. Stephen E. Bradley, Jr., 2001 Jeri Court, Virginia Beach, VA 23464
  VA residents add 4.5% sales tax.

G0758 Dee Ann Buck, 10814 Paynes Church Drive, Fairfax, VA 22032

G0759 Historical Publications, Inc., 15705 Hilcroft Cove, Austin, TX 78717-5331; tel. 800-880-6789
  TX residents add 8% sales tax.

G0760 N O Inc., c/o Ed Eisley 415 Corrydale Drive, Pensacola, FL 32506
  FL residents add 7% sales tax.

G0761 Tammy L. Smallen, 1110 Grove Street, Loudon, TN 37774

G0762 Margaret C. Snider, 633 Lake Spring Road, Franklin, KY 42134

G0763 Nelle J. Berry, Route 1, Box 190, Iron City, TN 38463

G0764 Vandegrift Research, 797 S. 350 W., PO Box 952, Bountiful, UT 84011-0952

G0765 Eve Nicholson, 925 Northwood #9203, Baytown, TX 77521

G0766 Boone County Genealogical Society, PO Box 306, Madison, WV 25130

G0767 W. W. Hoffman, 6364 Cliffside Drive, Florence, KY 41042

G0774 Ashtabula County Genealogical Society, 117 West Main, Geneva, OH 44041-1227
  OH residents add 6% sales tax.

G0783 Nebraska State Genealogical Society, PO Box 5608, Lincoln, NE 68505-0608

G0784 Lower Delmarva Genealogical Society, PO Box 3602, Salisbury, Maryland 21802-3602
  MD residents add $1.75 sales tax.

G0786 Uptown Press, 2903 Grindon Avenue, Baltimore, MD 21214; tel. 410-254-2294; Fax: 410-254-2395
  Shipping and handling: Add $4.50. MD residents must pay 5% sales tax.

G0866 Nadine Billingsley, 706 Pershing, College Station, TX 77840

G0867 Joanne Dominik Glowski, 4131 Bethel, Houston, TX 77092

G0868 Rosemary DePasquale Boykin, 8407 Shadow Oaks, College Station, TX 77845

G0869 Kankakee Valley Genealogical Society, PO Box 442, Bourbonnais, IL 60914
Maximum postage and handling per single order within the continental United States: $4.00.

G0872 Harford County (Maryland) Genealogical Society, PO Box 15, Aberdeen, Maryland 21001

Shipping and handling: $1.50 for the first book, $.50 for each additional book. Make checks payable, in U.S. funds only, to the Harford County Genealogical Society.

List of Vendors

(organized alphabetically)

Aceto Bookman, Vendor G0691
AGLL, Vendor G0552
AKB Publications, Annette K. Burgert, Vendor G0458
ALDean Enterprises, Vendor G0534
Alexander, Susan R., Vendor G0028
Allegheny Regional Family History Society, Vendor G0662
Altamonte Springs City Library, Vendor G0542
-ana Publishing, Norma R. Lantz, Vendor G0199
Ancestor Publishers, Vendor G0478
Ancestor Shoppe, The, Vendor G0191
Ancestry, Inc., Vendor G0570
Archive Publishing/Microform Books, Vendor G0148
Arkansas Research, Vendor G0064
Arkansas Ancestors, Vendor G0675
Ashtabula County Genealogical Society, Vendor G0774
Avotaynu, Inc., Vendor G0559
Baccus, Janet Nixon, Vendor G0456
Bailey, Lloyd R., Vendor G0631
Barrington Public Library Trustees, Vendor G0664.
Bartlesville Genealogical Society, Vendor G0278
Bates, Mrs. Melvin J., Vendor G0750
Baxter County, Arkansas Historical and Genealogical Society, Vendor G0626
Bedford Historical Society, Vendor G0495
Berry, Nelle J., Vendor G0763
Billingsley, Nadine, Vendor G0866
Bland Books, Vendor G0387
Bogardus, William B., Vendor G0486
Bookmark, The, Vendor G0531
Book Shelf, The, Vendor G0522
Boone County Genealogical Society, Vendor G0766
Bouknecht, Carol Cox, Vendor G0019
Boykin, Rosemary DePasquale, Vendor G0868
Boyd, C. L., Vendor G0677
Bradley, Dr. Stephen E., Jr., Vendor G0757
Brazos Genealogical Association, Vendor G0665
Broadfoot Publishing Company, Vendor G0590
Broken Arrow Genealogical Society, Vendor G0059
Bryan County Heritage Association, Vendor G0710
Buck, Dee Ann, Vendor G0758
Buffalo & Erie County Historical Society, Vendor G0085
Burgert, Annette K., Vendor G0458
Burgin, Edna Montgomery, Vendor G0746

Burns, Loretta E., Vendor G0747
California Genealogical Society, Vendor G0628
Camp County Genealogical Society, Vendor G0497
Carter County History Book Committee, Vendor G0088
Casilear, Ms. Connie Jean, Vendor G0480
Cass County Genealogical Society, Vendor G0595
Catoctin Press, Vendor G0126
Cawthon, Juanita Davis, Vendor G0715
Cemeteries of Oglethorpe County, Vendor G0738
Cemeteries [Grove, OK], Vendor G0544
Centre County Historical Society, Vendor G0493
Champ, Minnie Pitts, Vendor G0539
Champaign County Genealogical Society, Vendor G0080
Chicago Genealogical Society, Vendor G0742
Christ Church Parish Preservation Society, Inc., Vendor G0538
City of Keene Police Department, Vendor G0755
Clark County Historical Association, Vendor G0274
Clark County Genealogical Society, Vendor G0717
Clearfield Company, Vendor G0011
Closson Press, Vendor G0536
Coastal Bend Genealogical Society, Vendor G0016
Cobb County GA Genealogical Society, Inc., Vendor G0313
Coiny Publishing Co., Vendor G0527
Colorado Genealogical Society Inc., Vendor G0174
Confederate Research Center, The, Vendor G0744
Connecticut Society of Genealogists, Inc., Vendor G0578
Connecticut Historical Society, Vendor G0645
Connellsville Area Historical Society, Vendor G0499
Cottage Grove Genealogical Society, Vendor G0505
Counts, Mrs. William H,, Vendor G0170
Cowart, Margaret M., Vendor G0176
Darlington, Jane E., Vendor G0108
d'Armand, Virginia Carlisle, Vendor G0009
Darnell, Betty R., Vendor G0261
DeArmond, Rebecca, Vendor G0630
Deeter, Judy A., Vendor G0467
Delaware Genealogical Society, Vendor G0653
Delaware Public Archives, Vendor G0597
Delaware County Historical Alliance, Vendor G0095
Deschutes County Historical Society, Vendor G0713
Detroit Society for Genealogical Research, Inc., Vendor G0696
Doherty, Frank J., Vendor G0181
Dolores Rench, Vendor G0084
Dolph, M. P., Vendor G0464
Don Mills, Inc., Vendor G0087
DuPage County (IL) Genealogical Society, Vendor G0606
Eastern Washington Genealogical Society, Vendor G0733
Eldorado Historical Society, Vendor G0712
Elkhart County Genealogical Society, Vendor G0685
Evans, Henrietta C., Vendor G0079

Evans, Tad, Vendor G0532
Everton Publishers, Inc., Vendor G0618
Fair Printing Company, Vendor G0514
Fairfax Genealogical Society, Vendor G0543
Family History World®, Vendor G0504
Family Line Publications, Vendor G0140
Family Publications, Vendor G0061
Family History & Genealogy Center, Vendor G0238
Family Tree, Vendor G0506
Family History Library, Vendor G0629
Farley, Hilde Shuptrine, Vendor G0024
Farley, William S., Vendor G0004
Farmer, Michal Martin, Vendor G0312
Faulkinbury, Jim W., Vendor G0489
Ferguson, Herman W., Vendor G0056
Filler, Eunice J., Vendor G0469
Finnell, Arthur Louis, Books, Vendor G0256
Fletcher, Virginia B., Vendor G0332
Florida State Genealogical Society, Inc., Vendor G0567
Fort William Bent Chapter NSDAR, Vendor G0752
Frontier Press, Vendor G0611
Garr, Margie, Vendor G0655
Genealogical Publishing Co., Inc., Vendor G0010
Genealogical Society of North Brevard, Inc., Vendor G0509
Genealogical Institute, The, Vendor G0504
Genealogical Society of Pennsylvania, The, Vendor G0202
Genealogical Books in Print, Vendor G0081
Genealogical Forum of Oregon, Vendor G0633
Genealogical Society of Yuma Arizona, Vendor G0674
Genealogy Society of Southern Illinois, Vendor G0741.
General Society of Mayflower Descendants, Vendor G0620
GenLaw Resources, Patricia Andersen, Vendor G0483
Gentges, Margaret H., Vendor G0533
Georgia Historical Society, Vendor G0636
Gibson, Joyce M., Vendor G0701
Gilbert, Audrey, Vendor G0530
Gloucester County Historical Society, Vendor G0069
Glowski, Joanne Dominik, Vendor G0867
Glyndwr Resources, Vendor G0094
Goodenow Family Association, Vendor G0116
Grand Prairie Research, Vendor G0537
Gransee, Mrs. Dean, Vendor G0753
Grant County Historical Society, Vendor G0462
Greene County Historical & Genealogical Society, Vendor G0188
Greene County Chapter, OGS, Vendor G0702
Griffis, Joan A., Vendor G0683
GSNOCC, Vendor G0529
Guilford County Genealogical Society, Vendor G0730
Haid, John A., Vendor G0603
Haines, Jeffrey L., Vendor G0163

Hallgren, Jeanne, Vendor G0749
Hammond, G. P., Publishing, Vendor G0670
Harford County (Maryland) Genealogical Society, Vendor G0872
Hartmann Heritage Productions of Texas, Vendor G0612
Hathaway, Warrine, Vendor G0708
Haydon, Robert, Vendor G0372
Heart of the Lakes Publishing, Vendor G0093
Hempstead County Genealogical Society, Vendor G0676
Higginson Book Co., Vendor G0259
Historical Research Associates, Vendor G0520
Historical Publications, Inc., Vendor G0759
Historical Data Service, Vendor G0698
Historical & Genealogical Society of Indiana Co., PA, Vendor G0042
Hoenstine Rental Library, Vendor G0622
Hoffman, W. W., Vendor G0767
Holcomb, Brent H., Vendor G0602
Holston Territory Genealogical Society, Vendor G0089
Hope Farm Press & Bookshop, Vendor G0160
Horsman, Mrs. Barbara Knott, Vendor G0115
Howard County Genealogical Society, Vendor G0149
Humphrey, John T., Vendor G0117
Hunterdon County Historical Society, Vendor G0180
Hunterdon House, Vendor G0561
Hyde County Historical and Genealogical Society, Vendor G0700
Iberian Publishing Company, Vendor G0632
Idaho Genealogical Society, Vendor G0668
IDL Research, Vendor G0507
Illiana Genealogical & Historical Society, Vendor G0723
Illinois State Genealogical Society, Vendor G0488
Illinois State Historical Society, Vendor G0501
Indian River Genealogical Society, Vendor G0151
Indiana Historical Society, Vendor G0109
Infopreneur Publishing Co., Vendor G0440
InfoServ, Vendor G0517
Institute of Science and Public Affairs, Vendor G0659
Irish Genealogical Society, Intl., Vendor G0305
Jackson, Martha W., Vendor G0594
Jaussi Publications, Vendor G0465
Jenks, Mrs. Margaret R., Vendor G0599
Jerome, Brenda Joyce, Vendor G0686
Jones, Henry Z, Jr., Vendor G0581
Jones, Janice L., Vendor G0460
Joyce Hardy Cates, Vendor G0666
Kankakee Valley Genealogical Society, Vendor G0869
Kansas Statistical Publishing Co., Vendor G0571
Kentucky Department for Libraries and Archives, Vendor G0651
Kepple, Arnold, Vendor G0067
Kinney, Mrs. Shirley F., Vendor G0021
Kinsey, Margaret B., Vendor G0307
Kinship, Vendor G0450

Kusek, Joan, Vendor G0122
LaCrosse Public Library Archives, Vendor G0722
Lake County Genealogical Society, Vendor G0739
Lancaster County Historical Society, Vendor G0572
Lantz, Norma R., Vendor G0199
Laurel County Historical Society, Vendor G0688
Lea, Mrs. Joyce Ray, Vendor G0526
Ledoux, Rev. Albert H., Vendor G0511
Lewis & Clark County Genealogical Society, Vendor G0716
Libra Pipecreek Publications, Vendor G0697
Library of Virginia, The, Vendor G0553
Library Council of Metropolitan Milwaukee, Inc., Vendor G0510
Lincoln-Lancaster County Genealogical Society, Vendor G0477
Linn, Jo White, Vendor G0131
Long, Helen R., Vendor G0015
Looney, Janice Soutee, Vendor G0694
Lorain County Chapter, OGS, Vendor G0055
Los Banos Genealogical Society, Inc., Vendor G0573
Lower Delmarva Genealogical Society, Vendor G0784
Lowry, James W., Vendor G0035
Lucas County Chapter, OGS, Vendor G0703
Luxemberg Publications, Vendor G0461
Lycoming County Genealogical Society, Vendor G0635
Macoupin County Illinois Genealogical Society, Vendor G0740
Mahoning County Chapter, OGS, Vendor G0709
Maine State Archives, Vendor G0650
Mallory, Rudena Kramer, Vendor G0667
Marietta Publishing Company, Vendor G0492
Marin County Genealogical Society, Vendor G0679
Martin, Catherine Machan, Vendor G0756
Martin, Irene, Vendor G0718
Martin, Mrs. Pauline, Vendor G0681
Martin, William T. and Patricia Thomas, Vendor G0673
Martinet, Tom C., Vendor G0535
Maryland Acadian Studies, Vendor G0500
Maryland Historical Society, Vendor G0617
Maryland State Archives Publications, Vendor G0593
Masley, Betty J., Vendor G0507
Mathews, Barbara Stacy, Vendor G0430
Mathews, Nathan, Vendor G0399
Maydew, Randall C., Vendor G0007
McClain Printing Company, Vendor G0660
McClure, Diane K., Vendor G0157
McCraken County Genealogical & Historical Society, Vendor G0187
McKinney Memorial Public Library, Vendor G0528
McManus, Mrs. Thelma S., Vendor G0541
Mearse, Linda, Vendor G0498
Mechling Associates, Inc., Vendor G0468
Minnesota Veterinary Historical Museum, Vendor G0123
Mitchell, Susan L., Vendor G0068

Morebeck, Nancy Justus, Vendor G0172
Morris, Jean S., Vendor G0521
Morrison, W. E., & Co., Vendor G0112
Morrow, Patricia, Vendor G0167
Mount Holly Cemetery Association, Vendor G0039
Mountain Press, Vendor G0549
Murray, Joyce Martin, Vendor G0466
Muskingum County Footprints, Vendor G0494
N O Inc., Vendor G0760
Namaqua Chapter NSDAR, Vendor G0680
National Genealogical Society, Vendor G0627
NCOHA, Inc., Vendor G0524
Nebraska State Genealogical Society, Vendor G0783
New England Historic Genealogical Society, Vendor G0406
New York Genealogical and Biographical Society, Vendor G0182
New Hampshire Society of Genealogists, Vendor G0598
New Jersey State Archives, Vendor G0585
New York State Archives and Records Administration, Vendor G0587
Newton County Historical Commission, Vendor G0156
Nicholson, Eve, Vendor G0765
Nickell Genealogical Books, Vendor G0113
Nicklas, Laurie, Vendor G0678
Nodaway County Genealogical Society, Vendor G0695
North Carolina Genealogical Society, Vendor G0623
North Antelope County Genealogical Society, Vendor G0754
North Hills Genealogists, Vendor G0607
North Carolina Division of Archives and History, Vendor G0586
Northeast Michigan Genealogical and Historical Society, Vendor G0692
Northwest Missouri Genealogical Society, Vendor G0699
Ohio Historical Society, Vendor G0646
Ohio Genealogy Center, Vendor G0135
Ohio Genealogical Society, The, Vendor G0512
Oklahoma Genealogical Society, Vendor G0729
Old Jail Museum, Vendor G0476
Olson, Michael R., Vendor G0690
Olson, Roy F., Jr., Vendor G0077
Oregon Genealogical Society, Vendor G0634
Origins, Vendor G0195
Osborn, Donald Lewis, Vendor G0121
Ostertag, John and Enid, Vendor G0745
Ozarks Genealogical Society, Inc., Vendor G0175
Paradise Genealogical Society, Inc., Vendor G0736
Park Genealogical Books, Vendor G0583
Partin Publications, Vendor G0672
Pau Hana Press, Vendor G0154
Paulding County Chapter, OGS, Vendor G0704
Peabody Essex Museum, Vendor G0600
Pennsylvania Historical & Museum Commission, Vendor G0554
Peters, Bonnie, Vendor G0482
Peters, Joan W., Vendor G0074

Picton Press, Vendor G0082
Poestenkill Historical Society, Vendor G0058
Pollard, Louise K., Vendor G0517
Poplar Grove Press, Vendor G0471
Powell, E. S., Vendor G0607
Prince George's County Genealogical Society, Vendor G0075
Ptak, Diane Snyder, Vendor G0663
Remsen-Steuben Historical Society, Vendor G0070
Reprint Company, The, Vendor G0551
Reynolds, Marion Lavender, Vendor G0682
Richland County Genealogical Society, Vendor G0728
Riley County Genealogical Society, Vendor G0083
Robertson, Donna J., Vendor G0545
Rose Family Association, Vendor G0474
San Mateo County Genealogical Society, Vendor G0737
Sanders, Faye Sea, Vendor G0689
Scheuer Publications, Larry and Cynthia, Vendor G0684
Scholarly Resources, Vendor G0118
Schweitzer, Dr. George K., Vendor G0569
SFK Genealogy, Vendor G0021
Shiawassee County Historical Society, Vendor G0751
Shubert, Dwight, Vendor G0734
Sickel, Marilyn Hambrick, Vendor G0537
Simmons Historical Publications, Vendor G0687
Sisler, Janice Cale, Vendor G0719
Sistler, Byron, & Associates, Vendor G0577
Skipwith Historical & Genealogical Society, Vendor G0484
Smallen, Tammy L., Vendor G0761
Smith, Alma A., Vendor G0547
Smith, Patricia D., Vendor G0177
Smith, Peter, Publisher, Inc., Vendor G0648
Smoky Mountain Historical Society, Vendor G0654
Snell, William R., Vendor G0522
Snider, Margaret C., Vendor G0762
Solano County Genealogical Society, Inc., Vendor G0184
Sonoma County Genealogical Society, Inc., Vendor G0605
South Carolina Department of Archives and History, Vendor G0130
South Bend Area Genealogical Society, Vendor G0743
Southern California Genealogical Society (SCGS), Vendor G0656
Southern Historical Press., Inc., Vendor G0610
Southwest Oklahoma Genealogical Society, Vendor G0661
St. Clair County (IL) Genealogical Society, Vendor G0110
Stafford, Linda Berg, Vendor G0032
Starke County Genealogical Society, Vendor G0748
State Historical Society of Missouri, Vendor G0596
Steele, Patricia M., Vendor G0463
Stoddard, John H., Vendor G0319
Strickland, Ben, Vendor G0693
Stroh, Oscar H., Vendor G0333
Sutherland, Laine, Vendor G0624

T.L.C. Genealogy, Vendor G0609
Tabernacle Cemetery Trust Fund, Vendor G0459
Tallahassee Genealogical Society, Inc., Vendor G0036
Taylor, Richard H., Vendor G0525
Tazewell County Historical Society, Vendor G0649
TCI Genealogical Resources, Vendor G0496
Tedford, Sandra, Vendor G0711
Templin, Ronald R., Vendor G0096
Tennessee Valley Publishing, Vendor G0183
Tennessee Valley Genealogical Society, Vendor G0625
Terry, Rose Caudle, Vendor G0061
Texas State Archives, Vendor G0601
Thode, Ernest, Vendor G0197
Tice, Mrs. Helen, Vendor G0707
Uptown Press, Vendor G0786
Van Noy, Rosamond Houghton, Vendor G0245
Vandegrift Research, Vendor G0764
Venango County Historical Society, Vendor G0727
VESCO, Inc., Vendor G0724
Virginia Genealogical Society, Vendor G0582
Walters, David N., Vendor G0472
Warren Co. (OH) Genealogical Society, Vendor G0335
Washington County Historical Assoc., Vendor G0540
Waukesha County Genealogical Society, Vendor G0721
Weaver, Darlene F., Vendor G0519
Weber, Nancie Todd, Vendor G0337
West Central Wisconsin Genealogy, Vendor G0720
Westchester County Historical Society, Vendor G0479
Western Pennsylvania Genealogical Society, Vendor G0615
Westland Publications, Vendor G0491
Whatcom Genealogical Society, Vendor G0503
Williams County Genealogical Society, Vendor G0705
Williams, Gene L., Vendor G0613
Williams, James E., Vendor G0508
Willow Bend Books, Vendor G0669
Wise, William E., Vendor G0314
Wood County Chapter, OGS, Vendor G0706
Woolkoch Publishing, Vendor G0487
Worrel, S., Vendor G0057
Worthy-Brandenburg Index, Vendor G0190
Wright, Mildred S., Vendor G0145
Wright, Pauline Williams, Vendor G0076
Wynne, Frances H., Vendor G0040
Yakima Valley Genealogical Society, Vendor G0139
Ye Olde Genealogie Shoppe, Vendor G0574
Young, Connie L., Vendor G0470
Zimmerman, Elaine Obbink, Vendor G0103

Genealogical & Local History Books in Print

5th Edition

U.S. Sources & Resources Volume

A – N

New England

Anderson, Robert Charles. **The Great Migration Begins: Immigrants to New England 1620-1633**. 3 vols. 1995.
Cloth. $131.00. 717 + 645 + 700 pp. .... Vendor G0406

Austin, John Osborne. **One Hundred and Sixty Allied Families**. (1893) reprint 1982. Indexed.
    On the families of New England settlers, many of whom migrated to Rhode Island.
Cloth. $30.00. 288 pp. .... Vendor G0010

Banks, Charles Edward. **The English Ancestry and Homes of the Pilgrim Fathers** Who Came to Plymouth on the Mayflower in 1620, the Fortune in 1621, and the Anne and the Little James in 1623. (1929) reprint 1997. Indexed.
    Contains biographical sketches of 112 passengers who sailed on the first four ships to New England.
Cloth. $18.50. 187 pp. .... Vendor G0010

Banks, Charles Edward. **The Planters of The Commonwealth in Massachusetts, 1620-1640**. (1930) reprint 1997. Indexed. Illus.
Cloth. $20.00. xiii + 231 pp. .... Vendor G0010

Banks, Charles Edward. **Topographical Dictionary of 2885 English Emigrants to New England, 1620-1650**. (1937) reprint 1992. Indexed. Illus.
Cloth. $25.00. 333 pp. .... Vendor G0010

Banks, Charles Edward. **The Winthrop Fleet of 1630**. An Account of the Vessels, the Voyage, the Passengers and Their English Homes, from Original Authorities. (1930) reprint 1994. Indexed. Illus.
Cloth. $15.00. ix + 119 pp. .... Vendor G0010

Brown, George S. **Yarmouth, Nova Scotia, Genealogies**. Transcribed from the Yarmouth Herald. 1993. Indexed.
    Focuses almost exclusively on New England families who migrated to Nova Scotia around the time of the Revolutionary War, many of them descended from Mayflower colonists.
Cloth. $60.00. 956 pp. .... Vendor G0010

Chase, Theodore, and Laurel K. Gabel. **Gravestone Chronicles: Some Eighteenth-Century New England Carvers and Their Work**. 1990. Indexed. Illus.
Cloth. $28.50. .... Vendor G0406

Chipman, Scott. **New England Vital Records, 1831-1840**.
    Public records for this period are very sparse. This excellent source adds thousands of private records from a period of strong population growth.
Cloth. $27.50. .... Vendor G0598

MASS. & CONN. GENEALOGY

RECORDS OF THE TOWN OF PLYMOUTH [1636–1705, 1705–1743, 1743–1783]
Published By Order of the Town In Three Volumes
William T. Davis, ed.

These three volumes contain transcriptions of many of the official records of the town of Plymouth, Massachusetts. The published records pertain to formal actions of the town, such as the laying out of highways and grants of land, and cover important periods of local history. While marriage records were omitted from the volumes, each of them is full of land records, showing all parties to the transfer of land, lists of persons in attendance at town meetings, selectmen, jurymen, committee members, militiamen, etc.

3 vols. 1,193 pp. total, indexed, paper. (1889, 1892, 1903), repr. 1995. #9124.   **$75.00**

THE MAYFLOWER READER
A Selection of Articles from
The Mayflower Descendant
George Ernest Bowman

The Mayflower Reader consists of a comprehensive selection of articles from the first seven volumes of The Mayflower Descendant, an authoritative journal devoted to Pilgrim genealogy and history, discontinued in 1937 and now quite scarce. The seventy-eight articles selected for inclusion are of special significance to the descendants of the early Plymouth and Cape Cod settlers, now numbering in the hundreds of thousands and scattered to all points of the compass. They include transcriptions of wills, inventories, passenger lists, and memoirs, as well as a fair number of genealogies and historical sketches.

537 pp., illus., paper. (1899–1905), repr. 1996. #645.   **$39.95**

The Old Families of SALISBURY AND AMESBURY, Massachusetts
David W. Hoyt

Originally published in a dozen or more parts between 1897 and 1919, Hoyt's Families of Salisbury and Amesbury, like Jacobus' Families of Ancient New Haven, is not only the genealogical record of a New England town but the complete record of an entire region, that of the lower Merrimack Valley. Not content with publishing the genealogies of more than 300 families, each traced through at least five or six generations in accordance with the most rigid standards of documentation, Hoyt further provides us with hundreds of pages of source records, including thousands of baptism, marriage, and death records from the period 1720 to 1800.

1,097 pp., indexed, paper. (1897–1919), repr. 1996. #2935.   **$65.00**

THE HISTORY OF NEW ENGLAND From 1630 to 1649 by John Winthrop, Esq., First Governour of the Colony of The Massachusetts Bay, From His Original Manuscripts With Notes...
Revised ed.
James Savage

Winthrop's History of New England is arranged, journal entry–by–journal entry, from the patriarch's arrival in Massachusetts Bay in 1630 until 1648, the year before his death. In "Savage's Edition of Winthrop's Journal," as this work is usually referred to, the editor's notes on any given entry appear on the same page of the volume in smaller type. Turn to any page in the Savage edition and you will find nuggets of great genealogical value. In fact, Savage's notes frequently overshadow the entry they refer to, as when the editor marshals lists of oath takers or paragraphs of court records to develop one of Winthrop's observations.

2 vols. 514, 504 pp., indexed, paper. (revised ed., 1853), repr. 1996. #9445.   **$75.00**

A CATALOGUE OF THE NAMES OF THE FIRST PURITAN SETTLERS Of the Colony of Connecticut; With the Time of Their Arrival in the Colony and Their Standing in Society...
Royal R. Hinman

The standard dictionary of the "First Settlers" of Connecticut, this work consists of an alphabetically arranged list of about 2,000 persons, showing the time of their arrival, residence, station or occupation, and names of wives and children. It includes alphabetical lists of the first settlers of Enfield, Hartford, Saybrook, Wetherfield, and Windsor; a list of "A Part of the Early Marriages, Births, and Baptisms, in Hartford, Ct. from Record," and "Passengers of the Mayflower in 1620."

336 pp., paper. (1846), repr. 1996. #2720.   **$31.50**

HISTORY OF ANCIENT WOODBURY, CONNECTICUT
William Cothren

From 1,500 manuscript volumes of church, state, town, and society records, and from many thousands of rare manuscripts consulted during the course of seven years' labor, Mr. Cothren succeeded in developing an exhaustive chronicle of the persons, places, and events which most accurately characterized Woodbury's history up to the middle of the 19th century. The genealogies, of which there are some eighty-five, are a flesh and blood inventory of the families most intimately linked to the rise and progress of the town of Woodbury.

851 pp., illus., indexed, paper. (1854), repr. 1996. #1160.   **$65.00**

Chipman, Scott. **New England Vital Records, 1841-1846**.

Public records are still weak for this period. In these years hundreds of Revolutionary War veterans died and their obituaries, reproduced here, are often very informative.

Cloth. $27.50. .... Vendor G0598

Chipman, Scott. **New England Vital Records, 1847-1852**.

Covers the Gold Rush years, when thousands pushed West in search of easy fortunes. The unlucky ones ended up on the obituary pages.

Cloth. $27.50. .... Vendor G0598

Chipman, Scott. **New England Vital Records, 1853-1858**.

The Underground Railroad flourished in this period, as westward expansion continued. These last quiet years before the Civil War saw considerable population shifts.

Cloth. $27.50. .... Vendor G0598

Chipman, Scott. **New England Vital Records, 1859-1865**.

Features the Civil War years.

Contact vendor for information. .... Vendor G0598

Chipman, Scott Lee. **New England Vital Records from the Exeter News-Letter 1831-1840, Volume 1**. 1993. Indexed.

Book #1459.

Cloth. $30.00. 288 pp. .... Vendor G0082

Chipman, Scott Lee. **New England Vital Records from the Exeter News-Letter 1841-1846, Volume 2**. 1993. Indexed.

Book #1460.

Cloth. $30.00. 288 pp. .... Vendor G0082

Chipman, Scott L. **New England Vital Records from the Exeter News-Letter 1847-1852, Volume 3**. 1994. Indexed.

Book #1513.

Cloth. $30.00. 344 pp. .... Vendor G0082

Chipman, Scott Lee. **New England Vital Records from the Exeter News-Letter, 1853-1858**. 1994.

Book #1579.

Cloth. $30.00. 352 pp. .... Vendor G0082

Chipman, Scott Lee. **New England Vital Records, Volume 5**. 1995.

Book #1743.

Cloth. $30.00. .... Vendor G0082

The Colonial Society of Massachusetts. **Seventeenth-Century New England**. 1984.

A collection of essays relating to the social history of early New England.

Cloth. $28.95. 340 pp. .... Vendor G0611

Cook. **The Fathers of the Towns: Leadership and Community Structure in 18th-Century New England**. 1976.

Examines community structure in four New England colonies from 1700 to 1785. In a sample of seventy widely dispersed towns, lists of town and provincial officeholders, biographical data, church records, town meeting records, and tax lists provide material for analysis.

Paper. $15.95. 273 pp. .... Vendor G0611

Cutter, William Richard. **New England Families, Genealogical and Memorial**. Third Series. In 4 Volumes. (1915) reprint 1996. Indexed. Illus.

Paper. $200.00. 2,395 pp. total. .... Vendor G0011

Demos. **Entertaining Satan: Witchcraft and the Culture of Early New England**. 1982.

A fascinating study of witchcraft. Includes 121 pages of extensive footnotes.

Paper. $16.95. 543 pp. .... Vendor G0611

Drake, Samuel G. **The Annals of Witchcraft in New England & Elsewhere in the U.S., from Their First Settlement**. (1869) reprint 1994.

Cloth. $35.00. 306 pp. .... Vendor G0259

Eakle, Arlene H., Ph.D. **New England Genealogy**. (1992) revised 1996. Illus.

Includes sources to access data on 20,000 settlers to 1642, Mayflower ancestry projects, maps, bibliography of significant research.

Paper. $23.50. 80 pp. .... Vendor G0504

Family History Library. **Family History Centers: Northeastern States**.

Free. 2 pp. .... Vendor G0529

Farmer, John. **A Genealogical Register of the First Settlers of New England, 1620-1675**. With additions and corrections by Samuel G. Drake. (1829, 1847) reprint 1994.

Cloth. $25.00. 355 pp. .... Vendor G0010

Flagg, Ernest. **Genealogical Notes on the Founding of New England**. (1926) reprint 1996. Illus.

Paper. $39.95. 440 pp. .... Vendor G0011

General Society of Mayflower Descendants. **Mayflower Families Through Five Generations**.

This series traces descendants of the Pilgrims down through the fifth generation to the birth of the sixth generation children. The volumes are carefully researched and contain the best documented genealogical data that is available.

Volume 1: Francis Eaton, Samuel Fuller, William White, includes addendum & revised index.

Volume 2: James Chilton, Richard More, Thomas Rogers, includes addendum.

Volume 4: Second Edition: Edward Fuller.

Volume 5: Edward Winslow and John Billington.

Volume 6: Stephen Hopkins.

Volume 7: Peter Brown.

Volume 8: Degory Priest. Contact vendor for info. on Vols. 9-12.

Cloth. $20.00/Vols. 1, 5, 7 & 8. $25.00/Vols. 2 & 4. $35.00/Vol. 6. ... Vendor G0620

Holmes, Frank R. **Directory of the Ancestral Heads of New England Families, 1620-1700**. (1923) reprint 1989.

Contact vendor for information. 274 pp. .... Vendor G0010

Hubbard, B. F. **The History of Stanstead County, Province of Quebec**. 1874. Reprinted. Indexed.

Stanstead County lies just north of the Vermont border in Quebec. It was first settled in the early 1800s by families from New England, particularly from Vermont and New Hampshire.

Paper. $25.00. 367 pp. .... Vendor G0561

Karlsen. **The Devil in the Shape of a Woman: Witchcraft in Colonial New England**. 1987.

A richly detailed portrait of the women who were persecuted as witches.

Paper. $13.00. 360 pp. .... Vendor G0611

Kelly, Arthur C. M. **Vital Records of Remarkable Records of Rev. Gideon Bostwick: 1770-92, St. James Episcopal Church, Great Barrington, MA**. Indexed.

Over 2,000 baptisms, marriages, and death records. The ministry included the states of Connecticut, Massachusetts, New York, and Vermont.

Cloth. $25.00. 118 pp. .... Vendor G0450

Lainhart, Ann Smith. **Digging for Genealogical Treasure in New England Town Records**. 1996.

Paper. $17.00. ix + 203 pp. .... Vendor G0406

Ledogar, Edwin Richard. **Vital Statistics of Eastern Connecticut, Western Rhode Island, South Central Massachusetts**. 2 vols. 1995. Reprint on microfiche.

Organized alphabetically.

Order no. 867-868, $38.00/each or $69.00/set. 540 + 537 pp. .... Vendor G0478

Lindberg, Marcia Wiswall. **Genealogist's Handbook for New England Research**. 1993.

Cloth, $23.50. Paper, $18.50. 178 pp. .... Vendor G0406

Malone. **The Skulking Way of War: Technology and Tactics Among the New England Indians**. 1991.

Looks at combat in the 17th century and shows how Indians honed their skills, creatively adapting European military technology to fit their own needs.

Paper. $13.95. 172 pp. .... Vendor G0611

Martin. **Profits in the Wilderness: Entrepreneurship and the Founding of New England Towns in the Seventeenth Century**. 1991.

Reviewing some sixty towns and the activities of one hundred town founders, Martin takes a fresh look at the social and cultural history of early New England.

Paper. $14.95. 363 pp. .... Vendor G0611

The NEHG [New England Historical and Genealogical] Register, 1847-1994 (CD-ROM). 1996.

CD-ROM. $298.50. 9 disks. .... Vendor G0406

The New England Historical and Genealogical Register Index, Vol. 1. 1989. Indexed.

Book #1115.

Cloth. $20.00. .... Vendor G0082

O'Connor, Thomas, Marie E. Daly, and Edward L. Galvin. **Irish in New England.** 1985.
Paper. $4.95. 44 pp. .... Vendor G0406

Peirce, Ebenezer Weaver. **Peirce's Colonial Lists.** Civil, Military and Professional Lists of Plymouth and Rhode Island Colonies . . . 1621-1700. (1881) reprint 1995. Indexed.
Paper. $17.00. 156 pp. .... Vendor G0011

Roser, Susan E. **Mayflower Births and Deaths.** From the Files of George Ernest Bowman, at the Massachusetts Society of Mayflower Descendants. 2 vols. 1992. Indexed.
Contact vendor for information. 1,075 pp. total. .... Vendor G0010

Roser, Susan E. **Mayflower Deeds & Probates.** From the Files of George Ernest Bowman, at the Massachusetts Society of Mayflower Descendants. 1994. Indexed.
Paper. $44.95. 660 pp. .... Vendor G0010

Roser, Susan E. **Mayflower Increasings.** 2nd ed. (1995) reprint 1996.
Paper. $20.00. 170 pp. .... Vendor G0010

Roser, Susan E. **Mayflower Marriages.** From the Files of George Ernest Bowman, at the Massachusetts Society of Mayflower Descendants. (1990) reprint 1994. Indexed.
Paper. $29.95. 415 pp. .... Vendor G0010

Sanborn, Melinde Lutz. **[First] Supplement to Torrey's New England Marriages Prior to 1700.** (1991) reprint 1996. Indexed.
Cloth. $12.50. 80 pp. .... Vendor G0010

Sanborn, Melinde Lutz. **Second Supplement to Torrey's New England Marriages Prior to 1700.** (1995) reprint 1996. Indexed.
Cloth. $20.00. 124 pp. .... Vendor G0010

Savage, James. **A Genealogical Dictionary of the First Settlers of New England.** 4 vols. (1860-1862) reprint 1994.
Cloth. $125.00. 2,541 pp. total. .... Vendor G0010

Savage, James. **The History of New England,** from 1630 to 1649 by John Winthrop, Esq., First Governour of the Colony of The Massachusetts Bay from His Original Manuscripts With Notes . . . Rev. ed. 2 vols. (Rev. ed., 1853) reprint 1996. Indexed.
Paper. $75.00. 514 + 504 pp. .... Vendor G0011

Schutz, John A. **A Noble Pursuit: The Sesquicentennial History of the New England Historic Genealogical Society 1845-1995.** 1995.
Cloth. $28.50. xii + 281 pp. .... Vendor G0406

Southern California Genealogical Society. **Sources of Genealogical Help in New England.**
Paper. $4.50. 48 pp. .... Vendor G0656

Stoddard, Francis R. **The Truth About the Pilgrims.** (1952) reprint 1997. Indexed. Illus.
Paper. $22.50. 206 pp. .... Vendor G0011

Talcott, Sebastian V. **Genealogical Notes of New York and New England Families.** (1883) reprint 1994. Indexed.
Paper. $50.00. 786 pp. .... Vendor G0011

Taylor, John M. **The Witchcraft Delusion: The Story of the Witchcraft Persecutions in Seventeenth-Century New England, Including Original Trial Transcripts**. 1995.
   A study of witchcraft persecution in general and that which occurred in New England in particular.
Cloth. $14.95. 164 pp. .... Vendor G0611

Taylor, Richard H. **The Churches of Christ of the Congregational Way in New England**. 1989. Indexed.
   Church directory.
Cloth. $33.00. vii + 308 pp. .... Vendor G0525

Tenney, Jonathan. **New England in Albany**. 1883. Reprinted. Indexed.
   Traces the emigration of New Englanders to Albany. Includes the names of the earliest New England settlers (1780-1800) and provides more detailed information about residents with New England backgrounds during the mid-1800s.
Paper. $18.00. 89 pp. .... Vendor G0160

Tepper, Michael. **Passengers to America**. A Consolidation of Ship Passenger Lists from The New England Historical and Genealogical Register. (1847-1961) reprint 1988. Indexed.
Cloth. $25.00. 554 pp. .... Vendor G0010

Torrey, Clarence A. **New England Marriages Prior to 1700**. 6th printing. With an updated Introduction by Gary Boyd Roberts. (1985) reprint 1997. Indexed.
   See above under "Sanborn, Melinde Lutz" for the supplements to this book.
Cloth. $50.00. 1,009 pp. .... Vendor G0010

Ulrich. **Good Wives: Image and Reality in the Lives of Women in Northern New England, 1650-1750**. 1982.
   Well-researched social history. Lively with scandal and homely detail.
Paper. $11.00. 296 pp. .... Vendor G0611

Waters, Henry F. **Genealogical Gleanings in England**. Abstracts of Wills Relating to Early American Families. 2 vols. (1901) reprint 1997. Indexed. Illus.
Contact vendor for information. 1,779 pp. .... Vendor G0011

Weis, Frederick Lewis. **The Colonial Clergy and the Colonial Churches of New England**. (1936) reprint 1995.
Paper. $24.00. 280 pp. .... Vendor G0011

Mid-Atlantic

Bogardus, William Brower. **Directory of Genealogical and Historical Articles Published in "de Halve Maen" from 1923 to 1991**. 1992. Indexed.
   Contains hundreds of titles which identify date of issue, author, and page numbers from the quarterly journal of The Holland Society of New York.
Paper. $8.00. 27 pp. .... Vendor G0486

Burgert, Annette K., and Henry Z Jones, Jr. **Westerwald to America:** Some 18th Century German Immigrants. Indexed. Illus.

Documents the German origins of more than 265 individuals and/or families who immigrated to Pennsylvania, New Jersey, New York, Maryland, and Virginia.

Cloth. $29.95 + $2.50 p&h. 272 pp. .... Vendor G0581

Burgert, Annette K., and Henry Z Jones, Jr. **Westerwald to America:** Some 18th Century German Immigrants. 1989. Indexed. Illus.

Cloth. $32.45. 278 pp. .... Vendor G0458

Burgert, Annette K., and Henry Z Jones, Jr. **Westerwald to America**. 1989. Indexed. Illus.

Book #1132.

Cloth. $29.95. 284 pp. .... Vendor G0082

Dobson, David. **Scots on the Chesapeake, 1607-1830**. 1992.

Cloth. $20.00. 169 pp. .... Vendor G0010

Green, Karen M. **The Maryland Gazette, 1727-1761: Genealogical and Historical Abstracts**. 1990.

Over 40,000 entries pertaining to early residents. For genealogists studying families in Maryland during this period, the newspaper provides information on early residents, mostly ordinary farmers and artisans, that simply cannot be obtained from any other source. *The Maryland Gazette*, as the only newspaper in Maryland in that period, contained news of individuals from all over MD, as well as DE, VA and PA. Includes court and probate records, apprentices, marriages, obituaries, lost persons, heirs, divorce, land records, occupations, ads, military expeditions, former residences, estate settlements, seafaring vessels and captains, and much more. Complete index of persons, place names and subjects. Winner of the 1991 Norris Harris Award, Maryland Historical Society.

Cloth. $27.50. 324 pp. .... Vendor G0611

Johnson, Amandus. **The Swedish Settlements on the Delaware, 1638-1664**. 2 vols. (1911) reprint 1996. Indexed. Illus.

Paper. $80.00. 1,080 pp. in all. .... Vendor G0011

Jones, Henry Z, Jr. **More Palatine Families**. Indexed. Illus.

Some immigrants to the middle colonies from 1717-1776, and their European origins, plus new discoveries on German families who arrived in colonial New York in 1710. Long buried emigration materials found in Germany give ancestral origins of hundreds of New York, New Jersey, and Pennsylvania colonists.

Cloth. $65.00 + $4.50 p&h. 625 pp. .... Vendor G0581

Jones, Henry Z, Jr. **More Palatine Families**. 1991. Indexed. Illus.

Book #1161.

Cloth. $65.00. 625 pp. .... Vendor G0082

Keith, Charles P. **The Provincial Councillors of Pennsylvania Who Held Office Between 1733 and 1776,** and Those Earlier Councillors Who Were Some Time Chief Magistrates of the Province, and Their Descendants. (1883) reprint 1997. Indexed.

Covers many of the leading families of the mid-Atlantic region and includes the entire progeny of the councillors.

Cloth. $45.00. 628 pp. .... Vendor G0010

Ljungstedt, Milnor. **The County Court Note-book and Ancestral Proofs and Probabilities**. (1921-31, 1935-36) reprint 1995. Indexed.

The geographical coverage of the subject matter includes Maryland, Virginia, West Virginia, Georgia, the Carolinas, Delaware, Kentucky, and Pennsylvania.

Paper. $50.00. 788 pp. .... Vendor G0011

Parker, J. Carlyle. **Pennsylvania and Middle Atlantic States Genealogical Manuscripts:** A User's Guide to the Manuscript Collections of the Genealogical Society of Pennsylvania as Indexed in Its Manuscript Materials Index; Microfilmed by the Genealogical Department, Salt Lake City. 1986.

Strongest in coverage of eastern Pennsylvania and southern New Jersey.

Paper. $16.95. 45 pp. .... Vendor G0492

Tepper, Michael. **Immigrants to the Middle Colonies**. A Consolidation of Ship Passenger Lists and Associated Data from The New York Genealogical and Biographical Record. (1879-1970) reprint 1992. Indexed. Illus.

Cloth. $17.50. 191 pp. .... Vendor G0010

Van Voorhis, John S. **The Old and New Monongahela**. (1893) reprint 1991. Indexed.

Extracted from newspapers of the Monongahela and adjacent regions of Pennsylvania and West Virginia, this work's genealogical coverage features lengthy sketches of early families of the Monongahela Valley.

Contact vendor for information. 504 pp. .... Vendor G0011

Weis, Frederick Lewis. **The Colonial Clergy of Maryland, Delaware and Georgia**. (1950) reprint 1991.

Paper. $12.50. 104 pp. .... Vendor G0011

Weis, Frederick Lewis. **The Colonial Clergy of the Middle Colonies,** New York, New Jersey, and Pennsylvania 1628-1776. (1957) reprint 1995.

Paper. $20.00. 184 pp. .... Vendor G0011

Wright, Lauren. **1997 Pocket Guide to Genealogical Resource Centers of the Mid-Atlantic**.

Paper. $4.00. 40 pp. .... Vendor G0140

ঌ South ঌ

Armstrong, Zella. **Notable Southern Families**. In Six Volumes.
  Volume I: 247 pp., (1918) reprint 1993. Contact vendor for information.
  Volume II: 377 pp., (1922) reprint 1993. Contact vendor for information.
  Volume III: 369 pp., (1926) reprint 1993, $28.50.
  Volume IV: 325 pp., (1926) reprint 1993, $26.00.
  Volume V: 611 pp., indexed, (1928) reprint 1993, $45.00.
  Volume VI: 98 pp., indexed, (1933) reprint 1993, $12.50.
Paper. .... Vendor G0011

Bleser. **In Joy and Sorrow: Women, Family, and Marriage in the Victorian South**.
1991.
  Probing study of the Southern domestic experience. Extensive footnotes.
Paper. $16.95. 330 pp. .... Vendor G0611

Boddie, John Bennett, and Mrs. John Bennett Boddie. **Historical Southern Families**
Volumes I-XXIII. Indexed.
  Volume I, 385 pp., illus., (1957) reprint 1994, $30.00.
  Volume II, 315 pp., illus., (1958) reprint 1994, $25.00.
  Volume III, 255 pp., illus., (1959) reprint 1994, $22.50.
  Volume IV, 259 pp., (1960) reprint 1994, $23.00.
  Volume V, 320 pp., illus. (1960) reprint 1994, $26.00.
  Volume VI, 275 pp., (1962) reprint 1994, $24.00.
  Volume VII, 282 pp., (1963) reprint 1995, $25.00.
  Volume VIII, 254 pp., illus., (1964) reprint 1993, $22.50.
  Volume IX, 302 pp., illus., (1965) reprint 1993, $26.00.
  Volume X, 275 pp., illus., (1966) reprint 1993, $24.00.
  Volume XI, 287 pp., illus., (1967) reprint 1995, $25.00.
  Volume XII, 289 pp., illus., (1968) reprint 1995, $25.00.
  Volume XIII, 256 pp. (1969) reprint 1994, $22.50.
  Volume XIV, 240 pp., (1970) reprint 1994, $22.00.
  Volume XV, 272 pp. (1971) reprint 1994, $24.00.
  Volume XVI, 288 pp., (1971) reprint 1994, $25.00.
  Volume XVII, 248 pp., (1972) reprint 1994, $22.50.
  Volume XVIII, 240 pp., (1973) reprint 1994, $22.00.
  Volume XIX, 204 pp., (1974) reprint 1995, $21.00.
  Volume XX, 201 pp., (1975) reprint 1995, $21.00.
  Volume XXI, 226 pp., (1976) reprint 1995, $21.50.
  Volume XXII, 246 pp., (1978) reprint 1995, $22.50.
  Volume XXIII, 212 pp., (1980) reprint 1995, $21.00.
Paper. .... Vendor G0011

Broadfoot Publishing Company. **The Southern Historical Society Papers**. 55 vols.
Indexed.
  Includes a history of the Southern Historical Society, biographical sketches of its
founders, first-hand battle accounts, diaries, letters, articles, correspondence, and
reviews.
Cloth. $1,700.00. Contact vendor for pricing options. .... Vendor G0590

Bynum. **Unruly Women: The Politics of Social and Sexual Control in the Old South**. 1992.

Analyzing the complex and interrelated impact of gender, race, class, and region on the lives of black and white women, Bynum shows how their diverse experiences and behavior reflected and influenced the changing social order and political economy of the state and region. Extensive footnotes and bibliography.

Paper. $12.95. 233 pp. .... Vendor G0611

Cashin. **A Family Venture: Men & Women on the Southern Frontier**. 1991.

Explores the profoundly different ways that planter men and women experienced migration from the Southern seaboard to the antebellum Southern frontier.

Cloth, $32.50. Paper, $13.95. 198 pp. .... Vendor G0611

Clark, Murtie June. **Colonial Soldiers of the South, 1732-1774**. (1983) reprint 1986. Indexed.

Contact vendor for information. xxx + 1,245 pp. .... Vendor G0010

Clifford, Karen, ed. **Tidewater Families of the New World and Their Westward Migrations**. Case Studies in Southern States Research. 1996. Indexed. Illus.

Cloth. $109.95 + $9.95 p&h. 1,312 pp. .... Vendor G0759

Clinton. **The Plantation Mistress: Woman's World in the Old South**. 1982.

This pioneering study of the much-mythologized Southern belle offers the first serious look at the lives of white women and their harsh and restricted place in the slave society before the Civil War.

Paper. $13.00. 331 pp. .... Vendor G0611

Family History Library. **Family History Centers: Southern States**.

Free. 2 pp. .... Vendor G0629

Farley, William S. **Vanocaten: A Farley-Reid Genealogy**. 1993. Indexed. Illus.

Includes families in Virginia, North Carolina, and Tennessee.

Cloth. $48.75. 500 pp. .... Vendor G0004

Faust, Drew Gilpin. **Mothers of Invention: Women of the Slaveholding South in the American Civil War**. 1996.

A look at the experiences of southern white women in the South during the Civil War and the war's effect on their lives.

Contact vendor for information. .... Vendor G0611

Foster, Frances Smith. **Witnessing Slavery: The Development of Ante-Bellum Slave Narratives**. (1979) reprint 1994.

A classic study of the pre-Civil War American slave autobiography. A wonderful book for the students of the American South, slavery, the Civil War, and race issues.

Paper. $17.95. 194 pp. .... Vendor G0611

Fox-Genovese. **Within the Plantation Household: Black and White Women of the Old South**. 1988.

Whether your particular interest is the slave or the slaveholder, you will come away with a deep appreciation of this aspect of our social history.

Paper. $14.95. 544 pp. .... Vendor G0611

Friedman. **The Enclosed Garden: Women & Community in the Evangelical South, 1830-1900**. 1985.

How the church and family influenced Southern women's history. Making use of original diaries and letters, this book paints a vivid picture of women's lives during this period.
Paper. $13.95. 180 pp. .... Vendor G0611

Gallagher, Gary, ed. **The Southern Bivouac**. 6 vols. Indexed. Illus.
Sketches of soldiers and articles, stories, and letters related to the southern soldier, the Confederacy, and southern life.
Cloth. $300.00. Contact vendor for pricing options. 3,200+ pp. .... Vendor G0590

Heinegg, Paul. **Free African Americans of North Carolina and Virginia**. Including the Family Histories of More than 80% of Those Counted As "All Other Free Persons" in the 1790 and 1800 Census. Expanded 3rd ed. 1997. Indexed.
Contact vendor for information. 831 pp. .... Vendor G0011

Holcomb, Brent H. **Death and Obituary Notices from the** *Southern Christian Advocate* **1867-1878**. 1993. Indexed.
Cloth. $40.00. 515 pp. .... Vendor G0602

Holcomb, Brent H. **Marriage and Death Notices from Southern Christian Advocate, Vol. 1 (1837-1860)**. 1979. Indexed.
These notices cover the Southeastern United States, mainly the states of Georgia, Alabama, North and South Carolina, Florida, Mississippi, and Tennessee, and occasionally contain notices from other states. Vol. 1 contains the names of approximately 70,000 individuals.
Contact vendor for information. iv + 758 pp. .... Vendor G0610

Holcomb, Brent H. **Marriage and Death Notices from Southern Christian Advocate, Vol. 2 (1861-1867)**. 1980. Indexed.
These notices cover the Southeastern United States, mainly the states of Georgia, Alabama, North and South Carolina, Florida, Mississippi, and Tennessee, and occasionally contain notices from other states. Vol. 2 covers the Civil War period and contains the names of approximately 30,000 individuals.
Contact vendor for information. vi + 276 pp. .... Vendor G0610

Holcomb, Brent H. **Marriage Notices from the Southern Christian Advocate 1867-1878**. 1994. Indexed.
Cloth. $35.00. 427 pp. .... Vendor G0602

Holcomb, Brent H. **Southern Christian Advocate Death and Obituary Notices, 1867-1878**. 1993. Indexed.
Cloth. $40.00. 515 pp. .... Vendor G0610

Kirkham, E. Kay. **Index to Some of the Family Records of the Southern States**.
An index to 35,000 family Bibles, family records, and family histories of the southern states of the U.S. by surnames only.
Paper. $16.00. 234 pp. .... Vendor G0618

Lee, Eleanor Agnes. **Growing Up in the 1850's: The Journal of Agnes Lee**. 1984.
The journal of Eleanor Agnes Lee, Robert E. Lee's fifth child, from the age of twelve. Remarkable glimpse into a southern girl's life.
Paper. $9.95. 151 pp. .... Vendor G0611

Lester, Memory Aldridge. **Old Southern Bible Records**. Transcriptions of Births, Deaths and Marriages from Family Bibles, Chiefly of the 18th and 19th Centuries. (1974) reprint 1996. Indexed.
Paper. $37.50. 378 pp. .... Vendor G0011

Ljungstedt, Milnor. **The County Court Note-book and Ancestral Proofs and Probabilities**. (1921-31, 1935-36) reprint 1995.
The geographical coverage of the subject matter includes Maryland, Virginia, West Virginia, Georgia, the Carolinas, Delaware, Kentucky, and Pennsylvania.
Paper. $50.00. 788 pp. .... Vendor G0011

MacLeod, James. **The Great Doctor Waddel (Pronounced Waddle):** A Study of Moses Waddel, 1770-1840, as Teacher and Puritan. 1985. Indexed.
A study of the South's most famous antebellum educator, Mose Waddel of Willington Academy in South Carolina and fifth president of the University of Georgia. Includes fifty biographical sketches of famous Waddel alumni from Willington and forty from the University of Georgia.
Paper. $12.50. 194 pp. .... Vendor G0610

Mathews. **Religion in the Old South**. 1977.
"A major study in American cultural history . . . Professor Mathew's book is an explanation of what religion meant in the everyday lives of southern whites and blacks."—David H. Donald, Harvard.
Paper. $16.95. 274 pp. .... Vendor G0611

Morrill, Dan L. **Southern Campaigns of the American Revolution**. 1993.
Recounts the story of the "homespun" soldiers of the American Revolution in the South. The determining effects of the war in the South, Dr. Morrill maintains, were not the full-scale engagements "between armies and fleets but engagements between militia, often among neighbors."
Cloth. $29.95. 271 pp. .... Vendor G0611

Mullin, Michael. **Africa in America: Slave Acculturation and Resistance in the American South and the British Caribbean, 1736-1831**. (1992) reprint 1994.
Extensive archival and anecdotal sources support Mullin's description of slavery as it was practiced in Tidewater Virginia, on the rice coast of the Carolinas, and in Jamaica and Barbados. Through case histories, he offers new and definitive information about how Africans met and often overcame the challenges and deprivations of their new lives through religion, family life, and economic strategies.
Paper. $15.95. 412 pp. .... Vendor G0611

National Road—1828.
Document No. 209 filed with the 20th Congress of the U.S. from the Secretary of War as a report on the National Road from Zanesville, Ohio to Florence, Alabama. Discusses the route as it passes through Ohio, into Kentucky, through Tennessee, and ending in Alabama.
Paper. $8.50. .... Vendor G0549

Peters, Joan W. **Local Sources for African-American Family Historians: Using County Court Records and Census Returns**. 1993. Indexed. Illus.
Local Sources—covers the primary record base, using a local Virginia county as an illustration, found in a judicious use of census returns and court records including the often-overlooked entries found in local County Court Minute Books. The techniques

found in this volume can be applied anywhere researchers find county courts. In addition, there are courthouse record forms and pre-1850 federal census forms to help African-American family historians trace their ancestry.
Paper. $24.00. 142 pp. .... Vendor G0074

Potter, Dorothy Williams. **Passports of Southeastern Pioneers, 1770-1823**. Indian, Spanish and Other Land Passports for Tennessee, Kentucky, Georgia, Mississippi, Virginia, North and South Carolina. (1982) reprint 1994. Indexed. Illus.
Cloth. $32.50. 461 pp. .... Vendor G0010

Rouse, Parke, Jr. **The Great Wagon Road from Philadelphia to the South: How Scotch-Irish and Germanics Settled the Uplands**. (1973) reprint 1995.
This book is recognized for its insight into the birth of the American South, from the early 1700s until the Civil War. Countless Scotch-Irish, Germanic, and English settlers traveled the road southward from Philadelphia to settle the Appalachian uplands from Pennsylvania to Georgia.
Paper. 1995. 292 pp. .... Vendor G0611

Rowland, Dunbar. **History of the Mississippi, the Heart of the South**. 4 vols. (1925) reprint 1978. Indexed. Illus.
Volumes I and II contain the historical narrative. Volumes III and IV contain biographical material on leading citizens.
Cloth. $37.50/vol., $150.00/set. .... Vendor G0551

Sanders, Joanne McRee. **Barbados Records: Marriages, 1643-1800**. In Two Volumes. 1982. Indexed.
Many of the early settlers of Barbados eventually moved to the mainland and settled in Virginia, Georgia, the Carolinas, and other colonies.
Cloth. $60.00. 939 pp. .... Vendor G0011

Sanders, Joanne McRee. **Barbados Records: Wills, Vol. II: 1681-1700; Wills, Vol. III: 1701-1725**. 2 vols. 1980-81. Indexed.
Many of the early settlers of Barbados eventually moved to the mainland and settled in Virginia, Georgia, the Carolinas, and other colonies.
Cloth. $30.00/vol. 536 + 526 pp. .... Vendor G0011

Smith, Clifford N. **Deserters and Disbanded Soldiers from British, German, and Loyalist Military Units in the South, 1782**. British-American Genealogical Research Monograph Number 10. 1991.
ISBN 0-915162-36-9.
Paper. $20.00. 26 pp. double-columned. .... Vendor G0491

Steele. **Civil War in the Ozarks**. 1993.
The Ozarks were a volatile and strategically important region during the Civil War.
Paper. $8.95. 136 pp. .... Vendor G0611

Tadman, Michael. **Speculators and Slaves: Masters, Traders, and Slaves in the Old South**. (1989) reprint 1996.
Previously untapped manuscript sources are used in this book to establish that all levels of white society in the antebellum South were deeply involved in a massive interregional trade in slaves. Advances a major thesis of master-slave relationships.
Paper. $17.95. 317 pp. .... Vendor G0611

Taylor, Richard H. **Southern Congregational Churches**. 1994. Indexed.
  Church directory.
  Cloth. $33.00. x + 255 pp. .... Vendor G0525

Tennessee Valley Authority. **Complete TVA Burial Removal Records**.
  Cloth. $100.00 + $5.00 postage. .... Vendor G0549

Weis, Frederick Lewis. **The Colonial Clergy of Virginia, North Carolina and South
  Carolina**. (1955) reprint 1996.
  Paper. $16.00. 100 pp. .... Vendor G0011

Wilson, Theresa E., and Janice L. Grimes. **Marriage and Death Notices from The
  Southern Patriot 1815-1848, Vol. 1 (1815-1830)**. 1982. Indexed.
  These notices are not limited to the southern states but include many other states
  such as New York, Virginia, Pennsylvania, Ohio, Florida, Tennessee, Connecticut,
  Vermont, Massachusetts, and Rhode Island.
  Paper. $25.00. 262 pp. .... Vendor G0610

Wilson, Theresa E., and Janice L. Grimes. **Marriage and Death Notices from The
  Southern Patriot 1815-1848, Vol. 2 (1831-1848)**. 1986. Indexed.
  These notices are not limited to the southern states but include many other states
  such as New York, Virginia, Pennsylvania, Ohio, Florida, Tennessee, Connecticut,
  Vermont, Massachusetts, and Rhode Island.
  Paper. $25.00. 248 pp. .... Vendor G0610

ᎦᏍᎩ Mid-West ᏍᎦᎧ

Family History Library. **Family History Centers: North Central States**.
  Free. 2 pp. .... Vendor G0629

Smith, Clifford N. **Spanish and British Land Grants in Mississippi Territory, 1750-
  1784:** Selections from The American State Papers. 1996.
  Part 5: ISBN 0-915162-68-7.
  Part 6: ISBN 0-915162-58-X.
  Part 7: ISBN 0-915162-59-8.
  Additional parts forthcoming.
  Paper. $20.00. .... Vendor G0491

Tanner. **Atlas of Great Lakes Indian History**. 1987. Illus.
  A beautiful book with exquisite maps and illustrations accompanying a detailed
  text. 9" x 12".
  Paper. $45.00. 224 pp. .... Vendor G0611

🦋 West 🦋

Armitage and Jameson. **The Women's West**. 1987.
This collection of twenty-one articles creates a multi-dimensional portrait of pioneer western women.
Paper. $16.95. 323 pp. .... Vendor G0611

Blevins, Winfred. **Dictionary of the American West**. 1993.
This unique reference tool defines more than 5,000 terms and expressions of the American West.
Cloth. $40.00. 400 pp. .... Vendor G0611

Brown, John Henry, and William S. Speer. **Encyclopedia of the New West of Texas, Arkansas, Colorado, New Mexico and Indian Territory**. Also Biographical Sketches of Their Representative Men and Women. (1881) reprint 1978. Indexed. Illus.
Contact vendor for information. 1,180 pp. .... Vendor G0610

Butruille, Susan G. **Women's Voices from the Oregon Trail**. 2nd ed.
Part I of this book is a collection of diaries, songs, history, poetry, and recipes creating a masterful narration of women's roles in opening the West. Part II provides a guide to women's history along the trail, showing where to find markers, signposts, landmarks, and historical sites.
Paper. $14.95. 254 pp. .... Vendor G0611

Dutton, Bertha P. **American Indians of the Southwest**. (1983) reprint 1994.
This books covers the history and contemporary tribal affairs, arts and crafts, changing lifestyles, and cultural and social characteristics that set apart each Indian group in the Southwest.
Paper. $16.95. 285 pp. .... Vendor G0611

Family History Library. **Family History Centers: Mountain States**.
Free. 2 pp. .... Vendor G0629

Family History Library. **Family History Centers: Northwestern States and Hawaii**.
Free. 2 pp. .... Vendor G0529

Family History Library. **Family History Centers: Southwestern States**.
Free. 2 pp. .... Vendor G0529

Hampsten, Elizabeth. **Settlers' Children: Growing up on the Great Plains**. 1991.
An account of the experience of children in the earliest settlements of the American West after the Civil War.
Cloth. $19.95. 252 pp. .... Vendor G0611

Irwin, W. B. **Settling the West**.
Paper. $2.25. 10 pp. .... Vendor G0656

Josephy, Alvin M., Jr. **The Civil War in the American West**. 1991.
From Minnesota to Louisiana to Colorado to Texas, the Civil War as fought in the American West is frequently forgotten. Remarkably detailed.
Paper. $15.00. 448 pp. .... Vendor G0611

MacGregor, Greg. **Overland: The California Emigrant Trail of 1841-1870**. 1996.
A fascinating book contrasting memories of the trail between 1841-1870 with black and white present-day photographs of the trail. MacGregor has followed the California-Oregon Trail photographing both the beautiful and the ugly. He provides us with a remarkable glimpse into this portion of our history, and the few traces that remain of it.
Paper. $37.50. 168 pp. .... Vendor G0611

Milner, Clyde A., Carol A. O'Connor, and Martha A. Sandweiss, eds. **The Oxford History of the American West**. 1996. Indexed. Illus.
This book brings together twenty-eight leading historians to explore the West from a number of new perspectives. It explores many distinct western places from the earliest Indian Pueblos of the Southwest to the colonial frontier.
Paper. $25.00. 904 pp. .... Vendor G0611

Paul, Rodman, ed. **A Victorian Gentlewoman in the Far West: The Reminiscences of Mary Hallock Foote**. (1972) reprint 1992. Indexed. Illus.
The story of a young woman artist's life in the American West in the 1860s; includes Hallock/Foote genealogical tables.
Paper. $14.95. 416 pp. .... Vendor G0611

Taylor, Richard H. **The Congregational Churches of the West**. 1992. Indexed.
  Church directory.
Cloth. $29.00. viii + 216 pp. .... Vendor G0525

Terry, Rose Caudle. **Oregon Trail Sources, Queries & Reviews Volume 1**. 1993.
Indexed. Illus.
Paper. $8.95. 37 pp. .... Vendor G0061

Terry, Rose Caudle. **Oregon Trail Sources, Queries & Reviews Volume 2**. 1993.
Indexed. Illus.
Paper. $8.95. 43 pp. .... Vendor G0061

Terry, Rose Caudle. **Oregon Trail Sources, Queries & Reviews Volume 3**. 1994.
Indexed. Illus.
Paper. $8.95. 48 pp. .... Vendor G0061

Terry, Rose Caudle. **Oregon Trail Sources, Queries & Reviews Volume 4**. 1994.
Indexed. Illus.
  Queries published free.
Paper. $8.95. .... Vendor G0061

Utley, Robert M. **The Indian Frontier of the American West, 1846-1890**. (1984) reprint 1993.
A study of the conflicts between Indians and whites through half a century with perspectives from both sides. Utley recreates events from the Indian viewpoint while providing an objective appraisal of why the 19th-century white man acted as he did.
Paper. $15.95. 325 pp. .... Vendor G0611

Ward, Geoffrey C. **The West: An Illustrated History**. 1996. Illus.
A beautiful book that brings to life America's expansion to the Pacific. Drawn from first-person accounts and letters, commentaries by the best historians in the field, and diaries and journals. Includes maps and 450 photographs. This is the companion text to the PBS series *The West*. $9^{1}/4$" x $10^{7}/8$".
Cloth. $60.00. 464 pp. .... Vendor G0611

White, Richard. **It's Your Misfortune and None of My Own: A New History of the American West**. 1991.
Paper. $21.95. 614 pp. .... Vendor G0611

 Alabama

Statewide and Regional References

1905 Alabama Community and Business Directory.
An alphabetical listing of the communities in each county with names of merchants in each area.
Paper. $22.50. .... Vendor G0549

Abernethy. **The Formative Period in Alabama, 1815-1828**. 1990.
Traces the evolution of Alabama out of the Mississippi Territory, and the earliest years of statehood.
Paper. $17.95. 220 pp. .... Vendor G0611

Alabama Historical Quarterly, Vol. 6, No. 3. **Alabama Census Returns, 1820,** and an Abstract of Federal Census of Alabama, 1830. (1944) reprint 1996. Illus.
Paper. $20.00. 192 pp. .... Vendor G0011

Black, Clifford. **Alabama—S.A.R. Members & Ancestors 1903-1996**.
Cloth. $45.00. 272 pp. .... Vendor G0549

Brewer, W. **Alabama: Her History, Resources, War Record, and Public Men from 1540 to 1872**. (1872) reprint 1995. Indexed.
Paper. $47.50. 712 pp. .... Vendor G0011

Douthat, James L. **Robert Armstrong—Plat Book of Those Indians Given Reservations After the 1817 Treaty**. Indexed.
Over 100 plats are given in their original drawing as presented in Robert Armstrong's Plat Book. The plats are found in North Carolina, Tennessee, and Alabama.
Paper. $10.00. .... Vendor G0549

DuBose, Hon. Joel C. **Notable Men of Alabama: Personal & Genealogical**. 1904.
Reprint on microfiche. Indexed.
Order no. 928. $22.00. 476 pp. .... Vendor G0478

England, Flora D. **Alabama Notes**. Volumes 1 and 2. 2 vols in 1. (1977) reprint 1997. Indexed.
Contact vendor for information. 240 pp. in all. .... Vendor G0011

England, Flora D. **Alabama Notes**. Volumes 3 and 4. 2 vols. in 1. (1978) reprint 1997. Indexed.
Contact vendor for information. 280 pp. in all. .... Vendor G0011

Family History Library. **Research Outline: Alabama**.
Leaflet. $.25. 7 pp. .... Vendor G0629

Foley, Helen S. **Marriage and Death Notices from Alabama Newspapers and Family Records, 1819-1890**. 1981. Indexed.
Cloth. $27.50. 200 pp. + index. .... Vendor G0610

Foscue. **Place Names in Alabama**. 1989.
    Includes obsolete names as well as present-day places.
Paper. $17.50. 174 pp. .... Vendor G0611

Gandrud, Pauline Jones. **Marriage, Death, and Legal Notices from Early Alabama Newspapers, 1818-1880**. (1981) reprint 1994. Indexed.
Hard-cover. $45.00. 728 pp. .... Vendor G0610

Liahona Research. **Alabama Marriages, Early to 1825**. 1990.
Cloth. $35.00. 158 pp. .... Vendor G0552

McMillan. **Indian Place Names in Alabama**. 1984.
Paper. $11.50. 107 pp. .... Vendor G0611

Owen, Thomas M. **Revolutionary Soldiers in Alabama**. (1911) reprint 1990.
Cloth. $16.00. 131 pp. .... Vendor G0011

Penny, Morris M., and J. Gary Laine. **Law's Alabama Brigade in the War Between the Union and the Confederacy**. 1996.
    The gripping personal stories of the five Alabama regiments known as "Law's Brigade" formed by men from twenty-five of Alabama's sixty-seven counties.
Cloth. $37.50. 480 pp. .... Vendor G0611

Potter, Johnny L. T. N. **Vidette Cavalry**.
    The roster of the First Tennessee and Alabama Independent Vidette Cavalry is listed alphabetically, with the addition of the *Official Records* entries for the unit.
$12.50 (perfect bound). 42 pp. .... Vendor G0549

Rogers, William Warren, Robert David Ward, Leah Rawls Atkins, and Wayne Flynt. **Alabama: The History of a Deep South State**. 1994.
    This comprehensive history presents, explains, and interprets the major events that occurred during Alabama's history within the larger context of the South and the nation.
Cloth, $49.95. Paper, $29.95. 735 pp. .... Vendor G0611

Saunders, J. E. **Early Settlers of Alabama**. With Notes and Genealogies by E. S. B. Stubbs. (1899) reprint 1991.
Contact vendor for information. 530 pp. .... Vendor G0010

Saunders, James Edmonds. **Early Settlers of Alabama, with Notes and Genealogies,** Parts 1 & 2. (1899) reprint 1994. Indexed.
Hard-cover. $40.00. 566 pp. .... Vendor G0610

Sifakis. **Compendium of the Confederate Armies: Alabama**. 1992.
    Describes each regiment, the officers, and lists the battles in which they fought.
Cloth. $24.95. 160 pp. .... Vendor G0611

Southerland and Brown. **The Federal Road Through Georgia, the Creek Nation, and Alabama, 1806-1836**. 1989.
    This fascinating book tells the story of the Federal Road, "possibly the longest stretch of back road in American history."
Paper. $16.50. 198 pp. .... Vendor G0611

Strickland, Jean, and Patricia N. Edwards. **Residents of the Mississippi Territory**. 3 vols.
The Mississippi Territory covered the later states of Mississippi and Alabama. Contact vendor for information. .... Vendor G0693

Thorndale, William, and William Dollarhide. **County Boundary Map Guides to the U.S. Federal Censuses, 1790-1920: Alabama, 1800-1920**. 1987. $5.95. .... Vendor G0552

Volunteer Soldiers in the Cherokee War—1836-1839.
An alphabetical listing of over 11,000 volunteers from Tennessee, Georgia, North Carolina, and Alabama who volunteered in the Cherokee Wars and Removal. $35.00 (perfect bound). 210 pp. .... Vendor G0549

Barbour County

Foley, Helen S. **The 1833 State Census for Barbour County, Alabama**. 1976. Indexed.
Paper. $9.00. 66 pp. .... Vendor G0610

Foley, Helen S. **Abstracts of Wills and Estates, O.C.R. Books, Barbour County, Alabama, 5-6, 1852-1856,** Vol. 3. 1976. Indexed.
Paper. $17.00. 122 pp. .... Vendor G0610

Foley, Helen S. **Barbour County, Alabama Marriage Records, 1838-1859**. 1990.
Paper. $20.00. Approx. 100 pp. .... Vendor G0610

Foley, Helen S. **Barbour County, Alabama Obituaries from Newspapers, 1890-1905**. 1976. Indexed.
Paper. $15.00. 146 pp. .... Vendor G0610

Godfrey, Marie H. **Early Settlers of Barbour County, Alabama, Vols. 1 and 2**. Indexed.
Cloth. $35.00. 379 pp. .... Vendor G0610

Godfrey, Marie H. **Rural Landowners of Barbour County, Alabama**. 1990. Indexed.
Paper. $20.00. 164 pp. .... Vendor G0610

Hathaway, Warrine. **Barbour County Marriages 1838-1930**. Indexed.
Cloth. $33.50. 326 pp. .... Vendor G0708

Blount County

Brown, Albert. **Blount County, Alabama Marriages 1821-1844**.
Paper. $10.00. .... Vendor G0549

Clarke County

Graham, John Simpson. **History of Clarke County, Alabama**. 1923. Indexed. Illus. Hard-Cover. $35.00. 352 pp. + index. .... Vendor G0610

Colbert County

Cowart, Margaret Matthews. **Old Land Records of Colbert County, Alabama**. 1985. Indexed.
8½" x 11". Complete transcription and comparison of the state and county copies of Government Tractbook dating from the first land sales in 1818, also information from several old ledgers from the District Land Office (Huntsville) found in Tuscumbia and Montgomery. Shows original owner (and/or assignee) of each tract of land in county. Paper. $18.00. 240 pp. .... Vendor G0176

Douthat, James L. **Pickwick Landing Reservoir Cemeteries**.
Cemeteries found in Hardin County, TN; Tishomingo County, MS; and Lauderdale and Colbert counties, AL.
Cloth. $12.00. .... Vendor G0549

Conecuh County

Ellis, Robert, and Lucy Wiggins Colson. **Marriages, Monroe & Conecuh Counties, Alabama, 1833-1880**. 1983. Indexed.
Cloth. $20.00. 172 pp. .... Vendor G0610

Riley, Benjamin Franklin. **History of Conecuh County, Alabama**. (1881) reprint 1994. Indexed.
Hard-cover. $28.50. 246 pp. .... Vendor G0610

Coosa County

Brewer, Rev. George E. **History of Coosa County, Alabama**. 1987. Indexed.
Cloth. $35.00. 314 pp. .... Vendor G0610

Dekalb County

Black, Clifford D. **1880 Dekalb County, Alabama Census Index**.
Paper. $15.00. .... Vendor G0549

Elmore County

Muckleroy, D. V., comp. **Elmore County, Alabama Marriage Records 1881-1893**. Edited, produced, and foreword written by SheRita Kae Partin. 1996.
Spiral binding. $22.00. 65 pp. .... Vendor G0672

Etowah County

Martin, William T., and Patricia Thomas Martin. **The Gadsden Times, 1867-1871**. Indexed. Illus.
   Includes brief abstracts of news items through 1871, including births and deaths, wills, legislation, business plans, and more.
Cloth. $55.00. 367 pp. .... Vendor G0673

Franklin County

Cowart, Margaret Matthews. **Old Land Records of Franklin County, Alabama**. 1986. Indexed.
   8½" x 11". Complete transcription and comparison of the state, county, and BLM copies of Government Tractbook dating from the first land sales in 1818, plus data from the early township plats. Shows original owner (and/or his assignee) of each tract of land in the county.
Paper. $18.00. 280 pp. .... Vendor G0176

Jackson County

Black, Clifford D. **1880 Jackson County, Alabama Census Index**.
Paper. $30.00. .... Vendor G0549

Cowart, Margaret Matthews. **Old Land Records of Jackson County, Alabama**. 1980. Indexed.
   Contact vendor for details about reprint. 439 pp. .... Vendor G0176

Douthat, James L. **Guntersville Reservoir Cemeteries**.
Paper. $17.50. .... Vendor G0549

Tennessee Valley Genealogical Society. **Minutes of the Baptist Church on Paint Rock River & Larkin Fork in Jackson County, Alabama**.
Paper. $16.00. .... Vendor G0625

Jefferson County

DuBose, John W., ed. **Jefferson County & Birmingham: Historical & Biographical**. (1887) reprint 1994.
Cloth. $62.50. 595 pp. .... Vendor G0259

Lauderdale County

Cowart, Margaret Matthews. **Old Land Records of Lauderdale County, Alabama**. 1995. Indexed.
   8½" x 11". Complete transcription and comparison of the state, county, and BLM copies of Government Tractbook dating from the first land sales in 1818.
Paper. $24.00. 393 pp. + 11 pp. explanations. .... Vendor G0176

Douthat, James L. **Pickwick Landing Reservoir Cemeteries**.
  Cemeteries found in Hardin County, TN; Tishomingo County, MS; and Lauderdale and Colbert counties, AL.
Cloth. $12.00. .... Vendor G0549

Lawrence County

Cowart, Margaret Matthews. **Old Land Records of Lawrence County, Alabama**.
1991. Indexed.
  8½" x 11". Complete transcription and comparison of the state, county, and BLM copies of Government Tractbook dating from the first land sales in 1818. Shows original owner (and/or assignee) of each tract of land in the county.
Paper. $23.00. 444 pp. .... Vendor G0176

Tennessee Valley Genealogical Society. **Lawrence County, Alabama, 1820 State Census**.
Paper. $10.00. .... Vendor G0625

Limestone County

Cowart, Margaret Matthews. **Old Land Records of Limestone County, Alabama**.
1984.
  8½" x 11". Fully indexed. Complete transcription and comparison of two copies of Government Tractbook dating from first land sales in 1809, plus added data from Limestone County Plat Book. Shows original owner (or his assignee) of each tract of land in the county.
Paper. $18.00. 265 pp. .... Vendor G0176

Douthat, James L. **Wheeler Reservoir Cemeteries**.
Paper. $7.50. .... Vendor G0549

Tennessee Valley Genealogical Society. **1907 Confederate Census of Limestone, Madison, & Morgan Counties**.
Paper. $8.00. .... Vendor G0625

Wellden, Eulalia Y. **1840 Limestone County Census**.
Paper. $15.00. 195 pp. .... Vendor G0625

Wellden, Eulalia Y. **Death Notices in Limestone County Newspapers, 1829-1891**.
Paper. $18.00. .... Vendor G0625

Madison County

Cowart, Margaret Matthews. **Old Land Records of Madison County, Alabama**.
1979. Indexed.
Contact vendor for information about reprint. 292 pp. .... Vendor G0176

Douthat, James L. **Wheeler Reservoir Cemeteries**.
Paper. $7.50. .... Vendor G0549

Tennessee Valley Genealogical Society. **1907 Confederate Census of Limestone, Madison, & Morgan Counties**.
Paper. $8.00. .... Vendor G0625

Marshall County

Cowart, Margaret Matthews. **Old Land Records of Marshall County, Alabama**. 1988. Indexed.
    8½" x 11". Complete transcription and comparison of the state, county, and BLM copies of Government Tractbook dating from the early 1830s, plus data from the plat book. Shows original owner (and/or assignee) of each tract of land in the county and some surrounding areas.
Paper. $22.00. 432 pp. .... Vendor G0176

Douthat, James L. **Guntersville Reservoir Cemeteries**.
Paper. $17.50. .... Vendor G0549

Douthat, James L. **Wheeler Reservoir Cemeteries**.
Paper. $7.50. .... Vendor G0549

Mobile County

Bergeron. **Confederate Mobile**. 1991.
    A descriptive account of the vital role played by Mobile, a Gulf Coast city that served as the back door into the Confederacy.
Cloth. $29.50. 271 pp. .... Vendor G0611

Higginbotham. **Old Mobile: Fort Louis de la Louisiane, 1702-1711**. 1991.
    Fascinating, well-documented history of early Mobile.
Paper. $25.00. 585 pp. .... Vendor G0611

Monroe County

Ellis, Robert, and Lucy Wiggins Colson. **Marriages, Monroe & Conecuh Counties, Alabama, 1833-1880**. 1983. Indexed.
Cloth. $20.00. 172 pp. .... Vendor G0610

Morgan County

Cowart, Margaret Matthews. **Old Land Records of Morgan County, Alabama**. 1981.
    8½" x 11". Fully indexed. Complete transcription and comparison of three copies of Government Tractbook dating from first land sales in 1818, plus added data from Morgan County Map Book. Shows original owner (or his assignee) of each tract of land in the county.
Paper. $17.00. 295 pp. .... Vendor G0176

Tennessee Valley Genealogical Society. **1907 Confederate Census of Limestone, Madison, & Morgan Counties**.
Paper. $8.00. .... Vendor G0625

Tennessee Valley Genealogical Society. **Marriages of Morgan County, Alabama, 1818-1896**.
Paper. $22.00. .... Vendor G0625

Pickens County

Smith, Nelson F. **History of Pickens County, Alabama, from Its First Settlement in 1817-1856**. (1856) reprint 1994. Indexed.
Cloth. $28.50. 272 pp. .... Vendor G0610

Smith, Nelson F. **History of Pickens County, Alabama, from Its First Settlement in 1817 to 1856**. (1856) reprint 1980. Indexed.
Cloth. $20.00. 283 pp. .... Vendor G0551

St. Clair County

Wright, Mildred S. **St. Clair County, Alabama Genealogical Notes**. 1974.
  Marriage returns 1855-1864, tombstone inscriptions.
Paper. $12.50. 83 pp. .... Vendor G0145

Wright, Mildred S. **St. Clair County, Alabama Genealogical Notes No. 2**. 1981. Indexed.
  Index wills 1819-1827, marriage licenses 1866-1871, tombstone inscriptions.
Paper. $17.50. 67 pp. .... Vendor G0145

Washington County

Washington County Historical Society. **The History of Washington County, Alabama, Vol. II**. 1989. Indexed.
Cloth. $50.00. 400 pp. .... Vendor G0610

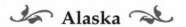

ᘐᗘ Alaska ᗘᘔ

Statewide and Regional References

Delorme. **Alaska Atlas and Gazetteer**.
  Very detailed atlas; 11" x 16".
Paper. $19.95. .... Vendor G0611

Family History Library. **Research Outline: Alaska**.
Leaflet. $.25. 6 pp. .... Vendor G0629

Thorndale, William, and William Dollarhide. **County Boundary Map Guides to the U.S. Federal Censuses, 1790-1920: Alaska, 1880-1920**. 1987. $5.95. .... Vendor G0552

Arizona

Statewide and Regional References

Family History Library. **Research Outline: Arizona.**
Leaflet. $.25. 7 pp. .... Vendor G0629

Thorndale, William, and William Dollarhide. **County Boundary Map Guides to the U.S. Federal Censuses, 1790-1920: Arizona, 1860-1920**. 1987. $5.95. .... Vendor G0552

Yuma County

Genealogical Society of Yuma Arizona. **The Arizona Sentinel Newspaper Death Notices and Obituaries 1872-1899.**
Paper. $3.95. 12 pp. .... Vendor G0674

Genealogical Society of Yuma Arizona. **The Johnson Mortuary Death Records 1904-1937.**
Paper. $16.45. 153 pp. .... Vendor G0674

Arkansas

Statewide and Regional References

Allen, Desmond Walls. **1918 Camp Pike, Arkansas, Index to Soldiers' Naturalizations**. 1988. Indexed.
Paper. $21.00. 134 pp. .... Vendor G0064

Allen, Desmond Walls. **The Twenty-seventh Arkansas Confederate Infantry**. 1987. Indexed.
   Roster and regimental history.
Paper. $17.00. 101 pp. .... Vendor G0064

Allen, Desmond Walls. **The Thirty-eighth Arkansas Confederate Infantry**. 1988. Indexed. Illus.
Paper. $19.00. 73 pp. .... Vendor G0064

Allen, Desmond Walls. **Arkansas Death Record Index, 1914-1923.** 1996.
Paper. $52.50. 572 pp. .... Vendor G0064

Allen, Desmond Walls. **Arkansas Death Record Index, 1924-1933.** 1997.
Paper. $52.50. 500 pp. .... Vendor G0064

Allen, Desmond Walls. **Arkansas Death Record Index, 1934-1940.** 1996.
Paper. $52.50. 475 pp. .... Vendor G0064

Allen, Desmond Walls, and Bobbie Jones McLane. **Arkansas Land Patents: Eastern Arkansas Counties (Clay, Craighead, Crittenden, Cross, Greene, Lee, Mississippi, Monroe, Phillips, Poinsett, and St. Francis Counties, granted through 30 June 1908).** 1991. Indexed.
Paper. $27.00. 232 pp. .... Vendor G0064

Allen, Desmond Walls. **Arkansas Township Digest: Minor Civil Divisions, 1820-1990.** 1994. Indexed.
Cloth, $46.00. Paper, $35.00. 276 pp. .... Vendor G0064

Allen, Desmond Walls. **Arkansas Union Soldiers Pension Application Index.** 1987.
Cloth, $35.00. Paper, $23.00. 182 pp. .... Vendor G0064

Allen, Desmond Walls. **Arkansas' Damned Yankees: Index to Union Soldiers in Arkansas Regiments.** 1987.
Cloth, $37.00. Paper, $25.00. 220 pp. .... Vendor G0064

Allen, Desmond Walls. **Arkansas' Mexican War Soldiers.** 1988. Indexed.
Paper. $21.00. 135 pp. .... Vendor G0064

Allen, Desmond Walls. **Arkansas' Spanish American War Soldiers.** 1988. Indexed.
Paper. $27.00. 200 pp. .... Vendor G0064

Allen, Desmond Walls. **Central Arkansas Death Record Index, 1914-1923: Garland, Grant, Hot Spring, Lonoke, Perry, Prairie, Pulaski, and Saline Counties.** 1996.
Paper. $21.00. 128 pp. .... Vendor G0064

Allen, Desmond Walls. **Central Arkansas Death Record Index, 1934-1940: Garland, Grant, Hot Spring, Lonoke, Perry, Prairie, Pulaski, and Saline Counties.** 1996.
Paper. $19.00. 94 pp. .... Vendor G0064

Allen, Desmond Walls. **Eastern Arkansas Death Record Index, 1914-1923: Clay, Craighead, Crittenden, Cross, Greene, Lee, Mississippi, Monroe, Phillips, Poinsett, and St. Francis Counties.** 1996.
Paper. $19.00. 109 pp. .... Vendor G0064

Allen, Desmond Walls. **Eastern Arkansas Death Record Index, 1934-1940: Clay, Craighead, Crittenden, Cross, Greene, Lee, Mississippi, Monroe, Phillips, Poinsett, and St. Francis Counties.** 1996.
Paper. $19.00. 105 pp. .... Vendor G0064

Allen, Desmond Walls. **First Arkansas Confederate Mounted Rifles.** 1988. Indexed. Illus.
Paper. $19.00. 104 pp. .... Vendor G0064

Allen, Desmond Walls. **Forty-fifth Arkansas Confederate Cavalry.** 1988. Indexed.
Paper. $17.00. 40 pp. .... Vendor G0064

Allen, Desmond Walls. **The Fourteenth Arkansas Confederate Infantry.** 1988. Indexed. Illus.
Paper. $19.00. 58 pp. .... Vendor G0064

Allen, Desmond Walls. **Index to Arkansas Confederate Pension Applications.** 1991.
Cloth, $52.00. Paper, $40.00. 324 pp. .... Vendor G0064

Allen, Desmond Walls. **Index to Arkansas Confederate Soldiers.** 3 vols. 1990.
Cloth, $108.00. Paper, $72.00. 656 pp./3 vols. .... Vendor G0064

Allen, Desmond Walls. **North Central Arkansas Death Record Index, 1914-1923: Baxter, Cleburne, Conway, Faulkner, Fulton, Independence, Izard, Jackson, Lawrence, Randolph, Sharp, Stone, Van Buren, White, and Woodruff Counties.** 1996.
Paper. $19.00. 74 pp. .... Vendor G0064

Allen, Desmond Walls. **North Central Arkansas Death Record Index, 1934-1940: Baxter, Cleburne, Conway, Faulkner, Fulton, Independence, Izard, Jackson, Lawrence, Randolph, Sharp, Stone, Van Buren, White, and Woodruff Counties.** 1996.
Paper. $18.00. 55 pp. .... Vendor G0064

Allen, Desmond Walls. **Northwestern Arkansas Death Record Index, 1914-1923: Benton, Boone, Carroll, Madison, Marion, Newton, Searcy, and Washington Counties.** 1996.
Paper. $18.00. 53 pp. .... Vendor G0064

Allen, Desmond Walls. **Northwestern Arkansas Death Record Index, 1934-1940: Benton, Boone, Carroll, Madison, Marion, Newton, Searcy, and Washington Counties.** 1996.
Paper. $18.00. 40 pp. .... Vendor G0064

Allen, Desmond Walls. **The Seventh Arkansas Confederate Infantry**. 1988. Indexed. Illus.
Paper. $17.00. 52 pp. .... Vendor G0064

Allen, Desmond Walls. **Southeastern Arkansas Death Record Index, 1914-1923: Arkansas, Ashley, Bradley, Chicot, Cleveland, Desha, Drew, Jefferson, and Lincoln Counties**. 1996.
Paper. $18.00. 54 pp. .... Vendor G0064

Allen, Desmond Walls. **Southeastern Arkansas Death Record Index, 1934-1940: Arkansas, Ashley, Bradley, Chicot, Cleveland, Desha, Drew, Jefferson, and Lincoln Counties**. 1996.
Paper. $18.00. 56 pp. .... Vendor G0064

Allen, Desmond Walls. **Southwestern Arkansas Death Record Index, 1914-1923: Calhoun, Clark, Columbia, Dallas, Hempstead, Howard, Lafayette, Little River, Miller, Nevada, Ouachita, Pike, Sevier, and Union Counties**. 1996.
Paper. $19.00. 72 pp. .... Vendor G0064

Allen, Desmond Walls. **Southwestern Arkansas Death Record Index, 1934-1940: Calhoun, Clark, Columbia, Dallas, Hempstead, Howard, Lafayette, Little River, Miller, Nevada, Ouachita, Pike, Sevier, and Union Counties**. 1996.
Paper. $18.00. 61 pp. .... Vendor G0064

Allen, Desmond Walls. **Western Arkansas Death Record Index, 1914-1923: Crawford, Franklin, Johnson, Logan, Montgomery, Polk, Pope, Scott, Sebastian, and Yell Counties**. 1996.
Paper. $18.00. 61 pp. .... Vendor G0064

Allen, Desmond Walls. **Western Arkansas Death Record Index, 1934-1940: Crawford, Franklin, Johnson, Logan, Montgomery, Polk, Pope, Scott, Sebastian, and Yell Counties**. 1996.
Paper. $18.00. 51 pp. .... Vendor G0064

Allsop, Fred W. **History of the Arkansas Press for a Hundred Years and More**. (1922) reprint 1978. Indexed. Illus.
Cloth. $25.00. 688 pp. .... Vendor G0610

Arnold. **Colonial Arkansas, 1686-1804:** A Social and Cultural History. 1991.
    A history of colonial Arkansas.
Cloth, $28.00. Paper, $20.00. 232 pp. .... Vendor G0611

Atlas of Arkansas, 75 county maps.
    Includes detailed maps of individual counties, all the back roads, streams, lakes, towns, etc. 11" x 16".
$14.95. .... Vendor G0611

Chism, Stephen J. **The Arkansas Gazette Obituaries Index, 1819-1879**. 1990.
Cloth. $27.50. 120 pp. .... Vendor G0610

Christ. **Rugged and Sublime: The Civil War in Arkansas**. 1994.
    A well-documented history of the Civil War period in Arkansas.
Paper. $14.00. 207 pp. .... Vendor G0611

Craig, Marion S. **Early Arkansas Residents, 1814-1816**. (1984) reprint 1992. Indexed.
Paper. $13.00. 41 pp. .... Vendor G0064

Dougan. **Confederate Arkansas: The People and Policies of a Frontier State in Wartime**. Reprint 1991.
    Interesting study of the situation in Arkansas prior to and during the Civil War.
Paper. $14.95. 165 pp. .... Vendor G0611

Family History Library. **Research Outline: Arkansas**.
Leaflet. $.25. 7 pp. .... Vendor G0629

Finley, Randy. **From Slavery to Uncertain Freedom: The Freedmen's Bureau in Arkansas, 1865-1869**. 1996.
    A collection of accounts taken from the Freedmen's Bureau in Arkansas, an organization formed after the Civil War to ensure that some measure of freedom was being granted to the new citizens.
Cloth. $28.00. 229 pp. .... Vendor G0611

Goodspeed Publishing Company. **Biographical & Historical Memoirs of Arkansas: General History of Arkansas**. (1884) reprint 1984.
Cloth. $20.00. 128 pp. .... Vendor G0610

Goodspeed Publishing Company. **History of Central Arkansas**. (1889) reprint 1984. Indexed.
Cloth. $40.00. 760 pp. .... Vendor G0610

Goodspeed Publishing Company. **History of Eastern Arkansas**. (1890) reprint 1984. Indexed.
Cloth. $40.00. 792 pp. .... Vendor G0610

Goodspeed Publishing Company. **History of Northeast Arkansas**. (1884) reprint 1984. Indexed.
Cloth. $42.50. 1,040 pp. .... Vendor G0610

Goodspeed Publishing Company. **History of Northwestern Arkansas**. (1889) reprint 1984. Indexed.
Cloth. Contact vendor for price. 1,512 pp. .... Vendor G0610

Goodspeed Publishing Company. **History of South Arkansas**. (1884) reprint 1984. Indexed.
Cloth. $47.50. 1,112 pp. .... Vendor G0610

Goodspeed Publishing Company. **History of Western Arkansas**. (1891) reprint 1984. Indexed.
Cloth. $37.50. 592 pp. .... Vendor G0610

Goodspeed Publishing Company. **A Reminiscent History of the Ozark Region of Arkansas and Missouri**. (1894) reprint 1988. Indexed.
Cloth. $45.00. 784 pp. .... Vendor G0610

Hallum, John. **Biographical and Pictorial History of Arkansas**. (1887) reprint 1978. Indexed. Illus.
Cloth. $37.50. 760 pp. .... Vendor G0610

Hanson and Moneyhon. **Historical Atlas of Arkansas**. 1989.
"The maps in this well-designed book provide an enormous amount of information on every imaginable aspect of Arkansas history."—*Journal of Southern History*
Paper. $19.95. 91 pp. .... Vendor G0611

Hempstead, Fay. **Historical Review of Arkansas: Its Commerce, Industry, and Modern Affairs,** Volume 1: General History. (1911) reprint 1977. Indexed.
Cloth. $40.00. 640 pp. .... Vendor G0610

Hempstead, Fay. **Historical Review of Arkansas: Its Commerce, Industry, and Modern Affairs,** Volume 2. (1911) reprint 1977.
Cloth. $40.00. 624 pp. .... Vendor G0610

Hempstead, Fay. **Historical Review of Arkansas: Its Commerce, Industry, and Modern Affairs,** Volume 3. (1911) reprint 1977.
Cloth. $40.00. 704 pp. .... Vendor G0610

Hempstead, Fay. **A Pictorial History of Arkansas from Earliest Times to 1890**. (1890) reprint 1978. Indexed. Illus.
Cloth. $26.50. 1,256 pp. .... Vendor G0610

Herndon, Dallas T. **The Arkansas History Commission Bulletin of Information, Nos. 13, 14, 15, 16**. (1915) reprint 1977.
Cloth. $20.00. 168 pp. .... Vendor G0610

Ingmire, Frances. **Arkansas Confederate Veterans & Widows Home Records**.
Paper. $8.50. 30 pp. .... Vendor G0549

Ingmire, Frances T., comp. **Arkansas Confederate Veterans and Widows Pension Applications**. 1985.
Hard-cover. $32.50. xii + 442 pp. .... Vendor G0632

Liahona Research. **Arkansas Marriages, Early to 1850**. 1992. Illus.
Cloth. $60.00. 249 pp. .... Vendor G0552

McLane, Bobbie Jones, and Desmond Walls Allen. **1850 Census of Central Arkansas: Hot Spring, Jefferson, Montgomery, Perry, Prairie, Pulaski, Saline, Scott, and Yell Counties**. 1995. Indexed.
Paper. $23.00. 119 pp. .... Vendor G0064

McLane, Bobbie Jones, and Desmond Walls Allen. **1850 Census of Eastern Arkansas: Arkansas, Chicot, Crittenden, Desha, Greene, Mississippi, Monroe, Phillips, Poinsett, and St. Francis Counties**. 1995. Indexed.
Paper. $23.00. 112 pp. .... Vendor G0064

McLane, Bobbie Jones, and Desmond Walls Allen. **1850 Census of North Central Arkansas: Conway, Fulton, Independence, Izard, Jackson, Lawrence, Marion, Randolph, Searcy, Van Buren, and White Counties**. 1995.
Paper. $25.00. 153 pp. .... Vendor G0064

McLane, Bobbie Jones, and Desmond Walls Allen. **1850 Census of Northwest Arkansas: Benton, Carroll, Crawford, Franklin, Johnson, Madison, Newton, Pope, and Washington Counties**. 1995. Indexed.
Paper. $27.00. 170 pp. .... Vendor G0064

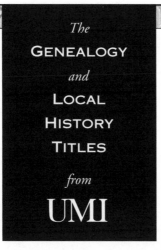

McLane, Bobbie Jones, and Desmond Walls Allen. **1850 Census of Southern Arkansas: Ashley, Bradley, Clark, Dallas, Drew, Hempstead, Lafayette, Ouachita, Pike, Polk, Sevier, and Union Counties**. 1995. Indexed.
Paper. $27.00. 182 pp. .... Vendor G0064

McLane, Bobbie Jones, and Desmond Walls Allen. **Arkansas 1850 Census Every-Name Index**. 1995. Indexed.
Cloth. $52.50. 480 pp. .... Vendor G0064

McNeil, W. K., and William M. Clements. **An Arkansas Folklore Sourcebook**. 1992.
Starting with a working description of folklore as "cultural material that is traditional and unofficial," the authors survey in detail a wide array of folk objects, activities, beliefs, and customs.
Cloth. $34.00. 281 pp. .... Vendor G0611

Morgan, James Logan. **1820 Census of the Territory of Arkansas (Reconstructed)**. (1984) reprint 1992. Indexed.
Paper. $19.00. 108 pp. .... Vendor G0064

Morgan, James Logan. **Arkansas Marriage Notices, 1819-1845**. (1984) reprint 1992. Indexed.
From extant issues of twenty newspapers.
Paper. $17.00. 86 pp. .... Vendor G0064

Morgan, James Logan. **Arkansas Marriage Records, 1808-1835**. (1981) reprint 1994. Indexed.
Paper. $18.00. 90 pp. .... Vendor G0064

Morgan, James Logan. **Arkansas Newspaper Abstracts, 1819-1845**. (1981) reprint 1992. Indexed.
Cloth, $45.00. Paper, $35.00. 364 pp. .... Vendor G0064

Payne, Dorothy. **Arkansas Pensioners, 1818-1900: Records of Some Arkansas Residents Who Applied to the Federal Government for Benefits Arising from Services in Federal Military Organizations** (Revolutionary War, War of 1812, Indian and Mexican Wars). 1985. Indexed.
Cloth. $26.50. 226 pp. .... Vendor G0610

Pope, William F. **Early Days in Arkansas: Being for the Most Part the Personal Recollections of an Old Settler**. (1895) reprint 1978. Indexed. Illus.
Contact vendor for information. 368 pp. .... Vendor G0610

Reeves, Lucy Marion. **Arkansas Families: Glimpses of Yesterday Columns from the Arkansas Gazette**. Edited by Desmond Walls Allen. 1996. Indexed.
Free surname index available from Arkansas Research.
Paper. $27.50. 228 pp. .... Vendor G0064

Riggins, J. H. **Lest We Forget, or Character Gems Gleaned from South Arkansas**. (1910) reprint 1978. Indexed.
Cloth. $20.00. 224 pp. .... Vendor G0610

Roberts, Lewis E. **The By-Name Index to the Centennial History of Arkansas**. 1994.
Includes 37,876 names from Dallas Herndon's three volumes.
Cloth, $41.50. Paper, $31.50. 260 pp. .... Vendor G0064

Shinn, Josiah H. **Pioneers and Makers of Arkansas**. (1908) reprint 1991. Indexed.
Cloth. $30.00. 423 pp. .... Vendor G0011

Sifakis. **Compendium of the Confederate Armies: Florida and Arkansas**. 1992.
Describes each regiment, the officers, and lists the battles in which they fought.
Cloth. $24.95. 144 pp. .... Vendor G0611

Thorndale, William, and William Dollarhide. **County Boundary Map Guides to the
U.S. Federal Censuses, 1790-1920: Arkansas, 1810-1920**. 1987.
$5.95. .... Vendor G0552

Turnbo, Silas Claborn. **History of the Twenty-seventh Arkansas Confederate In-
fantry**. 2nd ed. 1993. Indexed. Illus.
First-hand account.
Paper. $31.00. 159 pp. .... Vendor G0064

Arkansas County

Allen, Desmond Walls, and Bobbie Jones McLane. **Arkansas Land Patents: Arkansas, Chicot, and Desha Counties (granted through 30 June 1908)**. 1991. Indexed.
Paper. $19.00. 124 pp. .... Vendor G0064

Halliburton, W. H. **History of Arkansas County, Arkansas, from 1541-1875**. (1903)
reprint 1978. Indexed.
Cloth. $25.00. 98 pp. .... Vendor G0610

Ashley County

Allen, Desmond Walls, and Bobbie Jones McLane. **Arkansas Land Patents: Ashley
County (granted through 30 June 1908)**. 1991. Indexed.
Paper. $17.00. 87 pp. .... Vendor G0064

DeArmond, Rebecca. **Beyond Bartholomew: The Portland [AR] Area History**.
1996. Indexed. Illus.
Contains over 100 old photographs, as well as photographs of people who were
interviewed. Includes family histories of early settlers, and subject and surname
indexes.
Cloth. $33.00. 492 + 20 pp. .... Vendor G0630

Baxter County

Allen, Desmond Walls, and Bobbie Jones McLane. **Arkansas Land Patents: Baxter
County (granted through 30 June 1908)**. 1991. Indexed.
Paper. $17.00. 78 pp. .... Vendor G0064

Baxter Co. Arkansas Historical and Genealogical Society. **Baxter County Ancestors,
Volume I**.
A collection of pedigrees and family group charts of Baxter County families. The
collection of materials for Volume 2 is in progress.
Contact vendor for information. .... Vendor G0626

Baxter Co. Arkansas Historical and Genealogical Society. **Early Marriages of Baxter County**.
   A transcript of Marriage Book B and some records from Book A, which was burned in a fire in the 1890s.
Contact vendor for information. .... Vendor G0626

Baxter Co. Arkansas Historical and Genealogical Society. **Of Grave Importance**.
   Inventories of seventy-eight active cemeteries of Baxter County.
Contact vendor for information. .... Vendor G0626

Garr, Margie, comp. **Hatch, Match & Dispatch, Book 1. Index to** *The Baxter Bulletin*, Mountain Home, Arkansas: Dec. 20, 1901 thru Dec. 31, 1915.
   Includes births, marriages, and deaths.
Paper. $20.50. 140 pp. .... Vendor G0655

Garr, Margie, comp. **Hatch, Match & Dispatch, Book 2. Index to** *The Baxter Bulletin*, Mountain Home, Arkansas.
   Includes births, marriages, and deaths.
Paper. $18.50. 81 pp. .... Vendor G0655

Garr, Margie, comp. **Index to** *The Cotter Courier,* **Cotter, Arkansas:** Dec. 11, 1903 thru May 30, 1918.
   Includes births, marriages, and deaths.
Paper. $18.50. 89 pp. .... Vendor G0655

Garr, Margie, comp. **Index to** *The Cotter Record,* **Cotter, Arkansas:** Jan. 15, 1909 thru Dec. 30, 1937.
   Includes births, marriages, and deaths.
Paper. $19.50. 135 pp. .... Vendor G0655

Messick, Mary Ann. **History of Baxter County, 1873-1973**. (1973) reprint 1994.
Cloth. $54.00. 506 pp. .... Vendor G0259

Benton County

Allen, Desmond Walls, and Bobbie Jones McLane. **Arkansas Land Patents: Benton County (granted through 30 June 1908)**. 1991. Indexed.
Paper. $21.00. 154 pp. .... Vendor G0064

Boone County

Allen, Desmond Walls, and Bobbie Jones McLane. **Arkansas Land Patents: Boone County (granted through 30 June 1908)**. 1991. Indexed.
Paper. $19.00. 114 pp. .... Vendor G0064

Bradley County

Allen, Desmond Walls, and Bobbie Jones McLane. **Arkansas Land Patents: Bradley County (granted through 30 June 1908)**. 1991. Indexed.
Paper. $17.00. 95 pp. .... Vendor G0064

Calhoun County

Allen, Desmond Walls, and Bobbie Jones McLane. **Arkansas Land Patents: Calhoun County (granted through 30 June 1908)**. 1991. Indexed.
Paper. $17.00. 77 pp. .... Vendor G0064

Carroll County

Allen, Desmond Walls, and Bobbie Jones McLane. **Arkansas Land Patents: Carroll County (granted through 30 June 1908)**. 1991. Indexed.
Paper. $19.00. 114 pp. .... Vendor G0064

Chicot County

Allen, Desmond Walls, and Bobbie Jones McLane. **Arkansas Land Patents: Arkansas, Chicot, and Desha Counties (granted through 30 June 1908)**. 1991. Indexed.
Paper. $19.00. 124 pp. .... Vendor G0064

Clark County

Allen, Desmond Walls, and Bobbie Jones McLane. **Arkansas Land Patents: Clark County (granted through 30 June 1908)**. 1991. Indexed.
Paper. $17.00. 81 pp. .... Vendor G0064

Arnold, H. B., Jr., Norma S. Arnold, and Wendy Bradley Richter, eds. **We Were There, Clark Countians in World War II**. Compiled by the Clark County Book Committee. 1995. Indexed.
Cloth. $22.00. 280 pp. .... Vendor G0274

Clark County Historical Journal. Published annually since 1973. Indexed. Illus.
Paper. $12.00. Approx. 175 pp. .... Vendor G0274

Dennis, Pamela, Angela Nation, and Lori Hoggard. **1880 Census Index: Clark County, Arkansas**. 1989. Indexed.
Paper. $12.00. 81 pp. .... Vendor G0274

Dennis, Pamela, Angela Nation, and Lori Hoggard. **1900 Census Index: Clark County, Arkansas**. 1989. Indexed.
Paper. $12.00. 116 pp. .... Vendor G0274

Dennis, Pamela, Angela Nation, and Lori Hoggard. **1910 Census Index: Clark County, Arkansas**. 1989. Indexed.
Paper. $12.00. 134 pp. .... Vendor G0274

Etchieson, Meeks. **Index to Clark County, Arkansas Court Records: 1834-1839**. 1994. Indexed.
Paper. $10.00. 80 pp. .... Vendor G0274

Etchieson, Meeks. **Index to Clark County, Arkansas Court Records: 1840-1844**. 1994. Indexed.
Paper. $12.00. 110 pp. .... Vendor G0274

Etchieson, Meeks. **Index to Clark County, Arkansas Court Records: 1845-1858**. 1993. Indexed.
Paper. $12.00. 192 pp. .... Vendor G0274

Etchieson, Meeks. **Index to Probate Book B (1847-1851): Clark County, Arkansas**. 1993. Indexed.
Paper. $10.00. 79 pp. .... Vendor G0274

Marriage Licenses of Clark County, Arkansas (Unclaimed). 1988. Indexed.
Paper. $12.00. 78 pp. .... Vendor G0274

Newberry, W. L. **1890 "Census" of Clark County, Arkansas**. 1988. Indexed.
Paper. $12.00. 123 pp. .... Vendor G0274

Richter, Wendy, ed. **Clark County, Arkansas: Past and Present**. 1992. Indexed. Illus.
Cloth. $45.00. 857 pp. .... Vendor G0274

Syler, Allen B., and Bobbie Jones McLane, comps. **Clark County, Arkansas Obituaries and Death Notices 1914-1921, Volume 3**. 1995. Indexed.
Paper. $21.00. 116 pp. .... Vendor G0675

Wright, Pauline Williams, and Barbara McDow Caffee. **Clark County, Arkansas: A Genealogical Source Book**. 1982. Indexed. Illus.
   Marriage, early probate records.
Cloth. $20.00. 314 pp. .... Vendor G0076

Wright, Pauline Williams, and Barbara McDow Caffee. **Clark County, Arkansas: A Genealogical Source Book, v. II**. 1994. Indexed. Illus.
   Abstracted loose probate records and early court records in Clark County Courthouse.
Cloth. $35.00. 392 pp. .... Vendor G0076

Cleburne County

Allen, Desmond Walls, and Bobbie Jones McLane. **Arkansas Land Patents: Cleburne County (granted through 30 June 1908)**. 1991. Indexed.
Paper. $17.00. 76 pp. .... Vendor G0064

Cleveland County

Allen, Desmond Walls, and Bobbie Jones McLane. **Arkansas Land Patents: Cleveland County (granted through 30 June 1908)**. 1991. Indexed.
Paper. $17.00. 70 pp. .... Vendor G0064

Columbia County

Allen, Desmond Walls, and Bobbie Jones McLane. **Arkansas Land Patents: Columbia County (granted through 30 June 1908)**. 1991. Indexed.
Paper. $19.00. 113 pp. .... Vendor G0064

Conway County

Allen, Desmond Walls, and Bobbie Jones McLane. **Arkansas Land Patents: Conway, Faulkner, and Perry Counties (granted through 30 June 1908)**. 1991. Indexed.
Paper. $21.00. 142 pp. .... Vendor G0064

McFall, Pat. **Index to Conway County, Arkansas, Deed Books A & B, 1825-1843**. 1989. Indexed.
Paper. $17.00. 50 pp. .... Vendor G0064

Craighead County

Williams, Harry Lee. **The History of Craighead County, Arkansas**. (1977) reprint 1986.
Cloth. $48.50. 752 pp. .... Vendor G0610

Williams, Harry Lee. **History of Craighead County**. With genealogies. (1930) reprint 1993.
Cloth. $67.50. 654 pp. .... Vendor G0259

Crawford County

Allen, Desmond Walls, and Bobbie Jones McLane. **Arkansas Land Patents: Crawford County (granted through 30 June 1908)**. 1991. Indexed.
Paper. $17.00. 66 pp. .... Vendor G0064

Dallas County

Allen, Desmond Walls, and Bobbie Jones McLane. **Arkansas Land Patents: Dallas County (granted through 30 June 1908)**. 1991. Indexed.
Paper. $17.00. 55 pp. .... Vendor G0064

Desha County

Allen, Desmond Walls, and Bobbie Jones McLane. **Arkansas Land Patents: Arkansas, Chicot, and Desha Counties (granted through 30 June 1908)**. 1991. Indexed.
Paper. $19.00. 124 pp. .... Vendor G0064

Drew County

Allen, Desmond Walls, and Bobbie Jones McLane. **Arkansas Land Patents: Drew County (granted through 30 June 1908)**. 1991. Indexed.
Paper. $17.00. 88 pp. .... Vendor G0064

DeArmond, Rebecca. **Old Times Not Forgotten: A History of Drew County [AR]**. 1980. Indexed. Illus.
   A realistic picture of "life as it was" during settlement days. Emphasis is on the people and their adaptation of the natural resources of the county. Includes forty-five old photographs, as well as photos of those interviewed during the research process. Also contains family histories and subject and surname indexes.
Cloth. $22.00. 418 pp. .... Vendor G0630

Faulkner County

Allen, Desmond Walls, and Bobbie Jones McLane. **Arkansas Land Patents: Conway, Faulkner, and Perry Counties (granted through 30 June 1908)**. 1991. Indexed.
Paper. $21.00. 142 pp. .... Vendor G0064

Allen, Desmond Walls, and Henryetta Walls Vanaman. **Guide to Faulkner County, Arkansas, Loose Probate Packets, 1873-1917**. 1985. Indexed.
Paper. $13.00. 57 pp. .... Vendor G0064

Allen, Desmond Walls. **Pence Funeral Home, Conway, Arkansas, Volume I, 1881-1904**. 1986. Indexed.
   Faulkner and surrounding counties.
Paper. $21.00. 154 pp. .... Vendor G0064

Allen, Desmond Walls. **Pence Funeral Home, Conway, Arkansas, Volume II**. 1986. Indexed.
Paper. $25.00. 212 pp. .... Vendor G0064

Shubert, Dwight, comp. **Faulkner County Marriage Index 1873-1925, Volume I**. 1996.
Cloth, $32.50. Paper, $18.50. 372 pp. .... Vendor G0734

Voyles, Edsel F. **Pence Funeral Home, Conway, Arkansas, Volume III, 1926-1945**. 1989. Indexed.
Paper. $25.00. 202 pp. .... Vendor G0064

Franklin County

Allen, Desmond Walls, and Bobbie Jones McLane. **Arkansas Land Patents: Franklin County (granted through 30 June 1908)**. 1991. Indexed.
Paper. $17.00. 71 pp. .... Vendor G0064

Fulton County

Allen, Desmond Walls, and Bobbie Jones McLane. **Arkansas Land Patents: Fulton County (granted through 30 June 1908)**. 1991. Indexed.
Paper. $17.00. 97 pp. .... Vendor G0064

Allen, Desmond Walls, and Henryetta Walls Vanaman. **Fulton County, Arkansas, Folks, 1890-1893**. 1987. Indexed.
Paper. $21.00. 137 pp. .... Vendor G0064

Allen, Desmond Walls. **Fulton County, Arkansas, Tax Records 1849-1868**. 1987. Indexed.
Paper. $18.00. 104 pp. .... Vendor G0064

Garland County

Allen, Desmond Walls, and Bobbie Jones McLane. **Arkansas Land Patents: Garland County (granted through 30 June 1908)**. 1991. Indexed.
Paper. $17.00. 97 pp. .... Vendor G0064

Grant County

Allen, Desmond Walls, and Bobbie Jones McLane. **Arkansas Land Patents: Grant and Saline Counties (granted through 30 June 1908)**. 1991. Indexed.
Paper. $19.00. 126 pp. .... Vendor G0064

Greene County

Addison, Norma, and Ellen Lacey (extracted by). **Marriage Records: Greene County, Arkansas 1876-1881.** Compiled and indexed by Dawn Linden. 1989. Indexed.
Paper. $12.00. 52 pp. .... Vendor G0188

Greene County Historical & Genealogical Society. **1890 Reconstructed Census of Greene County, Arkansas from Personal Property Taxlist**. 1989. Indexed.
Paper. $12.00. 47 pp. .... Vendor G0188

Moody, Lillian (extracted by). **Veterans Discharge Extractions: Greene County,** mostly World War I era. 1990.
    Organized alphabetically.
Paper. $17.00. 111 pp. .... Vendor G0188

Rowland, George. **Fathers of the Ridge**. 4 vols. 1978-1984.
    Profiles 706 families. Organized alphabetically.
Paper. $52.00. 325 pp. .... Vendor G0188

Wood, Charles, and Helen Wood. **1880 Federal Census Greene County, Arkansas**. (1988) reprint 1996. Indexed.
Paper. $22.00. 143 pp. .... Vendor G0188

Wood, Charles, Helen Wood, and Carol Queen (extracted by). **1900 Federal Census Greene County, Arkansas**. (1990) reprint 1996. Indexed.
Paper. $32.00. 316 pp. .... Vendor G0188

Wood, Charles, and Helen Wood (extracted by). **1910 Federal Census Greene County, Arkansas**. (1991) reprint 1996. Indexed.
Paper. $42.50. 463 pp. .... Vendor G0188

Wood, Charles, and Helen Wood (extracted by). **1920 Federal Census Greene County, Arkansas**. 1994. Indexed.
Cloth, $63.00. Paper, $47.50. 505 pp. .... Vendor G0188

Wood, Charles, and Helen Wood. **Cemeteries of Greene County, Arkansas**. 2 vols. (1989) reprint 1996. Indexed.
Paper. $78.50. 828 pp. .... Vendor G0188

Hempstead County

Allen, Desmond Walls, and Bobbie Jones McLane. **Arkansas Land Patents: Hempstead County (granted through 30 June 1908)**. 1991. Indexed.
Paper. $17.00. 89 pp. .... Vendor G0064

Hempstead County Genealogical Society. **Hempstead County, Arkansas Marriages January 1, 1900 Through December 31, 1912**. Indexed.
Paper. $20.00. 210 pp. .... Vendor G0676

Hempstead County Genealogical Society. **Hempstead County, Arkansas United States Census of 1830, 1840, 1850 and Tax Lists of 1828, 1829, 1830, 1831, 1832, 1839, 1841, 1842, 1847, 1848, 1849**. Indexed.
Paper. $15.00. 137 pp. .... Vendor G0676

Hot Spring County

Allen, Desmond Walls, and Bobbie Jones McLane. **Arkansas Land Patents: Hot Spring County (granted through 30 June 1908)**. 1991. Indexed.
Paper. $17.00. 60 pp. .... Vendor G0064

Howard County

Allen, Desmond Walls, and Bobbie Jones McLane. **Arkansas Land Patents: Howard County (granted through 30 June 1908)**. 1991. Indexed.
Paper. $17.00. 100 pp. .... Vendor G0064

Independence County

Allen, Desmond Walls. **Arkansas Land Patents: Independence County (granted through 30 June 1908)**. 1991.
Paper. $17.00. 109 pp. .... Vendor G0064

Izard County

Allen, Desmond Walls, and Bobbie Jones McLane. **Arkansas Land Patents: Izard County (granted through 30 June 1908)**. 1991. Indexed.
Paper. $17.00. 106 pp. .... Vendor G0064

Allen, Desmond Walls. **Izard County, Arkansas, Tax Records 1829-1866**. 1985. Indexed.
Paper. $25.00. 178 pp. .... Vendor G0064

Jackson County

Allen, Desmond Walls, and Bobbie Jones McLane. **Arkansas Land Patents: Jackson, Lawrence, and Woodruff Counties (granted through 30 June 1908)**. 1991. Indexed.
Paper. $17.00. 79 pp. .... Vendor G0064

Jefferson County

Allen, Desmond Walls, and Bobbie Jones McLane. **Arkansas Land Patents: Jefferson County (granted through 30 June 1908)**. 1991. Indexed.
Paper. $17.00. 78 pp. .... Vendor G0064

Johnson County

Allen, Desmond Walls. **Arkansas Land Patents: Johnson County (granted through 30 June 1908)**. 1991. Indexed.
Paper. $17.00. 70 pp. .... Vendor G0064

Dewberry, Jimmie, and Doris Evans Dewberry. **Johnson County, Arkansas, 1880 Federal Census**. 1996. Indexed.
Paper. $31.00. 305 pp. .... Vendor G0064

Lafayette County

Allen, Desmond Walls, and Bobbie Jones McLane. **Arkansas Land Patents: Lafayette County (granted through 30 June 1908)**. 1991. Indexed.
Paper. $17.00. 71 pp. .... Vendor G0064

Lawrence County

Allen, Desmond Walls, and Bobbie Jones McLane. **Arkansas Land Patents: Jackson, Lawrence, and Woodruff Counties (granted through 30 June 1908)**. 1991. Indexed.
Paper. $17.00. 79 pp. .... Vendor G0064

Craig, Marion S. **Early Lawrence County, Arkansas, Records, 1817-1830**. 1996. Indexed.
  Circuit court records and Deed Book B.
Paper. $18.00. 52 pp. .... Vendor G0064

Craig, Marion S. **Lawrence County, Arkansas, Loose Probate Papers, 1815-1890**. (1986) reprint 1992.
Paper. $31.00. 300 pp. .... Vendor G0064

Knotts, Burton Ray. **Lawrence County, Arkansas, Tax Records, 1829-1838**. 1996. Indexed.
Paper. $25.00. 160 pp. .... Vendor G0064

Lincoln County

Allen, Desmond Walls, and Bobbie Jones McLane. **Arkansas Land Patents: Lincoln County (granted through 30 June 1908)**. 1991. Indexed.
Paper. $17.00. 62 pp. .... Vendor G0064

Little River County

Allen, Desmond Walls,. **Arkansas Land Patents: Little River County (granted through 30 June 1908)**. 1991. Indexed.
Paper. $17.00. 64 pp. .... Vendor G0064

Logan County

Allen, Desmond Walls and Bobbie Jones McLane. **Arkansas Land Patents: Logan County (granted through 30 June 1908)**. 1991. Indexed.
Paper. $17.00. 89 pp. .... Vendor G0064

Lonoke County

Allen, Desmond Walls. **Arkansas Land Patents: Lonoke and Prairie Counties (granted through 30 June 1908)**. 1991. Indexed.
Paper. $17.00. 73 pp. .... Vendor G0064

Martinet, Tom C. **Lonoke County Arkansas Cemetery Inscriptions**. 5 vols. 1996. Indexed. Illus.
  Every cemetery, fully indexed; any cemetery may be purchased individually. Send S.A.S.E. for a current price list.
Paper. $135.00/set. 1,995 pp. .... Vendor G0535

Martinet, Tom C. **Master Index to Lonoke County Arkansas Cemetery Inscriptions**. 1996.
Spiral bound. $25.00. 310 pp. .... Vendor G0535

Shubert, Dwight, comp. **Lonoke County [Arkansas] Marriage Index 1921-1951, Volume 2**. 1996. Indexed.
Cloth, $32.50. Paper, $18.50. 372 pp. .... Vendor G0734

Madison County

Allen, Desmond Walls, and Bobbie Jones McLane. **Arkansas Land Patents: Madison County (granted through 30 June 1908)**. 1991. Indexed.
Paper. $21.00. 149 pp. .... Vendor G0064

Marion County

Allen, Desmond Walls, and Bobbie Jones McLane. **Arkansas Land Patents: Marion County (granted through 30 June 1908)**. 1991. Indexed.
Paper. $17.00. 105 pp. .... Vendor G0064

Allen, Desmond Walls. **Marion County, Arkansas, Tax Records 1841-1866**. 1988. Indexed.
Paper. $25.00. 179 pp. .... Vendor G0064

Weber, Nancie Todd. **1870 Marion County, Arkansas Census (Edited/Annotated)**. 1994. Indexed.
   Some spousal surnames, family locations 1860/1880.
Paper. $15.00. 87 pp. .... Vendor G0337

Miller County

Allen, Desmond Walls, and Bobbie Jones McLane. **Arkansas Land Patents: Miller County (granted through 30 June 1908)**. 1991. Indexed.
Paper. $17.00. 61 pp. .... Vendor G0064

Montgomery County

Allen, Desmond Walls, and Bobbie Jones McLane. **Arkansas Land Patents: Montgomery County (granted through 30 June 1908)**. 1991. Indexed.
Paper. $17.00. 71 pp. .... Vendor G0064

Nevada County

Allen, Desmond Walls, and Bobbie Jones McLane. **Arkansas Land Patents: Nevada County (granted through 30 June 1908)**. 1991. Indexed.
Paper. $17.00. 79 pp. .... Vendor G0064

Hempstead County Genealogical Society. **Nevada County, Arkansas United States Census of 1880**. Indexed. Illus.
Paper. $20.00. 163 pp. .... Vendor G0676

Newton County

Allen, Desmond Walls, and Bobbie Jones McLane. **Arkansas Land Patents: Newton County (granted through 30 June 1908)**. 1991. Indexed.
Paper. $17.00. 97 pp. .... Vendor G0064

Lackey, Walter F. **History of Newton County**. (1950) reprint 1991.
Cloth. $47.00. 423 pp. .... Vendor G0259

Ouachita County

Allen, Desmond Walls, and Bobbie Jones McLane. **Arkansas Land Patents: Ouachita County (granted through 30 June 1908)**. 1991. Indexed.
Paper. $17.00. 99 pp. .... Vendor G0064

Ozark Region

Turnbo, Silas Claborn. **Turnbo's Tales of the Ozarks: Bear Stories**. Edited by Desmond Walls Allen. 1988. Indexed.
Paper. $18.00. 148 pp. .... Vendor G0064

Turnbo, Silas Claborn. **Turnbo's Tales of the Ozarks: Biographical Stories**. Edited by Desmond Walls Allen. (1987) rev. ed. 1989. Indexed.
  Free surname index for all Turnbo volumes available from Arkansas Research
Paper. $21.00. 180 pp. .... Vendor G0064

Turnbo, Silas Claborn. **Turnbo's Tales of the Ozarks: Deer Hunting Stories**. Edited by Desmond Walls Allen. 1989. Indexed.
Paper. $18.00. 101 pp. .... Vendor G0064

Turnbo, Silas Claborn. **Turnbo's Tales of the Ozarks: Incidents, Mean Tricks and Fictitious Stories**. Edited by Desmond Walls Allen. (1988) rev. ed. 1990. Indexed.
Paper. $18.00. 99 pp. .... Vendor G0064

Turnbo, Silas Claborn. **Turnbo's Tales of the Ozarks: Panther Stories**. Edited by Desmond Walls Allen. 1989.
Paper. $21.00. 142 pp. .... Vendor G0064

Turnbo, Silas Claborn. **Turnbo's Tales of the Ozarks: Schools, Indians, Hard Times and More Stories**. Edited by Desmond Walls Allen. (1987) rev. ed. 1989. Indexed.
Paper. $21.00. 138 pp. .... Vendor G0064

Turnbo, Silas Claborn. **Turnbo's Tales of the Ozarks: Snakes, Birds and Insect Stories**. Edited by Desmond Walls Allen. 1989. Indexed.
Paper. $18.00. 96 pp. .... Vendor G0064

Turnbo, Silas Claborn. **Turnbo's Tales of the Ozarks: War and Guerrilla Stories**. Edited by Desmond Walls Allen. (1987) rev. ed. 1989. Indexed.
Paper. $21.00. 165 pp. .... Vendor G0064

Turnbo, Silas Claborn. **Turnbo's Tales of the Ozarks: Wolf Stories**. Edited by Desmond Walls Allen. 1989. Indexed.
Paper. $21.00. 141 pp. .... Vendor G0064

Perry County

Allen, Desmond Walls, and Bobbie Jones McLane. **Arkansas Land Patents: Conway, Faulkner, and Perry Counties (granted through 30 June 1908)**. 1991. Indexed.
Paper. $21.00. 142 pp. .... Vendor G0064

Pike County

Allen, Desmond Walls, and Bobbie Jones McLane. **Arkansas Land Patents: Pike County (granted through 30 June 1908)**. 1991. Indexed.
Paper. $17.00. 83 pp. .... Vendor G0064

Polk County

Allen, Desmond Walls. **Arkansas Land Patents: Polk County (granted through 30 June 1908)**. 1991. Indexed.
Paper. $17.00. 93 pp. .... Vendor G0064

Pope County

Allen, Desmond Walls, and Bobbie Jones McLane. **Arkansas Land Patents: Pope County (granted through 30 June 1908)**. 1991. Indexed.
Paper. $17.00. 81 pp. .... Vendor G0064

Ballard, James, and Alta Ballard. **Cemeteries of the Dwight Mission, London and Scotia Areas of Pope County, Arkansas**. 1996. Indexed.
Paper. $12.50. vi + 187 pp. .... Vendor G0677

Prairie County

Allen, Desmond Walls. **Arkansas Land Patents: Lonoke and Prairie Counties (granted through 30 June 1908)**. 1991. Indexed.
Paper. $17.00. 73 pp. .... Vendor G0064

Sickel, Marilyn Hambrick. **Prairie County Arkansas Cemetery Inscriptions**. 1989. Indexed.
Paper. $25.00. 275 pp. .... Vendor G0537

Sickel, Marilyn Hambrick, comp. **Prairie County, Arkansas Pioneer Family Interviews**. 1989. Indexed.
Paper. $30.00. 320 pp. .... Vendor G0537

Sickel, Marilyn Hambrick, comp. **White River Journal—Des Arc, Arkansas, Abstracts of Death Notices**. 1996. Indexed.
The first fifty years, August 1907-August 1957.
Paper. $15.00. .... Vendor G0537

Pulaski County

Allen, Desmond Walls, and Bobbie Jones McLane. **Arkansas Land Patents: Pulaski County (granted through 30 June 1908)**. 1991. Indexed.
Paper. $17.00. 80 pp. .... Vendor G0064

Counts, Mrs. William H. **A Compendium of Arkansas Genealogy**. 2 vols. in 1. Indexed.
Over 20,000 listings; Little Rock (Pulaski County) area.
Cloth. $30.00. 575 pp. .... Vendor G0170

Crawford, Sybil F. **Jubilee: Mount Holly Cemetery, Little Rock, Arkansas, Its First 150 Years**. 1993. Indexed. Illus.
History of the "Westminster Abbey of Arkansas" includes valuable genealogical data.
Cloth. $39.00. 142 pp. .... Vendor G0039

Crawford, Sybil F., and Mary F. Worthen. **Mount Holly Cemetery, Little Rock, Arkansas, Burial Index, 1843-1993**. 1993. Indexed.
Full-name index (approximately 5,000 entries) giving name of deceased, vital data, parentage, spouse, military service, fraternal and social relationships, special distinctions, occupation.
Paper. $20.00. 274 pp. .... Vendor G0039

Martinet, Tom C. **Location and Driving Directions to All Known Cemeteries,** Plus Their Records We Have Found. 2 vols.
This is an on-going project, with two books finished for cemeteries in Pulaski County.
Send a S.A.S.E. for a current price sheet. .... Vendor G0535

Randolph County

Allen, Desmond Walls, and Bobbie Jones McLane. **Arkansas Land Patents: Randolph County (granted through 30 June 1908)**. 1991. Indexed.
Paper. $17.00. 82 pp. .... Vendor G0064

Knotts, Burton Ray. **1890 Census of Randolph County, Arkansas, Reconstructed from the Personal Property Tax List**. (1988) reprint 1996. Indexed.
Paper. $21.00. 113 pp. .... Vendor G0064

Knotts, Burton Ray. **Randolph County, Arkansas, Marriages, 1821-1893**. 1996. Indexed.
Paper. $27.00. 170 pp. .... Vendor G0064

Knotts, Burton Ray. **Randolph County, Arkansas, Marriages, 1893-1923**. 1996. Indexed.
Paper. $27.00. 170 pp. .... Vendor G0064

Saline County

Allen, Desmond Walls, and Bobbie Jones McLane. **Arkansas Land Patents: Grant and Saline Counties (granted through 30 June 1908)**. 1991. Indexed. Paper. $19.00. 126 pp. .... Vendor G0064

Bruce, Virginia M. **Original Land Entries Saline County Arkansas**. 1982. Indexed. Paper. $22.50. 64 pp. .... Vendor G0191

Scott County

Allen, Desmond Walls, and Bobbie Jones McLane. **Arkansas Land Patents: Scott County (granted through 30 June 1908)**. 1991. Indexed. Paper. $17.00. 75 pp. .... Vendor G0064

Searcy County

Allen, Desmond Walls, and Bobbie Jones McLane. **Arkansas Land Patents: Searcy County (granted through 30 June 1908)**. 1991. Indexed. Paper. $17.00. 85 pp. .... Vendor G0064

Sebastian County

Allen, Desmond Walls, and Bobbie Jones McLane. **Arkansas Land Patents: Sebastian County (granted through 30 June 1908)**. 1991. Indexed. Paper. $17.00. 78 pp. .... Vendor G0064

Lester, Gary, and Tina Lester. **Fort Smith, Arkansas, National Cemetery**. 1995. Indexed. Paper. $28.00. 165 pp. .... Vendor G0064

Sevier County

Allen, Desmond Walls, and Bobbie Jones McLane. **Arkansas Land Patents: Sevier County (granted through 30 June 1908)**. 1991. Indexed. Paper. $17.00. 86 pp. .... Vendor G0064

Sharp County

Allen, Desmond Walls, and Bobbie Jones McLane. **Arkansas Land Patents: Sharp County (granted through 30 June 1908)**. 1991. Indexed. Paper. $17.00. 95 pp. .... Vendor G0064

Allen, Desmond Walls. **Index to the Sharp County Record Newspaper, Evening Shade, Arkansas 1877-1883**. (1986) 2nd ed. 1993. Indexed.
Paper. $23.00. 113 pp. .... Vendor G0064

Stone County

Allen, Desmond Walls and Bobbie Jones McLane. **Arkansas Land Patents: Stone County (granted through 30 June 1908)**. 1991. Indexed.
Paper. $17.00. 73 pp. .... Vendor G0064

Union County

Allen, Desmond Walls, and Bobbie Jones McLane. **Arkansas Land Patents: Union County (granted through 30 June 1908)**. 1991. Indexed.
Paper. $21.00. 138 pp. .... Vendor G0064

Van Buren County

Allen, Desmond Walls, and Bobbie Jones McLane. **Arkansas Land Patents: Van Buren County (granted through 30 June 1908)**. 1991. Indexed.
Paper. $17.00. 81 pp. .... Vendor G0064

Washington County

Allen, Desmond Walls, and Bobbie Jones McLane. **Arkansas Land Patents: Washington County (granted through 30 June 1908)**. 1991. Indexed.
Paper. $25.00. 197 pp. .... Vendor G0064

Lester, Gary, and Tina Lester. **Fayetteville, Arkansas, National Cemetery**. 1995. Indexed.
Paper. $23.00. 92 pp. .... Vendor G0064

White County

Allen, Desmond Walls, and Bobbie Jones McLane. **Arkansas Land Patents: White County (granted through 30 June 1908)**. 1991. Indexed.
Paper. $17.00. 75 pp. .... Vendor G0064

Woodruff County

Allen, Desmond Walls, and Bobbie Jones McLane. **Arkansas Land Patents: Jackson, Lawrence, and Woodruff Counties (granted through 30 June 1908)**. 1991. Indexed.
Paper. $17.00. 79 pp. .... Vendor G0064

Yell County

Allen, Desmond Walls, and Bobbie Jones McLane. **Arkansas Land Patents: Yell County (granted through 30 June 1908)**. 1991. Indexed.
Paper. $17.00. 83 pp. .... Vendor G0064

California

Statewide and Regional References

Bancroft, Hubert H. **California Pioneer Register and Index, 1542-1848,** Including Inhabitants . . . 1769-1800 and a List of Pioneers. (1884-90) reprint 1990.
Cloth. $20.00. 392 pp. .... Vendor G0011

Banvard, Theodore James Fleming. **Goodenows Who Originated in Sudbury, Massachusetts 1638 A.D.** 1994. Indexed. Illus.
Cloth. $78.50. 952 pp. .... Vendor G0116

Bolton, Herbert E. **The Spanish Borderlands: A Chronicle of Old Florida and the Southwest**. (1921) reprint 1996.
   In narrative prose, Bolton recounts the Spanish exploration and the permanent settlement of Old Florida, New Mexico, Texas, Louisiana, and California.
Paper. $22.50. 320 pp. .... Vendor G0611

California Genealogical Society. **Genealogy Success Stories: Personal Problem-solving Accounts That Encourage, Enlighten and Inspire You**. 1995. Indexed.
Paper. $12.00. 134 pp. .... Vendor G0628

Carr, Peter E. **San Francisco Passenger Departure Lists—Vols. I-IV**. 1991-1993. Indexed.
Paper. $15.95/vol. 138 + 160 + 204 pp. .... Vendor G0496

Church, Madeline. **Emma LeDoux and the Trunk Murder**. 1995. Illus.
Paper. $11.45. 70 pp. .... Vendor G0461

Deeter, Judy A. **Veterans Who Applied for Land in Southern California 1851-1911**. 1993.
Paper. $8.00. 32 pp. .... Vendor G0467

Dilts, Bryan Lee, comp. **1860 California Census Index: Heads of Households and Other Surnames in Household Index**. 2nd ed. 1984.
Cloth. $175.00. 960 pp. .... Vendor G0552

Family History Library. **Family History Centers: California**.
Free. 3 pp. .... Vendor G0629

Family History Library. **Research Outline: California**.
Leaflet. $.25. 9 pp. .... Vendor G0629

Faulkinbury, Jim W., CGRS. **The Foreign-Born Voters of California in 1872**. 1994.
  Alphabetized statewide listing from voter rolls. Includes name, age, nativity, and date, place and court of naturalization; 61,691 voters listed.
Microfiche, $45.00. 1,168 pp. .... Vendor G0489

Genealogical Society of North Orange County California. **The Yorba Linda Star: Death Notices & Obituaries, Volume I, 1920-1929**. 1993. Indexed.
Paper. $24.00. 192 pp. .... Vendor G0529

Kot and Thomson. **California Cemetery Inscription Sources: Print and Microform**. 1994.
  A comprehensive bibliography including books, periodicals, and manuscript sources as well as LDS Family History Library microfilm and microfiche numbers. A valuable resource for California researchers.
$29.95. 291 pp. .... Vendor G0611

Morebeck, Nancy Justus. **Northern California Marriage Index 1850-1860**. 1993. Indexed.
Paper. $22.00 incl. p&h; CA tax $1.45. 203 pp. .... Vendor G0172

Nicklas, Laurie. **The California Locator. A Directory of Public Records for Locating People Dead or Alive in California**. 1996 edition.
Paper. $27.00. 152 pp. .... Vendor G0678

Books from the Rose Family Association
Christine Rose, C.G., C.G.L., F.A.S.G.
1474 Montelegre Drive, San Jose, California 95120

Nicknames: Past & Present, 2nd ed., by Christine Rose. 1995. v + 41 pp., paper.

Family Associations: Organization & Management, 2nd ed., by Christine Rose. 1994. xii + 71 pp., paper.

Robert Rose of Wethersfield and Branford, Connecticut Who Came on the Ship Francis in 1634, by Christine Rose. 1983. xvi + 512 pp., cloth.

The Brothers Rev. Robert Rose and Rev. Charles Rose of Colonial Virginia and Scotland, by Christine Rose. 1985. xvi + 318 pp., cloth.

Declarations of Intention of Santa Clara County, California 1850–1870, by Christine Rose. iii + 76 pp., paper.

Preliminary Inventory of the Land Entry Papers of the General Land Office, by Harry B. Yoshpe and Philip P. Brower. 1996. v + 77 pp., paper.

Abstracts of Early Virginia Rose Estates to 1850, by Christine Rose. 1972. 48 pp., paper.

Frederick Rose Family of Wayne and Hardin Cos., Tennessee, North Carolina, and Virginia. 1980. 77 pp., paper.

Family of Rose of Kilravock [Scotland]. (1848) reprint 1981. viii + 531 pp., cloth.

Rose War Files: Land Bounty Records, by Christine Rose. x + 210 pp., paper.

Paradise Genealogical Society. **Genealogical Library Collection Shelf List, Paradise Genealogical Society**. 1995.

This is a list of the holdings of the Paradise Society as of December 15, 1995; includes publications from across the United States.

Spiral binding. $6.00 postpaid. 71 pp. .... Vendor G0736

Parker, J. Carlyle. **An Index to the Biographies in 19th Century California County Histories**. (1979) reprint 1994.

Microfiche, $15.95. 279 pp. .... Vendor G0492

Parker, J. Carlyle. **A Personal Name Index to Orton's "Records of California Men in the War of the Rebellion, 1861 to 1867."** (1978) reprint 1994.

Microfiche, $10.95. 153 pp. .... Vendor G0492

Shumway, Burgess McK. **California Ranchos: Patented Private Land Grants Listed by County**. Edited by Michael and Mary Burgess. 1941. Indexed.

A listing of the Spanish and Mexican grants and the subsequent patents granted by the U.S. authorities.

Paper. $19.95. 144 pp. .... Vendor G0632

Smith, Clifford N. **Gold! German Transcontinental Travelers to California, 1849-1851**. German-American Genealogical Research Monograph Number 24. 1988.
ISBN 0-915162-76-8.

Paper. $20.00. iii + 62 pp. .... Vendor G0491

Solano County Genealogical Society, Inc. **Index to the DAR "Records of the Families of the California Pioneers," Volumes 1-27**. 1988. Indexed.

Paper. $10.00 + $1.50 p&h. 55 pp. .... Vendor G0184

Southern California Genealogical Society. **American Indian Related Books in the SCGS Library**.

Paper. $.75. 4 pp. .... Vendor G0656

Southern California Genealogical Society. **Sources of Genealogical Help in California Libraries**. Rev. ed. 1996.

Paper. $2.00. 7 pp. .... Vendor G0656

Southern California Genealogical Society. **UCLA Library: Sources of Genealogical Help**.

Paper. $1.75. 9 pp. .... Vendor G0656

Thorndale, William, and William Dollarhide. **County Boundary Map Guides to the U.S. Federal Censuses, 1790-1920: California, 1850-1920**.

$5.95. .... Vendor G0552

Dr. Frank L. & Odette J. Kaufman
2794 Hyannis Way
Sacramento CA 95827
Northern California

Alameda County

Baker, Joseph E., ed. **Past & Present of Alameda County.** 2 vols. (1914) reprint 1993.
 Volume I: History.
 Volume II: Biography.
 Cloth. $47.00/Vol. I. $59.50/Vol. II. $99.50/Both in 1 vol. 463 +
 594 pp. .... Vendor G0259

Munro-Fraser, J. P. **History of Alameda County,** Including . . . the Early History &
Settlement; a Full Political History; Separate History of Each Township; and Incidents
of Pioneer Life. (1883) reprint 1993.
Cloth. $99.50. 1,001 pp. .... Vendor G0259

Amador County

Cissna, Catherine A., and Madeline Church. **A Few of Our Friends in the Amador
County Cemeteries.** 1994.
Paper. $14.45. 87 pp. .... Vendor G0461

Butte County

Gilbert, Frank T. (Vol. I), and Harry L. Wells (Vol. II). **History of Butte County.**
Volume I, History of California from 1513 to 1850. Volume II, History of Butte
County. 2 vols in 1. (1881) reprint 1994.
Cloth. $34.50. 305 pp. .... Vendor G0259

Paradise Genealogical Society. **Bangor Cemetery, Bangor, Butte County, California.** 1994.
Paper. $3.50. 16 pp. .... Vendor G0736

Paradise Genealogical Society. **Butte County Cemetery 1862-1980 Oroville, Butte
County, California.** 1994.
Paper. $5.00. 33 pp. .... Vendor G0736

Paradise Genealogical Society. **Cherokee Cemetery 1863-1993, Butte County, California.** 1993.
Paper. $5.00. 32 pp. .... Vendor G0736

Paradise Genealogical Society. **Upham Cemetery 1858-June 1993, Butte County,
California.** 1993.
Paper. $3.50. 16 pp. .... Vendor G0736

Colusa County

McComish, Charles Davis, and Rebecca T. Lambert. **History of Colusa & Glenn
Counties,** with Biographical Sketches of Leading Men & Women of the Counties.
(1918) reprint 1993.
Cloth. $99.50. 1,074 pp. .... Vendor G0259

Rogers, Justus H. **Colusa County:** Its History Traced from a State of Nature Through the Early Period of Settlement & Development to the Present Day [1891]. With Biographical Sketches of Pioneers & Prominent Residents. (1891) reprint 1993. Cloth. $49.50. 473 pp. .... Vendor G0259

Contra Costa County

History of Contra Costa County, with Biographical Sketches of Leading Men & Women of the County . . . from the Early Days to [1926]. (1926) reprint 1993. Cloth. $105.00. 1,102 pp. .... Vendor G02509

Fresno County

Memorial & Biographical History of the Counties of Fresno, Tulare & Kern. 1892. Cloth. $84.50. 822 pp. .... Vendor G0259

Glenn County

McComish, Charles Davis, and Rebecca T. Lambert. **History of Colusa & Glenn Counties,** with Biographical Sketches of Leading Men & Women of the Counties. (1918) reprint 1993. Cloth. $99.50. 1,074 pp. .... Vendor G0259

Kern County

Memorial & Biographical History of the Counties of Fresno, Tulare & Kern. 1892. Cloth. $84.50. 822 pp. .... Vendor G0259

Lake County

Menefee, C. A. **Historical and Descriptive Sketchbook of Napa, Sonoma, Lake, and Mendocino.** (1873) reprint 1993. Indexed. Illus. Cloth. $29.95 + $3.50 p&h. 268 pp. .... Vendor G0184

Palmer, Lyman L. **History of Napa & Lake Counties,** Comprising Their Geography, Geology, Topography . . . Also Extended Sketches of the Milling, Mining, Pisciculture & Wine Interests. With Biographical Sketches. (1881) reprint 1995. Cloth. $92.50. 600 + 291 pp. .... Vendor G0259

Lassen County

Fairfield, Asa Merrill. **Fairfield's Pioneer History of Lassen County,** Containing Everything That Can Be Learned About It from the Beginning of the World . . . to 1870. (1916) reprint 1993. Cloth. $55.00. 506 pp. .... Vendor G0259

Los Angeles County

Clary, Jeanne B. **Indexes to Los Angeles County Marriages, Book 1: August 1851-March 1870**.
Paper. $5.00. 94 pp. .... Vendor G0656

Clary, Jeanne B. **Los Angeles County Marriages, Book 2: March 1870-December 1872**.
Paper. $2.25. 30 pp. .... Vendor G0656

Clary, Jeanne B. **Los Angeles County Marriages, Book 3: January 1873-July 1875**.
Paper. $3.50. 61 pp. .... Vendor G0656

Clary, Jeanne B. **Los Angeles County Marriages, Book 4: July 1875-May 1877**.
Paper. $3.50. 62 pp. .... Vendor G0656

Schulz, Peggy. **Los Angeles County Cemeteries to 1940**.
Paper. $2.00. 9 pp. .... Vendor G0656

Marin County

Gowdy, Catherine Lutes, comp. **Coroner's Inquest Book Number 1, Marin County, California 1857-1910**. 1993.
Paper. $12.00. 40 pp. .... Vendor G0679

Marin County Genealogical Society. **Great Register of Marin County, California 1890**. Photocopied from microfilm at California State Library. 1992.
Spiral binding. $6.00. Approx. 40 pp. .... Vendor G0679

Mendocino County

Menefee, C. A. **Historical and Descriptive Sketchbook of Napa, Sonoma, Lake, and Mendocino**. (1873) reprint 1993. Indexed. Illus.
Cloth. $29.95 + $3.50 p&h. 268 pp. .... Vendor G0184

Merced County

Los Banos Genealogical Society. **Cemetery Index—1862-1989**. (1994) reprint 1996.
Paper. $15.00. CA residents add $1.09 tax. 103 pp. .... Vendor G0573

Los Banos Genealogical Society. **Cemetery Index—1990-1995**. 1996.
Paper. $10.00. CA residents add $.73 tax. 50 pp. .... Vendor G0573

Napa County

History of Solano & Napa County. Volume II, Biographical. (1926) reprint 1995.
Cloth. $52.50. 495 pp. .... Vendor G0259

Menefee, C. A. **Historical and Descriptive Sketchbook of Napa, Sonoma, Lake, and Mendocino**. (1873) reprint 1993. Indexed. Illus.
Cloth. $29.95 + $3.50 p&h. 268 pp. .... Vendor G0184

Palmer, Lyman L. **History of Napa & Lake Counties,** Comprising Their Geography, Geology, Topography . . . Also Extended Sketches of the Milling, Mining, Pisciculture & Wine Interests. With Biographical Sketches. (1881) reprint 1995.
Cloth. $92.50. 600 + 291 pp. .... Vendor G0259

Orange County

Genealogical Society of North Orange County California. **The Yorba Linda Star: Death Notices & Obituaries, Volume I, 1920-1929**. 1993. Indexed.
Paper. $24.00. 192 pp. .... Vendor G0529

San Francisco County

Annals of San Francisco . . . with Biographical Memoirs of Some Prominent Citizens. (1855) reprint 1993.
Cloth. $84.50. 824 pp. .... Vendor G0259

Beals, Kathleen C. **Index to San Franciso Marriage Returns 1850-1858**. 1992.
Paper. $15.00. 109 pp. .... Vendor G0628

Beals, Kathleen C. **San Francisco Probate Index 1880-1906: A Partial Reconstruction**. 1996.
Paper. $15.00. 239 pp. .... Vendor G0628

Beals, Kathleen C. **A Useful Guide to Researching San Francisco Ancestry**. 1994.
Paper. $12.00. 60 pp. .... Vendor G0628

Carr, Peter E. **San Francisco Passenger Departure Lists—Vols. I-IV**. 1991-1993. Indexed.
Paper. $15.95/vol. 138 + 160 + 204 pp. .... Vendor G0496

Young, John Philip. **San Francisco: A History of the Pacific Coast Metropolis**. 2 vols. (1912) reprint 1993.
Cloth. $99.50. xxx + 969 pp. .... Vendor G0259

San Mateo County

Tessendorf, Kenneth R., comp. **A Finding Aid for Naturalization Documents of San Mateo County, California**. Edited by Helen M. Graves. 1995.
Spiral binding. $8.00. 50 pp. .... Vendor G0737

Santa Barbara County

History of Santa Barbara & Ventura Counties, with Illustrations & Biographical Sketches of Its Prominent Men & Pioneers. (1883) reprint 1993.
Cloth. $49.50. 477 pp. .... Vendor G0259

Santa Clara County

Rose, Christine. **Declarations of Intention of Santa Clara County, California 1850-1870**. Indexed.
Paper. Contact vendor for information. iii + 76 pp. .... Vendor G0474

Solano County

Cowart, Cordell. **Resources at the Library of the Solano County Genealogical Society, Inc.—December 1992**. 1994.
Paper. $12.50 + $2.50 p&h. 176 pp. .... Vendor G0184

Cowart, Cordell. **Solano County, California—1852 State Census Index**. 1992. Indexed.
Paper. $12.50 + $2.50 p&h. 60 pp. .... Vendor G0184

Cowart, Cordell. **Solano County, California—1993 Pioneer File Index**. 1993. Indexed.
Paper. $5.00 + $1.50 p&h. 26 pp. .... Vendor G0184

Cunningham, Rosalie S. (Neall), and Dolores (Vega) McLean. **Solano County Cemeteries Volume II—Vacaville, Elmira & Surrounding Areas**. 1989. Indexed.
See below under "Setterquist, Ruth" for Volume I.
Paper. $15.00 + $2.50 p&h. 138 pp. .... Vendor G0184

Hayes, Michael J. **Solano County Cemeteries Volume III—Benicia City Cemetery Burials**. 1994. Indexed.
Paper. $17.00 + $2.50 p&h. 162 pp. .... Vendor G0184

History of Solano & Napa County. Volume II, Biographical. (1926) reprint 1995.
Cloth. $52.50. 495 pp. .... Vendor G0259

Setterquist, Ruth. **Solano County Cemeteries Volume I—Rockville Cemetery**. 1986. Indexed.
Paper. $9.50 + $1.50 p&h. 93 pp. .... Vendor G0184

Smith, Gloria, and Pat Cook. **Marriages of Solano County, California, 1853-1893 (Marriage License Applications)**. 1982. Indexed.
Paper. $10.50 + $2.50 p&h. 100 pp. .... Vendor G0184

Solano County Genealogical Society, Inc. **Index to the Great Register of Solano County, California, 1890**. Compiled by Corky Cowart. 1996.
Paper. $12.00 + $2.50 p&h. 96 pp. .... Vendor G0184

Solano County Genealogical Society, Inc. **Ninth U.S. Census—1870 Index of Solano County, California**. 1988. Indexed.
Paper. $17.00 + $2.50 p&h. 164 pp. .... Vendor G0184

Solano County Genealogical Society, Inc. **Solano County, California Will Book I, 1856-1876**. 1988. Indexed.
Paper. $12.50 + $2.50 p&h. 64 pp. .... Vendor G0184

Wood, Alley & Co. (J. P. Munro Fraser). **History of Solano County.** (1879) reprint 1995. Indexed. Illus.
Cloth. $34.95 + $3.50 p&h. 540 pp. .... Vendor G0184

Sonoma County

Hively, Emma A. Street. **The Patriarch of the Valley—Isaac W. Sullivan.** 1977. Indexed. Illus.
Paper. $5.00 + $1.50 p&h. 115 pp. .... Vendor G0184

Menefee, C. A. **Historical and Descriptive Sketchbook of Napa, Sonoma, Lake, and Mendocino.** (1873) reprint 1993. Indexed. Illus.
Cloth. $29.95 + $3.50 p&h. 268 pp. .... Vendor G0184

Sonoma County Genealogical Society. **1890 Census Sonoma County California Reconstructed.**
  Alphabetical listing of 18,008 people; 55% of all 1890 Sonoma Co. residents. Includes surname, given name, age, occupation, birthplace, and residence. Entries keyed to source of information.
Paper. $25.00. .... Vendor G0605

Sonoma County Genealogical Society. **1895 Map of Sonoma County.**
  Location of old and extinct towns and schools when given. Includes typed lists of all county school districts and towns with map coordinates. 2' x 3', sepia toned.
Map. $3.50. .... Vendor G0605

Sonoma County Genealogical Society. **Amended Index Sonoma County Homestead Declarations 1860-1920.** 3rd printing.
  Alphabetical listing, date and Recorder's official page number; 4,600 entries.
Paper. $8.00. 60 pp. .... Vendor G0605

Sonoma County Genealogical Society. **Great Register of Voters Sonoma County 1890.**
  Includes 8,500 names. Gives full name, nativity, residence, age, occupation, and place of naturalization if applicable.
Paper. $12.00. 204 pp. plus appendices. .... Vendor G0605

Sonoma County Genealogical Society. **Index to the Sonoma Searcher V 1, #1-V 15, #4 (1973-1988).**
  Includes names, cemeteries, churches, cities/towns, lodges, schools, etc. Approximately 8,100 listings under 5,800 entries.
Microfiche (set of 3). Postpaid $4.50. .... Vendor G0605

Sonoma County Genealogical Society. **Sonoma County Coroner's Inquests 1852-1896.** Indexed.
  Summaries of approximately 800 cases heard in Coroner's proceedings, each outlined as it appears in the official record. Family information and witnesses.
Paper. $5.50. 115 pp. .... Vendor G0605

Sonoma County Genealogical Society. **Sonoma County Death Records 1873-1905.**
  Includes 11,000 names. Alphabetical listing by years. Name, date, marital status, nativity and burial site. Recorder's Office reference numbers.
Paper. $11.00. 165 pp. .... Vendor G0605

Sonoma County Genealogical Society. **Sonoma County Delayed Birth Certificates 1855-1971**.
  Approximately 11,000 names. Lists alphabetically principal name, date and place of birth, and county reference page. Family members; 3,350 principal entries.
Paper. $10.00. 152 pp. .... Vendor G0605

Sonoma County Genealogical Society. **Sonoma County Marriages 1847-1902**.
  Includes 7,600 marriages listed alphabetically by both groom and bride's maiden name. Book and page number for Recorder's Office reference. Attending officials and their affiliations.
Paper. $15.00. 300 pp. .... Vendor G0605

Sonoma County Genealogical Society. **Surname Directory of Sonoma County Genealogical Society 1991-1992**.
  Alphabetical listing of 3,950 surnames being researched by Society members. Gives country of origin, dates and migration path, and member searching each name.
Paper. $4.50. 90 pp. .... Vendor G0605

Stanislaus County

History of Stanislaus County, with Illustrations Descriptive of Its Scenery, Farms, Residences, Public Buildings, Etc., with Biographical Sketches of Prominent Citizens. (1881) reprint 1994.
Cloth. $35.00. 254 pp. .... Vendor G0259

Tulare County

Memorial & Biographical History of the Counties of Fresno, Tulare & Kern. 1892.
Cloth. $84.50. 822 pp. .... Vendor G0259

Tuolumne County

Lang, Herbert O. **History of Tuolumne County.** With Biographies. (1882) reprint 1994.
Cloth. $57.50. 509 + 48 pp. .... Vendor G0259

Ventura County

History of Santa Barbara & Ventura Counties, with Illustrations & Biographical Sketches of Its Prominent Men & Pioneers. (1883) reprint 1993.
Cloth. $49.50. 477 pp. .... Vendor G0259

Yuba County

Mathews, Barbara Stacy. **The Great Register. 1880 Voter Registration of Yuba County, California**. 1993. Self-indexed.
  Eighteen-eighty voter register of Yuba County, California. Some deaths and/or place of relocations are documented.
Paper. $37.50. 212 pp. .... Vendor G0430

Mathews, Barbara Stacy. **Miscellaneous Record Book, Yuba County, California. Book I**. 1994. Indexed.
Paper. $40.00. 290 pp. .... Vendor G0430

Mathews, Barbara Stacy. **Probate Court Records, Yuba County, California, June 3, 1850-March 29, 1852**. 1994. Indexed.
Paper. $21.50. 72 pp. .... Vendor G0430

 Colorado

Statewide and Regional References

Colorado Genealogical Society, Inc. **Colorado Families, Vol. I-A**. 1981. Indexed.
This valuable collection contains biographies and genealogical information on 134 families who were pioneers in Colorado prior to statehood in 1876. Includes maps, early family photographs, plus an every-name index of over 40,000 names.
Cloth. $20.50. 752 pp. .... Vendor G0174

Colorado Genealogical Society, Inc. **Genealogical Index to the Records of the Society of Colorado Pioneers**. 1990. Indexed.
Includes records of meetings from the 1850s to the 1900s when the Society ceased to meet.
Paper. $17.50. 120 pp. .... Vendor G0174

Colorado Genealogical Society, Inc. **Subject Index to the Colorado Genealogist, Vols. 1-42 (1939-1981), Parts I and II**. 1982.
Microfiche. $3.00. .... Vendor G0174

Colorado Genealogical Society, Inc. **Surname Index to the Colorado Genealogist, Vols. 1-10 (1939-1949), Parts I and II**. 1969.
Microfiche. $8.00. .... Vendor G0174

Colorado Genealogical Society, Inc. **Surname Index to the Colorado Genealogist, Vols. 11-20 (1950-1959), Parts I and II**. 1974.
Microfiche. $8.00. .... Vendor G0174

Colorado Genealogical Society, Inc. **Surname Index to the Colorado Genealogist, Vols. 21-41 (1960-1980)**. 1984.
Microfiche. $8.00. .... Vendor G0174

Family History Library. **Research Outline: Colorado**.
Leaflet. $.25. 7 pp. .... Vendor G0629

Namaqua Chapter NSDAR. **Daughters of the American Revolution, Lineage of Namaqua Chapter Members, Loveland, Colorado, January 8, 1914 Through October 31, 1994**. Indexed.
Presents a record of all application papers of members of this chapter of the NSDAR.
Paper. $30.00. 495 pp. .... Vendor G0680

Root, Frank A., and William E. Connelley. **Overland Stage to California:** Personal Reminiscences & Authentic History of the Great Overland Stage Line & Pony Express from the Missouri River to the Pacific Ocean. (1901) reprint 1992.
A wonderful book covering a fascinating chapter of American history, it focuses on Denver and other Colorado and Kansas locations.
Cloth. $52.50. 631 pp. .... Vendor G0259

Thorndale, William, and William Dollarhide. **County Boundary Map Guides to the U.S. Federal Censuses, 1790-1920: Colorado, 1860-1920**. 1987.
$5.95. .... Vendor G0552

Arapahoe County

Colorado Genealogical Society, Inc. **Declaration of Intention (First Papers) to Become a Citizen of the United States: Arapahoe (Denver) County Court**. 1992. Indexed.
Books A-F, 1880-1906.
Contact vendor for information. 115 pp. .... Vendor G0174

Colorado Genealogical Society, Inc. **Marriages of Arapahoe County, Colorado 1859-1901:** Including Territory That Became Adams, Denver and Other Counties. 1986. Indexed. Illus.
Groom index chronological, alphabetically organized.
Paper. $33.00. 483 pp. .... Vendor G0174

Baca County

Fort William Bent Chapter NSDAR. **Baca County, Colorado, Probate Index 1910-1992**.
Paper. $12.00. .... Vendor G0752

Fort William Bent Chapter NSDAR. **Burial Record, Baca County, Colorado**. Indexed.
Paper. $23.00. .... Vendor G0752

Logan County

Conklin, Emma B., comp. **A Brief History of Logan County**. (1928) reprint 1995.
Cloth. $45.00. 354 pp. .... Vendor G0259

Connecticut

Statewide and Regional References

Atwater, Edward E., et al. **History of the Colony of New Haven to Its Absorption into Connecticut, with Supplementary History & Personnel of the Towns of Branford, Guilford, Milford, Stratford, Norwalk, Southold, Etc.** 2 vols. in 1. (1902) reprint 1994.
Cloth. $75.00. 767 pp. .... Vendor G0259

Bailey, Frederic W. **Early Connecticut Marriages** As Found on Ancient Church Records Prior to 1800. 7 books in 1. (1896-1906) reprint 1997. Indexed.
Cloth. $55.00. Approx. 1,000 pp. .... Vendor G0010

Bates, Alfred C., ed. **Rolls of Connecticut Men in the French and Indian War, 1755-1762**. 2 vols. Collections of the Connecticut Historical Society, Volumes IX & X. (1903, 1905) reprint 1997. Indexed.
Contact vendor for information. 364 + 488 pp. .... Vendor G0011

Bickford, Christopher P., and J. Bard McNulty. **John Warner Barber's Views of Connecticut Towns, 1834-36**. 1990. Illus.
Cloth. $22.00. 123 pp. .... Vendor G0645

Bolles, J. R., and Anna B. Williams. **The Rogerenes: Some Hitherto Unpublished Annals Belonging to the Colonial History of Connecticut**. With Appendix of Rogerene writings. (1904) reprint 1990.
A fascinating history of an important but little-known 17th-century sect, this book contains much useful information on early Connecticut history, as well as genealogical material on early New London.
Cloth. $42.50. 396 pp. .... Vendor G0259

Connecticut Society Daughters of the American Revolution. **Connecticut Revolutionary Pensioners**. (1919) reprint 1997.
Paper. $17.50. 169 pp. .... Vendor G0011

Cutter, William Richard, et al. **Genealogical and Family History of the State of Connecticut**. A Record of the Achievements of Her People in the Making of a Commonwealth and the Building of a Nation. In Four Volumes. Partially indexed. (1911) reprint 1995. Illus.
Contact vendor for information. 2,842 pp. .... Vendor G0011

Dayton, Cornelia Hughes. **Women Before the Bar: Gender, Law, & Society in Connecticut: 1639-1789**. 1995.
Explores women's role in the court system in the early 18th century. Includes study of their participation in a range of legal actions such as debt, divorce, illicit sex, rape, and slander.
Paper. $18.95. 382 pp. .... Vendor G0611

Dilts, Bryan Lee, comp. **1860 Connecticut Census Index: Heads of Households and Other Surnames in Household Index**. 1985.
Cloth. $190.00. 707 pp. .... Vendor G0552

Family History Library. **Research Outline: Connecticut**.
Leaflet. $.25. 9 pp. .... Vendor G0629

The First Laws of the State of Connecticut. (1784) reprint 1982.
Cloth. $62.50. 307 pp. .... Vendor G0118

Goodwin, Nathaniel. **Genealogical Notes,** Or Contributions to the Family History of Some of the First Settlers of Connecticut and Massachusetts. (1856) reprint 1995.
Cloth. $25.00. xx + 362 pp. .... Vendor G0010

Hinman, Royal R. **A Catalogue of the Names of the First Puritan Settlers of the Colony of Connecticut;** with the Time of Their Arrival in the Colony and Their Standing in Society . . . . (1846) reprint 1996.
Paper. $31.50. 336 pp. .... Vendor G0011

Holbrook, Jay Mack. **Connecticut 1670 Census**. 1977.
Microfiche. $6.00. 84 pp. on 1 fiche. .... Vendor G0148

Jacobus, Donald Lines. **Families of Ancient New Haven**. With an Index Vol. by Helen L. Scranton. 9 vols. in 3. (1922-32, 1939) reprint 1997. Indexed.
Contact vendor for information. .... Vendor G0010

Jacobus, Donald Lines. **Lists of Officials ... of Connecticut Colony ... 1636 through ... 1677 and of New Haven Colony ... [with] Soldiers in the Pequot War ...** (1935) reprint 1996.
Paper. $12.50. 69 pp. .... Vendor G0011

Ledogar, Edwin Richard. **Vital Statistics of Eastern Connecticut, Western Rhode Island, South Central Massachusetts**. 2 vols. 1995. Reprint on microfiche.
   Organized alphabetically.
Order no. 867-868, $38.00/each or $69.00/set. 540 + 537 pp. .... Vendor G0478

Long, John H., ed. **Connecticut, Maine, Massachusetts, and Rhode Island Atlas of Historical County Boundaries**. 1994.
   A beautiful and extremely useful book detailing the changes in county boundaries from colonial times to 1990. 8½" x 11".
Cloth. $92.00. 412 pp. .... Vendor G0611

Manwaring, Charles William. **A Digest of the Early Connecticut Probate Records**. 3 vols. (1904-1906) reprint 1995. Indexed.
Cloth. $150.00. 2,224 pp. total. .... Vendor G0010

Manwaring, Charles William. **A Digest of the Early Connecticut Probate Records 1635-1750**. 3 vols. 1904. Reprint on microfiche. Indexed.
Order nos. 453-459—Vol. 1, $42.00; order nos. 522-526—Vol. 2, $40.00; order nos. 918-919—Vol. 3, $44.00. .... Vendor G0478

Morrison, Betty Jean. **Connecting to Connecticut**. 1995.
   Reference guide to records held in each of Connecticut's 169 towns.
Paper. $24.95. 350 pp. .... Vendor G0578

Pease, J., and J. Niles. **Gazetteer of the States of Connecticut & R.I.** Consisting of Two Parts: I, Geogr. & Statistical Desc. of Each State; II, General Geogr. View of Each County, & a Minute & Ample Topographical Desc. of Each Town, Village, Etc. (1819) reprint 1990.
Cloth. $35.00. 339 pp. .... Vendor G0259

Record of Service of Connecticut Men in the Army and Navy of the United States, During the War of the Rebellion. (1889) reprint 1996.
Cloth. $105.00. 1,071 pp. .... Vendor G0259

Southern California Genealogical Society. **Sources of Genealogical Help in Connecticut**.
Paper. $1.50. 9 pp. .... Vendor G0656

Sperry, Kip. **Connecticut Sources for Family Historians and Genealogists**.
   Genealogical and historical sources for genealogical research in Connecticut are found in this book, including manuscript collections, indexes, published works, etc.
Paper. $9.95. 112 pp. .... Vendor G0618

Thorndale, William, and William Dollarhide. **County Boundary Map Guides to the U.S. Federal Censuses, 1790-1920: Connecticut, Massachusetts, Rhode Island, 1790-1920.** 1987.
$5.95. .... Vendor G0552

United States Bureau of the Census. **Heads of Families at the First Census of the United States Taken in the Year 1790: Connecticut.** (1908) reprint 1992. Indexed. Illus.
Paper. $22.50. 227 pp. .... Vendor G0010

United States Bureau of the Census. **Heads of Families at the First Census of the United States Taken in the Year 1790: Connecticut.**
Cloth, $35.00. Paper, $20.00. .... Vendor G0552

Volkel, Lowell. **Connecticut 1800 Census Index.** 3 vols.
   Volume I: Fairfield & Hartford Cos., 87 pp.
   Volume II: Litchfield, New Haven, Tolland, & Windham Cos., 125 pp.
   Volume III: Middlesex & New London, 64 pp.
Paper. $10.00/Vols. I & III. $12.00/Vol. II. $25.00/set. 276 pp. .... Vendor G0574

White, Lorraine Cook. **The Barbour Collection of Connecticut Town Vital Records.** Andover, 1848-1879; Ashford, 1710-1851; Avon, 1830-1851. 1994.
Paper. $25.00. 297 pp. .... Vendor G0010

White, Lorraine Cook. **The Barbour Collection of Connecticut Town Vital Records.** Barkhamsted, 1779-1854; Berlin, 1785-1850; Bethany, 1832-1853; Bethlehem, 1787-1851; Bloomfield, 1835-1853; Bozrah, 1786-1850. 1995.
Paper. $25.00. 282 pp. .... Vendor G0010

White, Lorraine Cook. **The Barbour Collection of Connecticut Town Vital Records.** Branford, 1644-1850; Bridgeport, 1821-1854. 1995.
Paper. $30.00. 326 pp. .... Vendor G0010

White, Lorraine Cook. **The Barbour Collection of Connecticut Town Vital Records.** Bristol, 1785-1854; Brookfield, 1788-1852; Brooklyn, 1786-1850; Burlington, 1806-1852. 1996.
Paper. $25.00. 236 pp. .... Vendor G0010

White, Lorraine Cook. **The Barbour Collection of Connecticut Town Vital Records.** Canaan, 1739-1852; Canterbury, 1703-1850. 1996.
Paper. $30.00. 309 pp. .... Vendor G0010

White, Lorraine Cook. **The Barbour Collection of Connecticut Town Vital Records.** Canton, 1806-1853; Chaplin, 1822-1851; Chatham, 1767-1854; Cheshire, 1780-1840; Chester, 1836-1852; Clinton, 1838-1854; Diary of Aaron G. Hurd, Clinton, 1809-1878. 1996.
Paper. $30.00. 335 pp. .... Vendor G0010

White, Lorraine Cook. **The Barbour Collection of Connecticut Town Vital Records.** Colchester, 1699-1850; Colebrook, 1779-1810; Columbia, 1804-1852; Cornwall, 1740-1854. 1996.
Paper. $35.00. 412 pp. .... Vendor G0010

Berlin

Camp, David N. **History of New Britain, with Sketches of Farmington & Berlin**. (1889) reprint 1994.
Cloth. $56.00. 534 pp. .... Vendor G0259

Bridgewater

Orcutt, S. **History of the Towns of New Milford & Bridgewater, 1703-1882** [Including cemetery records & genealogies]. (1882) reprint 1992.
Cloth. $89.00. 909 pp. .... Vendor G0259

Ellsworth

Goodenough, G. F., ed. **Ellsworth. A Gossip About a Country Parish of the Hills, and Its People, a Century After Its Birth**. (1900) reprint 1992.
Cloth. $16.00. 129 pp. .... Vendor G0259

Fairfield County

Ancient Historical Records of Norwalk. With Genealogical Register. (1865) reprint 1993.
Cloth. $38.00. 320 pp. .... Vendor G0259

Bedini, Sylvio A. **Ridgefield in Review**. With a Foreword by Prof. Allan Nevins. (1958) reprint 1994.
Cloth. $44.50. 396 pp. .... Vendor G0259

Child, Frank Samuel. **(Fairfield) An Old New England Town: Sketches of Life, Scenery, Character**. (1895) reprint 1994.
Cloth. $32.50. xvi + 230 pp. .... Vendor G0259

Hawley, Emily C. **Annals of Brookfield, Fairfield County**. With Genealogies. (1929) reprint 1993.
Cloth. $68.00. 656 pp. .... Vendor G0259

Hill, S. B., from research by James Montgomery Bailey. **History of Danbury, 1684-1896**. (1896) reprint 1992.
Cloth. $59.50. 583 pp. .... Vendor G0259

Hubbard, F. A. **Other Days in Greenwich, or Tales & Reminiscences of an Old New England Town**. (1913) reprint 1988.
   A charming and informative history of the town of Greenwich, with many illustrations and photographs.
Cloth. $39.50. 363 pp. .... Vendor G0259

Huntington, E. B. **History of Stamford Connecticut**. (1868) reprint 1992. Indexed. Illus.
   Book #1347.
Cloth. $45.00. 576 pp. .... Vendor G0082

Huntington, E. B. **History of Stamford from Its Settlement in 1641 to 1868, Including Darien.** (1868) reprint 1987.
Cloth. $49.95. 492 pp. .... Vendor G0259

Hurd, D. H., ed. **History of Fairfield County, with Illustrations & Biographical Sketches of Its Prominent Men & Pioneers.** (1881) reprint 1987.
Cloth. $89.00. 847 pp. .... Vendor G0259

Jacobus, Donald Lines. **History and Genealogy of the Families of Old Fairfield.** With Additions and Corrections from The American Genealogist. 2 vols in 3. (1930-1932, 1943) reprint 1991. Indexed.
Cloth. $150.00. 2,051 pp. .... Vendor G0010

Johnson, Jane Eliza. **Newtown's History, and Historical Ezra Kevan Johnson.** With additional material. Includes genealogies. (1917) reprint 1992.
Cloth. $41.00. 365 pp. .... Vendor G0259

Lathrop, Cornelia P. **Black Rock, Seaport of Old Fairfield. 1644-1870.** (1930) reprint 1995.
Cloth. $32.00. 214 pp. .... Vendor G0259

Mead, Daniel M. **History of Greenwich, Fairfield Co., with Many Important Statistics.** (1857) reprint 1993.
Cloth. $37.00. 318 pp. .... Vendor G0259

Mead, Spencer P. **Historie of Ye Town of Greenwich, Connecticut.** (1911) reprint 1992. Indexed.
   Book # 1348.
Cloth. $49.50. 862 pp. .... Vendor G0082

Mead, Spencer P. **Ye Historie of Ye Town of Greenwich, Co. of Fairfield and State of Conn., with Genealogcal Notes on [many] Families.** Revision & Continuation of 1857 History of the Town of Greenwich by Daniel M. Mead. (1911) reprint 1995.
Cloth. $77.50. 768 pp. .... Vendor G0259

Norwalk After Two Hundred Fifty Years: An Account of the Celebration of the 250th Anniversary of the Charter of the Town, 1651-1901. (1902) reprint 1995.
   Includes historical sketches of churches, schools, old homes, institutions, eminent men, etc., along with military service records.
Cloth. $44.00. 387 pp. .... Vendor G0259

Orcutt, S. **History of the Old Town of Stratford & the City of Bridgeport.** 2 vols. (1886) reprint 1900.
Cloth. $69.50/vol. 692 + 700 pp. .... Vendor G0259

Perry, K. E. **Old Burying Ground of Fairfield: Memorial of Many Early Settlers & Transcript of the Inscriptions & Epitaphs on the Tombstones Found in the Oldest Burying Ground in Fairfield.** (1882) reprint 1988.
Cloth. $29.50. 241 pp. .... Vendor G0259

Rockwell, George L. **The History of Ridgefield Connecticut.** (1927) reprint 1979. Indexed. Illus.
   Book #1350.
Cloth. $39.50. 653 pp. .... Vendor G0082

Schenk, Elizabeth H. **The History of Fairfield, Volume I: 1639-1818**. (1889) reprint 1991.
Cloth. $45.00. 423 pp. .... Vendor G0259

Schenk, Elizabeth H. **The History of Fairfield, Volume II: 1700-1800**. (1905) reprint 1991.
Cloth. $45.00. 538 pp. .... Vendor G0259

Todd, C. B. **The History of Redding,** From Its First Settlement to the Present Time, with Notes on the Early Families. (1880) reprint 1988.
Cloth. $32.00. 248 pp. .... Vendor G0259

Waldo, George C., Jr., comp. **History of Bridgeport & Vicinity**. (1897) reprint 1993.
Cloth. $29.50. 203 pp. .... Vendor G0259

Waldo, George C., Jr. **"The Standard's" History of Bridgeport**. (1897) reprint 1993.
Cloth. $29.50. 203 pp. .... Vendor G0259

Farmington

Camp, David N. **History of New Britain, with Sketches of Farmington & Berlin**. (1889) reprint 1994.
Cloth. $56.00. 534 pp. .... Vendor G0259

Hartford County

Adams, Gladys S. **Buckland, the North West Section of Manchester**. 1995.
Paper. $17.50. 123 pp. .... Vendor G0259

Adams, Sherman W. **The History of Ancient Wethersfield, Volume I**. (1904) reprint 1990. Indexed. Illus.
  Book #1191.
Cloth. $65.00. 1,011 pp. .... Vendor G0082

Allen, Francis O., ed. **History of Enfield** . . . from the Beginning to 1850, Together with Graveyard Inscriptions and Those Hartford, Northampton and Springfield Records Which Refer to the People of Enfield. 3 vols. (1900) reprint 1994.
Cloth. $89.50/vol., $225.00/set. 2,652 pp. .... Vendor G0259

Andrews, A. **Genealogical & Ecclesiastical History of New Britain**. (1867) reprint 1987.
Cloth. $55.00. 538 pp. .... Vendor G0259

Andrews, Charles M. **The River Towns of Connecticut: A Study of Wethersfield, Hartford & Windsor**. (1889) reprint 1994.
Paper. $19.50. 126 pp. .... Vendor G0259

Atwater, Francis. **History of Southington**. (1924) reprint 1995.
Cloth. $57.50. 549 pp. .... Vendor G0259

Barbour, Lucius Barnes. **Families of Early Hartford, Connecticut**. (1977) reprint 1996. Indexed.
Paper. $50.00. 736 pp. .... Vendor G0011

Camp, David N. **History of New Britain, with Sketches of Farmington & Berlin**. (1889) reprint 1994.
Cloth. $56.00. 534 pp. .... Vendor G0259

Cemetery Inscriptions in Windsor. (1929) reprint 1992.
Paper. $18.00. 178 pp. .... Vendor G0259

Chapin, Alonzo B. **Glastenbury for Two Hundred Years: A Centennial Discourse, May 18th, 1853**. (1853) reprint 1994.
Cloth. $32.50. 252 pp. .... Vendor G0259

Dewey and Barbour, comps. **Inscriptions from Gravestones in Glastonbury**.
Paper. $15.00. 101 pp. .... Vendor G0259

Goodwin, Joseph O. **East Hartford: Its History and Traditions**. (1879) reprint 1992. Indexed. Illus.
    Book #1409.
Cloth. $25.00. 280 pp. .... Vendor G0082

Grant, Ellsworth S., and Marion H. Grant. **The City of Hartford 1784-1984: An Illustrated History**. 1986. Indexed. Illus.
Cloth. $29.95. .... Vendor G0645

Grant, Marion Hepburn. **In and About Hartford: Its People and Places**. Rev. 5th ed. 1989. Illus.
Paper. $10.00. 393 pp. .... Vendor G0645

Historical Catalog of the First Church in Hartford, 1633-1885 (includes members, births and bapts., marriages & deaths). Published by the Church. (1885) reprint 1994.
Paper. $27.50. 274 pp. .... Vendor G0259

Holbrook, Jay Mack. **Connecticut Colonists: Windsor 1635-1703**. 1986.
    Alphabetizes over 9,500 entries of 17th-century births, marriages, and deaths. Compiled from vital records and supplementary sources, including the Loomis Copy from the Windsor Town Hall; Matthew Grant's records; Hartford County probate records; births, marriages, and deaths in the Windsor land records; church records; and census, freeman, ratable, and petition lists.
Cloth. $35.00. 317 pp. .... Vendor G0148

Hosley, William. **By Their Markers Ye Shall Know Them: A Chronicle of the History and Restorations of Hartford's Ancient Burying Ground**. Published by the Ancient Burying Ground Association, Inc. With Introduction, synopsis, epitaphs, and map by Shepherd M. Holcomb, Sr. 1994. Indexed. Illus.
Cloth, $27.50. Paper, $18.75. 173 pp. .... Vendor G0645

Little, Henry G. **Early Days in Newington, 1833-1836**. (1937) reprint 1994.
Paper. $17.50. 122 pp. .... Vendor G0259

Love, William DeLoss. **Colonial History of Hartford, Gathered from the Original Records**. (1914) reprint 1993.
Cloth. $41.50. 369 pp. .... Vendor G0259

North, C. M. **History of Berlin**. (1916) reprint 1987.
Cloth. $38.00. 294 pp. .... Vendor G0259

Norton, F. C. et al. **Bristol, Connecticut ("In Olden Time New Cambridge"), Which Includes Forestville**. (1907) reprint 1994.
Cloth. $41.00. 362 pp. .... Vendor G0259

Only More So: The History of East Hartford 1783-1976. (1976) reprint 1992. Illus.
    Book #1410.
Cloth. $30.00. 372 pp. .... Vendor G0082

Peck, Epaphroditus. **History of Bristol**. (1931) reprint 1994.
Cloth. $41.00. 362 pp. .... Vendor G0259

Ransom, Stanley A. **History of Hartland, the 69th Town in the Colony of Connecticut**. (1961) reprint 1995.
Cloth, $29.00. Paper, $19.00. 189 pp. .... Vendor G0259

Rose, Christine. **Robert Rose of Wethersfield and Branford, Connecticut Who Came on the Ship Francis in 1634**. 1983. Indexed.
Cloth. Contact vendor for information. xvi + 512 pp. .... Vendor G0474

Sheldon, Hezekiah Spencer. **Documentary History of Suffield, in the Colony & Province of Massachusetts Bay in New England, 1660-1749**. (1879) reprint 1992.
Cloth. $39.00. 342 pp. .... Vendor G0259

Stiles, Henry R. **History of Ancient Wethersfield**. 2 vols. (1904) reprint 1987.
    Volume I: History.
    Volume II: Genealogy.
Cloth. $95.00/vol., $179.50/set. 995 + 946 pp. .... Vendor G0259

Stiles, Henry R. **The History and Genealogies of Ancient Windsor 1635-1891 Vol. I**. (1892) reprint 1976. Indexed. Illus.
    Book #1194.
Cloth. $60.00. 1,012 pp. .... Vendor G0082

Stiles, Henry R. **The History and Genealogies of Ancient Windsor 1635-1891 Vol. II**. (1893) reprint 1992. Indexed. Illus.
    Book #1316.
Cloth. $65.00. 960 pp. .... Vendor G0082

Stiles, Henry R. **History and Genealogies of Ancient Windsor,** Including E. Windsor, S. Windsor, Bloomfield, Windsor Locks & Ellington, 1635-1891. 2 vols. (1859, 1892) reprint 1992.
Cloth. $89.50/vol., $175.00/set. 922 + 867 pp. .... Vendor G0259

Timlow, Heman R. **Sketches of Southington: Ecclesiastical & Others**. (1875) reprint 1992.
    Part I: Sketches, 570 pp.
    Part II: Genealogies, 275 pp.
Cloth. $57.00/Part I. $33.50/Part II. The set in one volume/$84.00. ... Vendor G0259

Trumbuss, J. Hammond, ed. **Memorial History of Hartford County, 1633-1884**. 2 vols. (1886) reprint 1994.
    Volume I: General county history; town and city of Hartford.
    Volume II: History of individual towns in Hartford County.
Cloth. $119.00/set. $71.00/Vol. 1; $57.50/Vol. 2. 704 + 569 pp. .... Vendor G0259

Welles, Edwin Stanley. **Some Early Records & Documents of and Relating to Windsor, 1639-1703**. (1898, 1930) reprint 1993.
Cloth. $29.50. 227 pp. .... Vendor G0259

Welles, R., ed. **Early Annals of Newington**. (1874) reprint 1991.
Cloth. $25.00. 204 pp. .... Vendor G0259

Litchfield County

Addington, Robert M. **History of Litchfield County,** with Illustrations and Biographical Sketches of Its Prominent Men and Pioneers. (1881) reprint 1994.
Cloth. $77.50. 730 pp. .... Vendor G0259

Atwater, F. **History of the Town of Plymouth,** with an Account of the Centennial Celebration & a Sketch of Plymouth, Ohio, Settled by Local Families. (1895) reprint 1988.
Cloth. $49.00. 447 pp. .... Vendor G0259

Atwater, Francis. **History of Kent,** Including Biographical Sketches of Many of Its Present or Former Inhabitants. (1897) reprint 1994.
Cloth. $27.50. 176 pp. .... Vendor G0259

Boswell, G. C., ed. **The Litchfield Book of Days:** A Collation of the Historical, Biographical & Literary Reminiscences of Litchfield. (1900) reprint 1992.
Cloth. $29.50. 221 pp. .... Vendor G0259

Boyd, J. **Annals & Family Records of Winchester**. (1873) reprint 1988.
Cloth. $65.00. 632 pp. .... Vendor G0259

Chipman, R. Manning. **History of Harwinton**. (1860) reprint 1992.
Cloth. $22.00. 152 pp. .... Vendor G0259

Cothren, W. **History of Ancient Woodbury**. (1854) reprint 1990.
Cloth. $83.50. 833 pp. .... Vendor G0259

Cothren, William. **History of Ancient Woodbury, Connecticut**. (1854) reprint 1996. Indexed. Illus.
Paper. $65.00. 851 pp. .... Vendor G0011

Eldridge, J., and T. W. Crissey. **History of Norfolk, 1744-1900, Litchfield County**. (1900) reprint 1992.
Cloth. $67.00. 648 pp. .... Vendor G0259

Gold, Theodore S. **Historical Record of the Town of Cornwall, Litchfield Co.** (1877) reprint 1994.
Cloth. $59.50. 339 pp. .... Vendor G0259

Grafton Press, ed. **Two Centuries of New Milford,** with An Account of the Bi-Centennial Celebration. (1907) reprint 1994.
Cloth. $37.00. xii + 307 pp. .... Vendor G0259

Hibbard, A. G. **History of the Town of Goshen, with Genealogies & Biographies**. Based upon the Records of Dea. L. M. Norton. (1897) reprint 1988.
Cloth. $61.50. 602 pp. .... Vendor G0259

Hibbard, Rev. A. G. **Marriages in Goshen, Connecticut**. Excerpted from the author's *History of Goshen*, 1897. Reprinted. Indexed.
  Covers 1740-1785 and 1821-1896 (records for 1786-1820 are missing).
Paper. $7.00. 54 pp. .... Vendor G0561

Kilbourne, Payne Kenyon. **Sketches & Chronicles of the Town of Litchfield**. (1859) reprint 1992.
Cloth. $34.50. 265 pp. .... Vendor G0259

Lee, Wallace. **Barkhamsted & Its Centennial, 1879, to Which Is Added an Historical Appendix**. (1881) reprint 1994.
Cloth. $27.50. 178 pp. .... Vendor G0259

Old Woodbury Historical Society. **Homes of Old Woodbury**. (1959) reprint 1995.
  Includes towns of Washington, Woodbury, Bethlehem, Southbury, Roxbury.
Cloth. $35.00. 262 pp. .... Vendor G0259

Orcutt, S. **History of Torrington,** from Its First Settlement in 1737, with Biographies and Genealogies. (1878) reprint 1988.
Cloth. $85.00. 817 pp. .... Vendor G0259

Orcutt, S. **History of the Towns of New Milford & Bridgewater, 1703-1882** [Including cemetery records & genealogies]. (1882) reprint 1992.
Cloth. $89.00. 909 pp. .... Vendor G0259

Russell, Donna Valley. **Salisbury, Connecticut, Records: Vital, Gravestones, Deeds, Taxpayers**. 1983. Illus.
Paper. $28.00. 271 pp. .... Vendor G0126

Russell, Donna Valley. **Sharon [District], Connecticut, Probate Records, 1757-1783**. 1984. Indexed.
Paper. $12.00. 106 pp. .... Vendor G0126

Salisbury Association. **Historical Collections Relating to the Town of Salisbury, Litchfield County**. (1913) reprint 1992.
Paper. $19.00. 154 pp. .... Vendor G0259

Starr, Edward Comfort. **History of Cornwall: A Typical New England Town**. (1926) reprint 1992.
Cloth. $58.00. 547 pp. .... Vendor G0259

VanAlstyne, L. **Burying Grounds of Sharon, Conn., and Amenia & North East, NY**. (1903) reprint 1983. Indexed.
  Contains all the cemeteries not listed in Poucher's "Gravestones of Old Dutchess County."
Cloth. $15.00. 256 pp. .... Vendor G0093

White, Alain C. **History of the Town of Litchfield, 1720-1920**. (1920) reprint 1992.
Cloth. $42.50. 360 pp. .... Vendor G0259

Wiek, Laura C., comp. **"One Hundred Years": History of Morris, 1859-1959**. (1959) reprint 1994.
Cloth. $33.00. 250 pp. .... Vendor G0259

Woodruff, George C. **A Genealogical Register of the Inhabitants of the Town of Litchfield, Conn**. from the Settlement of the Town, A.D. 1720 to the Year 1800 . . . (1845) reprint 1997.
Paper. $25.00. 267 pp. .... Vendor G0011

Madison

Steiner, B. C. **History of the Plantation of Menunkatuck, and the Original Town of Guilford (including Madison)**. (1897) reprint 1992.
Cloth. $56.00. 538 pp. .... Vendor G0259

Middlesex County

Fowler, W. C. **History of Durham, from Its First Grant of Land in 1662 to 1866**. (1866) reprint 1991.
Cloth. $49.00. 460 pp. .... Vendor G0259

Gates, Gilman C. **Saybrook at the Mouth of the Connecticut River: The First One Hundred Years**. (1935) reprint 1995.
Cloth. $32.50. 246 pp. .... Vendor G0259

Knowles, Rev. William C. **By-Gone Days in Ponsett-Haddam, Middlesex Co.: A Story**. (1914) reprint 1994.
Paper. $14.00. 65 pp. .... Vendor G0259

New Haven County

Abbott, Susan Woodruff. **Families of Early Milford, Connecticut**. (1979) reprint 1996.
Paper. $55.00. 875 pp. .... Vendor G0011

Atwater, Edward E., et al. **History of the Colony of New Haven to Its Absorption into Connecticut, with Supplementary History & Personnel of the Towns of Branford, Guilford, Milford, Stratford, Norwalk, Southold, Etc**. 2 vols. in 1. (1902) reprint 1994.
Cloth. $75.00. 767 pp. .... Vendor G0259

Beach, Joseph P. **History of Cheshire from 1694 to 1840,** Including Prospect, Which as Columbia Parish Was a Part of Cheshire Until 1829. (1912) reprint 1994.
Cloth. $59.50. 574 pp. .... Vendor G0259

Blake, William P., ed. **History of the Town of Hamden, with an Account of the Centennial Celebration**. (1888) reprint 1994.
Cloth. $39.50. 350 pp. .... Vendor G0259

Breckenridge, Frances A. **(Meriden) Recollections of a New England Town**. (1899) reprint 1994.
Cloth. $31.50. 222 pp. .... Vendor G0259

Bronson, Henry. **History of Waterbury,** with an Appendix of Biography, Genealogy & Statistics. (1858) reprint 1992.
Cloth. $59.00. 583 pp. .... Vendor G0259

Campbell, Hollis A., William C. Sharpe, and Frank G. Bassett. **Seymour, Past & Present.** (1902) reprint 1995.
Cloth. $64.00. 613 pp. .... Vendor G0259

Davis, Charles Henry Stanley. **Early Families of Wallingford, Connecticut** With a New Index. (1870) reprint 1995. Indexed.
Paper. $31.50. 363 pp. .... Vendor G0011

Dickerman, J. **Colonial History of the Parish of Mount Carmel,** as Read in its Geologic Formations, Records & Traditions. (1904) reprint 1994.
Paper. $17.50. 109 pp. .... Vendor G0259

Dodd, Stephen. **East Haven Register, in Three Parts (History & Vital Records).** (1824) reprint 1994.
Cloth. $28.00. 198 pp. .... Vendor G0259

Gillespie, C. B., and G. C. Munson. **A Century of Meriden: An Historic Record & Pictorial Description of the Town of Meriden.** (1906) reprint 1992.
Cloth. $109.00. 1,226 pp. .... Vendor G0259

Hill, Everett G. **Modern History of New Haven & Eastern New Haven County.** 2 vols. (1918) reprint 1994.
Volume I: Historical.
Volume II: Biographical.
Cloth. $129.00/set. $47.50/Vol. I. $89.50/Vol. II. 436 + 907 pp. .... Vendor G0259

Hughes, Sarah E. **History of East Haven.** (1908) reprint 1992.
Cloth. $38.00. 324 pp. .... Vendor G0259

Inscriptions from the Gravestones of Derby, with Additions & Corrections. 1987.
Paper. $6.00. 31 pp. .... Vendor G0259

Jacobus, Donald Lines. **Families of Ancient New Haven.** With an Index Vol. by Helen L. Scranton. 9 vols. in 3. (1922-32, 1939) reprint 1997. Indexed.
Contact vendor for information. .... Vendor G0010

Jacobus, Donald Lines. **Lists of Officials . . . of Connecticut Colony . . . 1636 through . . . 1677 and of New Haven Colony . . . [with] Soldiers in the Pequot War . . .** (1935) reprint 1996.
Paper. $12.50. 69 pp. .... Vendor G0011

New Haven Vital Records, 1649-1850. Parts I & II. 2 vols. (1917) reprint 1994.
Cloth. $119.50/set. Part I, $59.00. Part II, $69.00. 599 + 690 pp. .... Vendor G0259

Old Woodbury Historical Society. **Homes of Old Woodbury.** (1959) reprint 1995.
Includes towns of Washington, Woodbury, Bethlehem, Southbury, Roxbury.
Cloth. $35.00. 262 pp. .... Vendor G0259

Orcutt, S. **History of the Town of Wolcott, from 1731 to 1874.** (1874) reprint 1991.
Cloth. $59.50. 608 pp. .... Vendor G0259

Orcutt, S., and A. Beardsley. **History of the Old Town of Derby, 1642-1880, with Biographies & Genealogies**. (1880) reprint 1987.
Cloth. $87.00. 843 pp. .... Vendor G0259

Prichard, K. A., scr. **Ancient Burying-Grounds of the Town of Waterbury,** Together with Other Records of Church and Town. (1917) reprint 1988.
Cloth. $38.00. 338 pp. .... Vendor G0259

Prichard, K. A., scr. **Proprietors' Records of the Town of Waterbury, 1677-1761**. 1988.
Cloth. $34.00. 260 pp. .... Vendor G0259

Proceedings at the Celebration of the 250th Anniversary of the Settlement of Guilford, 1639-1889. (1889) reprint 1994.
Cloth. $39.50. 288 pp. .... Vendor G0259

Rose, Christine. **Robert Rose of Wethersfield and Branford, Connecticut Who Came on the Ship Francis in 1634**. 1983. Indexed.
Cloth. Contact vendor for information. xvi + 512 pp. .... Vendor G0474

Scott, Kenneth, and Rosanne Conway. **Genealogical Data from Colonial New Haven Newspapers**. 1979. Indexed.
Cloth. $22.50. 547 pp. .... Vendor G0011

Sharpe, W. C. **History of Seymour, with Biographies and Genealogies**. (1879) reprint 1993.
Contact vendor for information. 244 pp. .... Vendor G0259

Sharpe, W. C. **Sketches & Records of South Britain**. (1898) reprint 1987.
Cloth. $23.00. 167 pp. .... Vendor G0259

Smith, R. D. (from the manuscripts of). **History of Guilford, from Its First Settlement in 1639**. (1877) reprint 1988.
Cloth. $25.00. 219 pp. .... Vendor G0259

Steiner, B. C. **History of the Plantation of Menunkatuck, and the Original Town of Guilford (including Madison)**. (1897) reprint 1992.
Cloth. $56.00. 538 pp. .... Vendor G0259

Thorpe, Sheldon B. **North Haven Annals: History of the Town from Its Settlement, 1680, to Its First Centennial, 1886**. (1892) reprint 1994.
Cloth. $47.00. 422 pp. .... Vendor G0259

Townsend, Charles Delmar. **Connecticut Inscriptions New Haven County, Guilford—North Guilford**.
Paper. $22.00. 101 pp. .... Vendor G0691

New London County

Allyn, Charles. **The Battle of Groton Heights: A Collection of Narratives, Official Reports, Records, Etc., of the Storming of Ft. Griswold**. (1882) reprint 1992.
Cloth. $45.00. 399 pp. .... Vendor G0259

Avery, Rev. J. **History of the Town of Ledyard, 1650-1900**. (1901) reprint 1992.
Cloth. $38.00. 334 pp. .... Vendor G0259

Baker, Henry A. **History of Montville, Formerly the North Parish of New London, 1640-1896 [with genealogies]**. (1896) reprint 1992.
Cloth. $75.00. 726 pp. .... Vendor G0259

Caulkins, Frances M. **History of Norwich, from Its Possession by Indians to 1866**. (1866) reprint 1991.
Cloth. $72.00. 704 pp. .... Vendor G0259

Caulkins, Frances M. Edited by E. S. Gilman. **The Stone Records of Groton**. (1903) reprint 1994.
Includes gravestone and monument inscriptions, along with the history of Arnold's Expedition in the Revolutionary War.
Paper. $18.00. 96 pp. .... Vendor G0259

Celebration of the 150th Anniversary of the Organization of the Congregational Church & Society in Franklin, 1868. (1869) reprint 1994.
Contact vendor for information. 151 pp. .... Vendor G0259

Diary of Joshua Hempstead 1711-1758. (1901) reprint 1985. Indexed. Illus.
Book #1432.
Cloth. $45.00. 766 pp. .... Vendor G0082

First Congregational Church of Preston, 1698-1898, Together with Statistics of the Church Taken from Church Records. (1900) reprint 1990.
Cloth. $21.00. 201 pp. .... Vendor G0259

Greenhalgh, Kathleen. **A History of West Mystic, 1600-1985**. (1985) reprint 1995.
Cloth, $35.00. Paper, $25.00. 248 pp. .... Vendor G0259

Haynes, Williams. **Stonington Chronology, 1649-1949, Being a Year-By-Year Record of the American Way of Life in a Connecticut Town**. (1949) reprint 1994.
Cloth. $25.00. 151 pp. .... Vendor G0259

History of New London, CT.
Book #1768.
Cloth. $49.50. .... Vendor G0082

Hurd, D. H., ed. **History of New London County,** with Biographical Sketches of Many of Its Pioneers & Prominent Men. (1882) reprint 1990.
Cloth. $79.00. 768 pp. .... Vendor G0259

Milne, George M. **Lebanon: Three Centuries in a Conn. Hilltop Town**. (1986) reprint 1995.
Cloth. $39.00. 287 pp. .... Vendor G0259

Miscellaneous History of New London, from the Records & Papers of the New London Historical Society. (1895) reprint 1994.
Includes the early whaling industry of New London, famous old taverns, facts and reminiscences, and more.
Paper. $15.00. 110 pp. .... Vendor G0259

Perkins, M. E. **Old Houses of the Ancient Town of Norwich, 1660-1800**. With Maps, Illustrations, Portraits & Genealogies. (1895) reprint 1991.
Cloth. $67.00. 621 pp. .... Vendor G0259

Phillips, Daniel L. **Griswold—A History,** Being a History of the Town of Griswold, from the Earliest Times to the Entrance of Our Country in the World War in 1917. (1929) reprint 1995.
Cloth. $49.00. 456 pp. .... Vendor G0259

Picturesque New London and Its Environs—Groton—Mystic—Montville—Waterford. (1901) reprint 1991.
A fine picture history of life in New London.
Cloth. $30.00. 192 pp. .... Vendor G0259

Prentice, Edward, comp. **Ye Ancient Burial Place of New London**. (1899) reprint 1990.
Alphabetically arranged inscriptions from the oldest cemetery in eastern Connecticut, from 1652.
Paper. $8.50. 40 pp. .... Vendor G0259

The Society of Colonial Wars in the State of Connecticut. **Vital Records of Norwich 1659-1848**. 1913. Reprint on microfiche. Indexed.
Order nos. 887-889, $54.00. 1,015 pp. + index .... Vendor G0478

Trask, John J. **Stonington Houses: A Panorama of New England Architecture, 1750-1900**. (1976, reprinted by permission) reprint 1994.
A wonderful book of photographs and text, showing the finest historic houses of one of New England's most scenic towns.
Cloth. $29.95. 120 pp. .... Vendor G0259

Vital Records of Norwich, 1649-1848, Parts I & II. (1913) reprint 1992.
Cloth. $109.00. 1,180 pp. .... Vendor G0259

Wheeler, Grace Denison. **Old Homes in Stonington, with Additional Chapters & Graveyard Inscriptions**. (1903, 1930) reprint 1993.
Cloth. $39.50. 336 pp. .... Vendor G0259

Wheeler, Richard A. **History of the First Congregational Church of Stonington, 1674-1874,** with the Report of Bi-Centennial Proceedings and Appendix Containing Statistics of the Church. (1875) reprint 1900.
Includes thousands of admissions, baptisms, marriages, and death records.
Paper. $30.00. 299 pp. .... Vendor G0259

Wheeler, Richard A. **History of the Town of Stonington, Connecticut**. With a Genealogical Register of Stonington Families. (1900) reprint 1993. Indexed.
Paper. $49.95. 754 pp. .... Vendor G0011

Wheeler, Richard A. **History of the Town of Stonington, County of New London, 1649-1900**. (1900) reprint 1987.
Cloth. $69.50. 754 pp. .... Vendor G0259

Tolland County

Brookes, George S. **Cascades & Courage: The History of the Town of Vernon & the City of Rockville.** (1955) reprint 1992.
Cloth. $55.00. 529 pp. .... Vendor G0259

Cole, J. R. **History of Tolland County.** (1888) reprint 1992.
Cloth. $99.50. 992 pp. .... Vendor G0259

Lawson, Harvey M., et al. **History of Union.** Founded on material gathered by Rev. Charles Hammond. (1893) reprint 1995.
Cloth. $53.00. 509 pp. .... Vendor G0259

Windham County

Bowen, C. W. **History of Woodstock.** (1926) reprint 1990.
Cloth. $75.00. xxxvi + 691 pp. .... Vendor G0259

Griggs, Susan Jewett. **Folklore and Firesides of Pomfret and Hampton, and Vicinity.** (1950) reprint 1992.
A delightful history of a large section of Windham County.
Cloth. $36.00. 161 + 118 pp. .... Vendor G0259

Larned, Ellen D. **Church Records of Killingly, Connecticut.** Excerpted from *Putnam's Genealogical Magazine*. Reprinted. Indexed.
Contains marriages, baptisms, and members 1715-1741, as well as marriages and members 1754-1775.
Paper. $8.00. 56 pp. .... Vendor G0561

Larned, Ellen D. **History of Windham County.** 2 vols. (1874) reprint 1992.
Cloth. $59.50/vol., $109.00/set. 1,181 pp. .... Vendor G0259

 Delaware

Statewide and Regional References

Arellano, Fay Louise Smith, scr. **Delaware Trails: Some Tribal Records, 1842-1907.** 1996.
Cloth. $55.00. 527 pp. .... Vendor G0011

Atlas of Maryland and Delaware, Topographical.
This present-day atlas provides the researcher with the detail needed to conduct a proper search. It is the size of a Rand McNally atlas of the entire U.S. 11" x 15½".
$16.95. .... Vendor G0611

Atlases & Gazetteers: Maryland/Delaware. Illus.
Paper. $16.95. 80 pp. .... Vendor G0632

Bendler, Bruce. **Colonial Delaware Records: 1681-1713**. 1992. Indexed.
Paper. $7.00. 80 pp. .... Vendor G0140

Boyer, Carl, 3rd. **Ship Passenger Lists: Pennsylvania and Delaware (1641-1825)**.
1980. Indexed.
Paper. $24.00. 289 pp. .... Vendor G0140

de Valinger, Leon, Jr. **Reconstructed 1790 Census of Delaware**.
Paper. $9.50. 83 pp. .... Vendor G0627

Dilts, Bryan Lee, comp. **1860 Delaware Census Index: Heads of Households and
Other Surnames in Household Index**. 1984.
Cloth. $59.00. 153 pp. .... Vendor G0552

Dilts, Bryan Lee, comp. **1870 Delaware Census Index: Heads of Households and
Other Surnames in Household Index**. 1985.
Cloth. $59.00. 153 pp. .... Vendor G0552

Doherty, Thomas P., ed. **Delaware Genealogical Research Guide**. 1989, with 1996
Update.
Paper. $9.50. 44 pp. .... Vendor G0653

Family History Library. **Research Outline: Delaware**.
Leaflet. $.25. 8 pp. .... Vendor G0629

The First Laws of the State of Delaware. 4 vols. (1797) reprint 1981.
Cloth. $242.50. .... Vendor G0118

Frazier. **Delaware Advertiser, 1827-1831: Genealogical Extracts**. 1987.
    From the "Delaware Advertiser and Farmer's Journal," Wilmington, Del. Marriages,
deaths, ads, election results, meetings, tax lists, legal notices, school news, heirs,
estate settlements, etc.
Cloth. $26.00. 272 pp. .... Vendor G0611

Gannett, Henry. **A Gazetteer of Maryland and Delaware**. 2 vols. in 1. (1904) reprint
1994.
Paper. $12.50. 99 pp. .... Vendor G0011

Hart, Matilda Spicer. **The Delaware Historical and Genealogical Recall**. With index
by Mary Fallon Richards. (1936) reprint 1984. Indexed.
    Births, marriages, deaths, etc., from various obscure sources; all three counties.
Paper. $7.00. 59 pp. .... Vendor G0653

Maddus, Gerald, and Dorris Maddux. **1800 Census of Delaware**. (1964) reprint 1996.
Indexed.
Paper. $22.50. 200 pp. .... Vendor G0011

Peden, Henry C., Jr. **Colonial Delaware Soldiers and Sailors, 1638-1776**. 1995.
Indexed.
Paper. $19.00. 235 pp. .... Vendor G0140

Peden, Henry C., Jr. **Revolutionary Patriots of Delaware, 1775-1783**. 1996.
Cloth. $42.00. 301 pp. .... Vendor G0140

Redden, Robert, ed. **Delaware Genealogical Society Surname Index**. 1995.
Paper. $6.00. 370+ pp. .... Vendor G0653

Thorndale, William, and William Dollarhide. **County Boundary Map Guides to the U.S. Federal Censuses, 1790-1920: Maryland, Delaware, District of Columbia 1790-1920**. 1987.
$5.95. .... Vendor G0552

Weinberg et al. **Index to 1759 Warrants and Surveys of Province of Pennsylvania Including Three Lower Counties (Delaware)**. (1965) reprint 1975. Indexed.
Paper. $9.00. 91 pp. .... Vendor G0531

Kent County

Brewer, Mary Marshall. **Kent County, Delaware, Land Records, 1680-1701**. 1996. Indexed.
Paper. $16.00. 186 pp. .... Vendor G0140

Brewer, Mary Marshall. **Kent County, Delaware, Land Records, Volume 2, 1702-1722**. 1997. Indexed.
Paper. $14.00. 167 pp. .... Vendor G0140

Brewer, Mary Marshall. **Kent County, Delaware, Land Records, Volume 3, 1723-1734**. 1997. Indexed.
Paper. $18.00. 228 pp. .... Vendor G0140

Delaware State Archives. **An Index to Kent County Probates 1680-1925**.
Paper. $25.00. 373 pp. .... Vendor G0597

Wright, F. Edward. **Vital Records of Kent and Sussex Counties, Delaware, 1686-1800**. 1986. Indexed.
Paper. $16.00. 206 pp. .... Vendor G0140

New Castle County

Burr, Horace, trans. **Records of the Holy Trinity (Old Swedes) Church from 1697 to 1773,** with abstracts of the English records, 1773-1810. (1890) reprint 1988.
   The Old Swedes Church was the first built at what would become Wilmington. These records include birth, baptism, marriage, and death records for the early settlers of the area, both Swedish and otherwise.
Cloth. $79.50. 772 pp. .... Vendor G0259

Records of the Holy Trinity (Old Swedes) Church from 1697 to 1773—Index & Errata. (1919) reprint 1988.
   May be ordered bound with the above book.
Paper. $17.00. 166 pp. .... Vendor G0259

Burr, Horace, trans. **Early Church Records of New Castle County, DE, Vol. 2: Old Swedes Church 1713-1799**. 1994. Indexed.
Paper. $32.00. 410 pp. .... Vendor G0140

Colonial Dames of Delaware. **A Calendar of Delaware Wills, New Castle County, 1682-1800**. (1911) reprint 1996. Indexed.
Paper. $25.00. 218 pp. .... Vendor G0011

Public Archives Commission of the State of Delaware. **Inventory of the County Archives of Delaware: #1—New Castle County**. (1941) reprint 1994.
  Contains virtually every record that existed in New Castle County up to 1941.
Paper. $41.00. 327 pp. .... Vendor G0653

Wright, F. Edward. **Early Church Records of New Castle County, DE, Vol. 1: 1701-1800**. 1994. Indexed.
Paper. $24.50. 329 pp. .... Vendor G0140

Sussex County

de Valinger, Leon. **Calendar of Sussex County, Delaware Probate Records 1680-1800**. (1964) reprint 1984. Indexed.
  Names, relationships, witnesses, and dates of wills and administrations.
Paper. $31.00. 310 pp. .... Vendor G0653

Mason, Elaine Hastings, and F. Edward Wright. **Land Records of Sussex County, Delaware, 1782-1789**. 1990. Indexed.
Paper. $12.00. 121 pp. .... Vendor G0140

Wright, F. Edward. **Land Records of Sussex County, Delaware, 1769-1782**. 1994. Indexed.
Paper. $22.00. 275 pp. .... Vendor G0140

Wright, F. Edward. **Vital Records of Kent and Sussex Counties, Delaware, 1686-1800**. 1986. Indexed.
Paper. $16.00. 206 pp. .... Vendor G0140

District of Columbia

Angevine, Erma Miller. **Research in the District of Columbia**.
Paper. $6.50. 23 pp. .... Vendor G0627

Dilts, Bryan Lee, comp. **1860 District of Columbia Census Index: Heads of Households and Other Surnames in Household Index**. 1983.
Cloth. $50.00. 109 pp. .... Vendor G0552

Dilts, Bryan Lee, comp. **1870 District of Columbia Census Index: Heads of Households and Other Surnames in Household Index**. 1985.
Cloth. $52.00. 180 pp. .... Vendor G0552

Family History Library. **Research Outline: District of Columbia.**
Leaflet. $.25. 7 pp. .... Vendor G0629

Higgins, Margaret Elliott. **Marriages and Deaths from the National Intelligencer (Washington, D.C.) 1800-1850 (Microfilm)**; 471-page name index prepared.
Microfilm. $85.00/ 3-reel sets. 3 reels .... Vendor G0627

Liahona Research. **District of Columbia Marriages, Early to 1825**. 1993.
Cloth. $30.00. .... Vendor G0552

Parks, Gary W. **Index to the 1820 Census of Maryland and Washington, D.C.** 1986.
Cloth. $19.00. 274 pp. .... Vendor G0011

Pippenger, Wesley E. **District of Columbia Marriage Licenses: 1811-1858**. 1994.
Paper. $47.00. 665 pp. .... Vendor G0140

Pippenger, Wesley E. **District of Columbia Probate Records: 1801-1852**. 1996. Indexed.
Paper. $39.50. 326 pp. .... Vendor G0140

Provine, Dorothy S. **Index to District of Columbia Wills, 1801-1920**. 1992.
Paper. $18.50. 218 pp. .... Vendor G0011

Schaefer, Christina K. **The Center:** A Guide to Genealogical Research in the National Capital Area. 1996. Indexed. Illus.
Paper. $19.95. 160 pp. .... Vendor G0010

Thorndale, William, and William Dollarhide. **County Boundary Map Guides to the U.S. Federal Censuses, 1790-1920: Maryland, Delaware, District of Columbia, 1790-1920**. 1987.
$5.95. .... Vendor G0552

ꙮ Florida ꙮ

Statewide and Regional References

Atlas of Florida, Detailed Back Roads.
  This present-day atlas provides the researcher with the detail needed to conduct a proper search. It is the size of a Rand McNally atlas of the entire U.S. 11" x 15½".
$16.95. .... Vendor G0611

Atlases & Gazetteers: Florida. Illus.
Paper. $16.95. 80 pp. .... Vendor G0632

Banvard, Theodore James Fleming. **Goodenows Who Originated in Sudbury, Massachusetts 1638 A.D.** 1994. Indexed. Illus.
Cloth. $78.50. 952 pp. .... Vendor G0116

Bolton, Herbert E. **The Spanish Borderlands: A Chronicle of Old Florida and the Southwest**. (1921) reprint 1996.
  In narrative prose, Bolton recounts the Spanish exploration and the permanent settlement of Old Florida, New Mexico, Texas, Louisiana, and California.
Paper. $22.50. 320 pp. .... Vendor G0611

Bouknecht, Carol Cox. **Florida Prison Records, 1875 through 1899**. 1993.
  Alphabetical listing of 5,100+ names, with race, sex, birth state, age, date of sentence, crime.
Paper. $14.95. 152 pp. .... Vendor G0019

Davidson, Dianne Hatcher. **The Florida Genealogist, Index, Volumes I-X, 1977-1987**. 1992. Indexed.
Cloth. $26.50. 321 pp. .... Vendor G0567

Dilts, Bryan Lee, comp. **1860 Florida Census Index: Heads of Household and Other Surnames in Household Index**. 1984.
Cloth. $46.00. 93 pp. .... Vendor G0552

Family History Library. **Research Outline: Florida**.
Leaflet. $.25. 8 pp. .... Vendor G0629

Florida Bureau of Historic Sites and Properties, Department of State. **Delegates to the Saint Joseph Constitutional Convention, 1838-1839. Final Report**. 1989.
Paper. $25.00. 388 pp. .... Vendor G0567

Hartman, David W., and David Coles. **Biographical Rosters of Florida's Confederate & Union Soldiers 1861-1865**. 6 vols. Illus.
Cloth. $400.00. Contact vendor for pricing options. .... Vendor G0590

Institute of Science and Public Affairs. **Florida County Atlas and Municipal Fact Book**. (1988) reprint 1994.
  Includes up-to-date information on each of Florida's sixty-seven counties.
$20.00. .... Vendor G0659

Kleback, Linda Pazics. **Florida State Genealogical Society, Inc., Surname Directory 1995**. Indexed.
Paper. $12.00. 126 pp. .... Vendor G0567

Michaels, Brian E. **Florida Voters in Their First Statewide Election, May 26, 1845**. 1987. Indexed.
Cloth. $20.00. 114 pp. .... Vendor G0567

Nulty. **Confederate Florida: The Road to Olustee**. 1992.
An exhaustive look at Confederate Florida and in particular at the Olustee Campaign.
Paper. $19.95. 273 pp. .... Vendor G0611

Oesterreicher, Michel. **Pioneer Family: Life on Florida's Twentieth-Century Frontier**. 1996.
A personal account of Florida in the early part of the century and the hardships encountered away from the big cities in the long-gone wilderness of Florida.
Paper. $24.95. 174 pp. .... Vendor G0611

Secretary of the Treasury. **1830 Private Land Claims in East Florida**. Report No. 25 to the 21st Congress of the United States. Indexed. Illus.
$30.00 (perfect bound). 178 pp. .... Vendor G0549

Sifakis. **Compendium of the Confederate Armies: Florida and Arkansas**. 1992.
Describes each regiment, the officers, and lists the battles in which they fought.
Cloth. $24.95. 144 pp. .... Vendor G0611

Tallahassee Genealogical Society, Inc. **Florida Voter Registration Lists 1867-68**. 1992. Indexed. Illus.
Includes 13,800+ names of male citizens (first time blacks could register to vote). Most records list name, race, length of time in state and county, place of birth (if foreign born, the place and date of naturalization), and the date of registration. Transcribed from original handwritten lists at Florida State Archives. Includes historical background, map, photos, statistical analysis by county and race. 60# acid-free paper.
Cloth. $34.50. 379 pp. .... Vendor G0036

Taylor, Anne Wood, and Mary Lee Barnes Harrell. **Florida Connections Through Bible Records. Volume I**. 1993. Indexed.
Cloth. $44.50. 522 pp. .... Vendor G0567

Thorndale, William, and William Dollarhide. **County Boundary Map Guides to the U.S. Federal Censuses, 1790-1920: Florida, 1830-1920**. 1987.
$5.95. .... Vendor G0552

Wolfe, William A., and Janet Bingham Wolfe. **Names and Abstracts from the Acts of the Legislative Council of the Territory of Florida, 1822-1845**. 1991.
Cloth. $35.00. 190 pp. .... Vendor G0567

Brevard County

Genealogical Society of North Brevard, Inc. **Index to Mortuary Records of North Brevard County Florida 1946-1980**. 1984.
Paper. $14.00. 110 pp. .... Vendor G0509

Wooley, Rose. **Index to Mortuary Records Koon's Funeral Home North Brevard County Titusville, Florida Nov. 1924-Jun. 1946**. 1992.
Paper. $5.00. 13 pp. .... Vendor G0509

Hillsborough County

Bouknecht, Carol Cox. **Florida Juror and Witness Certificates, Hillsborough Co. 1848-1860, 1862, 1885 and Holmes Co. 1848-1852, 1854-1855, 1857-1862, 1879, 1880, 1884**. 1993. Indexed.
Names from original certificates.
Paper. $11.95. 79 pp. .... Vendor G0019

Holmes County

Bouknecht, Carol Cox. **Florida Juror and Witness Certificates, Hillsborough Co. 1848-1860, 1862, 1885 and Holmes Co. 1848-1852, 1854-1855, 1857-1862, 1879, 1880, 1884**. 1993. Indexed.
Names from original certificates.
Paper. $11.95. 79 pp. .... Vendor G0019

Indian River County

Indian River Genealogical Society, Inc. **Cemeteries of Indian River County FL**. 1987. Indexed.
Cloth. $25.00 incl. postage. 252 pp. .... Vendor G0151

Jackson County

Bouknecht, Carol Cox. **Florida Juror and Witness Certificates, Jackson County 1848-64, 1866, 1870-77**. 1994. Indexed.
Names from original certificates.
Paper. $16.95. 154 pp. .... Vendor G0019

Jefferson County

Bouknecht, Carol Cox. **Florida Juror and Witness Certificates, Jefferson Co. 1849-1860, 1873, 1875, 1881 and Lafayette Co. 1859-1860, 1871, 1874-1875, 1877, 1879, 1881, 1884**. 1992. Indexed.
Names from original certificates.
Paper. $9.95. 49 pp. .... Vendor G0019

Lafayette County

Bouknecht, Carol Cox. **Florida Juror and Witness Certificates, Jefferson Co. 1849-1860, 1873, 1875, 1881 and Lafayette Co. 1859-1860, 1871, 1874-1875, 1877, 1879, 1881, 1884**. 1992. Indexed.
Names from original certificates.
Paper. $9.95. 49 pp. .... Vendor G0019

Levy County

Bouknecht, Carol Cox. **Florida Juror and Witness Certificates, Levy County 1852-1854, 1856-1857, 1861 and Liberty County 1859-1862, 1879-1881**. 1992. Indexed. Names from original certificates.
Paper. $9.50. 30 pp. .... Vendor G0019

Liberty County

Bouknecht, Carol Cox. **Florida Juror and Witness Certificates, Levy County 1852-1854, 1856-1857, 1861 and Liberty County 1859-1862, 1879-1881**. 1992. Indexed. Names from original certificates.
Paper. $9.50. 30 pp. .... Vendor G0019

Seminole County

Shofner, Jerrell H. **A History of Altamonte Springs, Florida**. 1975. Indexed. Illus.
Cloth. $33.90. 303 pp. .... Vendor G0542

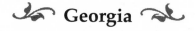 Georgia

Statewide and Regional References

1904 Georgia Community and Business Directory.
An alphabetical listing of the communities in each county with the names of merchants in each community.
Paper. $25.00. .... Vendor G0549

Alexander. **Ambiguous Lives: Free Women of Color in Rural Georgia, 1789-1879**. 1991.
Here's an excellent example of the social historian making appropriate use of genealogical methods in her research. The result is a well-written narrative history of a family, which also accomplishes her historical purpose.
Paper. $15.00. 268 pp. .... Vendor G0611

Arnold, H. Ross, and Hank Burnham, comps. **Georgia Revolutionary War Soldiers' Graves**. 2 vols. 1993. Indexed.
Paper. $39.95/set. vii + 803 pp. .... Vendor G0632

Austin, Jeannette Holland. **Georgia Intestate Records**. (1986) reprint 1995. Indexed.
Abstracts of intestate records from the fifty-seven counties formed before 1832.
Cloth. $30.00. 433 pp. .... Vendor G0010

Austin, Jeannette Holland. **The Georgians**. Genealogies of Pioneer Families. (1984) reprint 1986. Indexed.
Cloth. $30.00. 479 pp. .... Vendor G0010

Austin, Jeannette Holland. **Index to Georgia Wills**. (1976) reprint 1985. Indexed.
Cloth. Contact vendor for information. 169 pp. .... Vendor G0610

Austin, Jeannette Holland. **30,638 Burials in Georgia**. 1995.
Cloth. $50.00. 708 pp. .... Vendor G0010

Blair, Ruth. **Some Early Tax Digests of Georgia**. (1926) reprint 1971. Indexed.
Cloth. Contact vendor for information. 316 pp. + 174-p. index .... Vendor G0610

Bragg. **Joe Brown's Army: The Georgia State Line, 1862-1865**. 1987.
    Traces the history of the State Line regiments as they participated in every Confederate campaign waged in Georgia during their existence.
Cloth. $29.95. 175 pp. .... Vendor G0611

Brandenburg, John David, and Rita Binkley Worthy. **Index to Georgia's 1867-1868 Returns of Qualified Voters and Registration Oath Books (White)**. 1995.
    Full-name index to more than 103,000 white males in Georgia contained in two records. Oaths are sources for signatures. Some vital data given.
Cloth. $65.00. 600 pp. .... Vendor G0190

Bryan, Mary G. **Passports Issued by Governors of Georgia, 1785 to 1809**.
    Transcripts of documents relating to individuals and families wishing to settle in the Indian lands west of Georgia, east of the Mississippi, in present Alabama, Mississippi, and Louisiana. Places of origin are stated.
Paper. $8.00. 58 pp. .... Vendor G0627

Bryan, Mary G, and William H. Dumont. **Passports Issued by Governors of Georgia, 1810 to 1829**. Indexed.
    Continuation of the above book, with an index to both.
Paper. $8.00. 112 pp. .... Vendor G0627

Campbell, Jesse H. **Georgia Baptists: Historical and Biographical**. (1847) reprint 1993. Indexed.
Cloth. $33.00. 307 pp. .... Vendor G0610

Coulter, E. Merton, and Albert B. Saye. **A List of the Early Settlers of Georgia**. (1949, 1967) reprint 1996.
Paper. $14.00. 111 pp. .... Vendor G0011

Davis. **The Fledgling Province: Social and Cultural Life in Colonial Georgia, 1733-1776**. 1976.
    Detailed account of everyday life in colonial Georgia. Extensive footnotes.
Cloth. $32.50. 306 pp. .... Vendor G0611

Davis, Robert Scott, Jr. **The 1833 Land Lottery of Georgia and Other Missing Names of Winners in the Georgia Land Lotteries**. Indexed.
Paper. $20.00. Approx. 100 pp. .... Vendor G0610

Davis, Robert Scott, Jr. **The Georgia Black Book, Volume I: Morbid, Macabre, and Disgusting Records of Genealogical Value**. (1982) reprint 1992. Indexed. Illus.
Cloth. $42.50. 456 pp. .... Vendor G0610

Davis, Robert Scott, Jr. **The Georgia Black Book, Volume II: More Morbid, Maca-**

bre, and Sometimes Disgusting Records of Genealogical Value—Just When You Thought It Was Safe to Get Back into Genealogy. 1987. Indexed.
Cloth. $40.00. 435 pp. .... Vendor G0610

Davis, Robert Scott, Jr. **Georgia Citizens and Soldiers of the American Revolution**. (1979) reprint 1983. Indexed.
Paper. $27.00. 266 pp. .... Vendor G0610

Davis, Robert Scott, Jr. **Research in Georgia: With a Special Emphasis Upon the Georgia Department of Archives and History**. (1981) reprint 1991. Indexed. Illus.
Paper. $30.00. 268 pp. .... Vendor G0610

Davis, Robert Scott, Jr. **A Researcher's Library of Georgia History, Genealogy, and Records Sources, Vol. I**. 1987. Indexed. Illus.
Cloth. $42.50. 450 pp. .... Vendor G0610

Davis, Robert Scott, Jr. **A Researcher's Library of Georgia History, Genealogy, and Records Sources, Vol. II**. 1991. Indexed. Illus.
Cloth. $42.50. Approx. 500 pp. .... Vendor G0610

De Lamar, Marie, and Elisabeth Rothstein. **The Reconstructed 1790 Census of Georgia,** Substitutes for Georgia's Lost 1790 Census. (1976) reprint 1989. Indexed.
Cloth. $20.00. 235 pp. .... Vendor G0010

Dorsey, James E. **Georgia Genealogy and Local History: A Bibliography**. 1983. Indexed.
Paper. $15.00. vii + 384 pp. .... Vendor G0551

Dumont, William H. **Colonial Georgia Genealogical Data 1748-1783**. Indexed.
   Contains data unindexed in Georgia colonial records, e.g., marriage agreements from eight volumes of "Miscellaneous Bonds," grants, wills, deeds, list of stock owners, etc.
Paper. $7.50. 77 pp. .... Vendor G0627

Evans, Tad. **Genealogical Abstracts from Georgia Journal (Milledgeville), Newspaper 1809-1840: Vol. 5, 1836-1840**. 1995. Indexed. (See page 90-1 for vols. 1-4.)
Cloth. $64.00. 1,115 pp. .... Vendor G0532

Evans, Tad. **Milledgeville, Georgia, Newspaper Clippings (Southern Recorder), Vol. I, 1820-1827**. 1995. Indexed.
Cloth. $44.00. 504 pp. .... Vendor G0532

Evans, Tad. **Milledgeville, Georgia, Newspaper Clippings (Southern Recorder), Vol. II, 1828-1832**. 1995.
Cloth. $44.00. 535 pp. .... Vendor G0532

Evans, Tad. **Milledgeville, Georgia, Newspaper Clippings (Southern Recorder), Vol. III, 1833-1835**. 1995. Indexed.
Cloth. $44.00. 532 pp. .... Vendor G0532

Evans, Tad. **Milledgeville, Georgia, Newspaper Clippings (Southern Recorder), Vol. IV, 1836-1838**. 1996. Indexed.
Cloth. $44.00. 507 pp. .... Vendor G0532

Family History Library. **Research Outline: Georgia.**
Leaflet. $.25. 10 pp. .... Vendor G0629

Farmer, Michal Martin. **The Macon [Georgia] Telegraph (v.1 #1-v.7 #13; Nov. 1, 1826-Dec. 26, 1832) Abstracts of Marriage, Divorce, Death, and Legal Notices.** 1991. Indexed.
   An abstraction of the notices of genealogical value for this important paper for central Georgia.
Paper. $20.00. iv + 137 pp. .... Vendor G0632

The First Laws of the State of Georgia. 2 vols. (1800) reprint 1981.
Cloth. $122.50. .... Vendor G0118

Fries, Adelaide L. **The Moravians in Georgia, 1735-1740.** (1905) reprint 1993. Illus.
Contact vendor for information. 252 pp. .... Vendor G0011

Genealogical Material from Legal Notices in Early Georgia Newspapers. 1989. Indexed.
Cloth. $37.50. 310 pp. + index. .... Vendor G0610

Gentry, Lelia Thornton. **Historical Collections of the Georgia Chapters Daughters of the American Revolution. Vol. 4: Old Bible Records and Land Lotteries.** (1932) reprint 1995.
Paper. $35.00. 441 pp. .... Vendor G0011

Georgia Historical Society. **Index to United States Census of Georgia for 1820.** 2nd ed. (1969) reprint 1995.
Paper. $22.00. 167 pp. .... Vendor G0011

Georgia Scenes. Characters, Incidents &c, in the First Half Century of the Republic by a Native Georgian.
$18.50 (perfect bound). 220 pp. .... Vendor G0549

Gilmer, Gov. George R. **Gilmer's Georgians (Sketches of Early Settlers of Upper Georgia, the Cherokees and the Author).** 1855, 1926. Reprinted. Indexed. Illus.
Hard-cover. $35.00. 526 pp. .... Vendor G0632

Gilmer, George R. **Sketches of Some of the First Settlers of Upper Georgia, of the Cherokees, and the Author.** Revised and Corrected Edition with an Added Index. (1926, 1965) reprint 1995. Indexed. Illus.
Paper. $35.00. 463 pp. .... Vendor G0011

Gnann, Pearl Rahn, and Mrs. Charles LeBey. **Salzburgers and Allied Families, Georgia.** (1956) reprint 1983. Indexed.
Cloth. $35.00. 880 pp. .... Vendor G0610

Hartz, Fred R., and Emilie Hartz. **Genealogical Abstracts from Georgia Journal (Milledgeville), Newspaper 1809-1840: Vol. 1, 1809-1818.** 1990. Indexed.
Cloth. $64.00. 1,164 pp. .... Vendor G0532

Hartz, Fred R., and Emilie Hartz. **Genealogical Abstracts from Georgia Journal (Milledgeville), Newspaper 1809-1840: Vol. 2, 1819-1823.** 1992. Indexed.
Cloth. $64.00. 1,233 pp. .... Vendor G0532

Hartz, Fred R., and Emilie Hartz. **Genealogical Abstracts from Georgia Journal (Milledgeville), Newspaper 1809-1840: Vol. 3, 1824-1828**. 1994. Indexed.
Cloth. $64.00. 1,226 pp. .... Vendor G0532

Hartz, Fred R., Emilie K. Hartz, and Tad Evans. **Genealogical Abstracts from Georgia Journal (Milledgeville), Newspaper 1809-1840: Vol. 4, 1829-1835**. 1994. Indexed.
Cloth. $64.00. 1,108 pp. .... Vendor G0532

Harwell, Richard Barksdale, comp. **Confederate Imprints at the Georgia Historical Society**. 1975.
Paper. $5.00. 29 pp. .... Vendor G0636

Hawes, Lilla M., and Karen E. Osvald, comps. **Checklist of Eighteenth Century Manuscripts in the Georgia Historical Society**. 1976.
Paper. $5.00. 68 pp. .... Vendor G0636

Hawes, Lilla M., ed. **The Journal of the Reverend John Guaiacum Zubley, A.M., D.D., March 5, 1770 through June 22, 1781**. 1989.
Cloth. $17.50. 131 pp. .... Vendor G0636

Hawes, Lilla Mills, and Albert S. Britt, Jr., eds. **The Search for Georgia's Colonial Records**. 1976.
Paper. $10.00. 250 pp. .... Vendor G0636

Higgins, Margaret Elliott, ed. **Georgia Genealogical Gems**. Indexed.
    Contains twelve articles by five authors; provides information on some French marriages, taxpayers, legal notices, tax defaulters, slave owners, court records, and more.
Paper. $15.00. 190 pp. .... Vendor G0627

Historical Collections of the Georgia Chapters Daughters of the American Revolution. Vol. 1: Seventeen Georgia Counties. Published with an Index by Lelia Thornton Gentry. (1926, 1931) reprint 1995. Indexed.
Paper. $35.00. 439 pp. .... Vendor G0011

Houston, Martha Lou. **Reprint of Official Register of Land Lottery of Georgia 1827**. (1928) reprint 1992. Indexed.
Paper. $25.00. 308 pp. .... Vendor G0011

Johnson. **Militiamen, Rangers, and Redcoats: The Military in Georgia, 1754-1776**. 1992.
    Thorough examination of the military establishment in colonial Georgia. Extensive annotated bibliography.
Cloth. $25.00. 208 pp. .... Vendor G0611

Jones, George F. **The Germans of Colonial Georgia, 1733-1783**. Rev. ed. 1996. Indexed.
Paper. $17.50. 161 pp. .... Vendor G0011

Knight, Lucian L. **Georgia's Roster of the Revolution** Containing a List of the State's Defenders; Officers and Men; Soldiers and Sailors; Partisans and Regulars; Whether Enlisted from Georgia or Settled in Georgia After the Close of Hostilities. (1920) reprint 1996. Indexed.
Paper. $45.00. 658 pp. .... Vendor G0011

Liahona Reseach. **Georgia Marriages, Early to 1800**. 1990.
Cloth. $25.00. 55 pp. .... Vendor G0552

Liahona Research. **Georgia Marriages, 1801 to 1825**. 1992.
Cloth. $105.00. 613 pp. .... Vendor G0552

Lucas, Silas Emmett, Jr. **Index to the Headright and Bounty Grants in Georgia from 1756-1909, Revised Edition**. (1970) reprint 1992. Illus.
Cloth. $47.50. 786 pp. .... Vendor G0610

Lucas, Silas Emmett, Jr. **The Second or 1807 Land Lottery of Georgia**. (1968) reprint 1987. Illus.
Contact vendor for information. 170 pp. .... Vendor G0610

Lucas, Silas Emmett, Jr. **The Third or 1820 Land Lotteries of Georgia**. (1973) reprint 1986.
Cloth. $35.00. 382 pp. .... Vendor G0610

Lucas, Silas Emmett, Jr. **The Fourth or 1821 Land Lotteries of Georgia**. (1973) reprint 1986.
Cloth. $32.50. 262 pp. .... Vendor G0610

Lucas, Silas Emmett, Jr. **The 1827 Land Lottery of Georgia**. (1975) reprint 1986. Indexed. Illus.
Cloth. $30.00. 326 pp. .... Vendor G0610

Lucas, Silas Emmett, Jr. **The 1832 Gold Lottery of Georgia**. (1976) reprint 1987. Illus.
Cloth. $42.50. 568 pp. .... Vendor G0610

Lucas, Silas Emmett, Jr., and Robert Scott Davis, Jr., eds. **The Georgia Land Lottery Papers, 1805-1914**. (1979) reprint 1987. Indexed.
Cloth. $37.50. 366 pp. .... Vendor G0610

Lucas, Silas Emmett, Jr. **Some Georgia County Records, Vol. 1**. (1977) reprint 1994. Indexed.
    Contains abstracts of legal records for Columbia, Hancock, Jefferson, and Warren counties. Includes the names of more than 40,000 persons listed in these records.
Cloth. $40.00. 432 pp. .... Vendor G0610

Lucas, Silas Emmett, Jr. **Some Georgia County Records, Vol. 2**. (1981) reprint 1994. Indexed.
    Contains abstracts of legal records for Clark, Greene, Jasper, Morgan, Oglethorpe, and Putnam counties. Includes the names of more than 40,000 persons listed in these records.
Cloth. $40.00. 488 pp. .... Vendor G0610

Lucas, Silas Emmett, Jr. **Some Georgia County Records, Vol. 3**. (1978) reprint 1990. Indexed.
    Contains abstracts of legal records for Bibb, Butts, Fayette, Henry, Monroe, and Newton counties. Includes the names of more than 40,000 persons listed in these records.
Cloth. $40.00. 368 pp. .... Vendor G0610

Lucas, Silas Emmett, Jr. **Some Georgia County Records, Vol. 4**. 1991. Indexed.
  Contains abstracts of legal records for Burke, Butts, Columbia, Emanuel, Greene, Hancock, Jasper, Morgan, and Richmond counties. Includes the names of more than 35,000 persons listed in these records.
Cloth. $40.00. 430 pp. .... Vendor G0610

Lucas, Silas Emmett, Jr. **Some Georgia County Records, Vol. 5**. 1991. Indexed.
  Contains abstracts of legal records for Baker, Bibb, Early, Jones, Monroe, Marion, Morgan, Randolph, and Talbot counties. Includes the names of more than 25,000 persons listed in these records.
Cloth. $40.00. 326 pp. .... Vendor G0610

Lucas, Silas Emmett, Jr. **Some Georgia County Records, Vol. 6**. 1993. Indexed.
  This is the sixth volume in the continuing series of miscellaneous records on various Georgia counties. Included are Cherokee, Cass, Cobb, Dawson, Forsyth, Gordon, Gwinnett, Gilmer, Hall, Lumpkin, Murrary, Pickens, Rabun, Walton, Whitfield.
Cloth. $45.00. Approx. 500 pp. .... Vendor G0610

Lucas, Silas Emmett, Jr. **Some Georgia County Records, Vol. 7**. 1993. Indexed. Illus.
  Contains abstracts of records from Clarke, Habersham, Franklin, Lincoln, and Oglethorpe counties. Includes the names of approximately 38,000 persons.
Cloth. $45.00. Approx. 475 pp. .... Vendor G0610

Marriages and Obituaries from Early Georgia Newspapers. 1989. Indexed.
Cloth. $40.00. 464 pp. + index. .... Vendor G0610

Mathews, Nathan, and Kaydee Mathews. **Abstracts of Georgia Land Plat Books A & B**. 1995. Indexed. Illus.
Cloth. $33.00. 294 pp. .... Vendor G0399

McCall, Mrs. Howard H. **Roster of Revolutionary Soldiers in Georgia**. In Three Volumes. (1941, 1968, 1969) reprint 1996.
Paper. $27.00/Vol. I. $24.00/Vol. II. $38.00/Vol. III. 294 + 215 +
463 pp. .... Vendor G0011

Precision Indexing. **Georgia 1870 Census Index**. 1991.
Cloth. $350.00. 3,344 pp. .... Vendor G0552

Register, Alvaretta K. **Index to the 1830 Census of Georgia**. (1974) reprint 1982.
Cloth. $26.50. 520 pp. .... Vendor G0011

Rocker, Willard. **Marriages and Obituaries from the Macon Messenger, 1818-1865**. 1988. Indexed.
  Because of the centrality of the city of Macon in the state of Georgia, this newspaper was a natural focal point for people all over Georgia to have marriages and deaths recorded.
Cloth. $42.50. 588 pp. .... Vendor G0610

Rowland, Arthur Ray, and James E. Dorsey. **A Bibliography of the Writings on Georgia History 1900-1970**. 1966. Rev. ed. 1978.
Cloth. $20.00. xii + 531 pp. .... Vendor G0551

Schweitzer, George K. **Georgia Genealogical Research**. 1994. Illus.

History of the state, types of records (Bible through will), record locations, research techniques, listings of county records.

Paper. $15.00. 238 pp. .... Vendor G0569

Shaw, Aurora. **1850 Georgia Mortality Schedules or Census**. (1970) reprint 1982. Indexed.

Paper. $15.00. 87 pp. .... Vendor G0610

Sifakis. **Compendium of the Confederate Armies: South Carolina and Georgia**. 1995.

Describes each regiment and the officers, and lists the battles in which they fought.

Cloth. $24.95. 311 pp. .... Vendor G0611

Smith, George Gillman. **The Story of Georgia and the Georgia People, 1732 to 1860**. 2nd ed. (ca. 1901) reprint 1968. Indexed. Illus.

Cloth. $25.00. 684 pp. .... Vendor G0011

Smith, James F. **The Cherokee Land Lottery,** Containing a Numerical List of the Names of the Fortunate Drawers in Said Lottery, with an Engraved Map of Each District. With an Added Index of Names and a Map. (1838, 1969) reprint 1994. Indexed. Illus.

The upwards of 20,000 persons listed in this work were fortunate drawers in the 1832 (sixth and last) Land Lottery held in the original Cherokee County, Georgia. Cherokee County would ultimately become the parent county for all or part of twenty-five contemporary Georgia counties.

Paper. $45.00. 579 pp. in all. .... Vendor G0011

Smith, James F. **The 1832 Cherokee Land Lottery of Georgia**. (1838) reprint 1991. Indexed. Illus.

Cloth. $40.00. 504 pp. .... Vendor G0610

Southerland and Brown. **The Federal Road Through Georgia, the Creek Nation, and Alabama, 1806-1836**. 1989.

This fascinating book tells the story of the Federal Road, "possibly the longest stretch of back road in American history."

Paper. $16.50. 198 pp. .... Vendor G0611

Southern California Genealogical Society. **Land! Georgia Land Lotteries; Oregon Donation Land; Oklahoma Land Rushes**.

Paper. $2.00. 10 pp. .... Vendor G0656

Stewart, William C. **Gone to Georgia**. Indexed.

Continuation of 1800 Census of Pendleton District, South Carolina. Examines people who followed the Great Road from Virginia and North Carolina's Yadkin County into South Carolina and northeastern Georgia.

Paper. $18.00. 326 pp. .... Vendor G0627

Strobel, P.A. **Salzburgers and Their Descendants, Being the History of a Colony of German, Lutheran, Protestants Who Emigrated to Georgia in 1734**. (1855) reprint 1980. Indexed.

Cloth. $15.00. 320 pp. .... Vendor G0610

Thorndale, William, and William Dollarhide. **County Boundary Map Guides to the U.S. Federal Censuses, 1790-1920: Georgia, 1790-1920**. 1987.

$5.95. .... Vendor G0552

Volunteer Soldiers in the Cherokee War—1836-1839.
An alphabetical listing of over 11,000 volunteers from Tennessee, Georgia, North Carolina, and Alabama who volunteered in the Cherokee Wars and Removal.
$35.00 (perfect bound). 210 pp. .... Vendor G0549

Warren, Mary Bondurant. **1832 Cherokee Gold Lottery**. Indexed. Illus.
Alphabetical list of the winners of Georgia's last lottery.
Hard-cover. $15.00. 272 pp. .... Vendor G0632

Warren, Mary Bondurant, and Jack Moreland Jones. **Georgia Governor and Council Journal, 1753-1760**. 1991. Indexed. Illus.
Hard-cover. $28.50. xiv + 207 pp. .... Vendor G0632

Warren, Mary Bondurant, and Jack Moreland Jones. **Georgia Governor and Council Journal, 1761-1767**. 1992. Indexed. Illus.
Hard-cover. $28.50. xiv + 232 pp. .... Vendor G0632

Warren, Mary Bondurant, and Sarah Fleming White. **[Georgia] Marriages and Deaths, 1820 to 1830, Abstracted from Extant Georgia Newspapers**. (1972) reprint 1983. Indexed.
Hard-cover. $31.00. vi + 191 pp. .... Vendor G0632

Warren, Mary Bondurant, and Eve B. Weeks. **Whites Among the Cherokees**. Indexed. Illus.
Includes censuses, leases of Indian lands, oaths of allegiance, school rolls, militia musters, letters, newspaper accounts, and laws regarding the white families living among the Cherokees before the Trail of Tears.
Hard-cover. $26.00. 312 pp. .... Vendor G0632

White, George. **Historical Collections of Georgia**. Containing the Most Interesting Facts, Traditions, Biographical Sketches, Etc., Relating to Its History and Antiquities, from Its First Settlement to the Present Time. Third Edition. [Bound With] **Name Index of Persons Mentioned in the Historical Collections of Georgia**, by A. C. Dutton (1920). (1855, 1920) reprint 1996. Indexed. Illus.
Paper. $59.95. 803 pp. .... Vendor G0011

White, Rev. George. **Historical Collections of Georgia**. 1854. Reprinted. Indexed. Illus.
Hard-cover. $26.00. 746 pp. .... Vendor G0632

Williams. **The Georgia Gold Rush: Twenty-Niners, Cherokees, and Gold Fever**. 1993.
A study of the Georgia Gold Rush of the late 1820s.
Paper. $14.95. 178 pp. .... Vendor G0611

Wood, Virginia Steele, and Ralph Van Wood, eds. **The Reuben King Journal, 1800-1806**. 1971.
Paper. $10.00. 159 pp. .... Vendor G0636

WPA. **Georgia: The WPA Guide to Its Towns & Countryside**.
An interesting and thorough guide to the state.
Paper. $19.95. 578 pp. .... Vendor G0611

Baker County

Evans, Tad. **Albany, Georgia, Newspaper Clippings, Vol. I, 1845-1852**. 1996. Indexed.
Cloth. $44.00. 497 pp. .... Vendor G0532

Baldwin County

Cook, Mrs. Anna Maria Green. **History of Baldwin County, Georgia**. (1925) reprint 1992. Indexed. Illus.
Cloth. $30.00. 521 pp. .... Vendor G0551

Evans, Tad. **Baldwin County, Georgia, Newspaper Clippings (Union Recorder), Volume I, 1830-1833**. 1994. Indexed.
Cloth. $44.00. 548 pp. .... Vendor G0532

Evans, Tad. **Baldwin County, Georgia, Newspaper Clippings (Union Recorder), Volume II, 1834-1836**. 1995. Indexed.
Cloth. $44.00. 518 pp. .... Vendor G0532

Evans, Tad. **Baldwin County, Georgia, Newspaper Clippings (Union Recorder), Volume III, 1837-1839**. 1995. Indexed.
Cloth. $44.00. 537 pp. .... Vendor G0532

Evans, Tad. **Baldwin County, Georgia, Newspaper Clippings (Union Recorder), Volume IV, 1840-1842**. 1995. Indexed.
Cloth. $44.00. 495 pp. .... Vendor G0532

Evans, Tad. **Baldwin County, Georgia, Newspaper Clippings (Union Recorder), Volume V, 1843-1847**. 1995. Indexed.
Cloth. $44.00. 507 pp. .... Vendor G0532

Evans, Tad. **Baldwin County, Georgia, Newspaper Clippings (Union Recorder), Volume VI, 1848-1853**. 1996. Indexed.
Cloth. $44.00. 514 pp. .... Vendor G0532

Brooks County

Evans, Tad. **Brooks County, Georgia, Newspaper Clippings, Vol. I, 1866-1889**. 1995. Indexed.
Cloth. $44.00. 476 pp. .... Vendor G0532

Bryan County

White, George. **Georgia County Biographical Series, Bryan County**. Indexed.
Paper. $3.50. .... Vendor G0549

Burke County

Davis, Robert, Jr., and Silas Emmett Lucas, Jr. **The Families of Burke County, Georgia, 1755-1855,** A Census. 1981. Indexed. Illus.
Cloth. $48.50. 816 pp. .... Vendor G0610

Davis, Robert Scott, Jr. **Georgians in the Revolution: At Kettle Creek (Wilkes Co.) and Burke County**. 1987. Indexed. Illus.
Cloth. $35.00. 272 pp. .... Vendor G0610

Hillhouse, Albert M. **A History of Burke County, Georgia, 1777-1950**. 1985. Indexed. Illus.
Cloth. $30.00. x + 339 pp. .... Vendor G0551

Powell, Lillian Lewis, Dorothy Collins Odom, and Albert M. Hillhouse. **Grave Markers in Burke County, Georgia, with Thirty-nine Cemeteries in Four Adjoining Counties**. (1974) reprint 1988. Indexed.
Cloth. $32.50. 384 pp. .... Vendor G0610

White, George. **Georgia County Biographical Series, Burke County**. Indexed.
Paper. $4.50. .... Vendor G0549

Charlton County

McQueen, Alex S. **History of Charlton County**. (1932) reprint 1988. Indexed. Illus.
Cloth. $25.00. x + 295 pp. .... Vendor G0551

McQueen, Alex. S. **History of Charlton County**. With Genealogical Sketches. (1932) reprint 1993.
Cloth. $34.50. 269 pp. .... Vendor G0259

Chatham County

Georgia Historical Society. **The 1860 Census of Chatham County, Georgia**. 1979.
Cloth. $10.00. 436 pp. .... Vendor G0636

Georgia Historical Society. **Early Deaths in Savannah, GA 1763-1803: Obituaries and Legal Notices from Savannah Newspapers**. 1993.
Paper. $17.50. 280 pp. .... Vendor G0636

Georgia Historical Society. **Laurel Grove Cemetery, Savannah, Georgia**. Volume I, 12th October 1852-30th November 1861.
Paper. $27.50. 474 pp. .... Vendor G0636

Georgia Historical Society. **Marriages in Chatham County, Georgia: Volume I, 1748-1852**. 1993.
Paper. $20.00 (available as a set with Volume II for $45.00).
314 pp. .... Vendor G0636

Georgia Historical Society. **Marriages in Chatham County, Georgia: Volume II, 1852-1877**. 1993.
Paper. $27.50 (available as a set with Volume I for $45.00). 481 pp. . Vendor G0636

Georgia Historical Society. **Register of Deaths in Savannah, GA**. 1984-89.
  Volume I: 29th October 1803-1806. 73 pp., $6.50.
  Volume II: 1807-July 1811. 127 pp., $11.50.
  Volume III: August 1811-August 1818. 254 pp., $17.50.
  Volume IV: September 1818-1832. 326 pp., $20.00.
  Volume V: 1833-1847. 315 pp., $20.00.
  Volume VI: 1848-June 1853. 176 pp., $13.50.
  Index to Volumes I-VI: 29th of October 1803-June 1853. 171 pp., $17.50.
Paper. $100.00/set. .... Vendor G0636

LaFar, Mable Freeman, and Caroline Price Wilson. **Abstracts of Wills, Chatham County, Georgia, 1773-1817**. Indexed.
Paper. $8.50. 160 pp. .... Vendor G0627

Chattahoochee County

Rogers, N. K. **History of Chattahoochee County, Georgia**. (1933) reprint 1976. Indexed. Illus.
Cloth. Contact vendor for price. 402 pp. .... Vendor G0610

Chattooga County

White, George. **Georgia County Biographical Series, Chattooga County**. Indexed.
Paper. $3.50. .... Vendor G0549

Clarke County

Davis, Robert Scott, Jr. **Clarke County, Georgia Records, 1801-1892**. 1993. Indexed. Illus.
Cloth. $35.00. 264 pp. .... Vendor G0610

Cobb County

Butler, Mimi Jo, ed. **Cobb County GA Cemeteries, Vol. III**. 1994. Indexed. Illus.
  All 17,000 burials of Marietta National Cemetery, including 10,000 Union troops with original burial sites, and family of Henry Green Cole who gave property.
Cloth. $50.00. 504 pp. .... Vendor G0313

Butler, Mimi Jo., and Mary Hancock, eds. **Cobb County GA Family Tree Quarterly**. 1991. Indexed. Illus.
  Extensive Cobb County family and governmental records.
$25.00/yr. 200 pp./yr. .... Vendor G0313

Hancock, Mary, ed. **Cobb Co. GA Marriage Book 1865-1937 Whites, 1865-1966 Colored**. 1995. Indexed.
  All marriages since 1865 with full bride index.
  Cloth. $29.00. 504 pp. .... Vendor G0313

Lister, Betty, ed. **Cobb County Georgia Deed Book A, Vol. I**. 1989. Indexed.
  First deeds of Cobb Co., GA, many refiled after 1865 due to Court House fire in 1864.
  Paper. $13.00. 60 pp. .... Vendor G0313

Parker, Betty, ed. **Cobb County GA Cemeteries, Vol. II**. 1991. Indexed. Illus.
  Includes all cemeteries in the western portion of Cobb Co., GA with maps of cemeteries for entire county.
  Cloth. $50.00. 655 pp. .... Vendor G0313

Waters, Eleanor, ed. **Cobb County Georgia 1840 Census**. 1986. Indexed.
  Complete 1840 census.
  Paper. $13.00. 55 pp. .... Vendor G0313

Coffee County

Ward, Warren P. **Ward's History of Coffee County**. (1930) reprint 1985. Indexed. Illus.
  Cloth. $25.00. xiv + 388 pp. .... Vendor G0551

Coweta County

Jones, Mary G., and Lily Reynolds, eds. & comps. **Coweta County Chronicles for One Hundred Years.** With Lineages. (1929) reprint 1993.
  Cloth. $87.00. 869 pp. .... Vendor G0259

Jones, Mary G., and Lily Reynolds. **Coweta County, Georgia Chronicles**. (1928) reprint 1984. Indexed. Illus.
  Cloth. $40.00. 888 pp. .... Vendor G0610

Crisp County

Fleming, W. P. **Crisp County, Georgia: Historical Sketches, Volume I**. (1932) reprint 1980. Indexed. Illus.
  Cloth. $25.00. xiv + 228 pp. .... Vendor G0551

Dade County

White, George. **Georgia County Biographical Series, Dade County**. Indexed.
  Paper. $3.50. .... Vendor G0549

Decatur County

Jones, Frank S. **History of Decatur County, Georgia**. (1971) reprint 1980. Indexed. Cloth. $35.00. xi + 463 pp. .... Vendor G0551

Dodge County

Cobb, Mrs. Wilton Philip. **History of Dodge County**. (1932) reprint 1993. Indexed. Illus.
Cloth. $30.00. xii + 296 pp. .... Vendor G0551

Evans, Tad. **Dodge County Newspaper Clippings, Vol. I, 1873-1892**. 1991. Indexed. Cloth. $44.00. 557 pp. .... Vendor G0532

Evans, Tad. **Dodge County Newspaper Clippings, Vol. II, 1893-1907**. 1992. Indexed.
Cloth. $44.00. 503 pp. .... Vendor G0532

Evans, Tad. **Dodge County Newspaper Clippings, Vol. III, 1908-1919**. 1992. Indexed.
Cloth. $44.00. 577 pp. .... Vendor G0532

Evans, Tad. **Dodge County Newspaper Clippings, Vol. IV, 1920-1928**. 1992. Indexed.
Cloth. $44.00. 535 pp. .... Vendor G0532

Dougherty County

D.A.R., Thronateeska Chapter, Albany, Georgia. **History and Reminiscences of Dougherty County, Georgia**. (1924) reprint 1978. Indexed. Illus.
Cloth. $30.00. xvi + 444 pp. .... Vendor G0551

Evans, Tad. **Albany, Georgia, Newspaper Clippings, Vol. I, 1845-1852**. 1996. Indexed.
Cloth. $44.00. 497 pp. .... Vendor G0532

Effingham County

Farley, Hilde Shuptrine, and Alfred Earl Farley, Jr. **The Schubdrein-Schibendrein Family in Germany, 1668-1751**. 1992. Indexed. Illus.
    The ancestors of the Shuptrine Family from Georgia.
Paper. $18.00. 130 pp. .... Vendor G0024

Jones, George F., and Sheryl Exley. **Ebenezer Record Book, 1754-1781**. Births, Baptisms, Marriages and Burials of Jerusalem Evangelical Lutheran Church of Effingham, Georgia, More Commonly Known as Ebenezer Church. 1991. Indexed.
Cloth. $15.00. 187 pp. .... Vendor G0011

Lucas, Silas Emmett, and Caroline Price Wilson. **Records of Effingham County, Georgia**. (1976) reprint 1984.
Cloth. $30.00. 410 pp. .... Vendor G0610

White, George. **Georgia County Biographical Series, Effingham County**. Indexed.
Paper. $4.00. .... Vendor G0549

Elbert County

Davidson, Grace Gillam. **Historical Collections of the Georgia Chapters Daughters of the American Revolution. Vol. 3: Records of Elbert County, Georgia**. (1930) reprint 1995. Indexed.
Paper. $30.00. 348 pp. .... Vendor G0011

Floyd County

Kinney, Shirley F. **Floyd Co., Ga. Marriages - Vol. I, The Early Years 1834-1884 2nd Ed.** (1983) reprint 1989. Indexed.
Cloth. $33.50. 135 pp. .... Vendor G0021

Kinney, Shirley F. **Floyd Co., Ga. Marriages - Vol. II, 1883-1900**. 1984. Indexed.
Cloth. $33.50. 145 pp. .... Vendor G0021

Kinney, Shirley F. **Floyd Co., Ga. Miscellany - Vol. III, 2nd Ed**. 1986, 1991. Indexed.
Cloth. $38.50. 194 pp. .... Vendor G0021

Kinney, Shirley F. **Floyd Co., Ga. Marriages - Vol. IV, 3rd Ed**. (1987) reprint 1988, 1994. Indexed.
Cloth. $43.50. 172 pp. .... Vendor G0021

Kinney, Shirley F. **Floyd Co., Ga. Vital Statistics - Vols. V & VI**. 1988. Indexed.
Cloth. $49.50. 288 pp. .... Vendor G0021

Kinney, Shirley Foster, and James P. Kinney, Jr. **Floyd Co., Ga. 1890 - A Census Substitute - Vol. VII**. 1990. Indexed.
Cloth. $59.50. 345 pp. .... Vendor G0021

Kinney, Shirley Foster, and James P. Kinney, Jr. **Floyd Co., Ga. Confederates - Vol. VIII**. 1992. Indexed.
Cloth. $59.50. 380 pp. .... Vendor G0021

White, George. **Georgia County Biographical Series, Floyd County**. Indexed.
Paper. $6.00. .... Vendor G0549

Franklin County

Banks County, Georgia Hebron Historical Society. **Hebron Presbyterian Church God's Pilgrim People 1796-1996**. Indexed.
    The 200-year history of one of the first Presbyterian churches in Georgia, in one of the original counties.
Cloth. $38.00. 541 pp. .... Vendor G0681

Darnell, Ermina Jett. **Forks of Elkhorn Church**. With Genealogies of Early Members Reprinted with Numerous Additions and Corrections. (1946) reprint 1995. Indexed. Illus.

Situated near the conjunction of Franklin, Woodford, and Scott counties, the Elkhorn Church was a magnet for persons of the Baptist faith who had suffered under the established church in Virginia.

Paper. $29.50. xvii + 322 pp. .... Vendor G0011

Fulton County

Cooper, Walter G. **Official History of Fulton County**. (1934) reprint 1978. Indexed. Illus.

Cloth. $30.00. xvi + 912 pp. .... Vendor G0551

Gilmer County

Gilmer County Heritage Book Committee. **Gilmer County, Georgia Heritage 1832-1996**. Indexed. Illus.

One of the prestigious Georgia County Heritage Book series. Nearly 900 family stories, genealogies, and family photos in this most comprehensive Northern Georgia county book. Also included are stories of Gilmer County churches, clubs, schools, medical and military history, census records, and numerous other topics. All are combined in an impressive 9" x 12" hardbound book. Surname index.

Cloth. $63.60. 512 pp. .... Vendor G0087

Greene County

Smith, Mrs. Herschel W. **Historical Collections of the Georgia Chapters Daughters of the American Revolution. Vol. 5: Marriages of Greene County, Georgia (1787-1875) and Oglethorpe County, Georgia (1795-1852)**. (1949) reprint 1995.

Paper. $20.00. 210 pp. .... Vendor G0011

Hancock County

Houston, Martha Lou. **Marriages of Hancock County, Georgia, 1806 to 1850**. Reprinted with: **Land Lottery List of Hancock County, Georgia, 1806**. (1947, 1928) reprint 1995. Indexed.

Paper. $13.50. 115 pp. .... Vendor G0011

Jasper County

Davis, Robert Scott, Jr. **Records of Jasper County, Georgia, 1801-1922**. 1990. Indexed.

Cloth. $40.00. 485 pp. + index. .... Vendor G0610

Lamar County

Lambdin, Mrs. Augusta, and Mrs. Edward A. Fish. **The History of Lamar County 1825-1932**. (1932) reprint 1976, 1993. Indexed. Illus.
Cloth. $30.00. 573 pp. .... Vendor G0476

Liberty County

Stacy, James. **History and Published Records of the Midway Congregational Church, Liberty County, Georgia.** With addenda by Elizabeth Walker Quarterman and a new index prepared for this edition. 3 vols. in 1. (1903) reprint 1987. Indexed. Illus.
Cloth. $35.00. Approx. 500 pp. .... Vendor G0551

Lumpkin County

Cain, Andrew W. **History of Lumpkin County for the First Hundred Years: 1832-1932**. (1932) reprint 1992. Indexed.
Cloth. $40.00. ii + 530 pp. .... Vendor G0551

Lumpkin County Heritage Book Commission. **Heritage of Lumpkin County, Georgia 1832-1996**. Indexed. Illus.
   One of the prestigious Georgia County Heritage Book series. Nearly 700 family stories, genealogies, and family photos are included. Also of importance are the topical chapters on gold mining and Dahlongea Gold Museum, churches, clubs, organizations, and historic buildings. All combine to make this an impressive 9" x 12" hardbound book. Surname index.
Cloth. $61.50. 282 pp. .... Vendor G0087

Macon County

Hays, Mrs. Louise Frederick. **History of Macon County, Georgia**. (1933) reprint 1993. Indexed. Illus.
Cloth. $40.00. 808 pp. .... Vendor G0551

Meriwether County

Turner, Priscilla. **Meriwether County, Georgia, Cemeteries**. 1993. Indexed. Illus.
Cloth. $60.00. xvi + 616 pp. .... Vendor G0551

Montgomery County

Dorsey, James E., and John K. Derden. **Montgomery County, Georgia: A Source Book of Genealogy and History**. 1983. Indexed. Illus.
Cloth. $25.00. vi + 292 pp. .... Vendor G0551

Evans, Tad. **Montgomery County, Georgia, Newspaper Clippings, Vol. I, 1886-1905**. 1993. Indexed.
Cloth. $44.00. 570 pp. .... Vendor G0532

Evans, Tad. **Montgomery County, Georgia, Newspaper Clippings, Vol. II, 1906-1919**. 1994. Indexed.
Cloth. $44.00. 503 pp. .... Vendor G0532

Graves of Montgomery, Treutlen, and Wheeler. Indexed.
Cemetery survey of three south Georgia counties.
Cloth. $40.00. 582 pp. .... Vendor G0724

Oglethorpe County

Historic Oglethorpe County, Inc. **Cemeteries of Oglethorpe County, Georgia**. 1995.
Cloth. $39.00. .... Vendor G0738

Smith, Mrs. Herschel W. **Historical Collections of the Georgia Chapters Daughters of the American Revolution. Vol. 5: Marriages of Greene County, Georgia (1787-1875) and Oglethorpe County, Georgia (1795-1852)**. (1949) reprint 1995.
Paper. $20.00. 210 pp. .... Vendor G0011

Pulaski County

Barrow, Lee G. **Early Court Records of Pulaski County, Georgia 1809-1825**. Indexed.
Cloth. $32.50. 296 pp. .... Vendor G0610

Richmond County

Cashin. **Colonial Augusta: "Key of the Indian Country"**. 1986.
Fascinating look at colonial Augusta.
Paper. $8.95. 129 pp. .... Vendor G0611

Davidson, Grace Gillam. **Historical Collections of the Georgia Chapters Daughters of the American Revolution. Vol. 2: Records of Richmond County, Georgia (formerly Saint Paul's Parish)**. (1929) reprint 1995. Indexed.
Paper. $35.00. 402 pp. .... Vendor G0011

Jones, Charles Colcock, Jr., and Salem Dutcher. **Memorial History of Augusta, Georgia**. (1890) reprint 1980. Indexed. Illus.
Cloth. $30.00. Approx. 604 pp. .... Vendor G0551

Stephens County

Stephens County Heritage Book Committee. **Stephens County, Georgia and Its People, Vol. 1**. Indexed. Illus.

One of the prestigious Georgia County Heritage Book series. Nearly 750 modern and pioneer family stories, genealogies, and accompanying photos. Also of interest to researchers are the chapters on military history, historic markers, monuments and historic homes, transportation, early industry, churches and clubs. Hardbound collector's edition, 9" x 12". Surname index.
Cloth. $61.50. 368 pp. .... Vendor G0087

Taliaferro County

Lunceford, A. Mell, Jr. **Taliaferro County, Georgia, Records and Notes**. 1988. Indexed. Illus.
Cloth. $45.00. x + 670 pp. .... Vendor G0551

Terrell County

Kilbourne, Elizabeth Evans. **Terrell County, Georgia, Newspaper Clippings, Volume I, 1866-1872**. 1996. Indexed.
Cloth. $44.00. 525 pp. .... Vendor G0532

Thomas County

Evans, Tad. **Thomas County, Georgia, Newspaper Clippings, Vol. I, 1857-1875**. 1995. Indexed.
Cloth. $44.00. 518 pp. .... Vendor G0532

Evans, Tad. **Thomas County, Georgia, Newspaper Clippings, Vol. II, 1876-1881**. 1995. Indexed.
Cloth. $44.00. 534 pp. .... Vendor G0532

Evans, Tad. **Thomas County, Georgia, Newspaper Clippings, Vol. III, 1882-1888**. 1995. Indexed.
Cloth. $44.00. 499 pp. .... Vendor G0532

Toombs County

Cemeteries of Toombs County, Georgia. Indexed.
Cloth. $40.00. 390 pp. .... Vendor G0724

Treutlen County

Graves of Montgomery, Treutlen, and Wheeler. Indexed.
Cemetery survey of three south Georgia counties.
Cloth. $40.00. 582 pp. .... Vendor G0724

Turner County

Pate, John Ben. **History of Turner County**. (1933) reprint 1980. Indexed. Illus.
Cloth. $25.00. 222 pp. .... Vendor G0551

Upson County

Nottingham, Carolyn Walker, and Evelyn Hannah. **The Early History of Upson County, Georgia**. (1930) reprint 1982. Indexed. Illus.
Cloth. Contact vendor for information. 1,122 pp. .... Vendor G0610

Walker County

White, George. **Georgia County Biographical Series, Walker County**. Indexed.
Paper. $3.50. .... Vendor G0549

Ware County

Walker, L. J., and Marcia McDonald Black. **The History of Ware County, Georgia (revised)**. 1934. Rev. ed. 1990. Illus.
Cloth. $45.00. 704 pp. .... Vendor G0610

Washington County

De Lamar, Marie, and Elisabeth Rothstein. **Records of Washington County, Georgia**. (1975) reprint 1985. Indexed.
Cloth. $18.50. 184 pp. .... Vendor G0010

Evans, Tad. **Washington County, Georgia, Newspaper Clippings, Vol. I, 1852-1866**. 1994. Indexed.
Cloth. $44.00. 514 pp. .... Vendor G0532

Evans, Tad. **Washington County, Georgia, Newspaper Clippings, Vol. II, 1867-1880**. 1994. Indexed.
Cloth. $44.00. 514 pp. .... Vendor G0532

Evans, Tad. **Washington County, Georgia, Newspaper Clippings, Vol. III, 1881-1889**. 1994. Indexed.
Cloth. $44.00. 503 pp. .... Vendor G0532

Warren, Mary Bondurant, and Jack Moreland Jones. **Washington County, GA Land Warrants, 1784-1787**. 1992. Indexed.
Paper. $12.50. iv + 92 pp. .... Vendor G0632

Wheeler County

Graves of Montgomery, Treutlen, and Wheeler. Indexed.
Cemetery survey of three south Georgia counties.
Cloth. $40.00. 582 pp. .... Vendor G0724

Wilcox County

Young, Pauline. **Abstracts of Old Ninety-Six and Abbeville District Wills and Bonds**.
(1950) reprint 1996. Indexed.
Cloth. $50.00. 677 pp. .... Vendor G0610

Wilkes County

Davidson, Grace Gillam. **Early Records of Georgia: Wilkes County**. 2 vols. 1932.
Indexed.
Paper. $70.00. 409 + 421 pp. .... Vendor G0011

Davidson, Grace Gilliam. **Early Records of Georgia (Wilkes County), Vols. 1 & 2**.
(1933) reprint 1992. Indexed. Illus.
Cloth. $47.50. 844 pp. .... Vendor G0610

Davis, Robert Scott, Jr. **Georgians in the Revolution: At Kettle Creek (Wilkes Co.)
and Burke County**. 1987. Indexed. Illus.
Cloth. $35.00. 272 pp. .... Vendor G0610

Davis, Robert Scott, Jr. **The Wilkes County Papers, 1777-1833**. (1979) reprint 1983.
Indexed. Illus.
Paper. $28.50. 338 pp. .... Vendor G0610

Farmer, Michal Martin. **Wilkes Co., GA Deed Books A-VV 1784-1806**. 1996. Indexed. Illus.
Complete abstracts, index includes every-name and item. Maps of original and
present Wilkes Co. & Washington, GA in 1805.
Cloth. $50.00. TX residents add .0825 sales tax. 974 pp. .... Vendor G0312

Smith, Sarah Quinn. **Early Georgia Wills and Settlements of Estates: Wilkes County**.
(1959) reprint 1996. Indexed.
Paper. $12.50. 81 pp. .... Vendor G0011

Smith, Sarah Quinn. **Early Georgia Wills and Settlements of Estates, Wilkes County,
Georgia**. (1959) reprint 1994. Indexed.
Paper. $15.00. 114 pp. .... Vendor G0632

White, George. **Georgia County Biographical Series, Wilkes County**. Indexed.
Paper. $3.50. .... Vendor G0549

Wilkinson County

Davidson, Victor. **History of Wilkinson County [Georgia]**. (1930) reprint 1997.
Indexed. Illus.
Contact vendor for information. 645 pp. .... Vendor G0011

ᎏ Hawaii Ꮑ

Statewide and Regional References

British Commission Land Claims, 1843. 1995. Indexed. Illus.
Personal and land name index. The 1995 edition is out of print; a revised edition is
planned for late 1997.
Paper. $23.50. iv + 236 pp. .... Vendor G0154

Family History Library. **Research Outline: Hawaii**.
Leaflet. $.25. 6 pp. .... Vendor G0629

Thorndale, William, and William Dollarhide. **County Boundary Map Guides to the
U.S. Federal Censuses, 1790-1920: Hawaii, 1900-1920**. 1987.
$5.95. .... Vendor G0552

Honolulu

1889 Honolulu Business Directory. Self-indexed.
Paper. $14.50. ii + 82 pp. .... Vendor G0154

List of British Subjects at Honolulu, 1856. 1995. Self-indexed.
Paper. $3.65. ii + 16 pp. .... Vendor G0154

List of Foreigners Residing in Honolulu, 1847. Self-indexed.
Paper. $4.25. ii + 24 pp. .... Vendor G0154

 Idaho

Statewide and Regional References

Family History Library. **Research Outline: Idaho**.
Leaflet. $.25. 6 pp. .... Vendor G0629

Idaho Genealogical Society. **Footprints Through Idaho**. 3 vols.
Volume III includes a cumulative index for all three volumes.
Contact vendor for information. .... Vendor G0668

Southern California Genealogical Society. **Sources of Genealogical Help in Idaho**.
Paper. $1.50. 9 pp. .... Vendor G0656

Thorndale, William, and William Dollarhide. **County Boundary Map Guides to the U.S. Federal Censuses, 1790-1920: Idaho, 1870-1920**. 1987.
$5.95. .... Vendor G0552

Thousands of Idaho Surnames. 5 vols.
Volume I: $15.45.
Volume II: $24.95.
Volume III: $26.50.
Volume IV: $17.95.
Volume V: $10.50.
Contact vendor for information. .... Vendor G0633

Upper Snake River Valley Family History Center. **1910 Idaho Census Index**. 1993.
Cloth. $175.00. 1,245 pp. .... Vendor G0552

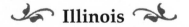 Illinois

Statewide and Regional References

Adams, James N. **Illinois Place Names**. (1969) reprint 1989.
Cloth. $21.50. .... Vendor G0501

Alvord. **The Illinois Country, 1673-1818**. 1987.
History of Illinois during this formative period.
Cloth. $29.95. 524 pp. .... Vendor G0611

Atlas of Illinois Topographical.
This present-day atlas provides the researcher with the detail needed to conduct a proper search. It is the size of a Rand McNally atlas of the entire U.S. 11" x 15½".
$16.95. .... Vendor G0611

Atlases & Gazetteers: Illinois. Illus.
Paper. $16.95. 80 pp. .... Vendor G0632

Bateman, Newton, and Paul Selby. **1904 Historical Encyclopedia of Illinois**. (1904) reprint 1978. Illus.
Many biographies.
Cloth. $35.00. 616 pp. .... Vendor G0531

Bateman, Newton, and Paul Selby. **Illinois & Effingham County,** Historical & Biographical. 2 vols. (1910) reprint 1993.
Volume I: Encyclopedia of Illinois.
Volume II: Effingham County.
Cloth. $62.00/Vol. I. $33.00/Vol. II. 616 + 272 pp. .... Vendor G0259

Carrier, Lois A. **Illinois: Crossroads of a Continent**. 1993.
Chronicles major events in Illinois history from prehistoric times to the present. A very readable history of the state.
Cloth. $29.95. 293 pp. .... Vendor G0611

Cole, Arthur Charles. **The Era of the Civil War: 1848-1870**. (1919) reprint 1987.
The history of the state of Illinois during this period.
Cloth. $29.95. 499 pp. .... Vendor G0611

Crowder. **Early Kaskaskia, Illinois, Newspapers: 1814-1832**. 1994. Indexed.
These abstracts of extant newspapers of Kaskaskia are filled with information on people from the entire region, both prominent and ordinary. This volume is jam-packed with marriages, obituaries, court and probate records, early ads, heirs, militia, land disputes, occupations, former residences, estate settlements, local events and disputes, military expeditions, divorces, and much more. Each abstract contains enough detail to explain the context of the advertisement or article. Thousands of early residents are mentioned and indexed.
Paper. $19.95. 121 pp. .... Vendor G0611

Family History Library. **Research Outline: Illinois**.
Leaflet. $.25. 9 pp. .... Vendor G0629

Ford, Governor Thomas. **A History of Illinois from Its Commencement as a State in 1818 to 1847**. Introduction by Rodney O. Davis. (1854) reprint 1995.
An outstanding early survey of Illinois history written by Illinois' seventh governor.
Cloth. $39.95. 343 pp. .... Vendor G0611

Gill, James, and Maryan Gill. **Illinois 1830 Census Index**. 4 vols.
Paper. $8.00/vol., $25.00/set. 57 + 50 + 50 + 60 pp. .... Vendor G0574

Gooldy, Pat, and Ray Gooldy. **Manual for Illinois Genealogical Research**. 1994.
Paper. $12.00. 74 pp. .... Vendor G0574

Griffis, Joan A. **Illiana Ancestors Volume 5, 1993, 1994, 1995, Genealogy Column in the Commercial News, Danville, Illinois**. 1996. Indexed.

A compilation of columns that appeared in the Danville, Illinois newspaper dealing mainly with eastern Illinois-western Indiana area.
Paper. $12.00. 97 pp. .... Vendor G0683

Hicken. **Illinois in the Civil War**. 1991.
Indispensable for studying the Illinois soldier in the Civil War.
Paper. $15.95. 415 pp. .... Vendor G0611

Historical Encyclopedia of Illinois, Edited by Bateman & Selby, & History of St. Clair Co. 2 vols. (1907) reprint 1993.
Volume I: Illinois.
Volume II: St. Clair County.
Cloth. $62.50/Vol. I. $55.00/Vol. II. $109.50/set. 616 + 522 pp. .... Vendor G0259

Illinois State Genealogical Society. **Ancestor Charts of Members—Volume 1**. 1988. Indexed.
Volume 2 is out of print.
Paper. $10.00 members/$12.00 nonmembers. 134 pp. .... Vendor G0488

Illinois State Genealogical Society. **Ancestor Charts of Members—Volume 3**. 1990. Indexed.
Paper. $10.00 members/$12.00 nonmembers. 190 pp. .... Vendor G0488

Illinois State Genealogical Society. **Ancestor Charts of Members—Volume 4**. 1990. Indexed.
Paper. $10.00 members/$12.00 nonmembers. 190 pp. .... Vendor G0488

Illinois State Genealogical Society. **Ancestor Charts of Members—Volume 5**. 1990. Indexed.
Paper. $10.00 members/$12.00 nonmembers. 192 pp. .... Vendor G0488

Illinois State Genealogical Society. **Ancestor Charts of Members—Volume 6**. 1991. Indexed.
Paper. $10.00 members/$12.00 nonmembers. 192 pp. .... Vendor G0488

Illinois State Genealogical Society. **Ancestor Charts of Members—Volume 7**. 1991. Indexed.
Paper. $10.00 members/$12.00 nonmembers. 174 pp. .... Vendor G0488

Illinois State Genealogical Sociey. **Family Bible Records—Volume 1**. 1990. Indexed.
Paper. $10.00 members/$12.00 nonmembers. 120 pp. .... Vendor G0488

Illinois State Genealogical Society. **Family Bible Records—Volume 2**. 1994. Indexed.
Paper. $10.00 members/$12.00 nonmembers. 159 pp. .... Vendor G0488

Illinois State Genealogical Society. **Guide to IL Researchers & Local Societies**. 1996.
Alphabetical listing.
Paper. $5.00 members/$6.00 nonmembers. 29 pp. .... Vendor G0488

Illinois State Genealogical Society. **Hames Collection: Pre-Statehood Land Records**. 2 reels.
Microform, $38.00 members/$45.00 nonmembers. .... Vendor G0488

Illinois State Genealogical Society. **IL Libraries with Genealogical Collections**. 1993 reprint.
Paper. $10.00 members/$12.00 nonmembers. 102 pp. .... Vendor G0488

Illinois State Genealogical Society. **IL Marriage Records Index (Pre-Statehood to at least 1900), Third Edition**.
   Consists of 95+ fiche containing over 800,000 records from 82 out of 102 counties, with 33 already completed.
Write to vendor for information. .... Vendor G0488

Illinois State Genealogical Society. **ISGS Celebrates 25 Years (1968-1993)**. 1993. Indexed.
Paper. $10.00 members/$12.00 nonmembers. 48 pp. .... Vendor G0488

Illinois State Genealogical Society. **ISGS Quarterly, Volumes I-XXV & 25 Year Index**. 4 reels. Indexed.
Microform. $76.00 members/$91.00 nonmembers. .... Vendor G0488

Illinois State Genealogical Society. **ISGS Quarterly—25-Year Index**. 1993.
   Alphabetical listing; indexed by county and subject, yearly contents; miscellaneous aids.
Paper. $12.00 members/$14.00 nonmembers. 84 pp. .... Vendor G0488

Illinois State Genealogical Society. **Prairie Pioneers, Volume 1**. 1986. Indexed.
Cloth, $28.00 members/$34.00 nonmembers. Paper, $15.00. Paper also available as a set with Vol. 2 for $25.00—see next listing. 380 pp. .... Vendor G0488

Illinois State Genealogical Society. **Prairie Pioneers, Volume 2**. 1988. Indexed.
Cloth, $28.00/members/$34.00 nonmembers. Paper, $15.00. Paper also available as a set with Vol. 1 for $25.00—see previous listing. 331 pp. .... Vendor G0488

Illinois State Genealogical Society. **Prairie Pioneers—Index to 2,830 Ancestors** (2,002 through 2,830 are not yet published).
Contact vendor for information. .... Vendor G0488

Illinois State Genealogical Society. **Remembering IL Veterans**. 1992.
   Alphabetical listing.
Paper. $6.00 members/$8.00 nonmembers. 40 pp. .... Vendor G0488

Liahona Research. **Illinois Marriages, Early to 1825**. 1990.
Cloth. $25.00. 87 pp. .... Vendor G0552

Norton, Margaret Cross. **Illinois Census Returns, 1810 [and] 1818**. (1935) reprint 1996. Indexed. Illus.
Paper. $32.50. xxxii + 329 pp. .... Vendor G0011

Norton, Margaret Cross. **Illinois Census Returns, 1820**. (1934) reprint 1996. Indexed.
Paper. $36.00. 466 pp. .... Vendor G0011

Pease. **The Frontier State (IL), 1818-1848**.
   A history of Illinois from 1818 to 1848.
Cloth. $29.95. 475 pp. .... Vendor G0611

Pease, Theodore Calvin. **The County Archives in the State of Illinois**. 1915. Reprint on microfiche. Indexed.
Order no. 129, $38.00. 730 pp. .... Vendor G0478

Reener, Lynn (Boyd). **Montgomery Co. IL Cemeteries—Volume 1**. 1985.
  Alphabetical listing.
Paper. $6.00 members/$8.00 nonmembers. 32 pp. .... Vendor G0488

Schweitzer, George K. **Illinois Genealogical Research**. 1996. Illus.
  History of the state, types of records (Bible through will), record locations, research techniques, listings of county records.
Paper. $15.00. 179 pp. .... Vendor G0569

Smith and Volkel. **How to Research a Family with Illinois Roots**.
Paper. $5.00. 44 pp. .... Vendor G0574

Smith, John H. **Illinois Regiment**.
Paper. $7.00. 24 pp. .... Vendor G0574

Thorndale, William, and William Dollarhide. **County Boundary Map Guides to the U.S. Federal Censuses, 1790-1920: Illinois, 1800-1920**. 1987.
$5.95. .... Vendor G0552

Volkel, Lowell. **Illinois 1820 Census Index**.
Paper. $18.00. 79 pp. .... Vendor G0574

Volkel, Lowell. **Illinois 1850 Mortality Schedule with Index**. 3 vols.
  Volume I: Adams thru Iroquois, 105 pp.
  Volume II: Jackson thru Ogle, 113 pp.
  Volume III: Peoria thru Woodford, 91 pp.
Paper. $12.00/vol., $30.00/set. .... Vendor G0574

Volkel, Lowell. **Illinois 1860 Mortality with Index**. 5 vols.
  Volume I: Adams thru Effingham, 129 pp.
  Volume II: Fayette thru Knox, 101 pp.
  Volume III: Lake thru Ogle, 121 pp.
  Volume IV: Peoria thru Vermilion, 113 pp.
  Volume V: Wabash thru Woodford, 106 pp.
Cloth. $12.00/vol., $56.00/set. .... Vendor G0574

Volkel, Lowell. **Illinois 1870 Mortality Schedule with Index**. 5 vols.
  Volume I: Kendall thru Macon, 60 pp.
  Volume II: Macoupin thru McHenry, 40 pp.
  Volume III: McLean thru Moultrie, 40 pp.
  Volume IV: Ogle thru Saline, 48 pp.
  Volume V: Sangamon thru Union, 50 pp.
Cloth. $11.00/Vols. I-IV. $14.00/Vol. V. $50.00/set. .... Vendor G0574

Walker, Harriet J. **Revolutionary Soldiers Buried in Illinois**. (1918) reprint 1992. Indexed.
Contact vendor for information. 186 pp. .... Vendor G0011

War of 1812 Bounty Lands in Illinois. Index by Lowell Volkel.
Paper. $25.00. 647 pp. .... Vendor G0574

Warner and Beers. **1876 Atlas of Illinois**.
Paper. $17.00. 105 pp. .... Vendor G0574

Wormer, Maxine. **Illinois 1840 Census Index**. 5 vols.
   Volume I: Adams-DuPage, 89 pp.
   Volume II: Edgar-Jefferson, 86 pp.
   Volume III: Jersey-Marshall, 85 pp.
   Volume IV: McDonough-Rock Island, 87 pp.
   Volume V: Sangamon-Winnebago, 124 pp.
Paper. $12.00/Vols. I-IV. $15.00/Vol. V. $48.00/set. .... Vendor G0574

WPA. **Guide to Public Vital Statistics Records in Illinois**.
Paper. $18.00. 135 pp. .... Vendor G0574

Adams County

Asbury, Henry. **Reminiscences of Quincy,** Containing Historical Events, Anecdotes, Matters Concerning Old Settlers, and Old Times. (1882) reprint 1995.
Cloth. $32.50. 224 pp. .... Vendor G0259

Volkel, Lowell. **Illinois Soldiers & Sailors Home at Quincy**.
Paper. $16.00. 188 pp. .... Vendor G0574

Alexander County

Perrin, William Henry, ed. **History of Alexander, Union & Pulaski Counties**. (1883) reprint 1995.
Cloth. $87.00. 588 + 338 pp. .... Vendor G0259

Wormer, Maxine. **Alexander Co. 1850 Census Transcription**.
Paper. $9.00. 31 pp. .... Vendor G0574

Boone County

Kett & Co., H. F. **Past and Present of Boone County**. (1877) reprint 1979. Illus.
Cloth. $24.00. 414 pp. .... Vendor G0531

Bureau County

Bradsby, H. C., ed. **History of Bureau County**. (1935) reprint 1995.
Cloth. $44.50. 384 pp. .... Vendor G0259

Matson, N. **Reminiscences of Bureau County,** in Two Parts, with Illustrations. (1872) reprint 1993.
Cloth. $44.00. 401 pp. .... Vendor G0259

Carroll County

History of Carroll County, Containing a History of . . . Its Cities, Towns, Etc., and a Biographical Directory. (1878) reprint 1993.
Cloth. $53.50. 501 pp. .... Vendor G0259

Smith, Marjorie. **Carroll Co. 1850 Census Transcription & Mortality Schedule**.
Paper. $9.00. 60 pp. .... Vendor G0574

Cass County

Allison and Taylor. **Cass Co. 1855 State Census**.
Paper. $9.00. 19 pp. .... Vendor G0574

Champaign County

Cunningham, J. O. **The History of Champaign County**. (1905) reprint 1995.
Cloth. $47.00. 435 pp. .... Vendor G0259

Prairie Farmer's Directory of Champaign County. Complete Directory of the Farmers of Champaign County; Breeders Directory; Business Directory. Published by "Prairie Farmer." (1917) reprint 1994.
Paper. $25.00. 266 pp. .... Vendor G0259

Stewart, J. R., ed. **A Standard History of Champaign County:** An Authentic Narrative of the Past, with Particular Attention to the Modern Era . . . with Family Lineage and Memoirs. 2 vols. (1918) reprint 1995.
    Volume I: History.
    Volume II: Biography.
Cloth. $57.50/vol., $109.00/set. 1,072 pp. .... Vendor G0259

Clay County

Wormer, Maxine. **Clay Co. 1850 Census Transcription**.
Paper. $9.00. 50 pp. .... Vendor G0574

Clinton County

Wormer, Maxine. **Clinton Co. 1850 Census Transcription**.
Paper. $9.00. 63 pp. .... Vendor G0574

Cook County

Bateman and Selby, eds. **Historical Encyclopedia of Illinois, Cook Co. Edition.** 2 vols. (1905) reprint 1994.
    Volume I: Historic Encyclopedia of Illinois.

Volume II: History of Cook County (with biographies).
Cloth. $62.00/vol. $99.50/set. 1,030 pp. .... Vendor G0259

Chicago Genealogical Society. **Obituary Dates from the Denni Hlasatel 1891-1899**. 1995.
This and the following two volumes of obituary dates from the Chicago newspaper *Denni Hlasatel* are excellent sources of information for those researching Czech, Moravian, and Slovak ancestors from the Chicago area.
Paper. $3.00. 22 pp. .... Vendor G0742

Chicago Genealogical Society. **Obituary Dates from the Denni Hlasatel 1930-1939**. 1995.
Paper. $8.00. 105 pp. .... Vendor G0742

Chicago Genealogical Society. **Obituary Dates from the Denni Hlasatel 1940-1949**. 1995.
Paper. $9.00. 130 pp. .... Vendor G0742

Kenilworth—The First Fifty Years. (1947) reprint 1994.
Paper. $16.00. 116 pp. .... Vendor G0259

McClure, Diane K., and Loretto D. Szucs. **Probate Court Records, Cook County, Illinois, Docket Book A, 1871-1872**. 1994. Indexed.
First probate docket book following the Chicago Fire of 1871. Detailed entries of 633 estates. Includes pre-fire records, estate file numbers, claims and remarks, full name index. Over 6,000 Chicago and Cook County residents listed.
Paper. $19.95. 134 pp. .... Vendor G0157

Sawislak. **Smoldering City: Chicagoans and the Great Fire, 1871-1874**. 1996.
Detailed account of the Great Chicago Fire of 1871 and the conflict that occurred afterwards. Drawn from memoirs, letters, and other documents.
Paper. $14.95. 388 pp. .... Vendor G0611

Stoddard, John H., comp. **Chicago Area Death Notices from the Chicago Tribune**.
Death notices from Nov. 1988 to the present.
Send S.A.S.E. for cost of death notice. .... Vendor G0319

Szucs, Loretto Dennis. **Chicago and Cook County: A Guide to Research**. Rev. ed. 1996.
Paper. $19.95. 528 pp. .... Vendor G0570

Volp, John H. **The First Hundred Years, 1835-1936: Historical Review of Blue Island**. (1935) reprint 1995.
Cloth. $44.50. 384 pp. .... Vendor G0259

Cumberland County

Counties of Cumberland, Jasper & Richland, Historical & Biographical. Published by F. A. Battey Co. (1884) reprint 1993.
Cloth. $85.00. 839 pp. .... Vendor G0259

DeKalb County

Taylor, Violet. **DeKalb Co. 1855 State Census**.
Paper. $7.00. 25 pp. .... Vendor G0574

DeWitt County

Taylor, Violet. **DeWitt Co. History Index**.
Paper. $9.00. 54 pp. .... Vendor G0574

Douglas County

Dugan, Taylor, and Allison. **Douglas Co. Cemetery Inscriptions**.
Paper. $8.00. 47 pp. .... Vendor G0574

DuPage County

Gross, Rev. T. Johannes. **Zion Evangelical Lutheran Church Cemetery and Burial Records 1837-1988 and Souls Register 1888.** Translated by E. F. Rittmueller. Edited by M. Fawkes and K. Madsen. 1989. Indexed.
Paper. $10.00. 154 pp. .... Vendor G0606

Harmon, Ada Douglas. **Glen Ellyn—The Story of an Old Town**. With Genealogical Sketches. Edited by Audrie A. Chase. (1928) reprint 1993.
Cloth. $29.50. 208 pp. .... Vendor G0259

Madsen, Ken. **Addison Township Records**. 1992. Indexed.
   Four microfiche containing 15,000 entries from cemetery, funeral home, and church records.
Microfiche. $10.00. 4 pp. .... Vendor G0606

Madsen, Ken. **York Township Records**. 1994. Indexed.
   Four microfiche containing 15,000 entries from cemetery, funeral home, and church records.
Microfiche. $10.00. 4 pp. .... Vendor G0606

Peters, Marjorie Herlache. **DuPage Landowners**. 1984. Indexed.
   Index to names from public domain land purchases, 1862 Map of DuPage Co., 1874 Atlas Map of DuPage Co., biographies in 1904 Atlas & History of DuPage Co., and 1875 tax list for Lombard.
Paper. $9.00. 100 pp. .... Vendor G0606

Price, Clarence. **Bicentennial Citizens and Their Ancestors**. 1976. Indexed.
   Index of birth, death, and marriage dates taken from applications for Bicentennial Citizen certificates issued in 1976.
Paper. $6.00. 48 pp. .... Vendor G0606

Richmond, C. W., and H. F. Vallette. **History of the County of Du Page,** Containing an Account of Its Early Settlement & Present Advantages & a Separate History of the Several Towns. (1857) reprint 1994.
Cloth. $29.50. 212 pp. .... Vendor G0259

Robb, Ruth Flesher. **1840 DuPage County Federal Census**. (1978) reprint 1991. Indexed.
Paper. $6.00. 17 pp. .... Vendor G0606

Robb, Ruth Flesher. **1850 DuPage County Federal Census**. (1976) reprint 1991. Indexed.
Paper. $12.50. 211 pp. .... Vendor G0606

Robb, Ruth Flesher. **1860 DuPage County Federal Census**. (1987) reprint 1991. Indexed.
Paper. $17.00. 203 pp. .... Vendor G0606

Robb, Ruth Flesher. **1870 DuPage County Federal Census**. (1987) reprint 1995. Indexed.
Paper. $25.00. 234 pp. .... Vendor G0606

Stoddard, John H. **Du Page County, Illinois Genealogical Records**. 1992. Indexed.
   Genealogical records of DuPage County—where located in DuPage County repositories
Paper. $14.00. 83 pp. .... Vendor G0319

Edgar County

History of Edgar County. With Biographies. (1879) reprint 1993.
Cloth. $79.50. 798 pp. .... Vendor G0259

EDGAR COUNTY GENEALOGICAL SOCIETY
P. O. Box 304, Paris, Illinois 61944-0304
Annual year July 1st - June 30th
Dues - $12.50   Phone 217-463-4209

Edwards County

Flower, G., and E. Washburne. **History of the English Settlement of Edwards Co.,** Founded in 1817 & 1818. (1882) reprint 1987.
Cloth. $42.50. 402 pp. .... Vendor G0259

Schwartz, Elsie. **Edwards County 1825 State Census.**
Paper. $8.00. 41 pp. .... Vendor G0574

Smith, Marjorie. **Edwards Co. 1850 Census Transcription**.
Paper. $9.00. 41 pp. .... Vendor G0574

Effingham County

Bateman, Newton, and Paul Selby. **Illinois & Effingham County,** Historical & Biographical. 2 vols. (1910) reprint 1993.
    Volume I: Encyclopedia of Illinois.
    Volume II: Effingham County.
Cloth. Vol. I, $62.00. Vol. II, $33.00. 616 + 272 pp. .... Vendor G0259

Perrin, William Henry, ed. **History of Effingham County**. (1883) reprint 1993.
Cloth. $67.00. 640 pp. .... Vendor G0259

Ford County

Prairie Farmer's Directory of Ford County. Complete Directory of the Farmers of
Ford County; Breeders Directory; Business Directory. Published by "Prairie Farmer."
(1917) reprint 1994.
Paper. $17.00. 152 pp. .... Vendor G0259

Fulton County

History of Fulton County. With Biographies. (1878) reprint 1995.
Cloth. $105.00. 1,090 pp. .... Vendor G0259

Gallatin County

Volkel, Lowell. **Shawneetown Land District Records 1814-1820**.
Paper. $18.00. 152 pp. .... Vendor G0574

Greene County

Miner, Ed. **Past & Present of Greene County**. (1905) reprint 1995.
Cloth. $67.00. 645 pp. .... Vendor G0259

Prairie Farmer Publishing Co. **Prairie Farmer's Reliable Directory of Farmers and
Breeders in Greene and Jersey Cos**. (1918) reprint 1979.
Cloth. $19.00. 264 pp. .... Vendor G0531

Hardin County

Reynolds, Marion Lavender. **Hardin County, Illinois Deaths 1884-1919 and Notes
from the Pleasant Hill Church Register**. 1995. Indexed.
Cloth. $25.00. 177 pp. .... Vendor G0682

Henry County

History of Henry County, Its Taxpayers & Voters, Containing Also a Biographical Directory . . . (1877) reprint 1995.
Cloth. $59.50. 589 pp. .... Vendor G0259

Portrait & Biographical Album of Henry County, Containing Full-Page Portraits & Biographical Sketches of Citizens . . . of the County. (1885) reprint 1993.
Cloth. $85.00. 834 pp. .... Vendor G0259

Iroquois County

Ely, S. **Centennial History of the Villages of Iroquois & Montgomery,** & the Twp. of Concord, 1818-1918. (1918) reprint 1991.
Paper. $17.00. 142 pp. .... Vendor G0259

Jasper County

Counties of Cumberland, Jasper & Richland, Historical & Biographical. Published by F. A. Battey Co. (1884) reprint 1993.
Cloth. $85.00. 839 pp. .... Vendor G0259

Jasper Co. Cemetery Survey. **Jasper Cemeteries, Crooked Creek, and Fox Townships.**
Paper. $9.00. 69 pp. .... Vendor G0574

Jasper Co. Cemetery Survey. **Some Cemeteries of Jasper Co.**
Paper. $7.00. 38 pp. .... Vendor G0574

Jersey County

Cooper, Rev. Marshall M. **History of Jerseyville, 1822 to 1901.** (1901) reprint 1994.
Cloth. $34.50. 245 pp. .... Vendor G0259

Hamilton, Oscar B., ed. **History of Jersey County.** (1919) reprint 1994.
Cloth. $34.50. 245 pp. .... Vendor G0259

Prairie Farmer Publishing Co. **Prairie Farmer's Reliable Directory of Farmers and Breeders in Greene and Jersey Cos.** (1918) reprint 1979.
Cloth. $19.00. 264 pp. .... Vendor G0531

Witt, Elaine. **Abandoned Cemeteries of Jersey Co.**
Paper. $8.00. 45 pp. .... Vendor G0574

Jo Daviess County

History of Jo Daviess County, Containing a History of . . . Its Cities, Towns, Etc., & a Biographical Directory. (1878) reprint 1993.
Cloth. $87.00. 853 pp. .... Vendor G0259

Kankakee County

1860 Kankakee County Census.
Cloth. $28.00. .... Vendor G0869

1883 Kankakee County Atlas.
Paper. $25.00. .... Vendor G0869

1893 Portrait & Biographic Record of Kankakee County.
Cloth. $23.00. .... Vendor G0869

1900 Kankakee County Atlas.
Paper. $12.50. .... Vendor G0869

1915 Kankakee County Atlas.
Paper. $12.50. .... Vendor G0869

Kankakee County Civil War Veterans.
Paper. $10.00. .... Vendor G0869

St. Anne Catholic Church Marriage Records.
Paper. $18.50. .... Vendor G0869

Kendall County

Hicks, Rev. E. W. **History of Kendall County** from the Earliest Discoveries to the Present Time. (1877) reprint 1995.
Cloth. $47.50. 438 pp. .... Vendor G0259

Plano: Birthplace of the Harvester, 1854-1954. (1954) reprint 1992.
Paper. $6.50. 32 pp. .... Vendor G0259

Knox County

Chapman, Chas. C., & Co. **History of Knox County,** Together with Sketches of the Cities, Villages & Townships . . . and Biographical Sketches. (1878) reprint 1995.
Cloth. $75.00. 718 pp. .... Vendor G0259

Lake County

The Cemetery Committee, Lake County Genealogical Society. **Warren Cemetery Tombstone Inscriptions and Burial Records, Warren Township, Lake County, Illinois**. 1995. Indexed.
Paper. $20.00. 208 pp. .... Vendor G0739

Halsey, John J., ed. **A History of Lake County**. (1912) reprint 1996.
Cloth. $89.00. 872 pp. .... Vendor G0259

Lake County (IL) Genealogical Society. **Antioch Township Cemeteries**. 1988. Indexed.
Paper. $9.30. 147 pp. .... Vendor G0464

Lake County (IL) Genealogical Society. **Avon Township Cemeteries**. 1986. Indexed.
Paper. $7.50. 126 pp. .... Vendor G0464

Lake County (IL) Genealogical Society. **Fremont Township Cemeteries**. 1980. Indexed.
Paper. $5.10. 71 pp. .... Vendor G0464

Lake County (IL) Genealogical Society. **Grant Township Cemeteries**. 1980. Indexed.
Paper. $3.00. 39 pp. .... Vendor G0464

Lake County (IL) Genealogical Society. **Guide to Cemetery Names & Locations in Lake County IL**. 1980. Indexed. Illus.
Paper. $2.10. 14 pp. .... Vendor G0464

Lake County (IL) Genealogical Society. **Index to the 1862 Military Census of Lake County IL**. (1991) reprint 1994. Indexed.
Paper. $10.50. 96 pp. .... Vendor G0464

Lake County (IL) Genealogical Society. **Index to the Past & Present of Lake County IL**. 1985. Indexed.
Paper. $10.50. 80 pp. .... Vendor G0464

Lake County (IL) Genealogical Society. **Index to the Portrait & Biog. Album of Lake County IL**. (1981) reprint 1987. Indexed.
Paper. $8.50. 58 pp. .... Vendor G0464

Lake County (IL) Genealogical Society. **Index to the Public Domain Computer Conversion Project**. 1987. Indexed.
Paper. $4.50. 10 pp. .... Vendor G0464

Lake County (IL) Genealogical Society. **Lake Co. IL Fed. Census, 1870: Vol. 1 Antioch-Avon-Grant-Newport-Warren**. 1985. Indexed.
Paper. $7.20. 136 pp. .... Vendor G0464

Lake County (IL) Genealogical Society. **Lake Co. IL Fed. Census, 1870: Vol. 2 Benton-Waukegan**. 1985. Indexed.
Paper. $7.20. 138 pp. .... Vendor G0464

Lake County (IL) Genealogical Society. **Lake Co. IL Fed. Census, 1870: Vol. 3 Cuba-Ela-Fremont-Wauconda**. 1985. Indexed.
Paper. $7.20. 106 pp. .... Vendor G0464

Lake County (IL) Genealogical Society. **Lake Co. IL Fed. Census, 1870: Vol. 4 Deerfield-Libertyville-Shields-Vernon**. 1985. Indexed.
Paper. $7.20. 127 pp. .... Vendor G0464

Lake County (IL) Genealogical Society. **Lake Co. IL Fed. Census, 1880: Vol. 1 Deerfield**. 1987. Indexed.
Paper. $4.50. 59 pp. .... Vendor G0464

Lake County (IL) Genealogical Society. **Lake Co. IL Fed. Census, 1880: Vol. 2 Vernon-Ela**. 1987. Indexed.
Paper. $4.80. 64 pp. .... Vendor G0464

Lake County (IL) Genealogical Society. **Lake Co. IL Fed. Census, 1880: Vol. 3 Cuba-Wauconda-Fremont**. 1987. Indexed.
Paper. $5.10. 77 pp. .... Vendor G0464

Lake County (IL) Genealogical Society. **Lake Co. IL Fed. Census, 1880: Vol. 4 Libertyville-Shields**. 1988. Indexed.
Paper. $4.80. 66 pp. .... Vendor G0464

Lake County (IL) Genealogical Society. **Lake Co. IL Fed. Census, 1880: Vol. 5 Waukegan**. 1988. Indexed.
Paper. $8.40. 112 pp. .... Vendor G0464

Lake County (IL) Genealogical Society. **Lake Co. IL Fed. Census, 1880: Vol. 6 Warren-Avon-Grant**. 1988. Indexed.
Paper. $4.80. 65 pp. .... Vendor G0464

Lake County (IL) Genealogical Society. **Lake Co. IL Fed. Census, 1880: Vol. 7 Antioch-Newport-Benton**. 1988. Indexed.
Paper. $5.10. 80 pp. .... Vendor G0464

Lake County (IL) Genealogical Society. **Lake Co. IL Fed. Census, 1900: Vol. 1 Fremont-Wauconda-Grant**. 1993. Indexed.
Paper. $6.75. 68 pp. .... Vendor G0464

Lake County (IL) Genealogical Society. **Lake Co. IL Fed. Census, 1900: Vol. 2 Libertyville-Vernon**. 1993. Indexed.
Paper. $7.50. 82 pp. .... Vendor G0464

Lake County (IL) Genealogical Society. **Lake Co. IL Fed. Census, 1900: Vol. 3 Antioch-Avon**. 1993. Indexed.
Paper. $7.50. 83 pp. .... Vendor G0464

Lake County (IL) Genealogical Society. **Lake Co. IL Fed. Census, 1900: Vol. 4 Cuba-Ela**. 1993. Indexed.
Paper. $6.25. 58 pp. .... Vendor G0464

Lake County (IL) Genealogical Society. **Lake Co. IL Fed. Census, 1900: Vol. 5 Benton-Newport-Warren**. 1993. Indexed.
Paper. $7.50. 77 pp. .... Vendor G0464

Lake County (IL) Genealogical Society. **Lake Co. IL Fed. Census, 1900: Vol. 6 Shields**. 1994. Indexed.
Paper. $7.75. 89 pp. .... Vendor G0464

Lake County (IL) Genealogical Society. **Lake Co. IL Fed. Census, 1900: Vol. 7 Deerfield**. 1994. Indexed.
Paper. $12.00. 130 pp. .... Vendor G0464

Lake County (IL) Genealogical Society. **Lake Co. IL Fed. Census, 1900: Vol. 8 Waukegan**. 1995. Indexed.
Paper. $22.50. 253 pp. .... Vendor G0464

Lake County (IL) Genealogical Society. **Lake County IL Landowners Map 1873 Index**. 1995. Indexed. Illus.
Paper. $6.50. 49 pp. .... Vendor G0464

Lake County (IL) Genealogical Society. **Lake County IL Marriages Vol. 1 (1839-1859)**. (1993) reprint 1994. Indexed.
Paper. $9.50. 71 pp. .... Vendor G0464

Lake County (IL) Genealogical Society. **Lake County IL Marriages Vol. 2 (1860-1880)**. (1993) reprint 1994. Indexed.
Paper. $10.00. 101 pp. .... Vendor G0464

Lake County (IL) Genealogical Society. **Lake County IL Marriages Vol. 3 (1881-1901)**. (1993) reprint 1994. Indexed.
Paper. $12.50. 140 pp. .... Vendor G0464

Lake County (IL) Genealogical Society. **Lake Villa Township Cemeteries**. 1981. Indexed.
Paper. $4.50. 60 pp. .... Vendor G0464

Lake County (IL) Genealogical Society. **Peterson Funeral Home, Waukegan IL Index to Burials (1865-1945)**. (1993) reprint 1996. Indexed.
Paper. $12.00. 147 pp. .... Vendor G0464

Lake County (IL) Genealogical Society. **Warren Township Cemeteries**. 1995. Indexed.
Paper. $20.00. 208 pp. .... Vendor G0464

LaSalle County

Allison and Taylor. **Records of LaSalle Co**.
Paper. $9.00. 53 pp. .... Vendor G0574

Baldwin, Elmer. **History of LaSalle County** ... and a Sketch of the Pioneer Settlers of Each Town to 1840, with an Appendix. (1877) reprint 1993.
Cloth. $58.00. 552 pp. .... Vendor G0259

O'Byrne, Michael Cyprian. **History of LaSalle County.** 3 vols. in 2. 1924.
    Volume I: History.
    Volume II: Biography.
Cloth. $53.00/Vol. I. $68.00/Vol. II. $109.00/set. 495 + 653 pp. .... Vendor G0259

The Past & Present of La Salle County, Containing a History of the County, Its Cities, Towns, Etc., a Biographical Directory of Its Citizens. . . . (1877) reprint 1994.
Cloth. $67.00. 653 pp. .... Vendor G0259

Patriotic Roster of LaSalle County.
Paper. $10.00. .... Vendor G0869

Lee County

Allison and Taylor. **Records of Lee Co**.
Paper. $8.00. 66 pp. .... Vendor G0574

Cochran, Dr., et al. **History of Lee County,** Together with Biographical Matter, Etc. (1881) reprint 1993.
Cloth. $89.50. 873 pp. .... Vendor G0259

Smith, Marjorie. **Lee Co. 1850 Census Transcription**.
Paper. $9.00. 66 pp. .... Vendor G0574

Livingston County

1911 Livingston County Atlas.
Paper. $12.50. .... Vendor G0869

Patriotic Roster of Livingston County.
Paper. $10.00. .... Vendor G0869

Strawn, C. C., et al., eds. **History of Livingston County** (published without Volume I, Historical Encyclopedia of Illinois). (1909) reprint 1996.
Cloth. $52.00. 480 pp. .... Vendor G0259

Logan County

Stringer, Lawrence B. **History of Logan County:** A Record of Its Settlement, Organization, Progress and Achievement. 2 vols. (1911) reprint 1995.
    Volume I: History.
    Volume II: Biography.
Cloth. $66.00/Vol. I. $45.00/Vol. II. $105.00/set. 630 + 407 pp. .... Vendor G0259

Macon County

Past & Present of the City of Decatur and Macon County, History & Biographical. (1903) reprint 1995.
Cloth. $89.50. 884 pp. .... Vendor G0259

Macoupin County

History of Macoupin County, with Illustrations . . . and Biographical Sketches of Prominent Men & Pioneers. (1879) reprint 1994.
    Original oversized book has been reduced by approximately 20 percent to fit our 8¹/₂" x 11" format. The type is clear and legible.
Cloth. $37.50. 288 pp. .... Vendor G0259

Leonard, Cinda, and Mary McKenzie. **Old Settlers' Stories, Volume 2**. Compiled by Macoupin County Illinois Genealogical Society. 1995.
    Contains stories of those who settled in Macoupin County, Illinois prior to 1900.
Paper. $7.00. 25 pp. .... Vendor G0740

Portrait & Biographical Record of Macoupin County, Containing Biographical Sketches of Prominent & Representative Citizens (reprinted without biographies of presidents and governors). (1891) reprint 1995.
Cloth. $75.00. 720 pp. .... Vendor G0259

Madison County

History of Madison County, with Biographical Sketches of Many Prominent Men & Pioneers. Published by W. R. Brink. (1882) reprint 1992.
Cloth. $55.00. 503 pp. .... Vendor G0259

St. Clair Co. Genealogical Society. **Bethel Baptist Church Minutes 1806-1851, Excerpts from the Minutes 1851-1852, Membership Lists 1809-1909**. 1993. Indexed.
    Aid to establishing family groups (women, children) prior to 1850 census; deaths prior to county registrations in 1878. Over 4,000 names.
Paper. $15.50. 98 pp. .... Vendor G0110

Wormer, Maxine. **Madison Co. 1850 Census Transcription**. 2 vols.
Paper. $24.00. 248 pp. .... Vendor G0574

Marion County

Wormer, Maxine. **Marion Co. 1850 Census Transcription**.
Paper. $16.00. 142 pp. .... Vendor G0574

Mason County

Cochrane, Joseph. **Centennial History of Mason County,** Including a Sketch of the Early History of Illinois. (1876) reprint 1995.
Cloth. $42.50. 352 pp. .... Vendor G0259

McDonough County

Clark, J. J. **History of McDonough County,** Its Cities, Towns & Villages, with Early Reminiscences, Personal Incidents & Anecdotes. (1878) reprint 1993.
Cloth. $69.50. 692 pp. .... Vendor G0259

History of McDonough County, Together with Sketches of the Towns, Villages, & Townships . . . & Biographies of Representative Citizens. (1885) reprint 1993.
Cloth. $109.00. 1,158 pp. .... Vendor G0259

McHenry County

Allison and Taylor. **Records of McHenry Co.**
Paper. $9.00. 46 pp. .... Vendor G0574

McLean County

Duis, Dr. E. **Good Old Times in McLean County,** Containing Two Hundred & Sixty-One Sketches of Old Settlers & a Complete Historical Sketch of the Black Hawk War. (1874) reprint 1993.
Cloth. $85.00. 865 pp. .... Vendor G0259

Gerwick, V. **McLean Co., Burials in Lexington Cemetery**.
Paper. $8.00. 46 pp. .... Vendor G0574

Hasbrouck, Jacob L. **History of McLean County**. (1924) reprint 1995.
Cloth. $125.00. 1,295 pp. .... Vendor G0259

History of McLean County, Containing a History of the . . . Cities, Towns, Etc. . . . & Portraits of Early Settlers & Prominent Men. (1879) reprint 1993.
Cloth. $105.00. 1,078 pp. .... Vendor G0259

Portrait & Biographical Album of McLean County, Containing Full-Page Portraits & Biographical Sketches of Prominent & Representative Citizens. With History of McLean Co. (reprinted without the biographies of U.S. presidents & governors of Illinois). (1887) reprint 1995.
Cloth. $99.50. 1,030 pp. .... Vendor G0259

Stone, Charles. **McLean Co., Pleasant Hill Cemetery Records**.
Paper. $8.00. 30 pp. .... Vendor G0574

Monroe County

Combined History of Randolph, Monroe & Perry Cos., with Illustrations Descriptive of Their Scenery & Biographical Sketches of Some of Their Prominent Men & Pioneers. (1883) reprint 1995.
Cloth. $53.00. 504 pp. .... Vendor G0259

St. Clair Co. Genealogical Society. **Bethel Baptist Church Minutes 1806-1851, Excerpts from the Minutes 1851-1852, Membership Lists 1809-1909**. 1993. Indexed.
    Aid to establishing family groups (women, children) prior to 1850 census; deaths prior to county registrations in 1878. Over 4,000 names.
Paper. $15.50. 98 pp. .... Vendor G0110

Wormer, Maxine. **Monroe Co. 1850 Census Transcription**.
Paper. $11.00. 98 pp. .... Vendor G0574

Montgomery County

Litchfield Centennial, Inc., comp. **Centennial History of Litchfield, 1853-1953**. (1953) reprint 1994.
Paper. $19.50. 208 pp. .... Vendor G0259

Reener, Lynn (Boyd). **Montgomery Co. IL Cemeteries—Volume 1**. 1985.
    Alphabetical listing.
Paper. $6.00 members/$8.00 nonmembers. 32 pp. .... Vendor G0488

Reener, Lynn (Boyd). **Montgomery Co. IL—Hart Cemetery**. 1987.
  Alphabetical listing.
  Paper. $5.00 members/$6.00 nonmembers. 33 pp. .... Vendor G0488

Montgomery Village

Ely, S. **Centennial History of the Villages of Iroquois & Montgomery,** & the Twp.
of Concord, 1818-1918. (1918) reprint 1991.
Paper. $17.00. 142 pp. .... Vendor G0259

Ogle County

History of Ogle County, Containing a History of the County, Its Cities, Towns, Etc.
With a Biographical Directory of Its Citizens . . . and Portraits of Early Settlers &
Prominent Men. (1878) reprint 1992.
Cloth. $87.00. 858 pp. .... Vendor G0259

Peoria County

Allison, Linda. **Records of Peoria Co**.
Paper. $11.00. 80 pp. .... Vendor G0574

Portrait and Biographical Album of Peoria County, with Biographical Sketches of
Prominent and Representative Citizens. (1890) reprint 1994.
Cloth. $97.50. 990 pp. .... Vendor G0259

Perry County

Clark and Spurgeon. **Perry Co. Marriages, 1827-1850**.
Paper. $13.00. 48 pp. .... Vendor G0574

Combined History of Randolph, Monroe & Perry Cos., with Illustrations Descrip-
tive of Their Scenery & Biographical Sketches of Some of Their Prominent Men &
Pioneers. (1883) reprint 1995.
Cloth. $53.00. 504 pp. .... Vendor G0259

Wormer, Maxine. **Perry Co. 1850 Census Transcription**.
Paper. $13.00. 118 pp. .... Vendor G0574

Piatt County

Piatt, Emma C. **History of Piatt County,** Together with a Brief History of Illinois
from the Discovery of the Mississippi to the Present Time [1883]. With every-name
index courtesy of Piatt Co. Historical & Genealogical Society. (1883) reprint 1994.
Cloth. $69.50. 643 + 68 pp. .... Vendor G0259

Pope County

Schonert, Janet. **Pope Co. Marriages 1816-1839**.
Paper. $9.00. 38 pp. .... Vendor G0574

Pulaski County

McMann, Martha W., Margaret K. Black, and Ethel K. Harville. **"Where They Sleep," Cemetery Inscriptions of Pulaski County, Illinois Book V**. 1995. Indexed. Illus. Hard-cover, $20.00. Laminated cover, $15.00. 115 pp. + index .... Vendor G0741

Perrin, William Henry, ed. **History of Alexander, Union & Pulaski Counties**. (1883) reprint 1995.
Cloth. $87.00. 588 + 338 pp. .... Vendor G0259

Wormer, Maxine. **Pulaski Co. 1850 Census Transcription**.
Paper. $9.00. 53 pp. .... Vendor G0574

Putnam County

Wormer, Maxine. **Putnam Co. 1850 Census Transcription**.
Paper. $9.00. 47 pp. .... Vendor G0574

Randolph County

Combined History of Randolph, Monroe & Perry Cos., with Illustrations Descriptive of Their Scenery & Biographical Sketches of Some of Their Prominent Men & Pioneers. (1883) reprint 1995.
Cloth. $53.00. 504 pp. .... Vendor G0259

St. Clair Co. Genealogical Society. **Bethel Baptist Church Minutes 1806-1851, Excerpts from the Minutes 1851-1852, Membership Lists 1809-1909**. 1993. Indexed.
   Aid to establishing family groups (women, children) prior to 1850 census; deaths prior to county registrations in 1878. Over 4,000 names.
Paper. $15.50. 98 pp. .... Vendor G0110

Taylor, Violet. **Randolph Co. 1825 State Census**.
Paper. $8.00. 29 pp. .... Vendor G0574

Taylor, Violet. **Records of Randolph Co.**
Paper. $8.00. 36 pp. .... Vendor G0574

Richland County

Counties of Cumberland, Jasper & Richland, Historical & Biographical. Published by F. A. Battey Co. (1884) reprint 1993.
Cloth. $85.00. 839 pp. .... Vendor G0259

Rock Island County

Historic Rock Island County: History of the Settlement from the Earliest Known Period to the Present Time. Including Biographies. (1908) reprint 1993.
Cloth. $47.50. 230 + 184 pp. .... Vendor G0259

Past & Present of Rock Island County, Containing a History of the County, Its Cities, Towns, Etc., & a Biographical Directory of Its Citizens. (1877) reprint 1993.
Contact vendor for information. 474 pp. .... Vendor G0259

Portrait & Biographical Album of Rock Island County, Containing Full-Page Portraits & Biographical Sketches of Citizens of the County. (1885) reprint 1993.
Cloth. $84.50. 818 pp. .... Vendor G0259

Quaife, M. M., ed. **Early Days of Rock Island [IL] & Davenport [IA]:** The Narratives of J. W. Spencer (1872) & J. M. D. Burrows (1888). (1872, 1888, 1942) reprint 1994.
Cloth. $35.00. 315 pp. .... Vendor G0259

Saline County

Moore, Bernard. **Saline Co. Marriages 1847-1880**.
Paper. $19.00. 272 pp. .... Vendor G0574

Sangamon County

History of Sangamon County, Together with Sketches of Its Cities, Villages & Townships . . . and Biographies of Prominent Persons. (1881) reprint 1993.
Cloth. $99.50. 1,067 pp. .... Vendor G0259

Shelby County

Historic Sketch and Biographical Album of Shelby County. (1900) reprint 1994.
Cloth. $39.50. 320 pp. .... Vendor G0259

Prairie Farmer's Directory of Shelby County. Complete Directory of the Farmers of Shelby County; Breeders Directory; Business Directory. Published by "Prairie Farmer." (1918) reprint 1994.
Paper. $22.50. 239 pp. .... Vendor G0259

St. Clair County

Historical Encyclopedia of Illinois, Edited by Bateman & Selby, & History of St. Clair Co. 2 vols. (1907) reprint 1993.
   Volume I: Illinois.
   Volume II: St. Clair County.
Cloth. $62.50/Vol. I. $55.00/Vol. II. $109.50/set. 616 + 522 pp. .... Vendor G0259

St. Clair Co. Genealogical Society. **1890 Census Substitute, St. Clair Co., IL**. (1891-1892) reprint 1993. Indexed.
Over 29,000 adults, limited edition. New Index.
Paper. $18.00. 240 pp. .... Vendor G0110

St. Clair Co. Genealogical Society. **Bethel Baptist Church Minutes 1806-1851, Excerpts from the Minutes 1851-1852, Membership Lists 1809-1909**. 1993. Indexed.
Aid to establishing family groups (women, children) prior to 1850 census; deaths prior to county registrations in 1878. Over 4,000 names.
Paper. $15.50. 98 pp. .... Vendor G0110

St. Clair Co. Genealogical Society. **Index to St. Clair Co., IL Probated and Non-Probated Wills 1772-1964**. 1993. Indexed.
Over 20,000 testators, limited edition. Arranged alphabetically in two sections.
Paper. $21.00. 184 pp. .... Vendor G0110

St. Clair Co. Genealogical Society. **St. Paul United Church of Christ Records, 1839-1939**. 1994/5. Indexed.
Translated from German, Fatherland towns named in first 50 years of records. Baptisms, Marriages, Confirmands, and Deaths include sponsors, parents, witnesses. Formerly St. Paul Evangelical, one of our earliest churches. Located in Belleville, the county seat. People from surrounding communities often included. Over 21,000 events.
Cloth, $59.00. Paper, $46.00. 900+ pp. .... Vendor G0110

Stark County

Leeson, M. A. **Documents & Biography Pertaining to the Settlement & Progress of Stark Co.,** Containing an Authentic Summary of Records, Documents, Historical Works & Newspapers. (1887) reprint 1988.
Cloth. $74.00. 708 pp. .... Vendor G0259

Leeson, M. A. **Stark Co. Marriages 1839-1866**.
Paper. $9.00. 48 pp. .... Vendor G0574

Shallenberger, Mrs. E. H. **Stark County & Its Pioneers**. (1876) reprint 1994.
Cloth. $37.50. 328 pp. .... Vendor G0259

Stephenson County

History of Stephenson County, Containing a History of the County, Its Cities, Towns, Etc. . . . . With biographies. (1880) reprint 1994.
Cloth. $79.00. 786 pp. .... Vendor G0259

Tazewell County

History of Tazewell County, Together with Sketches of Its Cities, Villages & Townships. (1879) reprint 1993.
Cloth. $79.50. 794 pp. .... Vendor G0259

Union County

Jackson, Ernest. **Union Co. Marriages 1818-1880**.
Paper. $19.00. 324 pp. .... Vendor G0574

Perrin, William Henry, ed. **History of Alexander, Union & Pulaski Counties**. (1883)
reprint 1995.
Cloth. $87.00. 588 + 338 pp. .... Vendor G0259

Vermilion County

Beckwith, H. W. **History of Vermilion County,** Together with Historic Notes on the
Northwest. (1879) reprint 1993.
Cloth. $99.50. 1,041 pp. .... Vendor G0259

Gill, James, and Maryan Gill. **Vermilion Co. Pioneers**. 2 vols.
Paper. $13.00. 100 pp. .... Vendor G0574

Gilroy, Frank. **Obituary Records, Records from the Ministry, Family Histories**.
Indexed.
 Covers most families of Sidell and Indianola, Illinois.
Spiral binding. $34.50. 477 pp. .... Vendor G0723

Illiana Genealogical & Historical Society. **Cemeteries of Vermilion County**. Indexed.
 Descriptive locations to over 110 cemeteries
Spiral binding. $6.50. 80 pp. .... Vendor G0723

Illiana Genealogical & Historical Society. **Cemeteries of Vermilion County Volume
I, Bount & Newell Twp**. Indexed.
Spiral binding. $22.50. 208 pp. .... Vendor G0723

Illiana Genealogical & Historical Society. **Cemeteries of Vermilion County Volume
II, Elwood & Love Twp**. Indexed.
Spiral binding. $14.00. 96 pp. .... Vendor G0723

Illiana Genealogical & Historical Society. **Cemeteries of Vermilion County Volume
III, Danville Twp. Part I**. Indexed.
Spiral binding. $27.50. 295 pp. .... Vendor G0723

Illiana Genealogical & Historical Society. **Friends of Illiana, 1826**. Indexed.
 Abstracts of Society of Friends meetings.
Spiral binding. $29.50. 391 pp. .... Vendor G0723

Illiana Genealogical & Historical Society. **Marriage Applications, Vermilion County,
Illinois 1826-1852**. Indexed.
Spiral binding. $12.00. 97 pp. .... Vendor G0723

Illiana Genealogical & Historical Society. **Marriage Applications, Vermilion County,
Illinois 1853-1874**. Indexed.
Spiral binding. $17.00. 211 pp. .... Vendor G0723

Illiana Genealogical & Historical Society. **Marriage Applications, Vermilion County, Illinois 1875-1877**. Indexed.
Spiral binding. $12.00. 58 pp. .... Vendor G0723

Illiana Genealogical & Historical Society. **Marriage Applications, Vermilion County, Illinois 1878-1881**. Indexed.
Spiral binding. $22.50. 246 pp. .... Vendor G0723

Illiana Genealogical & Historical Society. **Marriage Applications, Vermilion County, Illinois 1882-1891**. Indexed.
Spiral binding. $28.00. 351 pp. .... Vendor G0723

Illiana Genealogical & Historical Society. **Master Index of Known Burials, Vermilion County, Illinois, Part I**. Indexed.
Spiral binding. $79.50. 1,000+ pp. .... Vendor G0723

Illiana Genealogical & Historical Society. **Master Index of Known Burials, Vermilion County, Illinois, Part II**. Indexed.
Spiral binding. $79.50. 1,000+ pp. .... Vendor G0723

Wabash County

Bateman, Newton, Paul Selby, and T. G. Risley, eds. **Illinois Historical, Wabash County Biographical**. (1911) reprint 1994.
Cloth. $83.50. 738 pp. .... Vendor G0259

Warren County

Past & Present of Warren County, Containing a History of the County, Its Cities, Towns, Etc.; a Biographical Directory of Its Citizens. . . . With Modern Every-Name Index. (1877) reprint 1994.
Cloth. $49.50. 352 + 119 pp. .... Vendor G0259

Snapp, William L. **Early Days in Greenbush,** With Biographical Sketches of the Old Settlers. (1905) reprint 1993.
Cloth. $26.00. 195 pp. .... Vendor G0259

Taylor, Violet, and Dorothy Dugan. **Records of Warren Co.**
Paper. $9.00. 55 pp. .... Vendor G0574

Wormer, Maxine. **Warren Co. 1850 Census Transcription**.
Paper. $11.00. 91 pp. .... Vendor G0574

Washington County

Wormer, Maxine. **Washington Co. 1850 Census Transcription**.
Paper. $10.00. 81 pp. .... Vendor G0574

Wayne County

Bland, Doris Ellen (Witter). **Wayne County, Illinois Cemetery Inscriptions, Volumes I-IV, VI-XI**. 1991-1993. Indexed. Illus.
Paper. $14.00. .... Vendor G0387

Bland, Doris Ellen (Witter). **Wayne County, Illinois Cemetery Inscriptions, Volume V**. 1975. Indexed. Illus.
Paper. $20.00. 264 pp. .... Vendor G0387

Bland, Doris Ellen (Witter). **Wayne County, Illinois Newspaper Gleanings, 1855-75**. 1974. Indexed.
   Includes births, deaths, marriages, and divorces.
Paper. $16.00. 129 pp. .... Vendor G0387

Bland, Doris Ellen (Witter). **Wayne County, Illinois Newspaper Gleanings, 1876-1879**. 1989.
   Includes births, deaths, marriages, and divorces not in burned courthouse.
Paper. $16.00. .... Vendor G0387

Whiteside County

Bent, Charles, ed. **History of Whiteside County,** from Its First Settlement to the Present Time, with Numerous Biographical & Family Sketches. (1877) reprint 1993.
Cloth. $55.00. 534 pp. .... Vendor G0259

Biographical Record of Whiteside County. (1900) reprint 1995.
Cloth. $54.50. 522 pp. .... Vendor G0259

Davis, William A. **History of Whiteside County,** from Its Earliest Settlement to 1908. With Biographical Sketches of Some Prominent Citizens. 2 vols. (1908) reprint 1993.
Cloth. $69.00/vol. $132.50/set. 628 + 689 pp. .... Vendor G0259

Portrait and Biographical Album of Whiteside County, Containing Full-Page Portraits & Biographical Sketches of Prominent & Representative Citizens of the County with . . . a History of the County, from Its Earliest Settlement to the Present [1885]. (1885) reprint 1995.
Cloth. $94.50. 942 pp. .... Vendor G0259

Smith, Dora. **Whiteside Co. 1850 Census Transcription**.
Paper. $9.00. 64 pp. .... Vendor G0574

Will County

History of Will County. (1878) reprint 1993.
Cloth. $97.50. 995 pp. .... Vendor G0259

Williamson County

Erwin, Mile. **History of Williamson County,** from the Earliest Times Down to the Present [1876]. (1876) reprint 1993.
Cloth. $35.00. 286 pp. .... Vendor G0259

Winnebago County

Churchman, Charles. **Past and Present of City of Rockford and Winnebago Co.** (1905) reprint 1977. Indexed. Illus.
　Over 475 biographies.
Cloth. $40.00. 927 pp. .... Vendor G0531

Woodford County

Perrin, W. H., and H. H. Hill, eds. **The Past & Present of Woodford County.** With Biographical Sketches. (1878) reprint 1995.
Cloth. $69.00. 660 pp. .... Vendor G0259

Yates City

Yates City Community Centennial, 1957. (1957) reprint 1995.
Paper. $24.50. 159 pp. .... Vendor G0259

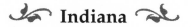 Indiana

Statewide and Regional References

1860 Indiana Census Index.
　This expanded every-name index for the 1860 census includes age, birthplace, township, county, and census page number for more than 3.4 million Hoosiers.
Microfiche. $300.00. 60 fiche. .... Vendor G0611

Alig, Leona Tobey. **Index, 1830 Federal Population Census for Indiana.** (1981) reprint 1991.
Paper. $22.75. 245 pp. .... Vendor G0109

Atlas of Indiana, 92 county maps.
　Includes detailed maps of individual counties, all the back roads, streams, lakes, towns, etc. 11" x 16".
$14.95 .... Vendor G0611

Ball, T. H. **Northwestern Indiana, from 1800 to 1900:** a View of Our Region Through the Nineteenth Century. (1900) reprint 1995.
Cloth. $59.00. 570 pp. .... Vendor G0259

Beatty, John D. **Research in Indiana**.
Paper. $6.50. 28 pp. .... Vendor G0627

Crowder. **Early Louisville, Kentucky, Newspaper Abstracts, 1806-1828**. 1995.
    These abstracts contain over 33,000 references to early residents of Louisville and the surrounding area (including Indiana), and much of Central Kentucky. An excellent source for both ordinary and prominent citizens. Contains information on marriages, obituaries, court and probate records, militia, occupations, former residences, early advertisements, lost persons, heirs, estate settlements, divorce, local events, and more.
Paper. $28.00. 283 pp. .... Vendor G0611

Dodd, Jordan R., and Norman L. Moyes, comps. **Indiana Marriages, Early to 1825**. 1991. Indexed. Illus.
Cloth. $80.00. 345 pp. .... Vendor G0552

Dorrel, Ruth, and Thomas D. Hamm. **Abstracts of the Records of the Society of Friends in Indiana,** Vol. 1. Rev. ed. 1996. Indexed.
Cloth. $62.75. 318 pp. .... Vendor G0109

Dorrel, Ruth. **Pioneer Ancestors of Members of The Society of Indiana Pioneers**. 1983.
Paper. $22.75. 246 pp. .... Vendor G0109

Esarey. **The Indiana Home**. (1953) reprint 1976.
    Details pioneer life in Indiana, yet will apply to all of the Midwest. Tells of early settlement, raising of cabins, farm life, artifacts of pioneer life, and more.
Paper. $12.95. 121 pp. .... Vendor G0611

Family History Library. **Research Outline: Indiana**.
Leaflet. $.25. 8 pp. .... Vendor G0629

Franklin, Charles. **Genealogical Atlas of Indiana**.
Paper. $10.00. 44 pp. .... Vendor G0574

Franklin, Charles. **Indiana Territorial Pioneer Records, Vol. I**.
Paper. $15.00. 101 pp. .... Vendor G0574

Franklin, Charles. **Indiana Territorial Pioneer Records, Vol. II**.
Paper. $15.00. 66 pp. .... Vendor G0574

Franklin, Charles. **Indiana Territorial Pioneer Records, Vol. III**.
Paper. $16.00. 91 pp. .... Vendor G0574

Franklin, Charles. **Indiana War of 1812 Soldiers**.
Paper. $15.00. 101 pp. .... Vendor G0574

Fraustein, Rebah M. **Census of Indiana Territory for 1807**. (1980) reprint 1990. Indexed.
Cloth. $22.75. 57 pp. .... Vendor G0109

Genealogy Division, Indiana State Library. **Index 1840 Federal Population Census, Indiana**. (1975) reprint 1991.
Paper. $32.75. 374 pp. .... Vendor G0109

Gibbs. **Indiana's African American Heritage**. 1993.
A collection of essays from "Black History News & Notes," including extensive footnotes.
Paper. $14.95. 243 pp. .... Vendor G0611

Gooldy, Pat, and Charles M. Franklin. **Indiana Wills Phase I (to 1850) and Phase II (1851-1898)**.
Cloth. $35.00/Phase I. $57.00/Phase II. 269 + 559 pp. .... Vendor G0574

Gooldy, Pat, and Ray Gooldy. **Manual for Indiana Genealogical Research**.
Paper. $15.00. 98 pp. .... Vendor G0574

Griffis, Joan A. **Illiana Ancestors Volume 5, 1993, 1994, 1995, Genealogy Column in the Commercial News, Danville, Illinois**. 1996. Indexed.
A compilation of columns that appeared in the Danville, Illinois newspaper dealing mainly with eastern Illinois-western Indiana area.
Paper. $12.00. 97 pp. .... Vendor G0683

Heiss, Willard. **1820 Federal Census for Indiana**. (1966) reprint 1975.
Cloth. $22.75. 461 pp. .... Vendor G0109

Indiana Gazetteer, or Topographical Dictionary of the State of Indiana. 3rd ed. (1850) reprint 1993.
In Indiana today there's one "Madison"; in 1850, there were eleven "Madison Townships." This book can help you find out which one you're really interested in. Very useful for early state research.
Cloth. $46.00. 440 pp. .... Vendor G0259

Indiana Source Book I; Genealogical Material from the Hoosier Genealogist, 1961-1966. By Willard Heiss. 1977.
Cloth. $22.75. 196 pp. .... Vendor G0109

Indiana Source Book II; Genealogical Material from the Hoosier Genealogist, 1967-72. By Willard Heiss. 1981.
Cloth, $22.75. Paper, $12.75. 280 pp. .... Vendor G0109

Indiana Source Book III; Genealogical Material from the Hoosier Genealogist, 1973-1979. By Willard Heiss. 1982.
Cloth, $22.75. Paper, $12.75. 352 pp. .... Vendor G0109

Indiana Source Books Index, Vols. 1-3. By Dorothy Riker. 1983.
Cloth. $27.75. 406 pp. .... Vendor G0109

Indiana Source Book IV; Genealogical Material from the Hoosier Genealogist, 1979-1981 By Rebah M. Fraustein and Willard Heiss. 1986. Indexed.
Cloth. $27.75. 366 pp. .... Vendor G0109

Indiana Source Book V; Genealogical Material from the Hoosier Genealogist, 1982-1984. By Rebah M. Fraustein. 1990. Indexed.
Paper. $17.75. 382 pp. .... Vendor G0109

Indiana Source Book VI; Genealogical Material from the Hoosier Genealogist, 1985-1988. By Ruth Dorrel. 1992. Indexed.
Cloth, $27.75. Paper, $17.75. 369 pp. .... Vendor G0109

Indiana Source Book VII; Genealogical Material from the Hoosier Genealogist, 1989-1990. By Ruth Dorrel. 1994. Indexed.
Cloth. $27.75. 500 pp. .... Vendor G0109

Maps of Indiana Counties in 1876. (1968) reprint 1979.
Paper. $18.75. 95 pp. .... Vendor G0109

Miller, Carolynne L. **Indiana Sources for Genealogical Research in the Indiana State Library**. 1984.
Cloth. $22.75. 200 pp. .... Vendor G0109

Morgan, Mary M. **Indiana 1820 Enumeration of Males**. 1988. Indexed.
Cloth. $14.75. 173 pp. .... Vendor G0109

Newman, John J. **Research in Indiana Courthouses: Judicial and Other Records**. (1981) reprint 1990.
Paper. $4.00. 15 pp. .... Vendor G0109

O'Byrne, Mrs. Roscoe C. **Roster of Soldiers and Patriots of the American Revolution Buried in Indiana**. (1938) reprint 1994.
Paper. $32.50. 407 pp. .... Vendor G0011

Pumroy, Eric, and Paul Brockman. **A Guide to Manuscript Collections of the Indiana Historical Society and Indiana State Library**. 1986. Indexed.
Cloth. $22.75. 513 pp. .... Vendor G0109

The Researchers. **Indiana, Her Counties, Her Townships, and Her Towns**.
Paper. $7.00. 33 pp. .... Vendor G0574

Riker, Dorothy. **Genealogical Sources Reprinted from the Genealogical Section, Indiana Magazine of History**. 1979. Indexed.
Cloth. $18.75. 456 pp. .... Vendor G0109

Robinson. **Who's Your Hoosier Ancestor?**. 1992.
    Loaded with information to aid in researching ancestors in the Hoosier state. Discusses both usual and unusual sources that can be employed in Indiana research.
Paper. $13.95. 2,215 pp. .... Vendor G0611

Rudolph. **Hoosier Faiths: A History of Indiana's Churches and Religious Groups**. 1995.
    This work surveys the history of more than fifty denominations and religious groups in Indiana from pioneer days to the present. 8½" x 11".
Cloth. $39.95. 710 pp. .... Vendor G0611

Schweitzer, George K. **Indiana Genealogical Research**. 1996. Illus.
    History of the state, types of records (Bible through will), record locations, research techniques, listings of county records.
Paper. $15.00. 184 pp. .... Vendor G0569

Smith, Clifford N., ed. **French and British Land Grants in the Post Vincennes (Indiana) District, 1750-1784**. Selections from The American State Papers. 1996.
    Part 1: ISBN 0-915162-64-4.
    Part 2: ISBN 0-915162-65-2.

Part 3: ISBN 0-915162-66-0.
Part 4: ISBN 0-915162-67-9.
Paper. $20.00/part. .... Vendor G0491

Southern California Genealogical Society. **Sources of Genealogical Help in Indiana**.
Paper. $3.50. 26 pp. .... Vendor G0656

Taylor, Robert M., Jr., Connie A. McBirney, eds. **Peopling Indiana: The Ethnic Experience**. 1996.
This massive volume is a collection of essays on the diverse ethnic groups that people the Hoosier state. Covers African Americans, Canadians, Chinese, English/Welsh, French, Germans, Greeks, Hispanics, Irish, Italians, Jews, Native Americans, Poles, Scandinavians, Scots, Slovaks, Southeast Asians, South Slavs, Swiss, and others. 8½" x 11".
Cloth. $39.95. 703 pp. .... Vendor G0611

Thorndale, William, and William Dollarhide. **County Boundary Map Guides to the U.S. Federal Censuses, 1790-1920: Indiana, 1800-1920**. 1987.
$5.95. .... Vendor G0552

Volkel, Lowell. **Indiana 1850 Mortality Schedule**. 3 vols.
    Volume I: Adams thru Harrison Cos., 119 pp.
    Volume II: Hendricks thru Posey Cos., 109 pp.
    Volume III: Pulaski thru Whitley Cos., 106 pp.
Paper. $12.00/vol., $30.00/set. .... Vendor G0574

Waters, Margaret R., Dorothy Riker, and Doris Leistner. **Abstracts of Obituaries in the Western Christian Advocate, 1834-1850**. 1988. Indexed.
Cloth. $27.75. 438 pp. .... Vendor G0109

Waters, Margaret R. **Indiana Land Entries—Vincennes District, 1807-1877**. (1948) reprint 1980. Indexed.
Cloth. $24.00. 275 pp. .... Vendor G0531

Waters, Margaret R. **Revolutionary Soldiers Buried in Indiana [Bound with:] Supplement**. 2 vols. in 1. (1949, 1954) reprint 1992.
Paper. $21.50. 165 pp. in all. .... Vendor G0011

Wilson, George R. **Early Indiana Trails and Surveys**. (1919) reprint 1991. Indexed. Illus.
Paper. $10.70. 114 pp. .... Vendor G0109

Wolfe, Barbara. **Index to Revolutionary Soldiers in Indiana**.
Paper. $18.00. 144 pp. .... Vendor G0574

Woolen, William Wesley, and Jacob Platt Dunn. **Executive Journal of Indiana Territory**. (1900) reprint 1985. Indexed.
Cloth. $25.25. 206 pp. .... Vendor G0109

WPA. **Guide to Vital Statistics Record in Indiana**.
Paper. $22.00. 180 pp. .... Vendor G0574

Adams County

Franklin, Charles. **Adams Co. Index to Testators to 1880**.
Paper. $9.00. 15 pp. .... Vendor G0574

Tyndall, John W., and O. E. Leah, eds. **Standard History of Adams & Wells Counties:** An Authentic Narrative of the Past, with an Extended Survey of Modern Developments in the Progress of the Town & Country. 2 vols. in 1. (1918) reprint 1992.
Cloth. $98.50. 985 pp. .... Vendor G0259

Allen County

Franklin, Charles. **Allen Co. Index to Testators to 1880**.
Paper. $10.00. 33 pp. .... Vendor G0574

Valley of the Upper Maumee River, with Historical Account of Allen County and the City of Ft. Wayne: The Story of Its Progress from Savagery to Civilization. 2 vols. (1889) reprint 1995.
Cloth. $52.50/vol., $97.50/set. 498 + 509 pp. .... Vendor G0259

Bartholomew County

Beers & Co, J. H. **1879 Landowner Atlas with History and Biographies**. (1879) reprint 1979. Indexed. Illus.
Paper. $11.00. 112 pp. .... Vendor G0531

Franklin, Charles. **Bartholomew Co. Index to Testators to 1880**.
Paper. $10.00. 19 pp. .... Vendor G0574

Slevin, Ruth. **Bartholomew Co. Marriages 1821-1850**.
Paper. $16.00. 93 pp. .... Vendor G0574

Benton County

Benton Co. Marriages 1840-1858.
Paper. $6.00. 9 pp. .... Vendor G0574

Biographical History of Tippecanoe, White, Jasper, Newton, Benton, Warren & Pulaski Counties. 2 vols. (1899) reprint 1992.
Cloth. $99.50. 1,074 pp. .... Vendor G0259

Birch, John Jesse Setlington. **History of Benton County & Historic Oxford**. (1928) reprint 1992.
Cloth. $43.50. 386 pp. .... Vendor G0259

Franklin, Charles. **Benton Co. Index to Testators to 1880**.
Paper. $7.00. 6 pp. .... Vendor G0574

Goodspeed, Weston A. **Counties of Warren, Benton, Jasper & Newton: Historical & Biographical.** (1883) reprint 1992.
Cloth. $83.00. 810 pp. .... Vendor G0259

Blackford County

Biographical and Historical Record of Jay and Blackford Counties. (1887) reprint 1995.
Cloth. $89.50. 901 pp. .... Vendor G0259

Blackford Co. Marriages 1839-1849.
Paper. $6.00. 9 pp. .... Vendor G0574

Franklin, Charles. **Blackford Co. Index to Testators to 1880.**
Paper. $8.00. 9 pp. .... Vendor G0574

Boone County

Boone & Clinton Counties. A Portrait & Biographical Record of Boone & Clinton Counties, Containing Biographical Sketches of Many Prominent & Representative Citizens. (1895) reprint 1992.
Cloth. $89.00. 908 pp. .... Vendor G0259

Franklin, Charles. **Boone Co. Index to Testators to 1880.**
Paper. $9.00. 16 pp. .... Vendor G0574

Harden, Samuel, and D. Spahr, comps. **Early Life & Times in Boone County,** from the First Down to 1886, with Biographical Sketches of Some of the Prominent Men & Women. (1887) reprint 1992.
Cloth. $51.50. 498 pp. .... Vendor G0259

Brown County

Blanchard, Charles, ed. **Counties of Morgan, Monroe & Brown,** Historical & Biographical. (1884) reprint 1992.
Cloth. $79.50. 800 pp. .... Vendor G0259

Franklin, Charles. **Brown Co. Index to Testators to 1880.**
Paper. $7.00. 8 pp. .... Vendor G0574

Carroll County

Burton, Ann Mullin. **Descendants of Noah and Margaret Crosby Mullin: A Scrapbook Family History.** 1994. Indexed. Illus.
Paper. $17.00. 205 pp. .... Vendor G0094

Burton, Ann, Conrad Burton, and Cheryl Burton. **Landowners on the 1897 (Wall) Map of Carroll County, Indiana**. 1993. Indexed. Illus.
Paper. $9.00. 30 pp. .... Vendor G0094

Franklin, Charles. **Carroll Co. Index to Testators to 1880**.
Paper. $10.00. 19 pp. .... Vendor G0574

Stewart, Dr. James Hervey. **Recollections of the Early Settlement of Carroll County**. (1872) reprint 1993.
Cloth. $41.50. 372 pp. .... Vendor G0259

Cass County

Biographical & Genealogical History of the Counties of Cass, Miami, Howard & Tipton. 2 vols. (1898) reprint 1992.
Cloth. $135.00. 1,395 pp. .... Vendor G0259

Franklin, Charles. **Cass Co. Index to Testators to 1880**.
Paper. $10.00. 20 pp. .... Vendor G0574

Powell, Jehun Z., ed. **History of Cass County,** from Its Earliest Settlement to the Present Time [1913]; with Biographical Sketches & References to Biographies Previously Compiled. 2 vols. (1913) reprint 1992.
Cloth. $109.00. 1,207 pp. .... Vendor G0259

Wolfe, Barbara. **Cass Co. Index of Estates**.
Paper. $13.00. 110 pp. .... Vendor G0574

Wolfe, Barbara. **Cass Co. Marriage Book I, 1829-1851**.
Paper. $13.00. 90 pp. .... Vendor G0574

Clark County

Clark Co. Marriages 1801-1849.
Paper. $19.00. 59 pp. .... Vendor G0574

Franklin, Charles. **Clark Co. Index to Testators to 1880**.
Paper. $10.00. 23 pp. .... Vendor G0574

Indiana Historical Society. **Census of Indiana Territory for 1807**. 1980.
    Reproduction of original lists for Indiana counties (Knox, Clark, and Dearborn) and Randolph Co., IL. Over 2,500 early settlers. 8½" x 11".
Cloth. $20.00. 57 pp. .... Vendor G0611

Lee, William. **1889 Biographical and Historical Souvenir of Clark Co.** (1889) reprint 1981. Indexed. Illus.
    Originally included eight counties. Two indexes.
Paper. $12.00. 158 pp. .... Vendor G0531

McCoy, W. H. **Pioneer Families of Clark County**. (1947) reprint 1987.
Paper. $4.50. 15 pp. t.s. .... Vendor G0259

Clay County

Blanchard, Charles, ed. **Counties of Clay & Owen, Historical & Biographical.** (1884) reprint 1992.
Cloth. $95.00. 966 pp. .... Vendor G0259

Franklin, Charles. **Clay Co. Index to Testators to 1880**.
Paper. $8.00. 12 pp. .... Vendor G0574

Franklin, Charles. **Clay Co. Will Abstracts 1848-1867**.
Paper. $10.00. 37 pp. .... Vendor G0574

Clinton County

Boone & Clinton Counties. A Portrait & Biographical Record of Boone & Clinton Counties, Containing Biographical Sketches of Many Prominent & Representative Citizens. (1895) reprint 1992.
Cloth. $89.00. 908 pp. .... Vendor G0259

Claybaugh, Hon. Joseph. **History of Clinton County,** with Historical Sketches of Representative Citizens & Genealogical Records of Many of the Old Families. (1913) reprint 1992.
Cloth. $97.00. 982 pp. .... Vendor G0259

Franklin, Charles. **Clinton Co. Index to Testators to 1880**.
Paper. $9.00. 17 pp. .... Vendor G0574

Slevin, Ruth. **Clinton Co. Marriage Book I, 1830-1849**.
Paper. $11.00. 59 pp. .... Vendor G0574

Crawford County

Crawford Co. Marriages 1818-1849.
Paper. $9.00. 26 pp. .... Vendor G0574

Franklin, Charles. **Crawford Co. Index to Testators to 1880**.
Paper. $7.00. 8 pp. .... Vendor G0574

Pleasant, Hazen H. **History of Crawford County**. (1926) reprint 1992.
Cloth. $67.00. 644 pp. .... Vendor G0259

Daviess County

Franklin, Charles. **Daviess Co. Index to Testators to 1880**.
Paper. $9.00. 15 pp. .... Vendor G0574

History of Knox & Daviess Counties, from the Earliest Time to the Present; with Biographical Sketches, Reminiscences, Notes, Etc. . . . with an Extended History of

the Colonial Days of Vincennes, and Its Progress Down to the Formation of the State Government. (1886) reprint 1995.
Cloth. $92.50. 914 pp. .... Vendor G0259

Dearborn County

Dearborn Co. Marriages 1803-1849.
Paper. $25.00. .... Vendor G0574

Fox, Dianne, and Lois Harper. **Cemeteries of the NE Section of Dearborn Co**.
Paper. $24.95. 250 pp. .... Vendor G0536

Franklin, Charles. **Dearborn Co. Index to Testators to 1880**.
Paper. $11.00. 36 pp. .... Vendor G0574

Harper, Lois. **Delayed Birth Records at Dearborn County, Indiana**.
Paper. $8.50. 67 pp. .... Vendor G0536

History of Dearborn & Ohio Counties, from Their Earliest Settlement. With Biographies. (1885) reprint 1993.
Cloth. $98.50. 1,072 pp. .... Vendor G0259

Indiana Historical Society. **Census of Indiana Territory for 1807**. 1980.
    Reproduction of original lists for Indiana counties (Knox, Clark, and Dearborn) and Randolph Co., IL. Over 2,500 early settlers. 8½" x 11".
Cloth. $20.00. 57 pp. .... Vendor G0611

Ross, W. B. **Manchester, Indiana**. Edited by Dolores Black Rench. Indexed. Illus.
    Reminiscences 1870 to 1935. Ross, Millikin, and other families. Churches, schools, societies; 1875 landowners map of Manchester Township. Fifty photographs.
Cloth. $13.00. .... Vendor G0084

Shaw, Archibald, ed. **History of Dearborn County,** Her People, Industries & Institutions, with Biographical Sketches of Representative Citizens & Genealogical Records of Old Families. (1915) reprint 1992.
Cloth. $99.00. 1,072 pp. .... Vendor G0259

Decatur County

Decatur Co. Marriages 1822-1849.
Paper. $18.00. .... Vendor G0574

Franklin, Charles. **Decatur Co. Index to Testators to 1880**.
Paper. $10.00. 24 pp. .... Vendor G0574

Harding, Lewis A. **History of Decatur County:** Its People, Industries & Institutions. (1915) reprint 1992.
Cloth. $109.00. 1,216 pp. .... Vendor G0259

DeKalb County

Carey, Dr. W. W. **History of Spencerville**. (1952) reprint 1996.
Cloth. $17.00. 125 pp. .... Vendor G0259

DeKalb Marriages 1837-1849.
Paper. $7.00. 16 pp. .... Vendor G0574

Ford, Stevens, McEwen, and McIntosh, eds. **History of Northeast Indiana:** LaGrange, Steuben, Noble & DeKalb Counties. 2 vols. (1920) reprint 1993.
Cloth. $105.00. 612 + 463 pp. .... Vendor G0259

Franklin, Charles. **DeKalb Co. Index to Testators to 1880**.
Paper. $8.00. 14 pp. .... Vendor G0574

History of DeKalb County, with Biographical Sketches of Representative Citizens and Genealogical Records of Old Families. (1914) reprint 1992.
Cloth. $97.00. 1,004 pp. .... Vendor G0259

Delaware County

Delaware County Historical Alliance. **Beech Grove Cemetery Records Muncie, Indiana from Office Records and Tombstone Inscriptions**. 1993. Indexed. Illus.
    History, pictures, over 7,200 records dating from 1828, alphabetical and lot print-outs, earliest known lot owners, detailed maps, all burials in Old Part and total cemetery up to 1899.
Paper. $27.50. 314 pp. .... Vendor G0095

Franklin, Charles. **Delaware Co. Index to Testators to 1880**.
Paper. $9.00. 19 pp. .... Vendor G0574

Griffin and Gordon. **1887 Landowner Atlas, Township, Town Plats, Business Directories**. (1887) reprint 1971.
Paper. $9.00. 26 pp. .... Vendor G0531

Haimbaugh, Frank D., ed. **History of Delaware County**. 2 vols. (1924) reprint 1992.
Cloth. $115.00. 578 + 687 pp. .... Vendor G0259

Portrait & Biographical Records of Delaware & Randolph Counties, Containing Biographical Sketches of Many Prominent & Representative Citizens. (1894) reprint 1992.
Cloth. $135.00. 1,445 pp. .... Vendor G0259

Rench, Dolores, and Nona Nunnelly. **Every Name Index to 1887 Atlas of Delaware County**. 1987.
    Atlas [published 1997 Griffing, Gordon & Co., reprinted 1971 by Mayhill Publications] not included. Map Guide to Cemeteries.
Cloth. $6.00. 34 pp. .... Vendor G0084

Rench, Dolores, and Nona Nunnelly. **Map of Delaware County, Indiana, 1874 (Atlas)**. 1994. Indexed. Illus.
  Thirty plat maps with 3,400-name index to landowners, churches, cemeteries, etc.
Cloth. $14.00. 43 pp. .... Vendor G0084

Dubois County

Franklin, Charles. **Dubois Co. Index to Testators to 1880**.
Paper. $9.00. 19 pp. .... Vendor G0574

Elkhart County

Biographical & Pictorial Memoirs of Elkhart & St. Joseph Counties. Together
with Biographies of Many Prominent Men of N. Indiana & of the Whole State. (1893)
reprint 1992.
Cloth. $79.50. 777 pp. .... Vendor G0259

Franklin, Charles. **Elkhart Co. Index to Testators to 1880**.
Paper. $9.00. 22 pp. .... Vendor G0574

History of Elkhart County, Together with Sketches of Its Cities, Villages & Townships and . . . Biographies of Representative Citizens. With the History of Indiana.
(1881) reprint 1992.
Cloth. $109.00. 1,181 pp. .... Vendor G0259

Skwiercz, Andrew L., and John L. Gold, comps. **Index to the Records of the Wally-Mills-Zimmerman Funeral Home, Elkhart, Indiana, April 1912-October 1988**.
1996.
Spiral binding. $14.50. .... Vendor G0685

Fayette County

Franklin, Charles. **Fayette Co. Index to Testators to 1880**.
Paper. $8.00. 17 pp. .... Vendor G0574

Lewis Publishing Co. **History of Wayne, Fayette, Union & Franklin Counties.** 2
vols. (1899) reprint 1992.
Cloth. $99.50. 1,073 pp. .... Vendor G0259

Slevin, Ruth. **Fayette Co. Will Records 1819-1895**.
Paper. $20.00. 146 pp. .... Vendor G0574

Walters, H. Max. Edited by David N. Walters. **The Making of Connersville and
Fayette County, Vol. 2**. 1989. Indexed.
  Stories about its people, places, and events.
Paper. $15.50. 290 pp. .... Vendor G0472

Floyd County

Franklin, Charles. **Floyd Co. Index to Testators to 1880**.
Paper. $9.00. 23 pp. .... Vendor G0574

Fountain County

Beckwith, H. W. **History of Fountain County (and Montgomery Co.),** Together
with Historic Notes on the Wabash Valley. (1881) reprint 1992.
Cloth. $95.00. History of Montgomery Co. only: $32.00, 224 pp. 982 pp. .... Vendor
G0259

Franklin, Charles. **Fountain Co. Index to Testators to 1880**.
Paper. $9.00. 21 pp. .... Vendor G0574

Volkel, Lowell. **Fountain Co. Biographical Abstracts**.
Paper. $9.00. 42 pp. .... Vendor G0574

Franklin County

Franklin, Charles. **Franklin Co. Index to Testators to 1880**.
Paper. $10.00. 32 pp. .... Vendor G0574

Lewis Publishing Co. **History of Wayne, Fayette, Union & Franklin Counties**. 2
vols. (1899) reprint 1992.
Cloth. $99.50. 1,073 pp. .... Vendor G0259

Fulton County

Franklin, Charles. **Fulton Co. Index to Testators to 1880**.
Paper. $7.00. 11 pp. .... Vendor G0574

Fulton Co. Marriages 1835-1849.
Paper. $8.00. 18 pp. .... Vendor G0574

Gibson County

Franklin, Charles. **Gibson Co. Index to Testators to 1880**.
Paper. $8.00. 17 pp. .... Vendor G0574

Grant County

Franklin, Charles. **Grant Co. Index to Testators to 1880**.
Paper. $8.00. 17 pp. .... Vendor G0574

Greene County

Franklin, Charles. **Greene Co. Index to Testators to 1880**.
Paper. $8.00. 14 pp. .... Vendor G0574

Franklin, Charles. **Greene Co. Marriages Vol. I 1821-1844**.
Paper. $9.00. 29 pp. .... Vendor G0574

Franklin, Charles. **Greene Co. Marriages Vol. II 1845-1852**.
Paper. $9.00. 31 pp. .... Vendor G0574

History of Greene & Sullivan Counties, from the Earliest Times to the Present,
Together with Interesting Biographical Sketches. (1884) reprint 1993.
Cloth. $85.00. 824 pp. .... Vendor G0259

Hamilton County

Franklin, Charles. **Hamilton Co. Index to Testators to 1880**.
Paper. $9.00. 19 pp. .... Vendor G0574

Ingmire, Frances. **Hamilton Co. Marriage Records 1833-1843**.
Paper. $17.00. 247 pp. .... Vendor G0574

Ingmire, Frances. **Hamilton Co. Naturalization Records 1855-1905**.
Paper. $14.00. 209 pp. .... Vendor G0574

Ingmire, Frances. **Hamilton Co. Will Records 1823-1834**.
Paper. $14.00. 143 pp. .... Vendor G0574

Ingmire, Frances. **Hamilton Co. Will Records 1835-1844**.
Paper. $14.00. 161 pp. .... Vendor G0574

Shirts, Augustus Finch. **History of the Formation, Settlement & Development of
Hamilton County** from the Year 1818 to the Close of the Civil War. (1901) reprint
1993.
Cloth. $39.50. 370 pp. .... Vendor G0259

Hancock County

Binford, J. H. **History of Hancock County,** from Its Earliest Settlement by the "Pale
Face" in 1818, Down to 1882. (1882) reprint 1992.
Cloth. $57.00. 536 pp. .... Vendor G0259

Franklin, Charles. **Hancock Co. Index to Testators to 1880**.
Paper. $8.00. 16 pp. .... Vendor G0574

Richman, George J. **History of Hancock County:** Its People, Industries & Institutions. With Biographical Sketches of Representative Citizens & Genealogical Records.
(1916) reprint 1992.
Cloth. $82.50. 815 pp. .... Vendor G0259

Williams, Dorothy June, and Thomas E. Q. Williams. **A History of Hancock Co. Indiana in the Twentieth Century**. 1995. Indexed.
Cloth. $27.50. 610 pp. .... Vendor G0527

Harrison County

Franklin, Charles. **Harrison Co. Index to Testators to 1880**.
Paper. $8.00. 16 pp. .... Vendor G0574

Harrison Co. Marriages 1809-1849.
Paper. $24.00. 160 pp. .... Vendor G0574

Hendricks County

Franklin, Charles. **Hendricks Co. Index to Testators to 1880**.
Paper. $9.00. 22 pp. .... Vendor G0574

Hadley, John V. **History of Hendricks County:** Its People, Industries & Institutions. With Biographical Sketches & Genealogical Records. (1914) reprint 1992.
Cloth. $86.50. 845 pp. .... Vendor G0259

Henry County

Cline and McHaffie. **1874 People's Guide, a Business, Political, Religious Directory**. (1874) reprint 1979. Indexed.
Cloth. $25.00. 398 pp. .... Vendor G0531

Franklin, Charles. **Henry Co. Index to Testators to 1880**.
Paper. $10.00. 28 pp. .... Vendor G0574

Harwood and Watson. **1857 Landowner Atlas Printed in Atlas Form From Original Wall Map**. (1857) reprint 1994. Illus.
   Town, township landowners, business directories.
Paper. $19.00. 42 pp. .... Vendor G0531

Hazzard, George. **Hazzard's History of Henry County, 1822-1906: Military Edition**. 2 vols. (1906) reprint 1993.
Cloth. $62.50/vol. $119.00/set. 1,236 pp. .... Vendor G0259

Higgins & Beldon & Co. **1875 Illustrated Historical Landowner Atlas**. (1875) reprint 1972. Illus.
   Township, county history, nativity of purchaser.
Paper. $10.00. 48 pp. .... Vendor G0531

Mayhill, R. Thomas. **1821-1849 Land Entry Atlas**. 1978. Indexed.
   Original landowners, date of purchase, location and number of acres, county of residence for each purchaser.
Paper. $14.00. 42 pp. .... Vendor G0531

Pleas, Edward. **History of Henry County,** Together with Sketches of Its Cities, Villages & Towns . . . and Biographies of Representative Citizens. With a Condensed History of Indiana. (1884) reprint 1992.
Cloth. $89.50. 912 pp. .... Vendor G0259

Howard County

Biographical & Genealogical History of the Counties of Cass, Miami, Howard & Tipton. 2 vols. (1898) reprint 1992.
Cloth. $135.00. 1,395 pp. .... Vendor G0259

Franklin, Charles. **Howard Co. Index to Testators to 1880**.
Paper. $7.00. 13 pp. .... Vendor G0574

Huntington County

Franklin, Charles. **Huntington Co. Index to Testators to 1880**.
Paper. $8.00. 14 pp. .... Vendor G0574

History of Huntington County from the Earliest Times to the Present, with Biographical Sketches, Etc. With a Short History of Indiana. (1887) reprint 1992.
Cloth. $89.00. 883 pp. .... Vendor G0259

Jackson County

Franklin, Charles. **Jackson Co. Index to Testators to 1880**.
Paper. $7.00. 13 pp. .... Vendor G0574

Jackson Co. Marriages 1817-1850.
Paper. $13.00. 62 pp. .... Vendor G0574

Jasper County

Biographical History of Tippecanoe, White, Jasper, Newton, Benton, Warren & Pulaski Counties. 2 vols. (1899) reprint 1992.
Cloth. $99.50. 1,074 pp. .... Vendor G0259

Franklin, Charles. **Jasper Co. Index to Testators to 1880**.
Paper. $6.00. 7 pp. .... Vendor G0574

Goodspeed, Weston A. **Counties of Warren, Benton, Jasper & Newton: Historical & Biographical**. (1883) reprint 1992.
Cloth. $83.00. 810 pp. .... Vendor G0259

Royalty, James H., comp. **History of the Town of Remington & Vicinity, Jasper County**. (1894) reprint 1992.
Cloth. $35.00. 271 pp. .... Vendor G0259

Jay County

Biographical and Historical Record of Jay and Blackford Counties. (1887) reprint 1995.
Cloth. $89.50. 901 pp. .... Vendor G0259

Franklin, Charles. **Jay Co. Index to Testators to 1880**.
Paper. $8.00. 14 pp. .... Vendor G0574

Jefferson County

Franklin, Charles. **Jefferson Co. Index to Testators to 1880**.
Paper. $11.00. 35 pp. .... Vendor G0574

Slevin, Ruth. **Jefferson Co. Marriages 1811-1849**.
Paper. $24.00. 168 pp. .... Vendor G0574

Jennings County

Jennings Co. Marriages 1818-1849.
Paper. $14.00. 68 pp. .... Vendor G0574

Franklin, Charles. **Jennings Co. Index to Testators to 1880**.
Paper. $9.00. 20 pp. .... Vendor G0574

Johnson County

Franklin, Charles. **Johnson Co. Index to Testators to 1880**.
Paper. $8.00. 16 pp. .... Vendor G0574

Knox County

Barekman, June. **Knox Co. Land and Court Records**.
Paper. $16.00. 227 pp. .... Vendor G0574

Cauthorn, Henry S. **History of the City of Vincennes, from 1702 to 1901**. (1901) reprint 1993.
Cloth. $29.50. 220 pp. .... Vendor G0259

Franklin, Charles. **Knox Co. Index to Testators to 1880**.
Paper. $10.00. 26 pp. .... Vendor G0574

History of Knox & Daviess Counties, from the Earliest Time to the Present; with Biographical Sketches, Reminiscences, Notes, Etc. . . . with an Extended History of the Colonial Days of Vincennes, and Its Progress Down to the Formation of the State Government. (1886) reprint 1995.
Cloth. $92.50. 914 pp. .... Vendor G0259

Indiana Historical Society. **Census of Indiana Territory for 1807**. 1980.
   Reproduction of original lists for Indiana counties (Knox, Clark, and Dearborn) and Randolph Co., IL. Over 2,500 early settlers. 8½" x 11".
Cloth. $20.00. 57 pp. .... Vendor G0611

Land Claims, Vincennes District, House Document No. 198. Claims, 1783-1812. (1835) reprint 1983.
   Transcripts of original claims list many early settlers.
Paper. $8.95. 107 pp. .... Vendor G0611

Kosciusko County

Franklin, Charles. **Kosciusko Co. Index to Testators to 1880**.
Paper. $9.00. 21 pp. .... Vendor G0574

Historical & Biographical Records of Kosciusko County . . . with Personal Histories of Many of the Leading Families. (1887) reprint 1993.
Cloth. $76.50. 734 pp. .... Vendor G0259

LaGrange County

Counties of LaGrange & Noble, Historical & Biographical. 2 vols. (1882) reprint 1993.
Cloth. $95.00. 441 + 502 pp. .... Vendor G0259

Ford, Stevens, McEwen, and McIntosh, eds. **History of Northeast Indiana:** LaGrange, Steuben, Noble & DeKalb Counties. 2 vols. (1920) reprint 1993.
Cloth. $105.00. 612 + 463 pp. .... Vendor G0259

Franklin, Charles. **LaGrange Co. Index to Testators to 1880**.
Paper. $7.00. 13 pp. .... Vendor G0574

Lake County

Ball, Rev. T. H. **Encyclopedia of Genealogy & Biography of Lake County,** with a Compendium of History, 1834-1904. (1904) reprint 1992.
Cloth. $69.50. 674 pp. .... Vendor G0259

Cannon, Thomas H., H. H. Loring, and C. J. Robb, eds. **History of the Lake & Calumet Region of Indiana,** Embracing the Counties of Lake, Porter & LaPorte: An Historical Account of Its People & Progress from the Earliest Times to [1927]. 2 vols. (1927) reprint 1993.
   Volume I: History.
   Volume II: Biography.
Cloth. $84.00/vol. $159.00/set. 840 + 827 pp. .... Vendor G0259

Franklin, Charles. **Lake Co. Index to Testators to 1880**.
Paper. $7.00. 11 pp. .... Vendor G0574

Lake Co. Marriages 1837-1850.
Paper. $7.00. 7 pp. .... Vendor G0574

LaPorte County

Cannon, Thomas H., H. H. Loring, and C. J. Robb, eds. **History of the Lake & Calumet Region of Indiana,** Embracing the Counties of Lake, Porter & LaPorte: An Historical Account of Its People & Progress from the Earliest Times to [1927]. 2 vols. (1927) reprint 1993.
   Volume I: History.
   Volume II: Biography.
Cloth. $84.00/vol. $159.00/set. 840 + 827 pp. .... Vendor G0259

Franklin, Charles. **LaPorte Co. Index to Testators to 1880.**
Paper. $9.00. 20 pp. .... Vendor G0574

History of LaPorte County. With Biographies (Reprinted Without General History of Indiana). (1880) reprint 1995.
Cloth. $62.50. 586 pp. .... Vendor G0259

Oglesbee, Rollo B., and Albert Hale. **History of Michigan City**. (1908) reprint 1995.
Cloth. $29.50. 201 pp. .... Vendor G0259

Packard, Jasper. **History of LaPorte County & Its Townships, Towns & Cities**. (1876) reprint 1993.
Cloth. $49.50. 467 pp. .... Vendor G0259

Lawrence County

Franklin, Charles. **Lawrence Co. Marriages Vol. I 1818-1834.**
Paper. $9.00. 31 pp. .... Vendor G0574

Franklin, Charles. **Lawrence Co. Marriages Vol. II 1835-1843**.
Paper. $9.00. 31 pp. .... Vendor G0574

Franklin, Charles. **Lawrence Co. Marriages Vol. III 1844-1851**.
Paper. $9.00. 32 pp. .... Vendor G0574

Franklin, Charles. **Lawrence Co. Will Abstracts 1819-1850**.
Paper. $9.00. 40 pp. .... Vendor G0574

History of Lawrence, Orange & Washington Counties, from the Earliest Times to the Present [1884], with Interesting Biographical Sketches, Etc. (1884) reprint 1992.
Cloth. $94.00. 937 pp. .... Vendor G0259

Lawrence Co. Atlas 1870.
Paper. $13.00. 47 pp. .... Vendor G0574

Madison County

Forkner, John L., and Byron H. Dyson. **Historical Sketches & Reminiscences of Madison County**. (1897) reprint 1993.
Cloth. $99.50. 1,038 pp. .... Vendor G0259

Forkner, John L. **History of Madison County:** A Narrative Account of Its Historical Progress, Its People, and Principal Interests. 2 vols. in 1. (1914) reprint 1992.
Cloth. $79.50. 791 pp. .... Vendor G0259

Franklin, Charles. **Madison Co. Index to Testators to 1880**.
Paper. $6.00. 6 pp. .... Vendor G0574

Marion County

Darlington, Jane E., C.G.R.S. **Marion Co., IN Birth Records 1882-1907**. 1987. Indexed.
Cloth. $40.00. 1,100 pp. .... Vendor G0108

Darlington, Jane E., C.G.R.S. **Marion Co., IN Complete Probate Records Jan. 1830-August 1852**. 1994. Indexed.
Cloth. $45.00. 515 pp. .... Vendor G0108

Darlington, Jane E., C.G.R.S. **Marion Co., IN, Indianapolis, Mortality Records 1872-1882**. 1989. Indexed.
Cloth. $35.00. 655 pp. .... Vendor G0108

Darlington, Jane E., C.G.R.S. **Parish Registers St. Paul's Episcopal Church, Indianapolis, IN, Vol. 1 1870-1910**. 1994. Indexed.
Paper. $10.00. 276 pp. .... Vendor G0108

Darlington, Jane E., C.G.R.S. **Parish Registers St. Paul's Episcopal Church, Indianapolis, IN, Vol. 2 1911-1954**. 1996. Indexed.
Paper. $10.00. 300 pp. .... Vendor G0108

Franklin, Charles. **Marion Co. Index to Testators to 1880**.
Paper. $12.00. 50 pp. .... Vendor G0574

Holloway, W. R. **A History & Statistical Sketch of the Railroad City: A Chronicle of Its Social, Municipal, Commercial & Manufacturing Progress**. (1870) reprint 1987.
Cloth. $42.50. 390 pp. .... Vendor G0259

Johnson, Oliver. **A Home in the Woods: Pioneer Life in Indiana**. (1951) reprint 1991.
  Oliver Johnson's reminiscences of early Indianapolis/Marion County in the 1820s and 1830s.
Paper. $9.95. 133 pp. .... Vendor G0611

Middleton, Wallace & Co. **1855 Landowner Atlas Printed From Original Wall Map**. (1855) reprint 1994.
Paper. $12.00. 15 pp. .... Vendor G0531

Sulgrove, Berry R. **History of Indianapolis & Marion County**. (1884) reprint 1992. Cloth. $75.00. 665 pp. .... Vendor G0259

Marshall County

Franklin, Charles. **Marshall Co. Index to Testators to 1880**. Paper. $7.00. 13 pp. .... Vendor G0574

Martin County

Franklin, Charles. **Martin Co. Index to Testators to 1880**. Paper. $7.00. 13 pp. .... Vendor G0574

Martin Co. Marriages 1820-1850. Paper. $10.00. 32 pp. .... Vendor G0574

Miami County

Biographical & Genealogical History of the Counties of Cass, Miami, Howard & Tipton. 2 vols. (1898) reprint 1992. Cloth. $135.00. 1,395 pp. .... Vendor G0259

Franklin, Charles. **Miami Co. Index to Testators to 1880**. Paper. $8.00. 17 pp. .... Vendor G0574

History of Miami County, from the Earliest Time to the Present [1887], with Biographical Sketches, Notes, Etc. With a History of Indiana. (1887) reprint 1992. Cloth. $83.00. 812 pp. .... Vendor G0259

Miami Co. Marriages 1843-1855. Paper. $11.00. 40 pp. .... Vendor G0574

Stephens, John H. **History of Miami County**. (1876) reprint 1993. Cloth. $43.50. 380 pp. .... Vendor G0259

Monroe County

Blanchard, Chas. **1884 History (Originally Included in History of Morgan, Monroe, Brown Cos.)**. (1884) reprint 1981. Indexed. Cloth. $25.00. 316 pp. .... Vendor G0531

Blanchard, Charles, ed. **Counties of Morgan, Monroe & Brown,** Historical & Biographical. (1884) reprint 1992. Cloth. $79.50. 800 pp. .... Vendor G0259

Franklin, Charles. **Monroe Co. Index to Testators to 1880**. Paper. $8.00. 17 pp. .... Vendor G0574

Montgomery County

Beckwith, H. W. **History of Fountain County (and Montgomery Co.),** Together
with Historic Notes on the Wabash Valley. (1881) reprint 1992.
Cloth. $95.00. History of Montgomery Co. only: $32.00, 224 pp.
982 pp. .... Vendor G0259

Cottage Grove Genealogical Society. **Obituary Dates and Family Ties:** Over 140
Years in Montgomery Co., Indiana, 1830's to 1970's, Deaths, Births and Ancestry into
the 1700's.
Paper. $23.50. 232 pp. .... Vendor G0505

Franklin, Charles. **Montgomery Co. Index to Testators to 1880**.
Paper. $10.00. 26 pp. .... Vendor G0574

Montgomery Co. Marriages 1823-1849.
Paper. $17.00. 99 pp. .... Vendor G0574

Shanklin, M. **Montgomery Co. Wills 1852-1869 and Marriages 1837-1847**.
Paper. $9.00. 85 pp. .... Vendor G0574

Shanklin, M. **Montgomery Co. Wills 1868-1883**.
Paper. $10.00. 80 pp. .... Vendor G0574

Morgan County

Blanchard, Charles, ed. **Counties of Morgan, Monroe & Brown,** Historical & Biographical. (1884) reprint 1992.
Cloth. $79.50. 800 pp. .... Vendor G0259

Franklin, Charles. **Morgan Co. Index to Testators to 1880**.
Paper. $7.00. 13 pp. .... Vendor G0574

Newton County

**Biographical History of Tippecanoe, White, Jasper, Newton, Benton, Warren &
Pulaski Counties**. 2 vols. (1899) reprint 1992.
Cloth. $99.50. 1,074 pp. .... Vendor G0259

Franklin, Charles. **Newton Co. Index to Testators to 1880**.
Paper. $6.00. 6 pp. .... Vendor G0574

Goodspeed, Weston A. **Counties of Warren, Benton, Jasper & Newton: Historical
& Biographical**. (1883) reprint 1992.
Cloth. $83.00. 810 pp. .... Vendor G0259

Noble County

Counties of LaGrange & Noble, Historical & Biographical. 2 vols. (1882) reprint 1993.
Cloth. $95.00. 441 + 502 pp. .... Vendor G0259

Ford, Stevens, McEwen, and McIntosh, eds. **History of Northeast Indiana:** LaGrange, Steuben, Noble & DeKalb Counties. 2 vols. (1920) reprint 1993.
Cloth. $105.00. 612 + 463 pp. .... Vendor G0259

Franklin, Charles. **Noble Co. Index to Testators to 1880**.
Paper. $8.00. 16 pp. .... Vendor G0574

Goodspeed, W. A., and C. Blanchard, eds. **Counties of Whitley & Noble: Historical & Biographical**. 2 vols. (1882) reprint 1992.
Volume I: Whitley County.
Volume II: Noble County.
Cloth. $49.00/vol. 428 + 502 pp. .... Vendor G0259

Ohio County

Franklin, Charles. **Ohio Co. Index to Testators to 1880**.
Paper. $7.00. 9 pp. .... Vendor G0574

History of Dearborn & Ohio Counties, from Their Earliest Settlement. With Biographies. (1885) reprint 1993.
Cloth. $98.50. 1,072 pp. .... Vendor G0259

Ohio Co. Marriages 1844-1849.
Paper. $6.00. 11 pp. .... Vendor G0574

Slevin, Ruth. **Ohio Co. Marriages 1844-1882**.
Paper. $14.00. 90 pp. .... Vendor G0574

Orange County

Franklin, Charles. **Orange Co. Index to Testators to 1880**.
Paper. $8.00. 16 pp. .... Vendor G0574

History of Lawrence, Orange & Washington Counties, from the Earliest Times to the Present [1884], with Interesting Biographical Sketches, Etc. (1884) reprint 1992.
Cloth. $94.00. 937 pp. .... Vendor G0259

Orange Co. Marriages 1816-1850.
Paper. $16.00. 91 pp. .... Vendor G0574

Owen County

Blanchard, Charles, ed. **Counties of Clay & Owen, Historical & Biographical.** (1884) reprint 1992.
Cloth. $95.00. 966 pp. .... Vendor G0259

Franklin, Charles. **Owen Co. Index to Testators to 1880.**
Paper. $8.00. 15 pp. .... Vendor G0574

Franklin, Charles. **Owen Co. Marriages Vol. I 1819-1844.**
Paper. $9.00. 35 pp. .... Vendor G0574

Franklin, Charles. **Owen Co. Marriages Vol. II 1845-1853.**
Paper. $9.00. 31 pp. .... Vendor G0574

Franklin, Charles. **Owen Co. Misc. Tax Lists 1819-1829 and Declarations of Intent.**
Paper. $10.00. 43 pp. .... Vendor G0574

Franklin, Charles. **Owen Co. Misc. Vol. II.**
Paper. $10.00. 33 pp. .... Vendor G0574

Franklin, Charles. **Owen Co. Tax Lists 1843.**
Paper. $14.00. 77 pp. .... Vendor G0574

Franklin, Charles. **Owen Co. Will Abstracts 1819-1861.**
Paper. $10.00. 57 pp. .... Vendor G0574

Parke County

Franklin, Charles. **Parke Co. Index to Testators to 1880.**
Paper. $9.00. 22 pp. .... Vendor G0574

History of Parke & Vermillion Counties, with Historical Sketches of Representative Citizens & Genealogical Records of Many Old Families. (1913) reprint 1992.
Cloth. $83.00. 816 pp. .... Vendor G0259

Sanders, Eva. **Parke Co. Marriages 1833-1844.**
Paper. $9.00. 37 pp. .... Vendor G0574

Perry County

Franklin, Charles. **Perry Co. Index to Testators to 1880.**
Paper. $8.00. 15 pp. .... Vendor G0574

History of Warrick, Spencer & Perry Counties, from the Earliest Time to the Present, Together with Interesting Biographical Sketches, Etc. (1885) reprint 1993.
Cloth. $86.00. 837 pp. .... Vendor G0259

Hunt, Thomas J. de la. **Perry County, A History.** (1916) reprint 1992.
Cloth. $43.00. 359 pp. .... Vendor G0259

Pike County

Franklin, Charles. **Pike Co. Index to Testators to 1880**.
Paper. $7.00. 12 pp. .... Vendor G0574

Porter County

Cannon, Thomas H., H. H. Loring, and C. J. Robb, eds. **History of the Lake & Calumet Region of Indiana,** Embracing the Counties of Lake, Porter & LaPorte: An Historical Account of Its People & Progress from the Earliest Times to [1927]. 2 vols. (1927) reprint 1993.
    Volume I: History.
    Volume II: Biography.
Cloth. $84.00/vol. $159.00/set. 840 + 827 pp. .... Vendor G0259

Franklin, Charles. **Porter Co. Index to Testators to 1880**.
Paper. $7.00. 12 pp. .... Vendor G0574

Hiday, Nellie. **Porter Co. 1850 Census Transcription**.
Paper. $10.00. 108 pp. .... Vendor G0574

Porter Co. Marriages 1836-1849.
Paper. $8.00. 19 pp. .... Vendor G0574

Posey County

Franklin, Charles. **Posey Co. Index to Testators to 1880**.
Paper. $9.00. 22 pp. .... Vendor G0574

Leffel, John C., ed. **History of Posey County**. (1913) reprint 1992.
Cloth. $44.00. 401 pp. .... Vendor G0259

Pulaski County

Biographical History of Tippecanoe, White, Jasper, Newton, Benton, Warren & Pulaski Counties. 2 vols. (1899) reprint 1992.
Cloth. $99.50. 1,074 pp. .... Vendor G0259

Franklin, Charles. **Pulaski Co. Index to Testators to 1880**.
Paper. $6.00. 8 pp. .... Vendor G0574

Goodspeed, W. A., ed. **Counties of White & Pulaski: Historical & Biographical**. (1883) reprint 1992.
Cloth. $79.50. 772 pp. .... Vendor G0259

Putnam County

Franklin, Charles. **Putnam Co. Index to Testators to 1880**.
Paper. $9.00. 22 pp. .... Vendor G0574

Franklin, Charles. **Putnam Co. Marriages Vol. I 1822-1837**.
Paper. $9.00. 34 pp. .... Vendor G0574

Franklin, Charles. **Putnam Co. Marriages Vol. II 1838-1847**.
Paper. $11.00. 55 pp. .... Vendor G0574

Weik, Jesse W. **Weik's History of Putnam County**. (1910) reprint 1992.
Cloth. $79.50. 785 pp. .... Vendor G0259

Randolph County

Franklin, Charles. **Randolph Co. Index to Testators to 1880**.
Paper. $9.00. 21 pp. .... Vendor G0574

Portrait & Biographical Records of Delaware & Randolph Counties, Containing
Biographical Sketches of Many Prominent & Representative Citizens. (1894) reprint
1992.
Cloth. $135.00. 1,445 pp. .... Vendor G0259

Randolph Co. Marriages 1819-1852.
Paper. $16.00. 111 pp. .... Vendor G0574

Ripley County

Franklin, Charles. **Ripley Co. Index to Testators to 1880**.
Paper. $10.00. 28 pp. .... Vendor G0574

Rush County

Franklin, Charles. **Rush Co. Index to Testators to 1880**.
Paper. $9.00. 21 pp. .... Vendor G0574

Wolfe, Barbara. **Rush Co. Marriages 1822-1849**.
Paper. $18.00. 125 pp. .... Vendor G0574

Scott County

Franklin, Charles. **Scott Co. Index to Testators to 1880**.
Paper. $7.00. 10 pp. .... Vendor G0574

Shelby County

Wolfe, Barbara. **Shelby Co. Index to Testators to 1880**.
Paper. $17.00. 96 pp. .... Vendor G0574

Wolfe, Barbara. **Shelby Co. Marriages 1822-1849**.
Paper. $17.00. 96 pp. .... Vendor G0574

Spencer County

Franklin, Charles. **Spencer Co. Index to Testators to 1880**.
Paper. $9.00. 21 pp. .... Vendor G0574

History of Warrick, Spencer & Perry Counties, from the Earliest Time to the Present, Together with Interesting Biographical Sketches, Etc. (1885) reprint 1993.
Cloth. $86.00. 837 pp. .... Vendor G0259

Young, Smith, and Hyde. **Spencer Co. Cemetery Inscriptions**. 13 vols. with index.
Paper. $65.00. 754 pp. .... Vendor G0574

Young, Smith, and Hyde. **Spencer Co. Marriages 1818-1855**.
Paper. $13.00. 109 pp. .... Vendor G0574

Young, Smith, and Hyde. **Spencer Co. Marriages 1855-1863**.
Paper. $9.00. 62 pp. .... Vendor G0574

Young, Smith, and Hyde. **Spencer Co. Wills 1818-1839**.
Paper. $8.00. 38 pp. .... Vendor G0574

St. Joseph County

Biographical & Pictorial Memoirs of Elkhart & St. Joseph Counties. Together with Biographies of Many Prominent Men of N. Indiana & of the Whole State. (1893) reprint 1992.
Cloth. $79.50. 777 pp. .... Vendor G0259

Franklin, Charles. **St. Joseph Co. Index to Testators to 1880**.
Paper. $9.00. 23 pp. .... Vendor G0574

Howard, Timothy Edward. **History of Saint Joseph County**. 2 vols. (1907) reprint 1992.
Cloth. $109.00. 1,157 pp. .... Vendor G0259

South Bend Area Genealogical Society. **St. Joseph County, Indiana Cemetery Inscriptions Volume 1: Greene, Liberty, Lincoln Townships**. 1992. Indexed.
Paper. $33.00. iv + 369 pp. .... Vendor G0743

South Bend Area Genealogical Society. **St. Joseph County, Indiana Cemetery Inscriptions Volume 2: Penn Township, Part 1 (Mishawaka City, St. Joseph, St. Francis, Laing, Smith, First Mishawaka Cemeteries)**. 1995. Indexed.
Paper. $38.00. iv + 312 pp. .... Vendor G0743

South Bend Area Genealogical Society. **St. Joseph County, Indiana Cemetery Inscriptions Volume 3: Penn Township, Part 2, Fairview (Partial), Pleasant Valley, Hebrew Orthodox, Eutzier-Hollingshead, Byrkit, Ferrisville Cemeteries**. 1995. Indexed.
Paper. $38.00. iv + 353 pp. .... Vendor G0743

Starke County

Franklin, Charles. **Starke Co. Index to Testators to 1880**.
Paper. $6.00. 6 pp. .... Vendor G0574

McCormick, Joseph N. **A Standard History of Starke County, Indiana 1915**. Indexed.
Cloth. $65.00. 747 pp. .... Vendor G0748

Steuben County

Ford, Stevens, McEwen, and McIntosh, eds. **History of Northeast Indiana:** LaGrange, Steuben, Noble & DeKalb Counties. 2 vols. (1920) reprint 1993.
Cloth. $105.00. 612 + 463 pp. .... Vendor G0259

Franklin, Charles. **Steuben Co. Index to Testators to 1880**.
Paper. $8.00. 14 pp. .... Vendor G0574

Sullivan County

Franklin, Charles. **Some Sullivan Co. Early Marriages 1815 to 1857**.
Paper. $9.00. 38 pp. .... Vendor G0574

Franklin, Charles. **Sullivan Co. Index to Testators to 1880**.
Paper. $8.00. 14 pp. .... Vendor G0574

Franklin, Charles. **Sullivan Co. Will Abstracts 1844-1864**.
Paper. $10.00. 38 pp. .... Vendor G0574

History of Greene & Sullivan Counties, from the Earliest Times to the Present, Together with Interesting Biographical Sketches. (1884) reprint 1993.
Cloth. $85.00. 824 pp. .... Vendor G0259

Switzerland County

Dufour, Perret. **Swiss Settlement of Switzerland County**. With Introduction by Harlow Lindley. (1925) reprint 1992.
Cloth. $49.00. 446 pp. .... Vendor G0259

Franklin, Charles. **Switzerland Co. Index to Testators to 1880**.
Paper. $8.00. 18 pp. .... Vendor G0574

Switzerland Co. Marriages 1814-1849.
Paper. $17.00. 114 pp. .... Vendor G0574

Tippecanoe County

Biographical History of Tippecanoe, White, Jasper, Newton, Benton, Warren & Pulaski Counties. 2 vols. (1899) reprint 1992.
Cloth. $99.50. 1,074 pp. .... Vendor G0259

Biographical Record & Portrait Album of Tippecanoe County. (1888) reprint 1993.
Cloth. $84.50. 825 pp. .... Vendor G0259

Franklin, Charles. **Tippecanoe Co. Index to Testators to 1880**.
Paper. $10.00. 24 pp. .... Vendor G0574

Tipton County

Biographical & Genealogical History of the Counties of Cass, Miami, Howard & Tipton. 2 vols. (1898) reprint 1992.
Cloth. $135.00. 1,395 pp. .... Vendor G0259

Franklin, Charles. **Tipton Co. Index to Testators to 1880**.
Paper. $7.00. 9 pp. .... Vendor G0574

Union County

Dean, Arnold L. **1st Land Entry Book of Union Co., IN**. 1994. Indexed. Illus.
Paper. $14.98 (IN residents pay $.62 tax). 108 pp. .... Vendor G0534

Franklin, Charles. **Union Co. Index to Testators to 1880**.
Paper. $8.00. 14 pp. .... Vendor G0574

Lewis Publishing Co. **History of Wayne, Fayette, Union & Franklin Counties**. 2 vols. (1899) reprint 1992.
Cloth. $99.50. 1,073 pp. .... Vendor G0259

Vanderburgh County

Franklin, Charles. **Vanderburgh Co. Index to Testators to 1880**.
Paper. $11.00. 40 pp. .... Vendor G0574

Vermillion County

Franklin, Charles. **Vermillion Co. Index to Testators to 1880**.
Paper. $7.00. 13 pp. .... Vendor G0574

History of Parke & Vermillion Counties, with Historical Sketches of Representative Citizens & Genealogical Records of Many Old Families. (1913) reprint 1992.
Cloth. $83.00. 816 pp. .... Vendor G0259

Volkel, Lowell. **Vermillion Co. Land & Marriage Records 1838-1844**.
Paper. $10.00. 53 pp. .... Vendor G0574

Volkel, Lowell. **Vermillion Co. Marriages 1844-1861**.
Paper. $10.00. 44 pp. .... Vendor G0574

Vigo County

Bradsby, Henry C. **History of Vigo County, with Biographical Selections**. (1891) reprint 1992.
Cloth. $99.50. 1,018 pp. .... Vendor G0259

Franklin, Charles. **Vigo Co. Index to Testators to 1880**.
Paper. $9.00. 21 pp. .... Vendor G0574

Franklin, Charles. **Vigo Co. Will Abstracts 1818-1860**.
Paper. $10.00. 37 pp. .... Vendor G0574

Wabash County

Franklin, Charles. **Wabash Co. Index to Testators to 1880**.
Paper. $8.00. 17 pp. .... Vendor G0574

Scheuer, Larry, and Cynthia Scheuer. **Wabash County, Indiana Marriages 1835-1899**. 1995.
Paper. $35.00. 194 pp. .... Vendor G0684

Weesner, Charles C. **History of Wabash County:** A Narrative Account of Its Historical Progress, Its People & Its Principal Interests. 2 vols. (1914) reprint 1992.
Cloth. $97.50. 970 pp. .... Vendor G0259

Warren County

Biographical History of Tippecanoe, White, Jasper, Newton, Benton, Warren & Pulaski Counties. 2 vols. (1899) reprint 1992.
Cloth. $99.50. 1,074 pp. .... Vendor G0259

Franklin, Charles. **Warren Co. Index to Testators to 1880**.
Paper. $7.00. 12 pp. .... Vendor G0574

Goodspeed, Weston A. **Counties of Warren, Benton, Jasper & Newton: Historical & Biographical**. (1883) reprint 1992.
Cloth. $83.00. 810 pp. .... Vendor G0259

Leath, Mrs. Warren. **Warren Co. Will Abstracts 1830-1858**.
Paper. $8.00. 26 pp. .... Vendor G0574

Warrick County

Franklin, Charles. **Warrick Co. Index to Testators to 1880**.
Paper. $8.00. 15 pp. .... Vendor G0574

History of Warrick, Spencer & Perry Counties, from the Earliest Time to the Present, Together with Interesting Biographical Sketches, Etc. (1885) reprint 1993.
Cloth. $86.00. 837 pp. .... Vendor G0259

Washington County

Franklin, Charles. **Washington Co. Index to Testators to 1880**.
Paper. $9.00. 20 pp. .... Vendor G0574

History of Lawrence, Orange & Washington Counties, from the Earliest Times to the Present [1884], with Interesting Biographical Sketches, Etc. (1884) reprint 1992.
Cloth. $94.00. 937 pp. .... Vendor G0259

Wayne County

Dean, Arnold L. **1910 Wayne Co., IN Census Index**. 1994. Indexed.
Paper. $35.00 (IN residents pay $1.53 tax). 450+ pp. .... Vendor G0534

Dean, Arnold L. **Early Naturalization Records—Wayne Co., IN**. 1995. Indexed. Illus.
Paper. $16.33 (IN residents pay $.67 tax). 125+ pp. .... Vendor G0534

Dean, Arnold L. **Early Wayne Co., IN Probate & Will Index**. 1995. Indexed.
Paper. $16.33 (IN residents pay $.67 tax). 132+ pp. .... Vendor G0534

Dean, Arnold L. **1st Land Entry Book of Wayne Co., IN**. 1994. Indexed. Illus.
Paper. $24.00 (IN residents pay $1.00 tax). 200 pp. .... Vendor G0534

Franklin, Charles. **Wayne Co. Index to Testators to 1880**.
Paper. $12.00. 52 pp. .... Vendor G0574

Griffing, Stevenson & Co. **1874 Landowner Atlas with Index**. (1874) reprint 1974.
Paper. $10.00. 77 pp. .... Vendor G0531

History of Wayne County, Together with Sketches of Its Cities, Village & Towns . . . and Biographies of Representative Citizens. 2 vols. (1884) reprint 1992.
Cloth. $125.00. 735 + 800 pp. .... Vendor G0259

Lewis Publishing Co. **History of Wayne, Fayette, Union & Franklin Counties.** 2 vols. (1899) reprint 1992.
Cloth. $99.50. 1,073 pp. .... Vendor G0259

Rerick Bros. **1893 Landowner Atlas.** (1893) reprint 1979. Illus.
  Town, township maps, many photos.
Paper. $19.00. 71 pp. .... Vendor G0531

Young, Andrew. **1872 History.** (1872) reprint 1976. Indexed. Illus.
Cloth. $26.00. 459 pp. .... Vendor G0531

Young, Andrew W. **History of Wayne County,** from Its First Settlement to the Present Time, with Biographical & Family Sketches. (1872) reprint 1993.
Cloth. $48.00. 459 pp. .... Vendor G0259

Yount, Beverly. **Wayne Co. Marriages 1811-1860**.
Paper. $25.00. 242 pp. .... Vendor G0574

Wells County

Franklin, Charles. **Wells Co. Index to Testators to 1880**.
Paper. $7.00. .... Vendor G0574

Tyndall, John W., and O. E. Leah, eds. **Standard History of Adams & Wells Counties:** An Authentic Narrative of the Past, with an Extended Survey of Modern Developments in the Progress of the Town & Country. 2 vols. in 1. (1918) reprint 1992.
Cloth. $98.50. 985 pp. .... Vendor G0259

White County

Biographical History of Tippecanoe, White, Jasper, Newton, Benton, Warren & Pulaski Counties. 2 vols. (1899) reprint 1992.
Cloth. $99.50. 1,074 pp. .... Vendor G0259

Franklin, Charles. **White Co. Index to Testators to 1880**.
Paper. $7.00. 12 pp. .... Vendor G0574

Goodspeed, W. A., ed. **Counties of White & Pulaski: Historical & Biographical.** (1883) reprint 1992.
Cloth. $79.50. 772 pp. .... Vendor G0259

Ogle, George (1896), and Kenyon Co. (1920). **1896 and 1920 Town and Township Atlases (Combined in One Book).** (1896, 1920) reprint 1976.
  Eighteen ninety-six reference directory of 900 names.
Paper. $15.00. 71 pp. .... Vendor G0531

White Co. Marriages 1834-1849.
Paper. $7.00. 13 pp. .... Vendor G0574

Whitley County

Franklin, Charles. **Whitley Co. Index to Testators to 1880**.
Paper. $7.00. 13 pp. .... Vendor G0574

Goodspeed, W. A., and C. Blanchard, eds. **Counties of Whitley & Noble: Historical & Biographical**. 2 vols. (1882) reprint 1992.
    Volume I: Whitley County.
    Volume II: Noble County.
Cloth. $49.00/vol. 428 + 502 pp. .... Vendor G0259

Kaler, S. P., and R. H. Maring. **History of Whitley County**. (1907) reprint 1992.
Cloth. $88.00. 861 pp. .... Vendor G0259

Iowa

Statewide and Regional References

Banvard, Theodore James Fleming. **Goodenows Who Originated in Sudbury, Massachusetts 1638 A.D.** 1994. Indexed. Illus.
Cloth. $78.50. 952 pp. .... Vendor G0116

Family History Library. **Research Outline: Iowa**.
Leaflet. $.25. 7 pp. .... Vendor G0629

Liahona Research. **Iowa Marriages, Early to 1850**. 1990.
Cloth. $65.00. 373 pp. .... Vendor G0552

Thorndale, William, and William Dollarhide. **County Boundary Map Guides to the U.S. Federal Censuses, 1790-1920: Iowa, 1840-1920**. 1987.
$5.95. .... Vendor G0552

Benton County

History of Benton County, Containing a History of the County . . . and a Biographical Directory of its Citizens. (1878) reprint 1993.
Cloth. $67.00. 641 pp. .... Vendor G0259

Boone County

Biographical Record of Boone County. (1902) reprint 1993.
Cloth. $68.00. 664 pp. .... Vendor G0259

History of Boone County, Containing a History of the County . . . and a Biographical
Directory of Its Citizens. (1880) reprint 1993.
Cloth. $69.00. 680 pp. .... Vendor G0259

Bremer County

Union Publishing Co. **History of Butler & Bremer Counties, Together with Biographies . . .** (1883) reprint 1993.
Cloth. $129.50. 1,323 pp. .... Vendor G0259

Butler County

Union Publishing Co. **History of Butler & Bremer Counties, Together with Biographies . . .** (1883) reprint 1993.
Cloth. $129.50. 1,323 pp. .... Vendor G0259

Carroll County

**History of Carroll County, A Record of Settlement, Organization, Progress &
Achievement.** (1912) reprint 1993.
Cloth. $34.50. 250 pp. .... Vendor G0259

Cedar County

History of Cedar County, Containing a History of the County, Its Cities, Towns, Etc.
[with a] Biographical Directory. (1878) reprint 1995.
Cloth. $75.00. 729 pp. .... Vendor G0259

Chickasaw County

Powers, J. H. **Historical & Reminiscences of Chickasaw County**. (1894) reprint
1992.
Cloth. $39.00. 332 pp. .... Vendor G0259

Clay County

Gillespie, Samuel, and James E. Steele. **History of Clay County,** from Its Earliest
Settlement to 1909. With Biographical Sketches. (1909) reprint 1995.
Cloth. $72.00. 682 pp. .... Vendor G0259

Clayton County

Price, Realto E., ed. **History of Clayton County,** from the Earliest Historical Times Down to the Present. With Genealogical & Biographical Records. 2 vols. in 1. (1916) reprint 1992.
Cloth. $94.00. 494 + 459 pp. .... Vendor G0259

Crawford County

Biographical History of Crawford, Ida & Sac Counties. (1893) reprint 1995.
Cloth. $69.00. 688 pp. .... Vendor G0259

Dallas County

Wood, Robert F. **Past & Present of Dallas County,** Together with Biographical Sketches of Many of Its Prominent & Leading Citizens . . . (1907) reprint 1992.
Cloth. $79.50. 795 pp. .... Vendor G0259

Delaware County

Merry, Capt. John F., ed. **History of Delaware County & Its People**. 2 vols. (1914) reprint 1994.
Cloth. $42.50/Vol. I. $52.50/Vol. II. 375 + 526 pp. .... Vendor G0259

Des Moines County

Antrobus, Augustine M. **History of Des Moines County and Its People**. 2 vols. (1915) reprint 1994.
Cloth. $55.00/vol., $105.00/set. 556 + 537 pp. .... Vendor G0259

Dickinson County

Smith, R. A. **A History of Dickinson County,** Together with an Account of the Spirit Lake Massacre and the Indian Troubles on the Northwestern Frontier. (1902) reprint 1995.
Cloth. $63.00. 598 pp. .... Vendor G0259

Doniphan County

Ford, Don L., comp. **Doniphan County Cemeteries and Burial Sites**. 1986.
Cloth. $28.00. 194 pp. .... Vendor G0259

Dubuque County

Oldt, Frank T., and P. J. Quigley. **History of Dubuque County,** Being a General Survey of Dubuque County History, Including a History of the City of Dubuque . . . from the Earliest Settlement to the Present Time. (1911) reprint 1993.
Cloth. $95.00. 943 pp. .... Vendor G0259

Fayette County

History of Fayette County, Containing . . . a Biographical Directory of Its Citizens. (1878) reprint 1993.
   With modern every-name index. Index also available separately in paperback for $16.00.
Cloth. $79.50. 758 pp. + 80-p. index. .... Vendor G0259

Greene County

Stillman, E. B., et al. **Past & Present of Greene County,** Together with Biographical Sketches of Many of Its Prominent & Leading Citizens. (1907) reprint 1993.
Cloth. $69.50. 664 pp. .... Vendor G0259

Grundy County

Portrait & Biographical Records of Jasper, Marshall & Grundy Counties, Containing Biographical Sketches of Prominent & Representative Citizens . . . (1894) reprint 1992.
Cloth. $69.50. 678 pp. .... Vendor G0259

Hardin County

Nichols, L. A. **History of Iowa Falls, 1900-1950**. (1956) reprint 1992.
Cloth. $43.50. 365 pp. .... Vendor G0259

Harrison County

History of Harrison County. 1891.
Cloth. $115.00. 978 + 160 pp. .... Vendor G0259

Hunt, Charles W., with W. L. Clark. **History of Harrison County,** Its People, Industries & Institutions. With Biographical Sketches of Representative Citizens & Genealogical Records of Many of the Old Families. (1915) reprint 1995.
Cloth. $95.00. 987 pp. .... Vendor G0259

Henry County

History of Henry County, Containing a History of the County, Its Cities,Towns, Etc. With Biographies. (1879) reprint 1995.
Cloth. $66.50. 637 pp. + 5-p. index. .... Vendor G0259

Ida County

Biographical History of Crawford, Ida & Sac Counties. (1893) reprint 1995.
Cloth. $69.00. 688 pp. .... Vendor G0259

Jackson County

History of Jackson County, Containing a History of the County . . . and Biographical Sketches of Its Citizens. (1879) reprint 1993.
Cloth. $79.50. 783 pp. .... Vendor G0259

Jasper County

Portrait & Biographical Records of Jasper, Marshall & Grundy Counties, Containing Biographical Sketches of Prominent & Representative Citizens . . . (1894) reprint 1992.
Cloth. $69.50. 678 pp. .... Vendor G0259

Weaver, James B. **Past & Present of Jasper County.** 2 vols. (1912) reprint 1994.
Cloth. $75.00/Vol. I. $62.50/Vol. II. $129.50/set. 752 + 613 pp. .... Vendor G0259

Jones County

Corbit, R. M. **History of Jones County, Past & Present.** 2 vols. (1910) reprint 1994.
Cloth. $75.00/Vol. I. $67.50/Vol. II. $135.00/set. 742 + 662 pp. .... Vendor G0259

History of Jones County, Containing a History of the County, Its Cities, Towns, Etc., with Biographical Sketches of Citizens . . . (1879) reprint 1993.
Cloth. $69.50. 705 pp. .... Vendor G0259

Keokuk County

History of Keokuk County. (1880) reprint 1994.
Cloth. $84.50. 822 pp. .... Vendor G0259

Lee County

History of Lee County: A History of the County, Its Cities, Towns; a Biographical Directory of Its Citizens, Etc. (1879) reprint 1992.
Cloth. $89.50. 887 pp. .... Vendor G0259

Linn County

Mitchell, William Ansel. **Linn County, A History**. (1928) reprint 1994.
Cloth. $42.50. 404 pp. .... Vendor G0259

Murray, Janette S., and Frederick G. Murray. **The Story of Cedar Rapids**. (1950) reprint 1994.
Cloth. $37.00. 284 pp. .... Vendor G0259

Louisa County

Portrait & Biographical Album of Louisa County, Containing Full Page Portraits & Biographical Sketches of Prominent . . . Citizens of the County. (1889) reprint 1993.
Cloth. $67.00. 658 pp. .... Vendor G0259

Mahaska County

History of Mahaska County. With Biographies. (1874) reprint 1994.
Cloth. $74.50. 724 pp. .... Vendor G0259

Phillips, Semira. **Proud Mahaska, 1843-1900**. (1900) reprint 1993.
Cloth. $42.50. 383 pp. .... Vendor G0259

Portrait & Biographical Album of Mahaska County, Containing Full Page Portraits & Biographical Sketches of Prominent & Representative Citizens of the County. (1887) reprint 1995.
Cloth. $58.50. 552 pp. .... Vendor G0259

"Roustabout" (Phil Hoffman). **Roustabout's History of Mahaska County**. (1916) reprint 1993.
Paper. $12.00. 102 pp. .... Vendor G0259

Marshall County

Battin, Judge William, and F. A. Moscrip. **Past & Present of Marshall County**. 2 vols. (1913) reprint 1993.
  Volume I: History.
  Volume II: Biography.
Cloth. $69.00/Vol. I. $51.00/Vol. II. $109/set. 672 + 500 pp. .... Vendor G0259

Iowa

History of Marshall County. (1878) reprint 1994.
Cloth. $69.50. 696 pp. .... Vendor G0259

Portrait & Biographical Records of Jasper, Marshall & Grundy Counties, Containing Biographical Sketches of Prominent & Representative Citizens . . . (1894) reprint 1992.
Cloth. $69.50. 678 pp. .... Vendor G0259

Mitchell County

History of Mitchell & Worth Counties. (1884) reprint 1993.
Cloth. $89.50. 886 pp. .... Vendor G0259

Monroe County

Hickenlooper, Frank. **Illustrated History of Monroe County:** A Complete Civil, Political & Military History of the County, from Its Earliest Period Down to 1896. With biographies. (1896) reprint 1993.
Cloth. $39.00. 360 pp. .... Vendor G0259

Montgomery County

Merritt, W. W., Sr. **History of the County of Montgomery,** from the Earliest Days to 1906. (1906) reprint 1994.
Cloth. $39.50. 343 pp. .... Vendor G0259

O'Brien County

Peck, J. L. E., O. H. Montzheimer, and William J. Miller. **Past & Present of O'Brien & Osceola Counties**. 2 vols. (1914) reprint 1994.
Cloth. $65.00/vol., $125.00/set. 690 + 629 pp. .... Vendor G0259

Perkins, D. A. W. **History of O'Brien County,** from Its Organization to the Present Time. (1897) reprint 1993.
Cloth. $49.50. 485 pp. .... Vendor G0259

Osceola County

Peck, J. L. E., O. H. Montzheimer, and William J. Miller. **Past & Present of O'Brien & Osceola Counties**. 2 vols. (1914) reprint 1994.
Cloth. $65.00/vol., $125.00/set. 690 + 629 pp. .... Vendor G0259

Perkins, D. A. W. **History of Osceola County,** from Its Organization to the Present Time. (1892) reprint 1992.
Cloth. $37.50. 267 + 27 pp. .... Vendor G0259

Page County

History of Page Co., Containing a History of the County, Its Cities, Towns, Etc. With a Biographical Directory. (1880) reprint 1995.
Cloth. $82.50. 806 pp. .... Vendor G0259

Kershaw, W. L. **History of Page County;** Also Biographical Sketches of Some Prominent Citizens of the County. 2 vols. (1909) reprint 1994.
Cloth. $49.50/Vol. I. $62.00/Vol. II. $107.00/set. 478 + 605 pp. .... Vendor G0259

Miller, E. **History of Page County,** from the Earliest Settlement, in 1843, to the First Centennial of American Independence, 1876. 1876.
Paper. $19.50. 114 pp. .... Vendor G0259

Plymouth County

Clark, W. L., J. E. Norris, et al. **History of the Counties of Woodbury & Plymouth,** Including an Extended Sketch of Sioux City . . . with Biographies of Many of the Representative Citizens. (1890-91) reprint 1993.
Cloth. $99.50. 1,022 pp. .... Vendor G0259

Pocahontas County

Flickinger, Robert E. **Pioneer History of Pocahontas County,** from the Time of Its Earliest Settlement to the Present, Including the Complete Hist. of Each Twp., Town & Important Business . . . & Biographical Sketches of the Leading Citizens. (1904) reprint 1993.
Cloth. $94.00. xxiv + 909 pp. .... Vendor G0259

Polk County

Andrews, L. F. **Pioneers of Polk County & Reminiscences of Early Days**. 2 vols. (1908) reprint 1993.
Cloth. $94.00. 456 + 472 pp. .... Vendor G0259

Brigham, Johnson. **Des Moines,** the Pioneer of Municipal Progress and Reform of the Middle West, Together with the History of Polk County. 2 vols. (1911) reprint 1994.
Cloth. $73.00/vol., $139.50/set. 746 + 702 pp. .... Vendor G0259

Porter, Will. **Annals of Polk County & the City of Des Moines**. (1898) reprint 1994.
Cloth. $99.50. 1,064 pp. .... Vendor G0259

Portrait & Biographical Album of Polk County, Containing Full Page Portraits & Biographical Sketches of Prominent & Representative Citizens (reprinted without biographies of presidents & governors). (1890) reprint 1995.
Cloth. $74.00. 690 pp. .... Vendor G0259

Pottawattamie County

Field, Homer H., and Joseph R. Reed. **History of Pottawattamie County,** from the Earliest Historic Times to 1907. 2 vols. (1907) reprint 1994.
Cloth. $57.50/Vol. I. $65.00/Vol. II. $115.00/set. 562 + 638 pp. .... Vendor G0259

Treynor Town & Country Club, comp. **History of the Community of Treynor.** (1961) reprint 1995.
Cloth. $35.00. 250 pp. .... Vendor G0259

Poweshiek County

History of Poweshiek County. (1880) reprint 1994.
Cloth. $95.00. 975 pp. .... Vendor G0259

Sac County

Biographical History of Crawford, Ida & Sac Counties. (1893) reprint 1995.
Cloth. $69.00. 688 pp. .... Vendor G0259

Scott County

Interstate Publishing Company. **The History of Scott County.** (1882) reprint 1993.
Cloth. $119.50. 1,265 pp. .... Vendor G0259

Quaife, M. M., ed. **Early Days of Rock Island [IL] & Davenport [IA]:** The Narratives of J. W. Spencer (1872) & J. M. D. Burrows (1888). (1872, 1888, 1942) reprint 1994.
Cloth. $35.00. 315 pp. .... Vendor G0259

Wilkie, Franc B. **Davenport Past & Present,** Including the Early History & Personal & Anecdotal Reminiscences of Davenport, Together with Biographies. (1858) reprint 1993.
Cloth. $38.50. 334 pp. .... Vendor G0259

Tama County

Caldwell, J. R. **History of Tama County.** 2 vols. (1910) reprint 1995.
Cloth. $105.00. 1,020 pp. .... Vendor G0259

Warren County

Union Hist. Co. **History of Warren County,** Containing a History of the County, Its Cities, Towns, Etc., with a Biographical Directory of Its Citizens . . . (1879) reprint 1993.
Cloth. $79.50. 800 pp. .... Vendor G0259

Winneshiek County

Bailey, Edwin C. **Past & Present of Winneshiek County:** A Record of Settlement, Organization, Progress & Achievement. 2 vols. (1913) reprint 1995.
  Volume I: History.
  Volume II: Biography
Cloth. $42.00/Vol. I. $59.00/Vol. II. $95.00/set. 354 + 580 pp. .... Vendor G0259

Woodbury County

Clark, W. L., J. E. Norris, et al. **History of the Counties of Woodbury & Plymouth,** Including an Extended Sketch of Sioux City . . . with Biographies of Many of the Representative Citizens. (1890-91) reprint 1993.
Cloth. $99.50. 1,022 pp. .... Vendor G0259

Worth County

History of Mitchell & Worth Counties. (1884) reprint 1993.
Cloth. $89.50. 886 pp. .... Vendor G0259

Wright County

Birdsall, B. P. **History of Wright County,** Its People, Industries & Institutions. (1914) reprint 1994.
Cloth. $105.00. 1,061 pp. .... Vendor G0259

Kansas

Statewide and Regional References

Armstrong, Ruth A., and R. Wayne Jennings. **1855 Territory of Kansas Census— Vol. I**. (1985) reprint 1996.
Paper. $21.50 (plus $1.40 KS tax). 259 pp. .... Vendor G0571

Armstrong, Ruth A., and R. Wayne Jennings. **1855 Territory of Kansas Census— Vol. II**. (1985) reprint 1996. Indexed.
Paper. $21.50 (plus $1.40 KS tax). 284 pp. .... Vendor G0571

Family History Library. **Research Outline: Kansas**.
Leaflet. $.25. 6 pp. .... Vendor G0629

Ford, Don L., comp. **Abandoned and Semi-Active Cemeteries**. 3 vols. 1985.
Cloth. $36.00/Vol. I. $70.00/Vol. II. $39.50/Vol. III. 360 + 784 +
399 pp. .... Vendor G0259

Kusek, Joan. **Federal Naturalizations for the 1st District of Kansas Northeast 1856-1902**. 1990. Indexed.
Paper. $20.95. 192 pp. .... Vendor G0122

Ostertag, John, and Enid Ostertag. **The Weekly Kansas Chief Volume 8, January 1892 thru December 31, 1893**. 1996.
Spiral binding. $17.45. Contact vendor about earlier volumes.
220 pp. .... Vendor G0745

Registration of Axis Aliens in Kansas January 1918 thru June 1918. Reprint 1996.
Paper. $15.00 (plus $.98 KS tax). .... Vendor G0571

Riley County Genealogical Society. **Pioneers of the Bluestem Prairie**. (1976) reprint 1991. Indexed. Illus.
    Clay, Geary, Marshall, Pottawatomie, Riley, Wabaunsee, and Washington counties.
Cloth. $53.95. 608 pp. .... Vendor G0083

Robertson, Clara Hamlett. **Kansas Territorial Settlers of 1860** Who Were Born in Tennessee, Virginia, North Carolina and South Carolina. (1976) reprint 1990. Illus.
Contact vendor for information. 215 pp. .... Vendor G0011

Smith, Patricia D. **Kansas Biographical Index: State-wide & Regional Histories**. 1994.
Paper. $30.00. 350 pp. .... Vendor G0177

Southern California Genealogical Society. **Sources of Genealogical Help in Kansas**.
Paper. $3.50. 25 pp. .... Vendor G0656

Thorndale, William, and William Dollarhide. **County Boundary Map Guides to the U.S. Federal Censuses, 1790-1920: Kansas, 1860-1920**. 1987.
$5.95. .... Vendor G0552

Brown County

Darby, Earl G. **1880 Federal Census: Brown County Kansas**. 1975. Indexed.
Paper. $22.00. 225 pp. .... Vendor G0083

Ford, Don L., comp. **Some Cemeteries of Brown County,** with Supplements. 1986.
Cloth. $48.00. 319 pp. .... Vendor G0259

Ostertag, John, and Enid Ostertag. **Township Maps of Brown County, Kansas 1887**. 1995.
Paper. $12.00. 82 pp. .... Vendor G0745

Butler County

Mooney, V. P. **History of Butler County**. (1916) reprint 1987.
Contact vendor for information. 869 pp. .... Vendor G0259

Clay County

Clay County Historical Society. **Rural Cemeteries, Clay County Kansas**. 1993. Indexed.
Paper. $19.50. 141 pp. .... Vendor G0083

Darby, Earl G. **1880 Federal Census: Clay County Kansas**. 1973. Indexed.
Paper. $22.00. 218 pp. .... Vendor G0083

Riley County Genealogical Society. **Pioneers of the Bluestem Prairie**. (1976) reprint 1991. Indexed. Illus.
    Clay, Geary, Marshall, Pottawatomie, Riley, Wabaunsee, and Washington counties.
Cloth. $53.95. 608 pp. .... Vendor G0083

Dickinson County

Darby, Earl G. **1880 Federal Census, Dickinson County Kansas**. 1975. Indexed.
Paper. $22.00. 219 pp. .... Vendor G0083

Douglas County

Cordley, R. **A History of Lawrence,** from First Settlement to the Close of the Rebellion. (1895) reprint 1987.
Cloth. $34.00. 269 pp. .... Vendor G0259

Ellsworth County

Darby, Earl G. **1880 Federal Census, Ellsworth County Kansas**. 1970. Indexed.
Paper. $22.00. 152 pp. .... Vendor G0083

Geary County

Brown, Evelyn J. **1870 Davis County Kansas Census**. 1982. Indexed.
Paper. $17.00. 55 pp. .... Vendor G0083

Darby, Earl G. **1880 Federal Census: Davis County Kansas**. 1970. Indexed.
Paper. $22.00. 131 pp. .... Vendor G0083

Riley County Genealogical Society. **Geary County Kansas Cemeteries Except Those in Junction City**. 1977. Indexed.
Paper. $17.00. 151 pp. .... Vendor G0083

Riley County Genealogical Society. **Pioneers of the Bluestem Prairie**. (1976) reprint 1991. Indexed. Illus.
    Clay, Geary, Marshall, Pottawatomie, Riley, Wabaunsee, and Washington counties.
Cloth. $53.95. 608 pp. .... Vendor G0083

Grant County

Wilson, R. R., and Ethel M. Sears. **History of Grant County**. (1950) reprint 1994.
Cloth. $34.00. 278 pp. .... Vendor G0259

Johnson County

Armstrong, Ruth A., and R. Wayne Jennings. **1860 Federal Census—Johnson Co., KS**. Reprint 1996. Indexed.
Paper. $16.50 (plus $1.07 KS tax). 149 pp. .... Vendor G0571

Leavenworth County

Moore, Henry Miles. **Early History of Leavenworth, City & County**. (1906) reprint 1993.
Cloth. $38.00. 339 pp. .... Vendor G0259

Marion County

Darby, Earl G. **1880 Federal Census, Marion County Kansas**. 1974. Indexed.
Paper. $22.00. 214 pp. .... Vendor G0083

Marshall County

Darby, Earl G. **1880 Federal Census, Marshall County Kansas**. 1973. Indexed.
Paper. $22.00. 278 pp. .... Vendor G0083

Riley County Genealogical Society. **Pioneers of the Bluestem Prairie**. (1976) reprint 1991. Indexed. Illus.
   Clay, Geary, Marshall, Pottawatomie, Riley, Wabaunsee, and Washington counties.
Cloth. $53.95. 608 pp. .... Vendor G0083

Meade County

Sullivan, Frank S. **A History of Meade County**. (1916) reprint 1994.
Cloth. $29.50. 184 pp. .... Vendor G0259

Mitchell County

Darby, Earl G. **1880 Federal Census, Mitchell County Kansas**. 1975. Indexed.
Paper. $22.00. 258 pp. .... Vendor G0083

Montgomery County

Darby, Earl G. **1880 Federal Census: Montgomery County Kansas**. 1971. Indexed.
Paper. $22.00. 313 pp. .... Vendor G0083

Morris County

Darby, Earl G. **1880 Federal Census, Morris County Kansas**. 1974. Indexed.
Paper. $22.00. 162 pp. .... Vendor G0083

Nemaha County

Crevecoeur, E. E. **Old Settlers' Tales, Pottawatomie & Nemaha Counties:** Historical & Biographical Sketches of the Early Settlement & Settlers of Northeastern
Pottawatomie & Southwestern Nemaha Cos., from Earliest Settlement to the Year
1877. (1901-2) reprint 1995.
Contact vendor for information. 162 pp. .... Vendor G0259

Darby, Earl G. **1880 Federal Census, Nemaha County Kansas**. 1976. Indexed.
Paper. $22.00. 168 pp. .... Vendor G0083

Pottawatomie County

Brown, Evelyn J. **1870 Census, Pottawatomie County, Kansas**. 1984. Indexed.
Paper. $17.00. 68 pp. .... Vendor G0083

Brown, Evelyn J. **Pottawatomie County Kansas 1900 Federal Census Abstract**.
1994. Indexed.
Paper. $39.00. 398 pp. .... Vendor G0083

Crevecoeur, E. E. **Old Settlers' Tales, Pottawatomie & Nemaha Counties:** Historical & Biographical Sketches of the Early Settlement & Settlers of Northeastern
Pottawatomie & Southwestern Nemaha Cos., from Earliest Settlement to the Year
1877. (1901-2) reprint 1995.
Contact vendor for information. 162 pp. .... Vendor G0259

Darby, Earl G. **1880 Federal Census, Pottawatomie County Kansas**. 1970. Indexed.
Paper. $22.00. 294 pp. .... Vendor G0083

Pinick, Merrie. **Pottawatomie County Kansas Marriages, 1856-1886**. 1981. Indexed.
Paper. $17.00. 107 pp. .... Vendor G0083

Riley County Genealogical Society. **Pioneers of the Bluestem Prairie**. (1976) reprint
1991. Indexed. Illus.
    Clay, Geary, Marshall, Pottawatomie, Riley, Wabaunsee, and Washington counties.
Cloth. $53.95. 608 pp. .... Vendor G0083

Reno County

Welsh, Willard. **Hutchinson, A Prairie City in Kansas**. (1946) reprint 1995.
Cloth, $25.00. Paper, $18.00. 166 pp. .... Vendor G0259

Republic County

Darby, Earl G. **1880 Federal Census Republic County Kansas**. 1977. Indexed.
Paper. $22.00. 266 pp. .... Vendor G0083

Riley County

Brown, Evelyn J. **1895 Kansas State Census, Riley County**. 1978. Indexed.
Paper. $17.00. 125 pp. .... Vendor G0083

Darby, Earl G. **1870 Federal Census, Riley County Kansas**. 1970. Indexed.
Paper. $17.00. 90 pp. .... Vendor G0083

Darby, Earl G. **1875 Kansas State Census, Riley County**. 1969. Indexed.
Paper. $17.00. 121 pp. .... Vendor G0083

Darby, Earl G. **1880 Federal Census, Riley County Kansas**. 1969. Indexed.
Paper. $22.00. 194 pp. .... Vendor G0083

Darby, Earl G. **1885 Kansas State Census, Riley County**. 1976. Indexed.
Paper. $22.00. 214 pp. .... Vendor G0083

Darby, Earl G. **Early Marriages Riley County, Kansas, 1855-1886**. 1960. Indexed.
Paper. $14.50. 71 pp. .... Vendor G0083

Riley County Genealogical Society. **1900 Riley County Kansas Census Index**. 1985.
Indexed.
Paper. $17.00. 68 pp. .... Vendor G0083

Riley County Genealogical Society. **Cemeteries of Riley County Kansas Excluding Manhattan City Cemeteries**. 1986. Indexed.
Paper. $27.00. 173 pp. .... Vendor G0083

Riley County Genealogical Society. **Guide to 1910 Federal Census of Riley County Kansas**. 1986. Indexed.
Paper. $14.50. 70 pp. .... Vendor G0083

Riley County Genealogical Society. **Manhattan Nationalist, Dec. 23, 1870-Dec. 30, 1871**. 1989. Indexed.
Paper. $12.00. 51 pp. .... Vendor G0083

Riley County Genealogical Society. **Pioneers of the Bluestem Prairie**. (1976) reprint 1991. Indexed. Illus.
   Clay, Geary, Marshall, Pottawatomie, Riley, Wabaunsee, and Washington counties.
Cloth. $53.95. 608 pp. .... Vendor G0083

Riley County Genealogical Society. **Sunset Cemetery, Manhattan, Kansas Including Inscriptions and Sexton's Records**. 1979. Indexed.
Paper. $27.00. 241 pp. .... Vendor G0083

Riley County Historical Society. **Riley County Kansas 1915 State Census Abstract**.
1990. Indexed.
Paper. $39.00. 459 pp. .... Vendor G0083

Riley County Historical Society. **Riley County Kansas Marriage License Index 1887-1897**. 1987. Indexed.
Paper. $14.50. 68 pp. .... Vendor G0083

Riley County Historical Society. **Riley County Kansas Marriage License Index 1898-1906**. 1988. Indexed.
Paper. $12.00. 46 pp. .... Vendor G0083

Riley County Historical Society. **Riley County Kansas Marriage License Index 1906-1914**. 1988. Indexed.
Paper. $12.00. 50 pp. .... Vendor G0083

Riley County Historical Society. **Riley County Kansas Marriage License Index 1914-1918**. 1995. Indexed.
Paper. $13.00. 56 pp. .... Vendor G0083

Smith County

Maydew, Randall C., ed. **A Kansas Farm Family**. 1993. Illus.
Cloth. $25.00. 313 pp. .... Vendor G0007

Wabaunsee County

Brown, Evelyn J. **1870 Census, Wabaunsee County Kansas**. 1984. Indexed.
Paper. $15.50. 30 pp. .... Vendor G0083

Darby, Earl G. **1880 Federal Census, Wabaunsee County Kansas**. 1970. Indexed.
Paper. $22.00. 153 pp. .... Vendor G0083

Riley County Genealogical Society. **Pioneers of the Bluestem Prairie**. (1976) reprint
1991. Indexed. Illus.
   Clay, Geary, Marshall, Pottawatomie, Riley, Wabaunsee, and Washington counties.
Cloth. $53.95. 608 pp. .... Vendor G0083

Soldan, Dick. **Wabaunsee Cemetery, Wabaunsee Kansas**. 1987. Indexed.
Paper. $12.00. 37 pp. .... Vendor G0083

Washington County

Darby, Earl G. **1880 Federal Census, Washington County Kansas**. 1971. Indexed.
Paper. $22.00. 256 pp. .... Vendor G0083

Riley County Genealogical Society. **Pioneers of the Bluestem Prairie**. (1976) reprint 1991. Indexed. Illus.
Clay, Geary, Marshall, Pottawatomie, Riley, Wabaunsee, and Washington counties.
Cloth. $53.95. 608 pp. .... Vendor G0083

Wyandotte County

Kusek, Joan. **Index to Wyandotte County, Kansas Final Naturalizations 1859-1947**. 1991. Indexed.
Paper. $30.95. 385 pp. .... Vendor G0122

Kusek, Joan. **Index to Wyandotte County, Kansas Petitions For Naturalization 1867-1906**. 1990. Indexed.
Paper. $18.95. 106 pp. .... Vendor G0122

Kusek, Joan. **Wyandotte County, Kansas Cemetery Records Volume I**. 1993. Indexed.
Paper. $32.95. 265 pp. .... Vendor G0122

Kentucky

Statewide and Regional References

Adjutant General State of Kentucky. **Kentucky Soldiers of the War of 1812**. (1891) reprint 1992. Indexed.
Cloth. $38.50. 460 pp. + index .... Vendor G0610

Ardery, Mrs. William Breckenridge. **Kentucky [Court and Other] Records [Vol. I]** Early Wills and Marriages, Old Bible Records and Tombstone Inscriptions. (1926) reprint 1986. Indexed.
Cloth. $17.50. 206 pp. .... Vendor G0010

J. M. Armstrong Company. **The Biographical Encyclopedia of Kentucky, of the Dead and Living Men of the Nineteenth Century**. (1876) reprint 1980. Indexed. Illus.
Cloth. $42.50. 820 pp. .... Vendor G0610

Atlas of Kentucky, 120 county maps.
Includes detailed maps of individual counties, all the back roads, streams, lakes, towns, etc. 11" x 16".
$14.95. .... Vendor G0611

Clark. **Historic Maps of Kentucky**.
Ten maps in facsimile, with a 96-page essay.
Oversized. $35.00. .... Vendor G0611

Clift, G. Glenn. **The Cornstalk Militia of Kentucky, 1792-1811**. (1957) reprint 1982. Indexed.
Contact vendor for information. 248 pp. .... Vendor G0610

Clift, G. Glenn. **Kentucky Marriages, 1797-1865**. (1938-1940) reprint 1995. Indexed.
Cloth. $20.00. 258 pp. .... Vendor G0010

Clift, G. Glenn. **Kentucky Obituaries, 1787-1854** from the Register of the Kentucky Historical Society. (1941-1943) reprint 1993. Indexed.
Cloth. $20.00. 254 pp. .... Vendor G0010

Clift, G. Glenn. **Remember the Raisin!** Kentucky and Kentuckians in the Battles and Massacre at Frenchtown, Michigan Territory, in the War of 1812. Published with **Notes on Kentucky Veterans of the War of 1812**. 2 vols. in 1. Partially indexed. (1961, 1964) reprint 1995.
Paper. $26.50. 339 pp. in all. .... Vendor G0011

Clift, G. Glenn. **"Second Census" of Kentucky 1800**. (1954) reprint 1993.
Cloth. $25.00. 333 pp. .... Vendor G0010

Collins, Lewis, and Richard H. Collins. **History of Kentucky** Embracing . . . Incidents of Pioneer Life, and Nearly Five Hundred Biographical Sketches of Distinguished Pioneers, Soldiers, Statesmen, Jurists, Lawyers, Surgeons . . . Etc. 2 vols. (1848, 1874) reprint 1995. Indexed. Illus.
Paper. $95.00. 804 + 683 pp. .... Vendor G0011

Crowder. **Early Louisville, Kentucky, Newspaper Abstracts, 1806-1828**. 1995.
These abstracts contain over 33,000 references to early residents of Louisville and the surrounding area (including Indiana), and much of Central Kentucky. An excellent source for both ordinary and prominent citizens. Contains information on marriages, obituaries, court and probate records, militia, occupations, former residences, early advertisements, lost persons, heirs, estate settlements, divorce, local events, and more.
Paper. $28.00. 283 pp. .... Vendor G0611

Dilts, Bryan Lee, comp. **1890 Kentucky Veterans Census Index**. 2nd ed. 1992. Illus.
Cloth. $48.00. 132 pp. .... Vendor G0552

Early Kentucky Settlers. The Records of Jefferson County, Kentucky, from the Filson Club History Quarterly. 1988. Indexed.
Cloth. $30.00. 505 pp. .... Vendor G0010

Ely, William. **The Big Sandy Valley**. A History of the People and Country. (1887) reprint 1993. Indexed. Illus.
The Big Sandy Valley, which is today situated mostly in Eastern Kentucky, encompasses all or part of sixteen counties in Kentucky, Virginia, and West Virginia.
Paper. $38.50. 500 pp. .... Vendor G0011

Family History Library. **Research Outline: Kentucky**.
Leaflet. $.25. 10 pp. .... Vendor G0629

Felldin, Jeanne Robey, and Gloria Kay Vandiver Inman. **Index to the 1820 Census of Kentucky**. (1981) reprint 1996.
Paper. $28.50. 318 pp. .... Vendor G0011

Fowler, I. E. **Kentucky Pioneers and Their Descendants**. (1951) reprint 1994.
Contact vendor for information. .... Vendor G0010

KENTUCKY BOOKS IN PRINT, 1996 Edition

Collected & Compiled by Betty Masley, of IDL Research

In its second printing & now published by IDL Research, this helpful 202-page catalog of **Kentucky** Genealogy Resource Materials lists 150 vendors, 1500 publications, plus resources for each county. Sources are locating: cemetery & funeral home records; 100+ family histories; microfilm of vital statistics, newspaper abstracts, census records, tax lists, manuscripts; military personnel & veterans' burial records; naturalization petitions; church records; African American genealogy, biographies & case studies; Records of the Bureau of Refugees, Freedmen & Abandoned Lands; Indian genealogy & Cherokee records. Also information about local & state societies' newsletters & publications.

202 pages $23.00 ppd.

OHIO BOOKS IN PRINT, 1994 Edition

Collected & Compiled by Betty Masley, of IDL Research

A helpful 125-page catalog of **Ohio** Genealogy Resource Materials listing 110 vendors, 1000 publications, and a resource directory for each county. Sources are shown for locating: cemetery & funeral home records; church records; Dutch, Italian & German emigrants' lists; Indian census rolls; microfilm of vital statistics, newspaper abstracts, census records, tax lists, manuscripts; military personnel records; veterans' burial records; naturalization petitions; plus valuable information for researching biographies of African Americans in the US Army. Forty individual family histories & contacts for local & state societies.

125 pages $15.75 ppd.

Order from IDL Research, Betty Masley,
PO Box 20654, Indianapolis, IN 46220-0654

Gooldy, Ray. **Kentucky: A Brief Genealogical Guide**.
Paper. $8.00. 34 pp. .... Vendor G0574

Green, Karen M. **The Kentucky Gazette, 1787-1800 & 1801-1820: Genealogical & Historical Abstracts**. 2 vols. 1984, 1985. Indexed.
Abstracts contain information on marriages, obituaries, court and probate records, militia, occupations, former residences, early advertisements, lost persons, heirs, estate settlements, divorce, local events, and more. A complete index to persons, place names, and subjects contains over 64,000 entries.
Cloth. $26.00/vol., $48.00/set. 706 pp. total. .... Vendor G0611

Green, Thomas Marshall. **Historic Families of Kentucky**. (1889) reprint 1996. Indexed.
Paper. $27.50. 304 pp. .... Vendor G0011

Gresham, John M. **Biographical Cyclopedia of the Commonwealth of Kentucky**. (1896) reprint 1980. Indexed. Illus.
Cloth. $40.00. 736 pp. .... Vendor G0610

The Guide to Kentucky Archival & Manuscript Repositories.
Locates 285 archival and manuscript repositories. Describes the holdings and published finding aids.
Paper. $20.00. 127 pp. .... Vendor G0611

A Guide to Kentucky Birth, Marriage and Death Records, 1852-1910. 1988.
What vital records are available and where they can be found.
Spiral bound. $13.50. 72 pp. .... Vendor G0611

Hall. **The Shane Manuscript Collection: A Genealogical Guide to the Kentucky and Ohio Papers**. 1990.
While many genealogists and historians are familiar with the collection of Rev. John Dabney Shane's papers in the Draper Manuscripts, it often comes as a surprise that half of Shane's papers are located at the Presbyterian Historical Association in Philadelphia, and not in Draper's collection. The collection (36 reels of microfilm) reflects his interest in the history of the Presbyterian Church in very early KY and OH, and the migration of congregations into IL, IN, MO.
Paper. $12.00. 133 pp. .... Vendor G0611

Harrison. **The Civil War in Kentucky**. 1975.
Describes the battles as well as the political climate in Kentucky during the War.
Cloth. $16.00. 123 pp. .... Vendor G0611

Heinemann, Charles B. **The "First Census" of Kentucky: 1790**. (1938) reprint 1992. Indexed.
Hard-cover. $27.50. 188 pp. .... Vendor G0610

Heinemann, Charles Brunk. **"First Census" of Kentucky, 1790**. (1940) reprint 1993. Illus.
Cloth. $17.50. 118 pp. .... Vendor G0010

Hogan, Roseann Reinemuth. **Kentucky Ancestry**. 1992.
An extensive guide to Kentucky genealogical and historical research.
Paper. $19.95. 400 pp. .... Vendor G0570

Hughes, Buckner L., and Nathaniel C. Hughes. **Kentucky Memories of Uncle Sam Williams**. Indexed.
 Sam Williams was born in Paris, KY in 1831. He became a newspaper man and worked on papers in Kentucky and Illinois until after the Civil War.
$15.50 (perfect bound). 112 pp. .... Vendor G0549

Ingmire, Frances T. **Pioneer Kentuckians with Missouri Cousins**. 2 vols.
 Missouri records showing over 65,000 persons born in Kentucky but who by 1850 are living in Missouri.
Paper. $35.00/vol. .... Vendor G0549

Jillson, Willard Rouse. **The Big Sandy Valley**. A Regional History Prior to the Year 1850. (1923) reprint 1994. Indexed. Illus.
 Deals with the region (mostly in Eastern Kentucky), which today encompasses all or part of sixteen counties in Kentucky, Virginia, and West Virginia.
Paper. $18.00. 183 pp. .... Vendor G0011

Jillson, Willard Rouse. **The Kentucky Land Grants**. A Systematic Index to All of the Land Grants Recorded in the State Land Office at Frankfort, Kentucky, 1782-1924. 2 vols. (1925) reprint 1994. Illus.
Cloth. $100.00. 1,844 pp. total. .... Vendor G0010

Johnson. **Slavery Days in Old Kentucky**. (1901) reprint 1994.
 A fascinating, first-hand account by a former slave.
Paper. $14.95. 69 pp. .... Vendor G0611

Kentucky Adjutant-General's Office. **Kentucky Soldiers of the War of 1812**. With an Added Index. (1891, 1969) reprint 1995. Indexed.
Paper. $49.95. 436 pp. .... Vendor G0011

Kentucky Department for Libraries and Archives. **The Guide to Kentucky Archival and Manuscript Repositories**. 1986.
Paper. $12.00. 127 pp. .... Vendor G0651

Kentucky Department for Libraries and Archives. **Guide to Kentucky Archival and Manuscript Collections, Vol. 1 (Albany-Burkesville)**. 1988.
Paper. $15.00. 222 pp. .... Vendor G0651

Kentucky Department for Libraries and Archives. **Guide to Kentucky Archival and Manuscript Collections, Vol. 2 (Cadiz-Eminence)**. 1992.
Paper. $10.00. 98 pp. .... Vendor G0651

Kentucky Department for Libraries and Archives. **A Guide to Kentucky Birth, Marriage, and Death Records (1852-1910)**. (1980) reprint 1988.
Paper. $8.00. 72 pp. .... Vendor G0651

Kentucky Department for Libraries and Archives. **Index to Confederate Pension Applications, Commonwealth of Kentucky**. 1978.
Paper. $5.00. 207 pp. .... Vendor G0651

Kentucky Department for Libraries and Archives. **Inventory of Confederate Pension Applications, Commonwealth of Kentucky**. (1978) reprint 1981.
Paper. $2.00. 10 pp. .... Vendor G0651

Kentucky Department for Libraries and Archives. **Inventory of the Early Records of the Kentucky Insurance Bureau and Department (1870-1936)**. 1977.
Paper. $3.00. 23 pp. .... Vendor G0651

Kentucky Department for Libraries and Archives. **Inventory of the Records of the Bank of Kentucky (1806-1835)**. 1976.
Paper. $3.00. 31 pp. .... Vendor G0651

Kentucky Department for Libraries and Archives. **Inventory of the Records of the Bank of the Commonwealth of Kentucky (1820-1830)**. 1976.
Paper. $3.00. 26 pp. .... Vendor G0651

Kentucky Department for Libraries and Archives. **Inventory of the Records of the Frankfort Bank (1818-1820)**. 1976.
Paper. $3.00. 8 pp. .... Vendor G0651

Kentucky Department for Libraries and Archives. **Register of Vietnam War Casualties from Kentucky**. 1988.
Paper. $12.00. 216 pp. .... Vendor G0651

Kentucky Historical Society. **Certificate Book of the Virginia Land Commission, 1779-1780,** The Register for 1923. (1923) reprint 1992. Indexed.
  The original records of Kentucky County, Virginia, 1776-1780, were lost in a fire in the 19th century, which makes this book quite important because it contains the names of most of the pioneer settlers of the state of Kentucky.
Cloth. $35.00. 344 pp. .... Vendor G0610

Kentucky Marriage Records from the Register of the Kentucky Historical Society. (1983) reprint 1996. Indexed.
Cloth. $55.00. 1,024 pp. .... Vendor G0010

Kentucky Pension Roll for 1835. Report from the Secretary of War, in Relation to the Pension Establishment of the United States. (1835) reprint 1994.
Paper. $15.00. 152 pp. .... Vendor G0011

King, Junie Estelle Stewart. **Abstract of Early Kentucky Wills and Inventories,** Copied from Original and Recorded Wills and Inventories. (1933) reprint 1996. Indexed.
Paper. $25.00. 298 pp. .... Vendor G0011

Kozee, William C. **Early Families of Eastern and Southeastern Kentucky and Their Descendants**. (1961) reprint 1994. Indexed. Illus.
Cloth. $45.00. 886 pp. .... Vendor G0010

Kozee, William C. **Pioneer Families of Eastern and Southeastern Kentucky**. (1957) reprint 1994.
Cloth. $25.00. 272 pp. .... Vendor G0010

Levin, H., ed. **Lawyers and Lawmakers of Kentucky**. (1897) reprint 1982. Indexed. Illus.
Cloth. $40.00. 808 pp. .... Vendor G0610

Liahona Research. **Kentucky Marriages, Early to 1800**. 1990. Illus.
Cloth. $60.00. 242 pp. .... Vendor G0552

Long, John H., ed. **Kentucky Atlas of Historical County Boundaries.** 1995. A beautiful and extremely useful book detailing the changes in county boundaries from colonial times to 1990. 8½" x 11".
Cloth. $120.00. 485 pp. .... Vendor G0611

Masley, Betty J., comp. **Kentucky Books in Print, 1996 Edition.** (1989) reprint 1996.
A 202-page catalogue of 150 Kentucky genealogy resource materials from 150 vendors. Advertisement on page 185.
Paper. $30.00. .... Vendor G0507

McAdams, Mrs. Harry Kennett. **Kentucky Pioneer and Court Records:** Abstracts of Early Wills, Deeds, and Marriages . . . (1929) reprint 1997. Indexed.
Paper. $35.00. 381 pp. .... Vendor G0011

Nickell, Joe. **Kentucky Genealogical Research: An Investigative Approach.** 1993.
Paper. $5.00. 31 pp. .... Vendor G0113

Peden, Henry C., Jr. **Marylanders to Kentucky, 1775-1825.** 1991. Indexed.
Paper. $15.00. 202 pp. .... Vendor G0140

Perrin, W. H., J. H. Battle, and G. C. Kniffin. **A History of the State of Kentucky: The General History.** (1885) reprint 1979. Indexed.
Cloth. $37.50. 652 pp. .... Vendor G0610

Perrin, W. H., J. H. Battle, and G. C. Kniffin. **A History of the State of Kentucky: The First Edition.** (1885) reprint 1979. Indexed. Illus.
Contains the precinct histories of the seven counties in the Jackson Purchase, and biographical sketches of individuals in Ballard, Calloway, Fulton, Graves, Hickman, McCraken, and Marshall counties.
Cloth. $32.50. 440 pp. .... Vendor G0610

Perrin, W. H., J. H. Battle, and G. C. Kniffin. **A History of the State of Kentucky: The Second Edition.** (1886) reprint 1979. Indexed. Illus.
Contains biographical sketches from Butler, Caldwell, Crittenden, Hancock, Hopkins, Livingston, Logan, Lyon, McLean, Muhlenberg, Ohio, Union, and Webster counties.
Cloth. Contact vendor for information. 613 pp. .... Vendor G0610

Perrin, W. H., J. H. Battle, and G. C. Kniffin. **A History of the State of Kentucky: The Third Edition.** (1886) reprint 1979. Indexed. Illus.
Contains biographical sketches of individuals from Allen, Barren, Breckenridge, Edmondson, Grayson, Hardin, Hart, Larue, Meade, Metcalfe, Monroe, Simpson, and Warren counties.
Cloth. Contact vendor for information. 613 pp. .... Vendor G0610

Perrin, W. H., J. H. Battle, and G. C. Kniffin. **A History of the State of Kentucky: The Fourth Edition.** (1887) reprint 1979. Indexed. Illus.
Contains biographical sketches on individuals from Adair, Boyle, Casey, Cumberland, Garrad, Green, Lincoln, Madison, Marion, Mercer, Nelson, Taylor, Trigg, and Washington counties.
Cloth. Contact vendor for information. 381 pp. .... Vendor G0610

Perrin, W. H., J. H. Battle, and G. C. Kniffin. **A History of the State of Kentucky: The Fifth Edition.** (1887) reprint 1979. Indexed. Illus.

Contains biographical sketches of individuals from Anderson, Franklin, Jessamine, and Woodford counties.

Cloth. $25.00. 163 pp. .... Vendor G0610

Perrin, W. H., J. H. Battle, and G. C. Kniffin. **A History of the State of Kentucky: The Sixth Edition**. (1887) reprint 1979. Indexed. Illus.

Contains biographical sketches on individuals from Henry, Oldham, Shelby, Spencer, and Trimble counties.

Cloth. $25.00. 184 pp. .... Vendor G0610

Perrin, W. H., J. H. Battle, and G. C. Kniffin. **A History of the State of Kentucky: The Seventh Edition**. (1887) reprint 1979. Indexed. Illus.

Contains biographical sketches on individuals from Boone, Campbell, Gallatin, Grant, Kenton, Owen, and Pendleton counties.

Cloth. $32.50. 211 pp. .... Vendor G0610

Perrin, W. H., J. H. Battle, and G. C. Kniffin. **A History of the State of Kentucky: The Eighth Edition**. (1888) reprint 1979. Indexed. Illus.

Contains biographical sketches on individuals from Jefferson County.

Cloth. $25.00. 209 pp. .... Vendor G0610

Perrin, W. H., J. H. Battle, and G. C. Kniffin. **A History of the State of Kentucky: The Eighth Edition, 8-B**. (1888) reprint 1992. Indexed. Illus.

Contains biographical sketches on individuals from Bath, Bracken, Breathitt, Carter, Clark, Clay, Estill, Flemming, Floyd, Greenup, Johnson, Knox, Laurel, Lawrence, Lee, Letcher, Lewis, Mogoffin, Mason, Montgomery, Morgan, Owsley, Pike, Pulaski, Robertson, Rockcastle, Russell, Wayne, and Whitley counties.

Cloth. $32.50. 311 pp. .... Vendor G0610

Quisenberry, Anderson Chenault. **Kentucky in the War of 1812**. (1915) reprint 1996. Indexed. Illus.

Paper. $25.00. 242 pp. .... Vendor G0011

Quisenberry, Anderson Chenault. **Revolutionary Soldiers in Kentucky; Also a Roster of the Virginia Navy**. (1896) reprint 1996. Indexed.

Paper. $22.00. 206 pp. .... Vendor G0011

Quisenberry, Anderson Chenault. **Revolutionary Soldiers in Kentucky: Also a Roster of the Virginia Navy**. (1896) reprint 1992. Indexed.

Hard-cover. $27.50. 248 pp. .... Vendor G0610

Rennick. **Kentucky Place Names**. 1984.

From Aaron to Zula, this book is interesting as well as a good reference.

Paper. $17.00. 375 pp. .... Vendor G0611

Robertson, James Rood, and John Frederick Dorman. **Petitions of the Early Inhabitants of Kentucky to the General Assembly of Virginia, 1769 to 1792** (Filson Club). (1914) reprint 1981. Indexed.

Cloth. $25.00. 292 pp. .... Vendor G0610

Schweitzer, George K. **Kentucky Genealogical Research**. 1995. Illus.

History of the state, types of records (Bible through will), record locations, research techniques, listings of county records.

Paper. $15.00. 154 pp. .... Vendor G0569

Sifakis. **Compendium of the Confederate Armies: Kentucky, Maryland, Missouri, the Confederate Units and the Indian Units.** 1995.
Describes the regiments, the officers, and the battles.
Cloth. $27.50. 234 pp. .... Vendor G0611

Sistler, Barbara, Byron Sistler, and Samuel Sistler. **1850 Census, South West Kentucky: Counties of Christian, Logan, Simpson, Todd, Trigg, and Warren.** 1993. Indexed.
Paper. $35.00. vii + 442 pp. .... Vendor G0632

Sistler, Barbara, Byron Sistler, and Samuel Sistler. **1850 Census, Kentucky.** 7 vols. 1991-95.
Volume 1: South Central Kentucky. Counties of Adair, Allen, Barren, Clinton, Cumberland, and Monroe. 382 pp., 48,000 names.
Volume 2: Southwest Kentucky. Counties of Christian, Logan, Simpson, Todd, Trigg, and Warren. 442 pp., 54,000 names.
Volume 3: Western Kentucky. Counties of Ballard, Caldwell, Calloway, Fulton, Graves, Hickman, Livingston, Marshall, and McCracken. 464 pp., about 55,000 names.
Volume 4: Southeastern Kentucky. Counties of Clay, Harlan, Knox, Laurel, Pulaski, Russell, Wayne, and Whitley. 409 pp., 52,000 names.
Volume 5: Eastern Kentucky. Counties of Breathitt, Carter, Floyd, Greenup, Johnson, Lawrence, Letcher, Morgan, Perry, and Pike. 423 pp., 52,000 names.
Volume 6: Northwest Kentucky. Counties of Crittenden, Daviess, Henderson, Hopkins, Muhlenberg, Ohio, and Union. 497 pp., 56,000 names.
Volume 7: Northeast Kentucky. Counties of Bath, Bourbon, Fleming, Lewis, Mason, and Nicholas. 58,500 names.
Paper. $33.00/Vol. 1. $35.00/all other vols. .... Vendor G0577

Sistler, Barbara, and Byron Sistler. **1850 Kentucky Census Series:** Volume 1, South Central.
Shows names and ages of all free persons arranged in order of the original schedules; has regional head of household index.
Paper. $33.00. .... Vendor G0577

Sistler, Barbara, and Byron Sistler. **1850 Kentucky Census Series:** Volume 2, Southwest.
Shows names and ages of all free persons arranged in order of the original schedules; has regional head of household index.
Paper. $35.00. .... Vendor G0577

Sistler, Barbara, and Byron Sistler. **1850 Kentucky Census Series:** Volume 3, Western.
Shows names and ages of all free persons arranged in order of the original schedules; has regional head of household index.
Paper. $35.00. .... Vendor G0577

Sistler, Barbara, and Byron Sistler. **1850 Kentucky Census Series:** Volume 4, Southeast.
Shows names and ages of all free persons arranged in order of the original schedules; has regional head of household index.
Paper. $35.00. .... Vendor G0577

Sistler, Barbara, and Byron Sistler. **1850 Kentucky Census Series:** Volume 5, Eastern.

Shows names and ages of all free persons arranged in order of the original schedules; has regional head of household index.
Paper. $35.00. .... Vendor G0577

Sistler, Barbara, and Byron Sistler. **1850 Kentucky Census Series:** Volume 6, Northwest.
Shows names and ages of all free persons arranged in order of the original schedules; has regional head of household index.
Paper. $35.00. .... Vendor G0577

Sistler, Barbara, and Byron Sistler. **1850 Kentucky Census Series:** Volume 7, Northeast.
Shows names and ages of all free persons arranged in order of the original schedules; has regional head of household index.
Paper. $35.00. .... Vendor G0577

Sistler, Barbara, and Byron Sistler. **1850 Kentucky Census Series:** Volume 8, East Central.
Shows names and ages of all free persons arranged in order of the original schedules; has regional head of household index.
Paper. $35.00. .... Vendor G0577

Sistler, Barbara, and Byron Sistler. **1850 Kentucky Census Series:** Volume 9, West Central.
Shows names and ages of all free persons arranged in order of the original schedules; has regional head of household index.
Paper. $35.00. .... Vendor G0577

Sistler, Barbara, and Byron Sistler. **1850 Kentucky Census Series:** Volume 10, Central.
Shows names and ages of all free persons arranged in order of the original schedules; has regional head of household index.
Paper. $35.00. .... Vendor G0577

Sistler, Barbara, and Byron Sistler. **1850 Kentucky Census Series:** Volume 11, North Central.
Shows names and ages of all free persons arranged in order of the original schedules; has regional head of household index.
Paper. $37.00. .... Vendor G0577

Sistler, Barbara, and Byron Sistler. **1850 Kentucky Census Series:** Volume 12, North Pt. 1.
Shows names and ages of all free persons arranged in order of the original schedules; has regional head of household index.
Paper. $35.00. .... Vendor G0577

Sistler, Barbara, and Byron Sistler. **1850 Kentucky Census Series:** Volume 13, North Pt. 2.
Shows names and ages of all free persons arranged in order of the original schedules; has regional head of household index.
Paper. $37.00. .... Vendor G0577

Sistler, Barbara, and Byron Sistler. **1850 Kentucky Census Series:** Volume 14, Jefferson County.

Shows names and ages of all free persons arranged in order of the original schedules; has regional head of household index.
Paper. $37.00. .... Vendor G0577

Smith, Clifford N. **Early Nineteenth-Century German Settlers in Ohio, Kentucky, and Other States**. German-American Genealogical Research Monograph Number 20. Parts 1-4C.
    Part 1 (1984; iv + 36 pp. double-columned). ISBN 0-915162-22-9.
    Part 2 (1988; ii + 56 pp. double-columned). ISBN 0-915162-23-7.
    Part 3 (1988; ii + 60 pp. double-columned). ISBN 0-915162-25-5.
    Part 4A: Surnames A Through J (1991; ii + 34 pp. double-columned). ISBN 0-915162-84-9.
    Part 4B: Surnames K Through Z (1991; ii + 37 pp. double-columned). ISBN 0-915162-85-7.
    Part 4C: Appendices (1991; ii + 26 pp. double-columned). ISBN 0-915162-85-7.
    Contact vendor for information about additional parts.
Paper. $20.00/part. .... Vendor G0491

Smith, Dora. **Kentucky 1830 Census Index**. 6 vols.
    Volume I: Adair thru Campbell Cos., 88 pp.
    Volume II: Casey thru Gallatin Cos., 89 pp.
    Volume III: Garrard thru Hopkins Cos., 89 pp.
    Volume IV: Jefferson thru Meade Cos., 78 pp.
    Volume V: Mercer thru Russell Cos., 81 pp.
    Volume VI: Scott thru Woodford Cos., 85 pp.
Paper. $10.00/vol., $54.00/set. 510 pp. .... Vendor G0574

Smith, W. T. **A Complete Index to the Names of Persons, Places and Subjects Mentioned in Littell's Laws of Kentucky** A Genealogical and Historical Guide. (1931) reprint 1996.
Paper. $22.50. 223 pp. .... Vendor G0011

Sprague, Stuart Seely. **Kentuckians in Illinois**. 1987. Indexed.
Cloth. $22.50. 306 pp. .... Vendor G0010

Sprague, Stuart Seely. **Kentuckians in Missouri,** Including Many Who Migrated by Way of Ohio, Indiana, or Illinois. (1983) reprint 1989. Indexed.
Cloth. $20.00. 209 pp. .... Vendor G0010

Sprague, Stuart Seely. **Kentuckians in Ohio and Indiana**. (1986) reprint 1992. Indexed.
Cloth. $22.50. 302 pp. .... Vendor G0010

Sutherland, James F. **Early Kentucky Householders, 1787-1811**. (1986) reprint 1997.
Paper. $24.00. 241 pp. .... Vendor G0011

Sutherland, James F. **Early Kentucky Landholders, 1787-1811**. (1986) reprint 1997.
Paper. $35.00. 428 pp. .... Vendor G0011

Swart, Shirley. **Index of "Kentucky Ancestors" Vol. 1-15 (1965-1980)**. 1981.
Paper. $14.00. 179 pp. .... Vendor G0139

T.L.C. Genealogy. **The 1795 Census of Kentucky**. 1991. Indexed.
    A statewide tax list constructed from all tax lists of the Kentucky counties that were in existence in 1795.
Paper. $18.00. 195 pp. .... Vendor G0609

Taylor, Philip Fall. **A Calendar of the Warrants for Land in Kentucky,** Granted for Service in the French and Indian War. (1917) reprint 1995. Indexed.
Paper. $10.00. 76 pp. .... Vendor G0011

Taylor, Philip Fall, and Samuel M. Wilson. **Kentucky Land Warrants, for the French and Indian Revolutionary Wars:** A Calendar of Warrants for Land in Kentucky, Granted for Service in the French and Indian Wars; and Land Bounty Land Warrants Granted for Military Service in the War for Independence. (1913) reprint 1917. Indexed.
Gives the researcher for both Kentucky and Virginia a much-needed source of information on early settlers. Contains the names of approximately 6,075 men who served in the Revolution from Virginia.
Hard-cover. $30.00. 164 pp. + index. .... Vendor G0610

Thorndale, William, and William Dollarhide. **County Boundary Map Guides to the U.S. Federal Censuses, 1790-1920: Kentucky, 1790-1920.** 1987.
$5.95. .... Vendor G0552

Volkel, Lowell. **Kentucky 1810 Census Index.** 4 vols.
  Volume I: Adair thru Cumberland, 77 pp.
  Volume II: Estill thru Hopkins Cos., 79 pp.
  Volume III: Jefferson thru Muhlenberg, 88 pp.
  Volume IV: Nelson thru Woodford, 82 pp.
Paper. $10.00/vol., $35.00/set. 316 pp. .... Vendor G0574

Volkel, Lowell. **Kentucky 1820 Census Index.** 4 vols.
  Volume I: Adair thru Cumberland, 100 pp.
  Volume II: Daviess thru Hopkins, 114 pp.
  Volume III: Jefferson thru Nicholas, 112 pp.
  Volume IV: Ohio thru Woodford, 91 pp.
Paper. $12.00/vol., $42.00/set. 417 pp. .... Vendor G0574

Wagstaff, Ann T. **Index to the 1810 Census of Kentucky.** (1980) reprint 1996.
Paper. $25.00. 230 pp. .... Vendor G0011

WPA. **Kentucky Guide to Vital Statistics.**
Paper. $16.00. 257 pp. .... Vendor G0574

Allen County

Jackson, Martha W. **Allen Co., KY Cemeteries Revisited, Vol. II.** Indexed.
Paper. $16.50. 174 pp. .... Vendor G0594

Jackson, Martha W. **Allen Co., KY Cemeteries & Graveyards Revisited, Vol. III.** Indexed.
Paper. $23.50. 196 pp. .... Vendor G0594

Jackson, Martha W. **Allen Co., KY Census for 1820.** Indexed.
Paper. $6.50. 29 pp. .... Vendor G0594

Jackson, Martha W. **Allen Co., KY Day Book 1826-1837.** Indexed.
Paper. $23.50. 214 pp. .... Vendor G0594

Jackson, Martha W. **Allen Co., KY Vital Statistics Revisited**. Indexed.
Paper. $16.50. 78 pp. .... Vendor G0594

Jackson, Martha W. **Earliest Tax Lists of Allen Co., KY 1815-1824**. Indexed.
Paper. $23.50. 205 pp. .... Vendor G0594

Jackson, Martha W. **The 1880 Census of Allen Co., KY**. 1996. Indexed.
Paper. $23.50. 80 pp. .... Vendor G0594

Anderson County

McKee, Lewis W., And Lydia K. Bond. **A History of Anderson County [Kentucky] 1780-1936**. (1936) reprint 1993.
Paper. $25.00. 288 pp. .... Vendor G0011

Barren County

T.L.C. Genealogy. **Barren County, Kentucky, Taxpayers, 1799**. 1990, revised 1995. Indexed.
Paper. $3.50. 12 pp. .... Vendor G0609

Boone County

Worrel, S., and A. Fitzgerald. **Boone County, Kentucky, Cemeteries**. 1996. Indexed.
Cloth. $45.00. 485 pp. .... Vendor G0057

Worrel, S., and A. Fitzgerald. **Boone County, Kentucky, County Court Orders 1799-1815**. 1994. Indexed.
Cloth. $35.00. 347 pp. .... Vendor G0057

Worrel, S., and A. Fitzgerald. **Boone County, Kentucky, Marriages, 1798-1850**. 1991. Indexed.
Cloth. $27.50. 233 pp. .... Vendor G0057

Bourbon County

Franklin, Charles. **Bourbon Co. Will Abstracts 1788-1816. Vol. I**.
Paper. $15.00. 84 pp. .... Vendor G0574

Franklin, Charles. **Bourbon Co. Will Abstracts 1816-1824, Vol. II**.
Paper. $12.00. 53 pp. .... Vendor G0574

Franklin, Charles. **Bourbon Co. Will Abstracts 1825-1831, Vol. III**.
Paper. $12.00. 46 pp. .... Vendor G0574

Perrin, William H., and Robert Peter. **History of Bourbon, Scott, Harrison, and Nicholas Counties, With a Brief Synopsis of the Blue Grass Region**. (1882) reprint 1979. Indexed.
Contact vendor for information. 815 pp. .... Vendor G0610

Schreiner-Yantis, Netti, and Florene Love. **1787 Census of Bourbon County**. 1987. Indexed.
Kentucky was part of Virginia in 1787. Information is from the 1787 Personal Property Tax Lists. In two of the three lists for Bourbon County, every male over 21 years is listed by name—with names of sons, brothers, fathers, and apprentices appearing under the name of the head of the household in which they were residing. The number of 16-21 year olds in the household was enumerated in all three lists.
Paper. $2.75. 20 pp. .... Vendor G0081

T.L.C. Genealogy. **Bourbon County, Kentucky, Court Orders, 1786-1793: An Every-Name Index**. 1995. Indexed.
Paper. $12.00. 88 pp. .... Vendor G0609

T.L.C. Genealogy. **Bourbon County, Kentucky Taxpayers, 1787-1799**. 1992. Indexed.
Paper. $12.00. 173 pp. .... Vendor G0609

Breckinridge County

Breckinridge County 1870 Census.
Paper. $35.00. .... Vendor G0549

Breckinridge County, Kentucky—Births 1852-1853, 1855-1859, 1861, 1874-1876, 1878, 1893-1894 and 1903-1904.
Paper. $18.50. .... Vendor G0549

Breckinridge County, Kentucky—Deaths 1852-1859, 1861, 1874-1878, 1894, 1903-1904.
Paper. $16.50. .... Vendor G0549

Breckinridge County, Kentucky—Marriages 1853-1859, 1861, 1875-1878, 1893-1894 and 1904.
Paper. $19.00. .... Vendor G0549

Bullitt County

Darnell, Betty R. **1810-1840 Census, Bullitt Co. KY**. 1989. Indexed.
Paper. $25.00. 122 pp. .... Vendor G0261

Darnell, Betty R. **1880 Census, Bullitt Co. KY**. 1991. Indexed.
Paper. $32.00. 186 pp. .... Vendor G0261

Darnell, Betty R. **Who Was Who in Bullitt Co. (in 1850)**. 1993. Indexed.
Paper. $14.00. 89 pp. .... Vendor G0261

T.L.C. Genealogy. **Bullitt County, Kentucky, Land Records, 1819-1825**. 1994. Indexed.
Paper. $20.00. 232 pp. .... Vendor G0609

Caldwell County

Jerome, Brenda Joyce (transcriber and indexer). **Caldwell County, Kentucky Vital Statistics—Births 1852-1910**. 1996. Indexed.
Cloth. $35.00. 214 pp. .... Vendor G0686

Calloway County

Douthat, James L. **Kentucky Lake Reservoir Cemeteries. Volume 1**.
Covers the Kentucky portion of the lake and includes Calloway and Lyon, Livingston, Marshall, and Trigg counties. Also available as a set with Volumes 2 and 3 (see Tennessee, Statewide and Regional References).
Paper. $35.00. .... Vendor G0549

Willis, Laura. **Calloway County, Kentucky Deed Books, Volume Three (Oct. 1834-June 1836)**. 1995. Indexed.
Paper. $10.00. Contact vendor for information about earlier volumes.
100 pp. .... Vendor G0687

Willis, Laura. **Calloway County, Kentucky Tax Lists 1829-1831-1833**. 1995.
Paper. $6.50. 69 pp. .... Vendor G0687

Willis, Laura. **Calloway County, Kentucky Tax Lists 1834-1835-1836**. 1995.
Paper. $9.00. 107 pp. .... Vendor G0687

Willis, Laura. **Calloway County, Kentucky Wills & Administrations Volume Two**. 1995. Indexed.
Paper. $10.00. Contact vendor about previous volume. 104 pp. .... Vendor G0687

Campbell County

Worrel, S. **Campbell County, Kentucky, Marriages 1795-1850**. 1992. Indexed.
Cloth. $32.50. 329 pp. .... Vendor G0057

Christian County

Perrin, W. H., ed. **County of Christian, Historical & Biographical**. 2 vols. in 1. (1884) reprint 1993.
Cloth. $67.00. 640 pp. .... Vendor G0259

Perrin, W. H. **History of Christian County, Kentucky: Historical and Biographical**. 1979. Indexed.
Contact vendor for information. 696 pp. .... Vendor G0610

T.L.C. Genealogy. **Christian County, Kentucky, Deed Book G (1816-1817)**. 1994. Indexed.
Paper. $15.00. 148 pp. .... Vendor G0609

T.L.C. Genealogy. **Christian County, Kentucky, Wills and Estates, 1815-1823**. 1993. Indexed.
Paper. $20.00. 223 pp. .... Vendor G0609

Taylor, Pete, scr. **Christian County, Kentucky Newspaper Abstracts, Volume Three (Kentucky New Era)**. 1996. Indexed.
Paper. $7.00. Contact vendor for information about earlier volumes.
84 pp. .... Vendor G0687

Taylor, Pete, scr. **Christian County, Kentucky Newspaper Abstracts, Volume Four (Kentucky New Era)**. 1996. Indexed.
Paper. $7.00. 74 pp. .... Vendor G0687

Clark County

T.L.C. Genealogy. **Clark County, Kentucky Taxpayers, 1793 thru 1799**. 1990. Indexed.
Paper. $7.50. 84 pp. .... Vendor G0609

Cumberland County

Wells, J. W. **History of Cumberland County**. (1947) reprint 1994.
Cloth. $49.50. 480 pp. .... Vendor G0259

Daviess County

History of Daviess County, Together with Sketches of Its Cities, Villages & Political History . . . and Biographies of Representative Citizens. (1883) reprint 1993.
Cloth. $89.50. 870 pp. .... Vendor G0259

Interstate Publishing Co., comp. **1883 History**. (1883) reprint 1978. Illus.
Cloth. $24.00. 870 pp. .... Vendor G0531

McDonough Co., Leo. **1876 Historical Atlas**. (1876) reprint 1978. Illus.
  Town, precinct (twp.) maps, history, biographies.
Paper. $10.50. 81 pp. .... Vendor G0531

Estill County

Wise, William E. **1920 Estill County Kentucky Census**. 1995. Indexed.
  Book contains 15,000 names; indexed 1,000 surnames.
Paper. $27.50 incl. sales tax. 158 pp. .... Vendor G0314

Fayette County

Franklin, Charles. **Fayette Co. Wills & Estates 1788-1822**.
Paper. $15.00. 122 pp. .... Vendor G0574

Perrin, W. H. **History of Fayette County, Kentucky: With an Outline Sketch of the Bluegrass Region**. (1882) reprint 1979. Indexed.
Contact vendor for information. 952 pp. .... Vendor G0610

Schreiner-Yantis, Netti, and Florene Love. **1787 Census of Fayette County**. 1987. Indexed.
Paper. $6.00. 48 pp. .... Vendor G0081

Fleming County

Franklin, Charles M. **Fleming Co. Wills & Estates 1798-1822, Vol. I**.
Paper. $10.00. 38 pp. .... Vendor G0574

Franklin, Charles. **Fleming Co. Wills & Estates 1822-1834, Vol. II**.
Paper. $10.00. 43 pp. .... Vendor G0574

T.L.C. Genealogy. **Fleming County, Kentucky, Taxpayers, 1798 & 1799**. 1995. Indexed.
Paper. $3.50. 14 pp. .... Vendor G0609

Garrard County

Franklin, Charles. **Garrard Co. Wills & Estates 1796-1819, Vol. I**.
Paper. $12.00. 47 pp. .... Vendor G0574

Franklin, Charles. **Garrard Co. Wills & Estates 1819-1833, Vol. II**.
Paper. $10.00. 39 pp. .... Vendor G0574

Grant County

Conrad, John B., ed. **History of Grant County Kentucky**. 1993. Indexed. Illus.
  Over 10,000 places and names alphabetically indexed.
Cloth. $38.50. 596 pp. .... Vendor G0462

Graves County

Simmons Historical Publications. **Graves County, Kentucky Tax Lists 1839 and 1840**. 1995.
Paper. $6.00. 49 pp. .... Vendor G0687

Green County

Green County, Kentucky Births 1852-1879 and 1904.
Paper. $35.00. 142 pp. .... Vendor G0549

Green County, Kentucky Deaths 1852-1879 and 1904.
Paper. $23.00. 84 pp. .... Vendor G0549

Green County, Kentucky Marriages 1852-1903.
Paper. $28.50. 110 pp. .... Vendor G0549

T.L.C. Genealogy. **Green County, Kentucky, Taxpayers, 1795-1799**. 1989, revised 1993. Indexed.
Paper. $5.00. 35 pp. .... Vendor G0609

Harlan County

Hiday, Nellie. **Harlan Co. 1850 Census**.
Paper. $7.00. 45 pp. .... Vendor G0574

Harrison County

Franklin, Charles. **Harrison Co. Marriage Register & Bonds 1794-1832**.
Paper. $15.00. 69 pp. .... Vendor G0574

Franklin, Charles. **Harrison Co. Wills 1795-1818, Vol. I**.
Paper. $12.00. 37 pp. .... Vendor G0574

Franklin, Charles. **Harrison Co. Wills 1819-1832, Vol. II**.
Paper. $12.00. 52 pp. .... Vendor G0574

Perrin, William H., and Robert Peter. **History of Bourbon, Scott, Harrison, and Nicholas Counties, With a Brief Synopsis of the Blue Grass Region**. (1882) reprint 1979. Indexed.
Contact vendor for information. 815 pp. .... Vendor G0610

T.L.C. Genealogy. **Harrison County, Kentucky Taxpayers, 1794 thru 1799**. 1990. Indexed.
Paper. $7.50. 36 pp. .... Vendor G0609

Henderson County

Sparling, Edmund L. **History of Henderson County**. (1887) reprint 1993.
Cloth. $85.00. 840 pp. .... Vendor G0259

Hickman County

Willis, Laura. **Hickman County, Kentucky Deeds Volume Three (1833-1834)**. 1995.
Indexed.
Paper. $10.00. Contact vendor for information about earlier volumes.
100 pp. .... Vendor G0687

Jackson County

1860 Jackson County, Kentucky Census.
Paper. $12.50. .... Vendor G0549

Jefferson County

Franklin, Charles. **Jefferson Co. Wills 1780-1814**.
Paper. $12.00. 46 pp. .... Vendor G0574

Newby, Nancy. **Jefferson Co. Wills 1814-1822**.
Paper. $12.00. 49 pp. .... Vendor G0574

Newby, Nancy. **Jefferson Co. Wills 1823-1837**.
Paper. $12.00. 97 pp. .... Vendor G0574

Newby, Nancy. **Jefferson Co. Wills 1838-1846**.
Paper. $12.00. 80 pp. .... Vendor G0574

Schreiner-Yantis, Netti, and Florene Love. **1787 Census of Jefferson County**. 1987.
Indexed.
   Unfortunately, the 1787 and 1788 Personal Property Lists for Jefferson County are
missing. The information in this booklet is from the 1789 Personal Property Tax Lists.
The information is the same as that supplied in the 1787 lists with the exception that
the number of cattle owned is missing.
Paper. $6.50. 60 pp. .... Vendor G0081

Sistler, Barbara, and Byron Sistler. **1850 Kentucky Census Series:** Volume 14,
Jefferson County.
   Shows names and ages of all free persons arranged in order of the original sched-
ules; has regional head of household index.
Paper. $37.00. .... Vendor G0577

Johnson County

Hall, Mitchel. **Johnson County:** History of the County & Genealogy of Its People to the Year 1927. 2 vols. (1928) reprint 1993.
Volume I: History.
Volume II: Genealogy.
Cloth. $55.00/Vol. I. $71.00/Vol. II. $119.00/set. 552 + 708 pp. .... Vendor G0259

Kenton County

Hoffman, W. W. **Kenton County, Kentucky Index #1**. Indexed.
Contains Marriage Bond Books #1 and #2; Abstracts of Will Book #1, Deed Book #1, and Inventory Book #1; Guardian Book #1 and Tavern Bond Book #1; Marriage Book #1, Covington Courthouse.
Cloth. $38.50. 520 pp. .... Vendor G0767

Worrel, S. **Kenton County, Kentucky, Marriages, 1840-50**.
Forecast for publication in 1997.
Contact vendor for information. .... Vendor G0057

Knott County

1900 Knott County, Kentucky Census.
Paper. $45.00. .... Vendor G0549

1910 Knott County, Kentucky Census.
Paper. $35.00. .... Vendor G0549

Laurel County

Laurel County Historical Society. **A Pictorial History of World War II Veterans from Laurel County, Kentucky**. 1995.
Cloth. $37.50. 228 pp. .... Vendor G0688

Leslie County

Cates, Joyce Hardy. **Leslie County, Kentucky Marriage Index, 1878-1982**.
Paper. $50.00. .... Vendor G0666

Letcher County

1850 & 1880 Letcher County, Kentucky Census.
Paper. $18.50. .... Vendor G0549

1860 Letcher County, Kentucky Census.
Paper. $12.00. .... Vendor G0549

1900 Letcher County, KY Census.
Paper. $25.00. .... Vendor G0549

Lincoln County

Franklin, Charles. **Lincoln Co. Wills & Estates 1781-1807**.
Paper. $12.00. 47 pp. .... Vendor G0574

Franklin, Charles. **Lincoln Co. Wills & Estates 1808-1822**.
Paper. $12.00. 40 pp. .... Vendor G0574

Schreiner-Yantis, Netti, and Florene Love. **1787 Census of Lincoln County**. 1987.
Indexed.
Paper. $3.00. 24 pp. .... Vendor G0081

Livingston County

Douthat, James L. **Kentucky Lake Reservoir Cemeteries. Volume 1**.
   Covers the Kentucky portion of the lake and includes Calloway and Lyon, Livingston, Marshall, and Trigg counties. Also available as a set with Volumes 2 and 3 (see Tennessee, Statewide and Regional References).
Paper. $35.00. .... Vendor G0549

Logan County

Murray, Joyce Martin. **Logan County, Kentucky Deed Abstracts, 1792-1813**.
Indexed.
   Area originally covered all of Logan and parts of present Simpson, Todd, Butler, Warren, Muhlenberg, Christian, Allen, Hopkins, Barren, Caldwell, Henderson, Livingston, and Union counties. Includes full-name, location, and slave indexes.
Paper. $25.00. 176 pp. .... Vendor G0466

Murray, Joyce Martin. **Logan County, Kentucky Deed Abstracts, 1813-1819**.
Indexed.
   Includes full-name, location, and slave indexes.
Paper. $25.00. 198 pp. .... Vendor G0466

Lyon County

Douthat, James L. **Kentucky Lake Reservoir Cemeteries. Volume 1**.
   Covers the Kentucky portion of the lake and includes Calloway and Lyon, Livingston, Marshall, and Trigg counties. Also available as a set with Volumes 2 and 3 (see Tennessee, Statewide and Regional References).
Paper. $35.00. .... Vendor G0549

Madison County

Franklin, Charles. **Madison Co. Wills & Estates 1785-1813**.
Paper. $12.00. 54 pp. .... Vendor G0574

Schreiner-Yantis, Netti, and Florene Love. **1787 Census of Madison County**. 1987.
Indexed.
Paper. $2.75. 20 pp. .... Vendor G0081

T.L.C. Genealogy. **Madison County, Kentucky Taxpayers, 1787-1799**. 1992.
Indexed.
Paper. $10.00. 119 pp. .... Vendor G0609

Marshall County

Douthat, James L. **Kentucky Lake Reservoir Cemeteries. Volume 1**.
   Covers the Kentucky portion of the lake and includes Calloway and Lyon, Livingston, Marshall, and Trigg counties. Also available as a set with Volumes 2 and 3 (see Tennessee, Statewide and Regional References).
Paper. $35.00. .... Vendor G0549

Freeman, Leon Lewis, and Edward C. Olds. **History of Marshall County**. 1933.
Cloth. $39.00. 252 + 52 + 40 pp. .... Vendor G0259

Mason County

T.L.C. Genealogy. **Mason County, Kentucky, County Clerk Court Orders, 1789-1800: An Every-Name Index**. 1995. Indexed.
Paper. $15.00. 127 pp. .... Vendor G0609

T.L.C. Genealogy. **Mason County, Kentucky, Court Orders, 1803-1816: An Every-Name Index**. 1994. Indexed.
Paper. $20.00. 107 pp. .... Vendor G0609

T.L.C. Genealogy. **Mason County, Kentucky, Taxpayers, 1790-1799**. 1993. Indexed.
Paper. $10.00. 159 pp. .... Vendor G0609

McCracken County

Olson, Roy F., Jr. **McCracken County Cemeteries, Vol. III, Expanded Version**.
1994. Indexed. Illus.
Paper. $21.75. 267 pp. .... Vendor G0077

Olson, Roy F., Jr. **McCracken County Cemeteries, Vol. IV (Mount Kenton)**. 1994.
Indexed. Illus.
Paper. $27.75. 329 pp. .... Vendor G0077

Olson, Roy F., Jr. **McCracken County School Records, for 1915-1916**.
Write for information. .... Vendor G0077

Tate, Bettie Bass, and Roy F. Olson, Jr. **McCracken Co., KY Newsletters, Vol. 1, 1984-88**. 1991. Indexed.
Paper. $16.50. 223 pp. .... Vendor G0187

Mercer County

Franklin, Charles. **Mercer Co. Wills & Estates 1786-1808**.
Paper. $12.00. 50 pp. .... Vendor G0574

Franklin, Charles. **Mercer Co. Wills & Estates 1808-1821**.
Paper. $12.00. 53 pp. .... Vendor G0574

Schreiner-Yantis, Netti, and Florene Love. **1787 Census of Mercer County**. 1987. Indexed.
  Only a fragment of one of three Mercer County lists survives (this is transcribed). It is fortunate that there are a number of contemporary records available to help determine the names of those who were on the tax lists that have been lost.
Paper. $6.00. 48 pp. .... Vendor G0081

Montgomery County

T.L.C. Genealogy. **Montgomery County, Kentucky Taxpayers, 1797 & 1799**. 1995. Indexed.
Paper. $5.00. 25 pp. .... Vendor G0609

Morgan County

Nickell, Joe, J. Wendell Nickell, and Ella T. Nickell. **Morgan County, Kentucky, Cemetery Records**. 1981. Indexed.
Paper. $25.00. 133 pp. .... Vendor G0113

Nickell, Joe, and Ella T. Nickell. **Morgan County, Kentucky, First Court Order Book 1823-30**. 1984. Indexed. Illus.
Paper. $20.00. 129 pp. .... Vendor G0113

Nickell, Joe, and Ella T. Nickell. **Morgan County, Kentucky, Genealogical Sourcebook with the 1830-40 Censuses**. 1980. Indexed.
Paper. $15.00. 75 pp. .... Vendor G0113

Muhlenberg County

Rothert, Otto A. **A History of Muhlenberg County [Kentucky]**. (1913) reprint 1996. Indexed.
Paper. $39.95. 496 pp. .... Vendor G0011

Nelson County

Franklin, Charles. **Nelson Co. Marriages 1785-1810**.
Paper. $12.00. 52 pp. .... Vendor G0574

Franklin, Charles. **Nelson Co. Marriages 1811-1830**.
Paper. $12.00. 73 pp. .... Vendor G0574

Franklin, Charles. **Nelson Co. Marriages 1831-1850**.
Paper. $12.00. 69 pp. .... Vendor G0574

Franklin, Charles. **Nelson Co. Wills & Estates 1785-1807**.
Paper. $12.00. 47 pp. .... Vendor G0574

Schreiner-Yantis, Netti, and Florene Love. **1787 Census of Nelson County**. 1987.
Indexed.
  Nelson County was in the farthest outreaches. Because of this, the tax commissioners chose to gather the tax information by using their militia districts. The information gathered is not as complete as for some of the other counties. There are, however, six tax lists available, and they appear to include most of the taxpayers. Besides these lists, eleven tithable lists (many of which overlap the tax lists) are included in this book.
Paper. $6.50. 56 pp. .... Vendor G0081

T.L.C. Genealogy. **Nelson County, Kentucky Taxpayers, 1793-1799**. 1995. Indexed.
Paper. $10.00. 100 pp. .... Vendor G0609

Nicholas County

Perrin, William H., and Robert Peter. **History of Bourbon, Scott, Harrison, and Nicholas Counties, With a Brief Synopsis of the Blue Grass Region**. (1882) reprint 1979. Indexed.
Contact vendor for information. 815 pp. .... Vendor G0610

Ohio County

Taylor, Harrison D. **Ohio County, Kentucky, in the Olden Days**. (1926) reprint 1989. Indexed. Illus.
Cloth. $14.00. 204 pp. .... Vendor G0011

Scott County

Franklin, Charles. **Scott Co. Marriages 1793-1850**.
Paper. $10.00. 29 pp. .... Vendor G0574

Franklin, Charles. **Scott Co. Wills & Estates 1795-1822**.
Paper. $12.00. 60 pp. .... Vendor G0574

Perrin, William H., and Robert Peter. **History of Bourbon, Scott, Harrison, and Nicholas Counties, With a Brief Synopsis of the Blue Grass Region**. (1882) reprint 1979. Indexed.
Contact vendor for information. 815 pp. .... Vendor G0610

T.L.C. Genealogy. **Scott County, Kentucky Taxpayers, 1794 thru 1799**. 1990. Indexed.
Paper. $7.50. 44 pp. .... Vendor G0609

Shelby County

Franklin, Charles. **Shelby Co. Wills & Estates 1792-1817**.
Paper. $12.00. 47 pp. .... Vendor G0574

Newby, Nancy. **Shelby Co. Wills & Estates 1817-1824**.
Paper. $12.00. 58 pp. .... Vendor G0574

Willis, Geo. L., Sr. **History of Shelby County, Kentucky**. (1929) reprint 1996. Illus.
Paper. $25.00. 268 pp. .... Vendor G0011

Simpson County

Jackson, Martha W. **Simpson Co., KY Census for 1820**. Indexed.
Paper. $10.50. 38 pp. .... Vendor G0594

Spencer County

Burgin, Edna Montgomery, comp. **Spencer County, Kentucky Cemeteries Then and Now Volume 2**. Indexed.
Paper. $18.00. Contact vendor for information about earlier volume.
90 pp. .... Vendor G0746

Darnell, Betty R. **1830 & 1840 Census, Spencer Co. KY**. 1990. Indexed.
Paper. $13.00. 64 pp. .... Vendor G0261

Darnell, Betty R. **1850 Census, Spencer Co. KY**. 1990. Indexed.
Paper. $11.50. 64 pp. .... Vendor G0261

Todd County

Battle, J. H., ed. **History of Todd County, Kentucky**. (1884) reprint 1979. Indexed.
Cloth. $35.00. 398 pp. .... Vendor G0610

Trigg County

Douthat, James L. **Kentucky Lake Reservoir Cemeteries. Volume 1**.
    Covers the Kentucky portion of the lake and includes Calloway and Lyon, Livingston,

Marshall, and Trigg counties. Also available as a set with Volumes 2 and 3 (see Tennessee, Statewide and Regional References).
Paper. $35.00. .... Vendor G0549

Perrin, W. H. **History of Trigg County, Kentucky: Historical and Biographical**. (1884) reprint 1979. Indexed.
Cloth. $32.50. 293 pp. .... Vendor G0610

Taylor, Pete. **Trigg County 1880 Families**. 1996. Indexed.
Paper. $15.00. 189 pp. .... Vendor G0687

Taylor, Pete. **Trigg County, Kentucky Newspaper Abstracts, Volume Twenty-eight**. 1996. Indexed.
Paper. $7.00. 72 pp. .... Vendor G0687

Willis, Laura, scr. **Trigg County, Kentucky Deeds, Volume One (1820-1824)**. 1996. Indexed.
Paper. $10.00. 96 pp. .... Vendor G0687

Warren County

Murray, Joyce Martin. **Deed Abstracts of Warren County, Kentucky, 1797-1812**. Indexed.
   Parts present Logan, Simpson, Barren, and Allen counties. Includes full-name, location, and slave indexes.
Cloth. $30.00. Microfiche, $7.00. 147 pp. .... Vendor G0466

Murray, Joyce Martin. **Deed Abstracts of Warren County, Kentucky, 1812-1821**. Indexed.
   Includes full-name, location, and slave indexes.
Paper. $30.00. Microfiche, $7.00. 203 pp. .... Vendor G0466

T.L.C. Genealogy. **Warren County, Kentucky, Deed Books, 1821-1825**. 1997. Indexed.
Paper. $20.00. .... Vendor G0609

Washington County

Sanders, Faye Sea, comp. **Washington County, Kentucky Court Order Book 1792-1800**. 1996. Indexed.
Paper. $22.00. 1,113 pp. .... Vendor G0689

T.L.C. Genealogy. **Washington County, Kentucky Taxpayers, 1792-1799**. 1992. Indexed.
Paper. $10.00. 78 pp. .... Vendor G0609

Wolfe County

Wolfe County Women's Club, comp. **Early and Modern History of Wolfe County**. (1958) reprint 1994.
Cloth. $39.50. 340 pp. .... Vendor G0259

Woodford County

Franklin, Charles. **Woodford Co. Wills & Estates 1789-1815**.
Paper. $12.00. 49 pp. .... Vendor G0574

Franklin, Charles. **Woodford Co. Wills & Estates 1815-1826**.
Paper. $12.00. 41 pp. .... Vendor G0574

Railey, William E. **History of Woodford County, Kentucky**. (1938) reprint 1990.
Indexed. Illus.
Cloth. $27.50. 449 pp. .... Vendor G0011

T.L.C. Genealogy. **Woodford County, Kentucky Taxpayers, 1790 thru 1799**. 1990.
Indexed.
Paper. $7.50. 85 pp. .... Vendor G0609

⊰⊱ Louisiana ⊰⊱

Statewide and Regional References

Ardoin, Robert Bruce L. **Louisiana Census Records. Volume I: Avoyelles and St. Landry Parishes, 1810 and 1820**. (1970) reprint 1995. Indexed.
Paper. $14.00. 114 pp. .... Vendor G0011

Ardoin, Robert Bruce L. **Louisiana Census Records. Volume II: Iberville, Natchitoches, Pointe Coupee, and Rapides Parishes, 1810 and 1820**. (1972) reprint 1995. Indexed. Illus.
Paper. $21.50. 216 pp. .... Vendor G0011

Arthur, Stanley Clisby. **Old Families of Louisiana, 1608-1929, Volume 1**. 1931. Reprint on microfiche. Indexed.
Order no. 950, $22.00. 432 pp. .... Vendor G0478

Bolton, Herbert E. **The Spanish Borderlands: A Chronicle of Old Florida and the Southwest**. (1921) reprint 1996.
  In narrative prose, Bolton recounts the Spanish exploration and the permanent settlement of Old Florida, New Mexico, Texas, Louisiana, and California.
Paper. $22.50. 320 pp. .... Vendor G0611

Booth, Andrew B., comp. **Records of Louisiana Confederate Soldiers and Louisiana Confederate Commands**. 4 vols. in 3. (1920) reprint 1996.
Cloth. $250.00/set + $5.00 p&h. 3,707 pp. .... Vendor G0551

Burns, Loretta E., comp. **Louisiana 1911 Census Confederate Veterans or Widows**. 1995.
Paper. $25.00. 97 pp. .... Vendor G0747

Conrad. **The Louisiana Purchase Bicentennial Series in Louisiana History, Volume I: The French Experience in Louisiana**. 1995.
  History of the French in Louisiana.
Cloth. $40.00. 666 pp. .... Vendor G0611

De Ville, Winston. **Gulf Coast Colonials**. A Compendium of French Families in Early Eighteenth Century Louisiana. Partially indexed. (1968) reprint 1995.
Paper. $8.50. 69 pp. .... Vendor G0011

De Ville, Winston. **Louisiana Colonials:** Soldiers and Vagabonds. (1963) reprint 1995. Indexed.
Paper. $9.00. 81 pp. .... Vendor G0011

De Ville, Winston. **Louisiana Troops 1720-1770**. (1965) reprint 1994. Illus.
Paper. $16.50. 136 pp. .... Vendor G0011

De Ville, Winston. **The New Orleans French, 1720-1733**. A Collection of Marriage Records Relating to the First Colonists of the Louisiana Province. (1973) reprint 1994. Indexed.
Paper. $13.50. 113 pp. .... Vendor G0011

Deiler, J. Hanno. **A History of the German Churches in Louisiana (1823-1893)**. Translated and edited by Marie Stella Condon. (1894, 1983) reprint 1995. Indexed.
Paper. $17.50. 155 pp. .... Vendor G0011

Dilts, Bryan Lee, comp. **1890 Louisiana Veterans Census Index**. 2nd ed. 1993. Illus.
Cloth. $32.00. 63 pp. .... Vendor G0552

Family History Library. **Research Outline: Louisiana**.
Leaflet. $.25. 9 pp. .... Vendor G0629

Goins and Caldwell. **Historical Atlas of Louisiana**. 1995.
    Historical atlases are important reference tools for the genealogist. This one contains ninety-nine pages of maps in color, each accompanied by descriptive essays.
Paper. $29.95. 240 pp. .... Vendor G0611

Hebert. **Acadian-Cajun Genealogy: Step by Step**. 1993.
    An essential guide to this special research. Maps, bibliography.
Paper. $10.00. 146 pp. .... Vendor G0611

Ingmire, Frances. **1840 Louisiana State Wide Index to the Census**.
Cloth, $45.00. Paper, $35.00. 270 pp. .... Vendor G0549

Inventory of the Louisiana Historical Association Collection on Deposit in the Howard-Tilton Memorial Library, Tulane University.
    Detailed guide to the Association's vast Civil War Collection.
Paper. $14.00. 201 pp. .... Vendor G0611

Louisiana Historical Association. **Louisiana History: The Journal of the Louisiana Historical Association**. Vols. 1-25, 1960-84. Vols. 26-30, 1985-89.
    Very useful indexes to the journal, 1960-1989.
Vols. 1-25, cloth, $21.00. Vols. 26-30, paper, $14.00. 331 + 120 pp. ... Vendor G0611

Lowrie, Walter, ed. **Land Claims in the Eastern District of the Orleans Territory,** Communicated to the House of Representatives, January 9, 1812. (1834) reprint 1986. Indexed.
Cloth. $27.50. 160 pp. .... Vendor G0610

Maduell, Charles R., Jr. **The Census Tables for the French Colony of Louisiana from 1699 Through 1732**. (1972) reprint 1995. Indexed. Illus.
Paper. $18.50. 181 pp. .... Vendor G0011

Books from Louisiana State University Press

Africans in Colonial Louisiana: The Development of Afro-Creole Culture in the Eighteenth Century, by Gwendolyn Midlo Hall.1992. 470 pp. $22.45 (paper)
Antebellum Natchez, by D. Clayton James. (1968) reprint 1993. 344 pp. $16.45 (paper)
The Canary Islanders of Louisiana, by Gilbert C. Din. 1988. 256 pp. $41.00 (cloth)
Confederate Cherokees: John Drew's Regiment of Mounted Rifles, by W. Craig Gaines. 1989. 200 pp. $26.45 (cloth)
Creole New Orleans: Race and Americanization, edited by Arnold R. Hirsch. 1992. 456 pp. $46.00 (cloth), $20.45 (paper)
Doctors in Gray: The Confederate Medical Service, by H. H. Cunningham. (1960) reprint 1993. 339 pp. $18.45 (paper)
Forgotten People: Cane River's Creole of Color, by Gary B. Mills. 1977. 278 pp. $18.45 (paper)
Founding of New Acadia: The Beginning of Acadian Life in Louisiana, 1765-1803, by Carl A. Brasseaux. 1987. 288 pp. $16.45 (paper)
French and Spanish Records of LA: A Bibliographical Guide to Archive and Manuscript Sources, by H. P. Beers. 1989. 368 pp. $53.50 (cloth)
Generals in Blue: Lives of the Union Commanders, by Ezra J. Warner. 1964. 680 pp. $38.45 (cloth)
Generals in Gray: Lives of the Confederate Commanders, by Ezra J. Warner. 1959. 420 pp. $33.45 (cloth)
Other Generals in Gray, by Bruck Allardice. 328 pp. $33.45 (cloth)
Guide to Louisiana Confederate Military Units, 1861-1865, by Arthur W. Bergeron, Jr. 1989. 256 pp. $16.45 (paper)
Historic Indian Tribes of Louisiana: From 1542 to the Present, by Fred B. Kniffen. (1987) reprint 1994. 344 pp. $18.45 (paper)
Life of Billy Yank: The Common Soldier of the Union, by Bell Irvin Wiley. (1952) reprint 1971. 454 pp. $33.45 (cloth), $15.45 (paper)
Life of Johnny Reb: The Common Soldier of the Confederacy, by Bell Irvin Wiley. (1943) reprint 1971. 444 pp. $33.45 (cloth), $18.45 (paper)
Mississippi Provincial Archives: French Dominion, 1729-1748, Volume IV, edited by Patricia Kay Galloway. 1984. 424 pp. $58.50 (cloth)
Mississippi Provincial Archives: French Dominion, 1749-1763, Volume V, edited by Patricia Kay Galloway. 1984. 424 pp. $58.50 (cloth)
Slave Testimony: Two Centuries of Letters, Speeches, Interviews, and Autobiographies, edited by John W. Blassingame. 1977. 777 pp. $23.45 (paper)
Tumult and Silence at Second Creek: An Inquiry into a Civil War Slave Conspiracy, by Winthrop D. Jordan. 1992. 408 pp. $20.45 (paper)

Many other books available. Send for a complete listing.

LSU Press
PO Box 25053, Baton Rouge, LA 70894-5053
800-861-3477
Payment must accompany orders from individuals. P&h: $3.50 for the first book, $.50 each additional book. LA residents add 4% sales tax; East Baton Rouge Parish residents add an additional 4% tax. MC and VISA accepted.

Malone. **Sweet Chariot: Slave Family and Household Structure in Nineteenth Century Louisiana**. 1992.
   Called "the best book ever written on slave family life in the American South," this fascinating book includes extensive footnotes and bibliography.
Cloth. $39.95. 369 pp. .... Vendor G0611

Sifakis. **Compendium of the Confederate Armies: Louisiana**. 1995.
   Describes each regiment, its officers, and its battles.
Cloth. $24.95. 144 pp. .... Vendor G0611

Thorndale, William, and William Dollarhide. **County Boundary Map Guides to the U.S. Federal Censuses, 1790-1920: Louisiana, 1810-1920**. 1987.
$5.95. .... Vendor G0552

Usner. **Indians, Settlers & Slaves in a Frontier Exchange Economy: The Lower Mississippi Valley Before 1783**. 1992.
   Economic and cultural interactions between Indians, Europeans, and African slaves of colonial Louisiana. Well documented.
Paper. $13.95. 294 pp. .... Vendor G0611

Wood, Gregory A. **A Guide to the Acadians in Maryland in the 18th and 19th Centuries**. 1995. Indexed. Illus.
   A comprehensive study of exile, migration to Louisiana in 1766-1769, and the growth of a merchant/shipping, "urban" Acadian community in Baltimore through 1830.
Cloth. $30.00. 408 pp. .... Vendor G0500

Ascension Parish

Marchand, Sidney A. **The Flight of a Century (1800-1900) in Ascension Parish**. (1936) reprint 1995.
Cloth. $32.50. 237 pp. .... Vendor G0259

Marchand, Sidney A. **The Story of Ascension Parish**. (1931) reprint 1995.
Cloth. $29.50. 193 pp. .... Vendor G0259

Attakapas County

Conrad. **Land Records of the Attakapas District, Vol. II, Part I: Conveyance Records of Attakapas County, 1804-1818**. 1992.
   Records of conveyances of land and slaves. A wealth of genealogical and historical information is included here.
Cloth. $24.95. 480 pp. .... Vendor G0611

Conrad. **Land Records of the Attakapas District, Vol. II, Part 2: Attakapas-St. Martin Estates, 1804-1818**. 1993.
   The estate records include wills, inventories, succession sales, legal emancipations, etc. Packed with information.
Cloth. $20.00. 304 pp. .... Vendor G0611

Avoyelles Parish

Ardoin, Robert Bruce L. **Louisiana Census Records. Volume I: Avoyelles and St. Landry Parishes, 1810 and 1820.** (1970) reprint 1995. Indexed.
Paper. $14.00. 114 pp. .... Vendor G0011

DeSoto Parish

DeSoto Parish, Louisiana—Loose Marriages 1837-1860 & Marriage Book A 1843-1860.
Paper. $6.00. 29 pp. .... Vendor G0549

Iberville Parish

Ardoin, Robert Bruce L. **Louisiana Census Records. Volume II: Iberville, Natchitoches, Pointe Coupee, and Rapides Parishes, 1810 and 1820.** (1972) reprint 1995. Indexed. Illus.
Paper. $21.50. 216 pp. .... Vendor G0011

Natchitoches Parish

Ardoin, Robert Bruce L. **Louisiana Census Records. Volume II: Iberville, Natchitoches, Pointe Coupee, and Rapides Parishes, 1810 and 1820.** (1972) reprint 1995. Indexed. Illus.
Paper. $21.50. 216 pp. .... Vendor G0011

Pointe Coupee Parish

Ardoin, Robert Bruce L. **Louisiana Census Records. Volume II: Iberville, Natchitoches, Pointe Coupee, and Rapides Parishes, 1810 and 1820.** (1972) reprint 1995. Indexed. Illus.
Paper. $21.50. 216 pp. .... Vendor G0011

Rapides Parish

Ardoin, Robert Bruce L. **Louisiana Census Records. Volume II: Iberville, Natchitoches, Pointe Coupee, and Rapides Parishes, 1810 and 1820.** (1972) reprint 1995. Indexed. Illus.
Paper. $21.50. 216 pp. .... Vendor G0011

St. Landry Parish

Ardoin, Robert Bruce L. **Louisiana Census Records. Volume I: Avoyelles and St. Landry Parishes, 1810 and 1820**. (1970) reprint 1995. Indexed.
Paper. $14.00. 114 pp. .... Vendor G0011

Maine

Statewide and Regional References

Annual Report of the Land Agent of the State of Maine, for the Year Ending Nov. 30, 1885. (1886) reprint 1994.
   Contains lands conveyed to settlers, esp. in Northern Maine; with detailed schedules for Madawaska, Ft. Kent, Frenchville, and other no. twps.
Paper. $13.00. 65 pp. .... Vendor G0259

Atlas of Maine, Detailed Back Roads.
   This present-day atlas provides the researcher with the detail needed to conduct a proper search. It is the size of a Rand McNally atlas of the entire U.S. 11" x 15½".
$16.95. .... Vendor G0611

Dilts, Bryan Lee, comp. **1890 Maine Veterans Census Index**. 2nd ed. 1993.
Cloth. $49.00. 128 pp. .... Vendor G0552

Family History Library. **Research Outline: Maine**.
Leaflet. $.25. 10 pp. .... Vendor G0629

Fisher, Maj. Gen. Carleton E., and Sue G. Fisher. **Soldiers, Sailors, & Patriots of the Revolutionary War—Maine**. 1982.
   Book # 1324.
Cloth. $45.00. 933 pp. .... Vendor G0082

Frost, John Eldridge. **Maine Probate Abstracts**. 2 vols. 1991. Indexed. Illus.
   Book # 1160.
Cloth. $145.00. 1,501 pp. .... Vendor G0082

Frost, John Eldridge. **Maine Probate Abstracts: 1687-1800**. 2 vols. 1991. Indexed.
Cloth. $149.75. 1,485 pp. .... Vendor G0406

Historical Sketch and Roster of Commissioned Officers and Enlisted Men [in the Aroostook War]. (1904) reprint 1989. Indexed.
Cloth. $12.00. 95 pp. .... Vendor G0011

House, Charles J. **Names of Soldiers of the American Revolution [from Maine]** Who Applied for State Bounty Under Resolves of March 17, 1835, March 24, 1836, and March 20, 1838, as Appears of Record in Land Office. (1893) reprint 1996.
Paper. $9.00. 50 pp. .... Vendor G0011

Jordan, William B., Jr. **Red Diamond Regiment: The 17th Maine Infantry, 1862-1865**. 1995.
This book traces the movements of this regiment, but goes beyond simple military history to show the soldiers' everyday life, their relationships to their home front state, and how their bravery and suffering related to the larger Civil War.
Cloth. $30.00. 438 pp. .... Vendor G0611

Long, John H., ed. **Connecticut, Maine, Massachusetts, and Rhode Island Atlas of Historical County Boundaries**. 1994.
A beautiful and extremely useful book detailing the changes in county boundaries from colonial times to 1990. 8½" x 11".
Cloth. $92.00. 412 pp. .... Vendor G0611

Maine Families in 1790, Volume I. By Ruth Gray. 1988. Indexed.
Book #1105.
Cloth. $35.00. 384 pp. .... Vendor G0082

Maine Families in 1790, Volume 2. By Ruth Gray. 1990. Indexed.
Book # 1172.
Cloth. $35.00. 416 pp. .... Vendor G0082

Maine Families in 1790, Volume 3. Edited by Ruth Gray and Joseph C. Anderson II. 1992. Indexed.
Book #1399.
Cloth. $35.00. 416 pp. .... Vendor G0082

Maine Families in 1790, Volume 4. By Joseph C. Anderson II and Lois Thurston. 1994. Indexed.
Book #1439
Cloth. $35.00. 416 pp. .... Vendor G0082

Maine Families in 1790, Volume 5. By Joseph C. Anderson II. 1996. Indexed.
  Book #1726.
Cloth. $35.00. .... Vendor G0082

Maine Genealogical Society. **1790 Census of Maine**. 1995. Indexed.
  Book #1440.
Paper. $17.50. 128 pp. .... Vendor G0082

Maine State Archives. **Agencies of State Government, 1820-1971, Parts I and II**.
Contact vendor for information. .... Vendor G0650

Maine State Archives. **Black House Papers—A Guide to Certain Microfilmed Land Records**.
Contact vendor for information. .... Vendor G0650

Maine State Archives. **Counties, Cities, Towns and Plantations of Maine**.
Contact vendor for information. .... Vendor G0650

Maine State Archives. **Dubros Times: Depositions of Revolutionary War Veterans**.
Contact vendor for information. .... Vendor G0650

Maine State Archives. **Maine Town Microfilm List: Town and Vital Records, and Census Reports**.
Contact vendor for information. .... Vendor G0650

Maine State Archives. **Public Record Repositories in Maine**.
Contact vendor for information. .... Vendor G0650

Massachusetts and Maine Families in the Ancestry of Walter Goodwin Davis. 3 vols. (1916-63) reprint 1996. Indexed. Illus.
  Vol. I: Allanson-French. 746 pp.
  Vol. II: Gardner-Moses. 717 pp.
  Vol. III: Neal-Wright. 732 pp.
Cloth. $50.00/vol., $135.00/set. 2,096 pp. in all. .... Vendor G0010

Noyes, Sybil, Charles T. Libby, and Walter G. Davis. **Genealogical Dictionary of Maine and New Hampshire**. 5 parts in 1. (1928-1939) reprint 1996.
Cloth. $40.00. 795 pp. .... Vendor G0010

Pope, Charles Henry. **The Pioneers of Maine and New Hampshire, 1623-1660**. (1908) reprint 1997.
Paper. $26.50. 263 pp. .... Vendor G0011

Porter, Joseph W., ed. **The Maine Historical Magazine (Formerly The Bangor Historical Magazine, 4 Volumes)**. (1885-1895) reprint 1993. Indexed. Illus.
  Book #1430.
Cloth. $195.00. 2,688 pp. .... Vendor G0082

Rimg, Elizabeth. **[Bibliographical] Reference List of Manuscripts Relating to the History of Maine**. (1938) reprint 1992.
Cloth. $89.50. 970 pp. .... Vendor G0259

Rohrbach, Lewis Bunker, ed. **Maine Marriages 1892-1966**. 1996.
  Item #1578.
CD-ROM. $99.00. .... Vendor G0082

Sargent, William M. **Maine Wills, 1640-1760**. (1887) reprint 1996. Indexed.
Paper. $60.00. 953 pp. .... Vendor G0011

Southern California Genealogical Society. **Sources of Genealogical Help in Maine**.
Paper. $1.00. 6 pp. .... Vendor G0656

Spencer, Wilbur D. **Pioneers on Maine Rivers**. With Lists to 1651. (1930) reprint
1995. Indexed. Illus.
Paper. $34.00. 414 pp. .... Vendor G0011

Taylor. **Liberty Men and Great Proprietors: The Revolutionary Settlement on the
Maine Frontier, 1760-1820**. 1990.
    A detailed exploration of the settlement of Maine, and how the settlers labored on
and defended their property.
Paper. $15.95. 381 pp. .... Vendor G0611

Thorndale, William, and William Dollarhide. **County Boundary Map Guides to the
U.S. Federal Censuses, 1790-1920: Maine, 1790-1920**. 1987.
$5.95. .... Vendor G0552

United States Bureau of the Census. **Heads of Families at the First Census of the
United States Taken in the Year 1790: Maine**.
Cloth, $31.50. Paper, $16.50. .... Vendor G0552

United States Bureau of the Census. **Heads of Families at the First Census of the
United States Taken in the Year 1790: Maine**. (1908) reprint 1992. Indexed. Illus.
Paper. $18.50. 105 pp. .... Vendor G0010

Williamson, Joseph. **Bibliography of the State of Maine**. 2 vols. (1896) reprint
1985.
    Book #1225.
Cloth. $65.00. 1,437 pp. .... Vendor G0082

Androscoggin County

Groves, Marlene Alma Hinkley, ed. **Lisbon, Maine Vital Records Prior to 1892**.
1995. Indexed.
    Book #1562.
Cloth. $39.95. 509 pp. .... Vendor G0082

Merrill, G. D. **History of Androscoggin County**. (1891) reprint 1988.
Cloth. $92.50. 893 pp. .... Vendor G0259

Mower, Walter L. **Sesquicentennial History of the Town of Greene, Androscoggin
Co., 1775 to 1900** with Some Matter Extending to a Later Date. (1938) reprint 1994.
Cloth. $59.50. 578 pp. .... Vendor G0259

Stackpole, E. S. **History of Durham,** with Genealogical Notes. (1899) reprint 1987.
Cloth. $39.50. 314 pp. .... Vendor G0259

Stinchfield, J. C., et al. **History of the Town of Leeds, Androscoggin Co.,** from Its
Settlement June 10, 1780. With many genealogies. (1901) reprint 1990.
Cloth. $45.00. Genealogies only: 227 pp., paper. $25.00. 419 pp. ...... Vendor G0259

Aroostook County

Ellis, C. H. **History of Fort Fairfield,** & Biographical Sketches with Illustrations. (1894) reprint 1992.
Cloth. $42.50. 382 pp. .... Vendor G0259

Wiggin, Edward. **History of Aroostook,** Comprising Facts, Names & Dates Relating to the Early Settlement of All . . . Towns & Plantations of the County. Vol. I. (1922) reprint 1994.
Cloth. $47.00. 306 + 122 pp. .... Vendor G0259

Augusta

North, James M. **The History of Augusta, Maine**. (1870) reprint 1981. Illus.
　　Book #1195. Separate index available.
Cloth. $60.00. 1,120 pp. .... Vendor G0082

Bethel

Lapham, William B. **History of Bethel Maine 1768-1890**. (1891) reprint 1986. Indexed. Illus.
　　Book #1199.
Cloth. $50.00. 827 pp. .... Vendor G0082

Cork

O'Brien, M. J. **The Lost Town of Cork**. (n.d.) reprint 1987.
Paper. $4.50. 12 pp. .... Vendor G0259

Cumberland County

Dole, Samuel Thomas. **Windham in the Past**. Edited by Frederick Howard Dole. (1916) reprint 1994.
Cloth. $63.00. 611 pp. .... Vendor G0259

Elwell, Edward H. **Portland & Vicinity**. (1876) reprint 1989. Illus.
　　History of the Portland area, including many illustrations of the city and the surrounding country and coast.
Cloth. $35.00. 142 pp. .... Vendor G0259

Gorhamtown: A Pictorial History. 1985. Illus.
　　Book #1420.
Paper. $5.00. 64 pp. .... Vendor G0082

Henry, Carl D. **Vital Records of North Yarmouth, Maine, Second Edition**. 1993. Indexed. Illus.
　　Book #1405.
Cloth. $39.50. 480 pp. .... Vendor G0082

History of Cumberland County, with Illustrations & Biographical Sketches of Prominent Men & Pioneers. (1880) reprint 1987.
Cloth. $49.00. 456 pp. .... Vendor G0259

Kellogg, Rev. Elijah. **Good Old Times**. (1878) reprint 1986. Illus.
　Book #1263.
Cloth. $20.00. 306 pp. .... Vendor G0082

King, Marquis F., comp. **Publishments, Marriages, Births, Deaths of Gorham, Maine**. 2nd ed. Edited by Russell S. Bickford. (1897) reprint 1991. Indexed. Illus.
　Book #1183.
Cloth. $29.50. 192 pp. .... Vendor G0082

McLellan, Hugh D. **The History of Gorham, Maine**. (1903) reprint 1992. Indexed. Illus.
　Book #1418.
Cloth. $59.50. 1,088 pp. .... Vendor G0082

Moulton, A., H. L. Sampson, and G. Fernald. **Centennial History of Harrison,** Containing the Celebration of 1905 and Historical and Biographical Matter. (1909) reprint 1995.
Cloth. $75.00. 727 pp. .... Vendor G0259

Rowe, Ernest R., et al. **Highlights of Westbrook History**. Edited by Marian B. Rowe. (1952) reprint 1995.
Cloth. $34.50. 242 pp. .... Vendor G0259

Rowe, William Hutchinson. **Ancient North Yarmouth & Yarmouth, 1636-1936,** A History. (1937) reprint 1995.
Cloth. $45.00. 427 pp. .... Vendor G0259

Spurr, W. S. **History of Otisfield, Cumberland Co.,** from the Original Grant to the Close of 1944. (1944) reprint 1990.
Cloth. $69.00. 661 pp. .... Vendor G0259

Franklin County

Biographical Review: Biographical Sketches of Leading Citizens of Oxford & Franklin Counties. (1897) reprint 1996.
Cloth. $65.00. 639 pp. .... Vendor G0259

Butler, Francis Gould. **A History of Farmington, Franklin County, Maine 1776-1885**. (1885) reprint 1983. Indexed. Illus.
　Book #1208.
Cloth. $55.00. 276 pp. .... Vendor G0082

Hatch, William Collins. **History of the Town of Industry Maine, 1787-1893**. (1893) reprint 1984. Indexed. Illus.
　Book #1211.
Cloth. $55.00. 932 pp. .... Vendor G0082

Gott's Island

Kenway, Rita Johnson. **Gott's Island, Maine: Its People 1880-1992**. 1993. Indexed. Illus.
  Book #1422.
  Cloth. $37.50. 352 pp. .... Vendor G0082

Hancock County

Hosmer, G. L. **An Historical Sketch of the Town of Deer Isle,** with Notices of Its Settlers & Early Inhabitants. (1886) reprint 1988.
  Contact vendor for information. 292 pp. .... Vendor G0259

Johnson, Murial Sampson. **Early Families of Gouldsboro Maine**. 1990. Indexed. Illus.
  Book #1154.
  Cloth. $32.50. 416 pp. .... Vendor G0082

Limeburner, Grace C., comp. **Stories of Brooksville**. (1924) reprint 1994.
  Paper. $16.00. 81 pp. .... Vendor G0259

Long, Alice MacDonald. **Marriage Records of Hancock County, Maine Prior to 1892**. 1992. Indexed.
  Book #1130.
  Cloth. $45.00. 576 pp. .... Vendor G0082

Long, Alice MacDonald. **Vital Records of Mount Desert Island and Nearby Islands 1776-1820**. 1990. Indexed. Illus.
  Book #1168.
  Cloth. $20.00. 96 pp. .... Vendor G0082

Thornton, Mrs. S. S. **Traditions & Records of Southwest Harbor & Somesville, Mt. Desert Island**. (1938) reprint 1994.
  Cloth. $39.50. 346 pp. .... Vendor G0259

Traditions & Records of Brooksville. Collected by the Brooksville Historical Society. (1936) reprint 1987.
  Cloth. $18.50. 132 pp. .... Vendor G0259

Wheeler, George Augustus. **History of Castine, Penobscot & Brooksville,** Including the Ancient Settlement of Pentagoet. (1875) reprint 1994.
  Cloth. $42.50. 401 pp. .... Vendor G0259

Isleboro County

Farrow, J. P. **History of Isleborough, 1764-1892**. (1893) reprint 1988.
  Cloth. $38.00. 325 pp. .... Vendor G0259

Kennebec County

Bicentennial Committee Members of Society. **History of Sidney, Maine**. 1992. Indexed. Illus.
   Book #1323.
Cloth. $25.00. 288 pp. .... Vendor G0082

Clark, W. H. **History of Winthrop, 1630-1952**. (1952) reprint 1990.
Cloth. $36.00. 313 pp. .... Vendor G0259

Fisher, C. E., ed. **Clinton Vital Records,** Births, Marriages & Deaths. (1967) reprint 1993.
Cloth. $38.00. 357 pp. .... Vendor G0259

Fisher, Maj. Gen. Carleton Edward. **History of Clinton, Maine**. 1971. Indexed. Illus.
   Book #1325.
Cloth. $35.00. 419 pp. .... Vendor G0082

Green, Clement M., comp. **Chronology of Municipal History and Election Statistics, Waterville, 1771-1908**. (1908) reprint 1995.
Cloth. $37.00. 282 pp. .... Vendor G0259

Hanson, J. W. **History of Gardiner, Pittston & W. Gardiner,** with a Sketch of the Kennebec Indians & New Plymouth Purchase, 1602-1852. (1852) reprint 1995.
Cloth. $42.00. 359 pp. .... Vendor G0259

History of Litchfield, and an Account of Its Centennial Celebration in 1895. (1895) reprint 1988.
Cloth. $58.00. 548 pp. .... Vendor G0259

Kingsbury, H. D., and S. L. Deyo. **Illustrated History of Kennebec County, 1625-1892**. 2 vols. (1892) reprint 1987.
Cloth. $63.00/vol., $122.50/set. 600 + 637 pp. .... Vendor G0259

Lang, S. D., ed. **Winslow Vital Records, to the Year 1892:** Births, Marriages & Deaths. (1937) reprint 1992.
Cloth. $37.50. 325 pp. .... Vendor G0259

Leadbetter, C. F., C. E. Wing, et al. **History of the Town of Wayne, Kennebec Co.,** from Its Settlement to 1898. With Genealogies. (1898) reprint 1993.
Cloth. $42.00. 354 pp. .... Vendor G0259

Ulrich. **A Midwife's Tale**. 1990.
   Based on Martha Ballard's diary of her midwifery and her life from 1785-1812 in Hallowell, Maine. Many locals mentioned, but this book is especially interesting for the portrait of the medical practices, religious squabbles, and sexual mores of the time.
Paper. $13.00. 444 pp. .... Vendor G0611

Webster, H. S., ed. **Farmingdale Vital Records to the Year 1892**. (1909) reprint 1993.
Cloth. $18.00. 96pp. .... Vendor G0259

Webster, H. S., ed. **Randolph Vital Records to the Year 1892**. (1910) reprint 1994.
Cloth. $22.50. 144 pp. .... Vendor G0259

Whitney, S. H. **The Kennebec Valley**. (1887) reprint 1993.
Cloth. $20.00. 122 pp. .... Vendor G0259

Wittemore, Edwin C., ed. **Centennial History of Waterville, Kennebec County, 1802-1902**. (1902) reprint 1988.
Cloth. $63.00. 592 pp. .... Vendor G0259

Knox County

Biographical Review: Life Sketches of Leading Citizens of Sagadahoc, Lincoln, Knox & Waldo Cos. (1897) reprint 1996.
Cloth. $47.00. 422 pp. .... Vendor G0259

Eaton, C. **History of Thomaston, Rockland & So. Thomaston,** from Their First Exploration, A.D. 1605. With Genealogies. 2 vols. (1865) reprint 1988.
Cloth. $49.00/vol. 468 + 472 pp. .... Vendor G0259

Hardy, Anna Simpson. **History of Hope Maine**. 1990. Indexed. Illus.
  Book # 1126.
Cloth. $45.00. 544 pp. .... Vendor G0082

Hill, Sally, and Arthur Spear, eds. **Remarks of My Life Pr Me Hezekiah Prince 1786-1792**. 1973. Indexed. Illus.
  Book #1169.
Cloth. $20.00. 125 pp. .... Vendor G0082

Locke, J. L. **Sketches of the History of the Town of Camden,** Including Incidental References to the Neighbouring Places & Adjacent Waters. (1859) reprint 1988.
Cloth. $32.00. 267 pp. .... Vendor G0259

Robinson, Reuel. **History of Camden & Rockport, Maine**. (1907) reprint 1994.
Cloth. $65.00. 644 pp. .... Vendor G0259

Sullivan, Steven E., scr. **Thomaston, Maine Vital Records from the Thomaston Recorder 1837-1846**. 1995. Indexed. Illus.
  Book #1610.
Cloth. $20.00. 128 pp. .... Vendor G0082

Lincoln County

Biographical Review: Life Sketches of Leading Citizens of Sagadahoc, Lincoln, Knox & Waldo Cos. (1897) reprint 1996.
Cloth. $47.00. 422 pp. .... Vendor G0259

Chase, F. S. **[History of] Wiscasset in Pownalborough**. (1941) reprint 1990.
Cloth. $67.00. 640 pp. .... Vendor G0259

Cushman, D. Q. **History of Ancient Sheepscot & Newcastle,** Including . . . Other

Contiguous Places from Earliest Discovery to the Present Time, with the Genealogy of More than Four Hundred Families. (1882) reprint 1992.
Cloth. $48.00. 458 pp. .... Vendor G0259

Greene, Francis B. **History of Boothbay, Southport & Boothbay Harbor, 1623-1905**. With Genealogies. (1906) reprint 1992.
Cloth. $59.00. 693 pp. .... Vendor G0259

Greene, Francis Byron. **History of Boothbay, Southport and Boothbay Harbor, Maine 1623-1905**. (1906) reprint 1984. Indexed. Illus.
  Book # 1202.
Cloth. $60.00. 771 pp. .... Vendor G0082

Johnston, J. **History of the Towns of Bristol & Bremen in the State of Maine,** Including the Pemaquid Settlement. (1873) reprint 1988.
Cloth. $54.50. 524 pp. .... Vendor G0259

Miller, S. L. **History of the Town of Waldoboro**. (1910) reprint 1987.
Cloth. $35.00. 281 pp. .... Vendor G0259

Patterson, William D. **The Probate Records of Lincoln County Maine 1760 to 1800**. (1895) reprint 1991. Indexed.
  Book #1177.
Cloth. $39.50. 448 pp. .... Vendor G0082

Rice, George Wharton. **The Shipping Days of Old Boothbay**. (1938) reprint 1984. Indexed. Illus.
  Book #1203.
Cloth. $45.00. 463 pp. .... Vendor G0082

Oxford County

Barrows, J. S. **Fryeburg, Maine:** An Historical Sketch. (1938) reprint 1990.
Cloth. $37.50. 309 pp. .... Vendor G0259

Biographical Review: Biographical Sketches of Leading Citizens of Oxford & Franklin Counties. (1897) reprint 1996.
Cloth. $65.00. 639 pp. .... Vendor G0259

Cole, A., and C. F. Whitman. **History of Buckfield, Oxford Co.,** from the Earliest Explorations to the Close of the Year 1900. (1915) reprint 1994.
Cloth. $77.00. 758 pp. .... Vendor G0259

King, Marquis F. **Annals of Oxford,** from Its Incorporation . . . in 1829 to 1850, with a Brief Account of the Settlement of Shepardsfield Plantation, Now Hebron and Oxford, and Genealogical Notes from . . . Both Towns. (1903) reprint 1994.
Cloth. $35.00. 298 pp. .... Vendor G0259

King, Marquis Fayette. **Annals of Oxford Maine from 1829 to 1850**. (1903) reprint 1986. Indexed. Illus.
  Book #1216.
Cloth. $45.00. 173 pp. .... Vendor G0082

Lapham, William B., and S. P. Maxim. **History of Paris,** from Its Settlement to 1880, with a History of the Grants of 1736 & 1771, with Personal Sketches, a Copious Genealogical Register, & an Appendix. (1884) reprint 1994.
Cloth. $89.50. 911 pp. .... Vendor G0259

Lapham, William Berry. **Centennial History of Norway, Oxford County, Maine 1786-1886**. (1886) reprint 1986. Indexed. Illus.
   Book #1215.
Cloth. $55.00. 822 pp. .... Vendor G0082

Lapham, William Berry. **History of Woodstock, Maine**. (1882) reprint 1983. Indexed. Illus.
   Book #1221.
Cloth. $35.00. 359 pp. .... Vendor G0082

McAllister, Rev. Donald, and Lucille Naas. **Marriage Returns of Oxford County Maine, Prior to 1892**. 1993. Indexed.
   Book #1455.
Cloth. $37.50. 352 pp. .... Vendor G0082

Paris Cape Historical Society. **Paris, Maine: The Second Hundred Years 1893-1993**. 1994. Indexed. Illus.
   Book #1512.
Cloth. $60.00. 1,216 pp. .... Vendor G0082

Turner, Hollis. **History of Peru, in the County of Oxford,** from 1789 to 1911. With Residents and Genealogies of the Families. (1911) reprint 1993.
Cloth. $37.00. 313 pp. .... Vendor G0259

Warren, Henry P., et al. **History of Waterford, Oxford County,** Comprising Historical Address, Record of Families, Centennial Proceedings. (1879) reprint 1994.
Cloth. $42.00. 371 pp. .... Vendor G0259

Penobscot County

Godfrey, John E. **Annals of Bangor, 1769-1882**. (1882) reprint 1990.
Cloth. $38.00. 304 pp. .... Vendor G0259

Gray, Ruth. **Abstracts of Penobscot County, Maine Probate Records 1816-1883**. 1993. Indexed.
   Book #1434.
Cloth. $94.50. 616 pp. .... Vendor G0082

Gray, Ruth, ed. **Penobscot County, Maine Marriage Returns Prior to 1892**. 2 vols. 1994. Indexed.
   Book #1452.
Cloth. $95.00. 704 pp. each. .... Vendor G0082

Oak, L. **History of Garland**. (1911) reprint 1990.
Cloth. $44.00. 401 pp. .... Vendor G0259

Swett, David Livingstone. **Orrington, Maine Cemetery Inscriptions**. 1996. Indexed.
   Book #1677.
Cloth. $95.00. 455 pp. .... Vendor G0082

Swett, David Livingstone. **Orrington, Maine Vital Records Prior to 1892**. 1995. Indexed.
    Book #1676.
Cloth. $95.00. 455 pp. .... Vendor G0082

Piscataquis County

Gerrish, Judson, and Henry Gerrish. **History of Brownville, 1824-1924**. (1924) reprint 1994.
Paper. $14.00. 71 pp. .... Vendor G0259

Saco Valley

Ridlon, G. T., Sr. **Saco Valley Settlements & Families,** Historical, Biographical, Genealogical, Traditional & Legendary. (1895) reprint 1993.
Cloth. $95.00. 1,224 pp. .... Vendor G0259

Sagadahoc County

Adams, Silas. **The History of the Town Of Bowdoinham, Maine**. (1912) reprint 1985. Indexed. Illus.
    Book #1200.
Cloth. $45.00. 376 pp. .... Vendor G0082

Biographical Review: Life Sketches of Leading Citizens of Sagadahoc, Lincoln, Knox & Waldo Cos. (1897) reprint 1996.
Cloth. $47.00. 422 pp. .... Vendor G0259

Lemont, Levi P. **Historical Dates of the Town & City of Bath,** and Town of Georgetown, from 1604 to 1874. (1874) reprint 1994.
Paper. $15.00. 104 pp. .... Vendor G0259

Owen, Henry Wilson. **The Edward Clarence Plummer History of Bath**. (1936) reprint 1995.
Cloth. $61.00. 575 pp. .... Vendor G0259

Reed, Parker McCobb. **History of Bath & Environs, Sagadahoc Co., 1607-1895,** with Illustrations. (1894) reprint 1993.
Cloth. $55.00. 526 pp. .... Vendor G0259

Somerset County

Coburn, Louise Helen, et al. **Skowhegan on the Kennebec**. 2 vols. (1941) reprint 1993.
Cloth. $99.50. 1,050 pp. .... Vendor G0259

Mitchell and Campbell, comps. **Norridgewock Register, 1903**. (1903) reprint 1993.
Paper. $15.00. 89 pp. .... Vendor G0259

Wood, Henrietta Danforth. **Early Days of Norridgewock**. (1933) reprint 1993.
Cloth. $21.50. 124 + 20 pp. .... Vendor G0259

Waldo County

Biographical Review: Life Sketches of Leading Citizens of Sagadahoc, Lincoln, Knox & Waldo Cos. (1897) reprint 1996.
Cloth. $47.00. 422 pp. .... Vendor G0259

Crosley, William George, John Lymburner Locke, and Herman Abbot. **Early Histories of Belfast Maine**. (1825,1827,1856,1874) reprint 1989. Indexed.
Book #1148.
Cloth. $29.50. 320 pp. .... Vendor G0082

Farrow, John Pendleton. **History of Islesborough, Maine**. (1893) reprint 1991. Indexed. Illus.
Book #1272.
Cloth. $35.00. 443 pp. .... Vendor G0082

Groves, Marlene A., scr. **Jackson and Brooks, Maine Church Records**. Indexed.
Book #1514.
Stapled booklet. $15.00. 72 pp. .... Vendor G0082

Hichborn, Faustina. **Historical Sketch of Stockton Springs**. Edited by Herbert C. Libby. (1908) reprint 1996.
Paper. $19.50. 133 pp. .... Vendor G0259

Hillman, Ralph E., ed. **Troy, Maine Vital Records Prior to 1892**. 1995. Indexed.
Book #1525.
Cloth. $24.95. 224 pp. .... Vendor G0082

Littlefield, Ada Douglas. **An Old River Town,** Being a History of Winterport (Old Frankfort). With 1993 addendum. (1907) reprint 1993.
Cloth. $36.00. $32.50 .... Vendor G0259

Maresh, Mosher, and Watts. **Vital Records of Lincolnville, Maine Prior to 1892**. 1993. Indexed. Illus.
Book #1130.
Cloth. $75.00. 394 pp. .... Vendor G0082

Mosher, Elizabeth M, scr. **Jackson, Maine Vital Records Prior to 1892**. 1989. Indexed.
Book #1128.
Cloth. $110.00. 249 pp. .... Vendor G0082

Norwood, Seth W. **Sketches of Brooks History**. (1935) reprint 1994.
Cloth. $48.50. 454 pp. .... Vendor G0259

Records of Rev. Edward F. Cutter of Maine 1833-1856. 1989. Indexed. Illus.
Book # 1119.
Cloth. $20.00. 96 pp. .... Vendor G0082

Williamson, Joseph, and Alfred Johnson. **The History of the City of Belfast, Volume II**. (1913) reprint 1982. Indexed. Illus.
   Book #1197.
Cloth. $55.00. 835 pp. .... Vendor G0082

Washington County

Drisko, G. W. **Narrative of the Town of Machias:** the Old & the New, the Early & the Late. (1904) reprint 1988.
Cloth. $62.00. 589 pp. .... Vendor G0259

Harmon, Wade F., comp. **Machias: Index of Surnames to George W. Drisko's "Narrative of the Town of Machias."** (1955) reprint 1995.
Cloth, $28.00. Paper, $18.00. 93 pp. .... Vendor G0259

Kilby, William Henry, comp. **Eastport & Passamaquoddy:** A Collection of Historical & Biographical Sketches. Incl. Weston's 1834 "History." (1988) reprint 1992.
Cloth. $49.50. 505 pp. .... Vendor G0259

Long, Alice MacDonald. **Marriage Returns of Washington County, Maine Prior to 1892**. 1993. Indexed.
   Book #1454.
Cloth. $24.50. 128 pp. .... Vendor G0082

Lubec, Maine Vital Records. 1996.
   Book #1738.
Cloth. $39.50. .... Vendor G0082

Willey, Kenneth L., scr. **Eastport, Maine Vital Records**. 1996.
   Index and tax listing. Book #1678.
Cloth. $54.50. 896 pp. .... Vendor G0082

York County

Albert, Fall, Goodrich, Hall, et al., comp. **The Story of Berwick**. (1963) reprint 1995.
Cloth. $29.50. 166 pp. .... Vendor G0259

Anderson, Joseph Crook II, and Lois Ware Thurston, eds. **Vital Records of Kittery, Maine Prior to 1892**. 1991. Indexed. Illus.
   Book #1173.
Cloth. $49.50. 640 pp. .... Vendor G0082

Bradbury, Charles. **History of Kennebunkport,** from Its First Discovery by Bartholomew Gosnold, 1602, to A.D. 1837. (1837) reprint 1992.
Cloth. $39.50. 338 pp. .... Vendor G0259

Bragdon, Lester MacKenzie, and John Eldridge Frost, scr. **Vital Records of York Maine Prior to 1892**. 1992. Indexed.
   Book #1187.
Cloth. $59.50. 831 pp. .... Vendor G0082

Cemetery Inscriptions of York County, Maine. 4 vols. 1995. Indexed.
  Book #1568.
Cloth. $250.00. 544 pp. .... Vendor G0082

Donahue, Marie. **The Old Academy on the Hill: A Bicentennial History 1791-1991**. 1992. Indexed. Illus.
  Book #1393.
Cloth. $35.00. 224 pp. .... Vendor G0082

Ernst, George. **New England Miniature: A History of York, Maine**. (1961) reprint 1993.
Cloth. $34.00. 284 pp. .... Vendor G0259

Folsom, George. **History of Saco and Biddeford**. (1830) reprint 1975. Indexed.
  Book #1218.
Cloth. $25.00. 379 pp. .... Vendor G0082

Freeman, Melville C. **History of Cape Porpoise**. (1955) reprint 1995.
Cloth. $22.50. 107 pp. .... Vendor G0259

Frost, John Eldridge, and Joseph Crook Anderson II. **Marriage Returns of York County, Maine Prior to 1892**. 1993. Indexed.
  Book #1423.
Cloth. $45.00. 576 pp. .... Vendor G0082

Frost, John Eldridge, and Joseph Crook Anderson II. **Vital Records of Berwick, South Berwick and North Berwick Maine**. 1993. Indexed. Illus.
  Book # 1337.
Cloth. $62.50. 862 pp. .... Vendor G0082

History of the First Century of Parsonsfield, Incorporated August 29, 1785. Includes Genealogies. By a Committee of the Town. (1888) reprint 1988.
Cloth. $55.00. 499 pp. .... Vendor G0259

History of York County, with Illustrations and Biographical Sketches of Prominent Men and Pioneers. (1880) reprint 1987.
Cloth. $48.00. 441 pp. .... Vendor G0259

The Old Gaol Museum Committee, and the Old York Historical and Improvement Society. **York Maine Then and Now: A Pictorial Documentation**. 1976. Illus.
  Book #1222.
Cloth. $12.00. 107 pp. .... Vendor G0082

Records of the Church of Christ in Buxton, Maine 1763-1817. (1868) reprint 1989. Indexed.
  Book #1102.
Cloth. $20.00. 104 pp. .... Vendor G0082

Remich, Daniel. **History of Kennebunk,** from Its Earliest Settlement to 1890, Including Biographical Sketches. (1890) reprint 1992.
Cloth. $58.00. 580 pp. .... Vendor G0259

Remick, Oliver Philbrick. **Record of Services of Officers and Enlisted Men, Kittery & Eliot**. (1901) reprint 1986. Illus.
Book #1217.
Cloth. $25.00. 235 pp. .... Vendor G0082

Spencer, W. D., comp. **Burial Inscriptions of Berwick to 1922**. (1922) reprint 1987.
Paper. $15.00. 133 pp. .... Vendor G0259

Spencer, W. D., comp. **List of Revolutionary Soldiers of Berwick**. (1898) reprint 1987.
Paper. $5.00. 18 pp. .... Vendor G0259

Stackpole, E. S. **Old Kittery and Her Families**. (1903) reprint 1988.
Cloth. $84.00. 822 pp. .... Vendor G0259

Stackpole, Everett S. **Old Kittery and Her Families**. (1903) reprint 1985. Indexed. Illus.
Book #1212.
Cloth. $55.00. 544 pp. .... Vendor G0082

Wills, John. **Old Eliot**. 3 vols. (1897-1909) reprint 1985. Indexed. Illus.
Book #1207.
Cloth. $119.00. 2,160 pp. .... Vendor G0082

 Maryland

Statewide and Regional References

Atlas of Maryland and Delaware, Topographical.
This present-day atlas provides the researcher with the detail needed to conduct a proper search. It is the size of a Rand McNally atlas of the entire U.S. 11" x 15½".
$16.95. .... Vendor G0611

Atlases & Gazetteers: Maryland/Delaware. Illus.
Paper. $16.95. 80 pp. .... Vendor G0632

Barnes, Robert W. **Maryland Marriages, 1634-1777**. (1978) reprint 1995. Indexed.
Cloth. $25.00. 233 pp. .... Vendor G0010

Barnes, Robert W. **Maryland Marriages, 1778-1800**. (1979) reprint 1993. Indexed.
Cloth. $25.00. 300 pp. .... Vendor G0010

Barnes, Robert W. **Maryland Marriages, 1801-1820**. 1993. Indexed.
Cloth. $25.00. 260 pp. .... Vendor G0010

Barnes, Robert W., and F. Edward Wright. **Colonial Families of the Eastern Shore of Maryland, Vol. 1**. 1996.
Paper. $36.00. 449 pp. .... Vendor G0140

Barnes, Robert W., and F. Edward Wright. **Colonial Families of the Eastern Shore of Maryland, Vol. 2**. 1996.
Paper. $33.50. 394 pp. .... Vendor G0140

Barnes, Robert W. **Marriages and Deaths from the Maryland Gazette, 1727-1839**. (1973) reprint 1994. Indexed.
Contact vendor for information. 234 pp. .... Vendor G0011

Brugger, Robert J. **Maryland: A Middle Temperament, 1634-1980**. (1988) reprint 1990.
The most comprehensive history of the state of Maryland ever to appear in a single volume. This is a very useful reference for anyone interested in Maryland history. 7¼" x 10¼".
Cloth. $35.95. 850 pp. .... Vendor G0611

Brumbaugh, Gaius Marcus. **Maryland Records:** Colonial, Revolutionary, County and Church from Original Sources. 2 vols. (1915, 1928) reprint 1993. Indexed. Illus.
Cloth. $75.00. 513 + 688 pp. .... Vendor G0010

Brumbaugh, Gaius Marcus, and Margaret R. Hodges. **Revolutionary Records of Maryland**. (1924) reprint 1996. Indexed. Illus.
Paper. $10.00. 56 pp. .... Vendor G0011

Callcott. **Mistress of Riversdale: The Plantation Letters of Rosalie Stier Calvert, 1795-1821**. 1991.
In letters to her European relatives, Calvert provided an uncommonly readable account of America's history and life in early 19th-century Maryland.
Paper. $15.95. 407 pp. .... Vendor G0611

Carothers, Bettie S., comp. **1776 Census of Maryland**. Rev. ed. 1989. Indexed.
Paper. $16.00. 214 pp. .... Vendor G0140

Carothers, Bettie S. **Maryland Oaths of Fidelity**. (1989) reprint 1995.
Paper. $9.00. 111 pp. .... Vendor G0140

Carr, Morgan, and Russo, eds. **Colonial Chesapeake Society**. 1988.
A fascinating collection of scholarly research essays on the social history of this region. Fully footnoted.
Paper. $18.95. 512 pp. .... Vendor G0611

Carr, Menard, and Walsh. **Robert Cole's World: Agriculture & Society in Early Maryland**. 1991.
Paints an intimate portrait of the social and economic life of a middling planter in the 17th-century Chesapeake by using the case study of the family of Robert Cole, an English Catholic, who moved with his family and servants in 1652 to St. Mary's County.
Paper. $19.95. 362 pp. .... Vendor G0611

Clements, S. Eugene, and F. Edward Wright. **Maryland Militia in the Revolutionary War**. 1987. Indexed.
Paper. $24.00. 351 pp. .... Vendor G0140

Coldham, Peter Wilson. **Settlers of Maryland, 1679-1700**. (1995) reprint 1996. Indexed.
Cloth. $25.00. 228 pp. .... Vendor G0010

Coldham, Peter Wilson. **Settlers of Maryland, 1701-1730**. 1996. Indexed.
Cloth. $25.00. 216 pp. .... Vendor G0010

Coldham, Peter Wilson. **Settlers of Maryland, 1731-1750**. 1996. Indexed.
Cloth. $30.00. 306 pp. .... Vendor G0010

Coldham, Peter Wilson. **Settlers of Maryland, 1751-1765**. 1996. Indexed.
Cloth. $32.50. 367 pp. .... Vendor G0010

Coldham, Peter Wilson. **Settlers of Maryland, 1766-1783**. 1996. Indexed.
Cloth. $25.00. 204 pp. .... Vendor G0010

Cotton, Jane Baldwin, and F. Edward Wright. **Maryland Calendar of Wills, Vols. 1-16 (complete set)**. (1904-1928) reprint 1988. Indexed.
See following listings for individual volumes.
Paper. $320.00. .... Vendor G0140

Cotton, Jane Baldwin. **Maryland Calendar of Wills, Vols. 1-8**. (1904-1928) reprint 1988. Indexed.
See below for individual volumes.
Paper. $160.00/set. .... Vendor G0140

Cotton, Jane Baldwin. **Maryland Calendar of Wills, Vol. 2: 1685-1702**. (1904) reprint 1988. Indexed.
Paper. $25.00. 327 pp. .... Vendor G0140

Cotton, Jane Baldwin. **Maryland Calendar of Wills, Vol. 3: 1703-1713**. (1904) reprint 1988. Indexed.
Paper. $25.00. 331 pp. .... Vendor G0140

Cotton, Jane Baldwin. **Maryland Calendar of Wills, Vol. 4: 1713-1720**. (1904) reprint 1988. Indexed.
Paper. $24.00. 306 pp. .... Vendor G0140

Cotton, Jane Baldwin. **Maryland Calendar of Wills, Vol. 5: 1720-1726**. (1904) reprint 1988. Indexed.
Paper. $24.00. 310 pp. .... Vendor G0140

Cotton, Jane Baldwin. **Maryland Calendar of Wills, Vol. 6: 1726-1732**. (1904) reprint 1988. Indexed.
Paper. $24.00. 322 pp. .... Vendor G0140

Cotton, Jane Baldwin. **Maryland Calendar of Wills, Vol. 7: 1732-1738**. (1904) reprint 1988. Indexed.
Paper. $24.00. 303 pp. .... Vendor G0140

Cotton, Jane Baldwin. **Maryland Calendar of Wills, Vol. 8: 1738-1743**. (1904) reprint 1988. Indexed.
Paper. $29.50. 368 pp. .... Vendor G0140

Cox, Richard J., and Larry E. Sullivan, eds. **Guide to the Research Collections of the Maryland Historical Society**. With contributions from Mary K. Meyer (genealogy) and Betty McKeever Key (oral history). Indexed.

Designed to be used with *Manuscript Collections of the Maryland Historical Society* (see "Pedley, Avril J. M., comp."), this reference volume includes manuscript collections accessioned between 1968 and 1981, as well as the genealogical and oral history collections of the Society.
Cloth. $22.00. 364 pp. .... Vendor G0617

Dilts, Bryan Lee, comp. **1890 Maryland Veterans Census Index**. 2nd ed. 1993.
Cloth. $34.00. 101 pp. .... Vendor G0552

Eisenberg, Gerson G. **Marylanders Who Served the Nation**.
A biographical dictionary of federal officials from Maryland.
Paper. $10.77. .... Vendor G0593

Ellis, Donna M., and Karen A. Stuart. **The Calvert Papers: Calendar and Guide to the Microfilm Edition**. With an Introduction by Richard J. Cox. Indexed. Illus.
Paper. $17.95. 214 pp. .... Vendor G0617

Family History Library. **Research Outline: Maryland**.
Leaflet. $.25. 15 pp. .... Vendor G0629

The First Laws of the State of Maryland. (1787) reprint 1981.
Cloth. $62.50. .... Vendor G0118

Gannett, Henry. **A Gazetteer of Maryland and Delaware**. 2 vols. in 1. (1904) reprint 1994.
Paper. $12.50. 99 pp. .... Vendor G0011

Genealogical Council of Maryland. **Inventory of Maryland Bible Records, Vol. 1**. 1989.
Paper. $26.50. 135 pp. .... Vendor G0140

Green, Karen M. **The Maryland Gazette, 1727-1761: Genealogical and Historical Abstracts**. 1990. Indexed.
Over 40,000 entries pertaining to early residents. For genealogists studying families in Maryland during this period, the newspaper provides information on early residents, mostly ordinary farmers and artisans, that simply cannot be obtained from any other source. *The Maryland Gazette*, as the only newspaper in Maryland in that period, contained news of individuals from all over MD, as well as DE, VA and PA. Includes court and probate records, apprentices, marriages, obituaries, lost persons, heirs, divorce, land records, occupations, ads, military expeditions, former residences, estate settlements, seafaring vessels and captains, and much more. Complete index of persons, place names, and subjects. Winner of the 1991 Norris Harris Award, Maryland Historical Society.
Cloth. $27.50. 324 pp. .... Vendor G0611

Hanson, George A. **Old Kent: The Eastern Shore of Maryland**. (1876) reprint 1996. Indexed. Illus.
Paper. $35.00. 383 pp. .... Vendor G0011

Hartsook, Elisabeth, and Gust Skordas. **Land Office and Prerogative Court Records of Colonial Maryland**. (1968) reprint 1996. Indexed.
Paper. $13.50. 124 pp. .... Vendor G0011

Hartzler, Daniel D. **Marylanders in the Confederacy**. 1986. Indexed.
Paper. $32.00. 415 pp. .... Vendor G0140

Heisey, John. **Maryland Research Guide**.
Paper. $12.00. 37 pp. .... Vendor G0574

Hooper, Debbie. **Abstracts of Chancery Court Records of Maryland, 1669-1782**. 1996. Indexed.
Paper. $12.50. 161 pp. .... Vendor G0140

Jones, Caleb, comp. **Orderly Book of the "Maryland Loyalists Regiment," June 18, 1778, to October 12, 1778,** Including General Orders Issued by Sir Henry Clinton, Baron Wilhelm von Kuyphausen, Sir William Erskine, Charles, Lord Cornwallis, General William Tryon and General Oliver De Lancey. Edited by Paul Leicester Ford. (1891) reprint 1996.
Paper. $12.50. 111 pp. .... Vendor G0011

Jourdan, Elise Greenup. **Early Families of Southern Maryland**. 5 vols. (1993-96) reprint 1995. Indexed.
    Vol. 1: 375 pp., $29.50.
    Vol. 2: 270 pp., $21.00.
    Vol. 3: 380 pp., $29.50.
    Vol. 4: 326 pp., $26.00.
    Vol. 5: 375 pp., $29.95.
Paper. .... Vendor G0140

Kanely, Edna A., comp. **Directory of Maryland Church Records**. Compiled under the auspices of the Genealogical Council of Maryland. 1987.
Paper. $16.00. 201 pp. .... Vendor G0140

Kenny, Hamill. **The Placenames of Maryland: Their Origin and Meaning**. Indexed.
    An alphabetical listing of the towns and villages, estates and other historic sites, and rivers and streams of Maryland and how they got their names.
Paper. $14.95. 364 pp. .... Vendor G0617

Kulikoff. **Tobacco and Slaves: The Development of Southern Cultures in the Chesapeake, 1680-1800**. 1986.
    Studies the changing social relations—among both blacks and whites. Extremely useful to understanding the family in Maryland during this period.
Paper. $14.95. 449 pp. .... Vendor G0611

Long, Helen R. **General History Section Index of Scharf's History of Western Maryland**. 1992.
Paper. $9.00. 65 pp. .... Vendor G0015

Maryland Genealogies. A Consolidation of Articles from the *Maryland Historical Magazine*. In Two Volumes. With an Introduction by Robert Barnes. (1980) reprint 1997. Indexed. Illus.
Cloth. $75.00. 549 + 548 pp. .... Vendor G0010

Maryland Hall of Records. **Calendar of Maryland State Papers:** No. 1—The Black Books. (1942) reprint 1995. Indexed.
Paper. $26.50. 297 pp. .... Vendor G0011

Maryland Historical Society. **Muster Rolls and Other Records of Service of Maryland Troops in the American Revolution, 1775-1783** (Archives of Maryland, XVIII). (1900) reprint 1996. Indexed.
Paper. $48.50. 736 pp. .... Vendor G0011

Maryland State Archives. **Archives of Maryland (original series).** 72 vols.
    Seventy-two volumes of original records from colonial Maryland, dating from 1635 through the Revolution.
Contact vendor for details of set and volume pricing. .... Vendor G0593

Maryland State Archives. **Archives of Maryland, New Series, Vol. I.** An Historical List of Public Officials of Maryland from 1662 to 1990.
Paper. $30.00. .... Vendor G0593

Maryland State Archives. **Guide to State Agency Records—Histories and Series Descriptions.**
    A history of every state agency and a description of each of their record series.
Paper. $25.00. .... Vendor G0593

Meyer, Mary Keyser. **Genealogical Research in Maryland: A Guide.** 4th ed.
    Contains information on archives in Maryland and state and county historical and genealogical societies and their holdings, as well as an extensive county by county bibliography of works useful to genealogists.
Paper. $12.00. 120 pp. .... Vendor G0617

Middleton. **Tobacco Coast: A Maritime History of Chesapeake Bay in the Colonial Era.** Reprint 1984.
    The history of how the Chesapeake Bay shaped the society and economy of an entire region. Its physical dominance created an "essential unity" of lands sharing its shores, despite the political decisions that created the separate colonies of Maryland and Virginia.
Paper. $16.95. 508 pp. .... Vendor G0611

Newman, Harry Wright. **The Flowering of the Maryland Palatinate.** (1961) reprint 1985. Indexed. Illus.
Cloth. $25.00. 359 pp. .... Vendor G0010

Newman, Harry Wright. **Maryland Revolutionary Records.** Data Obtained from 3,050 Pension Claims and Bounty Land Applications, Including 1,000 Marriages of Maryland Soldiers and a List of 1,200 Proved Services of Soldiers and Patriots of Other States. (1938) reprint 1993.
Cloth. $17.50. 155 pp. .... Vendor G0010

Newman, Harry Wright. **To Maryland from Overseas.** (1982) reprint 1991.
Cloth. $20.00. 190 pp. .... Vendor G0010

O'Neill, Francis P. **Index of Obituaries and Marriages in the [Baltimore] Sun, 1866-1870.** 2 vols. 1996.
    Name of bride/groom, date of marriage. Death notices include name, date of death, frequently includes age, cause of death. Entries arranged alphabetically.
Paper. $43.00. 539 pp. .... Vendor G0140

Oszakiewski, Robert A. **Maryland Naturalization Abstracts, Volume 2:** The County Court of Maryland, 1779-1851; The US Circuit Court for Maryland 1790-1851. Alphabetical listing. 1996.
Paper. $32.00. .... Vendor G0140

Owen, David R., and Michael C. Tolley. **Courts of Admiralty in Colonial America: The Maryland Experience, 1634-1776.** With a Foreword by Frank L. Wiswall, Jr. Indexed.
An examination of the admiralty law system as it was transmitted from England to America.
Cloth. $45.00. 458 pp. .... Vendor G0617

Parks, Gary W. **Index to the 1820 Census of Maryland and Washington, D.C.** 1986.
Cloth. $19.00. 274 pp. .... Vendor G0011

Parran, Alice. **Register of Maryland's Heraldic Families 1634-1935.** 2 vols.
Cloth. $25.00. 754 pp. .... Vendor G0574

Passano, Eleanor Phillips. **An Index of the Source Records of Maryland:** Genealogical, Biographical, Historical. (1940) reprint 1994.
Cloth. $28.50. 478 pp. .... Vendor G0010

Peden, Henry C., Jr. **Maryland Deponents, 1634-1799.** 1991.
Paper. $19.00. 241 pp. .... Vendor G0140

Peden, Henry C., Jr. **Marylanders to Carolina:** Migrations of Marylanders to North and South Carolina Prior to 1800. 1994. Indexed.
Paper. $17.00. 220 pp. .... Vendor G0140

Peden, Henry C., Jr. **Marylanders to Kentucky, 1775-1825.** 1991. Indexed.
Paper. $15.00. 202 pp. .... Vendor G0140

Peden, Henry C., Jr. **More Maryland Deponents, 1716-1799.** 1992.
Paper. $9.50. 123 pp. .... Vendor G0140

Peden, Henry C., Jr. **Quaker Records of Southern Maryland, 1658-1800.** 1992. Indexed.
Paper. $10.00. 120 pp. .... Vendor G0140

Pedley, Avril J. M., comp. **The Manuscript Collections of the Maryland Historical Society.** Indexed.
Cloth. $20.00. 392 pp. .... Vendor G0617

Retzer, Henry J. **German Regiment of Maryland and Pennsylvania.** 1991. Rev. ed. 1996.
Gives information on a little-known unit of Gen. Washington's army.
Paper. $15.00. 183 pp. .... Vendor G0140

Richardson, Hester Dorsey. **Side-lights on Maryland History** with Sketches of Early Maryland Families. 2 vols. (1913) reprint 1995. Indexed. Illus.
Cloth. $85.00. 482 + 508 pp. .... Vendor G0010

Russell, Donna Valley, ed. **Western Maryland Genealogy—a Quarterly Journal**. 1985. Indexed. Illus.
Paper. $19.00. 192 pp./yr. .... Vendor G0126

Scharf, J. Thomas. **History of Western Maryland**. With a New, Every-Name Index by Helen Long. 3 vols. (1882) reprint 1995. Indexed. Illus.
Paper. $125.00. 2,148 pp. in all. .... Vendor G0011

Scharf, J. Thomas. **History of Western Maryland**. 3 vols. (1882) reprint 1995. Indexed.
Cloth. $125.00. 1,929 pp. .... Vendor G0140

Schweitzer, George K. **Maryland Genealogical Research**. 1993. Illus.
   History of the state, types of records (Bible through will), record locations, research techniques, listings of county records.
Paper. $15.00. 208 pp. .... Vendor G0569

Sifakis. **Compendium of the Confederate Armies: Kentucky, Maryland, Missouri, the Confederate Units and the Indian Units**. 1995.
   Describes the regiments, the officers, and the battles.
Cloth. $27.50. 234 pp. .... Vendor G0611

Sketches of Maryland Eastern Shoremen. (1898) reprint 1992. Indexed.
   Genealogical extracts from Portrait and Biographical Record of the Eastern Shore of Maryland.
Paper. $15.00. 286 pp. .... Vendor G0140

Skirven, Percy G. **The First Parishes of the Province of Maryland,** Wherein Are Given Historical Sketches of the Ten Counties and of the Thirty Parishes in the Province at the Time of the Establishment of the Church of England in Maryland in 1692. (1923) reprint 1997. Indexed. Illus.
Paper. $29.95. 205 pp. .... Vendor G0011

Skordas, Gust. **The Early Settlers of Maryland**. An Index of Names of Immigrants Compiled from Records of Land Patents, 1633-1680, in the Hall of Records, Annapolis, Maryland. (1968) reprint 1995.
Cloth. $35.00. 525 pp. .... Vendor G0010

Smith, Daniel Blake. **Inside the Great House: Planter Family Life in Eighteenth-Century Chesapeake Society**. (1980) reprint 1994.
   The author explores all aspects of family life of the planters of the Chesapeake area in the 18th century.
Paper. $15.95. 303 pp. .... Vendor G0611

Southern California Genealogical Society. **Sources of Genealogical Help in Maryland**.
Paper. $1.50. 9 pp. .... Vendor G0656

Spencer, Richard Henry. **Genealogical and Memorial Encyclopedia of the State of Maryland**. A Record of the Achievements of Her People in the Making of a Commonwealth and the Founding of a Nation. 2 vols. (1919) reprint 1992. Indexed. Illus.
Paper. $59.95. 756 pp. .... Vendor G0011

Thomas, James Walter. **Chronicles of Colonial Maryland**. With Illustrations. (1900) reprint 1995. Illus.
Paper. $30.00. 323 pp. .... Vendor G0011

Thorndale, William, and William Dollarhide. **County Boundary Map Guides to the U.S. Federal Censuses, 1790-1920: Maryland, Delaware, District of Columbia, 1790-1920**. 1987.
$5.95. .... Vendor G0552

Torrence, Clayton. **Old Somerset on the Eastern Shore of Maryland**. A Study in Foundations and Founders. With an Added Prefatory Note by J. Millard Tawes, former Governor of Maryland. (1935) reprint 1996. Indexed.
At the time of its formation, Old Somerset included all the territory that is now Somerset, Wicomico, and Worcester counties.
Paper. $49.95. xvi + 583 pp. .... Vendor G0011

United States Bureau of the Census. **Heads of Families at the First Census of the United States Taken in the Year 1790: Maryland**. (1907) reprint 1992. Indexed. Illus.
Contact vendor for information. 189 pp. .... Vendor G0010

United States Bureau of the Census. **Heads of Families at the First Census of the United States Taken in the Year 1790: Maryland**.
Cloth, $36.00. Paper, $21.00. .... Vendor G0552

Volkel and Wilson. **Maryland 1800 Census**. 4 vols.
Paper. $10.00/vol., $35.00/set. 68 + 91 + 77 + 82 pp. .... Vendor G0574

White, Fr. John. **Briefe Relation of the Voyage Unto Maryland**.
A reprint of a first-hand account of the settlement of the colony.
Paper. $5.00. .... Vendor G0593

Wood, Gregory A. **A Guide to the Acadians in Maryland in the 18th and 19th Centuries**. 1995. Indexed. Illus.
A comprehensive study of exile, migration to Louisiana in 1766-1769, and the growth of a merchant/shipping, "urban" Acadian community in Baltimore through 1830.
Cloth. $30.00. 408 pp. .... Vendor G0500

Wright, F. Edward. **Citizens of the Eastern Shore of Maryland, 1659-1750**. 1986. Indexed.
Paper. $11.00. 145 pp. .... Vendor G0140

Wright, F. Edward. **Maryland Calendar of Wills, Vol. 9: 1744-1749**. 1988. Indexed.
Paper. $21.50. 257 pp. .... Vendor G0140

Wright, F. Edward. **Maryland Calendar of Wills, Vol. 10: 1748-1753**. 1988. Indexed.
Paper. $28.00. 350 pp. .... Vendor G0140

Wright, F. Edward. **Maryland Calendar of Wills, Vol. 11: 1753-1760**. 1988. Indexed.
Paper. $29.50. 370 pp. .... Vendor G0140

Wright, F. Edward. **Maryland Calendar of Wills, Vol. 12: 1759-1764**. 1988. Indexed.
Paper. $24.00. 297 pp. .... Vendor G0140

Wright, F. Edward. **Maryland Calendar of Wills, Vol. 13: 1764-1767**. 1988. Indexed.
Paper. $21.50. 260 pp. .... Vendor G0140

Wright, F. Edward. **Maryland Calendar of Wills, Vol. 14: 1767-1772**. 1988. Indexed.
Paper. $26.00. 325 pp. .... Vendor G0140

Wright, F. Edward. **Maryland Calendar of Wills, Vol. 15: 1772-1774**. 1988. Indexed.
Paper. $19.00. 241 pp. .... Vendor G0140

Wright, F. Edward. **Maryland Calendar of Wills, Vol. 16: 1774-1777**. 1988.
Indexed.
Paper. $24.00. 292 pp. .... Vendor G0140

Wright, F. Edward. **Maryland Eastern Shore Vital Records, Book 1: 1648-1725**.
1982. Indexed.
Paper. $16.00. 206 pp. .... Vendor G0140

Wright, F. Edward. **Maryland Eastern Shore Vital Records, Book 2: 1726-1750**.
1983. Indexed.
Paper. $14.00. 173 pp. .... Vendor G0140

Wright, F. Edward. **Maryland Eastern Shore Vital Records, Book 3: 1751-1775**.
1984. Indexed.
Paper. $11.00. 130 pp. .... Vendor G0140

Wright, F. Edward. **Maryland Eastern Shore Vital Records, Book 4: 1776-1800**.
1985. Indexed.
Paper. $11.00. 125 pp. .... Vendor G0140

Wright, F. Edward. **Maryland Eastern Shore Vital Records, Book 5: 1801-1825**.
1986. Indexed.
Paper. $11.00. 125 pp. .... Vendor G0140

Wright, F. Edward. **Newspaper Abstracts of Western Maryland, Vol. I: 1786-1798**.
1985. Indexed.
Paper. $11.00. 127 pp. .... Vendor G0140

Wright, F. Edward. **Newspaper Abstracts of Western Maryland, Vol. 2: 1799-1805**.
1986. Indexed.
Paper. $12.00. 165 pp. .... Vendor G0140

Wright, F. Edward. **Newspaper Abstracts of Western Maryland, Vol. 3: 1806-1810**.
1987. Indexed.
Paper. $12.00. 170 pp. .... Vendor G0140

Allegany County

Crosby, Anthony E., and Michael R. Olson, comps. **Commemorating Frostburg's Percy Cemetery: Restoration and Research**. 1995.
Spiral binding. $22.00. .... Vendor G0690

Fair, Patricia Stover. **Everyname Index to History of Allegany County Maryland.** 1990.
Paper. $15.00. 150+ pp. .... Vendor G0514

Genealogical Society of Allegany County, Maryland. **Allegany County, Maryland Rural Cemeteries.** 1990. Indexed.
Cloth. $25.00. Approx. 264 pp. .... Vendor G0660

Long, Helen R. **Allegany County Index to Scharf's History of Western Maryland.** 1990.
Paper. $8.00. 64 pp. .... Vendor G0015

Russell, Donna Valley. **Allegany and Garrett Counties, Maryland Genealogical Research Guide.** 1996. Indexed. Illus.
Paper. $12.00. 64 pp. .... Vendor G0126

Anne Arundel County

Barnes, Robert W. **Colonial Families of Anne Arundel County.** 1996. Indexed.
Paper. $24.50. 310 pp. .... Vendor G0140

Genealogical Council of Maryland. **Directory of Maryland's Burial Grounds, Vol. 1.** 1996.
Covers Anne Arundel, Carroll, Montgomery, and Prince George's counties.
Paper. $19.50. 241 pp. .... Vendor G0140

Hynson, Jerry M. **Maryland Freedom Papers: Volume I, Anne Arundel County.** 1996. Indexed.
Paper. $12.50. 124 pp. .... Vendor G0140

Luckenback, Al. **Providence-1649: The History & Archeology of Anne Arundel County, Maryland's 1st European Settlement.**
Reports and interpretation of the archeological digs of the Providence settlement on the Severn.
Paper. $7.00. .... Vendor G0593

Maryland Rent Rolls: Baltimore and Anne Arundel Counties, 1700-1707, 1705-1724. Reprinted with a New Index. (1924-31) reprint 1996. Indexed.
Paper. $25.00. 282 pp. .... Vendor G0011

Newman, Harry Wright. **Anne Arundel Gentry:** A Genealogical History of Twenty-two Pioneers of Anne Arundel County and Their Descendants. (1933) reprint 1995.
Cloth. $69.50. 668 pp. .... Vendor G0259

Newman, Harry Wright. **Anne Arundel Gentry, Early Families of Anne Arundel County, Maryland.** 2 vols. (1970) reprint 1996. Indexed.
Paper. $40.00/Vol. 1. $44.00/Vol. 2. $84.00/set. 500 + 550 pp. .... Vendor G0140

Peden, Henry C., Jr. **Revolutionary Patriots of Anne Arundel County.** 1992. Indexed.
Paper. $22.00. 288 pp. .... Vendor G0140

Reamy, Bill, and Martha Reamy. **Records of St. Paul's Parish, Vol. 1**. 1988. Indexed.
   Anglican-Episcopal records of births, marriages & deaths, early 1700s to 1800 of
Patapsco Parish (Baltimore City and Co., and Upper Anne Arundel County).
Paper. $18.50. 272 pp. .... Vendor G0140

Ridgely, David. **Annals of Annapolis,** Comprising Sundry Notices of That Old City
from the First Settlements in 1649 to the War of 1812. (1841) reprint 1992.
Cloth. $35.00. 283 pp. .... Vendor G0259

Riley, Elihu S. **"The Ancient City": History of Annapolis, in Maryland, 1649-
1887**. (1887) reprint 1995. Indexed.
Paper. $28.50. 396 pp. .... Vendor G0011

T.L.C. Genealogy. **Anne Arundel County, Maryland, Land Records, 1700-1702**.
1993. Indexed.
Paper. $12.00. 75 pp. .... Vendor G0609

T.L.C. Genealogy. **Anne Arundel County, Maryland, Land Records, 1703-1709**.
1994. Indexed.
Paper. $20.00. 156 pp. .... Vendor G0609

T.L.C. Genealogy. **Anne Arundel County, Maryland, Land Records, 1708-1712**.
1993. Indexed.
Paper. $14.00. 90 pp. .... Vendor G0609

T.L.C. Genealogy. **Anne Arundel County, Maryland, Land Records, 1712-1718**.
1993. Indexed.
Paper. $18.00. 150 pp. .... Vendor G0609

T.L.C. Genealogy. **Anne Arundel County, Maryland, Land Records, 1719-1724**.
1993. Indexed.
Paper. $16.00. 114 pp. .... Vendor G0609

T.L.C. Genealogy. **Anne Arundel County, Maryland, Land Records, 1724-1728**.
1993. Indexed.
Paper. $16.00. 116 pp. .... Vendor G0609

Warfield, J. D. **The Founders of Anne Arundel and Howard Counties, Maryland**.
(1905) reprint 1991. Indexed.
Contact vendor for information. 599 pp. .... Vendor G0011

Wright, F. Edward. **Anne Arundel Church Records of the 17th and 18th Centuries**.
1989. Indexed.
Paper. $22.00. 280 pp. .... Vendor G0140

Baltimore City and County

Baltimore County Genealogical Society. **Tombstone Inscriptions of Govans Pres-
byterian Church Cemetery**. 1996. Indexed.
   Lot by lot account of the tombstones in the Govans Presbyterian Church Cemetery.
Includes notes submitted by BCGS members on many of the families mentioned. Also
includes a short history of the cemetery and church.
Paper. $14.50. 118 pp. .... Vendor G0140

Barnes, Robert W., and Bettie S. Carothers. **1783 Tax List of Baltimore County**. 1978. Indexed. Illus.
Paper. $9.00. 117 pp. .... Vendor G0140

Barnes, Robert W. **Baltimore County Families, 1659-1759**. (1989) reprint 1996. Indexed.
Paper. $65.00. 924 pp. .... Vendor G0011

Barnes, Robert W. **Baltimore County, Maryland Deed Abstracts, 1659-1750**. 1996. Indexed.
   Tracing the descent of specific tracts of land has often revealed family relationships or clues to possible relationships that may not be apparent from other sources. Every name and relationship mentioned in the records is abstracted here. Records are arranged by name of tract with a chronological list of tracts. If a tract has been plotted on a map, the name of the map is given.
Paper. $34.50. 287 pp. .... Vendor G0140

Barnes, Robert W. **Guide to Research in Baltimore City and County**. Rev. ed. 1993.
Paper. $18.00. 160 pp. .... Vendor G0140

Brain, John. **Govans, Village and Suburb**. A Picture History. 1996. Illus.
   Traces the history of Govans from the granting of a tract of land by Frederick Calvert to William Govane in the mid-18th century to the city suburb it is today.
Paper. $15.00 + $4.50 p&h (MD residents must pay 5% sales tax).
96 pp. .... Vendor G0786

Coale, Joseph M. **Middling Planters of Ruxton Maryland, 1694-1850**. Illus.
Cloth. $21.00. 112 pp. .... Vendor G0617

Hoopes, E. Erick, and Christina Hoopes. **A Record of Interments at the Friends Burial Ground, Baltimore, Maryland**. (1995) reprint 1996.
Paper. $10.00. 66 pp. .... Vendor G0011

Horvath, George J., Jr. **The Particular Assessment Lists for Baltimore and Carroll Counties, 1798**. 1989. Indexed.
Paper. $14.00. 178 pp. .... Vendor G0140

Maguire, Joseph C., Jr. **Index of Obituaries and Marriages of the (Baltimore) Sun, 1861-1865**. 1992.
Paper. $28.50. 503 pp. .... Vendor G0140

Maryland Rent Rolls: Baltimore and Anne Arundel Counties, 1700-1707, 1705-1724. Reprinted with a New Index. (1924-31) reprint 1996. Indexed.
Paper. $25.00. 282 pp. .... Vendor G0011

O'Neill, Francis P. **Index of Obituaries and Marriages of the (Baltimore) Sun, 1871-1875**. 2 vols. 1995.
Paper. $45.50. 675 pp. .... Vendor G0140

Peden, Henry C., Jr. **Inhabitants of Baltimore County, 1763-1774**. 1989. Indexed.
Paper. $14.00. 184 pp. .... Vendor G0140

Peden, Henry C., Jr. **Methodist Records of Baltimore City, Vol. 1: 1799-1829**. 1994. Indexed.
Paper. $21.50. 271 pp. .... Vendor G0140

Peden, Henry C., Jr. **Methodist Records of Baltimore City, Vol. 2: 1830-1839**. 1994. Indexed.
Paper. $21.50. 281 pp. .... Vendor G0140

Peden, Henry C., Jr. **Presbyterian Records of Baltimore City, Maryland, 1765-1840**. 1995. Indexed.
Paper. $24.00. 326 pp. .... Vendor G0140

Peden, Henry C., Jr. **St. John's & St. George's Parish Registers, 1696-1851**. 1987. Indexed.
Paper. $18.50. 260 pp. .... Vendor G0140

Piet, Stanley. **Early Catholic Church Records in Baltimore, Maryland, 1782-1800**. 1989. Indexed.
Paper. $15.00. 202 pp. .... Vendor G0140

Power, Garrett. **Parceling Out Land in Baltimore, 1621-1796**. Illus.
Paper. $6.00. 56 pp. .... Vendor G0617

Reamy, Bill, and Martha Reamy. **Records of St. Paul's Parish, Vol. 1**. 1988. Indexed.
    Anglican-Episcopal records of births, marriages & deaths, early 1700s to 1800 of Patapsco Parish (Baltimore City and Co., and Upper Anne Arundel County).
Paper. $18.50. 272 pp. .... Vendor G0140

Reamy, Bill, and Martha Reamy. **St. George's Parish Records, 1689-1793**. 1988. Indexed.
Paper. $10.00. 150 pp. .... Vendor G0140

Reamy, Bill, and Martha Reamy. **St. Thomas' Parish Register, 1732-1850**. Indexed.
Paper. $8.00. 92 pp. .... Vendor G0140

Records of Old Otterbein Church, Baltimore, Maryland, 1785-1881. 1995. Indexed.
Paper. $17.00. 214 pp. .... Vendor G0140

Records of the First Reformed Church of Baltimore, 1768-1899. 1995. Indexed.
    A reprint of articles that originally appeared in the *Maryland Genealogical Society Bulletin*.
Paper. $28.00. 440 pp. .... Vendor G0140

Sisco, Louis Dow. **Baltimore County Land Records, 1665-1687,** from the Maryland Historical Magazine. With a New Introduction and Index by Robert Barnes. (1929-41) reprint 1995. Indexed.
Paper. $18.00. 113 pp. .... Vendor G0011

St. Thomas Parish Baptisms, Owings Mills, Maryland, 1732-1995. 1996.
   Data for St. Thomas Episcopal Church in Baltimore County. Arranged alphabetically.
   Paper. $23.00. 279 pp. .... Vendor G0140

St. Thomas Parish Deaths and Burials, Owings Mills, Maryland, 1728-1995. 1995.
   Paper. $10.00. 122 pp. .... Vendor G0140

St. Thomas Parish Marriage Records, Owings Mills, Maryland, 1738-1995. 1996.
   Data for St. Thomas Episcopal Church in Baltimore County. Arranged alphabetically.
   Paper. $14.50. 175 pp. .... Vendor G0140

Tepper, Michael H., ed. **Passenger Arrivals at the Port of Baltimore, 1820-1834**
from Customs Passenger Lists. Transcribed by Elizabeth P. Bentley. 1982.
   Cloth. $38.50. 768 pp. .... Vendor G0010

Watring, Anna Miller. **Civil War Burials in Baltimore's Loudon Park Cemetery**.
1996.
   Paper. $12.00. 81 pp. .... Vendor G0011

Wright, F. Edward. **Inhabitants of Baltimore County, 1692-1763**. 1987. Indexed.
   Paper. $10.00. 116 pp. .... Vendor G0140

Zimmerman, Elaine Obbink, and Kenneth Edwin Zimmerman. **Interment Records
1883-1929 Lorraine Cemetery & Mausoleum**. 1995. Indexed.
   Paper. $37.50. 473 pp. .... Vendor G0103

Zimmerman, Elaine Obbink, and Kenneth Edwin Zimmerman. **Records of St. Paul's
Cemetery 1855-1946, Located at Druid Hill Park**. 1992. Indexed.
   Paper. $9.50. 92 pp. .... Vendor G0103

Calvert County

Carothers, Bettie. **1783 Tax List of Maryland**. 1992. Indexed.
   Contains Cecil, Talbot, Harford, and Calvert counties.
   Paper. $15.00. 220 pp. .... Vendor G0140

Peden, Henry C. **Revolutionary Patriots of Calvert and St. Mary's Counties, Maryland, 1775-1783**. 1996. Indexed.
   Paper. $25.00. 307 pp. .... Vendor G0140

T.L.C. Genealogy. **Calvert County, Maryland, Rent Rolls, 1651-1776**. 1994.
Indexed.
   Paper. $14.00. 117 pp. .... Vendor G0609

Caroline County

Cochrane, Laura C., et al. **History of Caroline County, Maryland**. With an Added
Index. (1920) reprint 1994. Indexed. Illus.
   Paper. $28.00. 359 pp. .... Vendor G0011

Cranor, Henry Downes. **Marriage Licenses of Caroline County, Maryland, 1774-1815**. (1904) reprint 1994.
Paper. $7.50. 62 pp. .... Vendor G0011

Carroll County

Genealogical Council of Maryland. **Directory of Maryland's Burial Grounds, Vol. 1**. 1996.
    Covers Anne Arundel, Carroll, Montgomery, and Prince George's counties.
Paper. $19.50. 241 pp. .... Vendor G0140

Horvath, George J., Jr. **The Particular Assessment Lists for Baltimore and Carroll Counties, 1798**. 1989. Indexed.
Paper. $14.00. 178 pp. .... Vendor G0140

Long, Helen R. **Carroll County Index to Scharf's History of Western Maryland**. 1986.
Paper. $8.00. 46 pp. .... Vendor G0015

Stenley, Virginia D. **Chancery Books of Carroll County, 1837-1873**. 1994. Indexed.
Paper. $14.00. 200 pp. .... Vendor G0140

Stenley, Virginia D. **Chancery Books of Carroll County, 1873-1889**. 1997. Indexed.
Paper. $15.00. 182 pp. .... Vendor G0140

Cecil County

Beard, Alice L. **Births, Deaths and Marriages of the Nottingham Quakers, 1680-1889**. 1989. Indexed.
    East and West Nottingham Meetings, Little Britain, Deer Creek, and Eastland Meetings, and the Octorara Meeting, Cecil County, Maryland.
Paper. $24.00. 296 pp. .... Vendor G0140

Carothers, Bettie. **1783 Tax List of Maryland**. 1992. Indexed.
    Contains Cecil, Talbot, Harford, and Calvert counties.
Paper. $15.00. 220 pp. .... Vendor G0140

Johnston, George. **History of Cecil County, Maryland,** and the Early Settlements around the Head of Chesapeake Bay and on the Delaware River, with Sketches of Some of the Old Families of Cecil County. (1881) reprint 1989. Indexed. Illus.
Cloth. $25.00. 574 pp. .... Vendor G0010

Peden, Henry C., Jr. **Early Anglican Church Records of Cecil County**. 1990. Indexed.
Paper. $9.00. 105 pp. .... Vendor G0140

Peden, Henry C., Jr. **Inhabitants of Cecil County, 1649-1774**. 1993. Indexed.
Paper. $18.00. 250 pp. .... Vendor G0140

Peden, Henry C., Jr. **Revolutionary Patriots of Cecil County**. 1991. Indexed.
Paper. $11.50. 149 pp. .... Vendor G0140

Robertson, Donna J. **Tombstone Inscriptions of Cecil County, Maryland**. 1995. Indexed.
Spiral bound. $92.95. 486 pp. .... Vendor G0545

Robertson, Donna J. **Tombstone Inscriptions of Hopewell United Methodist Church Cemetery, Cecil County, Maryland**. 1995. Indexed.
Paper. $27.95. .... Vendor G0545

Robertson, Donna J. **Tombstone Inscriptions of West Nottingham Cemetery, Cecil County, Maryland**. 1995. Indexed.
Paper. $27.95. .... Vendor G0545

Charles County

Bates, Marlene Strawser, and F. Edward Wright. **Early Charles County, MD, Settlers, 1658-1745**. 1995. Indexed.
Paper. $28.00. 400 pp. .... Vendor G0140

Jourdan, Elise Greenup. **Abstracts of Charles County Court & Land Records, Vol. 1, 1658-1666**. 1992. Indexed.
Paper. $19.50. 278 pp. .... Vendor G0140

Jourdan, Elise Greenup. **Abstracts of Charles County Court & Land Records, Vol. 2: 1665-1695**. 1993. Indexed.
Paper. $14.00. 193 pp. .... Vendor G0140

Jourdan, Elise Greenup. **Abstracts of Charles County Court & Land Records, Vol. 3: 1694-1722**. 1994. Indexed.
Paper. $18.00. 246 pp. .... Vendor G0140

T.L.C. Genealogy. **Charles County, Maryland, Court Records, 1774-1778: An Every-Name Index**. 1995. Indexed.
Paper. $20.00. 124 pp. .... Vendor G0609

T.L.C. Genealogy. **Charles County, Maryland, Land Records, 1722-1733**. 1994. Indexed.
Paper. $20.00. 206 pp. .... Vendor G0609

T.L.C. Genealogy. **Charles County, Maryland, Land Records, 1733-1743**. 1993. Indexed.
Paper. $20.00. 169 pp. .... Vendor G0609

T.L.C. Genealogy. **Charles County, Maryland, Land Records, 1743-1752**. 1993. Indexed.
Paper. $20.00. 222 pp. .... Vendor G0609

T.L.C. Genealogy. **Charles County, Maryland, Land Records, 1752-1756**. 1996. Indexed.
Paper. $15.00. 120 pp. .... Vendor G0609

T.L.C. Genealogy. **Charles County, Maryland, Land Records, 1756-1761**. 1996. Indexed.
Paper. $15.00. 122 pp. .... Vendor G0609

T.L.C. Genealogy. **Charles County, Maryland, Land Records, 1761-1765**. 1996. Indexed.
Paper. $15.00. 140 pp. .... Vendor G0609

T.L.C. Genealogy. **Charles County, Maryland, Land Records, 1765-1775**. 1995. Indexed.
Paper. $20.00. 297 pp. .... Vendor G0609

T.L.C. Genealogy. **Charles County, Maryland, Land Records, 1790-1796**. 1994. Indexed.
Paper. $20.00. 292 pp. .... Vendor G0609

T.L.C. Genealogy. **Charles County, Maryland, Orphans Court Proceedings, 1791-1803: An Every-Name Index**. 1997. Indexed.
Paper. $20.00. 170 pp. .... Vendor G0609

T.L.C. Genealogy. **Charles County, Maryland, Wills, 1780-1791**. 1996. Indexed.
Paper. $20.00. 217 pp. .... Vendor G0609

T.L.C. Genealogy. **Charles County, Maryland, Wills, Administration Accounts, Inventories, and Orphans Court Proceedings, 1777-1780**. 1995. Indexed.
Paper. $20.00. 223 pp. .... Vendor G0609

Dorchester County

Jones, Elias. **Revised History of Dorchester County**. (1925) reprint 1994.
Cloth. $59.50. 603 pp. .... Vendor G0259

Mowbray, Calvin. **First Dorchester Families**. 1984. Indexed.
Paper. $15.00. 210 pp. .... Vendor G0140

Frederick County

Andersen, Patricia Abelard. **Frederick County Maryland Land Records, Liber B Abstracts, 1748-1752**. 1995. Indexed.
   Each volume's preface includes explanatory notes on the records found, and a listing of the active Justices of the Peace.
Paper. $15.00. 100+ pp. .... Vendor G0483

Andersen, Patricia Abelard. **Frederick County Maryland Land Records, Liber E Abstracts, 1752-1756**. 1995. Indexed.
   Each volume's full name index includes names of land tracts and slaves, as well as some occupations and miscellaneous acts.
Paper. $18.00. 120+ pp. .... Vendor G0483

Andersen, Patricia Abelard. **Frederick County Maryland Land Records, Liber F Abstracts, 1756-1761**. 1995. Indexed.
   This volume includes several militia discharges entitling the recorder to three years of property tax exemption.
Paper. $21.00. 154 pp. .... Vendor G0483

Andersen, Patricia Abelard. **Frederick County Maryland Land Records, Liber G & H Abstracts, 1761-1763**. 1996. Indexed.
These abstracts include cattle marks, estrays, misc. affidavits, naturalizations, bonds, supersedeas, indentures, leases, personal property sales as well as deeds and mortgages.
Paper. $21.00. 126 pp. .... Vendor G0483

Gilland, Steve. **Frederick County Backgrounds**. 1995. Indexed.
Paper. $10.50. 126 pp. .... Vendor G0140

Holdcraft, Jacob Mehrling. **Names in Stone**. 75,000 Cemetery Inscriptions from Frederick County, Maryland. 2 vols. (1966, 1972) reprint 1985. Illus.
Cloth. $56.50. 1,371 pp. .... Vendor G0011

Hood, Margaret Scholl. **Margaret Scholl Hood Diary 1851-1861**. 1992. Indexed. Illus.
   Book #1321.
Cloth. $25.00. 480 pp. .... Vendor G0082

Long, Helen R. **Frederick County Index to Scharf's History of Western Maryland**. 1985.
Paper. $9.00. 95 pp. .... Vendor G0015

Mallick, Sallie, and F. Edward Wright. **Frederick County Militia in the War of 1812**. 1992. Indexed.
Paper. $28.50. 450 pp. .... Vendor G0140

Myers, Margaret. **Marriage Licenses of Frederick County, 1778-1810**. 1986. Indexed.
Paper. $13.50. 166 pp. .... Vendor G0140

Myers, Margaret. **Marriage Licenses of Frederick County, 1811-1840**. 1987. Indexed.
Paper. $22.00. 278 pp. .... Vendor G0140

Myers, Margaret E. **Myersville, Maryland, Lutheran Baptisms, 1832-1849, 1861-1897**. 1986. Indexed. Illus.
Paper. $11.00. 68 pp. .... Vendor G0126

Peden, Henry C., Jr. **Revolutionary Patriots of Frederick County, MD, 1775-1783**. 1995. Indexed.
Paper. $30.00. 412 pp. .... Vendor G0140

Russell, Donna Valley. **Frederick County, Maryland, Genealogical Research Guide**. 1992. Illus.
Paper. $14.00. 64 pp. .... Vendor G0126

Russell, George Ely. **Moravian Families of Carroll's Manor, Frederick County, Maryland**. 1996. Indexed. Illus.
Paper. $19.00. 154 pp. .... Vendor G0126

Weiser, Frederick S. **Marriages and Burials from the Frederick, Maryland Evangelical Lutheran Church**. Indexed.

Earliest concentrated settlement of Germans in western Maryland. Burial records often give birthplaces in Europe and birth dates of early settlers.
Cloth. $19.00. 183 pp. .... Vendor G0627

Williams, T. J. C., and Folger McKinsey. **History of Frederick County, Maryland.** 2 vols. (1910) reprint 1997. Indexed. Illus.
Contact vendor for information. 1,724 pp. .... Vendor G0011

Young, Henry James, trans. **Moravian Families of Graceham, Maryland:** Church Records of Mainly German Families from Pennsylvania & Maryland Who Made Up the Congregation: 1759-1871. 1942. Indexed.
Paper. $11.00. 125 pp. .... Vendor G0140

Garrett County

Long, Helen R. **Garrett County Index for Scharf's History of Western Maryland.** 1986.
Paper. $4.00. 15 pp. .... Vendor G0015

Russell, Donna Valley. **Allegany and Garrett Counties, Maryland Genealogical Research Guide.** 1996. Indexed. Illus.
Paper. $12.00. 64 pp. .... Vendor G0126

Harford County

Abstracts of Death Certificates from the Files of Herbert S. Bailey, Funeral Director, Darlington, MD, 1921-1961, Vol. I, A-L Vol. II, M-Z.
Paper. $5.00/vol. 50+51 pp. .... Vendor G0872

Carothers, Bettie. **1783 Tax List of Maryland.** 1992. Indexed.
Contains Cecil, Talbot, Harford, and Calvert counties.
Paper. $15.00. 220 pp. .... Vendor G0140

Death Notices from the Bel Air Times, 1882-1899.
Paper. $4.00. 32 pp. .... Vendor G0872

Harford County, Maryland, Bible and Family Records, Vol. I.
Paper. $3.50. 27 pp. .... Vendor G0872

Harford County, Maryland, Bible and Family Records, Vols. II & III.
Paper. $3.50 ea. 27 pp. .... Vendor G0872

Index to Herrick's 1858 Map of Harford County, Maryland.
Paper. $2.50. 26 pp. .... Vendor G0872

Index to Naturalization Records of Harford County, Maryland, A-L.
Paper. $5.00. 50 pp. .... Vendor G0872

Index to Naturalization Records of Harford County, Maryland, M-Z.
Paper. $5.00. 51 pp. .... Vendor G0872

Livezey, Jon, and Helene Davis. **Harford County Marriage Licenses, 1777-1865**.
1993.
Paper. $20.00. 286 pp. .... Vendor G0140

Morgan, Ralph H., Jr. **Harford County Wills, 1774-1800**. 1990. Indexed.
Paper. $11.50. 153 pp. .... Vendor G0140

Preston, Walter W. **History of Harford County, Maryland**. (1901) reprint 1990.
Indexed.
Cloth. $20.00. 379 pp. .... Vendor G0011

Howard County

Howard County Maryland Records Volume I: Cemeteries. 1979. Indexed.
Paper. $4.00. 41 pp. .... Vendor G0149

Howard County Maryland Records Volume II: More Cemeteries. 1981. Indexed.
Paper. $6.00. 87 pp. .... Vendor G0149

Howard County Maryland Records Volume III: Even More Cemeteries. 1982.
Indexed.
Paper. $7.00. 87 pp. .... Vendor G0149

**Howard County Maryland Records Volume IV: Additional Cemeteries Plus
Manumission Records**. 1985. Indexed.
Paper. $7.00. 96 pp. .... Vendor G0149

**Howard County Maryland Records Volume V: More Cemetery Inscriptions Plus
Family Bible Data**. 1985. Indexed.
Paper. $7.00. 93 pp. .... Vendor G0149

**Howard County Maryland Records Volume VI: A Continuation of Howard County
Cemetery Records**. 1988. Indexed.
Paper. $7.00. 109 pp. .... Vendor G0149

**Howard County Maryland Records Volume VII: St. John's Cemetery and In-
scriptions from the St. John's Episcopal Church Columbarium**. 1991. Indexed.
Paper. $8.00. 132 pp. .... Vendor G0149

**Howard County Maryland Records Volume VIII: Additional Cemetery and In-
terment Information for Ten Howard County Grave Sites**. 1993. Indexed.
Contact vendor for information. 141 pp. .... Vendor G0149

Marriage Licenses in the Howard District of Anne Arundel County 1840-1851.
1966. Indexed.
   Originally published by Colonel Thomas Dorsey Chapter of DAR.
Paper. $5.00. 22 pp. .... Vendor G0149

Tombstone Inscriptions from a Few Cemeteries in Howard County Maryland.
1960. Indexed.
   Originally published by Colonel Thomas Dorsey Chapter of DAR.
Paper. $5.00. 29 pp. .... Vendor G0149

Warfield, J. D. **The Founders of Anne Arundel and Howard Counties, Maryland**. (1905) reprint 1991. Indexed.
Contact vendor for information. 599 pp. .... Vendor G0011

Kent County

Peden, Henry C., Jr. **Inhabitants of Kent County, Maryland**. 1994. Indexed.
Paper. $22.00. 275 pp. .... Vendor G0140

Peden, Henry C., Jr. **Revolutionary Patriots of Kent & Queen Anne's Counties**. 1995.
Paper. $24.00. 300 pp. .... Vendor G0140

Montgomery County

Barrow, Healan, and Kristine Stevens. **Olney: Echoes of the Past**. 1994. Indexed.
Paper. $12.00. 147 pp. .... Vendor G0140

Boyd, Thomas H. S. **The History of Montgomery County, Maryland**. (1879) reprint 1996. Indexed.
Paper. $18.00. 197 pp. .... Vendor G0011

Farquhar, Roger B. **Historic Montgomery County,** Old Homes & History. (1952) reprint 1993.
Cloth. $42.50. 373 pp. .... Vendor G0259

Genealogical Council of Maryland. **Directory of Maryland's Burial Grounds, Vol. 1**. 1996.
    Covers Anne Arundel, Carroll, Montgomery, and Prince George's counties.
Paper. $19.50. 241 pp. .... Vendor G0140

Long, Helen R. **Montgomery County Index to Scharf's History of Western Maryland**. 1991.
Paper. $8.00. 44 pp. .... Vendor G0015

Manuel, Janet D. **Montgomery County, Maryland, Marriage Licenses, 1798-1898**. 1987.
Paper. $19.50. 360 pp. .... Vendor G0140

Peden, Henry C., Jr. **Revolutionary Patriots of Montgomery County, Maryland, 1776-1783**. 1996. Indexed.
    A research tool for locating the men and women of Montgomery County who served in the military; rendered material aid to the army or navy; took the Oath of Allegiance and Fidelity; served in an office or on a committee at the town, county, or state level; or in some way contributed and supported the fight for freedom during the Revolutionary War. Most of the approximately 5,000 persons named herein also have genealogical data included with their respective entries.
Paper. $29.50. 369 pp. .... Vendor G0140

Prince George's County

Bowie, Effie Gwynn. **Across the Years in Prince George's County [Maryland]**. (1947) reprint 1996. Indexed. Illus.
Paper. $60.00. 904 pp. .... Vendor G0011

Brown, Helen W. **Index of Marriage Licenses, Prince George's County, Maryland 1777-1886**. (1971) reprint 1995.
Paper. $22.50. 249 pp. .... Vendor G0011

Genealogical Council of Maryland. **Directory of Maryland's Burial Grounds, Vol. 1**. 1996.
Covers Anne Arundel, Carroll, Montgomery, and Prince George's counties.
Paper. $19.50. 241 pp. .... Vendor G0140

Jourdan, Elise Greenup. **The Land Records of Prince George's County, Maryland, 1710-1717**. 1990. Indexed.
Paper. $8.00. 85 pp. .... Vendor G0140

Jourdan, Elise Greenup. **The Land Records of Prince George's County, Maryland, 1717-1726**. 1991. Indexed.
Paper. $12.00. 136 pp. .... Vendor G0140

Jourdan, Elise Greenup. **The Land Records of Prince George's County, Maryland, 1726-1733**. 1995.
Paper. $19.50. 245 pp. .... Vendor G0140

Jourdan, Elise Greenup. **The Land Records of Prince George's County, Maryland, 1733-1739**. 1996. Indexed.
Paper. $14.00. 168 pp. .... Vendor G0140

Jourdan, Elise Greenup. **The Land Records of Prince George's County, Maryland, 1739-1743**. 1997. Indexed.
Paper. $15.00. 152 pp. .... Vendor G0140

Prince George's County Genealogical Society. **1828 Tax List Prince George's County, Maryland**. 1985. Indexed.
Cloth. $12.00. 130 pp. .... Vendor G0075

Prince George's County Genealogical Society. **1850 Census Prince George's County, Maryland**. 1978. Indexed.
Cloth. $7.50. 160 pp. .... Vendor G0075

Prince George's County Genealogical Society. **A Bibliography of Published Genealogical Source Records, Prince George's County, Maryland**. (1975) reprint 1986.
Paper. $2.00. 28 pp. .... Vendor G0075

Prince George's County Genealogical Society. **Index to the Probate Records of Prince George's County, Maryland 1696-1900**. 1988. Indexed.
Cloth. $18.00. 238 pp. .... Vendor G0075

Prince George's County Genealogical Society. **Prince George's County Land Records, Volume A, 1696-1702**. (1976) reprint 1992. Indexed.
Cloth. $10.00. 98 pp. .... Vendor G0075

Prince George's County Genealogical Society. **Stones and Bones: Cemetery Records of Prince George's County, Maryland**. (1984) reprint 1988. Indexed.
Cloth. $28.00. 690 pp. .... Vendor G0075

T.L.C. Genealogy. **Prince George's County, Maryland, Land Records, 1739-1743**. 1996. Indexed.
Much more detailed and very accurate.
Paper. $20.00. 189 pp. .... Vendor G0609

Queen Anne's County

Peden, Henry C., Jr. **Revolutionary Patriots of Kent & Queen Anne's Counties**. 1995.
Paper. $24.00. 300 pp. .... Vendor G0140

Somerset County

Batchelder, Pauline Manning, comp. & ed. **A Somerset Sampler: Families of Old Somerset County, Maryland, 1700-1776**. Indexed.
Cloth. $38.50. 312 pp. .... Vendor G0784

Dryden, Ruth T. **Land Records of Somerset County, Maryland**. (1985) reprint 1992. Indexed. Illus.
Paper. $35.00. 537 pp. .... Vendor G0140

Dryden, Ruth T. **Rent Rolls of Somerset County, 1663-1723**. Indexed.
Paper. $12.00. 136 pp. .... Vendor G0140

Heise, David V. **Somerset County, Maryland Orphans Court Proceedings, 1777-1792 and 1811-1823**. 1996. Indexed.
The Orphans Court handled appointment of guardians for orphans, guardian accounts, apprenticeships, administrators' accounts of estates and disputes concerning these matters. Also, there are several accounts of Revolutionary Veterans seeking pensions. The main value of these records is the relationships they list, both stated and implied.
Paper. $17.50. 212 pp. .... Vendor G0140

Hume, Joan. **Maryland. Index to the Wills of St. Mary's County, 1662-1960 and Somerset County, 1664-1955**. (1970) reprint 1996.
Paper. $25.00. 277 pp. .... Vendor G0011

Torrence, Clayton. **Old Somerset on the Eastern Shore of Maryland,** "A Study in Foundations and Founders." (1935) reprint 1992. Indexed.
Paper. $35.00. 583 pp. .... Vendor G0140

St. Mary's County

Carr, Menard, and Walsh. **Robert Cole's World: Agriculture & Society in Early Maryland**. 1991.

Paints an intimate portrait of the social and economic life of a middling planter in the 17th-century Chesapeake by using the case study of the family of Robert Cole, an English Catholic, who moved with his family and servants in 1652 to St. Mary's County.
Paper. $19.95. 362 pp. .... Vendor G0611

Horsman, Mrs. Barbara Knott. **Reading Backwards On My Knott Heritage**. 1994. Indexed. Illus.
Cloth. $30.00. 432 pp. .... Vendor G0115

Hume, Joan. **Maryland. Index to the Wills of St. Mary's County, 1662-1960 and Somerset County, 1664-1955**. (1970) reprint 1996.
Paper. $25.00. 277 pp. .... Vendor G0011

O'Rourke, Timothy J. **Catholic Families of Southern Maryland**. Records of Catholic Residents of St. Mary's County in the Eighteenth Century. (1981) reprint 1985. Indexed.
Cloth. $17.50. 143 pp. .... Vendor G0010

Peden, Henry C. **Revolutionary Patriots of Calvert and St. Mary's Counties, Maryland, 1775-1783**. 1996. Indexed.
Paper. $25.00. 307 pp. .... Vendor G0140

T.L.C. Genealogy. **St. Mary's County, Maryland, Administrative Accounts, 1674-1720**. 1994. Indexed.
Paper. $20.00. 224 pp. .... Vendor G0609

T.L.C. Genealogy. **St. Mary's County, Maryland, Rent Rolls, 1639-1771**. 1993. Indexed.
Paper. $14.00. 145 pp. .... Vendor G0609

Talbot County

Carothers, Bettie. **1783 Tax List of Maryland**. 1992. Indexed.
Contains Cecil, Talbot, Harford, and Calvert counties.
Paper. $15.00. 220 pp. .... Vendor G0140

Tilghman, Oswald, comp. **History of Talbot County, 1661-1861**. Data collected by Sam'l Alexander Harrison. 2 vols. (1915) reprint 1995.
Contact vendor for information. 649 + 555 pp. .... Vendor G0010

Washington County

Bell, Herbert C. **History of Leitersburg District, Washington Co.,** Including Its Original Land Tenure; First Settlement; Material Development; Biographical Sketches, Etc. (1898) reprint 1995.
Cloth. $39.00. 331 pp. .... Vendor G0259

Keller, Roger. **Events of the Civil War in Washington County, Maryland**. 1995.
The Civil War transformed the Potomac River into an international boundary, placing Washington County on a dangerous border. This is an engaging history of Wash-

ington County's lesser known battlefields including Hagerstown, Funktown, Boonsboro, Smithsburg, Williamsport, and the Falling River's Road.
Cloth. $29.95. 412 pp. .... Vendor G0611

Keller, Roger. **Roster of Civil War Soldiers from Washington County, Maryland**. 1993.
Paper. $22.50. 255 pp. .... Vendor G0011

Long, Helen R. **Washington County Index of Scharf's History of Western Maryland**. 1983.
Paper. $9.00. 90+ pp. .... Vendor G0015

Morrow, Dale, ed. **Washington County Cemetery Records**. 7 vols. Indexed.
   Volume 1: 200 pp., $14.50.
   Volume 2: 145 pp., $14.00.
   Volume 3: 160 pp., $14.00.
   Volume 4: 158 pp., $14.00.
   Volume 5: 162 pp., $14.00.
   Volume 6: 147 pp., $14.00.
   Volume 7: 170 pp., $14.50.
Paper. $99.00/set. .... Vendor G0140

Russell, George Ely. **Washington County, Maryland, Genealogical Research Guide**. 1993. Indexed. Illus.
Paper. $11.00. 48 pp. .... Vendor G0126

Williams, Thomas J. C. **A History of Washington County, Maryland** from the Earliest Settlements to the Present Time. Including a History of Hagerstown. 2 vols. (1906) reprint 1992. Indexed. Illus.
Cloth. $125.00. 1,347 pp. .... Vendor G0011

Williams, Thomas J. C. **A History of Washington County, Maryland**. From the Earliest Settlements to the Present Time, Including a History of Hagerstown. 2 vols. plus 295-page Index. (1919) reprint 1992. Indexed.
Cloth. $79.50/set. 1,352 pp. + index. .... Vendor G0140

Wright, F. Edward. **Washington County Church Records of the 18th Century, 1768-1800**. 1988. Indexed.
   Lutheran and Reformed records of Hagerstown, Clearspring, Williamsport, Leitersburg, Funkstown, and Cearfoss.
Paper. $11.00. 155 pp. .... Vendor G0140

Worcester County

Long, Mary Beth, and Vanessa Long. **Worcester County, Maryland Marriage Licenses, 1795-1865**. 1990.
   Earliest known marriage licenses issued in Worcester County, Maryland.
Paper. $16.00. 264 pp. .... Vendor G0140

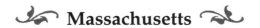

Massachusetts

Statewide and Regional References

Bailey, Frederic W. **Early Massachusetts Marriages Prior to 1800**. 3 vols. in 1. [Bound With] Plymouth County Marriages, 1692-1746. (1897, 1914) reprint 1996. Indexed.
Cloth. $40.00. 661 pp. .... Vendor G0010

Banks, Charles Edward. **The Planters of The Commonwealth in Massachusetts, 1620-1640**. (1930) reprint 1997. Indexed. Illus.
Cloth. $20.00. xiii + 231 pp. .... Vendor G0010

Barber, John W. **Historical Collections . . . Relating to the History and Antiquities of Every Town in Massachusetts**. With Geographical Descriptions Illustrated by 200 Engravings. (1839, 1844) reprint 1995. Illus.
Paper. $49.95. 631 pp. .... Vendor G0011

Barnes, Thomas G., ed. **The Book of the General Lawes and Libertyes Concerning the Inhabitants of Massachusetts**. 1975.
A reproduction of the earliest laws enacted in Massachusetts in 1648.
Paper. $6.00. 92 pp. .... Vendor G0611

Bodge, George Madison. **Soldiers in King Philip's War**. Official Lists of the Soldiers of Massachusetts Colony Serving in Philip's War, and Sketches of the Principal Officers, Copies of Ancient Documents and Records Relating to the War. (1906) reprint 1995. Indexed. Illus.
Paper. $35.00. 502 pp. .... Vendor G0011

Bowman, George Ernest. **The Mayflower Reader**. A Selection of Articles from *The Mayflower Descendant*. (1899-1905) reprint 1996. Illus.
Paper. $39.95. 537 pp. .... Vendor G0011

Broadfoot Publishing Company. **Papers of the Military Historical Society of Massachusetts**. 15 vols. Indexed.
Cloth. $500.00. Contact vendor for pricing options. .... Vendor G0590

Bushman. **King and People in Provincial Massachusetts**. 1992.
How colonial Massachusetts moved from the monarchy to republicanism in the years before the Revolutionary War.
Paper. $18.95. 280 pp. .... Vendor G0611

The Colonial Society of Massachusetts. **Medicine in Colonial Massachusetts, 1620-1820**. 1980.
A collection of essays covering various aspects of this subject.
Cloth. $23.50. 425 pp. .... Vendor G0611

The Colonial Society of Massachusetts. **Seafaring in Colonial Massachusetts**. 1980. Illus.
An interesting look at early seafaring with maps and illustrations.
Cloth. $27.50. 240 pp. .... Vendor G0611

Coquillette. **Law in Colonial Massachusetts, 1630-1800**. 1984.
  A comprehensive scholarly guide to Massachusetts law and legal records. Includes where to find them and how to use them.
Cloth. $24.95. 608 pp. .... Vendor G0611

Cutter, William Richard. **Genealogical and Personal Memoirs** Relating to the Families of Boston and Eastern Massachusetts. In Four Volumes. Partially indexed. (1908) reprint 1995. Illus.
Paper. $185.00. 2,201 pp. in all. .... Vendor G0011

Demos. **A Little Commonwealth: Family Life in Plymouth Colony**. 1970.
  Studies the family during the first two generations of the colony's existence.
Paper. $8.95. 201 pp. .... Vendor G0611

Dilts, Bryan Lee, comp. **1890 Massachusetts Veterans Census Index**. 2nd ed. 1993.
Cloth. $67.00. 281 pp. .... Vendor G0552

Donahue, Mary E. **Massachusetts Officers and Soldiers 1702-1722, Queen Anne's War to Dummer's War**. 1980.
Paper. $18.45. xxviii + 197 pp. .... Vendor G0406

Drake, Samuel G. **The Old Indian Chronicle**. Being a Collection of Exceeding Rare Tracts Written and Published in the Time of King Philip's War by Persons Residing in the Country. (1867) reprint 1995.
Cloth. $39.50. 333 pp. .... Vendor G0259

Family History Library. **Research Outline: Massachusetts**.
Leaflet. $.25. 10 pp. .... Vendor G0629

The First Laws of the Commonwealth of Massachusetts. (1788) reprint 1981.
Cloth. $62.50. 389 pp. .... Vendor G0118

Flagg, C. A. **An Index of Pioneers from Massachusetts to the West,** Especially to the State of Michigan. (1915) reprint 1997.
Contact vendor for information. 86 pp. .... Vendor G0011

Gannett, Henry. **A Geographic Dictionary of Massachusetts**. (1894) reprint 1978.
Cloth. $11.50. 126 pp. .... Vendor G0011

Goodwin, Nathaniel. **Genealogical Notes,** Or Contributions to the Family History of Some of the First Settlers of Connecticut and Massachusetts. (1856) reprint 1995.
Cloth. $25.00. xx + 362 pp. .... Vendor G0010

Goss, K. David, and David Zarowin. **Massachusetts Officers and Soldiers in the French and Indian Wars, 1755-56**. 1985.
Paper. $18.45. xxiv + 220 pp. .... Vendor G0406

Greenlaw, Lucy Hall. **The Genealogical Advertiser**. A Quarterly Magazine of Family History. 4 vols. in 1. (1898-1901) reprint 1994. Indexed. Illus.
Paper. $49.95. 677 pp. in all. .... Vendor G0011

Hills, Leon Clark. **History and Genealogy of the *Mayflower* Planters**. 2 vols. in 1. (1936, 1941) reprint 1996. Indexed.
Paper. $38.50. 461 pp. in all. .... Vendor G0011

Holbrook, Jay Mack. **Bibliography of Massachusetts Vital Records 1620-1905**. 1996.
This fiche identifies and describes the original manuscripts of vital and town records in the vaults of 324 Massachusetts towns.
Microfiche. $6.00. 617 pp. on 2 fiche. .... Vendor G0148

Holbrook, Jay Mack. **Guide to 1841-1895 Indexes of Massachusetts Vital Records**. 1989.
Paper. $3.00. 24 pp. .... Vendor G0148

Holbrook, Jay Mack. **Massachusetts Birth, Marriage, & Death Indexes 1841-1895**. 1989.
Microfiche. $6.00 each. 1,054 fiche. .... Vendor G0148

Holbrook, Jay Mack. **Massachusetts Cemetery Records: Quabbin Park 1741-1984**. 1985. Indexed.
Use this record to find former residents of Enfield, Greenwich, Prescott, and Dana—and their present burial places.
Microfiche. $6.00 each. 9 vols. on 79 fiche. .... Vendor G0148

Holbrook, Jay Mack. **Massachusetts Vital Record Transcripts 1620-1849**. 1995.
Microfiche. $6.00 each. 2,309 fiche. .... Vendor G0148

Holbrook, Jay Mack. **Massachusetts Vital Records 1620-1905 (originals)**. 1982+.
These are fiches of the original manuscripts of vital and town records. The vital records include births, marriage intentions, marriages, and deaths. Town records identify residents as they participate in town affairs, buy and sell property, attend church, pay taxes, serve in the military, vote, find stray animals, or receive town assistance.
Microfiche. $6.00 each. 20,000 fiche. .... Vendor G0148

Holbrook, Jay Mack. **Massachusetts Vital Records to 1850 (old printed series)**. 1993+.
Microfiche. $6.00 each. 287 fiche. .... Vendor G0148

Holbrook, Jay Mack. **The Mayflower Descendant 1620-1937**. 1995.
Thirty-four volumes of the quarterly magazine of Pilgrim genealogy and history, with one fiche per volume plus topical index.
Microfiche. $6.00 each or set of 35 fiche for $175.00. .... Vendor G0148

Jacobson, Judith. **Massachusetts Bay Connections**. (1992) reprint 1994. Indexed. Illus.
Paper. $20.00. 167 pp. .... Vendor G0011

Jones, Alfred E. **The Loyalists of Massachusetts,** Their Memorials, Petitions and Claims. (1930) reprint 1995. Indexed. Illus.
Paper. $29.95. 365 pp. .... Vendor G0011

Landis, John T. *Mayflower* **Descendants and Their Marriages for Two Generations After the Landing**. (1922) reprint 1990.
Paper. $5.00. 37 pp. .... Vendor G0011

Ledogar, Edwin Richard. **Vital Statistics of Eastern Connecticut, Western Rhode Island, South Central Massachusetts**. 2 vols. 1995. Reprint on microfiche.
Organized alphabetically.
Order no. 867-868, $38.00/each or $69.00/set. 540 + 537 pp. .... Vendor G0478

Long, John H., ed. **Connecticut, Maine, Massachusetts, and Rhode Island Atlas of Historical County Boundaries**. 1994.
A beautiful and extremely useful book detailing the changes in county boundaries from colonial times to 1990. 8½" x 11".
Cloth. $92.00. 412 pp. .... Vendor G0611

Massachusetts and Maine Families in the Ancestry of Walter Goodwin Davis. 3 vols. (1916-63) reprint 1996. Indexed. Illus.
Vol. I: Allanson-French. 746 pp.
Vol. II: Gardner-Moses. 717 pp.
Vol. III: Neal-Wright. 732 pp.
Cloth. $50.00/vol., $135.00/set. 2,096 pp. in all. .... Vendor G0010

Massachusetts Secretary of the Commonwealth, comp. **List of Persons Whose Names Have Been Changed in Massachusetts, 1780-1892**. (1893) reprint 1993.
Cloth. $49.50. 522 pp. .... Vendor G0259

Paige, L. **Freeman of Massachusetts, 1630-1691**. Extr. New England Hist. & Gen. Register. (1849) reprint 1990.
During this period, approximately 4,500 men were admitted as freeman; this complete list also gives the source of the data.
Contact vendor for information. 40 pp. .... Vendor G0010

Pearson, Gardner W. **Records of the Massachusetts Volunteer Militia** Called Out by the Governor of Massachusetts to Suppress a Threatened Invasion during the War of 1812-1814. (1913) reprint 1993. Indexed.
Paper. $35.00. 448 pp. .... Vendor G0011

Peirce, Ebenezer Weaver. **Peirce's Colonial Lists**. Civil, Military and Professional Lists of Plymouth and Rhode Island Colonies . . . 1621-1700. (1881) reprint 1995. Indexed.
Paper. $17.00. 156 pp. .... Vendor G0011

Pope, Charles Henry. **Pioneers of Massachusetts (1620-1650)**. (1900) reprint 1990.
Contact vendor for information. 550 pp. .... Vendor G0010

Schweitzer, George K. **Massachusetts Genealogical Research**. 1992. Illus.
History of the state, types of records (Bible through will), record locations, research techniques, listings of county records.

Shaw, H. K., comp. **Families of the Pilgrims.**
Paper. $15.00. 279 pp. .... Vendor G0569
Compiled for the Massachusetts Society of Mayflower Descendants. (1956) reprint 1994.
Contains biographical sketches and genealogies of several generations of Mayflower descendants, as well as an index to their wills and reference information.
Paper. $19.00. 178 pp. .... Vendor G0259

Simmons, C. H., Jr., scr. **Plymouth Colony Wills and Inventories, Vol 1, 1633-1669**. 1996. Indexed.
Book #1608.
Cloth. $59.50. 640 pp. .... Vendor G0082

Southern California Genealogical Society. **Sources of Genealogical Help in Massachusetts.**
Paper. $1.50. 8 pp. .... Vendor G0656

Stachwin, Myron O. **Massachusetts Officers and Soldiers 1723-1743, Dummer's War to War of Jenkin's Ear.** 1979.
Paper. $18.45. xxvii + 282 pp. .... Vendor G0406

Stark, J. H. **The Loyalists of Massachusetts,** and the Other Side of the American Revolution. (1910) reprint 1990.
Cloth. $54.00. 509 pp. .... Vendor G0259

Steele, Chris Ronald Poito. **A Directory of Massachusetts Photographers 1831-1900.** 1993. Indexed. Illus.
Book #1176.
Cloth. $89.50. 704 pp. .... Vendor G0082

Stevens, Cj. **The Massachusetts Magazine: Marriage and Death Notices, 1789-1796.** 1978.
Paper. $10.00. 315 pp. .... Vendor G0561

Stratton, Eugene Aubrey. **Plymouth Colony: Its History and People, 1620-1691.** 1986. Indexed. Illus.
The history and genealogy of Plymouth Colony, with more than 300 biographical sketches of the inhabitants.
Paper. $19.95. 481 pp. .... Vendor G0570

Subject Guide to Records in the Massachusetts Archives. 1992.
Index by Library of Congress subject heading to record series descriptions in the Research Libraries Information Network.
Contact vendor for information. .... Vendor G0647

Thorndale, William, and William Dollarhide. **County Boundary Map Guides to the U.S. Federal Censuses, 1790-1920: Connecticut, Massachusetts, Rhode Island, 1790-1920.** 1987.
Paper. $5.95. .... Vendor G0552

United States Bureau of the Census. **Heads of Families at the First Census of the United States Taken in the Year 1790: Massachusetts.** (1908) reprint 1992. Indexed. Illus.
Contact vendor for information. 363 pp. .... Vendor G0010

United States Bureau of the Census. **Heads of Families at the First Census of the United States Taken in the Year 1790: Massachusetts.**
Cloth, $50.00. Paper, $35.00. .... Vendor G0552

Voye, Nancy S. **Massachusetts Soldiers in the French and Indian Wars 1748-1763.** 1975.
Paper. $18.45. xviii + 220 pp. .... Vendor G0406

Young, Alexander. **Chronicles of the First Planters of the Colony of Massachusetts Bay, from 1623 to 1636.** (1846) reprint 1996. Indexed.
Paper. $45.00. 571 pp. .... Vendor G0011

Young, Alexander. **Chronicles of the Pilgrim Fathers of the Colony of Plymouth from 1602 to 1625**. 2nd ed. (1844) reprint 1995. Indexed. Illus.
Paper. $35.00. 518 pp. .... Vendor G0011

Barnstable County

Brown, G. E., comp. **Gravestone Records in the Ancient Cemetery & the Woodside Cemetery in Yarmouth**. (1906) reprint 1991.
Paper. $8.50. 46 pp. .... Vendor G0259

Brown, Oliver B. **Vital Records of Falmouth, Massachusetts**. (1976) reprint 1993. Book #1403.
Cloth. $22.50. 272 pp. .... Vendor G0082

Cape Cod Genealogical Society. **Dennis Vital Records, 1793-1900**. 3 vols.
Cloth. $100.00. .... Vendor G0620

Freeman, F. **The History of Cape Cod:** Annals of Barnstable Co., Incl. the District of Mashpee. 2 vols. (1858) reprint 1990.
Cloth. $79.00/vol., $149.00/set. 803 pp./vol. .... Vendor G0259

Jennings, Herman A. **Provincetown, or Odds & Ends from the Tip End:** A Brief Historical Description of Provincetown . . . with Thirty-Three Engravings. (1890) reprint 1993.
Cloth. $27.50. 212 pp. .... Vendor G0259

Kardell, Caroline Lewis, and Russell A. Lovell, Jr. **Vital Records of Sandwich, Massachusetts to 1885**. 1996. Indexed.
Cloth. $151.00. xxxviii + 686 pp. (Vol. 1), 848 pp. (Vol. 2),
viii + 276 pp. (Vol. 3). .... Vendor G0406

Keene, Betsey D. **History of Bourne, from 1622 to 1937**. (1937) reprint 1993.
Cloth. $32.00. 20 + 221 pp. .... Vendor G0259

Massachusetts Vital Records to the Year 1850: Brewster. 1904.
Cloth. $33.00. 281 pp. .... Vendor G0259

Massachusetts Vital Records to the Year 1850: Truro. 1910.
Cloth. $29.50. 244 pp. .... Vendor G0259

Otis, Amos. **Genealogical Notes of Barnstable Families**. 2 vols. in 1. (1888, 1890) reprint 1991. Indexed.
Cloth. $40.00. 536 + 291 pp. .... Vendor G0010

Paine, Josiah. **History of Harwich, Barnstable Co., 1620-1900,** Including the Early History of That Part Now Brewster. (1937) reprint 1995.
Cloth. $54.00. 503 pp. .... Vendor G0259

Rich, S. **Truro, Cape Cod: Landmarks & Seamarks**. (1883) reprint 1988.
Cloth. $58.00. 580 pp. .... Vendor G0259

Sherman, Robert M., and Ruth Wilder Sherman. **Vital Records of Yarmouth, Massachusetts**. (1979) reprint 1993. Indexed.
  Book #1402.
Cloth. $59.50. 992 pp. .... Vendor G0082

Smith, Leonard H. **Cape Cod Library of Local History and Genealogy**. A Facsimile Edition of 108 Pamphlets Published in the Early 20th Century. 2 vols. 1992. Indexed.
Cloth. $125.00. 2,066 pp. total .... Vendor G0010

Smith, William C. **History of Chatham,** Formerly the Constablewick or Village of Monomoit. With Numerous Genealogical Notes. 3 vols. in 1. (1909-17) reprint 1993.
Cloth. $42.00. 400 pp. .... Vendor G0259

Swift, C. F. **History of Old Yarmouth,** Comprising the Present Towns of Yarmouth & Dennis. (1884) reprint 1991.
Cloth. $35.00. 281 pp. .... Vendor G0259

Vital Records of the Town of Barnstable and Sandwich. An Authorized Facsimile Reproduction of Records Published Serially 1901-1937 in *The Mayflower Descendant*. With an Added Index of Persons. (1900-37, 1982) reprint 1996. Indexed.
Paper. $31.00. 238 pp. .... Vendor G0011

Vital Records of the Towns of Eastham and Orleans [Massachusetts]. An Authorized Facsimile Reproduction of Records Published Serially 1901-1935 in *The Mayflower Descendant*. With an Added Index of Persons. (1901-35) reprint 1993. Indexed.
Paper. $31.50. 250 pp. .... Vendor G0011

Berkshire County

Boltwood, Edw. **History of Pittsfield,** from the Year 1876 to 1916. (1916) reprint 1994.
Cloth. $43.00. 387 pp. .... Vendor G0259

Brooks, R. R., et al., eds. **Williamstown: The First Two Hundred Years, 1753-1953**. (1953) reprint 1996.
Cloth. $48.00. 458 pp. .... Vendor G0259

Fiske, Arthur D., comp. **Some Cemetery Records from North and South Egremont, Berkshire County, Massachusetts**. Facsimile reprint 1996. Indexed.
Paper. $10.00. 32 pp. .... Vendor G0691

History of Berkshire County, with Biographical Sketches of Its Prominent Men. 2 vols. (1885) reprint 1987.
Cloth. $72.00/vol. 701 + 708 pp. .... Vendor G0259

Hyde, C. M., and Alexander Hyde. **The Centennial Celebration & Centennial History of the Town of Lee**. (1878) reprint 1922.
Cloth. $38.50. 352 pp. .... Vendor G0259

Jones, Miss Electa F. **Stockbridge, Past & Present,** or Records of an Old Mission Station. (1854) reprint 1995.
Cloth. $35.00. 275 pp. .... Vendor G0259

Mallary, R. DeWitt. **Lenox and the Berkshire Highlands**. (1902) reprint 1994.
Cloth. $42.50. 363 pp. .... Vendor G0259

Massachusetts Vital Records to the Year 1850: Alford. 1902.
Cloth. $12.00. 32 pp. .... Vendor G0259

Massachusetts Vital Records to the Year 1850: Becket. 1903.
Cloth. $16.00. 98 pp. .... Vendor G0259

Massachusetts Vital Records to the Year 1850: Dalton. 1906.
Cloth. $16.00. 82 pp. .... Vendor G0259

Massachusetts Vital Records to the Year 1850: Great Barrington. 1904.
Cloth. $16.00. 89 pp. .... Vendor G0259

Massachusetts Vital Records to the Year 1850: Lee. 1903.
Cloth. $29.50. 239 pp. .... Vendor G0259

Massachusetts Vital Records to the Year 1850: New Ashford. 1916.
Cloth. $15.00. 43 pp. .... Vendor G0259

Massachusetts Vital Records to the Year 1850: Otis. 1941.
Cloth. $22.00. 159 pp. .... Vendor G0259

Massachusetts Vital Records to the Year 1850: Peru. 1902.
Cloth. $20.00. 122 pp. .... Vendor G0259

Massachusetts Vital Records to the Year 1850: Richmond. 1913.
Cloth. $19.50. 113 pp. .... Vendor G0259

Massachusetts Vital Records to the Year 1850: Tyringham. 1912.
Cloth. $16.50. 107 pp. .... Vendor G0259

Massachusetts Vital Records to the Year 1850: W. Stockbridge. 1907.
Cloth. $18.50. 115 pp. .... Vendor G0259

Massachusetts Vital Records to the Year 1850: Washington. 1904.
Cloth. $12.00. 57 pp. .... Vendor G0259

Massachusetts Vital Records to the Year 1850: Windsor. 1917.
Cloth. $22.50. 153 pp. .... Vendor G0259

Perry, Arthur Latham. **Origins of Williamstown**. (1896) reprint 1992.
Cloth. $65.00. 650 pp. .... Vendor G0259

Perry, Arthur Latham. **Williamstown & Williams College**. (1899) reprint 1995.
Cloth. $85.00. 847 pp. .... Vendor G0259

Raynor, Ellen M., and Emma L. Petitclerc. **History of the Town of Cheshire, Berkshire County**. (1885) reprint 1992.
Cloth. $28.00. 219 pp. .... Vendor G0259

Sedgwick, Sarah C., and Christina S. Marquand. **Stockbridge, 1739-1939: A Chronicle**. (1939) reprint 1995.
Cloth. $37.50. 306 pp. .... Vendor G0259

Smith, E. Y., comp. **Massachusetts Vital Records to the Year 1850: Sandisfield**. 1936.
Cloth. $19.50. 111 pp. .... Vendor G0259

Smith, J. E. A. **History of Pittsfield, Berkshire Co.,** from the Year 1734 to the Year 1800. (1869) reprint 1990.
Cloth. $54.00. 518 pp. .... Vendor G0259

Smith, J. E. A. **History of Pittsfield, Berkshire Co.,** from the Year 1800 to the Year 1876. (1876) reprint 1993.
Cloth. $73.00. 725 pp. .... Vendor G0259

Taylor, Charles J. **History of Great Barrington, Berkshire County**. (1882) reprint 1987.
Cloth. $53.00. 516 pp. .... Vendor G0259

Taylor, Charles J. **History of Great Barrington, 1676-1882** Extended to 1922 by George E. McLean. (1928) reprint 1992.
Cloth. $59.50. 620 pp. .... Vendor G0259

Vital Records of St. James Episcopal Church, Great Barrington, MA: 1827-1899. 1992. Indexed.
Cloth. $25.00. 114 pp. .... Vendor G0450

Bradford

Kingsbury, J. D. **Memorial History of Bradford,** from the Earliest Period to the Close of 1882. (1883) reprint 1993.
Cloth. $21.00. 144 pp. .... Vendor G0259

Massachusetts Vital Records to the Year 1850: Bradford. 1907.
Cloth. $32.50. 313 pp. .... Vendor G0259

Brighton

Winship, J. P. C. **Historical Brighton:** An Illustrated History of Brighton & Its Citizens. 2 vols. in 1. (1899, 1902) reprint 1987.
Cloth. $47.00. 240 + 222 pp. .... Vendor G0259

Bristol County

Arnold, J. N. **Massachusetts Vital Records to the Year 1850: Rehoboth, 1642-1896**. With Colonial Returns; Early Settlers, Purchasers & Freemen; Inhabitants & Soldiers. 1897.
Cloth. $89.00. 926 pp. .... Vendor G0259

Daggett, John. **Sketch of the History of Attleboro,** from Its Settlement to the Present Time. (1834) reprint 1993.
Cloth. $22.00. 136 pp. .... Vendor G0259

Daggett, John. **Sketch of the History of Attleboro,** from Its Settlement to the Present Time. 2nd ed. Edited by his daughter. (1894) reprint 1993.
Cloth. $79.50. 788 pp. .... Vendor G0259

Ellis, L. B. **History of New Bedford & Vicinity, 1602-1892**. (1892) reprint 1990.
Cloth. $89.50. 731 + 175 pp. .... Vendor G0259

Emery, S. H. **History of Taunton**. (1893) reprint 1987.
Cloth. $89.50. 768 + 110 pp. .... Vendor G0259

Federal Writers Project of Works Projects Admin. (WPA). **(New Bedford) Whaling Masters**. (1938) reprint 1992.
A fascinating look at the whaling industry of New Bedford, Nantucket, etc. Includes a directory of ship captains with home ports and a "roll of honor" of whaling men.
Cloth. $35.00. 314 pp. .... Vendor G0259

Hart, William A. **History of the Town of Somerset, Shawomet Purchase, 1677, Incorporated 1790**. (1940) reprint 1995.
Cloth. $35.00. 247 pp. .... Vendor G0259

History of the Town of Freetown. (1902) reprint 1991.
Cloth. $30.00. 287 pp. .... Vendor G0259

Lane, Helen H. **History of Dighton, the South Purchase, 1712**. (1962) reprint 1995.
Cloth. $35.00. 263 pp. .... Vendor G0259

Massachusetts Vital Records to the Year 1850: Dartmouth. 3 vols. 1929, 1930.
Volume I: Births.
Volume II: Marriages.
Volume III: Deaths.
Cloth. $35.00/Vol. I. $58.00/Vol. II. $16.00/Vol. II. 314 + 576
+ 82 pp. .... Vendor G0259

Massachusetts Vital Records to the Year 1850: New Bedford. 3 vols. 1932 (Vols. I & II), 1941 (Vol. III).
Volume I: Births.
Volume II: Marriages.
Volume III: Deaths.
Cloth. $54.50/Vol. I. $61.00/Vol. II. $24.00/Vol. III. $135.00/set. 544 + 615 +
191 pp. .... Vendor G0259

Massachusetts Vital Records to the Year 1850: Taunton. 3 vols. 1929.
Volume I: Births.
Volume II: Marriages.
Volume III: Deaths.
Cloth. $47.50/Vol. I. $55.00/Vol. II. $28.00/Vol. III. $125.00/set. 475 + 549 +
237 pp. .... Vendor G0259

Massachusetts Vital Records to the Year 1850: Westport. 1918.
Cloth. $34.00. 296 pp. .... Vendor G0259

Our County and Its People: Descriptive & Biographical Record of Bristol Co. Prepared for publ. by Fall River News & Taunton Gazette, with Alanson Borden. (1899) reprint 1993.
Cloth. $115.00. 1,217 pp. .... Vendor G0259

Rounds, H. L. Peter. **Abstracts of Bristol County, Massachusetts Probate Records, 1687-1745**. (1987) reprint 1996. Indexed.
Paper. $35.00. 392 pp. .... Vendor G0011

Rounds, H. L. Peter. **Abstracts of Bristol County, Massachusetts Probate Records, 1745-1762**. 1988. Indexed.
Cloth. $22.50. 365 pp. .... Vendor G0011

Sanford, E. **History of the Town of Berkley**. (1872) reprint 1987.
Paper. $10.00. 60 pp. .... Vendor G0259

Smith, Leonard H., Jr., and Dorothy Marvelle Boyer. **Vital Records of the Town of Fairhaven, Massachusetts to 1850**. (1986) reprint 1993. Indexed.
Paper. $24.95. 175 pp. .... Vendor G0011

Tilton, George H. **A History of Rehoboth:** Its History for 275 Years, 1643-1918. (1918) reprint 1990.
Cloth. $45.50. 417 pp. .... Vendor G0259

Wright, Otis O. **History of Swansea, 1667-1917**. (1917) reprint 1990.
Cloth. $31.00. 248 pp. .... Vendor G0259

Dana

Massachusetts Vital Records to the Year 1850: Dana. 1925.
Cloth. $15.00. 66 pp. .... Vendor G0259

Dukes County

The History of Martha's Vineyard, Dukes Co., Mass. 3 vols. (1911) reprint 1988.
 Volume I: General History. Volume II: Town Annals. Volume III: Genealogies.
Cloth. $53.50/Vol. I. $64.50/Vol. II. $56.50/Vol. III. $159.50/set. 535 + 645 + 565 pp.
Vendor G0259

Massachusetts Vital Records to the Year 1850: Chilmark. 1904.
Cloth. $16.00. 96 pp. .... Vendor G0259

Massachusetts Vital Records to the Year 1850: Edgartown. 1906.
Cloth. $32.50. 276 pp. .... Vendor G0259

Massachusetts Vital Records to the Year 1850: Tisbury. 1910.
Cloth. $29.50. 244 pp. .... Vendor G0259

Essex County

Abbot, A. **History of Andover from Its Settlement to 1829**. (1829) reprint 1993.
Cloth. $29.50. 204 pp. .... Vendor G0259

Allen, M. O. **The History of Wenham,** Civil & Ecclesiastical, from Its Settlement in 1639 to 1860. (1860) reprint 1988.
Cloth. $26.00. 220 pp. .... Vendor G0259

Archives Committee of Gloucester, comp. **Gloucester Town and City Records Guide,** Including Related Material. 1992.
Paper. $19.50. 150 pp. .... Vendor G0259

Authentic History of the Lawrence Calamity, Embracing a Description of the Pemberton Mill, a Detailed Account of the Catastrophe . . . Names of Killed & Wounded, Etc. (1860) reprint 1992.
Paper. $18.00. 98 pp. .... Vendor G0259

Babson, John J. **History of the Town of Gloucester,** Including the Town of Rockport. (1860) reprint 1993.
Cloth. $62.50. 610 pp. .... Vendor G0259

Babson, John J. **History of Gloucester, Notes & Additions,** First & Second Series. (1876, 1891) reprint 1992.
Cloth. $34.00. 94 + 187 pp. .... Vendor G0259

Bailey, S. L. **Historical Sketches of Andover**. (1880) reprint 1987.
Cloth. $65.00. 650 pp. .... Vendor G0259

Bayley, Capt. W. H., et al. **History of the Marine Society of Newburyport,** from Its Incorporation in 1772-1906. With Complete Roster & Narrative of the Important Events in the Lives of Its Members. (1906) reprint 1993.
Cloth. $49.50. 506 pp. .... Vendor G0259

Blodgett, George B. **Early Settlers of Rowley**. (1933) reprint 1994.
Cloth. $47.50. 472 pp. .... Vendor G0259

Blodgett, George B. **Record of Deaths in the First Church in Rowley, Massachusetts 1696-1777**. 1877. Facsimile reprint 1996. Indexed.
Paper. $17.00. 59 pp. .... Vendor G0691

Chase, George Wingate. **The History of Haverhill [Massachusetts],** from Its First Settlement, in 1640, to the Year 1860. (1861) reprint 1996. Indexed. Illus.
Paper. $55.00. 683 pp. .... Vendor G0011

Coffin, J. **A Sketch of the History of Newbury, Newburyport & West Newbury, from 1635-1845**. (1845) reprint 1987.
Cloth. $42.00. 416 pp. .... Vendor G0259

Cole, Adeline P., comp. **Notes on Wenham History, 1643-1943**. (1943) reprint 1993.
Cloth. $25.00. 157 pp. .... Vendor G0259

Crowell, R., and D. Choate. **History of the Town of Essex from 1634-1868,** with Sketches of the Soldiers in the War of the Rebellion. (1868) reprint 1987.
Cloth. $49.00. 488 pp. .... Vendor G0259

Currier, John J. **History of Newbury, 1635-1902**. (1902) reprint 1993.
Cloth. $75.00. 755 pp. .... Vendor G0259

Danvers: A Resume of Her Past History & Progress. (1899) reprint 1991. Illus.
    Contains over 200 pictures of people, homes, businesses, and landmarks.
Cloth. $25.00. 202 pp. .... Vendor G0259

Derby, P., comp. **Salem Inscriptions from the Charter Street Cemetery**.
Paper. $5.00. 22 pp. .... Vendor G0259

Dorgan, Maurice B. **Lawrence, Yesterday & Today (1845-1918)**. (1918) reprint 1992.
Cloth. $32.50. 263 pp. .... Vendor G0259

Dow, G. F. **History of Topsfield**. (1940) reprint 1987.
Cloth. $52.00. 517 pp. .... Vendor G0259

Dow, George F., ed. **The Probate Records of Essex County, 1635-1681**. Vol. I,
1635-1664; Vol. II, 1665-1674; Vol. III, 1675-1681. (1916) reprint 1990.
	Originally published in an edition of only 300, these records are one of the best
resources for early Massachusetts genealogical research. Taken from Probate Court
records, town deeds and records, and Shurtleff's 1854 Massachusetts Bay Colony
Records, these volumes reprint the original wills in full with abstracts of all documents relating to the estates.
Cloth. $47.50/vol., $130.00/set. .... Vendor G0259

Dow, George F., ed. **Records and Files of the Quarterly Courts of Essex County**. 8
vols. (1911-17) reprint 1995. Indexed.
	Complete record of wills, inventories, vital records, court cases, fines, depositions,
etc., abstracted but with all "particulars" needed for research.
	Volume I: 1636-56, 502 pp.
	Volume II: 1656-62, 506 pp.
	Volume III: 1662-67, 534 pp.
	Volume IV: 1667-71, 513 pp.
	Volume V: 1672-74, 501 pp.
	Volume VI: 1675-78, 517 pp.
	Volume VII: 1678-80, 489 pp.
	Volume VIII: 1680-83, 502 pp.
Cloth. $52.00/vol., $325.00/set. .... Vendor G0259

The Essex Institute. **The Probate Records of Essex County, Massachusetts**. 3 vols.
1917. Reprint on microfiche. Indexed.
	Vol. 1: 1635-1664.
	Vol. 2: 1665-1674.
	Vol. 3: 1675-1681.
Order no. 759—Vol. 1, $18.00; order no. 767—Vol. 2, $28.00; order no. 768—Vol. 3,
$24.00. 526 + 515 + 490 pp. .... Vendor G0478

The Essex Institute. **Vital Records of Salem,** to the End of the Year 1849. 3 vols.
(Births, Deaths & Marriages bound together). (1916) reprint 1991.
	Births, A-L: 536 pp., $49.00.
	Births, M-Z: 434 pp., $41.00.
	Marriages, A-L: 625 pp., $59.00.
	Marriages, M-Z: 529 pp., $49.00.
	Deaths, A-L: 412 pp., $39.00.
	Deaths, M-Z: 365 pp., $35.00.
Cloth. $225.00/set. .... Vendor G0259

Ewell, J. L. **The Story of Byfield,** a New England Parish. (1904) reprint 1987.
Cloth. $38.00. 344 pp. .... Vendor G0259

Felt, J. B. **Annals of Salem**. 2 vols. 2nd ed. (1845, 1849) reprint 1988.
Cloth. $54.00/Vol. I. $57.00/Vol. II. 535 + 563 pp. .... Vendor G0259

Felt, J. B. **History of Ipswich, Essex & Hamilton**. (1834) reprint 1987.
Cloth. $35.00. 304 pp. .... Vendor G0259

Floyd, Frank L. **Manchester-by-the-Sea**. (1945) reprint 1993.
Cloth. $27.50. 209 pp. .... Vendor G0259

Gage, T. **The History of Rowley,** Anciently Incl. Bradford, Boxford & Georgetown, from 1639-1840. (1840) reprint 1987.
Contact vendor for information. 483 pp. .... Vendor G0259

Gott, L., et al. **History of the Town of Rockport**. (1888) reprint 1987.
Cloth. $35.00. 295 pp. .... Vendor G0259

Hammatt, Abraham. **The Hammatt Papers:** Early Inhabitants of Ipswich, Massachusetts, 1633-1700. (1880-1899) reprint 1991. Indexed.
Cloth. $30.00. 448 pp. .... Vendor G0010

Hanson, J. W. **History of the Town of Danvers,** from Its Early Settlement to 1848. (1848) reprint 1987.
Cloth. $36.50. 304 pp. .... Vendor G0259

Hoffer, Peter Charles. **The Devil's Disciples: Makers of the Salem Witchcraft Trials**. 1996.
How could a settled community like Salem turn against itself so viciously? The author approaches the subject as a legal and social historian and provides us with a fresh view of one of the most frightening incidents in early American history.
Cloth. $29.95. 279 pp. .... Vendor G0611

Hoyt, David W. **The Old Families of Salisbury and Amesbury, Massachusetts**. (1897-1919) reprint 1996. Indexed.
Paper. $65.00. 1,097 pp. .... Vendor G0011

Hurd, D. H., comp. **History of Essex Co.,** with Biogr. Sketches of Many Pioneers & Prominent Men. 2 vols. (1888) reprint 1987.
Cloth. $95.00/Vol. I. $115.00/Vol. II. 957 + 1,173 pp. .... Vendor G0259

Johnson, A. W., and R. E. Ladd, Jr. **Momento Mori:** An Accurate Transcription of the [Memorials] in the Town of Ipswich . . . from 1634 to [1935]. (1935) reprint 1991.
Paper. $25.00. 264 pp. .... Vendor G0259

Kelly, Arthur C. M. **Vital Records of Hamilton, Massachusetts, to 1849**. 1907.
Cloth. $15.00. .... Vendor G0600

Lamson, Rev. D. F. **History of the Town of Manchester, 1645-1895**. (1895) reprint 1993.
Cloth. $47.50. 26 + 425 pp. .... Vendor G0259

Lapham, Alice G. **Old Planters of Beverly in Massachusetts,** and the Thousand Acre Grant of 1635. (1930) reprint 1995.
Paper. $19.50. 133 pp. .... Vendor G0259

Lewis, A., and J. R. Newhall. **History of Lynn, Essex Co.,** Including Lynnfield, Saugus, Swampscott & Nahant. 1865.
Cloth. $65.00. 620 pp. .... Vendor G0259

Lindsey, Benjamin J., comp. **Old Marblehead Sea Captains & the Ships in Which They Sailed.** (1915) reprint 1993.
Cloth. $25.00. 137 pp. .... Vendor G0259

Lynn in the Revolution. Compiled from notes gathered by Howard K. Sanderson. (1909) reprint 1993.
Cloth. $55.00. 503 + 50 pp. .... Vendor G0259

Massachusetts Vital Records to the Year 1850: Amesbury. 1913.
Cloth. $59.50. 600 pp. .... Vendor G0259

Massachusetts Vital Records to the Year 1850: Andover. 2 vols. 1912.
   Volume I: Births.
   Volume II: Marriages & Deaths.
Cloth. $41.00/Vol. I. $58.00/Vol. II. 391 + 575 pp. .... Vendor G0259

Massachusetts Vital Records to the Year 1850: Beverly. 2 vols. 1906, 1907.
   Volume I: Births.
   Volume II: Marriages & Deaths.
Cloth. $41.00/Vol. I. $63.00/Vol. II. 400 + 627 pp. .... Vendor G0259

Massachusetts Vital Records to the Year 1850: Boxford. 1905.
Cloth. $32.00. 274 pp. .... Vendor G0259

Massachusetts Vital Records to the Year 1850: Danvers. 2 vols. 1909, 1910.
   Volume I: Births.
   Volume II: Marriages & Deaths.
Cloth. $44.00/Vol. I. $49.50/Vol. II. 424 + 491 pp. .... Vendor G0259

Massachusetts Vital Records to the Year 1850: Essex. 1908.
Cloth. $15.00. 86 pp. .... Vendor G0259

Massachusetts Vital Records to the Year 1850: Georgetown. 1928.
Cloth. $16.00. 90 pp. .... Vendor G0259

Massachusetts Vital Records to the Year 1850: Gloucester 3 vols. 1917, 1923, 1924.
   Volume I: Births.
   Volume II: Marriages.
   Volume III: Deaths.
Cloth. $79.50/Vol. I. $59.50/Vol. II. $37.00/Vol. III. $150.00/set. 805 + 605 + 338 pp. .... Vendor G0259

Massachusetts Vital Records to the Year 1850: Hamilton. 1908.
Cloth. $18.00. 112 pp. .... Vendor G0259

Massachusetts Vital Records to the Year 1850: Haverhill. 2 vols. 1910, 1911.
   Volume I: Births.
   Volume II: Marriages & Deaths.
Cloth. $36.00/Vol. I. $49.50/Vol. II. 328 + 499 pp. .... Vendor G0259

Massachusetts Vital Records to the Year 1850: Ipswich. 2 vols. 1910.
Volume I: Births.
Volume II: Marriages & Deaths.
Cloth. $41.00/Vol. I. $72.00/Vol. II. 404 + 721 pp. .... Vendor G0259

Massachusetts Vital Records to the Year 1850: Lawrence. 1926.
Cloth. $18.50. 125 pp. .... Vendor G0259

Massachusetts Vital Records to the Year 1850: Lynn. 2 vols. 1905, 1906.
Volume I: Births.
Volume II: Marriages & Deaths.
Cloth. $44.00/Vol. I. $62.00/Vol. II. 429 + 621 pp. .... Vendor G0259

Massachusetts Vital Records to the Year 1850: Manchester. 1903.
Cloth. $34.00. 296 pp. .... Vendor G0259

Massachusetts Vital Records to the Year 1850: Marblehead. 2 vols. 1903, 1904.
Volume I: Births.
Volume II: Marriages & Deaths.
Cloth. $57.00/Vol. I. $71.00/Vol. II. $115.00/set. 564 + 708 pp. .... Vendor G0259

Massachusetts Vital Records to the Year 1850: Methuen. 1909.
Cloth. $36.00. 345 pp. .... Vendor G0259

Massachusetts Vital Records to the Year 1850: Middleton. 1904.
Cloth. $20.00. 143 pp. .... Vendor G0259

Massachusetts Vital Records to the Year 1850: Newbury. 2 vols. 1911.
Volume I: Births.
Volume II: Marriages & Deaths.
Cloth. $43.00/Vol. I. $81.00/Vol. II. 428 + 845 pp. .... Vendor G0259

Massachusetts Vital Records to the Year 1850: Newburyport. 2 vols. 1911.
Volume I: Births.
Volume II: Marriages & Deaths.
Cloth. $43.00/Vol. I. $81.50/Vol. II. 428 + 845 pp. .... Vendor G0259

Massachusetts Vital Records to the Year 1850: Rockport. 1924.
Cloth. $20.00. 120 pp. .... Vendor G0259

Massachusetts Vital Records to the Year 1850: Rowley. 1928.
Cloth. $54.00. 537 pp. .... Vendor G0259

Massachusetts Vital Records to the Year 1850: Salem. 6 vols.
Volume I: Births A-L (1916), 536 pp., $54.00.
Volume II: Births M-Z (1918), 454 pp., $46.00.
Volume III: Marriages A-L (1924), 625 pp., $63.00.
Volume IV: Marriages M-Z (1924), 529 pp., $54.00.
Volume V: Deaths A-L (1925), 412 pp., $43.00.
Volume VI: Deaths M-Z (1925), 365 pp., $38.00.
Cloth. The complete set in three volumes: $225.00. .... Vendor G0259

Massachusetts Vital Records to the Year 1850: Salisbury. 1915.
Cloth. $64.00. 636 pp. .... Vendor G0259

Massachusetts Vital Records to the Year 1850: Saugus. 1907.
Cloth. $15.00. 81 pp. .... Vendor G0259

Massachusetts Vital Records to the Year 1850: Topsfield. 1912.
Cloth. $29.50. 258 pp. .... Vendor G0259

Massachusetts Vital Records to the Year 1850: W. Newbury. 1918.
Cloth. $19.50. 122 pp. .... Vendor G0259

Massachusetts Vital Records to the Year 1850: Wenham. 1904.
Cloth. $27.00. 227 pp. .... Vendor G0259

Merrill, J. **History of Amesbury,** Including the First Seventeen Years of Salisbury to
Separation in 1654, and Merrimac from Incorporation in 1876. (1880) reprint 1987.
Cloth. $45.00. 431 pp. .... Vendor G0259

Perley, S. **History of Boxford,** from Its Settlement to 1875. (1880) reprint 1987.
Cloth. $42.00. 418 pp. .... Vendor G0259

Perley, Sidney. **History of Salem**. 3 vols. (1924, 1926, 1928) reprint 1987.
  Volume I: 1626-1637.
  Volume II: 1638-1670.
  Volume III: 1671-1716.
Cloth. $50.00/vol. 598 + 526 + 508 pp. .... Vendor G0259

Phillips, James D. **Salem in the Eighteenth Century**. 1969. Illus.
  This book covers the period from the time of Governor Phips to the American
Revolution, and represents a complete picture of commercial and social life during the
busy 1700s as Salem rose to its greatest heyday.
Cloth. $30.00. 533 pp. .... Vendor G0600

Pierce, Richard D., ed. **Records of the First Church in Salem, Massachusetts,
1629-1736**. 1974.
  Church records include members, births, deaths, communions, and excommunica-
tions.
Cloth. $30.00. 421 pp. .... Vendor G0600

[Danvers] Report of the Committee Appointed to Revise the Soldiers' Records.
(1895) reprint 1993.
  Contains list of soldiers in the Rev. War, with biographical information; also, lists
of soldiers from War of 1812, Mexican War, and militia.
Cloth. $19.50. 165 pp. .... Vendor G0259

Roads, S., Jr. **The History & Traditions of Marblehead**. Rev. ed. (1897) reprint
1987.
Cloth. $60.00. 595 pp. .... Vendor G0259

Rowley, Records of the First Church.
Cloth. $31.00. 220 pp. .... Vendor G0259

Rowley Town Records, 1639-1672. Vol. I.
Cloth. $32.00. 254 pp. .... Vendor G0259

Stone, Edwin M. **History of Beverly,** Civil & Ecclesiastical, from Its Settlement in 1630 to 1842. (1843) reprint 1992.
Contact vendor for information. 322 pp. .... Vendor G0259

Thresher, Mary G., ed. **Records and Files of the Quarterly Courts of Essex County, Massachusetts; Vol. 9: September 25, 1683-April 20, 1686.** 1975.
Cloth. $30.00. 663 pp. .... Vendor G0600

Townsend, Charles Delmar. **Proprietors Records, Newbury, Massachusetts 1720-1768.** 1994. Indexed.
Paper. $17.00. 101 pp. .... Vendor G0691

Vital Records of Lynnfield, Massachusetts, to 1849. 1907.
Cloth. $15.00. .... Vendor G0600

Vital Records of Manchester, Massachusetts, to the End of the Year 1849. 1903.
Cloth. $15.00. 298 pp. .... Vendor G0600

Vital Records of Saugus, Massachusetts, to 1849. 1904.
Cloth. $15.00. .... Vendor G0600

Vital Records of Wenham, Massachusetts, to the End of the Year 1849. 1904.
Cloth. $15.00. 227 pp. .... Vendor G0600

Wadsworth, H. A. **History of Lawrence,** with Portraits & Biographical Sketches of ex-Mayors to 1880, & Other Distinguished Citizens. (1880) reprint 1993.
Cloth. $24.50. 179 pp. .... Vendor G0259

Waters, T. F. **Ipswich in the Mass. Bay Colony,** Pt. I—Historical, Pt. II—Houses & Lands. (1905) reprint 1987.
Cloth. $62.00. 586 pp. .... Vendor G0259

Waters, T. F. **Ipswich in the Mass. Bay Colony, Volume II.** A History of the Town from 1700 to 1917. (1917) reprint 1993.
Cloth. $84.00. 837 pp. .... Vendor G0259

Waters, T. F. **[Ipswich] Jeffrey's Neck & the Way Leading Thereto,** with Notes on Little Neck. (1912) reprint 1987.
Paper. $10.00. 94 pp. .... Vendor G0259

Wellman, Thomas B. **History of Lynnfield, 1635-1785.** (1895) reprint 1990.
Cloth. $37.50. 283 pp. .... Vendor G0259

Wilson, Fred A. **Some Annals of Nahant.** (1928) reprint 1994.
Cloth. $42.50. 412 pp. .... Vendor G0259

Franklin County

Atkins, W. G. **History of the Town of Hawley, Franklin Co.,** from 1771 to 1887. With Family Records & Biographical Sketches. (1887) reprint 1987.
Cloth. $19.00. 132 pp. .... Vendor G0259

Baker and Coleman, comps. **Epitaphs in the Old Burying Ground of Deerfield.**
(1924) reprint 1987.
Paper. $9.00. 49 pp. .... Vendor G0259

Blake, Jonathan. **History of the Town of Warwick,** from Its First Settlement to 1854.
Brought Down to (1873) by Others. With Appendix. (1873) reprint 1993.
Cloth. $29.50. 240 pp. .... Vendor G0259

Crafts, J. M. **History of the Town of Whately,** Including Events from the First Planting of Hatfield, 1661-1899. (1899) reprint 1987.
Cloth. $64.00. 636 pp. .... Vendor G0259

Howes, F. G. **History of the Town of Ashfield, Franklin County,** from Settlement in
1742 to 1910. (1910) reprint 1987.
Cloth. $45.00. 425 pp. .... Vendor G0259

Kellogg, Lucy Cutler. **History of Greenfield, 1900-1929**. (1931) reprint 1991.
    Volume 3 of set (see Volumes 1 and 2 below, under Thompson, F. M.).
Cloth. $60.00. 629 pp. .... Vendor G0259

Kellogg, Lucy Cutler. **History of the Town of Bernardston, Franklin Co.,** 1736-
1900, with Genealogies. (1902) reprint 1992.
Cloth. $58.50. 581 pp. .... Vendor G0259

Massachusetts Vital Records to the Year 1850: Ashfield. 1942.
Cloth. $33.00. 273 pp. .... Vendor G0259

Massachusetts Vital Records to the Year 1850: Buckland. 1934.
Cloth. $26.00. 208 pp. .... Vendor G0259

Massachusetts Vital Records to the Year 1850: Charlemont. 1917.
Cloth. $23.00. 166 pp. .... Vendor G0259

Massachusetts Vital Records to the Year 1850: Conway. 1943.
Cloth. $32.00. 275 pp. .... Vendor G0259

Massachusetts Vital Records to the Year 1850: Deerfield. 1920.
Cloth. $36.00. 328 pp. .... Vendor G0259

Massachusetts Vital Records to the Year 1850: Gill. 1904.
Cloth. $18.00. 97 pp. .... Vendor G0259

Massachusetts Vital Records to the Year 1850: Greenfield. 1915.
Cloth. $34.00. 299 pp. .... Vendor G0259

Massachusetts Vital Records to the Year 1850: Heath. 1915.
Cloth. $21.00. 142 pp. .... Vendor G0259

Massachusetts Vital Records to the Year 1850: Montague. 1934.
Cloth. $22.00. 167 pp. .... Vendor G0259

Massachusetts Vital Records to the Year 1850: New Salem. 1927.
Cloth. $33.00. 283 pp. .... Vendor G0259

Massachusetts Vital Records to the Year 1850: Shelburne. 1931.
Cloth. $25.00. 190 pp. .... Vendor G0259

Morse, Charles A. **Warwick, Biography of a Town, 1763-1963**. (1963) reprint 1995. Cloth. $37.50. 288 pp. .... Vendor G0259

Severance, C. S. **History of Greenfield, 1930-1953**. (1954) reprint 1991.
  Volume 4 of set (see Volumes 1 and 2 below, under Thompson F. M., and Volume 3 above under Kellogg, Lucy C.).
Cloth. $55.00. 551 pp. .... Vendor G0259

Sheldon, G. **A History of Deerfield, 1636-1886**. 2 vols. (1895) reprint 1988.
  Volume I: Parts 1 and 2, History. Volume II: Genealogies.
Cloth. $89.50/Vol. I. $47.50/Vol. II. $132.50/set. 924 + 477 pp. .... Vendor G0259

Smith, J. M. **History of the Town of Sunderland,** Which Originally Embraced Within Its Limits the Towns of Montague & Leverett. With Genealogies. (1899) reprint 1988.
Cloth. $69.50. 696 pp. .... Vendor G0259

Sylvester, Nathaniel Bartlett, et al., comps. **History of the Connecticut Valley in Massachusetts,** with Illustrations & Biographical Sketches of Some of Its Prominent Men & Pioneers. (1879) reprint 1993.
  Volume I: Hampshire County.
  Volume II: Franklin and Hampden Counties.
Cloth. $57.50/vol., $105.00/set. 1,111 pp. .... Vendor G0259

Temple, J. H., and G. Sheldon. **History of the Town of Northfield for 150 Years,** with Genealogies. (1875) reprint 1987.
Cloth. $64.00. 636 pp. .... Vendor G0259

Temple, J. H. **History of the Town of Whately,** Including a Narrative of Leading Events from the First Planting of Hayfield,1660-1871. With Family Genealogies. (1872) reprint 1996.
Cloth. $42.00. 331 pp. .... Vendor G0259

Thompson, F. M. **History of Greenfield, 1682-1900**. 2 vols. (1904) reprint 1991.
Cloth. $98.00. 1,308 pp. .... Vendor G0259

Hampden County

Burt, Henry M. **The First Century of the History of Springfield:** The Official Records from 1636 to 1736, with an Historical Review & Biographical Mention of the Founders. 2 vols. (1899) reprint 1995.
Cloth. $51.00/Vol. I. $72.50/Vol. II. $115.00/set. 473 + 712 pp. .... Vendor G0259

Chapin, Charles W. **Sketches of the Old Inhabitants & Other Citizens of Old Springfield of the Present Century,** & Its Historic Mansions of "Ye Olden Tyme." With 124 Illustrations. (1893) reprint 1993.
Cloth. $45.00. 431 pp. .... Vendor G0259

Copeland, Alfred M. **A History of Hampden County:** Our County & Its People. 3 vols. (1902) reprint 1993.
Cloth. $52.50/vol., $145.00/set. 505 + 521 + 573 pp. .... Vendor G0259

Green, Mason A. **Springfield, 1636-1886,** History of Town and City, Including an Account of the Quarter-Millenial Celebration. (1888) reprint 1995.
Cloth. $67.50. 645 pp. .... Vendor G0259

Historical Celebration of the Town of Brimfield, Hampden Co. (1879) reprint 1987.
Cloth. $49.00. 487 pp. .... Vendor G0259

Ho, Joseph Carval, III. **Black Families in Hampden County, Massachusetts 1650-1855.** 1984. Indexed.
Cloth. $20.45. 211 pp. .... Vendor G0406

Lovering, M. **History of the Town of Holland.** (1915) reprint 1987.
Cloth. $75.00. 745 pp. .... Vendor G0259

Massachusetts Vital Records to the Year 1850: Brimfield. 1931.
Cloth. $35.00. 336 pp. .... Vendor G0259

Massachusetts Vital Records to the Year 1850: Chester. 1911.
Cloth. $29.50. 256 pp. .... Vendor G0259

Massachusetts Vital Records to the Year 1850: Granville. 1914.
Cloth. $29.00. 236 pp. .... Vendor G0259

Massachusetts Vital Records to the Year 1850: Montgomery. 1902.
Cloth. $15.00. 66 pp. .... Vendor G0259

Noon, A. **The History of Ludlow,** with Biogr. Sketches of Leading Citizens, Reminiscences, Genealogies, Farm History, and an Account of the Centennial Celebration, 1874. 2nd ed rev. and enlarged. (1912) reprint 1988.
Cloth. $63.00. 592 pp. .... Vendor G0259

Peck, Chauncey E. **History of Wilbraham.** (1913) reprint 1994.
Cloth. $47.50. 469 pp. .... Vendor G0259

Stebbins, Rufus P. **Historical Address, Delivered at the Centennial Celebration of the Incorporation of the Town of Wilbraham.** (1864) reprint 1994.
Cloth. $45.00. 317 pp. .... Vendor G0259

Storrs, R. S., et al. **Centennial Celebration of the Town of Longmeadow,** October 17th, 1883, with Numerous Historical Appendices & Town Genealogy. (1884) reprint 1993.
Cloth. $43.50. 321 + 97 pp. .... Vendor G0259

Sylvester, Nathaniel Bartlett, et al., comps. **History of the Connecticut Valley in Massachusetts,** with Illustrations & Biographical Sketches of Some of Its Prominent Men & Pioneers. (1879) reprint 1993.
    Volume I: Hampshire County.
    Volume II: Franklin and Hampden Counties.
Cloth. $57.50/vol., $105.00/set. 1,111 pp. .... Vendor G0259

Temple, J. H. **History of Palmer,** Early Known as the Elbow Tract, Incl. Records of the Plantation, District and Town, 1716-1889. (1889) reprint 1987.
Cloth. $67.00. 602 pp. .... Vendor G0259

Wood, S. G. **The Taverns & Turnpikes of Blandford, 1733-1833**. (1908) reprint 1991.
Interesting, well-illustrated social history.
Cloth. $39.00. 351 pp. .... Vendor G0259

Hampshire County

Barrus, H. **History of the Town of Goshen, Hampshire Co.,** from 1761-1881, with Family Sketches. (1881) reprint 1987.
Cloth. $33.50. 262 pp. .... Vendor G0259

Bicentennial Gen. Comm., comp. **History & Genealogy of the Families of Chester-field, 1762-1962**. (1962) reprint 1987.
Cloth. $48.50. 427 pp. .... Vendor G0259

Biographical Sketches of the Leading Citizens of Hampshire County. (1896) reprint 1993.
Cloth. $59.50. 581 pp. .... Vendor G0259

Boltwood, Lucius M. **Genealogies of Hadley [Massachusetts] Families** Embracing the Early Settlers of the Towns of Hatfield, South Hadley, Amherst and Granby. (1905) reprint 1996. Indexed.
Paper. $22.50. 205 pp. .... Vendor G0011

Carpenter and Morehouse, comps. **History of the Town of Amherst**. Part I, General History of the Town; Part II, Town Meeting Records. (1896) reprint 1993.
Cloth. $89.50. xxiii + 640 pp. .... Vendor G0259

Early Northampton. (1914) reprint 1996.
Cloth. $32.00. 231 pp. .... Vendor G0259

Judd, Sylvester. **History of Hadley**. (1863) reprint 1976. Indexed. Illus.
    Book #1229.
Cloth. $45.00. 768 pp. .... Vendor G0082

Knab, Frederick. **Northampton of Today, Depicted by Pen and Camera**. Edited by Charles F. Warner. (1902-3) reprint 1996. Illus.
    A description in text and many, many illustrations of Northampton at the dawn of the 20th century, including a number of very interesting old business advertisements.
Cloth, $27.50. Paper, $17.50. 96 pp. .... Vendor G0259

Kneeland, F. N., and L. P. Bryant. **Northampton, the Meadow City**. (1894) reprint 1996. Illus.
    Historical sketch of Northampton, with over 250 photographs and illustrations.
Cloth, $29.50. Paper, $19.50. 108 pp. .... Vendor G0259

Lyman, P. W. **History of Easthampton:** Its Settlement & Growth, with a Genealogical Record of Original Families. (1866) reprint 1987.
Cloth. $32.00. 194 pp. .... Vendor G0259

Massachusetts Vital Records to the Year 1850: Middlefield. 1907.
Cloth. $20.00. 138 pp. .... Vendor G0259

Massachusetts Vital Records to the Year 1850: Pelham. 1902.
Cloth. $24.00. 177 pp. .... Vendor G0259

Massachusetts Vital Records to the Year 1850: Worthington. 1911.
Cloth. $22.50. 159 pp. .... Vendor G0259

Parmenter, C. O. **History of Pelham, from 1738-1898,** Incl. the Early History of
Prescott. (1989) reprint 1990.
Cloth. $54.00. 531 pp. .... Vendor G0259

Rice, J. C. **The History of the Town of Worthington,** from Its First Settlement to
1874. 1988.
Cloth. $20.00. 123 pp. .... Vendor G0259

Smith, E. C., and P. M. Smith. **History of the Town of Middlefield**. With Genealogy.
(1924) reprint 1991.
Cloth. $67.50. 662 pp. .... Vendor G0259

Sylvester, Nathaniel Bartlett, et al., comps. **History of the Connecticut Valley in
Massachusetts,** with Illustrations & Biographical Sketches of Some of Its Prominent
Men & Pioneers. (1879) reprint 1993.
   Volume I: Hampshire County.
   Volume II: Franklin and Hampden Counties.
Cloth. $57.50/vol., $105.00/set. 1,111 pp. .... Vendor G0259

Trumbull, J. R. **The History of Northampton,** from Its Settlement in 1654. 2 vols.
(1898) reprint 1992.
Cloth. $65.00/vol., $125.00/set. 628 + 699 pp. .... Vendor G0259

Wells, D. W., and R. F. Wells. **History of Hatfield in 3 Parts,** Incl. Gen. of the
Families of the First Settlers. (1910) reprint 1987.
Cloth. $54.00. 536 pp. .... Vendor G0259

Middlesex County

Bacon, Oliver N. **A History of Natick** from Its First Settlement in 1651 to the Present
Time, with Notices of the First White Families. (1856) reprint 1990.
Cloth. $32.50. 261 pp. .... Vendor G0259

Barry, W. **A History of Framingham,** Incl. the Plantation, from 1640 to 1846. Also a
Register of Inhabitants before 1800, with Genealogical Sketches. (1847) reprint 1987.
Cloth. $45.50. 456 pp. .... Vendor G0259

Bigelow, Ella A. **Historical Reminiscences of Early Times in Marlborough,** and
Prominent Events from 1860 to 1910. (1910) reprint 1993.
Cloth. $49.50. 488 pp. .... Vendor G0259

Bolton, Ethel Stanley. **Shirley Uplands & Intervales:** Annals of a Border Town of
Old Middlesex, with Some Genealogical Sketches. (1914) reprint 1993.
Cloth. $41.00. 394 pp. .... Vendor G0259

Bond, Henry. **Genealogies of the Families & Descendants of the Early Settlers of Watertown,** Including Waltham & Weston; To Which Is Appended the Early History of the Town. 2 vols. in 1. (2nd ed. 1860) reprint 1991.
Cloth. $98.00. 1,094 pp. .... Vendor G0259

Brooks, C. **History of the Town Medford, Middlesex Co.,** from Its 1st Settlement in 1630 to 1855. Rev. by J. M. Usher. (1886) reprint 1988.
Cloth. $62.00. 592 pp. .... Vendor G0259

Brown, Abram English. **Glimpses of Old New England Life: Legends of Old Bedford.** (1892) reprint 1993.
Cloth. $25.00. 199 pp. .... Vendor G0259

Brown, Abram English. **History of the Town of Bedford,** from Its Earliest Settlement to the Year 1891, with a Genealogical Register of Old Families. (1891) reprint 1993.
Cloth. $22.50. 164 pp. .... Vendor G0259

Brown, Francis H. **Lexington Epitaphs:** A Copy of Epitaphs in the Old Burying Grounds of Lexington, Mass. (1905) reprint 1993.
Paper. $19.50. 169 pp. .... Vendor G0259

Bull, Sidney A. **History of the Town of Carlisle, 1754-1929**. (1920) reprint 1992.
Cloth. $39.50. 365 pp. .... Vendor G0259

Butler, Caleb. **History of the Town of Groton,** Including Pepperell & Shirley, from the First Grant of Groton Plantation in 1655. (1848) reprint 1993.
Cloth. $52.50. 29 + 499 pp. .... Vendor G0259

Chandler, S. **History of the Town of Shirley,** from Its Early Settlement to 1882. (1883) reprint 1987.
Cloth. $74.50. 744 pp. .... Vendor G0259

Concord Births, Marriages & Deaths, 1635-1850. (1891) reprint 1987.
Cloth. $50.00. 496 pp. .... Vendor G0259

Converse, Parker L. **Legends of Woburn, 1642-1892**. Now First Written and Pre-served in Collected Form . . . to Which is Added a Chrono-Indexical History of Woburn. (1892) reprint 1995.
Cloth. $27.50. 174 pp. .... Vendor G0259

Converse, Parker L. **Legends of Woburn, 1642-1892. Second Series**. (1896) reprint 1995.
Cloth. $35.00. 252 pp. .... Vendor G0259

Corey, D. P. **History of Malden, Mass., 1633-1785**. (1899) reprint 1988.
Cloth. $87.00. 870 pp. .... Vendor G0259

Cowley, Charles. **Illustrated History of Lowell**. Rev. ed. (1868) reprint 1993.
Cloth. $29.50. 235 pp. .... Vendor G0259

Cutter, B., and W. Cutter. **History of Arlington, 1635-1879**. (1880) reprint 1987.
Cloth. $39.00. 368 pp. .... Vendor G0259

Cutter, William Richard. **Historic Homes, Places, Genealogical . . . Memoirs . . . Families of Middlesex County, Massachusetts**. 4 vols. 1908. Reprint on microfiche.

Order no. 758—Vol. 1, $28.00; order no. 769—Vol. 2, $36.00; order No. 770—Vol. 3, $36.00; order no. 771—Vol. 4, $50.00. 2,026 pp. .... Vendor G0478

Eaton, L. **Genealogical History of the Town of Reading,** Incl. the Present Towns of Wakefield, Reading & No. Reading,with Chronological & Historical Sketches, from 1639-1874. (1874) reprint 1988.
Cloth. $82.00. 815 pp. .... Vendor G0259

Gozzaldi, Mary Isabella. **History of Cambridge, 1630-1930,** Supplement & Index, Comprising a Biographical & Genealogical Record of the Early Settlers & Their Descendants; with References to Their Wills & the Administration of Their Estates in the Middlesex Co. Registry of Probate. (1930) reprint 1995.
Cloth. $75.00. 860 pp. .... Vendor G0259

Green, Samuel A. **Boundary Lines of Old Groton**. 1885.
   Describes the "Groton Plantation," which includes all or part of Littleton, Shirley, Pepperell, Harvard, Ayer, Dunstable, and Tyngsborough.
Paper. $10.00. 103 pp. .... Vendor G0259

Green, Samuel A., comp. **Early Church Records of Groton, 1706-1830,** with a Register of Births, Deaths & Marriages, 1664-1830. (1896) reprint 1993.
Cloth. $29.00. 194+ 64 pp. .... Vendor G0259

Green, Samuel A. **Groton During the Indian Wars**. (1883) reprint 1987.
Cloth. $25.00. 214 pp. .... Vendor G0259

Green, Samuel A. **Groton During the Revolution,** with an Appendix. (1900) reprint 1988.
Cloth. $34.50. 343 pp. .... Vendor G0259

Green, Samuel Abbot. **Groton Historical Series:** A Collection of Papers Relating to the History of the Town of Groton. 4 vols. (1887-99) reprint 1995.
Cloth. $50.00/vol., $175.00/set. 490 + 471 + 489 + 520 pp. .... Vendor G0259

Gross, Elbridge H. **History of Melrose**. (1902) reprint 1993.
Cloth. $53.50. 18 + 508 pp. .... Vendor G0259

Hager, L. C. **Boxboro**. A New England Town & Its People, with Sketches & Illustrations. (1891) reprint 1987.
Cloth. $29.00. 218 pp. .... Vendor G0259

Hallowell, Henry C. **Vital Records of Townsend, Massachusetts**. 1992.
Cloth. $43.50. 588 + x pp. .... Vendor G0406

Hazen, H. A. **History of Billerica**. (1883) reprint 1987.
Cloth. $51.00. 513 pp. .... Vendor G0259

Hodgman, E. A. **History of the Town of Westford in the County of Middlesex, 1659-1883**. (1883) reprint 1987.
Cloth. $49.75. 494 pp. .... Vendor G0259

Hudson, Alfred S. **Annals of Sudbury, Wayland & Maynard, Middlesex Co**. (1891) reprint 1994.
Cloth. $32.50. 219 + 40 pp. .... Vendor G0259

Hudson, Alfred S. **History of Sudbury, 1638-1889**. (1889) reprint 1992.
Cloth. $66.00. 660 pp. .... Vendor G0259

Hudson, C. **History of the Town of Lexington, Middlesex Co.,** from Its First Settlement to 1868, with a Genealogical Register. (1868) reprint 1987.
Cloth. $74.00. 745 pp. .... Vendor G0259

Hudson, C. **History of the Town of Lexington, Middlesex Co.,** from Its First Settlement to 1868. Revised & Continued to 1912 by the Lexington Hist. Soc. 2 vols. (1913) reprint 1987.
Cloth. $59.00/History. $89.75/Genealogy. 583 + 897 pp. .... Vendor G0259

Hudson, Charles. **History of the Town of Marlborough, Middlesex Co.,** from Its First Settlement in 1657 to 1861, with a Brief Sketch of the Town of Northborough and a Genealogy of the Families in Marlborough to 1800. (1862) reprint 1995.
Cloth. $59.50. 544 pp. .... Vendor G0259

Illustrated History of Lowell & Vicinity. Done by "Divers Hands," published by the Courier Citizen. (1897) reprint 1993.
Cloth. $87.50. 881 pp. .... Vendor G0259

Jackson, F. **History of the Early Settlement of Newton from 1629-1800, with a Genealogical Register**. (1854) reprint 1987.
Cloth. $58.00. 555 pp. .... Vendor G0259

Johnson, Edward F. **Woburn Records of Births, Deaths, and Marriages from 1640-1873**. 1890. Reprint on microfiche.
Order nos. 498-501, $50.00. .... Vendor G0478

Johnson, Edward F. **Woburn Marriages, from 1640 to 1873** Pt. III of Woburn Records of Births, Deaths and Marriages. (1891) reprint 1996.
Cloth. $39.00. 338 pp. .... Vendor G0259

Lexington. Record of Births, Marriages & Deaths to Jan. 1, 1898. Pt. I: From Earliest Records to End of 1853. Pt. II: From 1854 to End of 1897.
Cloth. $28.00/Pt. I. $33.00/Pt. II. 213 + 269 pp. .... Vendor G0259

Littleton. From the Earliest Records in the Town Books, Begun in 1715. Births & Deaths; Some Marriages.
   Index to book available separately for $18.00.
Cloth. $54.00. 542 pp. .... Vendor G0259

Marlborough Burial Ground Inscriptions: Old Common, Spring Hill & Brigham Cemeteries. (1908) reprint 1987.
Cloth. $29.00. 218 pp. .... Vendor G0259

Massachusetts Vital Records to the Year 1850: Acton. 1923.
Cloth. $36.00. 311 pp. .... Vendor G0259

Massachusetts Vital Records to the Year 1850: Arlington. 1904.
Cloth. $22.50. 162 pp. .... Vendor G0259

Massachusetts Vital Records to the Year 1850: Bedford. 1903.
Cloth. $23.00. 141 pp. .... Vendor G0259

Massachusetts Vital Records to the Year 1850: Billerica. 1908.
Cloth. $41.00. 405 pp. .... Vendor G0259

Massachusetts Vital Records to the Year 1850: Boxboro. 1915.
Cloth. $15.00. 78 pp. .... Vendor G0259

Massachusetts Vital Records to the Year 1850: Burlington. 1915.
Cloth. $18.00. 100 pp. .... Vendor G0259

Massachusetts Vital Records to the Year 1850: Cambridge. 2 vols. 1914.
Volume I: Births.
Volume II: Marriages & Deaths.
Cloth. $91.00/Vol. I. $79.50/Vol. II. 936 + 806 pp. .... Vendor G0259

Massachusetts Vital Records to the Year 1850: Carlisle. 1918.
Cloth. $20.00. 100 pp. .... Vendor G0259

Massachusetts Vital Records to the Year 1850: Chelmsford. 1914.
Cloth. $47.00. 460 pp. .... Vendor G0259

Massachusetts Vital Records to the Year 1850: Dracut. 1907.
Cloth. $32.00. 302 pp. .... Vendor G0259

Massachusetts Vital Records to the Year 1850: Dunstable. 1913.
Cloth. $29.50. 238 pp. .... Vendor G0259

Massachusetts Vital Records to the Year 1850: Framingham. 1911.
Cloth. $48.00. 474 pp. .... Vendor G0259

Massachusetts Vital Records to the Year 1850: Groton. 2 vols. 1926, 1927.
Volume I: Births.
Volume II: Marriages & Deaths.
Cloth. $32.50/Vol. I. $33.50/Vol. II. 271 + 284 pp. .... Vendor G0259

Massachusetts Vital Records to the Year 1850: Holliston. 1908.
Cloth. $39.00. 358 pp. .... Vendor G0259

Massachusetts Vital Records to the Year 1850: Hopkinton. 1911.
Cloth. $47.00. 462 pp. .... Vendor G0259

Massachusetts Vital Records to the Year 1850: Lincoln. 1908.
Cloth. $24.00. 179 pp. .... Vendor G0259

Massachusetts Vital Records to the Year 1850: Lowell. 4 vols. 1930.
Volume I: Births. $41.00.
Volume II: Marriages A-L. $55.00.
Volume III: Marriages M-Z. $43.00.
Volume IV: Deaths. $35.00.
Cloth. $159.00/set. 404 + 543 + 427 + 324 pp. .... Vendor G0259

Massachusetts Vital Records to the Year 1850: Malden. 1903.
Cloth. $39.50. 393 pp. .... Vendor G0259

Massachusetts Vital Records to the Year 1850: Marlborough. 1908.
Cloth. $41.00. 404 pp. .... Vendor G0259

Massachusetts Vital Records to the Year 1850: Medford. 1907.
Cloth. $47.00. 469 pp. .... Vendor G0259

Massachusetts Vital Records to the Year 1850: Natick. 1910.
Cloth. $29.50. 249 pp. .... Vendor G0259

Massachusetts Vital Records to the Year 1850: Newton. 1905.
Cloth. $53.00. 521 pp. .... Vendor G0259

Massachusetts Vital Records to the Year 1850: Reading. 1912.
Cloth. $59.00. 586 pp. .... Vendor G0259

Massachusetts Vital Records to the Year 1850: Sherborn. 1911.
Cloth. $27.00. 229 pp. .... Vendor G0259

Massachusetts Vital Records to the Year 1850: Shirley. 1918.
Cloth. $26.00. 211 pp. .... Vendor G0259

Massachusetts Vital Records to the Year 1850: Stoneham. 1918.
Cloth. $25.00. 191 pp. .... Vendor G0259

Massachusetts Vital Records to the Year 1850: Stow. 1911.
Cloth. $32.00. 270 pp. .... Vendor G0259

Massachusetts Vital Records to the Year 1850: Sudbury. 1903.
Cloth. $36.00. 332 pp. .... Vendor G0259

Massachusetts Vital Records to the Year 1850: Tewksbury. 1912.
Cloth. $29.50. 246 pp. .... Vendor G0259

Massachusetts Vital Records to the Year 1850: Tyngsboro. 1912.
Cloth. $19.00. 119 pp. .... Vendor G0259

Massachusetts Vital Records to the Year 1850: Wakefield. 1912.
Cloth. $36.00. 341 pp. .... Vendor G0259

Massachusetts Vital Records to the Year 1850: Waltham. 1904.
Cloth. $34.00. 298 pp. .... Vendor G0259

Massachusetts Vital Records to the Year 1850: Westford. 1915.
Cloth. $35.00. 325 pp. .... Vendor G0259

Morse, Abner. **Genealogical Register of the Inhabitants & History of Sherborn & Holliston.** (1856) reprint 1993.
Cloth. $37.50. 347 pp. .... Vendor G0259

Nason, E. **A History of the Town of Dunstable,** from Its Earliest Settlement to the Year 1873. (1877) reprint 1987.
Cloth. $37.00. 316 pp. .... Vendor G0259

Paige, Lucius R. **History of Cambridge, 1630-1877,** with a Genealogical Register. (1877) reprint 1995.
Cloth. $77.00. Genealogies only: 251 pp., paper, $32.50. 731 pp. .... Vendor G0259

Peirce, Mary F., ed. **Town of Weston** Births, Deaths, & Marriages,1707-1850; Gravestones, 1703-1900; Church Records, 1709-1825. With Appendix & Addenda. (1901) reprint 1993.
Cloth. $65.00. 649 pp. .... Vendor G0259

Plimton, Oakes. **Stories of Early 20th Century Life**. 1992. Illus.
   Book #1388.
Cloth. $12.00. 192 pp. .... Vendor G0082

Records of the Town of Cambridge, 1630-1703: The Records of the Town Meetings and the Selectmen, Comprising All of the First Volume of Records and Being Volume II of the Printed Records of the Town. (1901) reprint 1996.
Cloth. $42.00. 397 pp. .... Vendor G0259

Ritter, Priscilla, and Thelma Fleishman. **Newton, Massachusetts, 1679-1779: A Biographical Directory**. 1982.
Paper. $15.45. 152 pp. .... Vendor G0406

Sawtelle, Ithamar B. **History of Townsend** from the Grant of Hathorn's Farm, 1676-1878. (1878) reprint 1991.
Cloth. $45.00. 455 pp. .... Vendor G0259

Sawtelle, Ithamar B. **Marriage Records of Townsend, Massachusetts 1737-1830**. Excerpted from the author's *History of Townsend*, 1878. Reprinted. Indexed.
Paper. $7.00. 60 pp. .... Vendor G0561

Service Men from North Reading in the Revolution.
Paper. $4.00. 8 pp. .... Vendor G0259

Sewall, Samuel. **History of Woburn, Middlesex Co.,** from the Grant of Its Territory to Charlestown in 1640 to the Year 1860. (1868) reprint 1991.
Cloth. $65.00. 677 pp. .... Vendor G0259

Shattuck, L. **History of the Town of Concord, Middlesex Co.,** from Earliest Settlement to 1832, and of the Adjoining Towns of Bedford, Acton, Lincoln & Carlisle. (1834) reprint 1987.
Cloth. $43.00. 412 pp. .... Vendor G0259

Smith, S. F. **History of Newton,** Town & City, from Its Earliest Settlement to the Present Time, 1630-1880. (1880) reprint 1988.
Cloth. $86.00. 851 pp. .... Vendor G0259

Stevens, William B. **History of Stoneham, Massachusetts,** with Biographical Sketches of Many of Its Prominent Men. (1891) reprint 1993. Illus.
Paper. $29.00. 352 pp. .... Vendor G0011

Strong, Isabel L. **Waban: Early Days, 1781-1918**. Edited by Jane B. McIntire. (1944) reprint 1995.
Cloth. $39.00. 294 pp. .... Vendor G0259

Temple, Josiah Howard. **History of Framingham, Massachusetts**. (1887) reprint 1988. Indexed. Illus.
   Book #1228.
Cloth. $55.00. 810 pp. .... Vendor G0082

Vital Records of Westford to the End of the Year 1849. (1915) reprint 1991.
Cloth. $34.00. 325 pp. .... Vendor G0259

Walcott, Charles H. **Concord in the Colonial Period,** Being a History of the Town of
Concord from Earliest Settlement to the Overthrow of the Andros Government, 1685-
1689. (1884) reprint 1993.
Cloth. $25.00. 186 pp. .... Vendor G0259

Nantucket County

Farnham, Joseph E. C. **Fascinating Old Town on the Island in the Sea:** Brief Historical Data & Memories of My Boyhood Days in Nantucket. 2nd ed. (1923) reprint
1992.
Cloth. $36.00. 319 pp. .... Vendor G0259

Hinchman, Lydia S. **The Early Settlers of Nantucket,** Their Associates and Descendants. (1896) reprint 1993.
Contact vendor for information. 330 pp. .... Vendor G0011

Macy, Obed, with William C. Macy. **History of Nantucket,** Being a Compendious
Acct. of the First Settlement of the Island by the English, Together with the Rise and
Progress of the Whale Fishery, and Other Historical Facts . . . (1880) reprint 1994.
Cloth. $39.50. 313 pp. .... Vendor G0259

Massachusetts Vital Records to the Year 1850: Nantucket. 5 vols. 1925-28.
    Volume I: Births A-F, 520 pp., $52.00.
    Volume II: Births G-Z, 643 pp., $64.00.
    Volume III: Marriages A-G, 566 pp., $57.00.
    Volume IV: Marriages H-Z, 543 pp., $55.00.
    Volume V: Deaths, 626 pp., $63.00.
Cloth. $250.00/set. .... Vendor G0259

Starbuck, Alexander. **The History of Nantucket County, Island & Town,** Including
Genealogies of the First Settlers. (1924) reprint 1992.
Cloth. $75.00. 871 pp. .... Vendor G0259

Norfolk County

Bates, S. A., ed. **Records of the Town of Braintree, 1640-1793**. (1886) reprint 1988.
    Includes government and vital records.
Cloth. $94.00. 939 pp. .... Vendor G0259

Bigelow, W. Victor. **A Narrative History of the Town of Cohasset**. (1898) reprint
1992.
Cloth. $56.50. 561 pp. .... Vendor G0259

Chamberlain, George Walter. **Genealogies of the Early Families of Weymouth,
Massachusetts**. (1923) reprint 1984.
Cloth. $34.00. 846 pp. .... Vendor G0011

Clark, G. K. **History of Needham, Mass., 1711-1911,** Including West Needham, now Wellesley, to Its Deparation in 1881 with Some References to Its Affairs to 1911. (1913) reprint 1988.
Cloth. $75.00. 746 pp. .... Vendor G0259

Davenport, G. L., et al., comps. **Genealogies of the Families of Cohasset.** (1909) reprint 1993.
Supplement to *A Narrative History of the Town of Cohasset* (see Bigelow, W. Victor).
Cloth. $65.00. 631 pp. .... Vendor G0259

Davenport, George Lyman, and Elizabeth Osgood Davenport. **The Genealogies of the Families of Cohasset Massachusetts.** (1909) reprint 1984. Illus.
Book #1227.
Cloth. $55.00. 707 pp. .... Vendor G0082

de Lue, Willard. **The Story of Walpole, 1724-1924:** A Narrative History. (1925) reprint 1993.
Cloth. $39.50. vii + 374 pp. .... Vendor G0259

(Needham) **Epitaphs from Graveyards,** in Wellesley, No. Natick, & St. Mary's Churchyards in Newton Lower Falls, with Genealogical & Biographical Notes. (1900) reprint 1993.
Paper. $24.00. 241 pp. .... Vendor G0259

Hanson, Robert B. **Dedham, 1635-1890:** "Examples of Things Past." With 1996 Index. (1976) reprint 1996.
Cloth. $39.00. 250 + 23 pp. .... Vendor G0259

History of the Town of Franklin, from Its Settlement to the Completion of Its 1st Century. (1878) reprint 1987.
Cloth. $33.00. 263 pp. .... Vendor G0259

Hurd, D. H., comp. **The History of Norfolk Co.,** with Biogr. Sketches of Many of Its Pioneers & Prominent Men. (1884) reprint 1987.
Cloth. $99.00. 1,001 pp. .... Vendor G0259

Jameson, E. O. **Biographical Sketches of Prominent Persons** & the Genealogical Records of Many Early & Other Families in Medway, 1713-1886. (1886) reprint 1987.
Cloth. $28.00. 208 pp. .... Vendor G0259

Lewis, I. N. **A History of Walpole, from Its Earliest Times.** (1905) reprint 1987.
Cloth. $25.00. 217 pp. .... Vendor G0259

Mann, Herman. **Historical Annals of Dedham,** from Its Settlement in 1635 to 1847. (1847) reprint 1994.
Paper. $22.50. 136 pp. .... Vendor G0259

Massachusetts Vital Records to the Year 1850: Brookline. 1929.
Cloth. $29.50. 244 pp. .... Vendor G0259

Massachusetts Vital Records to the Year 1850: Cohasset. 1916.
Cloth. $29.00. 237 pp. .... Vendor G0259

Massachusetts Vital Records to the Year 1850: Dedham Town Records. 2 vols. 1886-88.
Includes births, baptisms, marriages, deaths, and miscellaneous records.
Cloth. $64.50. 286 + 347 pp. .... Vendor G0259

Massachusetts Vital Records to the Year 1850: Dover. 1908.
Cloth. $17.00. 107 pp. .... Vendor G0259

Massachusetts Vital Records to the Year 1850: Foxborough. 1911.
Cloth. $31.00. 249 pp. .... Vendor G0259

Massachusetts Vital Records to the Year 1850: Medfield. 1903.
Cloth. $29.50. 243 pp. .... Vendor G0259

Massachusetts Vital Records to the Year 1850: Medway. 1909.
Cloth. $38.00. 345 pp. .... Vendor G0259

Massachusetts Vital Records to the Year 1850: Sharon. 1909.
Cloth. $25.00. 193 pp. .... Vendor G0259

Massachusetts Vital Records to the Year 1850: Walpole. 1902.
Cloth. $26.50. 216 pp. .... Vendor G0259

Massachusetts Vital Records to the Year 1850: Weymouth. 2 vols. 1910.
Volume I: Births.
Volume II: Marriages & Deaths.
Cloth. $38.00/Vol. I. $39.50/Vol. II. 359 + 376 pp. .... Vendor G0259

Massachusetts Vital Records to the Year 1850: Wrentham. 2 vols. 1910.
Volume I: Births.
Volume II: Marriages & Deaths.
Cloth. $28.50/Vol. I. $52.00/Vol. II. 237 + 518 pp. .... Vendor G0259

Pattee, W. S. **A History of Old Braintree & Quincy,** with a Sketch of Randolph & Holbrook. (1878) reprint 1990.
Cloth. $66.00. 660 pp. .... Vendor G0259

Smith, F. **Dover Farms,** in Which Is Traced the Development of the Territory from the First Settlement in 1640 to 1900. (1914) reprint 1993.
Cloth. $22.50. 160 pp. .... Vendor G0259

Smith, F. **The Genealogical History of Dover,** Tracing All Families Previous to 1850 & Many Families That Have Lived in the Town Since. (1917) reprint 1987.
Cloth. $30.00. 298 pp. .... Vendor G0259

Smith, F. **A Narrative History of Dover** as a Precinct, Parish, District & Town. (1897) reprint 1987.
Cloth. $40.00. 354 pp. .... Vendor G0259

Teele, A. K., ed. **The History of Milton, 1640-1887**. (1887) reprint 1987.
Cloth. $68.00. 668 pp. .... Vendor G0259

Tilden, W. S. **History of the Town of Medfield, 1650-1886,** with Gen. of the Families That Held Real Estate or Made Any Considerate Stay in the Town During the First 2 Centuries. (1887) reprint 1987.
Cloth. $58.00. 556 pp. .... Vendor G0259

Weymouth Historical Society. **History of Weymouth**. 2 vols. in 1. (1923) reprint 1993.
Cloth. $97.50. 996 pp. .... Vendor G0259

Woods, H. F. **Historical Sketches of Brookline**. (1874) reprint 2988.
Cloth. $43.00. 431 pp. .... Vendor G0259

Plymouth County

Bailey, Frederic W. **Early Massachusetts Marriages Prior to 1800**. 3 vols. in 1. [Bound With] Plymouth County Marriages, 1692-1746. (1897, 1914) reprint 1996. Indexed.
Cloth. $40.00. 661 pp. .... Vendor G0010

Barry, John S. **Historical Sketches of the Town of Hanover,** with Family Genealogies. (1853) reprint 1993.
Cloth. $46.50. 448 pp. .... Vendor G0259

Bradford, Laurence. **Historic Duxbury in Plymouth County**. (1902) reprint 1993.
Cloth. $21.00. 128 pp. .... Vendor G0259

Briggs, L. V. **Hanover**. First Congregational Church & Cemetery Records, 1727-1895. (1895) reprint 1987.
Cloth. $23.00. 216 pp. .... Vendor G0259

Davis, W. T. **Genealogical Register of Plymouth Families**. Part II of Ancient Landmarks of Plymouth. (1889) reprint 1994.
Contact vendor for information. 363 pp. .... Vendor G0010

Davis, William T., ed. **Records of the Town of Plymouth [1636-1705, 1705-1743, 1743-1783]**. Published By Order of the Town. In Three Volumes. (1889, 1892, 1903) reprint 1995. Indexed.
Paper. $75.00. 1,193 pp. in all. .... Vendor G0011

Deane, S. **History of Scituate** from First Settlement to 1831. (1831) reprint 1991.
  About half of the book consists of genealogies.
Cloth. $40.00. 408 pp. .... Vendor G0259

Deane, Samuel. **History of Scituate, Massachusetts,** from Its First Settlement to 1831. (1831) reprint 1995.
Paper. $31.50. 408 pp. .... Vendor G0011

(Middleboro) **Descriptive Catalog of Members of the 1st Congregational Church**. With Index to Surnames. Ext. from "200th Anniversary of 1st Cong. Church." (1895) reprint 1991.
Paper. $5.00. 16 pp. .... Vendor G0259

Drew, Benjamin. **Burial Hill, Plymouth, Massachusetts:** Its Monuments and Gravestones Numbered and Briefly Described, and the Inscriptions and Epitaphs Thereon Carefully Copied. (1894) reprint 1994. Indexed.
Paper. $25.00. 332 pp. .... Vendor G0011

Dwelley and Simmons. **The History of the Town Hanover,** with Family Genealogies. 2 vols. (1910) reprint 1988.
 Volume I: History.
 Volume II: Genealogy.
Cloth. $32.00/Vol. I. $47.50/Vol. II. 291 + 474 pp. .... Vendor G0259

Griffith, Henry S. **History of the Town of Carver**. (1913) reprint 1991.
Cloth. $40.00. 366 pp. .... Vendor G0259

History of Plymouth County, with Biographical Sketches of Many of Its Pioneers & Prominent Men. Comp. under supervision of D. H. Hurd. (1884) reprint 1987.
Cloth. $98.00. 1,198 pp. .... Vendor G0259

History of the Town of Hingham. 2 vols. (1893) reprint 1992.
 Volume I: Historical.
 Volume II: Genealogical.
Cloth. $77.50/Vol. I. $62.50/Vol. II. 805 + 915 pp. .... Vendor G0259

Hobart, B. **History of the Town of Abington, Plymouth Co., from Its First Settlement**. (1866) reprint 1987.
Cloth. $49.00. 452 pp. .... Vendor G0259

Holbrook, Jay Mack. **Massachusetts Church Records: Scituate 1695-1871**. 1990.
Microfiche. $6.00 each. 19 fiche. .... Vendor G0148

Kingman, B. **History of North Bridgewater, Plymouth Co.,** from Its First Settlement to 1866, with Family Register. (1866) reprint 1987.
Cloth. $73.00. 696 pp. .... Vendor G0259

Kingman, Bradford. **Epitaphs from Burial Hill, Plymouth, Massachusetts, from 1657 to 1892**. (1892) reprint 1994. Indexed. Illus.
Paper. $27.50. 330 pp. .... Vendor G0011

Krusell, Cynthia Hagar, and Betty Magoun Bates. **Marshfield: A Town of Villages 1640-1990**. 1990. Indexed. Illus.
 Contains genealogical material on many Plymouth Colony/Pilgrim families. Includes material on Daniel Webster.
Cloth. $44.00. 244 pp. .... Vendor G0520

Krusell, Cynthia Hagar; assisted by Betty Magoun Bates. **Winslows of Careswell in Marshfield**. (1975) enlarged & revised 1992. Indexed. Illus.
 Pilgrim Edward Winslow and his descendants with genealogical charts.
Cloth. $14.45. 75 pp. .... Vendor G0520

Lazell, T. S. **Death Records from the Ancient Burial Ground at Kingston**. (1905) reprint 1991.
Paper. $6.50. 31 pp. .... Vendor G0259

Lincoln, George. **Hingham, Massachusetts History of the Town**. 1987. Indexed.
 Book #1231.
Cloth. $60.00. 927 pp. .... Vendor G0082

Long, E. Waldo, ed. **The Story of Duxbury, 1637-1937**. 1937.
Cloth. $29.00. 1992 .... Vendor G0259

Massachusetts Vital Records to the Year 1850: Abington. 2 vols. 1912.
Volume I: Births.
Volume II: Marriages & Deaths.
Cloth. $32.00/Vol. I. $41.00/Vol. II. 251 + 381 pp. .... Vendor G0259

Massachusetts Vital Records to the Year 1850: Bridgewater. 2 vols. 1916.
Volume I: Births.
Volume II: Marriages & Deaths.
Cloth. $39.50/Vol. I. $62.00/Vol. II. 360 + 588 pp. .... Vendor G0259

Massachusetts Vital Records to the Year 1850: Brockton. 1911.
Cloth. $39.00. 371 pp. .... Vendor G0259

Massachusetts Vital Records to the Year 1850: Carver. 1911.
Cloth. $25.00. 179 pp. .... Vendor G0259

Massachusetts Vital Records to the Year 1850: Duxbury. 1911.
Cloth. $45.00. 446 pp. .... Vendor G0259

Massachusetts Vital Records to the Year 1850: E. Bridgewater. 1917.
Cloth. $42.00. 406 pp. .... Vendor G0259

Massachusetts Vital Records to the Year 1850: Halifax. 1905.
Cloth. $27.00. 211 pp. .... Vendor G0259

Massachusetts Vital Records to the Year 1850: Hanover Records, 1727-1857. 1898.
Cloth. $35.00. 318 pp. .... Vendor G0259

Massachusetts Vital Records to the Year 1850: Hanson. 1911.
Cloth. $21.00. 110 pp. .... Vendor G0259

Massachusetts Vital Records to the Year 1850: Hull. 1911.
Cloth. $15.00. 75 pp. .... Vendor G0259

Massachusetts Vital Records to the Year 1850: Kingston. 1911.
Cloth. $41.00. 396 pp. .... Vendor G0259

Massachusetts Vital Records to the Year 1850: Pembroke. 1911.
Cloth. $47.00. 465 pp. .... Vendor G0259

Massachusetts Vital Records to the Year 1850: Plympton. 1923.
Cloth. $55.00. 540 pp. .... Vendor G0259

Massachusetts Vital Records to the Year 1850: Rochester. 2 vols. 1914.
Volume I: Births.
Volume II: Marriages & Deaths.
Cloth. $35.00/Vol. I. $45.00/Vol. II. 319 + 450 pp. .... Vendor G0259

Massachusetts Vital Records to the Year 1850: Scituate. 2 vols. 1909, 1926.
Volume I: Births.
Volume II: Marriages & Deaths.
Cloth. $44.00/Vol. I. $48.00/Vol. II. 436 + 473 pp. .... Vendor G0259

Massachusetts Vital Records to the Year 1850: W. Bridgewater. 1911.
Cloth. $27.00. 222 pp. .... Vendor G0259

Mattapoisett & Old Rochester Being a History of These Towns, & Also in Part of Marion & a Portion of Wareham. Prepared under direction of Committee of Town of Mattapoisett. 3rd ed. (1907) reprint 1992.
Cloth. $44.00. 426 pp. .... Vendor G0259

Merritt, J. F. **A Narrative History of South Scituate/Norwell**. (1938) reprint 1987.
Cloth. $24.00. 203 pp. .... Vendor G0259

Mitchell, Nahum. **History of the Early Settlement of Bridgewater,** in Plymouth Co., Including an Extensive Family Register. (1840) reprint 1992.
Cloth. $44.50. 424 pp. .... Vendor G0259

Plymouth County Marriages, 1692-1746. Transcribed from Records of the Court of Common Pleas & Court of General Session. (1900) reprint 1993.
    Contains records not found in Bailey's Early Mass. Marriages.
Paper. $10.00. 54 pp. .... Vendor G0259

Pratt, H. H. **Early Planters of Scituate**. A History of the Town of Scituate, from Its Establishment to the End of the Rev. War. (1929) reprint 1990.
Cloth. $44.00. 386 pp. .... Vendor G0259

Richards, Lysander S. **History of Marshfield,** Vol. II, Old Historic Families. (1905) reprint 1993.
Cloth. $32.50. 247 pp. .... Vendor G0259

Sherman, Robert M. **Marshfield, Massachusetts Vital Records**. 1993. Indexed.
    Book #1401.
Cloth. $39.50. 502 pp. .... Vendor G0082

Smith, Col. Leonard H., Jr., and Norma H. Smith. **Records of the First Church of Wareham, Massachusetts, 1739-1891**. (1974) reprint 1993. Indexed.
Paper. $24.95. 164 pp. .... Vendor G0011

Smith, Leonard H., Jr., and Norma H. Smith. **Vital Records of the Town of Middleborough**. An Authorized Facsimile Reproduction of Records Published Serially 1899-1937 in *The Mayflower Descendant*. With an Added Index of Persons. (1899-37, 1981) reprint 1993. Indexed.
Contact vendor for information. 245 pp. .... Vendor G0011

Thacher, James. **History of the Town of Plymouth** from Its Earliest Settlement in 1620 to the Present Time; with a Precise History of the Aborigines of New England & Their Wars with the English. (1835) reprint 1991.
Cloth. $40.00. 401 pp. .... Vendor G0259

vanAntwerp, Lee D., comp. **Vital Records of Plymouth, Massachusetts to the Year 1850**. Edited by Ruth Wilder Sherman. 1993. Indexed. Illus.
    Book #1406.
Cloth. $59.50. 864 pp. .... Vendor G0082

Weston, Thomas. **History of the Town of Middleboro**. (1906) reprint 1992.
Cloth. $73.00. 724 pp. .... Vendor G0259

Winsor, Justin. **History of the Town of Duxbury, Massachusetts with Genealogical Registers**. (1849) reprint 1995. Indexed.
Paper. $30.00. 360 pp. .... Vendor G0011

Quabbin Reservoir Area

Coolidge, Lillian P. **History of Prescott,** One of Four Townships in the Swift River Valley Which Was "Born, Lived & Died" to Make Way for Metro. Water Basin (Quabbin Reservoir). With Genealogies and Biographies. (n.d.) reprint 1994.
Cloth. $39.50. 288 pp. .... Vendor G0259

Howe, Donald W., comp. **Quabbin: The Lost Valley**. Edited by Roger Nye Lincoln. (1951) reprint 1992.
    A fascinating look at the area of western Massachusetts that was inundated to create the Quabbin Reservoir, now a major water source for Boston. Contains biographical and historical information on the lost towns of Enfield, Smith's Village, Greenwich and Greenwich Village, Prescott, Dana and No. Dana, and Millington. Of special interest are the photographs of many lost scenes and landmarks.
Cloth. $65.00. 631 pp. .... Vendor G0259

Suffolk County

Appleton, William S. **Boston Births, Baptisms, Marriages, and Deaths, 1630-1699 and Boston Births, 1700-1800**. 2 vols. in 1. (1883, 1894) reprint 1994. Indexed.
Paper. $49.95. 661 pp. in all. .... Vendor G0011

Boston Marriages. A Volume of Records Relating to the Early History of Boston, Containing Boston Marriages, 1752-1809. 1903.
Cloth. $71.00. 712 pp. .... Vendor G0259

Boston Records: The Statistics of the U.S. Direct Tax of 1798, as Assessed on Boston, & the Names of the Inhabitants of Boston in 1790 as Collected for the First National Census. (1890) reprint 1987.
    All properties are described and owners listed.
Cloth. $54.00. 537 pp. .... Vendor G0259

Chamberlain, M. **A Documentary History of Chelsea,** Including the Boston Precincts of Wimmisimmet Rumney Marsh & Pullen Point, 1624-1824. 2 vols. (1908) reprint 1988.
Cloth. $74.00/Vol. I. $79.50/Vol. II. $149.50/set. 712 + 793 pp. .... Vendor G0259

Commission of the Dorchester Antiquarian & Historical Society, comp. **History of the Town of Dorchester**. (1859) reprint 1991.
Cloth. $65.00. 671 pp. .... Vendor G0259

Drake, F. S. **The Town of Roxbury:** Its Memorable Persons & Places, Its History & Antiquities, with Numerous Illustrations of Old Landmarks & Noted Personages. (1905) reprint 1987.
Cloth. $48.00. 475 pp. .... Vendor G0259

Drake, S. G. **History & Antiquities of Boston,** from Its Settlement in 1630 to the Year 1770. Also, an Introductory History of the Discovery & Settlement of New England. (1856) reprint 1987.
Cloth. $85.00. 840 pp. .... Vendor G0259

Dunkle, Robert J., and Ann S. Lainhart, eds. **The New North Church, Boston [1714-1799]**. Compiled by Thomas Bellows Wyman. (1867) reprint 1995. Paper. $18.95. 143 pp. .... Vendor G0011

Frothingham, E., Jr. **The History of Charlestown**. (1845) reprint 1987. Cloth. $37.00. 368 pp. .... Vendor G0259

Holbrook, Jay Mack. **Boston Beginnings 1630-1699**. 1980.
Over 16,000 entries identify Boston's first settlers through records of allegiance, church, estate, land, indenture, occupation, petition, residence, or taxes.
Cloth. $35.00. 320 pp. .... Vendor G0148

Joslyn, Roger D. **Charlestown (MA) Vital Records**. 3 vols. 1984, 1995. Indexed.
Cloth. $33.50/Vol. 1. $64.75/ Vol. 2, Parts 1 & 2. 919 pp. (Vol. 1), xvi + 1,231 pp. (Vol. 2) .... Vendor G0406

Knights. **Yankee Destinies: The Lives of Ordinary Nineteenth-Century Bostonians**. 1991.
A fascinating look at Boston and Bostonians that is part genealogy and part sociology. A unique study of 2,808 men of Boston in the 19th century.
Cloth. $37.50. 281 pp. .... Vendor G0611

Kuhns, Maude Pinney. **The "Mary & John": A Story of the Founding of Dorchester, MA, 1630**. (1943) reprint 1991.
Authoritative genealogical study on the passengers of the *Mary & John* and their descendants.
Cloth. $32.00. 254 pp. .... Vendor G0259

Lainhart, Ann Smith. **First Boston City Directory (1789) Including Extensive Annotations by John Haven Dexter (1791-1876)**. 1989.
Cloth. $23.50. 152 pp. .... Vendor G0406

Massachusetts Vital Records to the Year 1850: Chelsea. 1916.
Cloth. $56.00. 558 pp. .... Vendor G0259

Massachusetts Vital Records to the Year 1850: Roxbury. 2 vols. 1925-26.
Volume I: Births.
Volume II: Marriages & Deaths.
Cloth. $41.00/Vol. I. $69.00/Vol. II. 398 + 682 pp. .... Vendor G0259

Note-Book Kept by Thomas Lechford, Lawyer in Boston. (1885) reprint 1988. Indexed.
Book #1106.
Cloth. $49.50. 512 pp. .... Vendor G0082

Porter, Edward G. **Rambles in Old Boston**. Illustrations by G. R.Tolam. (1887) reprint 1991.
Concentrates on the history and buildings of the old North End of Boston.
Cloth. $49.00. 439 pp. .... Vendor G0259

Pratt, William M. **The Burning of Chelsea**. With Numerous Illustrations. (1908) reprint 1993.
Cloth. $24.50. 149 pp. .... Vendor G0259

Rohrbach, Lewis Bunker. **Boston Taxpayers in 1821**. (1822) reprint 1988. Indexed. Book #1101.
Cloth. $25.00. 256 pp. .... Vendor G0082

Simonds, Thomas C. **History of South Boston,** Formerly Dorchester Neck, Now Ward XII of Boston. (1857) reprint 1993.
Cloth. $35.00. 331 pp. .... Vendor G0259

Sumner, William H. **History of East Boston,** with Biographical Sketches of Its Early Proprietors and Appendix. (1858) reprint 1995.
Cloth. $82.50. 801 pp. .... Vendor G0259

Whitmore, W. H. **The Graveyards of Boston**. First Vol.: Copp's Hill Epitaphs. (1878) reprint 1987.
Paper. $12.50. 114 pp. .... Vendor G0259

Whitmore, William H. **Port Arrivals and Immigrants to the City of Boston, 1715-1716 and 1762-1769**. (1900) reprint 1996. Indexed.
Paper. $12.50. 111 pp. .... Vendor G0011

Wyman, Thomas Bellows. **Genealogies & Estates of Charlestown, 1629-1818**. (1879) reprint 1992.
Cloth. $82.50. 1,208 pp. .... Vendor G0259

Worcester County

Ballou, A. **History of the Town Milford** from Its First Settlement to 1881, in 2 Parts. (1882) reprint 1988.
    Part 1, History. Part 2, Biogr. & Gen.
Cloth. $52.00/Pt. 1. $65.00/Pt. 2. 511 + 646 pp. .... Vendor G0259

Benedict, W. A., and H. A. Tracy. **History of the Town of Sutton, 1704-1876,** Incl. Grafton until 1735; Millbury until 1813; and Parts of Northbridge, Upton & Auburn. (1878) reprint 1993.
Cloth. $83.00. 837 pp. .... Vendor G0259

Bill, Ledyard. **History of Paxton**. (1889) reprint 1995.
Paper. $19.50. 121 pp. .... Vendor G0259

Biographies of the First Settlers of Rutland. From History of Rutland. (1836) reprint 1987.
Paper. $11.00. 76 pp. .... Vendor G0259

Blake, F. W. **The History of the Town of Princeton,** in the County of Worcester & the Commonwealth of Massachusetts. 2 vols. 1915.
    Volume I: History.
    Volume II: Genealogies.
Cloth. $44.00/Vol. I. $34.00/Vol. II. 426 + 336 pp. .... Vendor G0259

Centennial History of the Town of Millbury, Including Vital Statistics, 1850-1899. Edited by Committee of the Town. (1915) reprint 1994.
    See *Massachusetts Vital Records to the Year 1850: Millbury* for vital records to 1850.
Cloth. $81.50. 814 pp. .... Vendor G0259

Daniels, G. **History of the Town of Oxford,** with Genealogies. (1892) reprint 1987.
Cloth. $87.00. 856 pp. .... Vendor G0259

Davis, Walter A. **Early Records of the Town of Lunenburg,** Including That Part Which Is Now Fitchburg, 1719-1764. (1896) reprint 1994.
  Includes town and selectmen's records; vital statistics.
Cloth. $42.50. 384 pp. .... Vendor G0259

DeForest, Heman P., and Edw. C. Bates. **History of Westborough:** Part I, Early History; Part II, Later History. (1891) reprint 1994.
Cloth. $52.00. 504 pp. .... Vendor G0259

Draper, J. **History of Spencer,** from Its Early Settlement to the Year 1860, Incl. a Sketch of Leicester to 1753. 2nd ed. (1860) reprint 1987.
Cloth. $34.00. 276 pp. .... Vendor G0259

Emerson, William A. **Fitchburg, Past & Present**. (1887) reprint 1993.
Cloth. $39.50. 38 + 312 pp. .... Vendor G0259

Emerson, William A. **History of the Town of Douglas,** from the Earliest Period to the Close of 1878. (1879) reprint 1992.
Cloth. $38.50. 359 pp. .... Vendor G0259

Emerson, William A. **Leominster Traditions:** Incidents, Anecdotes, Reminiscences, Etc., Connected with the History of Leominster, Mass., & Vicinity. (1891) reprint 1993.
Paper. Contact vendor for price. 99 pp. .... Vendor G0259

Forbes, Harriette M. **The Hundredth Town: Glimpses of Life in Westborough, 1717-1817**. (1889) reprint 1993.
Cloth. $27.50. 209 pp. .... Vendor G0259

Ford, Andrew E. **History of the Origin of the Town of Clinton, 1653-1865**. (1896) reprint 1992.
Cloth. $69.50. 696 pp. .... Vendor G0259

Freeland, Mary DeWitt. **Records of Oxford,** Including Chapter on Nipmuck, Huguenot & English History from the Earliest Date, 1630, with Manners & Fashions of the Time. (1894) reprint 1993.
Cloth. $45.00. 429 pp. .... Vendor G0259

Heywood, W. S. **History of Westminster,** from 1728-1893, with a Biographical and Genealogical Register of Its Principle Families. (1893) reprint 1987.
Cloth. $96.00. 963 pp. .... Vendor G0259

History of the Town of Sutton, Vol. II, 1876-1950. Compiled by the Town Hist. Comm., John C. Dudley, Chair. (1952) reprint 1993.
Contact vendor for information. 634 pp. .... Vendor G0259

History of Worcester County, Embracing a Comprehensive History of the County from Its First Settlement to the Present Time with a History of Cities and Towns. 2 vols. 1879.
Cloth. $139.00. 662 + 710 pp. .... Vendor G0259

Holbrook, Jay Mack. **Massachusetts Church Records: Sutton, Warren**. 1990.
Microfiche. $6.00 each. 11 fiche. .... Vendor G0148

Holbrook, Jay Mack. **Massachusetts Vital Records to 1850: Southbridge**. 1981.
　　Taken from the original town records, this volume alphabetizes births, marriages, and deaths—and usually includes parents or spouse, marriage age and occupation, or death age and cause.
Cloth. $35.00. 312 pp. .... Vendor G0148

Holbrook, Jay Mack. **Massachusetts Vital Records to 1850: Webster**. 1980.
　　Taken from the original town records, this volume alphabetizes births, marriages, and deaths—and usually includes parents or spouse, marriage age and occupation, or death age and cause.
Cloth. $35.00. 333 pp. .... Vendor G0148

Houghton, William A. **History of the Town of Berlin, Worcester Co.,** from 1784 to 1795. (1895) reprint 1992.
　　Contains over 200 pages of genealogies.
Cloth. $59.00. 584 pp. .... Vendor G0259

Lincoln, William. **History of Worcester,** from Its Earliest Settlement to September, 1836, with Various Notices Relating to the History of Worcester County. (1837) reprint 1995.
Cloth. $42.50. 383 pp. .... Vendor G0259

Lord, William G. **History of Athol**. (1953) reprint 1996.
Cloth. $75.00. 745 pp. .... Vendor G0259

Marshall and Cox, comps. **Inscriptions from the Burial Grounds of Lunenburg**. (1902) reprint 1987.
Paper. $11.50. 100 pp. .... Vendor G0259

Marvin, A. P. **History of the Town of Lancaster, Mass.,** from the First Settlement to the Present Time, 1643-1879. (1879) reprint 1988.
Cloth. $79.00. 798 pp. .... Vendor G0259

Marvin, Rev. A. P. **History of the Town of Winchedon, Worcester Co.,** from the Grant of Ipswich Canada in 1735. (1868) reprint 1994.
Cloth. $55.00. 528 pp. .... Vendor G0259

Massachusetts Vital Records to the Year 1850: Ashburnham. 1909.
Cloth. $27.00. 215 pp. .... Vendor G0259

Massachusetts Vital Records to the Year 1850: Athol. 1910.
Cloth. $28.00. 230 pp. .... Vendor G0259

Massachusetts Vital Records to the Year 1850: Bolton. 1910.
Cloth. $27.00. 232 pp. .... Vendor G0259

Massachusetts Vital Records to the Year 1850: Boylston. 1900.
Cloth. $20.00. 124 pp. .... Vendor G0259

Massachusetts Vital Records to the Year 1850: Brookfield. 1909.
Cloth. $55.00. 549 pp. .... Vendor G0259

Massachusetts Vital Records to the Year 1850: Charlton. 1905.
Cloth. $23.50. 169 pp. .... Vendor G0259

Massachusetts Vital Records to the Year 1850: Douglas. 1906.
Cloth. $26.00. 192 pp. .... Vendor G0259

Massachusetts Vital Records to the Year 1850: Dudley. 1908.
Cloth. $34.00. 288 pp. .... Vendor G0259

Massachusetts Vital Records to the Year 1850: Grafton. 1906.
Cloth. $42.00. 377 pp. .... Vendor G0259

Massachusetts Vital Records to the Year 1850: Hardwick. 1917.
Cloth. $36.00. 336 pp. .... Vendor G0259

Massachusetts Vital Records to the Year 1850: Harvard. 1917.
Cloth. $35.00. 326 pp. .... Vendor G0259

Massachusetts Vital Records to the Year 1850: Hubbardston. 1907.
Cloth. $27.00. 226 pp. .... Vendor G0259

Massachusetts Vital Records to the Year 1850: Leominster. 1911.
Cloth. $37.50. 369 pp. .... Vendor G0259

Massachusetts Vital Records to the Year 1850: Mendon. 1920.
Cloth. $52.00. 518 pp. .... Vendor G0259

Massachusetts Vital Records to the Year 1850: Milford. 1917.
Cloth. $39.50. 378 pp. .... Vendor G0259

Massachusetts Vital Records to the Year 1850: Millbury. 1903.
Cloth. $21.00. 158 pp. .... Vendor G0259

Massachusetts Vital Records to the Year 1850: New Braintree. 1904.
Cloth. $22.50. 163 pp. .... Vendor G0259

Massachusetts Vital Records to the Year 1850: Northbridge. 1916.
Cloth. $27.00. 202 pp. .... Vendor G0259

Massachusetts Vital Records to the Year 1850: Oakham. 1905.
Cloth. $20.00. 133 pp. .... Vendor G0259

Massachusetts Vital Records to the Year 1850: Oxford. 1905.
Cloth. $35.00. 315 pp. .... Vendor G0259

Massachusetts Vital Records to the Year 1850: Petersham. 1904.
Cloth. $25.00. 193 pp. .... Vendor G0259

Massachusetts Vital Records to the Year 1850: Phillipston. 1906.
Cloth. $19.00. 121 pp. .... Vendor G0259

Massachusetts Vital Records to the Year 1850: Princeton. 1902.
Cloth. $25.00. 195 pp. .... Vendor G0259

Massachusetts Vital Records to the Year 1850: Royalston. 1906.
Cloth. $25.00. 196 pp. .... Vendor G0259

Massachusetts Vital Records to the Year 1850: Rutland. 1905.
Cloth. $28.00. 255 pp. .... Vendor G0259

Massachusetts Vital Records to the Year 1850: Shrewsbury. 1904.
Cloth. $31.00. 282 pp. .... Vendor G0259

Massachusetts Vital Records to the Year 1850: Southborough. 1903.
Cloth. $25.00. 187 pp. .... Vendor G0259

Massachusetts Vital Records to the Year 1850: Spencer. 1909.
Cloth. $31.00. 276 pp. .... Vendor G0259

Massachusetts Vital Records to the Year 1850: Sturbridge. 1906.
Cloth. $39.50. 393 pp. .... Vendor G0259

Massachusetts Vital Records to the Year 1850: Sutton. 1907.
Cloth. $48.00. 478 pp. .... Vendor G0259

Massachusetts Vital Records to the Year 1850: Templeton. 1907.
Cloth. $26.50. 212 pp. .... Vendor G0259

Massachusetts Vital Records to the Year 1850: Upton. 1904.
Cloth. $25.00. 190 pp. .... Vendor G0259

Massachusetts Vital Records to the Year 1850: Uxbridge. 1916.
Cloth. $43.00. 420 pp. .... Vendor G0259

Massachusetts Vital Records to the Year 1850: W. Boylston. 1911.
Cloth. $22.50. 153 pp. .... Vendor G0259

Massachusetts Vital Records to the Year 1850: Warren. 1910.
Cloth. $25.00. 196 pp. .... Vendor G0259

Massachusetts Vital Records to the Year 1850: Westborough. 1903.
Cloth. $31.00. 258 pp. .... Vendor G0259

Massachusetts Vital Records to the Year 1850: Westminster. 1908.
Cloth. $29.50. 258 pp. .... Vendor G0259

Massachusetts Vital Records to the Year 1850: Winchendon. 1909.
Cloth. $27.50. 223 pp. .... Vendor G0259

Metcalf, John G., comp. **Annals of the Town of Mendon, from 1659 to 1880**. (1880)
reprint 1993.
Cloth. $72.00. 723 pp. .... Vendor G0259

Milford, 1880-1930: A Chronological List of Events for Fifty Years, with Illustrations. (1930) reprint 1993.
Cloth. $29.50. 248 pp. .... Vendor G0259

Nourse, H. S. **Military Annals of Lancaster, 1740-1865**. (1889) reprint 1988.
    Includes lists of soldiers who served in the Colonial and Revolutionary Wars for
Berlin, Bolton, Harvard, Leominster, and Sterling.
Cloth. $42.50. 402 pp. .... Vendor G0259

Paige, L. R. **The History of Hardwick, Mass.,** with a Genealogical Register. (1883) reprint 1988.
Cloth. $57.50. 555 pp. .... Vendor G0259

Pierce, F. C. **History of Grafton, Worcester Co.,** from Early Settlement by the Indians in 1647-1879, Including Genealogies of 79 Older Families. (1879) reprint 1987.
Cloth. $68.00. 623 pp. .... Vendor G0259

Reed, Jonas. **A History of Rutland, Worcester County,** from Its Earliest Settlement, with a Biography of Its First Settlers. (1836) reprint 1992.
Cloth. $22.50. 168 pp. .... Vendor G0259

Stackpole, E. S. **History of Ashburnham,** from 1734-1886, with a Genealogical Register. (1887) reprint 1987.
Cloth. $92.00. 1,022 pp. .... Vendor G0259

Stanley, Dr. Josiah M. **Northborough History.** With 1994 Index Compiled by Christine K. Ellis. (1921) reprint 1995.
Cloth. $59.00. 529 + 62 pp. .... Vendor G0259

Stowe, Rev. J. M. **History of the Town of Hubbardston,** from the Time Its Territory Was Purchased of the Indians in 1686 to the Present. With the Genealogy of Residents. (1881) reprint 1993.
Cloth. $42.50. 383 pp. .... Vendor G0259

Temple, J. **History of North Brookfield,** with a Genealogical Register. (1887) reprint 1987.
Cloth. $85.00. 824 pp. .... Vendor G0259

Torrey, R. C. **History of the Town of Fitchburg,** Comprising Also a History of Lunenburg from Its 1st Settlement to the Year 1764. (1865) reprint 1988.
Cloth. $21.00. 128 pp. .... Vendor G0259

Tower, Henry M. **Historical Sketches Relating to Spencer.** Vol. IV. (1909) reprint 1993.
A variety of biographical and historical sketches.
Cloth. $28.50. 234 pp. .... Vendor G0259

Ward, Andrew H. **Family Register of the Inhabitants of Shrewsbury,** from Its Settlement in 1717 to 1829. (1847) reprint 1991.
Rare early genealogy of Shrewsbury.
Cloth. $35.00. 294 pp. .... Vendor G0259

Washburn, Emory. **Historical Sketch of the Town of Leicester,** during the First Century from Its Settlement. (1860) reprint 1993.
Cloth. $47.50. 467 pp. .... Vendor G0259

Wilder, D. **The History of Leominster,** or the Northern Half of the Lancaster New Grant, from 1701 to 1852. (1853) reprint 1987.
Cloth. $33.00. 263 pp. .... Vendor G0259

Worcester County Warnings 1737-1788. With an Introduction by Francis E. Blake. 1899. Indexed.
Book #1368.
Cloth. $24.50. 128 pp. .... Vendor G0082

Wright, Henry Parks. **Soldiers of Oakham,** in the Revolutionary War, the War of 1812, & the Civil War. (1914) reprint 1995.
Cloth. $37.50. 325 pp. .... Vendor G0259

✌ Michigan ✌

Statewide and Regional References

Atlas of Michigan, Detailed Back Roads.
   This present-day atlas provides the researcher with the detail needed to conduct a proper search. It is the size of a Rand McNally atlas of the entire U.S. 11" x 15½".
$16.95. .... Vendor G0611

Atlas of Michigan, 83 county maps.
   Includes detailed maps of individual counties, all the back roads, streams, lakes, towns, etc. 11" x 16".
$14.95. .... Vendor G0611

Blois, John T., and S. L. Hood & Co. **1838 Michigan Gazetteer.** (1838) reprint 1979.
Cloth. $26.00. 424 pp. .... Vendor G0531

Blois, John T. **Gazetteer of the State of Michigan,** in Three Parts. (1840) reprint 1993.
Cloth. $44.00. 418 pp. .... Vendor G0259

Burton, Ann, and Conrad Burton. **Born in Ohio and Living in Southwest Michigan in 1860.** (1986) reprint 1993. Indexed.
One Microfiche. $5.00. 78 pp. .... Vendor G0094

Burton, Ann, and Conrad Burton. **Finding Aid (Index) for Scrapbook History of Decatur, Michigan 1829-1976.** 1990. Indexed.
Paper. $2.75. 20 pp. .... Vendor G0094

Burton, Ann, and Conrad Burton. **Michigan Quakers: Abstracts of All Known Extant Records of Friends Meetings in Michigan (1831-1960).** 1989. Indexed.
Cloth. $50.00. 601 pp. .... Vendor G0094

Dilts, Bryan Lee, comp. **1890 Michigan Veterans Census Index.** 2nd ed. 1993.
Cloth. $53.00. 321 pp. .... Vendor G0552

Family History Library. **Research Outline: Michigan.**
Leaflet. $.25. 8 pp. .... Vendor G0629

Flagg, C. A. **An Index of Pioneers from Massachusetts to the West,** Especially to the State of Michigan. (1915) reprint 1997.
Contact vendor for information. 86 pp. .... Vendor G0011

Howland, Catherine. **Scrapbook History of Decatur, Michigan 1829-1976.** 1976. Illus.

Compilation of newspaper clippings covering Berrien, Cass, Van Buren and Kalamazoo counties.
Paper. $15.00. 1,531 pp. .... Vendor G0094

Jacobson, Judy. **Detroit River Connections**. Historical and Biographical Sketches of the Eastern Great Lakes Border Region. 1994. Indexed.
Paper. $22.50. 208 pp. .... Vendor G0011

Lewis, Helen. **Southeastern Michigan Pioneer Families,** Especially Lenawee County and New York Origins. Indexed.
A compendium of family information for an area largely settled by New Yorkers.
Cloth. $73.95. 426 pp. .... Vendor G0450

Lewis, Helen. **Southeastern Michigan Pioneer Families,** Especially Livingston County and New York Origins. Indexed.
A compendium of family information for an area largely settled by New Yorkers.
Cloth. $51.95. 302 pp. .... Vendor G0450

Pilon, Robert L. **The Genealogy of the French Families of the Detroit River Region 1701-1936**. 2 vols. Rev. ed. 1987.
Cloth. $48.00/set. 1,487 pp. .... Vendor G0696

Russell, Donna Valley, ed. **Michigan Censuses 1710-1830 Under the French, British, and Americans**. 1982.
Cloth. $17.00. 300 pp. .... Vendor G0696

Silliman, Sue Imogene. **Michigan Military Records**. The D.A.R. of Michigan Historical Collections: Records of the Revolutionary Soldiers Buried in Michigan; the Pensioners of Territorial Michigan; and the Soldiers of Michigan Awarded the "Medal of Honor." (1920) reprint 1996. Indexed.
Paper. $23.00. 244 pp. .... Vendor G0011

Thorndale, William, and William Dollarhide. **County Boundary Map Guides to the U.S. Federal Censuses, 1790-1920: Michigan, 1810-1920**. 1987.
$5.95. .... Vendor G0552

Allegan County

Hallgren, Jeanne. **Casco Township—Bounty by the Lake. The History of Casco Township, Allegan County, Michigan 1844-1995**. Illustrations by Jim Van Oss. 1996. Indexed.
Paper. $19.00. 192 pp. .... Vendor G0749

History of Allegan & Barry Counties. (1880) reprint 1990.
Cloth. $54.50. 512 pp. .... Vendor G0259

Alpena County

Northeast Michigan Genealogical and Historical Society. **St. Bernard Church Records, Alpena, Michigan, 1864-1925: Baptisms 1864-1894, Marriages 1870-1894, Funerals 1870-1925**.
Paper. $15.00. vi + 156 pp. .... Vendor G0692

Barry County

History of Allegan & Barry Counties. (1880) reprint 1990.
Cloth. $54.50. 512 pp. .... Vendor G0259

Berrien County

History of Berrien & Van Buren Counties, with Illustrations & Biographical Sketches
of Its Prominent Men & Pioneers. (1880) reprint 1993.
Contact vendor for information. 548 pp. .... Vendor G0259

Cass County

Burton, Ann, and Conrad Burton. **1860 Cass Co. Michigan Census Index**. (1986)
reprint 1993. Indexed.
One Microfiche. $5.00. 61 pp. .... Vendor G0094

Burton, Ann, and Conrad Burton. **1870 Cass Co., Michigan Census Index**. 1990.
Indexed.
Paper. $10.00. 81 pp. .... Vendor G0094

Burton, Ann, and Conrad Burton. **Charleston Cemetery in Volinia Township, Cass
County, Michigan**. 1993. Indexed.
Paper. $8.00. 15 pp. .... Vendor G0094

Burton, Ann, and Conrad Burton. **Crane Cemetery in Volinia Township, Cass County,
Michigan**. 1993. Indexed.
Paper. $10.00. 52 pp. .... Vendor G0094

Burton, Ann, and Conrad Burton. **Rose Hill Cemetery in Volinia Township, Cass
County, Michigan**. 1993. Indexed.
Paper. $12.00. 30 pp. .... Vendor G0094

Jackson County

Interstate Publishing Co., comp. **1881 History of Jackson Co., Michigan**. 2 vols.
(1881) reprint 1978. Indexed. Illus.
Cloth. $34.00/set. 1,156 pp. .... Vendor G0531

Kalamazoo County

History of Kalamazoo County with Illustrations & Biographical Sketches. (1880)
reprint 1993.
Cloth. $56.50. 552 pp. .... Vendor G0259

Kent County

Baxter, Albert. **History of the City of Grand Rapids**. (1891) reprint 1993.
Cloth. $87.00. 845 pp. .... Vendor G0259

Everett, Franklin. **Memorials of the Grand River Valley**. With Biographical Sketches.
(1877) reprint 1995.
Cloth. $65.00. 545 + 74 pp. .... Vendor G0259

Fisher, Ernest B., ed. **Grand Rapids & Kent County:** Historical Account of Their
Progress from First Settlement to the Present Time [1918]. 2 vols. (1918) reprint
1995.
Cloth. $55.00/vol., $105.00/set. 1,105 pp. .... Vendor G0259

Heiss, Betty L. **Solon Township: Out of the Wilderness**. 1995. Indexed. Illus.
Paper. $20.00. 152 pp. .... Vendor G0750

Lenawee County

Lewis, Helen. **Southeastern Michigan Pioneer Families,** Especially Lenawee County
and New York Origins. Indexed.
   A compendium of family information for an area largely settled by New Yorkers.
Cloth. $73.95. 426 pp. .... Vendor G0450

Livingston County

Lewis, Helen. **Southeastern Michigan Pioneer Families,** Especially Livingston
County and New York Origins. Indexed.
   A compendium of family information for an area largely settled by New Yorkers.
Cloth. $51.95. 302 pp. .... Vendor G0450

Mackinac County

Russell, D., ed. **Michigan Voyageurs: Notary Book of S. Abbot, Mackinac Island,
1807-1817**. 1982.
Paper. $4.00. 56 pp. .... Vendor G0696

Macomb County

Worrell, Donald E., Jr. **Index to 1880 Federal Population Census of Macomb County,
Michigan**. 1981.
Cloth. $11.00. 112 pp. .... Vendor G0696

Manistee County

History of Manistee County, with Illustrations & Biographical Sketches of Some of its Prominent Men & Pioneers. (1882) reprint 1994.
Cloth. $25.00. 154 pp. .... Vendor G0259

Midland County

Imperial Publishing Co., comp. **1897 History and Directory Including Portraits, Buildings, Township Directories**. (1897) reprint 1976. Illus.
Cloth. $19.00. 132 pp. .... Vendor G0531

Newaygo County

Newaygo City Bicentennial Commission. **The First Hundred Years, 1873-1973: White Cloud Area**. (1973) reprint 1995.
Cloth, $29.50. Paper, $22.50. 166 pp. .... Vendor G0259

Portrait & Biographical Album of Newaygo County, Containing Portraits and Biographical Sketches of Prominent and Representative Citizens. (Reprinted without biographies of Presidents of the U.S. & governors of Mich.) Incl. 1980 every-name index by Newaygo Co. Historical Society. (1884) reprint 1995.
Cloth. $51.00. 478 pp. .... Vendor G0259

Thompson, Robert I. **Newaygo White Pine Heritage:** A Pictorial History of the Lumbering Era along the Muskegon River in Newaygo Co., 1837-1899. (1976) reprint 1995.
Paper. $18.00. 91 pp. .... Vendor G0259

Shiawassee County

Han, Lila. **Echoes of Yesteryears: Shiawassee County Schools, Antrim and Perry Townships, 1837-1987 Volume 8**. Indexed.
Paper. $10.55. Contact vendor about earlier volumes. 104 pp. .... Vendor G0751

Han, Lila. **Echoes of Yesteryears: Shiawassee County Schools, Woodhull Township, Historical Records 1837-1962, County Rural School Teachers 1893-1934 Volume 9**. Indexed.
Paper. $10.55. 104 pp. .... Vendor G0751

Harrelson, Helen. **Owosso Michigan A to Z**. Edited by Charles S. Arvis. 1993.
Paper. $45.00. 582 pp. .... Vendor G0751

St. Clair County

Biographical Memoirs of St. Clair County. (1903) reprint 1993.
Cloth. $69.50. 695 pp. .... Vendor G0259

Van Buren County

Burton, Ann, and Conrad Burton. **1860 Van Buren County Michigan Census Index**. (1986) reprint 1993. Indexed.
One microfiche. $5.00. 81 pp. .... Vendor G0094

Burton, Ann, and Conrad Burton. **Anderson Cemetery in Decatur Township, Van Buren County, Michigan**. 1993. Indexed.
Paper. $8.00. 25 pp. .... Vendor G0094

Burton, Ann, and Conrad Burton. **Cuddeback Cemetery in Paw Paw Township, Van Buren County, Michigan**. 1993. Indexed.
Paper. $9.00. 33 pp. .... Vendor G0094

Burton, Ann, and Conrad Burton. **Hamilton Cemetery, Hamilton Township, Van Buren County, Michigan**. 1993. Indexed.
Paper. $14.00. 78 pp. .... Vendor G0094

Burton, Ann, and Conrad Burton. **Harrison Cemetery in Decatur Van Buren County, Michigan**. 1993. Indexed.
  Includes tombstone readings and sexton records.
Paper. $10.00. 56 pp. .... Vendor G0094

Burton, Ann, and Conrad Burton. **Kern Cemetery in Porter Township, Van Buren County, Michigan**. 1990. Indexed.
Paper. $9.00. 31 pp. .... Vendor G0094

Burton, Ann, and Conrad Burton. **Lakeside Cemetery in the Village of Decatur, Michigan**. 1992. Indexed.
  Includes tombstone readings and sexton records.
Paper. $30.00. 234 pp. .... Vendor G0094

History of Berrien & Van Buren Counties, with Illustrations & Biographical Sketches of Its Prominent Men & Pioneers. (1880) reprint 1993.
Contact vendor for information. 548 pp. .... Vendor G0259

Rowland, Oran W. **History of Van Buren County:** A Narrative Account of its Historical Progress, Its People, & Its Principal Interest. 2 vols. (1912) reprint 1993.
  Volume I: History.
  Volume II: Biography.
Cloth. $59.50/vol., $115.00/set. 1,158 pp. .... Vendor G0259

Washtenaw County

Colburn, Harvey C. **The Story of Ypsilanti**. (1923) reprint 1995.
Cloth. $39.00. 327 pp. .... Vendor G0259

Wayne County

Duncan, M. L. **Mt. Elliott Cemetery Burial Records, Detroit, 1845-1861**. 1994.
Paper. $6.00. 76 pp. .... Vendor G0696

Ibbotson, Patricia. **Record of the Juvenile Inmates of the Home for the Friendless 1862-1868, Detroit, MI**. 1995.
Paper. $8.00. 90 pp. .... Vendor G0696

Ibbotson, Patricia. **Reports of City Physicians 1860-1869: Detroit, Wayne County, Michigan**. 1995.
Paper. $12.00. 135 pp. .... Vendor G0696

Jackson, J. N., comp. **The Guide to the First Fifty Years of the Detroit Genealogical Magazine**. 1990.
Paper. $13.00. 196 pp. .... Vendor G0696

 Minnesota

Statewide and Regional References

Andreas, T. **Illustrated Historical Atlas of the State of Minnesota**. 1874. Reprint on microfiche.
Order no. 853, $46.00. 398 pp. .... Vendor G0478

Arnold, John P., D.V.M., and H. C. H. Kernkamp, D.V.M. **"100 Years of Progress." The History of Veterinary Medicine in Minnesota**. 1994. Indexed. Illus.
Cloth. $45.00. 309 pp. .... Vendor G0123

Atlas of Minnesota, Topographical.
This present-day atlas provides the researcher with the detail needed to conduct a proper search. It is the size of a Rand McNally atlas of the entire U.S. 11" x 15½".
$16.95. .... Vendor G0611

Bakeman, Mary Hawker. **Comprehensive Index to AT Andreas' Illustrated Historical Atlas of Minnesota—1874**. 1992. Indexed. Illus.
Cloth. $32.50. 332 pp. .... Vendor G0583

Bakeman, Mary Hawker. **Guide to the Minnesota State Census Microfilm**. 1992. Paper. $7.00. 12 pp. .... Vendor G0583

Bakeman, Mary Hawker. **Minnesota Land Owner Maps & Directories**. 1994. Indexed. Illus.
   Bibliography, covering 1860s-1994, with names of repositories.
Cloth. $23.00. 160 pp. .... Vendor G0583

Banvard, Theodore James Fleming. **Goodenows Who Originated in Sudbury, Massachusetts 1638 A.D.** 1994. Indexed. Illus.
Cloth. $78.50. 952 pp. .... Vendor G0116

Brown, Alonzo L. **History of the Fourth Regiment of Minnesota Infantry Volunteers During the Great Rebellion**. (1892) reprint 1995.
Cloth. $61.50. 592 pp. .... Vendor G0259

Compendium of History & Biography of Central & Northern Minnesota, Containing a History of the State of Minnesota . . . and a Compendium of Biography. (1904) reprint 1995.
Cloth. $84.50. 828 pp. .... Vendor G0259

Compendium of History & Biography of Northern Minnesota. Containing a History of the State of Minnesota. (1902) reprint 1994.
Cloth. $99.50. 1,039 pp. .... Vendor G0259

Dilts, Bryan Lee. **1890 Minnesota Veterans Census Index**. 2nd ed. 1993.
Cloth. $35.00. 141 pp. .... Vendor G0552

Easton, Augustus B., et al., eds. **History of the St. Croix Valley**. 2 vols. (1909) reprint 1996.
Cloth. $67.50/vol., $119.00/set. 1,289 pp. .... Vendor G0259

Edwards, Rev. Maurice Dwight. **History of the Synod of Minnesota—Presbyterian Church USA**. Introduction by Rev. Robt. Jeambey. (1927) reprint 1993. Indexed. Illus.
Paper. $15.00. 64 pp. .... Vendor G0583

Family History Library. **Research Outline: Minnesota**.
Leaflet. $.25. 7 pp. .... Vendor G0629

Finnell, Arthur Louis, Howard Stewart Kushman, Curtis John Oliver, and Charles A. Stuck, Jr. **Minnesota Society of the Sons of the American Revolution Centennial Registry**. 1989.
Cloth. $20.00. 154 pp. .... Vendor G0256

Folsom, W. H. C. **Fifty Years in the Northwest,** with an Introduction and Appendix Containing Reminiscences, Incidents and Notes. (1888) reprint 1994.
   A history of the settlement of Wisconsin and Minnesota, with town and county histories, and biographies of pioneers.
Cloth. $77.00. 763 pp. .... Vendor G0259

Green, Stina B. **Adoptions & Name Changes: Minnesota Territory & State, 1851-1881**. 1994. Indexed.
Paper. $11.00. 34 pp. .... Vendor G0583

Hage, Anne A. **Church Records in Minnesota: Guide to Parish Records of Congregational, Evangelical, Reformed & United Church of Christ Churches 1851-1981**. 1983.
Paper. $10.00. 36 pp. .... Vendor G0583

Hobart, Chauncey. **History of Methodism in Minnesota**. Introduction by Thelma Boeder. (1887) reprint 1992. Indexed. Illus.
Paper. $15.50. 102 pp. .... Vendor G0583

Illustrated Album of Biography of the Famous Valley of the Red River of the North and the Park Regions . . . Containing the Biogr. Sketches of Hundreds of Prominent Old Settlers and Representative Citizens . . . (1889) reprint 1996.
Cloth. $87.00. 844 pp. .... Vendor G0259

Memorial Record of Southwestern Minnesota. (1897) reprint 1994.
Cloth. $59.00. 560 pp. .... Vendor G0259

Minnesota Genealogical Journal.
   Semi-annual publication, record extracts and transcriptions from manuscripts, newspapers, courthouses.
Paper. $14.00. 100 pp. .... Vendor G0583

Minnesota in the Civil & Indian Wars, 1861-1865, Volume I: Narratives & Rosters of Minn. State Regiments, Companies and Batteries. Compiled and edited under the supervision of Minn. Bd. of Commissioners. (1890) reprint 1994.
Cloth. $85.00. Also available as a set with next 2 listings for $175.00.
843 pp. .... Vendor G0259

Minnesota in the Civil & Indian Wars, 1861-1865, Volume II: Official Reports & Correspondence on Battles, Campaigns, Expeditions, Skirmishes, Etc. (2nd ed. 1899) reprint 1994.
Cloth. $65.00. Also available as a set with Vol. I & Index (see next listing for information). 634 pp. .... Vendor G0259

Minnesotans in the Civil & Indian Wars, An Index to the Rosters in "Minnesotas in the Civil & Indian Wars, 1861-1865." Compiled under the direction of Irene B. Warming. A W.P.A. project for the Minnesota Historical Society. (1936) reprint 1994.
   Includes more than 25,000 Minnesotans who participated in both wars.
Cloth. $49.00. Also available as a set with previous 2 listings for
$175.00. .... Vendor G0259

Minnesota's World War II Army Dead. 1994.
Paper. $12.50. 40 pp. .... Vendor G0583

Minnesota's World War II Navy Casualties. 1996. Indexed.
Paper. $15.50. .... Vendor G0583

Neill, Rev. Edward D., and Charles S. Bryant. **History of the Minnesota Valley,** including the Explorers & Pioneers of Minnesota & History of the Sioux Massacre. (1882) reprint 1994.
Cloth. $99.50. 1,016 pp. .... Vendor G0259

Neill, Rev. Edward D. **History of the Upper Mississippi Valley,** Including Explorers & Pioneers of Minnesota, Outlines of the History of Minnesota, Exploration & Development Above the Falls of St. Anthony. (1881) reprint 1994.
Cloth. $74.50. 717 pp. .... Vendor G0259

Pensioners on the Rolls as of 1 January 1883 (Living in Minnesota) with Every Name Index. (1883) reprint 1994. Indexed.
Paper. $15.50. 84 pp. .... Vendor G0583

Pond Brothers. **Early Presbyterian Church Records from Minnesota 1835-1871.** Transcribed by Mary Hawker Bakeman. 1992. Indexed. Illus.
Paper. $13.00. 36 pp. .... Vendor G0583

Strand, A. E. **History of the Swedish-Americans of Minnesota.** 3 vols. (1910) reprint 1994.
Cloth. $115.00/set. 1,147 pp. .... Vendor G0259

Thorndale, William, and William Dollarhide. **County Boundary Map Guides to the U.S. Federal Censuses, 1790-1920: Minnesota, 1830-1920.** 1987.
$5.95. .... Vendor G0552

Warren, Paula Stuart. **Research in Minnesota.**
Paper. $6.50. 29 pp. .... Vendor G0627

Anoka County

Goodrich, Albert M. **History of Anoka County** and the Towns of Champlin & Dayton in Hennepin Co. (1905) reprint 1994.
Cloth. $38.50. 320 pp. .... Vendor G0259

Becker County

Wilcox, Alvin H. **A Pioneer History of Becker County,** Including a Brief Account of Its Natural History. (1907) reprint 1994.
Cloth. $77.00. 757 pp. .... Vendor G0259

Blue Earth County

Green, Stina B. **Index to Deaths in the Mankato City and Blue Earth County Minnesota Directories from 1892-1930.** 1991. Indexed.
Paper. $10.00. 32 pp. .... Vendor G0583

Cottonwood County

Richter, Gary, and Arthur L. Finnell, comps. **Sanborn, Minnesota 1881-1981 Centennial History, Including the Townships of Charlestown and Germantown.** 1981.
Paper. $4.25. 202 pp. .... Vendor G0753

Crow Wing County

Green, Stina B., comp. **Minnesota's Mining Accidents 1900-1920 and Mining Deaths 1889-1990**. 1995. Indexed.
Paper. $16.00. 55 pp. .... Vendor G0583

Dakota County

Curtiss-Wedge, Franklyn. **History of Dakota County**. Volume I of *History of Dakota & Goodhue Counties,* complete for Dakota Co. (1910) reprint 1993.
Cloth. $68.00. 662 pp. .... Vendor G0259

Irish Genealogical Society, Intl. **St. John the Baptist Cemetery, Burnsville, Dakota Co., MN**. 1983. Indexed.
Paper. $8.00. 51 pp. .... Vendor G0305

Neill, Rev. Edward D. **History of Dakota County & the City of Hastings,** Including the Explorers & Pioneers of Minnesota. (1881) reprint 1993.
Cloth. $58.00. 551 pp. .... Vendor G0259

Dodge County

Bowen, Jessie Marsh, ed. **A Chronicle of Claremont Township & Village**. A History of Claremont, Dodge County. (1937) reprint 1988.
Cloth. $18.50. 115 pp. .... Vendor G0259

Douglas County

Larson, Constant. **History of Douglas & Grant Counties,** Their People, Industries & Institutions. 2 vols. (1916) reprint 1994.
Cloth. $51.00/Vol. I. $69.50/Vol. II. $115.00/set. 509 + 693 pp. .... Vendor G0259

Fillmore County

Neill, Rev. Edward D., and Charles Bryan. **History of Fillmore County,** Including Explorers & Pioneers of Minnesota & the Sioux Massacre of 1862. (1882) reprint 1994.
Cloth. $65.00. 626 pp. .... Vendor G0259

Freeborn County

Curtiss-Wedge, Franklyn, ed. **History of Freeborn County**. (1911) reprint 1994.
Cloth. $89.00. 883 pp. .... Vendor G0259

Heideman, Marge. **Every Name Index to the 1895 Plat Book of Freeborn County with Reprints of Selected Maps**. 1995. Indexed. Illus.
Paper. $18.00. 80 pp. .... Vendor G0583

Goodhue County

Curtiss-Wedge, Franklyn, ed. **History of Goodhue County**. (1909) reprint 1994.
Cloth. $105.00. 1,074 pp. .... Vendor G0259

Grant County

Larson, Constant. **History of Douglas & Grant Counties,** Their People, Industries & Institutions. 2 vols. (1916) reprint 1994.
Cloth. $51.00/Vol. I. $69.50/Vol. II. $115.00/set. 509 + 693 pp. .... Vendor G0259

Swartz, Ginny. **Every Name Index to the 1900 Standard Atlas of Grant County Minnesota**. 1995. Indexed. Illus.
Paper. $15.00. 48 pp. .... Vendor G0583

Hennepin County

Atwater, Isaac. **History of the City of Minneapolis**. 2 vols. (1893) reprint 1994.
Cloth. $55.00/Vol. I. $47.50/Vol. II. $97.50/set. 544 + 466 pp. .... Vendor G0259

Dahlquist, Alfred J. **Grave Markers of Hennepin County Vol. 1**. 1981. Indexed.
  Maple Grove and West Osseo townships.
Paper. $9.00. 56 pp. .... Vendor G0583

Dahlquist, Alfred J. **Grave Markers of Hennepin County Vol. 2**. 1992. Indexed.
  Brooklyn Center, Brooklyn Park, Champlin, Dayton, and East Osseo townships.
Paper. $13.00. 60 pp. .... Vendor G0583

Goodrich, Albert M. **History of Anoka County** and the Towns of Champlin & Dayton in Hennepin Co. (1905) reprint 1994.
Cloth. $38.50. 320 pp. .... Vendor G0259

Green, Stina B., and Mary Melissa Lawrence. **Deaths Recorded in Minneapolis City Directories 1887-1900**. 1994. Indexed.
Paper. $26.00. 208 pp. .... Vendor G0583

Green, Stina B., and Mary Melissa Lawrence. **Deaths Recorded in Minneapolis City Directories 1901-1910**. 1994. Indexed.
Paper. $21.00. 116 pp. .... Vendor G0583

Holcombe, Maj. R. I., and W. H. Bingham. **Compendium of History & Biography of Minneapolis & Hennepin County**. (1914) reprint 1994.
Cloth. $59.50. 584 pp. .... Vendor G0259

Hudson, Horace B. **A Half-Century of Minneapolis**. (1908) reprint 1994.
Cloth. $59.00. 569 pp. .... Vendor G0259

Neill, Rev. Edward D. **History of Hennepin County & the City of Minneapolis,** Including the Explorers & Pioneers of Minnesota. (1881) reprint 1993. Cloth. $74.00. 713 pp. .... Vendor G0259

Itasca County

Green, Stina B., comp. **Minnesota's Mining Accidents 1900-1920 and Mining Deaths 1889-1990**. 1995. Indexed. Paper. $16.00. 55 pp. .... Vendor G0583

Lincoln County

Taker, A. E. **Early History of Lincoln County,** from the Early Writings of Old Pioneers, Historians & Later Writers. (1936) reprint 1994. Cloth. $39.50. 352 pp. .... Vendor G0259

Lyon County

Lyon County Minnesota Atlas 1926. 1926. Filmed 1995. Microfiche. $5.00. 1 fiche. .... Vendor G0256

Meeker County

Rosenow, Diane. **Meeker County Cemeteries**. 1993. Indexed.
    Includes 24,000 burials, 2 volumes.
Paper. $32.00. 268 pp. .... Vendor G0583

Mower County

Curtiss-Wedge, Franklyn, ed. **History of Mower County**. (1911) reprint 1993. Cloth. $99.50. 1,006 pp. .... Vendor G0259

Olmsted County

Leonard, Joseph A. **History of Olmsted County,** with Sketches of Many of Its Pioneers, Citizens, Families & Institutions. (1910) reprint 1993. Cloth. $69.50. 674 pp. .... Vendor G0259

Ramsey County

Bakeman, Mary Hawker, and Stina B. Green. **Calvary Cemetery, St. Paul, & Its Predecessors Vol. 1, 1850-1878**. 1995. Indexed. Illus.
    Includes 5,000+ Catholic burials.
Paper. $20.50. 72 pp. .... Vendor G0583

Bakeman, Mary Hawker, and Stina B. Green. **Calvary Cemetery, St. Paul, Vol. 2: 1879-1888**. 1996. Indexed. Illus.
Includes 6,400+ Catholic burials, ethnic parishes.
Paper. $25.50. .... Vendor G0583

Green, Stina B., and Minnie Gray Kendall. **Deaths Recorded in St. Paul City Directories 1888-1910**. 1990. Indexed.
Paper. $19.00. 196 pp. .... Vendor G0583

Hennesey, W. B. **Past & Present of St. Paul**. (1906) reprint 1994.
Cloth. $85.00. 814 pp. .... Vendor G0259

Neill, Rev. Edward D., and J. F. Williams. **History of Ramsey County & the City of St. Paul,** Including the Explorers & Pioneers of Minnesota. (1881) reprint 1994.
Cloth. $67.00. 650 pp. .... Vendor G0259

Newson, T. M. **Pen Pictures of St. Paul** & Biographical Sketches of Old Settlers, from the Earliest Settlement . . . to the Year 1857. (1886) reprint 1993.
Cloth. $77.00. 746 pp. .... Vendor G0259

Williams, J. Fletcher. **History of the City of St. Paul, & of the County of Ramsey**. (1876) reprint 1994.
Cloth. $49.50. 475 pp. .... Vendor G0259

Redwood County

Richter, Gary, and Arthur L. Finnell, comps. **Sanborn, Minnesota 1881-1981 Centennial History, Including the Townships of Charlestown and Germantown**. 1981.
Paper. $4.25. 202 pp. .... Vendor G0753

Renville County

Curtiss-Wedge, Franklyn, ed. **History of Renville County**. 2 vols. (1916) reprint 1994.
Cloth. $69.50/vol., $132.50/set. 675 + 701 pp. .... Vendor G0259

Rice County

Neill, Rev. Edward D., and C. S. Bryant. **History of Rice County,** Including Explorers & Pioneers of Minnesota & Outline History of the State of Minnesota. (1882) reprint 1994.
Cloth. $63.00. 603 pp. .... Vendor G0259

Scott County

Irish Genealogical Society, Intl. **St. Catherines Cemetery Transcription, Scott County, Minnesota (Spring Lake Twp)**. 1988. Indexed.
Paper. $8.00. 28 pp. .... Vendor G0305

Irish Genealogical Society, Intl. **St. Patricks Cemetery, Cedar Lake Twp., Scott Co. MN**. 1987. Indexed.
Paper. $8.00. 39 pp. .... Vendor G0305

Irish Genealogical Society, Intl. **St. Peters Cemetery Transcription, Credit River Twp., Scott County, Minnesota**. 1984. Indexed.
Paper. $8.00. 38 pp. .... Vendor G0305

Sibley County

Irish Genealogical Society, Intl. **Jessenland Burial & St. Thomas Cemetery, Sibley County, MN**. 1990. Indexed.
Paper. $11.00. 49 pp. .... Vendor G0305

Irish Genealogical Society, Intl. **Jessenland Civil Records: Birth & Death, Sibley Co., MN**. 1990. Indexed.
Paper. $15.00. 85 pp. .... Vendor G0305

Irish Genealogical Society, Intl. **Jessenland Marriage Records, Sibley County, Minnesota**. 1990. Indexed.
Paper. $9.50. 33 pp. .... Vendor G0305

St. Louis County

Green, Stina B., comp. **Minnesota's Mining Accidents 1900-1920 and Mining Deaths 1889-1990**. 1995. Indexed.
Paper. $16.00. 55 pp. .... Vendor G0583

Mershart, Ronald V. **Pioneers of Superior Wisconsin**. 1996. Indexed.
Paper. $27.95. 80 pp. .... Vendor G0583

Steele County

Anderson, George W., scr. **Early Records of the LeSueur River Church of Waseca and Steele Counties**. 1993. Indexed.
Paper. $10.50. 56 pp. .... Vendor G0583

Wabasha County

Curtiss-Wedge, Franklyn, ed. **History of Wabasha County**. (1920) reprint 1994.
Cloth. $79.00. 781 pp. .... Vendor G0259

Lamb, Harold, comp. **Gillford**. Biographical Sketch of People Buried in the Gillford Cemetery, Lincoln, Gillford Twp., Wabasha Co.
Paper. $5.50. 22 pp. .... Vendor G0259

Waseca County

Anderson, George W., scr. **Early Records of the LeSueur River Church of Waseca and Steele Counties**. 1993. Indexed.
Paper. $10.50. 56 pp. .... Vendor G0583

Washington County

Green, Stina B. **Washington County Miscellaneous Death Listings 1871-1930**. 1993. Indexed.
Paper. $21.00. 121 pp. .... Vendor G0583

Neill, Rev. Edward D., and J. F. Williams. **History of Washington County & the St. Croix Valley,** Including the Explorers & Pioneers of Minnesota. (1881) reprint 1993.
Cloth. $65.00. 636 pp. .... Vendor G0259

Winona County

Green, Stina B. **Index to Deaths in the Winona City and County Directories from 1906-1930**. 1991. Indexed.
Paper. $10.00. 26 pp. .... Vendor G0583

History of Winona County, Together with Biographical Matter, Statistics, Etc. (1883) reprint 1994.
Cloth. $95.00. 951 pp. .... Vendor G0259

Wright County

Curtiss-Wedge, Franklyn, ed. **History of Wright County**. (1915) reprint 1994.
Cloth. $55.00/vol., $105.00/set. 544 + 567 pp. .... Vendor G0259

Dassel Area Historical Society. **Stockholm Cemeteries, Wright County Minnesota**. 1995. Indexed.
Paper. $13.00. 32 pp. .... Vendor G0583

French, C. A., and F. B. Lamson. **Condensed History of Wright County, 1851-1935**. (1935) reprint 1992.
Cloth. $29.50. 228 pp. .... Vendor G0259

Mississippi

Statewide and Regional References

Carpenter. **Ethnic Heritage in Mississippi**. 1992.
   A scholarly study of the influence of diverse ethnic groups on Mississippi culture.
Paper. $18.95. 212 pp. .... Vendor G0611

Claiborne, J. F. H. **Mississippi as a Province, Territory, and State,** with Biographical Notices of Eminent Citizens. (1880) reprint 1996. Indexed. Illus.
Cloth. $45.00. vi + xxiii + 591 pp. .... Vendor G0551

Dilts, Bryan Lee. **1890 Mississippi Veterans Census Index**. 2nd ed. 1992.
Cloth. $19.00. 50 pp. .... Vendor G0552

Family History Library. **Research Outline: Mississippi**.
Leaflet. $.25. 8 pp. .... Vendor G0629

Goodspeed Publishing Company. **Biographical and Historical Memoirs of Mississippi,** Embracing an Authentic and Comprehensive Account of the Chief Events in the History of the State and a Record of the Lives of Many of the Most Worthy and Illustrious Families and Individuals, Volume I. (1891) reprint 1996. Indexed. Illus.
Cloth. $95.00. 1,271 pp. + 58 pp. illus. .... Vendor G0551

Goodspeed Publishing Company. **Biographical and Historical Memoirs of Mississippi,** Embracing an Authentic and Comprehensive Account of the Chief Events in the History of the State and a Record of the Lives of Many of the Most Worthy and Illustrious Families and Individuals, Volume II. (1891) reprint 1996. Indexed. Illus.
Cloth. $85.00. 1,124 pp. + 51 pp. illus. .... Vendor G0551

King, J. Estelle Stewart. **Mississippi Court Records, 1799-1835**. (1936, 1969) reprint 1995. Indexed.
Paper. $22.50. 205 pp. .... Vendor G0011

Liahona Research. **Mississippi Marriages, Early to 1825**. 1990.
Cloth. $30.00. 117 pp. .... Vendor G0552

Lipscomb. **Tracing Your Mississippi Ancestors**. 1994.
   An essential how-to guide for researching ancestral roots in the Magnolia State. Covers colonial, territorial, state, and local record sources.
Paper. $14.95. 201 pp. .... Vendor G0611

Long, John H., ed. **Mississippi Atlas of Historical County Boundaries**. 1993.
   A beautiful and extremely useful book detailing the changes in county boundaries from colonial times to 1990. 8½" x 11".
Cloth. $57.00. 249 pp. .... Vendor G0611

Lowrie, Walter, ed. **Land Claims in the Mississippi Territory**. (1834) reprint 1986. Indexed.
Cloth. Contact vendor for information. 304 pp. .... Vendor G0610

Lowry, Robert, and William H. McCardle. **A History of Mississippi** from the Discovery of the Great River by Hernando DeSoto, Including the Earliest Settlement Made by the French, Under Iberville, to the Death of Jefferson Davis. (1891) reprint 1978. Indexed.
Cloth. $30.00. vi + 698 pp. .... Vendor G0551

McBee, May Wilson. **Mississippi County Court Records**. (1958) reprint 1994. Indexed.
Paper. $13.50. 94 pp. .... Vendor G0011

McBee, May Wilson. **The Natchez Court Records, 1767-1805**. (1953) reprint 1994. Indexed.
Paper. $47.50. 635 pp. .... Vendor G0011

Rietti, J. C., comp. **Military Annals of Mississippi:** Military Organizations Which Entered the Service of the Confederate States of America from the State of Mississippi. (1976) reprint 1996. Indexed.
Cloth. $25.00. iii + 245 pp. .... Vendor G0551

Rowland, Dunbar. **History of Mississippi, the Heart of the South**. 2 vols. 1925.
A social and political history of the state, including individual county histories.
Cloth. $89.50/vol., $185.00/set. 933 + 904 pp. .... Vendor G0259

Rowland, Dunbar. **Military History of Mississippi, 1803-1898** (Taken from the Official and Statistical Register of the State of Mississippi, 1908). (1908) reprint 1996. Indexed.
Cloth. $47.50. vii + 650 pp. .... Vendor G0551

Rowland, Dunbar. **Mississippi:** Comprising Sketches of Counties, Towns, Events, Institutions, and Persons, Arranged in Cyclopedic Form. 4 vols. (1907) reprint 1976. Indexed.
Volumes I and II are historical volumes arranged in cyclopedic form. Volume III contains contemporary biography, with approximately 900 biographies and over 500 photographs of individuals important in Mississippi around the turn of the century. Volume IV is a supplementary volume, containing personal sketches of representative Mississippians.
Cloth. $37.50/vol., $150.00/set. .... Vendor G0551

Rowland, Dunbar. **Official & Statistical Register of the State of Mississippi, Military History Only**. (1908) reprint 1995.
The first, most comprehensive collection of Mississippi Civil War data includes regimental histories and officers. Also covers pre-Civil War Miss. military.
Cloth. $59.00. 565 pp. .... Vendor G0259

Rowland, Eron Opha. **Mississippi Territory in the War of 1812**. Partially indexed. (1921) reprint 1996.
Paper. $23.00. 249 pp. .... Vendor G0011

Strickland, Jean, and Patricia N. Edwards. **Residents of the Mississippi Territory**. 3 vols.
The Mississippi Territory covered the later states of Mississippi and Alabama.
Contact vendor for information. .... Vendor G0693

Thorndale, William, and William Dollarhide. **County Boundary Map Guides to the U.S. Federal Censuses, 1790-1920: Mississippi, 1800-1920**. 1987.
$5.95. .... Vendor G0552

Adams County

Polk. **Natchez Before 1830**. 1989.
A collection of essays revealing the cultural, historical, economic and political evolution of Old Natchez.
Cloth. $27.50. 165 pp. .... Vendor G0611

Copiah County

T.L.C. Genealogy. **Copiah County, Mississippi Taxpayers, 1825-1841**. 1990. Indexed.
Paper. $12.00. 123 pp. .... Vendor G0609

George County

Cain, Cyril Edward. **Four Centuries on the Pascagoula,** Volume 1: History, Story, and Legend of the Pascagoula Country. (1953) reprint 1983. Indexed. Illus.

The Pascagoula River Valley includes Jackson County and George County, which was part of Jackson County for a century. This volume covers the history of the territory up to 1817.

Cloth. $25.00. xii + 216 pp. .... Vendor G0551

Cain, Cyril Edward. **Four Centuries on the Pascagoula,** Volume 2: History and Genealogy of the Pascagoula River Country. (1953) reprint 1983. Indexed.

Covers the history of the region from 1812 to 1960. Includes names of immigrants coming into the region, the census of 1850, families of 1860, and cemetery and Bible records.

Cloth. $25.00. 255 pp. .... Vendor G0551

Jackson County

Cain, Cyril Edward. **Four Centuries on the Pascagoula,** Volume 1: History, Story, and Legend of the Pascagoula Country. (1953) reprint 1983. Indexed. Illus.

The Pascagoula River Valley includes Jackson County and George County, which was part of Jackson County for a century. This volume covers the history of the territory up to 1817.

Cloth. $25.00. xii + 216 pp. .... Vendor G0551

Cain, Cyril Edward. **Four Centuries on the Pascagoula,** Volume 2: History and Genealogy of the Pascagoula River Country. (1953) reprint 1983. Indexed.

Covers the history of the region from 1812 to 1960. Includes names of immigrants coming into the region, the census of 1850, families of 1860, and cemetery and Bible records.

Cloth. $25.00. 255 pp. .... Vendor G0551

Jasper County

Strickland, Jean, and Patricia N. Edwards. **Records of Jasper County, Mississippi. WPA Source Materials, Will Abstracts 1855-1914**. 1995. Indexed.

Paper. $26.50. 197 pp. .... Vendor G0693

Lafayette County

1870 Census of Lafayette County Mississippi. 1990. Indexed.

Paper. $42.00. 491 pp. .... Vendor G0484

Tate County, Mississippi, Genealogical & Historical Society, Inc.
P. O. Box 974, Senatobia, MS 38668-0974; 601-562-0390; Research Library
Publ'd: county history, many county records, quarterly since 1983, brochure

---

Lafayette County Legacy. 1990. Indexed.
Confederate military records of 1,785 men who enlisted in Lafayette County.
Paper. $37.00. 401 pp. .... Vendor G0484

Marriage Bonds of Lafayette County, MS, Vol. I. 1990. Indexed.
Paper. $24.00. 284 pp. .... Vendor G0484

Marion County

Williams, E. Russ. **Marion County, Mississippi, Miscellaneous Records** (Orphans
Ct. Recs., Wills and Ests., 1812-1859; Deeds 1812-1840; Territorial and Federal Census Recs. and Mortality Schedules; Old Road Books; 1813 Lawrence County Tax
Lists). (1962) reprint 1985. Indexed.
Paper. $32.50. 376 pp. .... Vendor G0610

Newton County

Brown, A. J. **History of Newton County, from 1834 to 1894**. (1894) reprint 1993.
Cloth. $49.50. 473 pp. .... Vendor G0259

Pike County

Williams, E. Russ, and, Luke W. Conerly. **Source Records from Pike County, Mississippi, 1798-1910**. (1909) reprint 1989. Indexed. Illus.
Cloth. $50.00. 588 pp. .... Vendor G0610

Tishomingo County

Douthat, James L. **Pickwick Landing Reservoir Cemeteries**.
Cemeteries found in Hardin County, TN; Tishomingo County, MS; and Lauderdale
and Colbert counties, AL
Cloth. $12.00. .... Vendor G0549

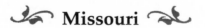

Missouri

Statewide and Regional References

Boeckman, Laurel, and Pat B. Weiner, comps. **Missouri Plat Books in the State
Historical Society of Missouri**. 1992. Indexed.
Paper. $5.00. 54 pp. .... Vendor G0596

Bryan, William S., and Robert Rose. **A History of the Pioneer Families of Missouri, with Numerous Sketches, Anecdotes, Adventures, Etc.** Relating to the Early Days in Missouri. Also the Lives of Daniel Boone and the Celebrated Indian Chief Black Hawk. (1876) reprint 1992. Indexed.
Hard-cover. $45.00. 592 pp. .... Vendor G0610

Bryan, William S., and Robert Rose. **A History of the Pioneer Families of Missouri.** (1876, 1935) reprint 1996. Indexed. Illus.
Paper. $45.00. 586 pp. .... Vendor G0011

Buss, Karen, comp. **An Every-Name Index to Revolutionary Soldiers and Their Descendants: Missouri Edition.** 1988.
Paper. $3.50. 26 pp. .... Vendor G0656

Concannon, Marie, and Josiah Parkinson. **Grand Army of the Republic—Missouri Division—Index to Death Rolls, 1882-1940.** 1995. Indexed.
    Lists many Union veterans' deaths in Missouri after the Civil War.
Paper. $10.00. 184 pp. .... Vendor G0596

Dilts, Bryan Lee, comp. **1890 Missouri Veterans Census Index.** 2nd ed. 1993.
Cloth. $87.00. 304 pp. .... Vendor G0552

Directory of Local Historical, Museum and Genealogical Agencies in Missouri. Rev. ed. 1996-97.
Paper. $7.00. .... Vendor G0596

Family History Library. **Research Outline: Missouri.**
Leaflet. $.25. 9 pp. .... Vendor G0629

Gentges, Margaret H. **Pioneer Settlers of Osage Co., Gasconade Co., and Maries Co., Missouri.** 1996.
    The author has created a database of 55,000 individuals, pioneer settlers and immigrants, their ancestors and descendants. Including families from St. Louis, Cole, Miller, Warren, and Calloway counties. Every Osage County marriage before 1900.
Spiral bound. $20.00 89 pp. .... Vendor G0533

Goodspeed Publishing Company. **General History of Missouri from Earliest Times to the Present.** (1888) reprint 1992.
Cloth. $25.00. 202 pp. .... Vendor G0610

Goodspeed Publishing Company. **The History of Southeast Missouri, Embracing an Historical Account of the Counties of St. Genevieve, St. Francois, Perry, Cape Girardeau, Bollinger, Madison, New Madrid, Pemiscot, Dunklin, Scott, Mississippi, Stoddard, Butler, Wayne, and Iron.** (1888) reprint 1990.
Cloth. $52.50. 1,126 pp. .... Vendor G0610

Goodspeed Publishing Company. **A Reminiscent History of the Ozark Region of Arkansas and Missouri.** (1894) reprint 1988. Indexed.
Cloth. $45.00. 784 pp. .... Vendor G0610

Ingmire, Frances T. **Pioneer Kentuckians with Missouri Cousins.** 2 vols.
    Missouri records showing over 65,000 persons born in Kentucky but who by 1850 are living in Missouri.
Paper. $35.00/vol. .... Vendor G0549

Kot and Thomson. **Missouri Cemetery Inscription Sources: Print & Microform**. 1995.
Over 15,000 entries citing the location of published listings of tombstone readings for cemeteries in Missouri. The vast number of references available here will save hundreds of hours of research.
$55.00. 850 pp. .... Vendor G0611

Liahona Research. **Missouri Marriages, Early to 1825**. 1991.
Cloth. $25.00. 67 pp. .... Vendor G0552

Liahona Research. **Missouri Marriages, 1826 to 1850**. 1993.
Cloth. $170.00. .... Vendor G0552

Lowrie, Walter, ed. **Land Claims in the Missouri Territory**. (1834) reprint 1986. Indexed.
Paper. $30.00. 232 pp. .... Vendor G0610

Missouri Confederate Pensions and Confederate Home Applications Index. 1996.
Spiral binding. $32.00 .... Vendor G0744

Missouri Newspapers on Microfilm at the State Historical Society of Missouri.
Revised annually.
Paper. $12.00. .... Vendor G0596

Missouri Plat Books in the State Historical Society of Missouri.
Paper. $5.00. .... Vendor G0596

Ormesher, Susan. **Missouri Marriages Before 1840**. (1982) reprint 1986. Indexed.
Cloth. $20.00. 317 pp. .... Vendor G0010

Parker, Ed, comp. **Union Burials—Missouri Units**. 3 vols. 1988, 1989, 1993. Indexed.
Paper. $16.00. 170 pp. .... Vendor G0596

Parker, Edward, comp. **Missouri Union Burials—Missouri Units**. 1989.
Paper. $6.00. (See above for 3-vol. set.) .... Vendor G0596

Parker, Edward, comp. **Selected Union Burials—Missouri Units**. 2 vols. 1988, 1993.
Paper. $5.00/vol. (See above for 3-vol. set.) .... Vendor G0596

Rafferty. **Historical Atlas of Missouri**. 1982.
The history of Missouri through maps.
Paper. $18.95. 129 pp. .... Vendor G0611

Sifakis. **Compendium of the Confederate Armies: Kentucky, Maryland, Missouri, the Confederate Units and the Indian Units**. 1995.
Describes the regiments, the officers, and the battles.
Cloth. $27.50. 234 pp. .... Vendor G0611

Southern California Genealogical Society. **Sources of Genealogical Help in Missouri**.
Paper. $3.00. 30 pp. .... Vendor G0656

Stanley, Lois, George F. Wilson, and Maryhelen Wilson. **Death Records from Missouri Newspapers, January 1854-December 1860**. (1982) reprint 1990.
Paper. $30.00. 274 pp. .... Vendor G0610

Stanley, Lois, George F. Wilson, and Maryhelen Wilson. **Death Records from the Missouri Newspapers: The Civil War Years, Jan. 1861-Dec. 1865**. (1983) reprint 1990.
Paper. $25.00. 198 pp. .... Vendor G0610

Stanley, Lois, George F. Wilson, and Maryhelen Wilson. **Death Records from Missouri Newspapers, Jan. 1866-Dec. 1870**. (1984) reprint 1990.
Paper. $30.00. 264 pp. .... Vendor G0610

Stanley, Lois, George F. Wilson, and Maryhelen Wilson. **Death Records of Missouri Men, 1808-1854**. (1981) reprint 1990.
Cloth. $25.00. 176 pp. .... Vendor G0610

Stanley, Lois, George F. Wilson, and Maryhelen Wilson. **Death Records of Pioneer Missouri Women, 1808-1853**. (1984) reprint 1990.
Paper. $18.50. 104 pp. .... Vendor G0610

Stanley, Lois, George F. Wilson, and Maryhelen Wilson. **Divorces and Separations in Missouri, 1808-1853**. 1990.
Paper. $12.00. 35 pp. .... Vendor G0610

Stanley, Lois, George F. Wilson, and Maryhelen Wilson. **Early Missouri Ancestors, Vol I:** From Newspapers, 1808-1822. (1985) reprint 1990. Indexed.
Paper. $25.00. 184 pp. .... Vendor G0610

Stanley, Lois, George F. Wilson, and Maryhelen Wilson. **Early Missouri Ancestors, Vol. II:** From Newspapers, 1823-1832. (1987) reprint 1990. Indexed.
Paper. $22.50. 124 pp. .... Vendor G0610

Stanley, Lois, George F. Wilson, and Maryhelen Wilson. **Early Missouri Marriages in the News, 1820-1853**. (1985) reprint 1990. Indexed.
Paper. $15.00. 64 pp. .... Vendor G0610

Stanley, Lois, George F. Wilson, and Maryhelen Wilson. **Missouri Marriages in the News, 1851-1865**. (1983) reprint 1990.
Paper. $18.50. 96 pp. .... Vendor G0610

Stanley, Lois, Goerge F. Wilson, and Maryhelen Wilson. **Missouri Taxpayers, 1819-1826**. (1979) reprint 1990. Indexed. Illus.
Paper. $23.00. 144 pp. .... Vendor G0610

Stanley, Lois, George F. Wilson, and Maryhelen Wilson. **More Death Records from Missouri Newspapers, 1810-1857**. (1985) reprint 1990.
Paper. $18.50. 128 pp. .... Vendor G0610

Stanley, Lois, George F. Wilson, and Maryhelen Wilson. **1300 "Missing" Missouri Marriage Records from Newspapers, 1812-1853**. (1979) reprint 1990.
Paper. $20.00. 112 pp. .... Vendor G0610

Stanley, Lois, George F. Wilson, and Maryhelen Wilson. **Missouri Marriages in the News, Vol. II, 1866-1870**. (1984) reprint 1990.
Paper. $18.50. 88 pp. .... Vendor G0610

State Historical Society of Missouri. **Directory of Local Historical, Museum and Genealogical Agencies in Missouri**. 1994. Indexed.
Paper. $7.00. 116 pp. .... Vendor G0596

State Historical Society of Missouri. **Historic Missouri: A Pictorial Narrative**. 1988. Indexed. Illus.
Paper. $11.45. 94 pp. .... Vendor G0596

State Historical Society of Missouri. **Missouri Newspapers on Microfilm at the State Historical Society**. 1993. Indexed.
All newspapers listed are available through interlibrary loan within the U.S.
Paper. $12.00. 225 pp. .... Vendor G0596

Stoddard, John H. **Rev. William Henry Johnston—His Ministry in Northeastern Missouri**. 1992. Indexed.
Approximately 2,000 baptisms, marriages, funerals, etc. performed 1872-1929.
Paper. $12.00. 54 pp. .... Vendor G0319

Terry, Rose Caudle. **Missouri Sources, Queries & Reviews Volume 1**. 1994. Indexed. Illus.
Queries published free.
Paper. $8.95. 39 pp. .... Vendor G0061

Thorndale, William, and William Dollarhide. **County Boundary Map Guides to the U.S. Federal Censuses, 1790-1920: Missouri, 1810-1920**. 1987.
$5.95. .... Vendor G0552

Adair County

Goodspeed Publishing Company. **The History of Adair, Sullivan, Putman and Schuyler Counties**. (1888) reprint 1990. Indexed.
Contact vendor for information. Approx. 1,255 pp. .... Vendor G0610

Andrew County

Goodspeed Publishing Company. **The History of Andrew and DeKalb Counties**. (1888) reprint 1990. Indexed.
Contact vendor for information. 591 pp. .... Vendor G0610

Atchison County

Northwest Missouri Genealogical Society. **Atchison County, Missouri Marriages 1863-1869**.
Paper. $4.00. 24 pp. .... Vendor G0699

Northwest Missouri Genealogical Society. **Atchison County, Missouri Atlas 1904**.
Paper. $5.00. 116 pp. .... Vendor G0699

Audrain County

History of Audrain County . . . Including a History of Its Townships, Towns and Villages . . . and Biographical Sketches. (1884) reprint 1995.
Cloth. $95.00. 973 pp. .... Vendor G0259

Ingmire, Frances. **Audrain County, Missouri—Grainger Furniture & Undertakers Company**.
Paper. $22.50. 98 pp. .... Vendor G0549

Barry County

Goodspeed Publishing Company. **The History of Newton, Lawrence, Barry and McDonald Counties**. (1888) reprint 1990. Indexed.
Contact vendor for information. 1,092 pp. .... Vendor G0610

Barton County

Goodspeed Publishing Company. **Hickory, Polk, Cedar, Dade and Barton Counties (Missouri)**. (1889) reprint 1990. Indexed.
Contact vendor for information. 1,096 pp. + index. .... Vendor G0610

Bates County

Christiansen, E. Joyce. **Bates County, Missouri Cemeteries**. (1980) reprint 1990. Indexed.
Paper. $32.95. 258 pp. .... Vendor G0122

Christiansen, E. Joyce. **Bates County, Missouri Marriages Volume 1 1860-1877**. 1990. Indexed.
Paper. $19.95. 167 pp. .... Vendor G0122

Christiansen, E. Joyce. **Bates County, Missouri Marriages Volume 2 1877-1883**. 1990. Indexed.
Paper. $18.95. 147 pp. .... Vendor G0122

Christiansen, E. Joyce. **Bates County, Missouri Marriages Volume 3 1883-1895**. 1990. Indexed.
Paper. $22.95. 275 pp. .... Vendor G0122

History of Bates County. With History of Missouri and Biographical Sketches. (1883) reprint 1994.
 Orig. published with *History of Cass County*.
Cloth. $74.50. 728 pp. .... Vendor G0259

Kusek, Joan, and E. Joyce Christiansen. **Bates County, Missouri Births & Deaths 1883-1886**. 1991. Indexed.
Paper. $20.95. 183 pp. .... Vendor G0122

Kusek, Joan. **Index to Bates County, Missouri Probate Papers 1850-1923**. 1994. Indexed.
Paper. $32.95. 342 pp. .... Vendor G0122

Benton County

Goodspeed Publishing Company. **History of Cole, Moniteau, Morgan, Benton, Miller, Maries, and Osage Counties Missouri**. (1889) reprint 1988. Indexed.
Cloth. $55.00. 972 pp. .... Vendor G0610

Boone County

History of Boone County, Including a History of the Townships, Towns & Villages . . . with Biographical Sketches. (1882) reprint 1993.
Cloth. $109.00. 1,144 pp. .... Vendor G0259

Buchanan County

History of Buchanan County. (1881) reprint 1994.
Cloth. $105.00. 1,073 pp. .... Vendor G0259

St. Joseph Publishing Co. **Daily News' History of Buchanan County & St. Joseph,** from the Time of the Platte Purchase to the End of 1898. With Biographical Sketches. (1898) reprint 1993.
Cloth. $59.00. 569 pp. .... Vendor G0259

Callaway County

History of Callaway County. (1884) reprint 1994.
Cloth. $95.00. 954 pp. .... Vendor G0259

Camden County

Goodspeed Publishing Company. **The History of Laclede, Camden, Dallas, Webster, Wright, Texas, Pulaski, Phelps and Dent Counties**. (1889) reprint 1974. Indexed. Cloth. $55.00. 1,326 pp. .... Vendor G0610

Cape Girardeau County

Gammon, William J. **A Belated Census of Earliest Settlers of Cape Girardeau County, Missouri**.
Paper. $8.00. 70 pp. .... Vendor G0627

Carroll County

History of Carroll County, Including a History of the Townships, Towns & Villages . . . with Biographical Sketches (reprinted without History of Missouri, which comprised first 200 pages of original ed). (1881) reprint 1993.
Cloth. $49.50. 490 pp. .... Vendor G0259

Carter County

McManus, Thelma S. **Grandin (Carter County), MO Records: 1888-1912**. 1984. Indexed.
If someone if your family "worked in timber" for the Missouri Lumber & Mining Company at Grandin, MO, the name may appear in this book, which includes abstracts of marriages, deaths, and births from *The Grandin-Herald*, the only newspaper published in Grandin from 1905-1909. Also included are listings of the Grandin Cemetery and several records from the Chief Surgeon's records of the Missouri Lumber & Mining Company. Information in this book has never been printed before.
Paper. $15.00. 114 pp. .... Vendor G0541

Cass County

History of Cass County. With Biographical Sketches and History of Missouri. (1883) reprint 1994.
Originally pub. with *History of Bates County*.
Cloth. $77.00. 757 pp. .... Vendor G0259

Osborn, Donald Lewis. **Tales of the Amarugia Highlands of Cass County, Missouri**. 1972.
Includes map.
Paper. $6.75. 20 pp. .... Vendor G0121

Cedar County

Goodspeed Publishing Company. **Hickory, Polk, Cedar, Dade and Barton Counties (Missouri)**. (1889) reprint 1990. Indexed.
Contact vendor for information. 1,096 pp. + index. .... Vendor G0610

Looney, Janice Soutee. **Cedar County, Missouri 1870 Federal Census**. Indexed.
Paper. $20.00. 115 pp. .... Vendor G0694

Chariton County

Smith, T. Berry, and Pearl Sims Gehrig. **History of Chariton & Howard Counties**. (1923) reprint 1994.
Cloth. $87.00. 856 pp. .... Vendor G0259

Clark County

Goodspeed Publishing Company. **The History of Knox, Lewis, Scotland, and Clark Counties**. (1887) reprint 1990. Indexed.
1,295 pp. .... Vendor G0610

Clay County

Mallory, Rudena Kramer. **Clay County, Missouri Marriages 1821-1881**. Indexed.
Cloth, $29.00. Paper, $24.00. 220 pp. .... Vendor G0667

Clinton County

Northwest Missouri Genealogical Society. **Clinton County, Missouri: Births 1883-1889 & Death Records 1883-1888**.
Paper. $6.00. 130 pp. .... Vendor G0699

Northwest Missouri Genealogical Society. **Clinton County, Missouri: Deaths from Area Newspapers 1876-1894**.
Paper. $7.00. 46 pp. .... Vendor G0699

Northwest Missouri Genealogical Society. **Clinton County, Missouri: Deaths from Area Newspapers 1895-1899**.
Paper. $9.00. 71 pp. .... Vendor G0699

Northwest Missouri Genealogical Society. **Clinton County, Missouri: Deaths from Area Newspapers 1900-1904**.
Paper. $9.00. 65 pp. .... Vendor G0699

Northwest Missouri Genealogical Society. **Clinton County, Missouri: Deaths from Area Newspapers 1905-1907**.
Paper. $9.00. 65 pp. .... Vendor G0699

Northwest Missouri Genealogical Society. **Clinton County, Missouri: Deaths from Area Newspapers 1908-1910**.
Paper. $10.00. 78 pp. .... Vendor G0699

Cole County

Ford, James E. **History of Jefferson City,** Missouri's State Capital, & of Cole Co. (1938) reprint 1994.
Cloth. $59.50. 600 pp. .... Vendor G0259

Goodspeed Publishing Company. **History of Cole, Moniteau, Morgan, Benton, Miller, Maries, and Osage Counties Missouri.** (1889) reprint 1988. Indexed.
Cloth. $55.00. 972 pp. .... Vendor G0610

Crawford County

Goodspeed Publishing Company. **(A History of) Franklin, Jefferson, Washington, Crawford and Gasconade Counties (Missouri).** (1888) reprint 1990. Indexed.
Contact vendor for information. 1,130 pp. + index. .... Vendor G0610

Dade County

Goodspeed Publishing Company. **Hickory, Polk, Cedar, Dade and Barton Counties (Missouri).** (1889) reprint 1990. Indexed.
Contact vendor for information. 1,096 pp. + index. .... Vendor G0610

Dallas County

Goodspeed Publishing Company. **The History of Laclede, Camden, Dallas, Webster, Wright, Texas, Pulaski, Phelps and Dent Counties.** (1889) reprint 1974. Indexed.
Cloth. $55.00. 1,326 pp. .... Vendor G0610

DeKalb County

Goodspeed Publishing Company. **The History of Andrew and DeKalb Counties.** (1888) reprint 1990. Indexed.
Contact vendor for information. 591 pp. .... Vendor G0610

Dent County

Goodspeed Publishing Company. **The History of Laclede, Camden, Dallas, Webster, Wright, Texas, Pulaski, Phelps and Dent Counties**. (1889) reprint 1974. Indexed. Cloth. $55.00. 1,326 pp. .... Vendor G0610

Douglas County

Coffman, Brenda Sutherland, David Coffman, and Laine Sutherland. **Gone But Not Forgotten: Cemetery Survey of the Eastern District, Douglas County, Missouri**. Indexed. Illus.
Paper. $30.00. 342 pp. .... Vendor G0624

Weber, Nancie Todd. **1860 Douglas County, Missouri Census (Edited/Annotated)**. 1982, projected reprint 1997. Indexed. Illus.
Genealogy, vignettes. Revision will include some spousal surnames, families located 1850/1870, contemporary map, Civil War participation.
Paper. $15.00. 147 pp. .... Vendor G0337

Weber, Nancie Todd. **1870 Douglas County, Missouri Census + Wood-Richland Townships in Texas County (Edited/Annotated)**. 1992. Indexed. Illus.
Some spousal surnames, family locations 1860/1880. Contemporary map.
Paper. $15.00. 76 pp. .... Vendor G0337

Weber, Nancie Todd. **Douglas County, Missouri 1880s Gazetteer**. 1996. Indexed. Illus.
Focus on 1800s county landmarks, multiple early maps.
Contact vendor for information. .... Vendor G0337

Weber, Nancie Todd. **Douglas County, Missouri Marriages 1840s-1900 (Reconstructed)**. 1996. Indexed.
Courthouse burned 1886. Reconstruction from genealogies, newspapers, surviving records.
Contact vendor for information. .... Vendor G0337

Franklin County

Goodspeed Publishing Company. **(A History of) Franklin, Jefferson, Washington, Crawford and Gasconade Counties (Missouri)**. (1888) reprint 1990. Indexed.
Contact vendor for information. 1,130 pp. + index. .... Vendor G0610

Gasconade County

Gentges, Margaret H. **Pioneer Settlers of Osage Co., Gasconade Co., and Maries Co., Missouri**. 1996.

The author has created a database of 55,000 individuals, pioneer settlers and immigrants, their ancestors and descendants. Including families from St. Louis, Cole, Miller, Warren, and Calloway counties. Every Osage County marriage before 1900.
Spiral bound. $20.00 89 pp. .... Vendor G0533

Goodspeed Publishing Company. **(A History of) Franklin, Jefferson, Washington, Crawford and Gasconade Counties (Missouri).** (1888) reprint 1990. Indexed.
Contact vendor for information. 1,130 pp. + index. .... Vendor G0610

Gentry County

History of Gentry & Worth Counties. (1882) reprint 1993.
Cloth. $84.00. 839 pp. .... Vendor G0259

Northwest Missouri Genealogical Society. **Gentry County, Missouri 1861 Tax Assessors Book.**
Paper. $7.00. 82 pp. .... Vendor G0699

Northwest Missouri Genealogical Society. **Gentry County, Missouri Birth Records, 1868-1900.**
Paper. $6.00. 90 pp. .... Vendor G0699

Northwest Missouri Genealogical Society. **Gentry County, Missouri Court Minute Records (Revised to One Vol.) 1845-1859.**
Paper. $10.00. 127 pp. .... Vendor G0699

Northwest Missouri Genealogical Society. **Gentry County, Missouri Deaths, 1868-1910.**
Paper. $10.00. 126 pp. .... Vendor G0699

Northwest Missouri Genealogical Society. **Gentry County, Missouri Marriage Index from Various Sources, 1885-1912 A-M.**
Paper. $8.00. 129 pp. .... Vendor G0699

Northwest Missouri Genealogical Society. **Gentry County, Missouri Marriage Index from Various Sources, 1885-1912 N-Z.**
Paper. $8.00. 90 pp. .... Vendor G0699

Northwest Missouri Genealogical Society. **Gentry County, Missouri Probate Index, 1885-1902.**
Paper. $5.95. 28 pp. .... Vendor G0699

Greene County

Fairbanks, Jonathan, and Clyde E. Tuck. **Past & Present of Greene County:** Early & Recent History & Genealogical Records of Many of the Representative Citizens. 2 vols. (1915) reprint 1995.
Volume I: History & Biography.
Volume II: Biography cont'd.
Cloth. $92.50/vol., $175.00/set. 1,933 pp. .... Vendor G0259

Ozarks Genealogical Society, Inc. **Funeral Records in Greene County, MO: Alma Lohmeyer-Jewell E. Windle Funeral Home 1919-1932**. 1994.
Paper. $18.00. 211 pp. .... Vendor G0175

Ozarks Genealogical Society, Inc. **Funeral Records in Greene County, MO: Paxson Funeral Home Records 1900-1926**. 1992.
Paper. $18.00. 242 pp. .... Vendor G0175

Ozarks Genealogical Society, Inc. **Funeral Records in Greene County, MO: Register of Interment in Hazelwood Cemetery 1868-1915**. 1988.
Paper. $12.00. 190 pp. .... Vendor G0175

Ozarks Genealogical Society, Inc. **Funeral Records in Greene County, MO: Republic Funeral Home 1908-1978**. 1994.
Paper. $18.00. 239 pp. .... Vendor G0175

Ozarks Genealogical Society, Inc. **Funeral Records in Greene County, MO: Will & Alma Lohmeyer Funeral Home Records 1904-1918**. 1991.
Paper. $10.00. 120 pp. .... Vendor G0175

Ozarks Genealogical Society, Inc. **Greene County, MO Cemeteries: Vol. 8 Pond Creek & Center Twps., Including White Chapel Cemetery in Campbell Twp.** 1990.
Paper. $24.00. 321 pp. .... Vendor G0175

Ozarks Genealogical Society, Inc. **Greene County, MO Cemeteries: Vol. 9 Campbell Twp. & Springfield (excluding large cemeteries)**. 1992.
Paper. $24.00. 303 pp. .... Vendor G0175

Ozarks Genealogical Society, Inc. **Greene County, MO Cemeteries: Vol. 10 Maple Park Cemetery**. 2 vols. 1993.
Paper. $40.00. 548 pp. .... Vendor G0175

Ozarks Genealogical Society, Inc. **Greene County, MO Federal Census: 1840 Census & Map**. 1986.
Paper. $17.00. 221 pp. .... Vendor G0175

Ozarks Genealogical Society, Inc. **Greene County, MO Federal Census: 1900 Census & Map, Vol. 1 Boone & Walnut Grove Twp**. 1992.
Paper. $12.00. 146 pp. .... Vendor G0175

Ozarks Genealogical Society, Inc. **Greene County, MO Federal Census: 1900 Census & Map, Vol. 2 Cass, Murray, Robberson, Franklin, & Jackson Townships**. 1992.
Paper. $15.00. 190 pp. .... Vendor G0175

Ozarks Genealogical Society, Inc. **Greene County, MO Marriages: Book D-E 1874-1881**. 1991.
Paper. $10.00. 121 pp. .... Vendor G0175

Ozarks Genealogical Society, Inc. **Greene County, MO Marriages: Book F-G 1881-1885**. 1992.
Paper. $10.00. 94 pp. .... Vendor G0175

Ozarks Genealogical Society, Inc. **Greene County, MO Marriages: Book H-I 1885-1891**. 1993.
Paper. $12.00. 158 pp. .... Vendor G0175

Ozarks Genealogical Society, Inc. **Greene County, MO Marriages: Book J-K 1891-1895**. 1994.
Paper. $12.00. 150 pp. .... Vendor G0175

Hickory County

Goodspeed Publishing Company. **Hickory, Polk, Cedar, Dade and Barton Counties (Missouri)**. (1889) reprint 1990. Indexed.
Contact vendor for information. 1,096 pp. + index. .... Vendor G0610

Howard County

Smith, T. Berry, and Pearl Sims Gehrig. **History of Chariton & Howard Counties**. (1923) reprint 1994.
Cloth. $87.00. 856 pp. .... Vendor G0259

Jackson County

Hickman, William Z. **The History of Jackson County, Missouri**. (1921) reprint 1990. Indexed. Illus.
Cloth. $30.00. 1,072 pp. .... Vendor G0610

Kusek, Joan. **Westport Cumberland Presbyterian Church Records Volume I 1865-1896**. 1989. Indexed.
Paper. $20.95. 192 pp. .... Vendor G0122

Kusek, Joan. **Westport Cumberland Presbyterian Church Records Volume II 1897-1908**. 1989. Indexed.
Paper. $20.95. 201 pp. .... Vendor G0122

Jasper County

McGregor, Malcolm G. **Biographical Record of Jasper County**. (1901) reprint 1993.
Cloth. $55.00. 526 pp. .... Vendor G0259

Jefferson County

Goodspeed Publishing Company. **(A History of) Franklin, Jefferson, Washington, Crawford and Gasconade Counties (Missouri)**. (1888) reprint 1990. Indexed.
Contact vendor for information. 1,130 pp. + index. .... Vendor G0610

Johnson County

History of Johnson County. (1881) reprint 1994.
Cloth. $97.50. 989 pp. .... Vendor G0259

Knox County

Goodspeed Publishing Company. **The History of Knox, Lewis, Scotland, and Clark Counties.** (1887) reprint 1990. Indexed.
1,295 pp. .... Vendor G0610

Laclede County

Goodspeed Publishing Company. **The History of Laclede, Camden, Dallas, Webster, Wright, Texas, Pulaski, Phelps and Dent Counties.** (1889) reprint 1974. Indexed.
Cloth. $55.00. 1,326 pp. .... Vendor G0610

Lafayette County

Frazier. **Missouri Ordeal, 1862-1864: Diaries of Willard Hall Mendenhall.** 1984.
This book is a unique documentary of the war years in Lafayette County, Missouri, naming most of the local families.
Cloth. $22.00. 224 pp. .... Vendor G0611

Lawrence County

Goodspeed Publishing Company. **The History of Newton, Lawrence, Barry and McDonald Counties.** (1888) reprint 1990. Indexed.
Contact vendor for information. 1,092 pp. .... Vendor G0610

Lewis County

Goodspeed Publishing Company. **The History of Knox, Lewis, Scotland, and Clark Counties.** (1887) reprint 1990. Indexed.
1,295 pp. .... Vendor G0610

Lincoln County

Goodspeed Publishing Company. **The History of Lincoln County, from Earliest Times to the Present.** (1888) reprint 1990. Indexed.
Contact vendor for information. 437 pp. + index .... Vendor G0610

Macon County

History of Randolph & Macon Counties . . . Including a History of Its Townships, Cities, Towns & Villages . . . with Biographical Sketches. (1884) reprint 1993. Cloth. $109.50. 1,123 pp. .... Vendor G0259

Madison County

Byerley, Donna, comp. **1860 Madison County, Missouri Census**. Paper. $7.00. 98 pp. .... Vendor G0536

Maries County

Gentges, Margaret H. **Pioneer Settlers of Osage Co., Gasconade Co., and Maries Co., Missouri**. 1996.
   The author has created a database of 55,000 individuals, pioneer settlers and immigrants, their ancestors and descendants. Including families from St. Louis, Cole, Miller, Warren, and Calloway counties. Every Osage County marriage before 1900.
Spiral bound. $20.00 89 pp. .... Vendor G0533

Goodspeed Publishing Company. **History of Cole, Moniteau, Morgan, Benton, Miller, Maries, and Osage Counties Missouri**. (1889) reprint 1988. Indexed. Cloth. $55.00. 972 pp. .... Vendor G0610

McDonald County

Goodspeed Publishing Company. **The History of Newton, Lawrence, Barry and McDonald Counties**. (1888) reprint 1990. Indexed. Contact vendor for information. 1,092 pp. .... Vendor G0610

Looney, Janice Soutee. **McDonald County, Missouri 1870 Federal Census**. 1996. Indexed. Paper. $20.00. 67 pp. .... Vendor G0694

Miller County

Goodspeed Publishing Company. **History of Cole, Moniteau, Morgan, Benton, Miller, Maries, and Osage Counties Missouri**. (1889) reprint 1988. Indexed. Cloth. $55.00. 972 pp. .... Vendor G0610

Mississippi County

Darnell, Betty R. **1850 Census, Mississippi Co. MO**. 1985. Indexed. Paper. $6.00. 28 pp. .... Vendor G0261

Darnell, Betty R. **1870 Census, Mississippi Co. MO**. 1987. Indexed.
Paper. $11.50. 63 pp. .... Vendor G0261

Darnell, Betty R. **Texas Bend Journal, Mississippi Co. MO**. 1989. Indexed.
Paper. $16.50. 77 pp. .... Vendor G0261

Moniteau County

Goodspeed Publishing Company. **History of Cole, Moniteau, Morgan, Benton, Miller, Maries, and Osage Counties Missouri**. (1889) reprint 1988. Indexed.
Cloth. $55.00. 972 pp. .... Vendor G0610

Morgan County

Goodspeed Publishing Company. **History of Cole, Moniteau, Morgan, Benton, Miller, Maries, and Osage Counties Missouri**. (1889) reprint 1988. Indexed.
Cloth. $55.00. 972 pp. .... Vendor G0610

New Madrid County

T.L.C. Genealogy. **New Madrid County, Missouri Court Orders, 1816-1825**. 1991. Indexed.
Paper. $11.00. 89 pp. .... Vendor G0609

Newton County

Goodspeed Publishing Company. **The History of Newton, Lawrence, Barry and McDonald Counties**. (1888) reprint 1990. Indexed.
Contact vendor for information. 1,092 pp. .... Vendor G0610

Nodaway County

Cooper, Martha L. **The Civil War and Nodaway County, MO—Volume 1**.
Paper. $33.00. 205 pp. .... Vendor G0549

Cooper, Martha L. **The Civil War and Nodaway County, MO—Volume 2**.
   Biographical data on over 3,000 Union and Confederate soldiers who served in the Civil War from Nodaway County or came in after the war ended.
Paper. $50.00. 349 pp. .... Vendor G0549

Cooper, Martha L. **Nodaway County Pension Records—Volume 1**. Indexed.
Contact vendor for information. 309 pp. .... Vendor G0549

Nodaway County Genealogical Society. **Monroe Township Cemeteries, Nodaway County, Missouri 1960**. 1966. Indexed.
Paper. $13.50. 120 pp. .... Vendor G0695

Nodaway County Genealogical Society. **Price Funeral Home Records, Maryville, Nodaway County, Missouri 1960**. Indexed.
Paper. $16.50. 200 pp. .... Vendor G0695

Osage County

Gentges, Margaret H. **Births/Baptisms in Osage County, Missouri,** Prior to the 1880 Federal Census of Children and Spouses of the Immigrant Families. 1995. Indexed.
Names 10,000 children, parents, and spouses.
Spiral bound. $30.00. 138 pp. .... Vendor G0533

Gentges, Margaret H. **Immigrants to Osage County Missouri and Their Immigrant Ships**. 1995. Indexed.
Names 9,000 immigrants to Osage, Maries, Gasconade, and Cole counties; father and spouse; place and date of birth; date of death; immigration date, ship, and ports, if known.
Spiral bound. $30.00. 135 pp. .... Vendor G0533

Gentges, Margaret H. **Pioneer Settlers of Osage Co., Gasconade Co., and Maries Co., Missouri**. 1996.
The author has created a database of 55,000 individuals, pioneer settlers and immigrants, their ancestors and descendants. Including families from St. Louis, Cole, Miller, Warren, and Calloway counties. Every Osage County marriage before 1900.
Spiral bound. $20.00 89 pp. .... Vendor G0533

Goodspeed Publishing Company. **History of Cole, Moniteau, Morgan, Benton, Miller, Maries, and Osage Counties Missouri**. (1889) reprint 1988. Indexed.
Cloth. $55.00. 972 pp. .... Vendor G0610

Ozark County

Weber, Nancie Todd. **1850 Ozark County, Missouri Census (Edited/Annotated)**. 1983, projected reprint 1997. Indexed. Illus.
Genealogy, 1850s map, some marriages. Revision will include some spousal identification, families located 1840/1860.
Paper. $15.00. 108 pp. .... Vendor G0337

Phelps County

Goodspeed Publishing Company. **The History of Laclede, Camden, Dallas, Webster, Wright, Texas, Pulaski, Phelps and Dent Counties**. (1889) reprint 1974. Indexed.
Cloth. $55.00. 1,326 pp. .... Vendor G0610

Polk County

Goodspeed Publishing Company. **Hickory, Polk, Cedar, Dade and Barton Counties (Missouri)**. (1889) reprint 1990. Indexed.
Contact vendor for information. 1,096 pp. + index. .... Vendor G0610

Pulaski County

Goodspeed Publishing Company. **The History of Laclede, Camden, Dallas, Webster, Wright, Texas, Pulaski, Phelps and Dent Counties**. (1889) reprint 1974. Indexed.
Cloth. $55.00. 1,326 pp. .... Vendor G0610

Putman County

Goodspeed Publishing Company. **The History of Adair, Sullivan, Putman and Schuyler Counties**. (1888) reprint 1990. Indexed.
Contact vendor for information. Approx. 1,255 pp. .... Vendor G0610

Randolph County

History of Randolph & Macon Counties . . . Including a History of Its Townships, Cities, Towns & Villages . . . with Biographical Sketches. (1884) reprint 1993.
Cloth. $109.50. 1,123 pp. .... Vendor G0259

Ripley County

McManus, Thelma S., comp. **Ripley County (MO) Records: Cemeteries, Part I**. (1973) reprint 1995. Indexed.
Paper. $5.00. 38 pp. .... Vendor G0541

McManus, Thelma S., comp. **Ripley County (MO) Records: Cemeteries, Part II**. (1977) reprint 1993.
Paper. $15.00. 136 pp. .... Vendor G0541

McManus, Thelma S., comp. **Ripley County (MO) Records: Cemeteries, Part III**. 1981. Indexed.
Paper. $15.00. 171 pp. .... Vendor G0541

McManus, Thelma S., comp. **Ripley County (MO) Records: Macedonia Cemetery**. 1987. Indexed.
Paper. $6.00. 20 pp. .... Vendor G0541

McManus, Thelma S., comp. **Ripley County (MO) Records: Marriages, 1860-1881, and Mortality Schedules, 1850-1880**. (1972) reprint 1991. Indexed.

Also contains list of officials performing marriages. Over 1,000 early marriages, many from NE Arkansas.
Paper. $5.50. 77 pp. .... Vendor G0541

McManus, Thelma S., comp. **Ripley County (MO) Records: Marriages, 1881-1887.** (1972) reprint 1991. Indexed.
Paper. $5.00. 42 pp. .... Vendor G0541

McManus, Thelma S., comp. **Ripley County (MO) Records: Obituaries, 1874-1910.** (1979) reprint 1991.
This book abstracts all obituaries/death notices that appeared in *The Prospect* and *The Prospect-News*, local newspapers published in Doniphan, MO since June 1874.
Paper. $17.50. 259 pp. .... Vendor G0541

McManus, Thelma S., comp. **Ripley County (MO) Records: Naylor (Masonic) Cemetery.** 1992. Indexed.
Paper. $15.00. 55 pp. .... Vendor G0541

McManus, Thelma S., comp. **Ripley County (MO) Records: Personal Tax Lists, 1873 and 1877.** 1994. Indexed.
Transcribed from the original, with an added index.
Paper. $12.00. 26 pp. .... Vendor G0541

McManus, Thelma S., and Joyce Richmond Beal. **Ripley County (MO) Records: Stephens-Richmond Cemetery.** Also includes a Sketch of the Families of J.B.S. Richmond and Zebediah W. Stephens. 1993. Indexed.
Paper. $12.50. 22 pp. .... Vendor G0541

Saint Francois County

Jones, Janice L. **Bonne Terre Cemetery Index, Bonne Terre, MO.** 1993.
Paper. $19.50. 26 pp. .... Vendor G0460

Jones, Janice L. **Boyer Funeral Home Records, 1882-1926, Bonne Terre, MO.** 1993. Indexed.
Paper. $35.00. 297 pp. .... Vendor G0460

Saline County

History of Saline County. (1881) reprint 1994.
Cloth. $97.50. 960 pp. .... Vendor G0259

Schuyler County

Goodspeed Publishing Company. **The History of Adair, Sullivan, Putman and Schuyler Counties.** (1888) reprint 1990. Indexed.
Contact vendor for information. Approx. 1,255 pp. .... Vendor G0610

Scotland County

Goodspeed Publishing Company. **The History of Knox, Lewis, Scotland, and Clark Counties**. (1887) reprint 1990. Indexed.
1,295 pp. .... Vendor G0610

Seward County

Cox, W. W. **History of Seward County,** Together with a Chapter of Reminiscences of the Early Settlement of Lancaster County. (1888) reprint 1993.
Cloth. $36.00. 290 pp. .... Vendor G0259

St. Charles County

Stanley, Lois, George F. Wilson, and Maryhelen Wilson. **Marriage Records of St. Charles County, Missouri, 1805-1844**. (1978) reprint 1990. Indexed.
Paper. $18.50. 96 pp. .... Vendor G0610

St. Louis

Precision Indexing. **St. Louis, Missouri 1870 Census Index**. 1989.
Cloth. $175.00. 1,181 pp. .... Vendor G0552

Stoddard County

1880-1887 Extracts, Bloomfield *Vindicator*, Stoddard Co. MO. 1996. Indexed.
Paper. $34.00. 182 pp. .... Vendor G0261

Jones, Janice L. **Chiles-Cooper Funeral Home Records, 1926-1982, Bloomfield, Stoddard Co., MO**. 1995. Indexed.
Paper. $49.00. 233 pp. .... Vendor G0460

Jones, Janice L. **Stoddard Co., MO 1883-1887 Birth Records**. 1996. Indexed.
Paper. $31.00. 112 pp. .... Vendor G0460

Jones, Janice L. **Stoddard Co., MO 1883-1887 Death Records**. 1996. Indexed.
Paper. $25.00. 52 pp. .... Vendor G0460

Sullivan County

Goodspeed Publishing Company. **The History of Adair, Sullivan, Putman and Schuyler Counties**. (1888) reprint 1990. Indexed.
Contact vendor for information. Approx. 1,255 pp. .... Vendor G0610

Taney County

Weber, Nancie Todd. **1840 Taney County, Missouri Census: A Study of 565 Pioneer Households (Edited/Annotated)**. 1994. Indexed. Illus.
Contemporary map. County creation legislation. Some early marriages (reconstruction).
Paper. $20.00. 135 pp. .... Vendor G0337

Weber, Nancie Todd. **1850 Taney County, Missouri Census (Edited/Annotated)**. 1994. Indexed. Illus.
Census initials extensively identified. Many spouses' surnames, families located before/after 1840 census. Contemporary map.
Paper. $15.00. 80 pp. .... Vendor G0337

Texas County

Goodspeed Publishing Company. **The History of Laclede, Camden, Dallas, Webster, Wright, Texas, Pulaski, Phelps and Dent Counties**. (1889) reprint 1974. Indexed.
Cloth. $55.00. 1,326 pp. .... Vendor G0610

Washington County

Goodspeed Publishing Company. **(A History of) Franklin, Jefferson, Washington, Crawford and Gasconade Counties (Missouri)**. (1888) reprint 1990. Indexed.
Contact vendor for information. 1,130 pp. + index. .... Vendor G0610

Webster County

Goodspeed Publishing Company. **The History of Laclede, Camden, Dallas, Webster, Wright, Texas, Pulaski, Phelps and Dent Counties**. (1889) reprint 1974. Indexed.
Cloth. $55.00. 1,326 pp. .... Vendor G0610

Worth County

History of Gentry & Worth Counties. (1882) reprint 1993.
Cloth. $84.00. 839 pp. .... Vendor G0259

Northwest Missouri Genealogical Society. **Worth County, Missouri: Death Notices from Area Newspapers 1874-1893**.
Paper. $6.00. 46 pp. .... Vendor G0699

Northwest Missouri Genealogical Society. **Worth County, Missouri: Death Notices from Area Newspapers 1894-1899**.
Paper. $7.00. 65 pp. .... Vendor G0699

Northwest Missouri Genealogical Society. **Worth County, Missouri: Death Notices from Area Newspapers 1900-1903**.
Paper. $7.00. 64 pp. .... Vendor G0699

Northwest Missouri Genealogical Society. **Worth County, Missouri: Death Notices from Area Newspapers 1904-1906**.
Paper. $6.00. 55 pp. .... Vendor G0699

Northwest Missouri Genealogical Society. **Worth County, Missouri: Death Notices from Area Newspapers 1907-1910**.
Paper. $7.00. 70 pp. .... Vendor G0699

Wright County

Goodspeed Publishing Company. **The History of Laclede, Camden, Dallas, Webster, Wright, Texas, Pulaski, Phelps and Dent Counties**. (1889) reprint 1974. Indexed.
Cloth. $55.00. 1,326 pp. .... Vendor G0610

Montana

Statewide and Regional References

Family History Library. **Research Outline: Montana**.
Leaflet. $.25. 6 pp. .... Vendor G0629

Southern California Genealogical Society. **Sources of Genealogical Help in Montana**.
Paper. $1.00. 4 pp. .... Vendor G0656

Thorndale, William, and William Dollarhide. **County Boundary Map Guides to the U.S. Federal Censuses, 1790-1920: Montana, 1860-1920**. 1987.
$5.95. .... Vendor G0552

Lewis and Clark County

Lewis & Clark County Genealogical Society. **Lewis & Clark County, Montana: Surname Directory, Volume 1, 1994**.
Paper. $9.00. .... Vendor G0716

Lewis & Clark County Genealogical Society. **Lewis & Clark County, Montana: Marriage Index, 1866-1985**. 5 vols.
    Volume 1: A-C.
    Volume 2: D-H.
    Volume 3: I-M.
    Volume 4: Mc-R.
    Volume 5: S-Z.
Cloth. $27.00/vol., $110.00/set. .... Vendor G0716

Lewis & Clark County Genealogical Society. **Lewis & Clark County, Montana Cemetery Records: Church of Sacred Heart, 1866-1908**.
Cloth. $27.00. .... Vendor G0716

Lewis & Clark County Genealogical Society. **Lewis & Clark County, Montana Cemetery Records: Forestvale Cemetery, 1890-1984**.
Cloth. $32.00. .... Vendor G0716

Lewis & Clark County Genealogical Society. **Lewis & Clark County, Montana Cemetery Records: Resurrection Cemetery, 1907-1990**.
Cloth. $32.00. .... Vendor G0716

Lewis & Clark County Genealogical Society. **Lewis & Clark County, Montana Cemetery Records: Rural County-wide Cemetery and Others**.
Cloth. $22.00. .... Vendor G0716

Lewis & Clark County Genealogical Society. **Lewis & Clark County, Montana Cemetery Records: Sunset Memorial Gardens, 1954-1986**.
Cloth. $27.00. .... Vendor G0716

✄ Nebraska ✄

Statewide and Regional References

Family History Library. **Research Outline: Nebraska**.
Leaflet. $.25. 8 pp. .... Vendor G0629

Index for Biographical and Genealogical History of Southwestern Nebraska 1904.
Contact vendor for information. .... Vendor G0477

Sittler, Melvin. **Sittler Index of Surnames from the Nebraska State Journal**. 5 vols. 1983-85.
   Information abstracted from issues from May 1873 through December 1900.
Contact vendor for information. .... Vendor G0477

Southern California Genealogical Society. **Sources of Genealogical Help in Nebraska**.
Paper. $2.50. 13 pp. .... Vendor G0656

Thorndale, William, and William Dollarhide. **County Boundary Map Guides to the U.S. Federal Censuses, 1790-1920: Nebraska, 1860-1920**. 1987.
$5.95. .... Vendor G0552

Antelope County

North Antelope County Genealogical Society. **Antelope County Cemetery Records,** Also Included are Florence, Lee and Lambert Cemeteries in Holt County, Hope/Enterprise and Grimpton Cemeteries in Knox County. 2 vols. 1995.
Paper. $17.50/vol., $30.00/set + postage. vi + 668 pp. .... Vendor G0754

Butler County

Memorial & Biographical Records & Illustrated Compendium of Biography,
Containing a Compendium of Local Biography, Including Biographical Sketches of
Hundreds of Prominent Old Settlers & Representative Citizens (reprinted without
"Compendium of National Biography"). (1899) reprint 1993.
 Covers Butler, Polk, Seward, York, and Fillmore counties.
Cloth. $89.50. 896 pp. .... Vendor G0259

Custer County

Gaston, W. L., and A. R. Humphrey. **History of Custer County:** A Narrative of the
Past, with Special Emphasis upon the Pioneer Period, Its Social . . . and Civic Devel-
opment from the Early Days to the Present Time [1919]. (1919) reprint 1993.
Cloth. $109.00. 1,175 pp. .... Vendor G0259

Douglas County

Bennett. **Mormons at the Missouri, 1846-1852.** 1987.
 This history of the Mormon community at Winter Quarters (Omaha, NE) names
many of the members as well.
Cloth. $28.95. 347 pp. .... Vendor G0611

Sorenson, Alfred. **History of Omaha,** from the Pioneer Days to the Present Time
[1889]. (2nd ed. 1889) reprint 1994.
Cloth. $39.00. 342 pp. .... Vendor G0259

Fillmore County

Memorial & Biographical Records & Illustrated Compendium of Biography,
Containing a Compendium of Local Biography, Including Biographical Sketches of
Hundreds of Prominent Old Settlers & Representative Citizens (reprinted without
"Compendium of National Biography"). (1899) reprint 1993.
 Covers Butler, Polk, Seward, York, and Fillmore counties.
Cloth. $89.50. 896 pp. .... Vendor G0259

Holt County

North Antelope County Genealogical Society. **Antelope County Cemetery Records,**
Also Included are Florence, Lee and Lambert Cemeteries in Holt County, Hope/Enter-
prise and Grimpton Cemeteries in Knox County. 2 vols. 1995.
Paper. $17.50/vol., $30.00/set + postage. vi + 668 pp. .... Vendor G0754

Johnson County

Portrait & Biographical Album of Johnson & Pawnee Counties, Containing Full Page Portraits & Biographical Sketches of Prominent & Representative Citizens of the Cos. (1885) reprint 1994.
Cloth. $65.00. 626 pp. .... Vendor G0259

Knox County

North Antelope County Genealogical Society. **Antelope County Cemetery Records,** Also Included are Florence, Lee and Lambert Cemeteries in Holt County, Hope/Enterprise and Grimpton Cemeteries in Knox County. 2 vols. 1995.
Paper. $17.50/vol., $30.00/set + postage. vi + 668 pp. .... Vendor G0754

Lancaster County

Cemetery Books: Vol. I. (1978) reprint 1983.
  SE Lancaster County (excluding Lincoln).
Contact vendor for information. 159 pp. .... Vendor G0477

Cemetery Books: Vol. II. 1979.
  SW Lancaster County.
Contact vendor for information. 172 pp. .... Vendor G0477

Cemetery Books: Vols. III-IV. 1980.
  North Lancaster County.
Contact vendor for information. 199 pp. .... Vendor G0477

DeVries, Ellen. **Lancaster County Nebraska District Court Records, Intention to Naturalize: 1867-1944.**
Contact vendor for information. .... Vendor G0477

Hayes, A. B., and Sam D. Cox. **History of the City of Lincoln.** (1889) reprint 1994.
Cloth. $42.50. 379 pp. .... Vendor G0259

Hickman Enterprise Index, 1900 through 1902.
  Births, marriages, deaths, anniversaries, business activities in Hickman and surrounding communities.
Contact vendor for information. .... Vendor G0477

Index for 1921 Atlas of Lancaster County, Nebraska.
  Lists rural residents and family members.
Contact vendor for information. .... Vendor G0477

Index for the 1903 Plat Book of Lancaster County, Nebraska.
Contact vendor for information. .... Vendor G0477

Index to the Early Marriage Records of Lancaster County Nebraska 1866-1912.
  Vol. I, 1866-July 1893. Vol. II, July 1893-June 1906.
Contact vendor for information. .... Vendor G0477

Pioneer Families of Lancaster County.
Surnames from applications for Pioneer Family recognition.
Contact vendor for information. .... Vendor G0477

Lincoln County

Cemetery Books: Vol. V. 1981.
Part 1: Wyuka A-K. Part 2: Wyuka L-Z. (Lincoln) Alphabetical index only.
Contact vendor for information. 330 pp. .... Vendor G0477

Cemetery Books: Vol. VI. 1981.
Fairview (Havelock) and Grasshopper Hill (Penitentiary) (Lincoln area).
Contact vendor for information. 133 pp. .... Vendor G0477

Cemetery Books: Vol. VII. 1982.
Calvary, College View (Cedar Lawn) and Mount Carmel (B'Nai Jehuda) (Lincoln area).
Contact vendor for information. .... Vendor G0477

Cemetery Books: Vol. VIII. 1983.
Lincoln Memorial Park. An alphabetical index.
Contact vendor for information. 105 pp. .... Vendor G0477

Coleman, Ruby Roberts, comp. **Marriages in Lincoln County, Nebraska, Volume 4 1886-1889**. 1995. Indexed.
Paper. $12.00. Contact vendor for information about earlier volumes.
71 pp. .... Vendor G0783

Pawnee County

Portrait & Biographical Album of Johnson & Pawnee Counties, Containing Full Page Portraits & Biographical Sketches of Prominent & Representative Citizens of the Cos. (1885) reprint 1994.
Cloth. $65.00. 626 pp. .... Vendor G0259

Polk County

Memorial & Biographical Records & Illustrated Compendium of Biography, Containing a Compendium of Local Biography, Including Biographical Sketches of Hundreds of Prominent Old Settlers & Representative Citizens (reprinted without "Compendium of National Biography"). (1899) reprint 1993.
Covers Butler, Polk, Seward, York, and Fillmore counties.
Cloth. $89.50. 896 pp. .... Vendor G0259

Richardson County

Edwards, Lewis C. **History of Richardson County,** Its People, Industries and Institutions. With Biographical Sketches of representative citizens and genealogical records of many of the old families. (1917) reprint 1996.
Cloth. $135.00. 1,417 pp. .... Vendor G0259

Seward County

Memorial & Biographical Records & Illustrated Compendium of Biography, Containing a Compendium of Local Biography, Including Biographical Sketches of Hundreds of Prominent Old Settlers & Representative Citizens (reprinted without "Compendium of National Biography"). (1899) reprint 1993.

  Covers Butler, Polk, Seward, York, and Fillmore counties.

Cloth. $89.50. 896 pp. .... Vendor G0259

Washington County

Carr, Daniel M., ed. **Men & Women of Nebraska:** A Book of Portraits, Washington Co. Edition, Containing an Historical Review of Washington Co., Compiled from Public & Private Records. (1903) reprint 1995.

Cloth. $29.50. 198 pp. .... Vendor G0259

York County

Memorial & Biographical Records & Illustrated Compendium of Biography, Containing a Compendium of Local Biography, Including Biographical Sketches of Hundreds of Prominent Old Settlers & Representative Citizens (reprinted without "Compendium of National Biography"). (1899) reprint 1993.

  Covers Butler, Polk, Seward, York, and Fillmore counties.

Cloth. $89.50. 896 pp. .... Vendor G0259

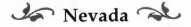

Nevada

Statewide and Regional References

Dilts, Bryan Lee, comp. **1910 Nevada Census Index: Heads of Households and Other Surnames in Households**. 1993.

Cloth. $63.00. .... Vendor G0552

Family History Library. **Family History Centers: Nevada and Utah**.

Free. 2 pp. .... Vendor G0629

Family History Library. **Research Outline: Nevada**.

Leaflet. $.25. 7 pp. .... Vendor G0629

History of Nevada, with Illustrations & Biographical Sketches of its Prominent Men & Pioneers. (1881) reprint 1992.

Cloth. $69.50. 680 pp. .... Vendor G0259

Parker, J. Carlyle, and Janet G. Parker. **Nevada Biographical and Genealogical Sketch Index**. 1986.

Cloth. $26.45. 96 pp. .... Vendor G0492

Thorndale, William, and William Dollarhide. **County Boundary Map Guides to the U.S. Federal Censuses, 1790-1920: Nevada, 1860-1920**. 1987. $5.95. .... Vendor G0552

✺ New Hampshire ✺

Statewide and Regional References

Atlas of New Hampshire, Detailed Roads.
This present-day atlas provides the researcher with the detail needed to conduct a proper search. It is the size of a Rand McNally atlas of the entire U.S. 11" x 15½". $16.95. .... Vendor G0611

Bent, Allen H. **Bent's Bibliography of the White Mountains**. (1911) reprint 1971. Illus.
Book #1239.
Cloth. $9.50. 134 pp. .... Vendor G0082

Crawford, L. **History of the White Mountains,** from the First Settlement of Upper Coos & Pequaket. (1883) reprint 1991.
Cloth. $30.00. 230 pp. .... Vendor G0259

Dean, John Ward, ed. **Captain John Mason, Founder of New Hampshire**. With Memoir by C. W. Tuttle. (1887) reprint 1991.
Cloth. $49.50. 491 pp. .... Vendor G0259

Dodge, Nancy L., comp. **Northern New Hampshire Graveyards & Cemeteries**. 1985.
Transcriptions and indexes of burial sites in the towns of Clarksville, Colebrook, Columbia, Dixville, Pittsburg, Stewartstown, and Stratford.
Cloth. $39.50. 443 pp. .... Vendor G0259

Drake, Samuel Adams. **The Heart of the White Mountains:** Their Legend and Scenery. Illustrations by W. Hamilton Drake. (1882) reprint 1995.
A pleasant narrative of travels through New Hampshire's spectacular White Mountains and many of its beautiful towns, with more than fifty engravings.
Cloth. $39.50. 318 pp. .... Vendor G0259

Family History Library. **Research Outline: New Hampshire**.
Leaflet. $.25. 10 pp. .... Vendor G0629

The First Laws of the State of New Hampshire. (1780) reprint 1981.
Cloth. $62.50. 235 pp. .... Vendor G0118

Gilmore, Geo. C. **Roll of New Hampshire Soldiers at the Battle of Bennington, August 16, 1777**. Published with **New Hampshire Men at Louisburg—1745**. (1891, 1896) reprint 1995.
Paper. $14.00. 55 + 63 pp. .... Vendor G0011

Green, Scott E. **Directory of Repositories of Family History in New Hampshire**. (1994) reprint 1997. Indexed.
Paper. $10.95. 61 pp. .... Vendor G0011

Hammond, Otis G. **Notices from the New Hampshire Gazette, 1765-1800**. Indexed.
Gives coverage to southern New Hampshire and nearby places in Maine and Massachusetts.
Cloth. $15.00. 246 pp. .... Vendor G0561

Hammond, Otis G. **Notices from the New Hampshire Gazette**. 1970. Indexed.
Contact vendor for information. 246 pp. .... Vendor G0011

Holbrook, Jay Mack. **New Hampshire 1732 Census**. 1981.
Cloth. $25.00. 75 pp. .... Vendor G0148

Holbrook, Jay Mack. **New Hampshire 1732 Census**. 1981.
Cloth. $25.00. 75 pp. .... Vendor G0011

Holbrook, Jay Mack. **New Hampshire 1776 Census**. 1976.
Microfiche. $6.00. 170 pp. on 1 fiche. .... Vendor G0148

Holbrook, Jay Mack. **New Hampshire Residents 1633-1699**. 1979.
Taken from over 100 lists of first settlers, church members, taxables, and land grantees; as well as estate valuations, minister rates, petitions, probates, and oaths of allegiance. The most inclusive list available of New Hampshire residents in the 1600s.
Cloth. $30.00. 234 pp. .... Vendor G0148

Long, John H., ed. **New Hampshire and Vermont Atlas of Historical Boundaries**. 1993.
A beautiful and extremely useful book detailing the changes in county boundaries from colonial times to 1990. 8½" x 11".
Cloth. $57.00. 216 pp. .... Vendor G0611

Noyes, Sybil, Charles T. Libby, and Walter G. Davis. **Genealogical Dictionary of Maine and New Hampshire**. 5 parts in 1. (1928-1939) reprint 1996.
Cloth. $40.00. 795 pp. .... Vendor G0010

Pope, Charles Henry. **The Pioneers of Maine and New Hampshire, 1623-1660**. (1908) reprint 1997.
Contact vendor for information. 263 pp. .... Vendor G0011

Southern California Genealogical Society. **Sources of Genealogical Help in New Hampshire**.
Paper. $1.50. 8 pp. .... Vendor G0656

Thorndale, William, and William Dollarhide. **County Boundary Map Guides to the U.S. Federal Censuses, 1790-1920: New Hampshire, Vermont, 1790-1920**. 1987.
$5.95. .... Vendor G0552

United States Bureau of the Census. **Heads of Families at the First Census of the United States Taken in the Year 1790: New Hampshire**. (1907) reprint 1992. Indexed. Illus.
Paper. $21.50. 146 pp. .... Vendor G0010

United States Bureau of the Census. **Heads of Families at the First Census of the United States Taken in the Year 1790: New Hampshire**.
Cloth, $35.00. Paper, $20.00. .... Vendor G0552

Wentworth, William Edgar. **Vital Records 1790-1829 from Dover, New Hampshire's First Newspaper**.
    More than 1,600 issues of a total of 2,000 of Dover's earliest newspaper were located, and all vital records were abstracted. Includes several thousand marriages and deaths.
Cloth. $36.00. .... Vendor G0598

Wilson, Emily S. **Inhabitants of New Hampshire, 1776**. (1983) reprint 1993.
Paper. $15.00. 124 pp. .... Vendor G0010

Belknap County

Hurd, D. H., ed. **History of Merrimac & Belknap Counties**. (1885) reprint 1987.
Cloth. $38.00. 915 pp. .... Vendor G0259

Lancaster, Daniel. **History of Gilmanton,** Embracing the . . . Civil, Biographical, Genealogical & Misc. History from the First Settlement to the Present Time [1845], Including What Is Now Guilford. (1845) reprint 1990.
Cloth. $37.50. 304 pp. .... Vendor G0259

Runnels, M. T. **History of Sanbornton**. 2 vols. (1881-2) reprint 1988.
    Volume I: Annals.
    Volume II: Genealogies.
Cloth. $57.00/Vol. I. $96.00/Vol. II. 570 + 1,022 pp. .... Vendor G0259

Vaughan, Charles W. **The Illustrated Laconian:** History & Industries of Laconia. (1899) reprint 1995.
Cloth. $32.50. 248 pp. .... Vendor G0259

Carroll County

Merrill, Georgia Drew, ed. **History of Carroll County**. (1889) reprint 1993.
Cloth. $97.50. 984 pp. .... Vendor G0259

Merrill, Georgia Drew. **History of Carroll County, New Hampshire**. (1889) reprint 1991. Illus.
    Book #1308.
Cloth. $59.50. 1,103 pp. .... Vendor G0082

Parker, B. F. **History of Wolfeborough**. (19091) reprint 1988.
Cloth. $59.50. 557 pp. .... Vendor G0259

Parker, Benjamin Franklin. **History of Wolfeborough, New Hampshire**. (1901) reprint 1986. Illus.
    Book #1369.
Paper. $14.50. 735 pp. .... Vendor G0082

Cheshire County

Aldrich, George. **Walpole As It Was and As It Is:** Containing the Complete Civil History of the Town from 1749 to 1879, Also . . . a History of the 150 Families That Settled in the Town Previous to 1820 . . . (1880) reprint 1995.
Cloth. $44.50. 404 pp. .... Vendor G0259

Bassett, William. **History of the Town of Richmond,** Cheshire Co., from Its First Settlement to 1882. (1884) reprint 1995.
Cloth. $62.00. 578 pp. .... Vendor G0259

Bemis, C. A. **History of the Town of Marlborough, Cheshire Co**. With Genealogical Register. (1881) reprint 1990.
Cloth. $69.50. 726 pp. .... Vendor G0259

Bemis, Charles A. **History of the Town of Marlborough, Cheshire County, NH**. (1881) reprint 1974. Indexed. Illus.
    Book #1241.
Cloth. $45.00. 792 pp. .... Vendor G0082

Brown, Capt. Hal G., L. Douglas K. Fish, and Mrs. Lorraine L. Madden, comp. **In Pursuit of Justice—A History of the Keene Police Department**. 1995.
Cloth. $35.00. xv + 422 pp. .... Vendor G0755

Caverly, A. M. **Historical Sketch of Troy and Her Inhabitants,** from the First Settlement in 1764 to 1855. (1859) reprint 1993.
Cloth. $36.50. 298 pp. .... Vendor G0259

Gill, James, and Maryan Gill. **New Hampshire 1800 Census Index**. 3 vols.
    Volume I: Cheshire Co., 54 pp.
    Volume II: Grafton & Hillsborough Cos., 88 pp.
    Volume III: Rockingham & Strafford Cos., 84 pp.
Paper. $8.00/vol., $21.00/set. .... Vendor G0574

Hayward, S. **History of Gilsum, from 1752 to 1879**. (1881) reprint 1988.
Cloth. $52.00. 468 pp. .... Vendor G0259

History of Dublin, with a Register of Families. (rev. ed. 1920) reprint 1991.
Cloth. $99.00. 1,018 pp. .... Vendor G0259

Kingsbury, F. B. **History of the Town of Surry, Cheshire Co.,** from the Date of Severance from Gilsum & Westmoreland, 1769-1922, with a Genealogical Reg. of the Town. (1925) reprint 1988.
Cloth. $98.00. 1,062 pp. .... Vendor G0259

Norton, John F., and Joel Wittemore. **History of Fitzwilliam,** from 1752 to 1887, with a Genealogical Record of Many Fitzwilliam Families. (1888) reprint 1995.
Cloth. $85.00. 829 pp. .... Vendor G0259

Randall, O. E. **History of Chesterfield, Cheshire County, 1736 to 1881,** with Family Histories. (1882) reprint 1987.
Cloth. $55.00. 525 pp. .... Vendor G0259

Read, Benjamin. **History of Swanzey, from 1734-1890**. (1892) reprint 1987.
Cloth. $59.50. 585 pp. .... Vendor G0259

Seward, J. L. **History of the Town of Sullivan, 1777-1917,** with Genealogies. 2 vols. (1921) reprint 1987.
Cloth. $79.50/vol. 816 + 820 pp. .... Vendor G0259

Stearns, E. S. **History of the Town of Rindge,** from the Date of the Rowley, Canada or Mass. Charter to the Present Time, 1736-1874, with Genealogical Register. (1875) reprint 1990.
Cloth. $79.00. 788 pp. .... Vendor G0259

Stone, M. T. **Historical Sketch of the Town of Troy & Her Inhabitants,** from the First Settlement of the Territory Now Within the Limits of the Town, 1764-1897. (1897) reprint 1988.
Cloth. $59.50. 587 pp. .... Vendor G0259

Whitcomb, F. H. **History of the Town of Keene, from 1732 to 1874**. (1904) reprint 1987.
Cloth. $84.00. 792 pp. .... Vendor G0259

Coos County

Dodge, Nancy L. **Gravestones of Guildhall, Vt. & Northumberland, N.H**. 1987.
Cloth. $39.00. 185 pp. .... Vendor G0259

Evans, George C. **History of the Town of Jefferson, 1773-1927**. (1927) reprint 1996.
Cloth. $39.00. 320 pp. .... Vendor G0259

History of Coos County. (1888) reprint 1992.
Cloth. $89.50. 956 pp. .... Vendor G0259

Somers, A. N. **History of Lancaster**. (1899) reprint 1987.
Cloth. $68.00. 652 pp. .... Vendor G0259

Grafton County

Bittinger, J. Q. **History of Haverhill**. (1888) reprint 1988.
Cloth. $47.00. 443 pp. .... Vendor G0259

Child, H. **Gazetteer of Grafton County, 1709-1886**. 2 vols. (1886) reprint 1990.
Part I: History.
Part II: Business Directory.
Cloth. $68.00/Part I. $39.50/Part II. 644 + 380 pp. .... Vendor G0259

Downs, C. A. **History of Lebanon, 1761-1887**. (1908) reprint 1990.
Cloth. $49.50. xiii + 459 pp. .... Vendor G0259

Gill, James, and Maryan Gill. **New Hampshire 1800 Census Index**. 3 vols.
Volume I: Cheshire Co., 54 pp.
Volume II: Grafton & Hillsborough Cos., 88 pp.
Volume III: Rockingham & Strafford Cos., 84 pp.
Paper. $8.00/vol., $21.00/set. .... Vendor G0574

Horton, L. S., E. H. Underhill, and E. D. Deal. **Piermont, New Hampshire, 1764-1947**. With Genealogies. (1947) reprint 1993.
Cloth. $32.50. 236 pp. .... Vendor G0259

Jackson, James R. **History of Littleton, in Three Volumes**. (1905) reprint 1991.
Cloth. $75.00/vol., $189.00/set. 771 + 733 + 706 pp. .... Vendor G0259

Johnson, Frances Ann. **History of Monroe, 1761-1954**. With Genealogical Records. (1955) reprint 1994.
Cloth. $67.00. 642 pp. .... Vendor G0259

Little, William. **History of Warren,** A Mountain Hamlet Located Among the White Hills of New Hampshire. (1870) reprint 1995.
Cloth. $59.50. 594 pp. .... Vendor G0259

Lord, John King. **History of the Town of Hanover**. (1928) reprint 1992.
Cloth. $42.50. 339 pp. .... Vendor G0259

Plummer, George F. **History of the Town of Wentworth**. (1930) reprint 1995.
Cloth. $45.00. xix + 401 pp. .... Vendor G0259

Stearns, Ezra S. **History of Plymouth, New Hampshire**. 2 vols. (1906) reprint 1987. Indexed. Illus.
  Book #1247.
Cloth. $95.00. 1,513 pp. .... Vendor G0082

Wallace, W. A. **History of Canaan**. Edited by J. B. Wallace. (1910) reprint 1988.
Cloth. $77.00. 757 pp. .... Vendor G0259

Whitcher, W. F. **History of the Town of Haverhill**. (1919) reprint 1993.
Cloth. $79.50. 781 pp. .... Vendor G0259

Whitcher, William F. **Some Things about Coventry-Benton**. (1905) reprint 1996.
Cloth. $36.00. 313 pp. .... Vendor G0259

Hillsborough County

Baldwin, Harrison C. **History of Hillsborough, 1921-1963**. (1963) reprint 1993.
Cloth. $29.50. 201 pp. .... Vendor G0259

Bedford Historical Society. **History of Bedford, New Hampshire 1737-1971**. 1972. Indexed. Illus.
  Book #1238.
Cloth. $45.00. 798 pp. .... Vendor G0082

Blood, Henry Ames. **History of Temple**. (1860) reprint 1993.
Cloth. $39.00. 352 pp. .... Vendor G0259

Chandler, C. H., and S. F. Lee. **History of New Ipswich, 1735-1914,** with Genealogical Records of the Principal Families. (1919) reprint 1993.
Cloth. $78.00. 782 pp. .... Vendor G0259

Cochrane, W. R. **History of Antrim,** from Its Earliest Settlement in 1727 to 1872. (1880) reprint 1987.
Cloth. $79.00. 791 pp. .... Vendor G0259

Cochrane, W. R., and G. K. Wood. **History of Francestown,** from Its Earliest Settlement, 1758-1891. (1895) reprint 1987.
Cloth. $95.00. 1,031 pp. .... Vendor G0259

Cogswell, Elliott C. **History of New Boston**. (1864) reprint 1993.
Cloth. $49.00. 470 pp. .... Vendor G0259

Dearborn, Helen E. **Town History of Weare, from 1888**. (1959) reprint 1993.
Cloth. $37.50. 305 + 44 pp. .... Vendor G0259

The Diary of Matthew Patten of Bedford, New Hampshire 1754-1788. (1903) reprint 1993. Indexed. Illus.
  Book #1424.
Cloth. $49.50. 640 pp. .... Vendor G0082

Farmer, John. **Historical Sketch of Amherst**. 2nd ed. (1837) reprint 1972.
  Book #1237.
Cloth. $15.00. 60 pp. .... Vendor G0082

Farmer, John. **Historical Sketch of Amherst,** in the Co. of Hillsborough, from Its First Settlement to the Year 1837 (2nd ed.). (1837) reprint 1995.
Cloth, $22.00. Paper, $12.00. 52 pp. .... Vendor G0259

Gill, James, and Maryan Gill. **New Hampshire 1800 Census Index**. 3 vols.
  Volume I: Cheshire Co., 54 pp.
  Volume II: Grafton & Hillsborough Cos., 88 pp.
  Volume III: Rockingham & Strafford Cos., 84 pp.
Paper. $8.00/vol., $21.00/set. .... Vendor G0574

Gould, A. A. **History of New Ipswich,** from Its First Grant in 1736, with Genealogical Notices of the Principal Families & the Proceedings of the Centennial Celebrations. (1852) reprint 1988.
Cloth. $49.50. 492 pp. .... Vendor G0259

Hadley, George Plummer. **History of the Town of Goffstown, 1733-1920**. 2 vols. (1923) reprint 1993.
  Volume I: History.
  Volume II: Genealogy.
Cloth. $59.50/vol. 601 + 586 pp. .... Vendor G0259

Hayward, W. W. **History of Hancock, 1764-1889**. With Genealogical Register. (1889) reprint 1987.
Cloth. $97.50. 1,070 pp. .... Vendor G0259

Hill, John B. **History of the Town of Mason,** from Its First Grant in 1749 to 1858 (incl. Greenville). (1858) reprint 1992.
Cloth. $38.00. 324 pp. .... Vendor G0259

History of Bedford, Being Statistics Compiled on the Occasion of the 100th Anniversary of the Town, May 19th, 1850. With Genealogies. (1851) reprint 1993.
Cloth. $39.50. 364 pp. .... Vendor G0259

History of Weare, 1735-1888. (1888) reprint 1988.
Cloth. $105.00. 1,064 pp. .... Vendor G0259

Hurd, D. H., ed. **History of Hillsborough County**. (1885) reprint 1989.
Cloth. $79.00. 748 pp. .... Vendor G0259

Livermore, A. A., and S. Putnam. **History of the Town of Wilton, Hillsborough Co.** with Genealogical Register. (1888) reprint 1988.
Cloth. $62.00. 575 pp. .... Vendor G0259

Parker, E. E. **History of Brookline,** formerly Raby, Hillsborough Co., with Tables of Family Records & Genealogies. (1913?) reprint 1988.
Cloth. $69.50. 664 pp. .... Vendor G0259

Potter, C. E. **History of Manchester,** Formerly Derryfield, in New Hampshire, Including That of Ancient Amoskeag, or the Middle Merrimack Valley. (1856) reprint 1994.
Cloth. $75.00. 764 pp. .... Vendor G0259

Ramsdell, G. A., and W. P. Colburn. **History of Milford, with Family Registers**. (1901) reprint 1990.
Cloth. $125.00. xii + 1,210 pp. .... Vendor G0259

Secomb, D. F. **History of the Town of Amherst, Hillsborough Co., from 1728 to 1882, with Genealogies**. (1883) reprint 1987.
Cloth. $95.00. 978 pp. .... Vendor G0259

Smith, Albert. **History of the Town of Peterborough, Hillsborough Co**. (1876) reprint 1992.
Cloth. $76.00. 735 pp. .... Vendor G0259

Smith, C. J. **History of the Town of Mont Vernon**. (1907) reprint 1988.
Cloth. $47.00. 443 pp. .... Vendor G0259

Spaulding, C. S. **West Dunstable, Monson & Hollis:** An Account of Some of the Early Settlers. (1915) reprint 1987.
Cloth. $35.00. 251 pp. .... Vendor G0259

Thorp, L. Ashton. **Manchester of Yesterday:** A Human Interest Story of Its Past, with One Hundred Illustrations, Including Rate Wood Engravings of Old Pioneers and Places. (1939) reprint 1996.
Cloth. $59.00. 561 pp. .... Vendor G0259

Webster, K. **History of Hudson (1673-1912),** Formerly a Part of Dunstable, Mass., Nottingham, Mass., & Nottingham West. Edited by G. W. Browne. (1913) reprint 1988.
Cloth. $69.00. 648 pp. .... Vendor G0259

Worcester, S. T. **History of the Town of Hollis,** from Its First Settlement to 1879. (1879) reprint 1987.
Cloth. $43.50. Family Register only: 32 pp., paper, $6.50. 394 pp. .... Vendor G0259

Isle of Shoals

Jenness, John Scribner. **The Isle of Shoals: An Historical Sketch**. (3rd ed. 1884) reprint 1993.
   Fascinating history of a group of small islands that began as a haven for colonial social outcasts and became a prominent summer resort in the Victorian era.
Cloth. $29.50. 214 pp. .... Vendor G0259

Merrimack County

Bouton, N. **History of Concord, from 1725 to 1853**. (1856) reprint 1987.
Cloth. $79.50. 786 pp. .... Vendor G0259

Cogswell, L. W. **History of the Town of Henniker, Merrimac Co.,** from the Date of the Canada Grant by the Province of Mass. in 1735 to 1880, with a Gen. Register. (1885) reprint 1989.
Cloth. $83.00. 807 pp. .... Vendor G0259

Cross, L. H. R. **History of Northfield, 1780-1905,** in Two Parts with Many Biographical Sketches & Portraits. 2 vols. (1905) reprint 1988.
   Part I: History.
   Part II: Genealogy.
Cloth. $34.00/Part I. $45.00/Part II. 293 + 410 pp. .... Vendor G0259

Dearborn, Adams, and Rolfe. **History of Salisbury,** from Date of Settlement to 1890. (1890) reprint 1987.
Cloth. $89.50. 892 pp. .... Vendor G0259

Eastman, J. R. **History of the Town of Andover, 1751-1906,** Including Genealogies. (1910) reprint 1987.
Cloth. $48.00. 450 pp. .... Vendor G0259

Harriman, Walter. **The History of Warner New Hampshire from 1735 to 1879**. (1879) reprint 1993. Indexed. Illus.
   Book #1255.
Cloth. $50.00. 680 pp. .... Vendor G0082

History of the Town of New London, Merrimac Co., 1779-1899. (1899) reprint 1991.
Cloth. $77.00. 774 pp. .... Vendor G0259

Hurd, D. H., ed. **History of Merrimac & Belknap Counties**. (1885) reprint 1987.
Cloth. $38.00. 915 pp. .... Vendor G0259

LeVarn, Caspar L. **The Early History of Wilmot**. (1957) reprint 1995.
Cloth. $32.50. 214 pp. .... Vendor G0259

Lord, C. C. **Life & Times in Hopkinton,** in Three Parts: Descriptive & Historical; Personal & Biographical; Statistical & Documentary. (1890) reprint 1992.
Cloth. $59.00. 583 pp. .... Vendor G0259

Lyford, J. O. **History of the Town of Canterbury, 1727-1912**. 2 vols. (1912) reprint 1990.
  Volume I: History.
  Volume II: Genealogy & Appendices.
Cloth. $49.50/vol., $95.00/set. 513 + 455 pp. .... Vendor G0259

Lyford, James O., ed. **History of Concord,** from the Original Grant in 1725 to the Opening of the 20th Century. 2 vols. (1903) reprint 1992.
Cloth. $135.00. 1,477 pp. .... Vendor G0259

Moore, Jacob B. **Annals of the Town of Concord,** in the County of Merrimack, from Its First Settlement in the Year 1726 to the Year 1823, with Several Biographical Sketches. (1824) reprint 1995.
Paper. $21.00. 112 pp. .... Vendor G0259

Stark, C. **History of the Town of Dunbarton, Merrimack Co.,** from 1751 to 1860. (1860) reprint 1987.
Cloth. $35.00. 272 pp. .... Vendor G0259

Worthen, Mrs. A. H., comp. **History of Sutton,** Consisting of the Historical Collections of Erastus Wadleigh & A. H. Worthen. 2 vols. (1890) reprint 1988.
Cloth. $56.50/vol. 595 + 510 pp. .... Vendor G0259

Young, E. Harold. **History of Pittsfield, New Hampshire**. (1953) reprint 1995.
Cloth. $62.00. 575 pp. .... Vendor G0259

Nottingham County

Cogswell, E. C. **History of Nottingham, Deerfield, Northwood,** Nottingham & Rockingham Cos., with Genealogical Sketches. (1878) reprint 1987.
Cloth. $79.00. 790 pp. .... Vendor G0259

Rockingham County

Adams, Nathaniel. **Annals of Portsmouth**. (1825; Index, 1940) reprint 1900.
Cloth. $39.00. 400 pp. .... Vendor G0259

Annis, Daniel Gage. **Vital Records of Londonderry, New Hampshire, 1719-1910**. (1914) reprint 1994.
Cloth. $17.50. 328 pp. .... Vendor G0011

Arseneault, Judith A. **The Vital Records of Kingston, New Hampshire 1694-1994**. 1995. Indexed.
Paper. $27.50. 315 pp. .... Vendor G0011

Bell, Charles H. **History of the Town of Exeter**. With a Family Register. (1888) reprint 1993.
Cloth. $58.00. 559 pp. .... Vendor G0259

Brentwood Hist. Society. **Brentwood's 225 Years, 1742-1967**. (1967?) reprint 1990.
Cloth. $19.50. 120 pp. .... Vendor G0259

Brewster, Charles W. **Rambles About Portsmouth**. (1869) reprint 1972. Indexed. Illus. Book #1298.
Cloth. $85.00. 912 pp. .... Vendor G0082

Brown, Warren. **History of the Town of Hampton Falls,** from the Time of the First Settlement Within Its Borders, 1640 to 1900. (1900) reprint 1993.
Cloth. $75.00. 637 pp. .... Vendor G0259

Chase, J. C. **History of Chester,** Including Auburn. Supplement to "History of Old Chester" (1869). (1926) reprint 1987.
Cloth. $57.00. 535 pp. .... Vendor G0259

Cogswell, E. C. **History of Nottingham, Deerfield, Northwood,** Nottingham & Rockingham Cos., with Genealogical Sketches. (1878) reprint 1987.
Cloth. $79.00. 790 pp. .... Vendor G0259

Dow, Joseph. **History of . . . Hampton, New Hampshire from . . . 1638-1892, with Genealogies**. 2 vols. 1893. Reprint on microfiche. Indexed.
Order nos. 583-584, 399, $62.00/set. .... Vendor G0478

Dow, Joseph. **History of the Town of Hampton,** from Its Settlement in 1638 to the Autumn of 1892. With a Genealogical Register. 2 vols. in 1. (1894) reprint 1993.
Cloth. $105.00. 1,104 pp. .... Vendor G0259

Eaton, F. B. **History of Candia,** Once Known as Charmingfare; with Notices of Some of the Early Families. (1852) reprint 1988.
Cloth. $21.00. 151 pp. .... Vendor G0259

Fitts, J. H. **History of Newfields, 1638-1911**. Edited by N. F. Carter. (1912) reprint 1990.
Cloth. $79.50. viii + 785 pp. .... Vendor G0259

Fullonton, Joseph. **History of Raymond**. (1875) reprint 1993.
Cloth. $44.50. 406 pp. .... Vendor G0259

George, Nellie Palmer. **Old Newmarket: Historical Sketches**. (1932) reprint 1995.
Cloth, $25.00. Paper, $18.00. 133 pp. .... Vendor G0259

Gilbert, E. **History of Salem**. (1907) reprint 1987.
Cloth. $79.50. 444 + 160 pp. .... Vendor G0259

Gill, James, and Maryan Gill. **New Hampshire 1800 Census Index**. 3 vols.
    Volume I: Cheshire Co., 54 pp.
    Volume II: Grafton & Hillsborough Cos., 88 pp.
    Volume III: Rockingham & Strafford Cos., 84 pp.
Paper. $8.00/vol., $21.00/set. .... Vendor G0574

Hazlett, Charles A. **History of Rockingham County & Representative Citizens**. (1915) reprint 1993.
Cloth. $125.00. 1,306 pp. .... Vendor G0259

Hurd, D. H., ed. **History of Rockingham & Strafford County,** with Biographical Sketches of Many of Its Prominent Men & Pioneers. (1882) reprint 1987.
Cloth. $92.00. 889 pp. .... Vendor G0259

Locke, Arthur. **Portsmouth & Newcastle Cemetery Inscriptions,** Abstracted from Some 2,000 Oldest Tombstones. (1907) reprint 1991.
Paper. $9.00. 44 pp. .... Vendor G0259

Moore, J. B. **History of the Town of Candia, Rockingham Co.,** from Its First Settlement to the Present Time [1893]. (1893) reprint 1991.
Cloth. $55.00. 528 pp. .... Vendor G0259

Morrison, L. A. **History of Windham, 1719-1883,** with the History & Genealogy of Its First Settlers & Descendants. (1883) reprint 1987.
Cloth. $88.00. 862 pp. .... Vendor G0259

Noyes, H. E. **Memorial of the Town of Hampstead,** Historic & Genealogical Sketches, Etc. (1899) reprint 1990.
Cloth. $52.00. xi + 468 pp. .... Vendor G0259

Noyes, H. E. **Memorial of the Town of Hampstead, Additions & Corrections.** From "Hist. of the Congregational Church of Hampstead". (1903) reprint 1990.
    May be ordered bound with the book in the previous listing.
Paper. $10.00. 50 pp. .... Vendor G0259

Noyes, Harriette Eliza. **Records of Hampstead, New Hampshire.** Excerpted from the author's *Memorial of the Town of Hampstead,* 1899. Reprinted. Indexed.
Paper. $7.00. 60 pp. .... Vendor G0561

Parker, E. L. **History of Londonderry,** Comprising the Towns of Derry & Londonderry. (1851) reprint 1988.
Cloth. $45.00. 418 pp. .... Vendor G0259

Parsons, L. B. **History of the Town of Rye, 1623-1903**. (1905) reprint 1987.
Cloth. $69.50. 675 pp. .... Vendor G0259

Varrell, W. M. **Rye on the Rocks:** The Tale of a Town; a Yankee Saga Told by a Yankee. (1962) reprint 1990.
Paper. $18.50. 149 pp. .... Vendor G0259

Strafford County

Barrington Public Library. **Traditions and Transitions: Every Person is a Book**. 1995. Illus.
    A collection of stories from members of this rural community, giving their memories of personal, family, and community life.
Paper. $10.00. 52 pp. .... Vendor G0664

Gill, James, and Maryan Gill. **New Hampshire 1800 Census Index**. 3 vols.
    Volume I: Cheshire Co., 54 pp.
    Volume II: Grafton & Hillsborough Cos., 88 pp.
    Volume III: Rockingham & Strafford Cos., 84 pp.
Paper. $8.00/vol., $21.00/set. .... Vendor G0574

Hurd, D. H., ed. **History of Rockingham & Strafford County,** with Biographical Sketches of Many of Its Prominent Men & Pioneers. (1882) reprint 1987.
Cloth. $92.00. 889 pp. .... Vendor G0259

McDuffee, Franklin. **Church Records of Rochester, New Hampshire**. Excerpted from the author's *History of Rochester,* 1892. Reprinted. Indexed.
    Contains baptisms 1737-1758 and 1764-1823; marriages 1745-1757 and 1776-1824.
Paper. $7.00. 52 pp. .... Vendor G0561

McDuffee, Franklin. **History of Rochester, from 1722 to 1890**. Edited by S. Hayward. 2 vols. in 1. (1892) reprint 1988.
Cloth. $69.50. 705 pp. .... Vendor G0259

McDuffee, Franklin. **History of the Town of Rochester, New Hampshire 1722-1890**. (1892) reprint 1988. Indexed. Illus.
  Book #1251.
Cloth. $60.00. 758 pp. .... Vendor G0082

Stackpole, E. S., and L. Thompson. **History of the Town of Durham (Oyster River Plantation) with Genealogical Notes**. 2 vols. (1913) reprint 1992.
  Volume I: Historical.
  Volume II: Genealogical.
Cloth. $45.00/Vol. I. $52.00/Vol. II. $93.50/set. 436 + 502 pp. .... Vendor G0259

Wentworth, William Edgar. **Dover, New Hampshire Vital Records**. 1995. Indexed.
  Book #1593.
Cloth. $37.50. 411 pp. .... Vendor G0082

Sullivan County

History of Washington, from 1768 to 1886, with Genealogies. By a Committee of the Town. (1886) reprint 1987.
Cloth. $69.50. 696 pp. .... Vendor G0259

Merrill, J. L. **History of Acworth,** with the Proceedings of the Centennial Anniversary, Gen. Records & Register of Farms. (1869) reprint 1988.
Cloth. $37.00. 306 pp. .... Vendor G0259

Nelson, W. R. **History of Goshen**. With Two Chapters of Genealogy. (1957) reprint 1991.
Cloth. $49.00. 471 pp. .... Vendor G0259

Waite, Otis F. R. **History of the Town of Claremont,** for a Period of 130 Years, from 1764 to 1894. (1895) reprint 1995.
Cloth. $57.00. 539 pp. .... Vendor G0259

Wheeler, Edmund. **History of Newport, from 1766 to 1878,** with Genealogical Register. (1879) reprint 1992.
Cloth. $59.50. 600 pp. .... Vendor G0259

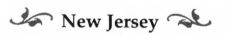

New Jersey

Statewide and Regional References

Armstrong, William C. **Pioneer Families of Northwestern New Jersey**. (1979) reprint 1996. Indexed.
Paper. $47.50. 616 pp. .... Vendor G0011

Bailey, Rosalie Fellows. **Dutch Systems in Family Naming, New York-New Jersey**. Paper. $6.50. 21 pp. .... Vendor G0627

Barber, John W., and Henry Howe. **Historical Collections of New Jersey: Past and Present,** Containing a General Collection of the Most Interesting Facts, Traditions, Biographical Sketches, Anecdotes, Etc. (Rev. ed. 1868) reprint 1995. Illus. Paper. $38.50. 544 pp. .... Vendor G0011

Bill. **New Jersey and the Revolutionary War**. (1964) reprint 1992.
A survey of the major military developments as well as the social and economic effects of the war in New Jersey.
Paper. $11.95. 117 pp. .... Vendor G0611

Boyer, Carl, 3rd. **Ship Passenger Lists: New York and New Jersey (1600-1825)**. 1980. Indexed.
Paper. $24.00. 333 pp. .... Vendor G0140

Chambers, T. F. **Early Germans of New Jersey, Their History, Churches, and Genealogy**. (1895) reprint 1991.
Contact vendor for information. 667 pp. .... Vendor G0010

Family History Library. **Research Outline: New Jersey**.
Leaflet. $.25. 24 pp. .... Vendor G0629

The First Laws of the State of New Jersey. (1783) reprint 1981.
Cloth. $62.50. 455 pp. .... Vendor G0118

Gannett, Henry. **Geographic Dictionary of New Jersey**. (1894) reprint 1993.
Contact vendor for information. 131 pp. .... Vendor G0011

Genealogies of New Jersey Families. From the Genealogical Magazine of New Jersey. 2 vols. 1996. Indexed. Illus.
  Vol. I: Contains family history articles arranged in alphabetical order.
  Vol. II: Contains Bible records and other miscellaneous family records.
Cloth. $75.00/vol., $150.00/set. 2,226 pp. .... Vendor G0010

Gordon, Thomas F. **A Gazetteer of the State of New Jersey**. (1834) reprint 1995. Illus.
Paper. $12.50. 174 pp. .... Vendor G0140

Haines, G., comp. **Early Quaker Marriages from Various Records in N.J**. (1902) reprint 1987.
Paper. $6.50. 32 pp. .... Vendor G0259

Hoelle, Edith. **Genealogical Resources in Southern New Jersey**. 1994.
Paper. $6.00. 35 pp. .... Vendor G0069

Koehler, Albert F. **The Huguenots or Early French in New Jersey**. (1955) reprint 1996. Indexed.
Paper. $9.00. 51 pp. .... Vendor G0011

Littell, John. **Family Records, or Genealogies of the First Settlers of Passaic Valley**. (1852) reprint 1981.
Cloth. $21.00. 512 pp. .... Vendor G0011

McCormick. **New Jersey from Colony to State, 1609-1789**. 1981.
   A history of the state.
Paper. $12.95. 191 pp. .... Vendor G0611

Mellick, Andrew D., Jr. **The Story of an Old Farm,** or, Life in N.J. in the 18th Century. With Genealogical Appendix (Mellick Family). (1889) reprint 1992.
   A well-written history of the state, as well as the story of the N.J. descendants of Johannes Moelich, who landed in Philadelphia in 1735 and settled on "the Old Farm" in Bedminster, Somerset Co., in 1751.
Cloth. $77.00. 742 pp. .... Vendor G0259

Nelson, William. **New Jersey Biographical and Genealogical Notes**. (1916) reprint 1997. Indexed.
Paper. $22.00. 222 pp. .... Vendor G0011

Nelson, William. **New Jersey Calendar of Wills, 1670-1780**. 1901. Reprint on microfiche. Indexed.
Order no. 871-872, $34.00. 660 pp. .... Vendor G0478

Nelson, William, ed. **New Jersey Marriages**. Documents Relating to the Colonial History of N.J.: Marriage Records, 1665-1800. (1900) reprint 1992.
Contact vendor for information. 678 pp. .... Vendor G0010

Nelson, William. **Patents and Deeds and Other Early Records of New Jersey 1664-1703**. (1899) reprint 1997. Indexed.
Paper. $49.95. 770 pp. .... Vendor G0011

New Jersey Adjutant-General's Office. **Records of Officers and Men of New Jersey in Wars 1791-1815**. (1909) reprint 1993. Indexed.
Paper. $42.50. 410 pp. .... Vendor G0011

New Jersey Historical Records Survey. **Index to Stryker's Register of New Jersey in the Revolution**. (1941) reprint 1995.
Paper. $15.00. 142 pp. .... Vendor G0011

New Jersey State Archives. **Colonial Marriage Bonds, 1711-1797**.
Microfilm. $35.00 each. 8 reels; Index, 2 reels. .... Vendor G0585

New Jersey State Archives. **Guide to Family History Sources in the New Jersey State Archives**. 3rd ed.
Paper. $7.00. .... Vendor G0585

New Jersey State Archives. **Index to Revolutionary War Manuscripts**.
   An alphabetical index to New Jerseyans involved in the American Revolution on the patriot side.
Microfilm. $25.00 each. 9 reels. .... Vendor G0585

New Jersey State Archives. **Laws of the Royal Colony of New Jersey 1703-1775, Volumes II-V**. Compiled with an introduction by Bernard Bush.

Compiled from various archival and manuscript depositories, this edition includes the text of all but two of the royal colonial laws. It is the most complete ever published. Genealogists will need to consult the colonial naturalization acts and the many other private bills passed during the period.

Cloth. $10.00/vol. .... Vendor G0585

New Jersey State Archives. **New Jersey State Census, 1855-1915**.

State censuses were enumerated in the middle of each decade, from 1855 to 1915. The 1855, 1865, and 1875 censuses do not include all counties. Contact vendor for details.

Microfilm. $25.00 each. 211 reels. .... Vendor G0585

Parker, J. Carlyle. **Pennsylvania and Middle Atlantic States Genealogical Manuscripts:** A User's Guide to the Manuscript Collections of the Genealogical Society of Pennsylvania as Indexed in Its Manuscript Materials Index; Microfilmed by the Genealogical Department, Salt Lake City. 1986.

Strongest in coverage of eastern Pennsylvania and southern New Jersey.

Paper. $16.95. 45 pp. .... Vendor G0492

Ricord, Frederick W. **General Index to the Documents Relating to the Colonial History of the State of New Jersey** First Series, in Ten Volumes. (1888) reprint 1994.

Cloth. $14.50. 198 pp. .... Vendor G0010

Sarapin. **Old Burial Grounds of New Jersey: A Guide**. 1994.

Not only does the author describe New Jersey burial grounds, she also introduces you to the history and lore of old graveyards, shows you how to read epitaphs, how to date gravestones by style, how to restore an abandoned graveyard, and how to find the stories of the people buried there.

Paper. $14.95. 224 pp. .... Vendor G0611

Shourds, Thomas. **History and Genealogy of Fenwick's Colony [N.J.]**. (1876) reprint 1991. Indexed. Illus.

Cloth. $29.95. 581 pp. .... Vendor G0011

Sinclair, Donald A. **A New Jersey Biographical Index,** covering some 100,000 biographies and associated portraits in 237 New Jersey cyclopedias, histories, yearbooks, periodicals, and other collective biographical sources published to about 1980. 1993.

Cloth. $60.00. 859 pp. .... Vendor G0010

Southern California Genealogical Society. **Sources of Genealogical Help in New Jersey**.

Paper. $3.00. 34 pp. .... Vendor G0656

Stillwell, John E., M.D. **Historical and Genealogical Miscellany:** Data Relating to the Settlement & Settlers of New Jersey, Volumes I-V. (1903-32) reprint 1993.

Volumes I and II of this meticulously researched reference set consist of historical articles that will be of great interest to many who are researching early New Jersey and Staten Island, including transcripts of court records and church registers, quit rents, Friends' records, cemetery inscriptions, and more. Areas covered are Monmouth, Burlington, and Cape May counties, and Staten Island, N.Y.

Volumes III-V contain hundreds of genealogical sketches of New Jersey families.

Contact vendor for information. 2,547 pp. in all. .... Vendor G0010

Stratford, Dorothy Agans, and Thomas B. Wilson. **Certificates and Receipts of Revolutionary New Jersey**. 1996. Indexed.
Names persons who provided goods and services for the Revolutionary War effort.
Cloth. $30.00. 337 pp. .... Vendor G0561

Stryker-Rodda, Kenn. **Given Name Index to the Genealogical Magazine of New Jersey. Volume III**. Indexed.
An every-name index to volumes 31-40 of GMNJ.
Cloth. $30.00. 511 pp. .... Vendor G0561

Stryker-Rodda, Kenn. **Given Name Index to the Genealogical Magazine of New Jersey. Volume IV**.
An every-name index to volumes 41-50 of GMNJ.
Cloth. $30.00. 580 pp. .... Vendor G0561

Stryker-Rodda, Kenn. **New Jersey Index of Wills, Inventories, Etc.** In the Office of the Secretary of State Prior to 1901. With a New Foreword. 3 vols. (1912-13) reprint 1994.
Paper. $120.00. 1,452 pp. .... Vendor G0011

Stryker-Rodda, Kenn. **Revolutionary Census of New Jersey: An Index Based on Rateables, of the Inhabitants of New Jersey During the Period of the American Revolution**. Rev. ed. 1986.
Cloth. $25.00. 414 pp. .... Vendor G0561

Thorndale, William, and William Dollarhide. **County Boundary Map Guides to the U.S. Federal Censuses, 1790-1920: New Jersey, 1790-1920**. 1987.
$5.95. .... Vendor G0552

Wilson, Thomas B. **Notices from New Jersey Newspapers, 1781-1790**. 1988. Indexed.
Contains thousands of public notices with some death and marriage notices.
Cloth. $30.00. 561 pp. .... Vendor G0561

WPA. **The WPA Guide to 1930's New Jersey**. (1939) reprint 1995.
Includes essays covering New Jersey's history, economics, social life, ethnic groups, arts, and recreation; descriptions of the state's most noteworthy cities and towns; and detailed road tours of New Jersey, covering towns, villages, and places of interest along the way.
Paper. $19.95. 735 pp. .... Vendor G0611

Atlantic County

Craig, H. Stanley. **Atlantic County, New Jersey Marriages**. (1935) reprint 1979. Indexed.
Prior to 1837 Atlantic Co. was part of Gloucester Co. Extracted from the County Clerk's books in Mays Landing.
Paper. $10.00. 85 pp. .... Vendor G0140

Hoelle, Edith. **Genealogical Resources in Southern New Jersey**. 1994.
Paper. $6.00. 35 pp. .... Vendor G0069

Wright, Barbara Epler. **Early Church Records of Atlantic and Cape May Counties, New Jersey**. 1995. Indexed.
Paper. $6.00. 83 pp. .... Vendor G0140

Bergen County

Clayton, W. Woodford, ed., with William Nelson. **History of Bergen & Passaic Counties,** with Biographical Sketches of Many of Its Pioneers & Prominent Men. With 1993 every-name index by Jerri Burket. (1882) reprint 1992.
Cloth. $67.00. Index available separately, paper, $16.00. 570 + 90 pp. Vendor G0259

Davis, John David. **Bergen County, New Jersey Deed Records, 1689-1801**. 1995. Indexed.
Paper. $32.00. 412 pp. .... Vendor G0160

Harvey, Cornelium B., ed. **Genealogical History of Hudson & Bergen Counties**. (1900) reprint 1992.
Cloth. $63.50. 617 pp. .... Vendor G0259

Meldrum, Charlotte. **Early Church Records of Bergen County, New Jersey, 1740-1800**. 1995. Indexed.
Paper. $13.00. 167 pp. .... Vendor G0140

New Jersey State Archives. **Revolutionary War Damages**.
Contains property owners' appraisals of damage by British troops in Bergen, Burlington, Essex, Middlesex, and Somerset counties; and by American troops in Bergen, Burlington, Hunterdon, Morris, and Somerset counties. Includes name index.
Microfilm. $35.00 each. 2 reels. .... Vendor G0585

Randolph, H. **Vital Records of Paramus, Bergen County, NJ, Reformed Church**. (1935) reprint 1992. Indexed.
Baptisms 1740-1850, together with records from the gravestones and a list of church members.
Cloth. $41.00. 224 pp. .... Vendor G0450

T.L.C. Genealogy. **Bergen County, New Jersey Taxpayers, 1777-1797**. 1991. Indexed.
Paper. $25.00. 470 pp. .... Vendor G0609

Van Valen, J. M. **History of Bergen County**. With 1994 Index, by Jerri Burket. (1900) reprint 1994.
Cloth. $76.50. Index available separately, paper, $14.00. 691 +
71 pp. .... Vendor G0259

Versteeg, Dingman, and Thomas Vermilye, Jr. **Bergen Records: Records of the Reformed Protestant Dutch Church of Bergen in New Jersey, 1666 to 1788**. 3 vols. in 1. (1913-15) reprint 1990. Indexed. Illus.
Includes baptism, marriage, and burial records of the Dutch Church of Bergen. Also included are histories of early New Jersey Dutch families and a history of Bergen.
Cloth. $20.00. 300 pp. in all. .... Vendor G0011

Westervelt, Frances A. **Families of Bergen County, New Jersey,** Excerpted from History of Bergen County, New Jersey, 1630-1923. (1923) reprint 1996. Indexed. Illus.
Paper. $49.95. 742 pp. in all. .... Vendor G0011

Burlingham County

Brown, Virginia Alleman. **New Jersey Heirs to Estates from Partitions and Divisions: Monmouth, Mercer & Burlington Counties**. (1993) reprint 1995. Indexed.
 Covers Monmouth County Partitions 1845-1862; Monmouth County Divisions 1793-1903; Mercer County Partitions 1838-1862; and Burlington County Divisions 1798-1896.
Paper. $15.00. 135 pp. .... Vendor G0011

Burlington County

Blackman, Leah. **History of Little Egg Harbor Township, Burlington Co.,** from Its First Settlement to the Present Time. (1880?) reprint 1994.
Cloth. $49.50. 468 pp. .... Vendor G0259

Craig, H. Stanley. **Burlington County Marriages**. (1932) reprint 1977. Indexed.
 Data from Friends Meetings, church records, and the County Clerk's office in Burlington from the late 1600s to 1880.
Paper. $19.50. 340 pp. .... Vendor G0140

Hoelle, Edith. **Genealogical Resources in Southern New Jersey**. 1994.
Paper. $6.00. 35 pp. .... Vendor G0069

Meldrum, Charlotte. **Early Church Records of Burlington County**. 3 vols. 1994, 1995. Indexed.
Paper. $24.00/Vols. 1 & 2 each. $16.00/Vol. 3. 292 + 298 +
201 pp. .... Vendor G0140

New Jersey State Archives. **Revolutionary War Damages**.
 Contains property owners' appraisals of damage by British troops in Bergen, Burlington, Essex, Middlesex, and Somerset counties; and by American troops in Bergen, Burlington, Hunterdon, Morris, and Somerset counties. Includes name index.
Microfilm. $35.00 each. 2 reels. .... Vendor G0585

Woodward, E. M., and J. F. Hageman. **History of Burlington & Mercer Counties,** with Biographical Sketches of Its Pioneers & Prominent Men. (1887) reprint 1988.
Cloth. $95.00. 888 pp. .... Vendor G0259

Camden County

Craig, H. Stanley. **Camden County Marriages**. (1932) reprint 1980. Indexed.
 Marriages from 1844 through 1890 comprise the bulk of this work.
Paper. $13.00. 196 pp. .... Vendor G0140

Hoelle, Edith. **Genealogical Resources in Southern New Jersey**. 1994.
Paper. $6.00. 35 pp. .... Vendor G0069

Prowell, George R. **History of Camden County**. (1886) reprint 1994.
Cloth. $79.00. 769 pp. .... Vendor G0259

Cape May County

Craig, H. Stanley, and Julias Way. **Cape May County Marriages**. (1931) reprint 1978. Indexed.
   Marriages from early 1700s to 1880.
Paper. $12.00. 131 pp. .... Vendor G0140

Hoelle, Edith. **Genealogical Resources in Southern New Jersey**. 1994.
Paper. $6.00. 35 pp. .... Vendor G0069

Howe, P. S. **Cape May County Mayflower Pilgrim Descendants**. (1921) reprint 1996.
Contact vendor for information. 464 pp. .... Vendor G0011

Stevens, Lewis Townsend. **The History of Cape May County, New Jersey,** from Aboriginal Times to the Present Day . . . (1897) reprint 1997.
Paper. $37.50. 480 pp. .... Vendor G0011

Wright, Barbara Epler. **Early Church Records of Atlantic and Cape May Counties, New Jersey**. 1995. Indexed.
Paper. $6.00. 83 pp. .... Vendor G0140

Cumberland County

Craig, H. Stanley, comp. **Cumberland County Genealogical Data:** Records Pertaining to Persons Residing in Cumberland County Prior to 1800. (n.d.) reprint 1996.
Paper. $27.00. 248 pp. .... Vendor G0259

Craig, H. Stanley. **Cumberland County, N.J. Marriages**. (1932) reprint 1987.
Paper. $19.50. 333 pp. .... Vendor G0140

Hoelle, Edith. **Genealogical Resources in Southern New Jersey**. 1994.
Paper. $6.00. 35 pp. .... Vendor G0069

Essex County

Atkinson, Joseph. **History of Newark,** Being a Narrative of Its Rise & Progress from the Settlement in May, 1666. (1878) reprint 1993.
Cloth. $39.50. 334 pp. .... Vendor G0259

Folsom, Joseph Fulford et al., ed. **Municipalities of Essex County, 1666-1924**. 4 vols. in 2. (1925) reprint 1993.
   Volumes I & II: History.
   Volumes III & IV: Biography.
Cloth. $89.00/Vols. I & II. $45.00/Vols. III & IV. $125.00/set. 888+ 409 pp. Vendor G0259

New Jersey State Archives. **Revolutionary War Damages**.
   Contains property owners' appraisals of damage by British troops in Bergen,

Burlington, Essex, Middlesex, and Somerset counties; and by American troops in Bergen, Burlington, Hunterdon, Morris, and Somerset counties. Includes name index.
Microfilm. $35.00 each. 2 reels. .... Vendor G0585

Shaw, William H., comp. **History of Essex & Hudson Counties**. 2 vols. 1884.
Volume I: Essex County.
Volume II: Hudson County.
Cloth. $68.00/Vol. I. $74.00/Vol. II. $135.00/set. 678 + 734 pp. .... Vendor G0259

Wickes, Stephen. **History of the Oranges, in Essex Co**. (1892) reprint 1992.
Cloth. $39.00. 334 pp. .... Vendor G0259

Gloucester County

Baker, Ruthe, ed. **The Diaries of Samuel Mickle, Woodbury, Gloucester County, New Jersey 1792-1829**. 2 vols. 1991. Indexed.
Thirty-seven years of local, state, and national events, including Revolution, War of 1812; 5,000 vital statistics of South Jersey.
Paper. $63.00. 834 pp. .... Vendor G0069

Craig, H. Stanley. **Atlantic County, New Jersey Marriages**. (1935) reprint 1979. Indexed.
Prior to 1837 Atlantic Co. was part of Gloucester Co. Extracted from the County Clerk's books in Mays Landing.
Paper. $10.00. 85 pp. .... Vendor G0140

Craig, H. Stanley. **Gloucester County Marriages**. (1930) reprint 1977. Indexed.
Paper. $19.50. 309 pp. .... Vendor G0140

Friel, Florence, ed. **The Diary of Job Whitall, Gloucester County, New Jersey 1775-1779**. 1992. Indexed.
Description of everyday life in the midst of opposing armies—"The Battle of Red Bank."
Paper. $16.50. 200 pp. .... Vendor G0069

Gibson, G., and F. Gibson. **Gloucester County Residents, 1850**. (n.d.) reprint 1993.
A combination of the genealogical parts of the 1850 census and 1849 maps showing 1,000 family locations. Very helpful for anyone with Gloucester Co. roots.
Cloth. $34.50. 337 pp. .... Vendor G0259

Hammell, Jeanne M. **South Jersey Church Records, Baptisms, Marriages, Deaths 1750-1900, Vol. 1**. 1990. Indexed.
Vital Statistics from seventeen churches in Gloucester County, never before published.
Paper. $20.50. 385 pp. .... Vendor G0069

Hammell, Jeanne M. **South Jersey Church Records, Baptisms, Marriages, Deaths 1750-1900, Vol. 2**. 1992. Indexed.
Vital Statistics from twelve more churches, never before published.
Paper. $22.50. 418 pp. .... Vendor G0069

Hoelle, Edith. **Genealogical Resources in Southern New Jersey**. 1994.
Paper. $6.00. 35 pp. .... Vendor G0069

Meldrum, Charlotte. **Early Church Records of Gloucester County, New Jersey**. 1996. Indexed.
Paper. $25.00. 306 pp. .... Vendor G0140

Steelman, James F., and Georgene L. Steelman. **Index of Land Documents in the Possession of the Gloucester County Historical Society**. 1993. Indexed.
   Includes almost 600 unrecorded deeds, providing rare information not in courthouses.
Paper. $11.50. 57 pp. .... Vendor G0069

Hudson County

Harvey, Cornelium B., ed. **Genealogical History of Hudson & Bergen Counties**. (1900) reprint 1992.
Cloth. $63.50. 617 pp. .... Vendor G0259

Shaw, William H., comp. **History of Essex & Hudson Counties**. 2 vols. 1884.
   Volume I: Essex County.
   Volume II: Hudson County.
Cloth. $68.00/Vol. I. $74.00/Vol. II. $135.00/set. 678 + 734 pp. .... Vendor G0259

Van Winkle, Daniel, ed. **History of the Municipalities of Hudson County, 1630-1923**. 3 vols. in 2. (1924) reprint 1995.
   Volume I: History.
   Volume II: Biography.
Cloth. $56.00/Vol. I. $83.00/Vol. II. $125.00/set. 534 + 803 pp. .... Vendor G0259

Van Winkle, Daniel. **Old Bergen History & Reminiscences,** with Maps & Illustrations. (1902) reprint 1993.
Cloth. $37.00. 319 pp. .... Vendor G0259

Winfield, C. H. **History of Hudson County,** from the Earliest Settlement to the Present Time. With 1993 Index by Jerri Burket. (1874) reprint 1990.
Cloth. $62.50. 568 + 40 pp. .... Vendor G0259

Hunterdon County

Beers, F. W. **Atlas of Hunterdon County New Jersey from Recent and Actual Surveys**. (1873) reprint 1987. Illus.
   Maps of fourteen townships and thirty-two towns showing owners' names.
Cloth. $42.00. 77 pp. .... Vendor G0180

D'Autrechy, Phyllis B. **Hunterdon County New Jersey Fisheries 1819-1820**. 1993. Indexed. Illus.
   History of shad fishing on the Delaware River with names, locations, and operators of fisheries within Hunterdon.
Paper. $9.50. 44 pp. .... Vendor G0180

Deats, Hiram E. **The Hunterdon County New Jersey Militia 1792**. (1936) reprint 1994.
   Alphabetical listing by township of "free and able-bodied white males between 18 and 45."
Paper. $14.00. 37 pp. .... Vendor G0180

Deats, Hiram E. **Marriage Records of Hunterdon County, New Jersey, 1795-1875**. (1917) reprint 1986 with additions & corrections.
Cloth. $25.00. 378 pp. .... Vendor G0561

New Jersey State Archives. **Hunterdon County Court of Common Pleas, Minutes, 1714-1908**.
Summaries of civil cases, which consist of litigants' names and court action taken.
Microfilm. $35.00 each. 12 reels. .... Vendor G0585

New Jersey State Archives. **Revolutionary War Damages**.
Contains property owners' appraisals of damage by British troops in Bergen, Burlington, Essex, Middlesex, and Somerset counties; and by American troops in Bergen, Burlington, Hunterdon, Morris, and Somerset counties. Includes name index.
Microfilm. $35.00 each. 2 reels. .... Vendor G0585

Snell, James P., comp. **History of Hunterdon & Somerset Counties,** with Illustrations & Biographical Sketches of Its Prominent Men & Pioneers. (1881) reprint 1992.
Cloth. $89.50. 864 pp. .... Vendor G0259

T.L.C. Genealogy. **Hunterdon County, New Jersey Taxpayers, 1778-1797**. 1990. Indexed.
Paper. $14.00. 203 pp. .... Vendor G0609

Wittwer, Norman C., Jr. **The Faithful and the Bold**. 1984. Indexed.
The story of the first service of the Zion Evangelical Lutheran Church, Oldwick, New Jersey.
Cloth. $12.00. 49 pp. .... Vendor G0180

Mercer County

Brown, Virginia Alleman. **New Jersey Heirs to Estates from Partitions and Divisions: Monmouth, Mercer & Burlington Counties**. (1993) reprint 1995. Indexed.
Covers Monmouth County Partitions 1845-1862; Monmouth County Divisions 1793-1903; Mercer County Partitions 1838-1862; and Burlington County Divisions 1798-1896.
Paper. $15.00. 135 pp. .... Vendor G0011

Cooley, Eli F., and William S. Cooley. **Genealogy of Early Settlers in Trenton and Ewing, "Old Hunterdon County," New Jersey**. (1883) reprint 1996. Indexed.
The majority of the genealogies in this collection trace families through successive generations of the 18th and 19th centuries in what is now mostly Mercer County.
Paper. $27.50. 336 pp. .... Vendor G0011

Hale, G. **History of the Old Presbyterian Congregation of the People of Maidenhead & Hopewell, at Pennington NJ**. (1876) reprint 1993.
Includes local history and genealogy, 1707-1876.
Cloth. $15.00. 128 pp. .... Vendor G0259

Raum, John O. **History of the City of Trenton,** Embracing a Period of Nearly Two Hundred Years. (1871) reprint 1992.
Cloth. $49.50. 448 pp. .... Vendor G0259

Woodward, E. M., and J. F. Hageman. **History of Burlington & Mercer Counties,** with Biographical Sketches of Its Pioneers & Prominent Men. (1887) reprint 1988.
Cloth. $95.00. 888 pp. .... Vendor G0259

Middlesex County

Benedict, William H. **New Brunswick in History**. Includes Genealogical Sketches. (1925) reprint 1993.
Cloth. $44.00. 391 pp. .... Vendor G0259

Brown, Virginia Alleman. **New Jersey Heirs to Estates from Partitions and Divisions: Middlesex County, 1780-1870**. 1988. Indexed.
Paper. $16.00. 107 pp. .... Vendor G0011

Clayton, W. Woodford, ed. **History of Union & Middlesex Counties,** with Biographical Sketches of Many of Their Prominent Men & Pioneers. 1882.
Cloth. $89.50. 885 pp. .... Vendor G0259

Dally, Rev. Joseph W. **Woodbridge and Vicinity: The Story of a New Jersey Township**. 1873. Reprinted.
  Includes the vital records from the ancient town books ca. 1680-1750.
Cloth. $27.50. 392 pp. .... Vendor G0561

Dutcher, Russell K., III. **Compiled Records of the Middlesex County, New Jersey Militia, 1791-1795**. With Biographical Sketches of the Officers of Selected Companies. Including a Roster of the Middlesex County Militia, 1775-1783. 1996. Indexed. Illus.
Paper. $26.50. 275 pp. .... Vendor G0011

McGinnis, William C. **History of Perth Amboy, 1651-1958**. 3 vols. in 1. (1958) reprint 1995.
Cloth. $49.50. 153 + 145 + 189 pp. .... Vendor G0259

New Jersey State Archives. **Revolutionary War Damages**.
  Contains property owners' appraisals of damage by British troops in Bergen, Burlington, Essex, Middlesex, and Somerset counties; and by American troops in Bergen, Burlington, Hunterdon, Morris, and Somerset counties. Includes name index.
Microfilm. $35.00 each. 2 reels. .... Vendor G0585

Whitehead, W. A. **Contributions to the Early History of Perth Amboy & Adjoining Country,** with Sketches of Men & Events in NJ During the Provincial Era. (1856) reprint 1991.
Cloth. $47.00. 428 pp. .... Vendor G0259

Monmouth County

Adelberg, Michael S. **Roster of the People of Revolutionary Monmouth County [New Jersey]**. 1997.
Paper. $32.50. 348 pp. .... Vendor G0011

Brown, Virginia Alleman. **New Jersey Heirs to Estates from Partitions and Divisions: Monmouth, Mercer & Burlington Counties**. (1993) reprint 1995. Indexed.
Covers Monmouth County Partitions 1845-1862; Monmouth County Divisions 1793-1903; Mercer County Partitions 1838-1862; and Burlington County Divisions 1798-1896.
Paper. $15.00. 135 pp. .... Vendor G0011

Ellis, Franklin. **History of Monmouth County**. (1885) reprint 1992.
Cloth. $89.50. 902 pp. .... Vendor G0259

Gibson, George, and Florence Gibson. **Marriages of Monmouth County, New Jersey, 1795-1843**. (1981) reprint 1995. Indexed.
Paper. $16.50. 143 pp. .... Vendor G0011

Hornor, William S. **This Old Monmouth of Ours**. (1932) reprint 1990. Indexed.
Cloth. $30.00. 444 pp. .... Vendor G0011

Salter, Edwin. **History of Monmouth & Ocean Counties**. Includes a Genealogical Register. (1890) reprint 1990.
Cloth. $53.00. 510 pp. .... Vendor G0259

Salter, Edwin, and George C. Beekman. **Old Times in Old Monmouth**. Historical Reminiscences of Old Monmouth County, New Jersey. (1887) reprint 1994. Indexed.
Paper. $38.00. 474 pp. .... Vendor G0011

Symmes, Rev. Frank R. **History of the Old Tennent Church**. With Historical Records, Genealogical Notes, Graveyard Transcriptions and Much Other Information About the History of the Town, as well as the Church. (1904) reprint 1994.
Cloth. $49.50. 472 pp. .... Vendor G0259

Morris County

Brown, Virginia Alleman. **New Jersey Heirs to Estates from Partitions and Divisions: Morris County, 1785-1900**. (1984) reprint 1992. Indexed.
Contact vendor for information. 357 pp. .... Vendor G0011

History of Morris County, with Illustrations & Biographical Sketches of Prominent Citizens & Pioneers. (1882) reprint 1992.
Cloth. $45.00. 407 pp. .... Vendor G0259

The Lewis Publishing Company. **Biographical and Genealogical History of Morris County, New Jersey**. Reprint on microfiche.
Order no. 472, $30.00. 416 pp. .... Vendor G0478

New Jersey State Archives. **Revolutionary War Damages**.
Contains property owners' appraisals of damage by British troops in Bergen, Burlington, Essex, Middlesex, and Somerset counties; and by American troops in Bergen, Burlington, Hunterdon, Morris, and Somerset counties. Includes name index.
Microfilm. $35.00 each. 2 reels. .... Vendor G0585

Wheeler, William O., and Edmund D. Halsey. **Inscriptions on the Tombstones and Monuments in the Graveyards at Whippany and Hanover, Morris County, New Jersey**. 1894. Reprinted.
Paper. $8.00. 100 pp. .... Vendor G0561

Ocean County

Hoelle, Edith. **Genealogical Resources in Southern New Jersey**. 1994.
Paper. $6.00. 35 pp. .... Vendor G0069

Salter, Edwin. **History of Monmouth & Ocean Counties**. Includes a Genealogical Register. (1890) reprint 1990.
Cloth. $53.00. 510 pp. .... Vendor G0259

Passaic County

Clayton, W. Woodford, ed., with William Nelson. **History of Bergen & Passaic Counties,** with Biographical Sketches of Many of Its Pioneers & Prominent Men. With 1993 every-name index by Jerri Burket. (1882) reprint 1992.
Cloth. $67.00. Index available separately, paper, $16.00. 570 + 90 pp. Vendor G0259

Kelly, Arthur C. M (for the Holland Society). **Vital Records of Acquackanonk Reformed Church, Passaic, NJ**. Indexed.
　Baptisms, marriages, members, deaths, 1727-1816.
Cloth. $49.00. 381 pp. .... Vendor G0450

Nelson, William. **History of the City of Paterson** & the County of Passaic. With 1994 Index by Jerri Burket. (1901) reprint 1994.
　N.B. This book was ended by the author on page 448, and in the middle of a sentence!
Cloth. $59.50. 448 + 132 pp. .... Vendor G0259

Pape, William J., ed., with William W. Scott. **The News' History of Passaic,** from the Earliest Settlement to the Present Day, Embracing a Descriptive History of Its Municipal, Religious, Social and Commercial Institutions, with Biographical Sketches. (1899) reprint 1996.
Cloth. $35.00. 320 pp. .... Vendor G0259

Whitehead, John. **The Passaic Valley in Three Centuries, Past & Present**. 2 vols. (n.d.) reprint 1993.
　Volume I: History.
　Volume II: Biography.
Cloth. $49.50/vol. 469 + 528 pp. .... Vendor G0259

Salem County

Craig, H. Stanley. **Salem County Marriage Records**. (1928) reprint 1978. Indexed.
　Marriage records from 1600s to 1880.
Paper. $17.00. 295 pp. .... Vendor G0140

Craig, H. Stanley. **Salem County Wills** Recorded in the Office of the Surrogate at Salem, 1804-1830. (1941?) reprint 1995.
Paper. $21.00. 214 pp. .... Vendor G0259

Gibson, Florence H. **Salem County, New Jersey Census 1860**. 1991. Indexed.
　This large volume contains over 19,500 Salem County names, plus ages, birthplace, etc.
Paper. $33.50. 659 pp. .... Vendor G0069

Hoelle, Edith. **Genealogical Resources in Southern New Jersey**. 1994.
Paper. $6.00. 35 pp. .... Vendor G0069

Meldrum, Charlotte. **Early Church Records of Salem County, N.J.**
Paper. $24.00. 308 pp. .... Vendor G0140

Shourds, Thomas. **History & Genealogy of Fenwick's Colony**. (1876) reprint 1992.
    Contains many family histories from this colony, which comprised one-tenth of western N.J.
Cloth. $49.00. 581 pp. .... Vendor G0259

Somerset County

Honeyman, A. Van Doren. **Somerset County Historical Quarterly**. 2 vols. (1912, 1913) reprint 1995.
Cloth. $37.50/vol., $69.50/set. 337 + 331 pp. .... Vendor G0259

New Jersey State Archives. **Revolutionary War Damages**.
    Contains property owners' appraisals of damage by British troops in Bergen, Burlington, Essex, Middlesex, and Somerset counties; and by American troops in Bergen, Burlington, Hunterdon, Morris, and Somerset counties. Includes name index.
Microfilm. $35.00 each. 2 reels. .... Vendor G0585

Snell, James P., comp. **History of Hunterdon & Somerset Counties,** with Illustrations & Biographical Sketches of Its Prominent Men & Pioneers. (1881) reprint 1992.
Cloth. $89.50. 864 pp. .... Vendor G0259

Somerset County Historical Quarterly. 8 vols. 1912-1919. Indexed.
    One of the mainstays of central New Jersey genealogy. Includes church registers dating from the colonial period, Somerset County marriage records 1795-1879, cemetery inscriptions, etc.
Cloth. $30.00 each/Vols. 1 & 2. $25.00 each/Vols. 3-8. .... Vendor G0561

Sussex County

Brown, Virginia Alleman. **New Jersey Heirs to Estates from Partitions and Divisions: Warren & Sussex Counties, 1789-1918**. (1978) reprint 1992. Indexed.
Paper. Contact vendor for information. 167 pp. .... Vendor G0011

History of Sussex & Warren Counties, with Illustrations & Biographical Sketches of Prominent Men & Pioneers. (1881) reprint 1992.
Cloth. $81.00. 748 pp. .... Vendor G0259

Schaeffer, Caspar, and William M. Johnson. **Memoirs & Reminscences,** Together with Sketches of the Early History of Sussex County, NJ, with Notes & Genealogical Record of the Schaeffer, Shaver, or Shafer family. (1907) reprint 1994.
Cloth. $29.50. 187 pp. .... Vendor G0259

Union County

Clayton, W. Woodford, ed. **History of Union & Middlesex Counties,** with Biographical Sketches of Many of Their Prominent Men & Pioneers. 1882.
Cloth. $89.50. 885 pp. .... Vendor G0259

Hatfield, Edwin F. **History of Elizabeth,** Including the Early History of Union County. (1868) reprint 1990.
Cloth. $73.00. 701 pp. .... Vendor G0259

Ricord, F. W., ed. **History of Union County**. (1897) reprint 1992.
Cloth. $68.00. 656 pp. .... Vendor G0259

Wheeler, W. O., and E. D. Halsey, comps. **Inscriptions on Tombstones & Monuments** in the Burying Grounds of the First Presbyterian Church & St. Johns Church at Elizabeth, 1664-1892. (1892) reprint 1994.
Cloth. $39.50. 355 pp. .... Vendor G0259

Warren County

Brown, Virginia Alleman. **New Jersey Heirs to Estates from Partitions and Divisions: Warren & Sussex Counties, 1789-1918**. (1978) reprint 1992. Indexed.
Paper. Contact vendor for information. 167 pp. .... Vendor G0011

History of Sussex & Warren Counties, with Illustrations & Biographical Sketches of Prominent Men & Pioneers. (1881) reprint 1992.
Cloth. $81.00. 748 pp. .... Vendor G0259

❧ New Mexico ❧

Statewide and Regional References

Bolton, Herbert E. **The Spanish Borderlands: A Chronicle of Old Florida and the Southwest**. (1921) reprint 1996.
  In narrative prose, Bolton recounts the Spanish exploration and the permanent settlement of Old Florida, New Mexico, Texas, Louisiana, and California.
Paper. $22.50. 320 pp. .... Vendor G0611

Family History Library. **Research Outline: New Mexico**.
Leaflet. $.25. 8 pp. .... Vendor G0629

Simons, Marc. **Coronado's Land: Daily Life in Colonial New Mexico**. 1996.
  A collection of essays detailing the social history of New Mexico in its infancy.
Paper. $10.95. 183 pp. .... Vendor G0611

Southern California Genealogical Society. **Sources of Genealogical Help in New Mexico**.
Paper. $2.25. 15 pp. .... Vendor G0656

Thorndale, William, and William Dollarhide. **County Boundary Map Guides to the U.S. Federal Censuses, 1790-1920: New Mexico, 1850-1920.** 1987. $5.95. .... Vendor G0552

Twitchell, Ralph Emerson. **Leading Facts of New Mexican History.** 2 vols. (1911) reprint 1994.
Cloth. $51.00/Vol. I. $64.00/Vol. II. $109.50/set. 506 + 631 pp. .... Vendor G0259

New York

Statewide and Regional References

Adams, Richard. **Delaware Indians: A Brief History.** Indexed.
A turn-of-the-century comprehensive history by a descendant of Chief White Eyes. Includes customs, folklore, religion, and first-person accounts of all their military involvement through the Civil War.
Paper. $8.95. 80 pp. .... Vendor G0160

All-Name Index to the 1860 Gazetteer of New York State. 1993.
Includes listing of geographic names not in original index. Included with paper version of the 1860 Gazetteer by J. H. French.
Paper. $15.00. 183 pp. .... Vendor G0093

Armstrong, Barbra Kay. **Index to the 1800 Census of New York.** (1984) reprint 1996.
Paper. $36.50. 432 pp. .... Vendor G0011

Atlas of New York State, Topographical.
This present-day atlas provides the researcher with the detail needed to conduct a proper search. It is the size of a Rand McNally atlas of the entire U.S. 11" x 15½".
$16.95. .... Vendor G0611

Bailey, Rosalie Fellows. **Dutch Systems in Family Naming, New York-New Jersey**. Paper. $6.50. 21 pp. .... Vendor G0627

Banvard, Theodore James Fleming. **Goodenows Who Originated in Sudbury, Massachusetts 1638 A.D.** 1994. Indexed. Illus.
Cloth. $78.50. 952 pp. .... Vendor G0116

Barbour, Hugh, Christopher Densmore, and Elizabeth Moger, eds. **Quaker Crosscurrents: Three Hundred Years of New York Yearly Meetings**. With Nancy Sorel, Alson Van Wagner, and Arthur Worrall. Foreword by Martin Marty. Indexed. Illus.
The first comprehensive history of the Religious Society of Friends or Quakers of New York, from their earliest appearance in the Dutch colony of New Netherlands in the 1650s to the present.
Paper. $19.95. 500 pp. .... Vendor G0160

Bayor, Ronald H., and Timothy J. Meagher, eds. **The New York Irish**. 1996.
A sweeping story of the Irish immigrants and the impact of their descendants on the history of New York. The history of the Irish in New York is almost as old as the city itself.
Cloth. $45.00. 743 pp. .... Vendor G0611

Bowman, Fred Q. **8,000 More Vital Records of Eastern New York State, 1804-1850**. 1991.
Marriage and death notices from newspapers, eastern New York, including Long Island.
Cloth. $24.00. 296 pp. .... Vendor G0450

Bowman, Fred Q. **10,000 Vital Records of Central New York, 1813-1850**. 1988. Indexed.
Cloth. $22.50. 338 pp. .... Vendor G0010

Bowman, Fred Q. **10,000 Vital Records of Eastern New York, 1777-1834**. 1989. Indexed.
Contact vendor for information. 356 pp. .... Vendor G0010

Bowman, Fred Q. **10,000 Vital Records of Western New York, 1809-1850**. (1985) reprint 1988. Indexed.
Cloth. $22.50. 318 pp. .... Vendor G0010

Bowman, Fred Q., and Thomas J. Lynch. **Directory to Collections of New York Vital Records, 1726-1989, with Rare Gazetteer**. 1995. Illus.
Identifies several hundred collections of newspaper-published vital records, 1726-1989.
Cloth. $31.00. 91 pp. .... Vendor G0160

Bowman, Fred Q. **Landholders of Northeastern New York, 1739-1802**. (1983) reprint 1987.
Cloth. $20.00. 228 pp. .... Vendor G0010

Brink, Benjamin Myer. **Militia: New York State Provincial & Revolutionary War Organizations**.
Describes uniforms, lists officers, and outlines involvement, especially the fall of Fort Montgomery.
Stapled booklet. $5.00. 26 pp. .... Vendor G0160

Calendar of Historical Manuscripts in the Office of the Secretary of State of N.Y. Part I, Dutch Mss., 1630-1664. (1865) reprint 1993.
   Includes council minutes, international commercial records, writs, patents, deeds, etc., trans. to English and fully indexed.
Cloth. $47.00. 423 pp. .... Vendor G0259

Crossing the Border. 1990.
   The syllabus of the GCNY 3-day conference held in Rochester, NY.
Paper. $10.00. .... Vendor G0093

Cutter, William Richard. **Families of Western New York** Excerpted from Genealogical and Family History of Western New York. A Record of the Achievements of Her People in the Making of a Commonwealth and the Building of a Nation. (1912) reprint 1996. Indexed. Illus.
Paper. $49.95. 511 pp. .... Vendor G0011

Cutter, William Richard. **Genealogical and Family History of Central New York**. A Record of the Achievements of Her People in the Making of a Commonwealth and the Building of a Nation. In Three Volumes. Partially indexed. (1912) reprint 1994.
Paper. $150.00. 1,612 pp. in all. .... Vendor G0011

Davis, Margaret P. **Honey Out of the Rafters**. (1976) reprint 1989. Illus.
Pictorial history of the settlement and growth of Steuben and Remsen, New York 1786-1940.
Paper. $12.95. 136 pp. .... Vendor G0070

Dilts, Bryan Lee, comp. **1890 New York Veterans Census Index**. 2nd ed. 1993.
Cloth. $112.00. 379 pp. .... Vendor G0552

Dixon, Nancy Wagoner. **Palatine Roots:** The 1710 German Settlement in NY as Experienced by Johann Peter Wagner. 1994. Indexed. Illus.
Book #1521. Tells the story of New York's Palatine settlers by focusing on the experiences of the author's ancestor Johann Peter Wagner and his family.
Cloth. $49.50. 352 pp. .... Vendor G0082

Epperson, Gwenn F. **New Netherland Roots**. (1994) reprint 1995. Illus.
Cloth. $20.00. 176 pp. .... Vendor G0010

Evjen, John O. **Scandinavian Immigrants in New York, 1630-1674**. (1916) reprint 1996. Illus.
Paper. $36.50. 464 pp. .... Vendor G0011

Family History Library. **Research Outline: New York**.
Leaflet. $.25. 32 pp. .... Vendor G0629

Fay, Loren V. **Quaker Census of 1828**. Illus.
Members of the New York Yearly Meeting, The Religious Society of Friends at the time of the Separation.
Cloth. $20.00. 329 pp. .... Vendor G0450

Fernow, Berthold, comp. **Calendar of Council Minutes 1668-1783**. (1902) reprint 1987.
Book #1362.
Cloth. $49.50. 726 pp. .... Vendor G0082

Fernow, Berthold. **[New York] Calendar of Wills** on File and Recorded in the Office of the Clerk of the Court of Appeals, of the County Clerk at Albany, and of the Secretary of State, 1626-1836. (1896) reprint 1991. Indexed.
Contact vendor for information. 672 pp. .... Vendor G0011

The First Laws of the State of New York. (1782) reprint 1984.
Cloth. $62.50. 255 pp. .... Vendor G0118

French, J. H. **Gazetteer of the State of New York (1860),** Reprinted with an Index of Names Compiled by Frank Place. (1860, 1983) reprint 1995. Indexed. Illus.
Cloth. $55.00. 926 pp. .... Vendor G0010

French, J. H. **Gazetteer (1860) of the State of New York**. (1860) reprint 1993. Indexed. Illus.
Long considered a Bible for New York research, which includes almost every place in New York; short histories and facts about events and early settlers; also many statistical tables. Cloth price does not include new, all-name index. Paper price includes new index.
Cloth, $35.00. Paper, $35.00. 784 pp. .... Vendor G0093

Gordon, T. F. **Gazetteer of the State of New York,** Comprehending Its Colonial History; General Geography, Geology, Internal Improvements; Its Political State; Minute Description of Its Several Counties, Towns, and Villages; Statistical Tables. (1836) reprint 1990.
Cloth. $79.50. 800 pp. .... Vendor G0259

Hagerty, Gilbert. **Wampum, War and Trade Goods West of the Hudson**. 1987. Indexed. Illus.
This book uses archaeology to document evidence of the history makers of the Mohawk Valley. A chronicle of Mohawk life during the 17th century. 9 maps, 250 illustrations.
Cloth. $40.00. 312 pp. .... Vendor G0093

Hall, Rev. Charles. **The Dutch and the Iroquois**. c. 1882.
Outlines the influence the Dutch had and its direct effect on relations with the Iroquois.
Paper. $8.95. 55 pp. .... Vendor G0160

Hastings, H., and H. H. Noble, comps. & eds. **Military Minutes of the Council of Appointment of the State of N.Y., 1783-1821**. 3 vols. + index. (1901) reprint 1993.
This invaluable set contains the complete military appointments for N.Y. by county, including appointments, promotions & resignations. Name Index represents all military commissions issued.
Cloth. $249.50. Index only (586 pp.), $59.50. 3,038 pp. .... Vendor G0259

Hayward, Elizabeth. **American Vital Records from the Baptist Register, 1824-1832 and the New York Baptist Register, 1832-1834**. Indexed.
Abstracts of deaths and marriages from a newspaper published in Utica, NY but area of interest embraces eastern United States. Includes a geographical locator.
Paper. $12.50. 105 pp. .... Vendor G0160

Herrick, Margaret. **A Civil War Soldier's Diary, Peter W. Funk, 150th NY Vol**. 1991. Indexed.
Diary of a foot soldier in the Union Army, 1862-1865; genealogical information and comment by Burton Coon.
Paper. $13.50. 54 pp. .... Vendor G0450

The Holland Society of New York. **Yearbook of the Holland Society of New York**. 1908. Reprinted. Indexed. Illus.
Paper. $27.00. 350 pp. .... Vendor G0160

Hough, Franklin B. **Gazetteer of the State of New York,** Embracing a Comprehensive Account of the History & Statistics of the State, with Geological & Topographical Descriptions of Each County, City, Town & Village. (1872) reprint 1993.
Many New York counties were divided several times, and town, township, and village names were often duplicated in every county. This book can help! Very useful for anyone researching New York.
Cloth. $75.00. 745 pp. .... Vendor G0259

Indexes of Hope Farm Press Publications.
Automatic search feature. DOS program for IBM-compatible computer.
IBM 3.5" diskette. $10.00 + shipping. .... Vendor G0160

James, Patricia R., comp. **Index to the "Black River and Northern New York Conference Memorial" Series**. 1996. Indexed.
Paper. $35.00. .... Vendor G0506

Jones, Henry Z, Jr. **The Palatine Families of New York - 1710**. 2 vols. Indexed. Illus.
    Winner of the Donald Lines Jacobus Award as Best Genealogical Work of the Year. Fully documented study of all 847 Palatine families who arrived in colonial New York from Germany in 1710. Includes illustrations, map, name and place index, and appendices.
Cloth. $85.00/set + $4.50 p&h. 1,350 pp. .... Vendor G0581

Jones, Henry Z, Jr. **The Palatine Families of New York**. 2 vols. 1985. Indexed. Illus.
    Book #1113
Cloth. $85.00. 1,374 pp. .... Vendor G0082

Jones, Henry Z, Jr. **More Palatine Families**. Indexed. Illus.
    A companion volume to *The Palatine Families of New York*. Some immigrants to the middle colonies from 1717-1776, and their European origins, plus new discoveries on German families who arrived in colonial New York in 1710. Long buried emigration materials found in Germany give ancestral origins of hundreds of New York, New Jersey, and Pennsylvania colonists.
Cloth. $65.00 + $4.50 p&h. 625 pp. .... Vendor G0581

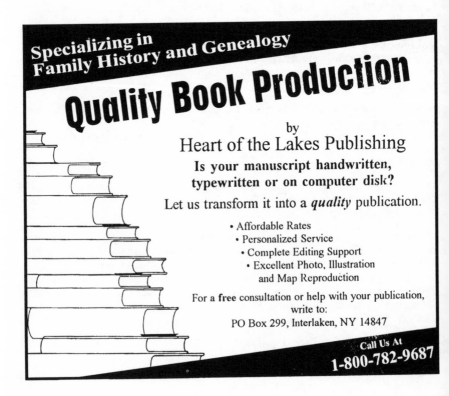

Jones, Henry Z, Jr. **More Palatine Families**. 1991. Indexed. Illus.
  Book #1161.
Cloth. $65.00. 625 pp. .... Vendor G0082

Kammen, Carol. **Lives Passed: Biographical Sketches from Central New York**. 1984. Illus.
  A series of mini-biographies of interesting and famous people from the past who lived in Central New York, including Irene Castle, silent movie star business; Charles Reed, a former slave; and many others who led fascinating lives.
Paper. $15.00. 176 pp. .... Vendor G0093

Kammen, Michael. **Colonial New York: A History**. 1975.
  Includes all the political, social, economic, cultural, and religious aspects of New York's formative centuries. Well-written, readable history.
Paper. $15.95. 426 pp. .... Vendor G0611

Kelby, William. **Orderly Book of the Three Battalions of Loyalists** Commanded by Brigadier-General Oliver De Lancey, 1776-1778. To Which is Appended a List of New York Loyalists in the City of New York During the War of the Revolution. (1917) reprint 1993. Indexed.
Contact vendor for information. 147 pp. .... Vendor G0011

Kelly, Arthur C. M. **Index to New York Wills, Volumes 9-15**. 1981.
Paper. $10.00. 45 pp. .... Vendor G0450

Kelly, Arthur C. M. **New York Revolutionary War Pensioners, 1840**. Extracted from the original 1841 government publication. Indexed.
Cloth. $27.00. 123 pp. .... Vendor G0450

Klos, Lloyd E. **A Resident's Recollections**. Illus.
  Almost anyone will relish and learn when they read these chatty, cheerful pieces of nostalgia. Klos tells tales about railroads, trolleys, and car ferries; he spins yarns about boyhood pursuits and meeting many of Central New York's famous folks. A collection of columns written during the 1970s and 1980s for Wolfe newspapers. Six volumes available with more promised; many photos.
Paper. $9.95/vol. 200 pp./vol. .... Vendor G0093

Lester, Eugenia Campbell, and Allegra Branson. **Frontiers Aflame**. 1987. Illus.
  This book follows each member of the Campbell family during the Revolutionary War.
Paper. $12.95. 304 pp. .... Vendor G0093

Lewis, Helen. **Southeastern Michigan Pioneer Families,** Especially Lenawee County and New York Origins. Indexed.
  A compendium of family information for an area largely settled by **New Yorkers**.
Cloth. $73.95. 426 pp. .... Vendor G0450

Lewis, Helen. **Southeastern Michigan Pioneer Families,** Especially Livingston County and New York Origins. Indexed.
  A compendium of family information for an area largely settled by **New Yorkers**.
Cloth. $51.95. 302 pp. .... Vendor G0450

Lewis, Helen F. **New York's Finger Lakes Pioneer Families, Especially Tompkins County**. 1991. Indexed.

Genealogical information on over seventy-five families, including Revolutionary soldiers in central New York.
Cloth. $69.95. 409 pp. .... Vendor G0450

Livsey, Karen E. **Western New York Land Transactions, 1804-1824** Extracted from the Archives of the Holland Land Company. 1991. Indexed.
Cloth. $35.00. 472 pp. .... Vendor G0010

Livsey, Karen E. **Western New York Land Transactions, 1825-1835** Extracted from the Archives of the Holland Land Company. 1996. Indexed.
Cloth. $60.00. 812 pp. .... Vendor G0010

Long, John H., ed. **New York Atlas of Historical County Boundaries**. 1993.
A beautiful and extremely useful book detailing the changes in county boundaries from colonial times to 1990. 8½" x 11".
Cloth. $57.00. 242 pp. .... Vendor G0611

MacWethy, Lou D. **The Book of Names** Especially Relating to the Early Palatines and the First Settlers in the Mohawk Valley. (1933) reprint 1985. Illus.
Cloth. $15.00. 209 pp. .... Vendor G0010

Macy, Harry, Jr. **Articles in *The New York Genealogical and Biographical Record* 1983-1995,** Indexed by Principal Surname or Location. 1995.
Supplements the 1870-1982 subject index to *The Record* by Mrs. Jean D. Worden.
Paper. $7.00. 20 pp. .... Vendor G0182

Mather, Frederic Gregory. **The Refugees of 1776 from Long Island to Connecticut**. (1913) reprint 1995. Indexed. Illus.
Following the Battle of Long Island (August 27, 1776), more than 5,000 refugees fled Long Island and New York City for the security of Connecticut. The account of their flight and subsequent adventures, their biographies and genealogies, and the history of New York in the Revolution form the main subject of this giant work.
Paper. $75.00. 1,204 pp. .... Vendor G0011

Merrill, Arch. **Arch Merrill's New York**. Illus.
A collection of twenty-three books by Western New York's most famous folk historian written between 1942 and 1973. A source for interesting information about the region. Some are indexed; all are illustrated.
Contact vendor for current listing of available titles. .... Vendor G0093

Military Bounty Lands: The Balloting Book & Other Documents Relating to Them in N.Y. (1825) reprint 1991.
Lists eligible soldiers by regiment, grants of land by townships, patent deliveries, and more.
Cloth. $19.50. 189 pp. .... Vendor G0259

Morrison, Patricia J. **Mrs. Morrison's A. B. C. Reader**. 1972. Illus.
Paper. $10.00. 32 pp. .... Vendor G0112

Morrison, Wayne E., Sr. **Morrison's Annals of Western New-York, 17 County History**. 1975. Illus.
Paper. $12.00. 72 pp. .... Vendor G0112

Morrison's Reprint. **The Balloting Book of the Military Tract 1825**. (1825) reprint 1983. Indexed. Illus.

Dispensation of Revolutionary War Military Bounty Lands in central New York State. Added map and index.

Cloth. $35.00. 214 pp. .... Vendor G0112

Narrett, David E. **Inheritance and Family Life in Colonial New York City**. 1992.

A detailed analysis of the inheritance practices in New York City from the Dutch settlements in the 1620s to the onset of the American Revolution.

Cloth. $42.50. 248 pp. .... Vendor G0611

Nestler, Harold. **A Bibliography of New York State Communities**. 3rd ed. 1990. Indexed.

A bibliography covering books and pamphlets on New York state history at the local or community level.

Paper. $25.50. 301 pp. .... Vendor G0160

Nestler, Harold. **Encyclopedia of New York State Ephemera & Americana**.

Twenty-one years of Harold Nestler's catalogues, March 1975-January 1996, almost 8MB of data, which is completely self-installing in its own directory and space on your hard drive. Over 21,000 entries from the 1,700 original pages; fully searchable ASCII text files. Nearly all the genealogical publications concerning New York are listed here.

IBM 3.5" diskette. $40.00 + shipping. 1,600 pp. .... Vendor G0160

New York Adjutant-General's Office. **[New York]: Index of Awards On Claims of the Soldiers of the War of 1812**. With an Added Introduction by Brigadier General Francis J. Higgins, Adjutant General. (1860, 1969) reprint 1994.

Paper. $42.50. 579 pp. .... Vendor G0011

New York Historical Society. **Muster Rolls of N.Y. Provincial Troops, 1755-1764**. (1897) reprint 1991.

Contains the muster rolls of all regiments & smaller organizations of troops, giving name, age, place of birth, and more; index lists 6,800 men.

Cloth. $52.00. 620 pp. .... Vendor G0259

New York State Archives and Records Administration. **Civil War Records in the New York State Archives**. 1986.

Paper. Free. 5 pp. .... Vendor G0587

New York State Archives and Records Administration. **County Clerks in New York State**. 1995.
Information Leaflet #7. Single copy free. .... Vendor G0587

New York State Archives and Records Administration. **Electronic Records**. 1994.
Information Leaflet #5. Single copy free. 2 pp. .... Vendor G0587

New York State Archives and Records Administration. **Genealogical Sources in the New York State Archives**. 1994.
Information Leaflet #1. Single copy free. 8 pp. .... Vendor G0587

New York State Archives and Records Administration. **A Guide to Records in the New York State Archives**. 1993.
Paper. $15.95. 497 pp. .... Vendor G0587

New York State Archives and Records Administration. **Guide to Records Relating to Native Americans [in the New York State Archives]**. 1988.
Paper. $2.00. 27 pp. .... Vendor G0587

New York State Archives and Records Administration. **Guide to Records Relating to the Revolutionary War [in the New York State Archives]**. 1994.
Paper. $2.00. 54 pp. .... Vendor G0587

New York State Archives and Records Administration. **Naturalization & Related Records**. 1994.
Information Leaflet #6. Single copy free. .... Vendor G0587

New York State Archives and Records Administration. **Probate Records**. 1993.
Information Leaflet #3. Single copy free. 9 pp. .... Vendor G0587

New York State Archives and Records Administration. **Vital Records**. 1993.
Information Leaflet #2. Single copy free. 2 pp. .... Vendor G0587

New York State Archives and Records Administration. **War Service Records & Searches**. 1994.
Information Leaflet #4. Single copy free. 2 pp. .... Vendor G0587

New York State County Atlases—Post Civil War—Complete set of the extensive Wehle reprint series. 46 vols. Illus.
    13" x 16"; each volume with county, town, village, and city land ownership maps, many with illustrations. (Some contain two or more counties.)
Cloth. Contact vendor for details. .... Vendor G0112

Noyes, J. O., and Morrison's Reprint. **Genesee Valley of Western New-York**. (1858) reprint 1972. Illus.
Paper. $12.00. 32 pp. .... Vendor G0112

Noyes, J. O., and Morrison's Reprint. **Lakes & Legends of Central New-York**. (1857) reprint 1972. Illus.
Paper. $12.00. 82 pp. .... Vendor G0112

O'Callaghan, Edmund B. **The Register of New Netherland, 1626-1674**. (1865) reprint 1996. Indexed.
Paper. $21.50. 198 pp. .... Vendor G0011

O'Callaghan, E. B., comp. **Calendar of New York Colonial Manuscripts 1643-1803**. (1864) reprint 1987. Indexed.
  Book #1363.
Cloth. $59.50. 1,096 pp. .... Vendor G0082

O'Callaghan, Edmund B. **Lists of Inhabitants of Colonial New York**. (1849-51) reprint 1989. Indexed.
Cloth. $20.00. 331 pp. .... Vendor G0010

Penrose, Maryly B. **Compendium of Early Mohawk Valley Families**. 2 vols. 1990. Indexed.
Cloth. $55.00. 1,173 pp. .... Vendor G0011

Phillips, Marion G., and Valerie Phillips Parsegian. **Richard and Rhoda, Letters from the Civil War**. 1981. Illus.
  Book #1462.
Cloth. $25.00. 128 pp. .... Vendor G0082

Reid, Arthur. **Reminiscences of the Revolution** or Le Loup's Bloody Trail.
  New York's Washington County General Burgoyne's barbarous Indian alliance and the death of Miss McCrea are described in this reprint of the 1859 booklet about the Indian atrocities that rallied the Patriots against the Crown.
Booklet. $6.50. 32 pp. .... Vendor G0160

Reynolds, Cuyler. **Genealogical and Family History of Southern New York and the Hudson River Valley**. A Record of the Achievements of Her People in the Making of a Commonwealth and the Building of a Nation. In Three Volumes. (1914) reprint 1997. Indexed. Illus.
Paper. $150.00. 1,482 pp. .... Vendor G0011

Reynolds, Cuyler. **Hudson-Mohawk Genealogical and Family Memoir:** A Record of Achievements of the People of the Hudson & Mohawk Valleys, Included Within the Present Counties of Albany, Rensselaer, Washington, Saratoga, Montgomery, Fulton, Schenectady, Columbia & Greene. With Historical Appendix & Index (Vol. IV). (1911) reprint 1994.
Contact vendor for information. .... Vendor G0011

Rice, Shirley A., ed. **Community: Birthplace of Popular Consent, A Salute to New York's Bicentennial Towns**. 1988. Illus.
  Published in cooperation with the New York State Commission on the Bicentennial of the United States Constitution.
Paper. $2.50. 56 pp. .... Vendor G0093

Roberts, James A., and Frederic G. Mather. **New York in the Revolution as Colony and State [Together with Supplement]**. 2 vols. in 1. (1898, 1901) reprint 1996. Indexed. Illus.
Cloth. $60.00. 900 pp. total. .... Vendor G0010

Roberts, James A. **New York in the Revolution as Colony and State**. (1898) reprint 1993. Indexed.
  Gives New York rolls of soldiers and sailors in the Revolutionary War.
Cloth. $53.50. 534 pp. .... Vendor G0450

Robison, Jeannie F-J., and Henrietta C. Bartlett, eds. **Genealogical Records:** Manuscript Entries of Births, Deaths and Marriages, Taken from Family Bibles, 1581-1917. (1917) reprint 1995. Indexed. Illus.
    Contains the genealogical records found in family Bibles of ninety Dutch and English New York families.
Paper. $28.50. 346 pp. .... Vendor G0011

Ruttenber, E. **Indian Tribes of Hudson's River Vol. I (to 1700)**. Indexed.
    The only complete history of all the tribes that were located in, or interacted with, New York State Native Americans.
Paper. $12.95. 208 pp. .... Vendor G0160

Ruttenber, E. **Indian Tribes of Hudson's River Vol. II (1700 to 1850)**. Indexed.
    Includes 100-page appendix of language and biographical data and complete 2-volume index.
Paper. $12.95. 246 pp. .... Vendor G0160

Sanford, L. **Membership Records of Seventh Baptists of Central New York State 1797-1940s**. Indexed. Illus.
Paper. $26.00. 127 pp. .... Vendor G0160

Schweitzer, George K. **New York Genealogical Research**. 1996. Illus.
    History of the state, types of records (Bible through will), record locations, research techniques, listings of county records.
Paper. $15.00. 252 pp. .... Vendor G0569

Scott, Kenneth. **Calendar of New York Colonial Commissions 1770-1776**. 1972. Indexed.
Paper. $6.50. 32 pp. .... Vendor G0182

Scott, Kenneth, and Kenn Stryker-Rodda. **Denizations, Naturalizations, and Oaths of Allegiance in Colonial New York**. (1975) reprint 1994. Indexed.
Contact vendor for information. 131 pp. .... Vendor G0011

Scott, Kenneth. **Genealogical Data from Colonial New York Newspapers**. A Consolidation of Articles from The New York Genealogical and Biographical Record. (1964-1976) reprint 1982. Indexed.
Cloth. $20.00. 278 pp. .... Vendor G0010

Scott, Kenneth, and James Owre. **Genealogical Data from Inventories of New York Estates 1666-1825**. 1970. Indexed.
Paper. $17.00. 220 pp. .... Vendor G0182

Scott, Kenneth. **Genealogical Data from New York Administration Bonds 1753-1799**. 1969. Indexed.
Cloth. $14.25. 194 pp. .... Vendor G0182

Scott, Kenneth. **Genealogical Data from the New York Post Boy, 1743-1773**. Indexed.
Abstracts covering New York and other colonies.
Cloth. $18.00. 188 pp. .... Vendor G0627

Scott, Kenneth. **Marriages and Deaths from the New Yorker (Double Quarto Edition) 1836-1841**. Indexed.
Approximately 5,000 deaths and 3,000 marriages excerpted. Events occurred not only in New York City and State, but throughout the United States and abroad.
Cloth. $19.95. 310 pp. .... Vendor G0627

Scott, Kenneth, and Rosanne Conway. **New York Alien Residents, 1825-1848**. (1978) reprint 1991.
Contact vendor for information. 122 pp. .... Vendor G0011

Shea, Ann M., and Marion R. Casey. **The Irish Experience in New York City: A Select Bibliography**. 1995.
An extensive research guide to non-archival source material that documents three centuries of the history of the Irish in New York City. Contains over 700 entries, including unpublished materials such as master's theses and doctorate dissertations, as well as published articles, chapters, books, and videos.
Cloth. $29.95. 140 pp. .... Vendor G0611

Simms, Jeptha R. **Frontiersmen of New York,** Showing Customs of the Indians, Vicissitudes of Pioneer White Settlers & Border Strife in Two Wars, with a Great Variety of Romantic & Thrilling Stories. 2 vols. 1883.
Cloth. $135.00. 712 + 759 pp. .... Vendor G0259

Singleton, Esther. **Dutch New York**. (1909) reprint 1994.
Fascinating social history of early New Amsterdam that is a must-read for anyone of Dutch background.
Cloth. $42.50. 360 pp. .... Vendor G0259

Southern California Genealogical Society. **Sources of Genealogical Help in New York**.
Paper. $3.00. 26 pp. .... Vendor G0656

Spafford, Horatio Gates. **Gazetteer (1824) of the State of New York**. (1824) reprint 1980.
Cloth. $35.00. 620 pp. .... Vendor G0093

Talcott, Sebastian V. **Genealogical Notes of New York and New England Families**. (1883) reprint 1994. Indexed.
Paper. $50.00. 786 pp. .... Vendor G0011

Thorndale, William, and William Dollarhide. **County Boundary Map Guides to the U.S. Federal Censuses, 1790-1920: New York, 1790-1920**. 1987.
$5.95. .... Vendor G0552

United States Bureau of the Census. **Heads of Families at the First Census of the U.S. Taken in the Year 1790: New York**. (1908) reprint 1990.
Paper. $30.00. 308 pp. .... Vendor G0259

United States Bureau of the Census. **Heads of Families at the First Census of the United States Taken in the Year 1790: New York**. (1908) reprint 1992. Indexed. Illus.
Contact vendor for information. 308 pp. .... Vendor G0010

United States Bureau of the Census. **Heads of Families at the First Census of the United States Taken in the Year 1790: New York**.
Cloth, $45.00. Paper, $30.00. .... Vendor G0552

Venables. **The Six Nations of New York, Mohawks, Oneidas, Onondagas, Senecas, Tuscaroras: The 1892 United States Extra Census Bulletin**. (1892) reprint 1995.
   A collection of census reports, observations, and photographs pertaining to the peoples of the Six Nations of New York.
Paper. $15.95. 89 pp. .... Vendor G0611

Western NY Genealogical Society, Inc. **Ancestors of Western New York Genealogical Society Members, Vol. I**. 1993.
   Book #1489.
Paper. $22.00. 336 pp. .... Vendor G0082

Wilson, Thomas B. **Inhabitants of New York, 1774-1776**. 1993. Indexed.
Cloth. $25.00. 358 pp. .... Vendor G0010

Albany County

Ballou and Morrison. **Meneely Bell Foundry of West Troy, Albany Co., N.Y**. (1855) reprint 1984. Illus.
Paper. $12.50. 20 pp. .... Vendor G0112

Christoph, Florence. **Upstate New York in the 1760s**. 1992. Indexed. Illus.
   Book #1328.
Cloth. $39.50. 320 pp. .... Vendor G0082

Davenport, David P. **1860 Albany County Mortality Schedule**. Indexed.
   Combines information from the 1860 Census of Albany with the Federal Mortality Schedule and City Directory information.
Cloth. $27.00. 133 pp. .... Vendor G0450

Dern, John P., ed. **The Albany Protocol 1731-1750**. (1971) reprint 1992. Indexed. Illus.
   Book #1364.
Cloth. $49.50. 704 pp. .... Vendor G0082

Giddings, Edward. **Coeymans and the Past**. Introduction by Raymond Beecher. Indexed.
   A 300-year history of this southern Albany County town on the Hudson River.
Paper. $18.95. 150 pp. .... Vendor G0160

Keefer, Donald. **Marriages of Rev. Harmanus Van Huysen, 1794-1825**. 1993. Indexed.
Helderberg (Guilderland), Jerusalem (Feura Bush), and Salem (New Salem).
Paper. $16.00. 85 pp. .... Vendor G0450

Kelly, Arthur C. M. **Baptism & Marriage Record, First Lutheran Chuch, Albany, NY: 1774-1842**. Indexed.
Paper (typescript). $52.00. 345 pp. .... Vendor G0450

Kelly, Arthur C. M. **Baptism Record, Albany Reformed Church, 1683-1809**.
Paper (typescript). $60.00. 660 pp. .... Vendor G0450

Kelly, Arthur C. M. **Baptism Records of Helderberg Reformed Church, Guilderland, NY: 1786-1860**. Indexed.
Cloth. $33.00. .... Vendor G0450

Kelly, Arthur C. M. **Marriage Record, Albany Reformed Church, 1683-1804**.
Paper (typescript). $20.00. 116 pp. .... Vendor G0450

Masten, Arthur M. **History of Cohoes** from Its Earliest Settlement to the Present Time [1877]. (1877) reprint 1994.
Cloth. $38.00. 327 pp. .... Vendor G0259

Myers, James T. **History of the City of Watervliet, 1630 to 1910**. 1910.
Paper. $18.50. 124 pp. .... Vendor G0259

Our Heritage: History of the Town of Berne in Albany County. Illus.
Paper. $10.00. 145 pp. .... Vendor G0160

Parker, Amasa J., ed. **Landmarks of Albany County**. Part I, Historical; Part II, Biographical. (1897) reprint 1994.
Cloth. $56.00/Part I. $45.00/Part II. $96.00/set. 557 + 418 pp. .... Vendor G0259

Pearson, Jonathan. **Contributions for the Genealogies of the First Settlers of the Ancient County of Albany, from 1630 to 1800**. (1872) reprint 1987. Indexed.
Contact vendor for information. 182 pp. .... Vendor G0010

Pearson, Jonathan. **Early Records . . . of Albany . . . Rensselaerswych (Mortgages and Wills 1652-1660)**. 1919. Indexed.
Order no. 933, $14.00. 220 pp. .... Vendor G0478

Ptak, Diane Snyder. **Cast in Stone, Selected Albany, Rensselaer and Saratoga County, NY, Cemetery Records**. Indexed.
Burials, 18th and 19th century; 8,500 people.
Cloth. $35.00. 169 pp. .... Vendor G0450

Ptak, Diane Snyder. **Lost and Found: Albany (New York) Area Church and Synagogue Records 1654-1925 and Supplement**. 1993.
Paper. $14.00. 35 pp. .... Vendor G0663

Scott, Kenneth. **New York: State Census of Albany County Towns in 1790**. (1975) reprint 1991.
Paper. $8.50. 68 pp. .... Vendor G0011

Tenney, Jonathan. **New England in Albany**. 1883. Reprinted. Indexed.
   Traces the emigration of New Englanders to Albany. Includes the names of the earliest New England settlers (1780-1800) and provides more detailed information about residents with New England backgrounds during the mid-1800s.
Paper. $18.00. 89 pp. .... Vendor G0160

Vital Records of Hamilton Union Presbyterian Chuch, Guilderland, Albany Co., NY: 1824-1899. Indexed.
Paper. $15.00. 67 pp. .... Vendor G0450

Vital Records of Jerusalem Reformed Church, Feura Bush, Albany County, NY: 1792-1890.
Cloth. $28.00. 140 pp. .... Vendor G0450

Weise, A. J. **History of the City of Albany,** from the Discovery of the Great River in 1524, by Verrazzano, to the Present [1884]. (1884) reprint 1988.
Cloth. $55.00. 528 pp. .... Vendor G0259

Allegany County

Beers & Co., F. W.—Morrison's Reprint. **History of Allegany County 1806-1879**. (1879) reprint 1979. Indexed. Illus.
Cloth. $81.00. 508 pp. .... Vendor G0112

French, Robert. **Name Index to Beers 1879 History of Allegany County**. 1978.
   Contains 6,500 names.
Paper. $10.00. 46 pp. .... Vendor G0093

Merrill, Georgia D., ed. **Allegany County & Its People:** A Centennial Memorial History of Allegany County; also, Histories of the Towns of the County. (1896) reprint 1995.
Cloth. $95.00. 951 pp. .... Vendor G0259

Sanford, L. **First Alfred Seventh Day Baptist Church Membership Records, Alfred, NY**. Indexed. Illus.
   From the archives of the Seventh Day Baptist Historical Society. Contains a wealth of biographical material concerning early Rhode Island families and the movement of Seventh Day Baptists as they migrated west.
Paper. $21.00. 107 pp. .... Vendor G0160

Town of Genesee Sesquicentennial 1830-1980. 1980. Illus.
Paper. $10.00. 116 pp. .... Vendor G0093

Broome County

Bridges, Robert L., and Ruth Keeler Lawrence. **One Room Schools of the Town of Chenango**. 1989. Illus.
   Memories of students of the Town of Chenango's one-room schoolhouses. Many actual documents, minutes, report cards, etc. are included. Photos.
Paper. $2.00. 171 pp. .... Vendor G0093

French, J. H., and Wayne E. Morrison, Sr. **Morrison's History of Broome County, Towns, Villages, &c., 1860**. Illus.
Contact vendor for availability. .... Vendor G0112

History of Broome Co., with Illustrations & Biographical Sketches of Some of Its Prominent Men & Pioneers. (1885) reprint 1991.
Cloth. $66.50. 630 pp. .... Vendor G0259

Tyne, John J. **Index of Names Appearing in Smith's 1885 History of Broom County**. (1885) reprint 1973.
Paper. $10.00. 131 pp. .... Vendor G0093

Cattaraugus County

Adams, William, ed. **Historical Gazetteer & Biographical Memorial of Cattaraugus Co., with Map and Illustrations**. (1893) reprint 1995.
Cloth. $115.00. 1,164 pp. .... Vendor G0259

French, J. H., and Wayne E. Morrison, Sr. **Morrison's History of Cattaraugus County, Towns, Villages, &c., 1860**. Illus.
Contact vendor for availability. .... Vendor G0112

History of Cattaraugus Co., with Illustrations & Biographical Sketches of Some of Its Prominent Men & Pioneers. (1879) reprint 1991.
Cloth. $65.00. 556 pp. .... Vendor G0259

Kilmer, Lawrence W. **Bradford & Foster Brook—The Peg Leg Railroad**. 1993. Illus.
    Information on five railroads in Cattaraugus Co., NY and McKean Co., PA; includes the history of the men that built them. Maps.
Paper. $20.00. 206 pp. .... Vendor G0093

Morrison, Wayne E., Sr. **Morrison's Annals of Western New-York, 17 County History**. 1975. Illus.
Paper. $12.00. 72 pp. .... Vendor G0112

Cayuga County

French, J. H., and Wayne E. Morrison, Sr. **Morrison's History of Cayuga County, Towns, Villages, &c., 1860**. Illus.
Contact vendor for availability. .... Vendor G0112

Gilbert, Frank, and Wayne E. Morrison, Sr. **Jethro Wood, Inventor of the Modern Plow**. 1882. Illus.
Paper. $14.00. 52 pp. .... Vendor G0112

History of Cayuga County, with Illustrations & Biographical Sketches of Some of Its Prominent Men & Pioneers. (1879) reprint 1991.
Cloth. $65.00. 556 pp. .... Vendor G0259

Meyer, Mary K., ed. **A Directory of Cayuga County Residents Who Supported Publication of the History of Cayuga County, New York**. (1879) reprint 1996. Indexed.
Paper. $16.00. 153 pp. .... Vendor G0697

Monroe, J. H. **Historical Records of a Hundred & Twenty-Five Years: Auburn**. (1913) reprint 1992.
Cloth. $35.00. 278 pp. .... Vendor G0259

Wright, James A. **Historical Sketches of the Town of Moravia, 1791 to 1853**. (1874) reprint 1993.
Cloth. $35.00. 289 pp. .... Vendor G0259

Champlain Valley

Watson, Winslow C. **Pioneer History of the Champlain Valley,** Being an Account of the Settlement of the Town of Willsborough by William Gilliland. (1863) reprint 1993.
Cloth. $29.50. 231 pp. .... Vendor G0259

Chautauqua County

Centennial History of Chautauqua County: Detailed & Entertaining Story of 100 Years of Development. 2 vols. (1904) reprint 1992.
Cloth. $69.50/Vol. I. $109.50/Vol. II. $169.50/set. 698 + 1,173 pp. ..... Vendor G0259

Child, Hamilton, ed., and W. E. Morrison & Co. **History of Chautauqua County 1808-1874**. 1965. Illus.
Cloth. $25.00. 96 pp. .... Vendor G0112

Hazeltin, G. W. **Early History of the Town of Ellicott [Part of Johnstown], Chautauqua Co**. (1887) reprint 1992.
Cloth. $58.00. 556 pp. .... Vendor G0259

Stewart, William. **1867 Topographical Atlas Including Town, Township Landowner Maps, Business Directories**. (1867) reprint 1985. Illus.
Paper. $17.50. 81 pp. .... Vendor G0531

Stewart, William. **Atlas of Chautauqua County 1867**. (1867) reprint 1980. Illus.
Cloth. $60.00. 81 pp. .... Vendor G0112

Ton, C. Edward, and Wayne E. Morrison, Sr. **History of Clymer, Chautauqua County 1821-1971**. 1971. Indexed. Illus.
Cloth. $28.00. 100 pp. .... Vendor G0112

Warren, Emory F., and Morrison's Reprint. **History of Chautauqua County 1846**. (1846) reprint 1976. Illus.
Cloth. $15.00. 159 pp. .... Vendor G0112

Young, Andrew W. **History of Chautauqua,** from Its First Settlement to the Present Time, with Numerous Biographical & Family Sketches. (1875) reprint 1995.
Cloth. $69.50. 667 pp. .... Vendor G0259

Chemung County

Cheney, T. Apoleon, and *The Havana Journal.* **Historical Sketch of the Chemung Valley 1867.** 1986. Illus.
Cloth. $24.00. 66 pp. .... Vendor G0112

Everts and Ensign—Morrison's Reprint. **History of Chemung County 1836-1879.** Edited by Pierce and Hurd. (1879) reprint 1979. Illus.
Cloth. $56.00. 288 pp. .... Vendor G0112

History of Tioga, Chemung, Tompkins & Schuyler Counties, with Illustrations & Biographical Sketches of Some of Their Prominent Men & Pioneers. (1879) reprint 1991.
Cloth. $78.50. 687 pp. .... Vendor G0259

Holmes, Clay W. **The Elmira Prison Camp:** A History of the Military Prison at Elmira, July 6, 1864 to July 10, 1865. With an Appendix Containing the Lists of Confederate Soldiers Buried in Woodlawn Nat'l Cemetery. (1912) reprint 1996.
Cloth. $69.50. 465 + 190 pp. .... Vendor G0259

Morrison, Wayne E., Sr. **The Contiguous Towns, Schuyler and Chemung Counties.** 1989. Illus.
   Veteran, Catlin, Catharine, Hector, Dix, Montour.
Cloth. $25.00. 92 pp. .... Vendor G0112

Morrison, Wayne E., Sr. **History of Havana 1788-1895.** 1986. Indexed. Illus.
   It is the design of this work to narrate in a clear, simple, and intelligible manner the leading events connected with the illustrious history of Havana. Incidents were related more to illustrate the past than to amuse the reader, the objective being to show and trace the advancement of progress in a concise, unpretentious manner. Only the printed page can now bear testimony to the existence and endurance of those whose traditions perished with and in them so very long ago. The voluminous files of *The Havana Journal* were indispensable in the preparation of this work, as were other essential documents, maps, pictures, portraits, etc. The whole, as compiled, contains a copious source of alphabetical information appearing in the appended index, and is handsomely bound in cloth.
Cloth. $36.00. 406 pp. .... Vendor G0112

Towner, Ausburn. **Our County & Its People:** A History of the Valley & County of Chemung from the Closing Years of the 18th Century. With Biographies & Personal References. (1892) reprint 1995.
Cloth. $88.00. 702 + 160 pp. .... Vendor G0259

Whitford and Morrison. **History of the Chemung Canal.** 1989. Illus.
Cloth. $28.00. 66 pp. .... Vendor G0112

Chenango County

French, J. H., and Wayne E. Morrison, Sr. **Morrison's History of Chenango County, Towns, Villages, &c., 1860**. Illus.
Contact vendor for availability.. .... Vendor G0112

Galpin, Henry J. **Annals of Oxford,** with Illustrations & Biographical Sketches of Some of Its Prominent Men & Early Pioneers. (1906) reprint 1992.
Cloth. $59.00. 568 pp. .... Vendor G0259

Smith, James H. **History of Chenango & Madison Counties,** with Illustrations & Biographical Sketches of Some of Its Prominent Men & Pioneers. (1880) reprint 1993.
Cloth. $79.50. 760 + 29 pp. .... Vendor G0259

Tyne, John J. **Name Index to Smith's 1880 History of Chenango & Madison Counties.** (1974) reprint 1978.
    Includes 29,100 entries.
Paper. $20.00. 210 pp. .... Vendor G0093

Clinton County

History of Clinton & Franklin Counties, with Illustrations & Biographical Sketches of Its Prominent Men & Pioneers. (1880) reprint 1995.
Cloth. $53.00. 508 pp. .... Vendor G0259

Columbia County

Collier, Edward A. **A History of Old Kinderhook,** from Aboriginal Days to the Present Time. (1914) reprint 1994.
Cloth. $59.50. 572 pp. .... Vendor G0259

Collin, John Francis. **History of Hillsdale, Columbia Co.,** a Memorabilia of Persons and Things of Interest, Passed and Passing. (1883) reprint 1995.
Cloth. $29.50. 195 pp. .... Vendor G0259

Divine, Al. **Columbia County, NY Gravestone Inscriptions**. A Guide to Understanding Them, with a Comprehensive Family Name Index. 1992. Indexed.
    A full name index showing about 80,000 individuals with location of gravesite in Columbia County (prior to 20th century).
Cloth. $39.50. 210 pp. .... Vendor G0450

Divine, Albert. **An Alphabetical First and Last Name Index to Ellis' History of Columbia County, NY.**
Cloth. $22.00. 106 pp. .... Vendor G0450

Divine, Gerta. **Old Tombstones & Unusual Cemeteries in Columbia County, NY.**
Volume 1: Eastern Columbia County. Indexed. Illus.

Many hard-to-find and unusual cemeteries.
Paper. $12.00. 148 pp. .... Vendor G0450

History of Columbia County, with Illustrations & Biographical Sketches of Some Prominent Men & Pioneers. (1878) reprint 1990.
Cloth. $47.00. 447 pp. .... Vendor G0259

Hunt, T. **Historical Sketch of the Town of Clermont.** (1928) reprint 1996.
Cloth, $29.50. Paper, $19.50. 149 pp. .... Vendor G0259

Hunt, Thomas. **Historical Sketch of Clermont, NY.** (1928) reprint 1984. Indexed. Illus.
History of Clermont with 1844 map of property owners.
Cloth. $20.00. 149 pp. .... Vendor G0450

Kelly, Arthur C. M. **Baptism Records of Christ Lutheran Church, Germantown, NY: 1746-1899.** Indexed.
Cloth. $29.00. 153 pp. .... Vendor G0450

Kelly, Arthur C. M. **Baptism Records of Claverack Reformed Church, Claverack, NY: 1727-1899.** Indexed.
Cloth. $72.00. 443 pp. .... Vendor G0450

Kelly, Arthur C. M. **Baptism Records of Gallatin Reformed Church, Gallatinville, NY: 1748-1899.** Indexed.
Cloth. $35.00. 169 pp. .... Vendor G0450

Kelly, Arthur C. M. **Baptism Records of Germantown Reformed Church, Germantown, NY (East Camp): 1729-1898.** Indexed.
Cloth. $59.00. 342 pp. .... Vendor G0450

Kelly, Arthur C. M. **Baptism Records of Hillsdale Reformed Church, Hillsdale, NY (defunct): 1776-1849.** Indexed.
Cloth. $16.00. 61 pp. .... Vendor G0450

Kelly, Arthur C. M. **Baptism Records of Kinderhook Reformed Church, Kinderhook, NY: 1718-1899.** Indexed.
Cloth. $67.50. 403 pp. .... Vendor G0450

Kelly, Arthur C. M. **Baptism Records of Linlithgo Reformed Church, Livingston, NY: 1722-1899.** Indexed.
Cloth. $40.00. 229 pp. .... Vendor G0450

Kelly, Arthur C. M. **Baptism Records of St. John's Lutheran Church, Manorton, NY: 1765-1872.** Indexed.
Cloth. $47.00. 267 pp. .... Vendor G0450

Kelly, Arthur C. M. **Baptism Records of St. Thomas' Lutheran Church, Churchtown, NY: 1760-1899.** Indexed.
Cloth. $52.00. 302 pp. .... Vendor G0450

Kelly, Arthur C. M. **Baptism Records of West Copake Reformed Church, Copake, NY: 1783-1899.** Indexed.
Cloth. $37.00. 189 pp. .... Vendor G0450

Kelly, Arthur C. M. **City of Hudson Burying Grounds, Interments 1829-73, Hudson, Columbia County, NY**. Indexed.
Cloth. $48.00. 274 pp. .... Vendor G0450

Kelly, Arthur C. M. **Hudson, NY Newspapers, Vol. 1, Deaths, 1802-1851**. Indexed.
Cloth. $32.00. 223 pp. .... Vendor G0450

Kelly, Arthur C. M. **Hudson, NY Newspapers, Vol. 2, Marriages, 1802-1851**. Indexed.
Cloth. $30.00. 208 pp. .... Vendor G0450

Kelly, Arthur C. M. **Marriage Records of Claverack Reformed Church, Claverack, NY: 1727-1899**. Indexed.
Cloth. $36.00. 198 pp. .... Vendor G0450

Kelly, Arthur C. M. **Marriage Records of Germantown, Gallatin, Copake, & Hillsdale Reformed Church: 1736-1899**. Indexed.
Cloth. $26.00. 121 pp. .... Vendor G0450

Kelly, Arthur C. M. **Marriage Records of Kinderhook Reformed Church, Kinderhook, NY: 1717-1899**. Indexed.
Cloth. $22.00. 103 pp. .... Vendor G0450

Kelly, Arthur C. M. **Marriage Records of Linlithgo Reformed Church, Livingston NY: 1723-1899**. Indexed.
Cloth. $16.00. 67 pp. .... Vendor G0450

Kelly, Arthur C. M. **Marriage Records of Manorton, Churchtown, Germantown, & Barrytown Lutheran Churches: 1794-1899**. Indexed.
Cloth. $24.00. 124 pp. .... Vendor G0450

Kelly, Arthur C. M. **Old Gravestones of Columbia County, NY**. 1996. Indexed.
Cloth. $29.00. 139 pp. .... Vendor G0450

Kelly, Arthur C. M., ed. **Southern Columbia County, New York Families**. A Genealogy by Peter Silvernail, 1896. 1996. Indexed.
Cloth. $46.00. 227 pp. .... Vendor G0450

Kelly, Arthur C. M. **Settlers and Residents, Town of Clermont, Columbia County, NY, Volume 2, Part 1: 1756-1899**.
Cloth. $34.00. 407 pp. .... Vendor G0450

Kelly, Arthur C. M. **Settlers and Residents, Town of Clermont, Columbia County, NY, Volume 2, Part 2, State-Federal Census**.
Cloth. $19.00. 212 pp. .... Vendor G0450

Kelly, Arthur C. M. **Settlers and Residents, Town of Germantown, Columbia County, NY, Volume 1, Part 1: 1710-1899**.
Cloth. $35.00. 394 pp. .... Vendor G0450

Kelly, Arthur C. M. **Settlers and Residents, Town of Germantown, Columbia County, NY, Volume 1, Part 2: 1790-1875**.
Cloth. $33.00. 229 pp. .... Vendor G0450

Kelly, Arthur C. M. **Settlers and Residents, Town of Livingston, Columbia County, NY, Volume 3, Part 1: 1710-1899**.
Cloth. $39.00. 338 pp. .... Vendor G0450

Kelly, Arthur C. M. **Settlers and Residents, Town of Livingston, Columbia County, NY, Volume 3, Part 2, State-Federal Census: 1790-1875**.
Cloth. $34.00. 449 pp. .... Vendor G0450

Kelly, Arthur C. M. **Settlers and Residents, Town of Livingston, Columbia County, NY, Volume 3, Part 3, Road Lists of Landowners: 1803-1850**.
Cloth. $38.00. 208 pp. .... Vendor G0450

Kelly, Arthur C. M. **Vital Records of Christ Lutheran Church, Ghent, Columbia Co., NY: 1801-1901**.
Cloth. $42.00. 234 pp. .... Vendor G0450

Kelly, Arthur C. M. **Vital Records of Emmanuel Evangelical Lutheran Church, Chatham Village, NY: 1874-1899**. Indexed.
Paper. $7.00. 32 pp. .... Vendor G0450

Kelly, Arthur C. M. **Vital Records of Ghent, W. Ghent, Mt. Pleasant, & Stuyvesant Falls, NY, Reformed Church: 1775-1899**.
Cloth. $32.00. 172 pp. .... Vendor G0450

Livingston Genealogical Register. 1995. Indexed.
Cloth. $55.00. 739 pp. .... Vendor G0450

Miller, Stephen B. **Sketches of Hudson**. (1862) reprint 1985. Indexed.
   A collection of stories and biographical sketches about the settlement of the City of Hudson.
Cloth, $12.50. Paper, $8.50. 120 pp. .... Vendor G0093

Shepard, E., and Rev. Churchill and Hand. **Marriage Records of New Lebanon, NY: 1795-1852**.
Paper. $8.00. 38 pp. .... Vendor G0450

Webb, Franklin H. **Claverick, Old and New**. 1892. Reprinted. Illus.
Paper. $6.00. 88 pp. .... Vendor G0160

Cortland County

Bracy, Isabel. **157th New York Volunteer (Infantry) Regiment - 1862-1865**. 1991. Indexed.
   See Madison County Listing.
Paper. $12.00. 128 pp. .... Vendor G0093

French, J. H., and Wayne E. Morrison, Sr. **Morrison's History of Cortland County, Towns, Villages, &c., 1860**. Illus.
Contact vendor for availability. .... Vendor G0112

Goodwin, H. C. **Pioneer History of Cortland County,** & the Border Wars of N.Y., from the Earliest Period. (1859) reprint 1992.
Cloth. $48.00. 456 pp. .... Vendor G0259

Delaware County

Briggs, Mary S., ed. **Ferguson-Jayne Papers**. 2 vols. 1981. Indexed. Illus.
  History of the Village of Fergusonville, Delaware County, New York, including Fergusonville Academy. Contains 750 family letters and three 19th-century diaries.
Cloth. $36.50. 1,392 pp. in all. .... Vendor G0093

Danforth, Edward. **Stones from the Walls of Jericho**. 1987. Illus.
  The bicentennial history of Bainbridge (1786-1986). Heavily illustrated.
Cloth. $25.00. 514 pp. .... Vendor G0093

Gould, Jay. **History of Delaware County** & Border Wars of New York, Containing a Sketch of Early Settlement. (1856) reprint 1993.
Cloth. $47.00. 426 pp. .... Vendor G0259

Munsell & Co, W. W.—Morrison's Reprint. **History of Delaware County 1797-1880**. (1880) reprint 1980. Illus.
Cloth. $81.00. 448 pp. .... Vendor G0112

Munsell, W., ed. **History of Delaware County,** with Illustrations, Biographical Sketches & Portraits of Some Pioneers & Prominent Residents. (1880) reprint 1993.
Cloth. $42.50. 363 pp. .... Vendor G0259

Murray, David, ed. **Delaware County: History of the Century, 1797-1897**. (1898) reprint 1993.
Cloth. $65.00. 604 pp. .... Vendor G0259

Sutch, G. E. **The Civil War: The Town of Prattsville**.
  Greene, Delaware, and Schoharie County enlistments and how the people left behind were affected.
Paper. $7.50. 41 pp. .... Vendor G0160

Dutchess County

Bathrick, M. **John Herrick Ledger, Pine Plains, Dutchess County, NY, 1852-1889**. Indexed.
  Payroll and accounts.
Paper. $15.50. 86 pp. .... Vendor G0450

Buck, Clifford. **1850 & 1865 Dutchess County Census Records: Amenia**.
Paper (typescript). $15.00 ea., $25.00 for both. .... Vendor G0450

Buck, Clifford. **1850 & 1865 Dutchess County Census Records: Beekman**.
Paper (typescript). $15.00 ea., $25.00 for both. .... Vendor G0450

Buck, Clifford. **1850 & 1865 Dutchess County Census Records: Clinton**.
Paper (typescript). $15.00 ea., $25.00 for both. .... Vendor G0450

Buck, Clifford. **1850 & 1865 Dutchess County Census Records: Dover**.
Paper (typescript). $15.00 ea., $25.00 for both. .... Vendor G0450

Buck, Clifford. **1850 & 1865 Dutchess County Census Records: E. Fishkill**.
Paper (typescript). $15.00 ea., $25.00 for both. .... Vendor G0450

Buck, Clifford. **1850 & 1865 Dutchess County Census Records: Hyde Park**.
Paper (typescript) $15.00 ea., $25.00 for both. .... Vendor G0450

Buck, Clifford. **1850 & 1865 Dutchess County Census Records: LaGrange**.
Paper (typescript). $15.00 ea., $25.00 for both. .... Vendor G0450

Buck, Clifford. **1850 & 1865 Dutchess County Census Records: Milan**.
Paper (typescript). $15.00 ea., $25.00 for both. .... Vendor G0450

Buck, Clifford. **1850 & 1865 Dutchess County Census Records: Northeast**.
Paper (typescript). $15.00 ea., $25.00 for both. .... Vendor G0450

Buck, Clifford. **1850 & 1865 Dutchess County Census Records: Pawling**.
Paper (typescript). $15.00 ea., $25.00 for both. .... Vendor G0450

Buck, Clifford. **1850 & 1865 Dutchess County Census Records: Pleasant Valley**.
Paper (typescript). $15.00 ea., $25.00 for both. .... Vendor G0450

Buck, Clifford. **1850 & 1865 Dutchess County Census Records: Stanford**.
Paper (typescript). $15.00 ea., $25.00 for both. .... Vendor G0450

Buck, Clifford. **1850 & 1865 Dutchess County Census Records: Washington**.
Paper (typescript). $15.00 ea., $25.00 for both. .... Vendor G0450

Buck, Clifford. **1850 Dutchess County Census Records: Fishkill**.
Paper (typescript). $30.00. .... Vendor G0450

Buck, Clifford. **1850 Dutchess County Census Records: Pine Plains**.
Paper (typescript). $15.00. .... Vendor G0450

Buck, Clifford. **1850 Dutchess County Census Records: Poughkeepsie**.
Paper (typescript). $40.00. .... Vendor G0450

Buck, Clifford. **1850 Dutchess County Census Records: Red Hook**.
Paper (typescript). $15.00, $25.00 with 1865 Census Records
(see below). .... Vendor G0450

Buck, Clifford. **1850 Dutchess County Census Records: Union Vale**.
Paper (typescript). $15.00. .... Vendor G0450

Buck, Clifford. **1865 Dutchess County Census Records: Rhinebeck**.
Paper (typescript). $15.00, $25.00 with 1850 Census Records
(see below). .... Vendor G0450

Buck, Clifford M. **Dutchess County, NY Tax Lists, 1718-1787**. With Rombout Precinct by William Reese.
Cloth. $55.00. 305 pp. .... Vendor G0450

Commemorative Biographical Record of Dutchess County. (1897) reprint 1994.
Cloth. $95.00. 950 pp. .... Vendor G0259

Doherty, Frank J. **The Settlers of the Beekman Patent: Volume I, Historical Records**.
1990. Indexed. Illus.

This important social history documents the 18th-century settlement of the Beekman Patent in the Hudson River Valley by Palatines, Dutch, and the English from Long Island and New England. The Beekman Patent was a major entry point from New England to New York and the West. There are three volumes available (see next two listings): any two volumes can be purchased for $150.00, all three volumes for $215.00 including p&h.
Cloth. $85.00; NY residents must pay sales tax. 819 pp. + index. ...... Vendor G0181

Doherty, Frank J. **The Settlers of the Beekman Patent: Volume II, Families Abbot - Burtch**. 1993. Indexed.
See description under Volume I, above.
Cloth. $85.00; NY residents must pay sales tax. 1,000 pp. + index. ... Vendor G0181

Doherty, Frank J. **The Settlers of the Beekman Patent: Volume III, Families Burtis - Dakin**. 1995. Indexed.
See description under Volume I, above.
Cloth. $85.00. 950 pp. + index. .... Vendor G0181

Dutchess County Genealogical Society. **1810 Census with Index, Dutchess County, NY**. (1978) reprint 1990. Indexed.
Paper. $20.00. 178 pp. .... Vendor G0450

Herrick, Margaret. **Early Settlements in Dutchess County, New York, A Compilation of the "Why . . . ?" Stories**. Indexed. Illus.
Articles originally written by Helen Myers for the *Poughkeepsie Journal* beginning 1962.
Cloth. $49.95. 213 pp. .... Vendor G0450

Herrick, Margaret. **Red Hook, Dutchess County, NY Newspapers, Deaths, 1859-1918**. Indexed.
Cloth. $56.00. 321 pp. .... Vendor G0450

Herrick, Margaret. **Red Hook, Dutchess County, NY Newspapers, Deaths, 1919-1936**. Indexed.
Paper. $23.00. 126 pp. .... Vendor G0450

Herrick, Margaret. **Red Hook, Dutchess County, NY Newspapers, Marriages, 1859-1936**. Indexed.
Cloth. $38.00. 206 pp. .... Vendor G0450

Huntting, Isaac. **(Dutchess Co.) History of "Little 9 Partners" of the N.E. Precinct & Pine Plains**. (1897) reprint 1987.
Cloth. $45.00. 411 pp. .... Vendor G0259

Huntting, Isaac. **Little Nine Partners: A History of Pine Plains, NY with Genealogies of the Early Settlers**. (1897) reprint 1974. Indexed. Illus.
Cloth. $41.00. 396 pp. .... Vendor G0450

Kelly, Arthur C. M. **Baptism Records of 8 Episcopal Congregations of the Rhinebeck Area: 1816-1899**. Indexed.
Cloth. $34.00. 181 pp. .... Vendor G0450

Kelly, Arthur C. M. **Baptism Records of Rhinebeck Reformed Church, Rhinebeck, NY: 1731-1899**. Indexed.

Cloth. $42.00. 229 pp. .... Vendor G0450

Kelly, Arthur C. M. **Baptism Records of St. Paul's (Zion's) Lutheran Church, Red Hook, NY: 1730-1899**. Indexed.
Cloth. $52.00. 301 pp. .... Vendor G0450

Kelly, Arthur C. M. **Baptism Records of St. Paul's Lutheran Church, Rhinebeck, NY (Wurtemburg): 1760-1899**. Indexed.
Cloth. $24.00. 112 pp. .... Vendor G0450

Kelly, Arthur C. M. **Baptism Records of St. Peter's Lutheran Church, Rhinebeck, NY (StoneCh): 1733-1899**. Indexed.
Cloth. $45.00. 245 pp. .... Vendor G0450

Kelly, Arthur C. M. **Baptism Records, Poughkeepsie Reformed Church, 1716-1824**.
Paper (typescript). $21.50. 127 pp. .... Vendor G0450

Kelly, Arthur C. M. **Dutchess County Probate Records: 1773-1865**. Wills, Letters Testamentary and of Administration. Indexed.
Cloth. $58.00. 326 pp. .... Vendor G0450

Kelly, Arthur C. M. **Index to Morse's Historic Old Rhinebeck**.
Reprint of index section of *Historic Old Rhinebeck* by Howard Morse (see page 402 under "Morse, Howard").
Paper. $3.00. 32 pp. .... Vendor G0450

Kelly, Arthur C. M. **Index to Smith's Documentary History of Rhinebeck**.
Reprint of index section of Smith's *Documentary History of Rhinebeck, NY* (see page 402 under "Smith, E.").
Paper. $4.00. 40 pp. .... Vendor G0450

Kelly, Arthur C. M. **Marriage Record, Poughkeepsie Reformed Church, 1746-1824**.
Paper (typescript). $7.50. .... Vendor G0450

Kelly, Arthur C. M. **Marriage Records of Four Reformed Congregations of Old Rhinebeck, NY: 1731-1899**. Indexed.
Cloth. $33.00. 168 pp. .... Vendor G0450

Kelly, Arthur C. M. **Marriage Records of Three Lutheran Congregations of Rhinebeck, NY: 1746-1899**. Indexed.
Cloth. $29.00. 152 pp. .... Vendor G0450

Kelly, Arthur C. M. **Poughkeepsie, Dutchess County, NY Newspapers: Marriages, 1826-1851**. Indexed.
Cloth. $49.50. 406 pp. .... Vendor G0450

Kelly, Arthur C. M. **Rhinebeck, NY, 18th and 19th Century Death Records**. 1992. Indexed. Illus.
Cemetery inscriptions, records, and church death records of the Town of Rhinebeck.
Cloth. $35.00. 190 pp. .... Vendor G0450

Kelly, Arthur C. M. **Rhinebeck, NY Newspapers, Vol. 1, Deaths, 1846-1899**. Indexed.
Cloth. $29.00. 214 pp. .... Vendor G0450

Kelly, Arthur C. M. **Rhinebeck, NY Newspapers, Vol. 2, Marriages, 1846-1899**. Indexed.
Cloth. $24.00. 160 pp. .... Vendor G0450

Kelly, Arthur C. M. **Vital Records of Up Red Hook, Tivoli, Mellenville, & Linlithgo NY Reformed Church: 1766-1899**.
Cloth. $29.00. 149 pp. .... Vendor G0450

Kelly, Nancy. **1850 Dutchess County Census Records: Rhinebeck**.
Paper (typescript). $15.00, $25.00 with 1865 Census Records (see page 398 listing under "Buck, Clifford"). .... Vendor G0450

Koehler, Linda. **Dutchess County, NY, Churches and Their Records: Historical Directory**. 1994.
The major portion of the book gives name and location of all known churches with a brief history of each. Appendices provide churches listed by denomination, in chronological order 1715-1901.
Cloth. $39.00. 200 pp. .... Vendor G0450

Losee, Clara. **1865 Dutchess County Census Records: Red Hook**.
Paper (typescript). $15.00, $25.00 with 1850 Census Records (see page 399 under "Buck, Clifford"). .... Vendor G0450

Lowry, James W. **Haskins Genealogy: The Descendants of Jonas Haskins (1788-1837) of Dutchess Co., New York, and Uhrichsville, Ohio**. 1992. Indexed. Illus.
Cloth. $29.95. 350 pp. .... Vendor G0035

Morse, Howard. **Historic Old Rhinebeck: History of Rhinebeck, NY with Genealogies of the Early Settlers**. (1908) reprint 1977. Indexed.
History of Rhinebeck with genealogies of the early settlers.
Cloth. $21.00. 443 pp. .... Vendor G0450

Platt, Edmund. **History of Poughkeepsie**. 328 pp. Indexed. Illus.
Contains biographical appendix.
Cloth. $25.00. 328 pp. .... Vendor G0093

Smith, E. **Documentary History of Rhinebeck, NY**. (1881) reprint 1974. Indexed.
Extensive documentation and genealogical information; map.
Cloth. $32.00. 240 pp. .... Vendor G0450

Smith, E. **History of Kipsbergen, Rhinebeck, NY,** with Supplemental Material by Margaret Herrick. (1894) reprint 1992. Indexed. Illus.
Cloth. $11.75. 58 pp. .... Vendor G0450

Smith, Edward M. **Documentary History of Rhinebeck, in Dutchess Co.,** Embracing Biographical Sketches & Genealogical Records of Our First Families & First Settlers, with a History of Its Churches & Other Public Institutions. (1881) reprint 1996.
Cloth. $32.00. 239 pp. .... Vendor G0259

Smith, James H. **History of Dutchess County,** with Illustrations & Biographical Sketches of Some of Its Prominent Men & Pioneers. (1882) reprint 1987.
Cloth. $59.50. 562 + 28 pp. .... Vendor G0259

Tower, M. **Vital Records of New Hackensack, Dutchess County, NY Reformed Church**. (1932) reprint 1993.
 Baptisms and marriages 1757-1906.
 Paper. $26.00. 347 pp. .... Vendor G0450

VanAlstyne, L. **Burying Grounds of Sharon, Conn., and Amenia & North East, NY**. (1903) reprint 1983. Indexed.
 Contains all the cemeteries not listed in Poucher's "Gravestones of Old Dutchess County."
 Cloth. $15.00. 256 pp. .... Vendor G0093

Vassar Bros. Institute. **(Dutchess Co.) Old Miscellaneous Records [of the Supervisors and Assessors, through 1742]**. (1909) reprint 1995.
 Includes apprentice contracts, wills, and administrations, assessments, Great Nine Partners Patent, makes, etc.
 Paper. $22.00. 195 pp. .... Vendor G0259

Vital Records of Hyde Park Reformed Church, Hyde Park, NY: 1810-1899.
 Cloth. $24.00. 114 pp. .... Vendor G0450

East Kill Valley

Woodworth, Olive Newell. **East Kill Valley Genealogy**. Indexed.
 A record of burials and genealogical data from 1620-1964.
 Stapled booklet. $5.00. 43 pp. .... Vendor G0160

Erie County

Briggs, Erasmus. **History of the Original Town of Concord**. (1883) reprint 1992. Indexed. Illus.
 Book #1365.
 Cloth. $59.50. 1,088 pp. .... Vendor G0082

Briggs, Erasmus. **History of the Original Town of Concord,** Being the Present Towns of Concord, Collins, N. Collins and Sardinia, Erie County. (1883) reprint 1996.
 Cloth. $95.00. 977 pp. .... Vendor G0259

Buffalo Historical Society, comp. **Picture Book of Earlier Buffalo**. (1912) reprint 1993.
 Cloth. $55.00. 508 pp. .... Vendor G0259

Eberle, Scott, and Joseph A. Grande. **Second Looks: A Pictorial History of Buffalo and Erie County**. (1987) reprint 1993. Indexed. Illus.
 Cloth. $42.95. 240 pp. .... Vendor G0085

French, J. H., and Wayne E. Morrison, Sr. **Morrison's History of Erie County, Towns, Villages, &c., 1860**. Illus.
 Contact vendor for availability. .... Vendor G0112

Johnson, Crisfield. **1876 Centennial History**. (1876) reprint 1980.
 Cloth. $24.00. 512 pp. .... Vendor G0531

Johnson, Crisfield. **Centennial History of Erie County,** Being Its Annals from the Earliest Recorded Events to the Hundredth Year of American Independence. (1876) reprint 1992.
Cloth. $55.00. 512 pp. .... Vendor G0259

Ketchum, William. **Authentic & Comprehensive History of Buffalo,** with Some Account of Its Early Inhabitants Both "Savage & Civilized." 2 vols. (1865) reprint 1994.
Cloth. $45.00/vol., $87.50/set. 432 + 443 pp. .... Vendor G0259

Morrison, Wayne E., Sr. **Morrison's Annals of Western New-York, 17 County History.** 1975. Illus.
Paper. $12.00. 72 pp. .... Vendor G0112

Smith, H. Perry. **History of Buffalo & Erie County,** with Illustrations & Biographical Sketches of Its Prominent Men & Pioneers. 2 vols. (1884) reprint 1993.
Cloth. $77.50/Vol. I. $69.50/Vol. II. 776 + 684 pp. .... Vendor G0259

Welch, Samuel M. **Home History:** Recollections of Buffalo During the Decade from 1830 to 1840, or Fifty Years Since. (1891) reprint 1993.
Cloth. $47.50. 423 pp. .... Vendor G0259

White, Truman C., ed. **Our County & Its People:** A Descriptive Work on Erie County. 2 vols. (1898) reprint 1990.
Cloth. $89.50/Vol. I. $63.00/Vol. II. $145.00/set. 906 + 617 pp. .... Vendor G0259

Witmer, Tobias. **1859 Deed Tables of Each Lot and Part of Lot as Sold by Holland Land Co.** (1859) reprint 1981. Indexed.
Cloth. $19.00. 236 pp. .... Vendor G0531

Essex County

Brown, George L. **Pleasant Valley: A History of Elizabethtown, Essex Co.** (1905) reprint 1995.
Cloth. $51.00. 480 pp. .... Vendor G0259

Watson, Winslow C. **Military & Civil History of the County of Essex.** (1869) reprint 1992.
Cloth. $52.50. 504 pp. .... Vendor G0259

Franklin County

History of Clinton & Franklin Counties, with Illustrations & Biographical Sketches of Its Prominent Men & Pioneers. (1880) reprint 1995.
Cloth. $53.00. 508 pp. .... Vendor G0259

Seaver, Frederick J. **Historical Sketches of Franklin County** & Its Several Towns, with Many Short Biographies. (1918) reprint 1994.
Cloth. $84.00. 819 pp. .... Vendor G0259

Fulton County

Beers & Co., F. W. **History of Montgomery & Fulton Counties 1772-1878**. (1878) reprint 1979. Indexed. Illus.
  Includes index by Al Chambers.
Cloth. $50.00. 432 pp. .... Vendor G0093

Kelly, Arthur C. M. **Grand Jurors of Montgomery County, New York, 1816-1850**. Indexed.
  Approximately 6,000 names from Montgomery, Fulton, Hamilton, and Herkimer counties. Residence town and occupation.
Cloth. $24.00. 109 pp. .... Vendor G0450

Vital Records of St. John's Episcopal Church, Johnstown, NY: 1815-1899.
Cloth. $27.00. 133 pp. .... Vendor G0450

Genesee County

French, J. H., and Wayne E. Morrison, Sr. **Morrison's History of Genesee County, Towns, Villages, &c., 1860**. Illus.
Contact vendor for availability. .... Vendor G0112

Morrison, Wayne E., Sr. **Morrison's Annals of Western New-York, 17 County History**. 1975. Illus.
Paper. $12.00. 72 pp. .... Vendor G0112

Greene County

Borthwick, William. **First Presbyterian Church of Durham**.
  A brief history of this little church.
Paper. $5.00. 26 pp. .... Vendor G0160

Bowman, Fred Q. **New York's Detailed Census of 1855, Greene County**.
Cloth. $21.95. 277 pp. .... Vendor G0450

History of Greene County, with Biographical Sketches of Its Prominent Men. (1884) reprint 1992.
Cloth. $55.00. 462 pp. .... Vendor G0259

Kelly, Arthur C. M. **Baptism Records of Coxsackie Reformed Church, Coxsackie, NY: 1738-1899**. Indexed.
Cloth. $37.00. 202 pp. .... Vendor G0450

Kelly, Arthur C. M. **Baptism Records of Zion Lutheran Church, Athens, NY: 1704-1899**. Indexed.
Cloth. $44.00. 254 pp. .... Vendor G0450

Kelly, Arthur C. M. **Marriage Records of 1st and 2nd Reformed Churches of Coxsackie, NY: 1797-1899**. Indexed.
Cloth. $24.00. 118 pp. .... Vendor G0450

Kelly, Arthur C. M. **Marriage Records of Lutheran Churches of Athens, NY & West Camp, NY: 1705-1899.** Indexed.
Cloth. $22.00. 99 pp. .... Vendor G0450

Kelly, Arthur C. M. **Vital Records of Prattsville Reformed Church, Prattsville, NY: 1798-1899.**
Cloth. $22.50. 111 pp. .... Vendor G0450

Morrow, Patricia. **Greene Genes: A Genealogical Quarterly About Greene County, New York.** 1988. Indexed. Illus.
Contains Bible, church, newspaper, and vital records; census schedules; land, military, and probate abstracts; gravestone inscriptions; government reports; book reviews; subscribers' queries, and much more for the towns of Ashland, Athens, Cairo, Catskill, Coxsackie, Durham, Greenville, Halcott, Hunter, Jewett, Lexington, New Baltimore, Prattsville, Windham. Subscription begins with first issue of the current year, binder included, back issues available. Annual supplement consisting of four-generation pedigree charts and family group sheets. SASE for submission guidelines.
Subscription. $20.00/yr. 120+ pp./yr. .... Vendor G0167

Pinckney, James. **Sketches of Catskill, NY.** (1868) reprint 1981. Indexed.
Reminiscences of early settlers and history of the Catskill area.
Cloth. $12.50. 84 pp. .... Vendor G0450

Sutch, G. E. **The Civil War: The Town of Prattsville**.
Greene, Delaware, and Schoharie County enlistments and how the people left behind were affected.
Paper. $7.50. 41 pp. .... Vendor G0160

Tompkins, Flora. **Ashland Collegiate Institute and Musical Academy**.
A history of the former Hedding Literary Institute with a glimpse of student life in Ashland from 1854 to 1861.
Paper. $6.00. 74 pp. .... Vendor G0160

Van Loan and Smith. **An Elegant Mistake**.
The architecture and history of the Haight/Gantley/Van Loan house in Athens in Greene County.
Paper. $6.00. 19 pp. .... Vendor G0160

Vedder, Jesse Van Vechten. **Official History of Greene County**. Vol. I (all published). (1927) reprint 1994.
Cloth. $19.50. 207 pp. .... Vendor G0259

Vedder, Jessie Van Vechten. **Historic Catskill**.
Paper. $12.95. 110 pp. .... Vendor G0160

Vedder, Jessie Van Vechten. **History of Greene County**. Indexed. Illus.
Reprinted village by village "official" history of Greene County from 1651-1800 with a statistical update to 1926.
Paper. $14.95. 207+ pp. .... Vendor G0160

Wiles, Richard C. **Windham**.
A history of this Greene County town.
Stapled booklet. $3.50. 20 pp. .... Vendor G0160

Hamilton County

Kelly, Arthur C. M. **Grand Jurors of Montgomery County, New York, 1816-1850**. Indexed.
Approximately 6,000 names from Montgomery, Fulton, Hamilton, and Herkimer counties. Residence town and occupation.
Cloth. $24.00. 109 pp. .... Vendor G0450

Herkimer County

Barker, William V. H. **Early Families of Herkimer County, New York**. 1986. Indexed.
Cloth. $25.00. 384 pp. .... Vendor G0010

Beers & Co., F. W.—Morrison's Reprint. **History of Herkimer County 1791-1879**. 1879. Indexed. Illus.
Cloth. $56.00. 352 pp. .... Vendor G0112

Benton, Nathaniel S. **History of Herkimer County,** Including the Upper Mohawk Valley from the Earliest Period to the Present Time [1856]. (1856) reprint 1993.
Cloth. $53.50. 497 pp. .... Vendor G0259

Hardin, George A., ed., with Frank H. Willard. **History of Herkimer County,** Illustrated with Portraits of Many of Its Citizens. With Several Hundred Pages of Family Sketches. (1893) reprint 1993.
Cloth. $83.00. 550 + 276 pp. .... Vendor G0259

Kelly, Arthur C. M. **Baptism Records of German Flats Reformed Church, Herkimer, NY: 1763-1899**. Indexed.
Cloth. $39.00. 219 pp. .... Vendor G0450

Kelly, Arthur C. M. **Baptism Records of Herkimer Reformed Church, Herkimer, NY: 1801-1899**. Indexed.
Cloth. $38.50. 211 pp. .... Vendor G0450

Kelly, Arthur C. M. **Grand Jurors of Montgomery County, New York, 1816-1850**. Indexed.
   Approximately 6,000 names from Montgomery, Fulton, Hamilton, and Herkimer counties. Residence town and occupation.
Cloth. $24.00. 109 pp. .... Vendor G0450

Kelly, Arthur C. M. **Marriage Record of German Flats and Herkimer Reformed Churches, Herkimer, NY: 1781-1899**. Indexed.
Cloth. $30.00. 154 pp. .... Vendor G0450

Hudson River Area

Elting, Irving. **Dutch Village Communities of the Hudson**.
   A reprint of the 1886 study of Dutch influence on the social and political development of Hudson River communities. Focuses on New Paltz.
Paper. $8.95. 68 pp. .... Vendor G0160

Hine, C. G. **Albany to Tappan**. The West Bank of the Hudson. 1906. Reprinted. Indexed.
Paper. $14.95. 174 pp. .... Vendor G0160

Letters About the Hudson River 1835-1837.
   A compilation of newspaper columns one eloquent traveler wrote about his rambles throughout the Hudson Valley in the 1830s.
Paper. $12.95. .... Vendor G0160

Lossing, Benson J. **The Hudson: From the Wilderness to the Sea**. (1866) reprint 1972. Illus.
   Book #1267.
Cloth. $39.50. 484 pp. .... Vendor G0082

Jefferson County

Haddock, John A. **Haddock's Centennial History of Jefferson County,** from 1793 to 1894. (1894) reprint 1993.
Cloth. $85.00. 843 pp. .... Vendor G0259

History of Jefferson County, with Illustrations & Biographical Sketches of Some of Its Prominent Men & Pioneers. (1878) reprint 1993.
Cloth. $65.00. 593 pp. .... Vendor G0259

Horton, W. H., ed. **Geographical Gazetteer & Business Directory of Jefferson Co., 1684-1890**. 2 parts. Compiled by H. Child. (1890) reprint 1993.
   Part I, Gazetteer & History. Part II, Business Directory.
Cloth. $89.00/Part I. $36.50/Part II. 887 + 340 pp. .... Vendor G0259

Hough, F. B. **History of Jefferson County** from the Earliest Period to the Present Time [1854]. (1854) reprint 1988.
Cloth. $63.00. 601 pp. .... Vendor G0259

Hough, Franklin B.—Morrison's Reprint. **History of Jefferson County 1854**. (1854) reprint 1976. Illus.
Cloth. $56.00. 601 pp. .... Vendor G0112

Hough, Franklin B. **History of Jefferson County, New York**. (1854) reprint 1991. Illus.
Paper. $35.00. 600 pp. .... Vendor G0506

James, Patricia R., ed. **Genealogical Journal of Jefferson Co., New York**. 1989. Indexed.
   Was a quarterly, now an annual publication devoted to listing and indexing all types of records, 1800 to 1880.
Paper. $20.00. 136 pp. .... Vendor G0506

James, Patricia R., comp. **Index to the DAR Bible Records of Jefferson County, NY**. 1992. Indexed.
   Every-name index of 2,400 entries includes birth and death dates if recorded in original work. Three unique appendices.
Paper. $12.50. 55 pp. .... Vendor G0506

James, Patricia R., comp. **Index to Hough's 1854 *History of Jefferson County, NY*.** 1987. Indexed.
   Includes 1,750 surnames; 4,200 given name entries. Five innovative appendices, such as "Place Names" and "Surname-Sounding Given Names."
Paper. $20.00. 175 pp. .... Vendor G0506

Kings County

Bergen, Teunis G. **Register . . . Early Settlers of Kings County, New York from . . . First Settlement**. 1881. Reprint on microfiche. Indexed.
Order no. 191, $18.00. 452 pp. .... Vendor G0478

Bergen, Teunis G. **Register . . . of the Early Settlers of Kings County, Long Island, N.Y.,** from Its First Settlement by Europeans to 1700. (1881) reprint 1994. Indexed.
Paper. $35.00. 452 pp. .... Vendor G0011

Furman, Gabriel. **Notes Geographical and Historical,** Relating to the Town of Brooklyn in Kings County on Long Island. (1824) reprint 1995.
Paper. $21.00. 116 pp. .... Vendor G0259

Stiles, H. R. **History of the City of Brooklyn,** Including the Old Town & Village of Brooklyn, the Town of Bushwick & the Village & City of Williamsburgh. 3 vols. (1869) reprint 1987.
Cloth. $49.00/vol., $135.00/set. 464 + 500 + 485 pp. .... Vendor G0259

Stiles, H. R., et al. **Kings County**. Civil, Political, Professional & Ecclesiastical History, & Commercial & Industrial Record of the County of King's & the City of Brooklyn, 1638-1884. 2 vols. (1884) reprint 1987.
Cloth. $67.00/Vol. I. $79.00/Vol. II. $139.00/set. 632 + 770 pp. .... Vendor G0259

Lewis County

French, J. H., and Wayne E. Morrison, Sr. **Morrison's History of Lewis County, Towns, Villages, &c., 1860**. Illus.
Contact vendor for availability. .... Vendor G0112

Hough, Franklin B. **History of Lewis County** in the State of New York, from the Beginning of Its Settlement to the Present Time. (1860) reprint 1993.
Cloth. $38.00. 320 pp. .... Vendor G0259

Hough, Franklin B. **History of Lewis County** in the State of New York, from the Beginning of Its Settlement to the Present Time, with Biographical Sketches. (1883) reprint 1993.
Cloth. $68.00. 606 + 37 pp. .... Vendor G0259

Livingston County

Boyd, William P. **History of the Town of Conesus, Livingston Co.,** from Its First Settlement in 1793 to 1887, with a Brief Genealogical Record of the Conesus Families. (1887) reprint 1995.
Cloth. $32.50. 207 pp. .... Vendor G0259

Bunnell, A. O., ed. **Dansville, 1789-1902:** Historical, Biographical, Descriptive. Compiled by F. N. Quick. (1902) reprint 1993.
Cloth. $55.00. 270 + 267 pp. .... Vendor G0259

French, J. H., and Wayne E. Morrison, Sr. **Morrison's History of Livingston County, Towns, Villages, &c., 1860**. Illus.
Contact vendor for availability. .... Vendor G0112

Hand, H. Wells., ed. **Centennial History of the Town of Nunda, 1808-1908,** with a Preliminary Recital of the Winning of Western N.Y. (1908) reprint 1993.
Cloth. $66.00. 637 pp. .... Vendor G0259

History of Livingston County, from Its Earliest Traditions to Its Part in the War for Our Union; with an Account of Seneca Nation of Indians. (1876) reprint 1991.
Cloth. $69.50. 685 pp. .... Vendor G0259

Morrison, Wayne E., Sr. **Morrison's Annals of Western New-York, 17 County History**. 1975. Illus.
Paper. $12.00. 72 pp. .... Vendor G0112

Long Island
(*see also* Kings, Queens, Nassau, and Suffolk counties)

Adams, James Truslow. **History of the Town of Southampton** (East of Canoe Place). (1918) reprint 1993.
Cloth. $45.00. 424 pp. .... Vendor G0259

Bunker, M. **Long Island Genealogies,** Being Kindred Desc. of Thomas Powell of Bethpage, Long Island, 1688. With Genealogical Material on over 60 Early Families. #24 in Munsell Series. (1895) reprint 1988.
Contact vendor for information. 350 pp. .... Vendor G0011

Genealogies of Long Island Families. From The New York Genealogical and Biographical Record. 2 vols. 1987. Indexed.
   Vol. I: Albertson-Polhemius. 787 pp.
   Vol. II: Praa-Youngs. 872 pp.
Cloth. $45.00/vol., $90.00/set. 1,659 pp. .... Vendor G0010

Hagman, Harlan L. **Nathan Hale and John Andre, Reluctant Heroes of the American Revolution**. 1992. Indexed. Illus.
   These two men, soldiers in opposing armies, typify the heroes of many wars where death cuts short the lives of the young and promising.
Cloth. $20.00. 149 pp. .... Vendor G0093

Howell, George Rogers. **Early History of Southampton, Long Island, with Genealogies**. 2nd ed. (1887) reprint 1993.
Cloth. $49.50. 473 pp. .... Vendor G0259

Jacobson, Judy. **Southold Connections**. Historical and Biographical Sketches of Northeastern Long Island. (1991) reprint 1997. Indexed. Illus.
Contact vendor for information. 113 pp. .... Vendor G0011

Long Island Source Records from *The New York Genealogical and Biographical Record*. Selected and Introduced by Henry B. Hoff. 1987. Indexed.
Cloth. $45.00. 737 pp. .... Vendor G0010

Monk, William. **Theodore and Alice: A Love Story**. 1994.
   The story of Theodore Roosevelt and his first wife, Alice Lee. Includes the genealogical background of both families.
Cloth. $20.00. 80 pp. .... Vendor G0093

Naylor, Natalie A., Douglas Brinkley, and John Allen Gable, eds. **Theodore Roosevelt, Many-Sided American**. 1992. Indexed. Illus.
   Forty-two essays on the many and diverse sides of the 26th president of the United States. Includes family genealogy.
Cloth. $55.00. 676 pp. .... Vendor G0093

Precision Indexing. **Long Island, New York 1870 Census Index**. 2 vols. 1989. Indexed. Illus.
Cloth. $195.00. 1,760 pp. .... Vendor G0552

Ross, Peter. **History of Long Island,** from Its Earliest Settlement to the Present Time [1902]. 2 vols. (1902) reprint 1995.
   Volume I: History.
   Volume II: Biography.
Cloth. $105.00/Vol. I. $65.00/Vol. II. $149.00/set. 1,080 + 562 pp. .... Vendor G0259

Seversmith, Herbert F., and Kenn Stryker-Rodda. **Long Island Genealogical Source Material**.
Cloth. $18.00. 121 pp. .... Vendor G0627

Madison County

Bracy, Isabel. **Immigrants in Madison County, New York 1815-1860**. 1990.
   An alphabetical listing of Italian and German immigrants to Madison County with a description of the industries in which they worked.
Paper. $10.00. 120 pp. .... Vendor G0093

Bracy, Isabel. **Records of Revolutionary War Veterans Who Lived in Madison County**. 1988.
   An alphabetical listing of Revolutionary War veterans from Madison County, includes some extensive biographies.
Paper. $10.00. 112 pp. .... Vendor G0093

French, J. H., and Wayne E. Morrison, Sr. **Morrison's History of Madison County, Towns, Villages, &c., 1860**. Illus.
Contact vendor for availability. .... Vendor G0112

Smith, James H. **History of Chenango & Madison Counties,** with Illustrations & Biographical Sketches of Some of Its Prominent Men & Pioneers. (1880) reprint 1993.
Cloth. $79.50. 760 + 29 pp. .... Vendor G0259

Tuttle, William H., comp. **Names and Sketches of the Pioneer Settlers of Madison County**. Edited by Isabel Bracy. 1981. Indexed. Illus.
   Contains countless bits and pieces of information from civil, census, military, church, and newspaper records. Transcribed into a book commonly known as "Tuttle's 10,000 Names," these records are now presented with additions from the 1894 "Biographical

Review." Fully cross-indexed and often serve as the only indication of residence in Madison County.

Cloth. $25.00. 292 pp. .... Vendor G0093

Tyne, John J. **Name Index to Smith's 1880 History of Chenango & Madison Counties**. (1974) reprint 1978.
  29,100 entries.

Paper. $20.00. 210 pp. .... Vendor G0093

Whitney, Mrs. L. M. Hammond. **History of Madison County,** State of New York. (1872) reprint 1994.

Cloth. $81.50. 774 pp. .... Vendor G0259

Mohawk Valley

Daily, W. N. P. **History of the Montgomery Classis,** to Which Is Added Sketches of Mohawk Valley Men & Events of Early Days, Etc. (1915?) reprint 1991.

The "classis" is the regional organization of the Dutch Reformed Church. This history of the Church and the region also contains valuable genealogical & biological information about early families.

Paper. $24.50. 198 pp. .... Vendor G0259

Diefendorf, Mary Riggs. **The Historic Mohawk**. (1910) reprint 1993.

Cloth. $38.50. 331 pp. .... Vendor G0259

Greene, Nelson. **The Story of Old Fort Plain & the Middle Mohawk Valley**. A Review of Mohawk Valley History from 1609 to 1912-14. (1915) reprint 1993.

Cloth. $45.00. 399 pp. .... Vendor G0259

Reid, W. Max, with photographs by J. Arthur Maney. **Mohawk Valley: Its Legends & History**. (1907) reprint 1993.

Cloth. $49.50. 455 pp. .... Vendor G0259

Monroe County

Barber, Gertrude A. **Abstracts of Wills of Monroe County, New York from 1821 to 1847**. 1940. Reprint on microfiche. Indexed.

Order no. 764, $10.00. 103 pp. .... Vendor G0478

McIntosh, Prof. W. H.—Morrison's Reprint. **History of Monroe County 1788-1877**. Everts, Ensign & Everts. (1877) reprint 1976. Illus.

Cloth. $56.00. 460 pp. .... Vendor G0112

Morrison, Wayne E., Sr. **History of Fairport, Monroe County 1877**. 1976. Illus.

Cloth. $25.00. 44 pp. .... Vendor G0112

Morrison, Wayne E., Sr. **History of Perinton, Monroe County 1812-1877**. 1976. Illus.

Cloth. $25.00. 66 pp. .... Vendor G0112

Morrison, Wayne E., Sr. **History of The Farm, Mendon, Monroe County 1828-1958**. 1966. Indexed. Illus.

Includes general history and genealogy of the Zebedee Bond, John Yorks, etc., families.
Cloth. $25.00. 88 pp. .... Vendor G0112

Peck, William F. **History of Rochester, & Monroe County,** from Earliest Historic Times to the Beginning of 1907. 2 vols. (1908) reprint 1992.
Cloth. $119.50. 1,434 pp. .... Vendor G0259

Montgomery County

Beers & Co., F. W. **History of Montgomery & Fulton Counties 1772-1878**. (1878) reprint 1979. Indexed. Illus.
Includes index by Al Chambers.
Cloth. $50.00. 432 pp. .... Vendor G0093

Chambers, Al. **Name Index to Beer's 1878 History of Montgomery & Fulton Counties**. 1979.
Included with above listing.
Cloth. $15.00. 72 pp. .... Vendor G0093

Davenport, David P. **1855 Census of Montgomery County, NY, Heads of Household**. Indexed.
Cloth. $38.00. 314 pp. .... Vendor G0450

Frothingham, Washington, ed. **History of Montgomery County**. With Biographies and Family Sketches. (1892) reprint 1993.
Cloth. $81.50. 450 + 349 pp. .... Vendor G0259

Keefer, Donald. **Vital Records of Amsterdam Reformed Church at Manny's Corners: 1799-1828**.
Paper. $13.50. 59 pp. .... Vendor G0450

Keefer, Donald. **Vital Records of Glen Reformed Chuch, Glen, NY: 1805-1882**.
Cloth. $25.00. 106 pp. .... Vendor G0450

Keefer, Donald. **Vital Records of Mapletown Reformed Church (Middletown) Canajoharie, NY: 1803-1901**.
Cloth. $29.50. 150 pp. .... Vendor G0450

Kelly, Arthur C. M. **Baptism Records of Caughnawaga Reformed Church, Fonda, NY: 1758-1899**. Indexed.
Cloth. $64.00. 378 pp. .... Vendor G0450

Kelly, Arthur C. M. **Baptism Records of Stone Arabia Reformed Church, Stone Arabia, NY: 1739-1899**. Indexed.
Cloth. $45.00. 250 pp. .... Vendor G0450

Kelly, Arthur C. M. **Baptism Records of Trinity Lutheran Church, Stone Arabia, NY: Pre-1751-1899**. Indexed.
Cloth. $55.00. 319 pp. .... Vendor G0450

Kelly, Arthur C. M. **Grand Jurors of Montgomery County, New York, 1816-1850**. Indexed.

Approximately 6,000 names from Montgomery, Fulton, Hamilton, and Herkimer counties. Residence town and occupation.

Cloth. $24.00. 109 pp. .... Vendor G0450

Kelly, Arthur C. M. **Marriage Records of Caughnawaga Reformed Church, Fonda, NY: 1772-1899**. Indexed.

Cloth. $28.00. 140 pp. .... Vendor G0450

Kelly, Arthur C. M. **Marriage Records of Lutheran & Reformed Churches, Stone Arabia, NY: 1739-1899**. Indexed.

Cloth. $27.00. 134 pp. .... Vendor G0450

Nassau County

Burke, Jeanne M. **Cumulative Index to Nassau County Historical Society Journal (1958-1988)**. 1989.

Paper. $5.00. 32 pp. .... Vendor G0093

New York City

Ernst, Robert. **Immigrant Life in New York City, 1825-1863**. 1994.

An important historical study of acculturation in New York City. Extensive footnotes and bibliography.

Paper. $14.95. 331 pp. .... Vendor G0611

Ernst, Robert. **Immigrant Life in New York City, 1825-1863**. Indexed.

One of the few comprehensive studies on immigration and acculturation in New York.

Cloth. $32.50. 352 pp. .... Vendor G0160

Fisher, William Scott. **New York City Methodist Marriages 1785-1893**. 2 vols. 1994.

Book #1526.

Cloth. $89.50. 765 + 735 pp. .... Vendor G0082

Franks, David, comp. **New York [City] Directory from 1786,** Prefaced by a General Description of N.Y. by Noah Webster & an Appendix of the Annals of N.Y.C., 1786. 1994 reprint.

Cloth. $29.50. xxii + 216 pp. .... Vendor G0259

Guzik, Estelle M. **Genealogical Resources in the New York Metropolitan Area**. Published by Jewish Genealogical Society, Inc.

Definitive resource book for those with ancestors who lived in the New York City area. More than 100 facilities identified. It has one of the most complete annotated lists of yizkor books.

Cloth. $29.95. 404 pp. .... Vendor G0559

Inskeep, Carolee. **The Children's Aid Society of New York:** An Index to the Federal, State, and Local Census Records of Its Lodging Houses (1855-1925). 1996.

Includes the names of 5,000 children who lived in one of the dozen or so lodging houses of the Children's Aid Society long enough to be counted as a resident in one of the federal, state, or city enumerations conducted between 1855 and 1925.
Paper. $20.00. 166 pp. .... Vendor G0011

Inskeep, Carolee. **The New York Foundling Hospital:** An Index to the Federal, State, and Local Census Records [1870-1925]. 1995.
Between 1853 and 1929, an estimated 200,000 poor, abandoned, and orphaned children were shipped from New York City orphanages to western families for adoption. The names in this volume represent 13,000 children who lived in the Roman Catholic New York Foundling Hospital between 1870 and 1925.
Paper. $27.50. 350 pp. .... Vendor G0011

Kelly, Arthur C. M. **Index to Colonial New York Wills, Volumes 1-8**. 1981.
Index to the New York Historical Society Collections 1892-1899, which contain the abstracts of wills on file in the City of New York 1665-1776.
Paper. $10.00. 63 pp. .... Vendor G0450

Kelly, Arthur C. M. **Index to New York State Wills, Volumes 9-15, 1981 Index to the New York Historical Society Collection, 1900-1906,** Which Contains the Abstracts of Wills on File in the City of New York, 1777-1800.
Paper. $10.00. 45 pp. .... Vendor G0450

Kessner. **The Golden Door: Italian and Jewish Immigrant Mobility in New York City, 1880-1915**. 1977.
A fascinating closely documented study tracing these New York City immigrants.
Paper. $14.95. 224 pp. .... Vendor G0611

McKay. **The Civil War and New York City**. 1990.
A comprehensive history of New York City and the Civil War.
Paper. $15.95. 377 pp. .... Vendor G0611

Phillip's Elite Directory of Private Families, 1881-1882, Containing the Names of 25,000 Householders. (1881) reprint 1993.
Family and business directory of Manhattan.
Cloth. $54.50. 515 pp. .... Vendor G0259

Precision Indexing. **1703 Masters of Families: New York City, New York**.
Contains a listing of heads of households.
Paper. $7.95. 9 pp. .... Vendor G0552

Precision Indexing. **Passenger Ships Arriving in New York Harbor: Vol. 1, 1820-1850**. 1991.
Cloth. $79.95. 352 pp. .... Vendor G0552

Riker, James. **Harlem (City of New York), Its Origin and Early Annals . . . Also Sketches of Numerous Families and the Recovered History of the Land-titles. Revised from the Author's Notes and Enlarged by Henry P. Toler.** (1904) reprint 1996. Indexed. Illus.
Paper. $50.00. 928 pp. .... Vendor G0011

Scott, Kenneth. **New York City Court Records, 1684-1760**.
Cloth. $22.75. 161 pp. .... Vendor G0627

Scott, Kenneth. **New York City Court Records, 1760-1797**. Indexed.
Cloth. $22.00. 250 pp. .... Vendor G0627

Scott, Kenneth. **New York City Court Records, 1797-1801**. Indexed.
Cloth. $24.95. 148 pp. .... Vendor G0627

Scott, Kenneth. **New York City Court Records, 1801-1804**.
Cloth. $24.95. 160 pp. .... Vendor G0627

Scott, Kenneth. **Nineteenth Century Apprentices in New York City**. Indexed.
Cloth. $27.00. 474 pp. .... Vendor G0627

Scott, Kenneth. **Petitions for Name Changes in New York City, 1848-1899**.
Indexed.
    All genealogical data pertaining to legal name changes of more than 890 persons.
Cloth. $19.95. 144 pp. .... Vendor G0627

Stevens, John Austin. **British Occupation of New York City 1781-1783**. Indexed.
    Reprinted from the 1885 Centennial Celebration with a new index and introduction.
Paper. $6.50. 40 pp. .... Vendor G0160

Valentine, David T. **History of the City of New York**. (1853) reprint 1996.
Cloth. $47.50. 404 pp. + 5 folding maps. .... Vendor G0259

Wittmeyer, Alfred V. **Registers of the Births, Marriages, and Deaths of the "Eglise Francoise a la Nouvelle York" [French Church of New York], from 1688 to 1804**.
(1886) reprint 1994. Indexed.
Paper. $25.00. 366 pp. .... Vendor G0011

New York County

Innes, J. H. **New Amsterdam and Its People, 1626-1902**. 1902. Reprint on microfiche. Indexed.
Order no. 529, $22.00. 365 pp. .... Vendor G0478

The New York Historical Society. **The Burghers of New Amsterdam and the Freemen of New York 1675-1866**. 1885. Reprint on microfiche. Indexed.
Order no. 628-629, $38.00. 622 pp. + index. .... Vendor G0478

Scott, Kenneth. **Coroners' Reports, New York City, 1823-1842**. 1989. Indexed.
    Deaths under unusual or suspicious circumstances.
Cloth. $21.50. 263 pp. .... Vendor G0182

Scott, Kenneth. **Coroners' Reports, New York City, 1843-1849**. 1991. Indexed.
Cloth. $25.75. 320 pp. .... Vendor G0182

Scott, Kenneth. **Naturalizations in the Marine Court, New York City, 1827-1835**.
1990. Indexed.
Cloth. $20.00. 192 pp. .... Vendor G0182

Scott, Kenneth. **Naturalizations in the Marine Court, New York City, 1834-1840**.
1991. Indexed.
Cloth. $20.00. 192 pp. .... Vendor G0182

Wittmeyer, Rev. Alfred V. **Births, Marriages, Deaths . . . "Eglise Francoise a la Nouvelle York," 1688-1806**. 1866. Reprint on microfiche.
Order no. 671-672, $34.00. 431 + index .... Vendor G0478

Niagara County

French, J. H., and Wayne E. Morrison, Sr. **Morrison's History of Niagara County, Towns, Villages, &c., 1860**. Illus.
Contact vendor for availability. .... Vendor G0112

Morrison, Wayne E., Sr. **Morrison's Annals of Western New-York, 17 County History**. 1975. Illus.
Paper. $12.00. 72 pp. .... Vendor G0112

Parish, Dr. Charles Carlin. **Queen of the Mist**. 1987. Indexed.
    The story of Annie Edson Taylor, first person ever to go over Niagara Falls and survive.
Paper. $9.95. 148 pp. .... Vendor G0093

Oneida County

Baggs, M. M., M.D. **Pioneer Settlers of Utica,** Being Sketches of Its Inhabitants & Its Institutions, with the Civil History of the Place, from the Earliest Settlement to 1825. (1877) reprint 1993.
Cloth. $68.50. 665 pp. .... Vendor G0259

French, J. H., and Wayne E. Morrison, Sr. **Morrison's History of Oneida County, Towns, Villages, &c., 1860**. Illus.
Contact vendor for availability.. .... Vendor G0112

Gridley, Rev. A. D. **History of the Town of Kirkland**. (1874) reprint 1993.
Cloth. $32.00. xiv + 232 pp. .... Vendor G0259

History of Oneida County, with Illustrations & Biographical Sketches of Some of Its Prominent Men & Pioneers. (1878) reprint 1992.
Cloth. $69.50. 678 pp. .... Vendor G0259

Jones, Pomroy. **Annals & Recollections of Oneida County**. (1851) reprint 1993.
Cloth. $88.00. 893 pp. .... Vendor G0259

Pioneer History of Camden, Oneida County. (1897) reprint 1992.
Cloth. $58.00. 559 pp. .... Vendor G0259

Rogers, Henry C. **History of the Town of Paris & the Valley of the Sauquoit: Anecdotes & Reminiscences**. (1881) reprint 1992.
Cloth. $44.00. 398 pp. .... Vendor G0259

Wager, Daniel, ed. **Our County & Its People:** A Descriptive Work on Oneida County. 2 vols. (1896) reprint 1991.
    Volume I (Parts I & II), History & Biography.
    Volume II (Part III), Family Sketches.
Cloth. $88.00/Vol. I. $44.00/Vol. II. $125.00/set. 851 + 411 pp. .... Vendor G0259

Onondaga County

Beauchamp, Rev. W. M. **Revolutionary Soldiers Resident or Dying in Onondaga Co.,** with Supplementary List of Possible Veterans. (1912) reprint 1993.
Cloth. $34.50. 307 pp. .... Vendor G0259

Cheney, T. C. **Reminiscences of Syracuse [Onondaga County, NY].** Indexed.
   Early history of Syracuse related by one of the original settlers.
Paper. $12.00. 117 pp. .... Vendor G0160

Collons, G. K. **Mortuary Records, with Genealogical Notes of the Town of Spafford, Onondaga Co.** (1917) reprint 1993.
Paper. $28.00. 280 pp. .... Vendor G0259

French, J. H., and Wayne E. Morrison, Sr. **Morrison's History of Onondaga County, Towns, Villages, &c., 1860.** Illus.
Contact vendor for availability. .... Vendor G0112

Smith, Carroll E. **Pioneer Times in the Onondaga Country.** Edited by Charles Carroll Smith. (1904) reprint 1994.
Cloth. $45.00. 415 pp. .... Vendor G0259

Ontario County

Aldrich, Lewis C., comp. **History of Ontario County,** with Illustrations and Family Sketches of Some of the Prominent Men & Families. Edited by George S. Conover. (1893) reprint 1996.
Cloth. $92.00. Family sketches only, $47.50. 519 + 396 pp. .... Vendor G0259

Burnisky, David L. **The Personalities of Melvin Hill Cemetery, Phelps, Ontario County, New York.** 1995. Indexed. Illus.
Paper. $28.50. 269 pp. .... Vendor G0160

Colf, Mary Loeper, John I. Loepe, and Ruth Nightingale. **All-Name Index to MacIntosh's 1876 History of Ontario County.** 1988.
Paper. $10.00. 68 pp. .... Vendor G0093

McIntosh, Prof. W. H.—Morrison's Reprint. **History of Ontario County 1788-1876.** Everts, Ensign, and Everts. (1876) reprint 1976. Illus.
Cloth. $56.00. 330 pp. .... Vendor G0112

Orange County

Coleman, Charles C. **The Early Records of the First Presbyterian Church at Goshen, New York, from 1767 to 1885.** (1933) reprint 1990. Indexed.
Cloth. $15.00. 215 pp. .... Vendor G0011

Corning, Rev. Elwood. **The Concise History of Orange County.** Indexed. Illus.
Paper. $13.95. Approx. 130 pp. .... Vendor G0160

Hand, Juliana Free. **The Andre Trail Book! Westchester County Treasure Hunt Tour: Treason in the American Revolution**. 1980. Illus.
Paper. $12.95. 93 pp. .... Vendor G0479

Headley, Russel, ed. **History of Orange County**. (1908) reprint 1993.
Cloth. $98.00. 997 pp. .... Vendor G0259

Ruttenber, E. M., and L. H. Clark. **History of Orange County,** with Illustrations & Biographical Sketches of Many of Its Pioneers & Prominent Men. 2 vols. (1881) reprint 1992.
Cloth. $69.00. 820 pp. .... Vendor G0259

Ruttenber, E. M. **History of the Town of Newburgh**. (1859) reprint 1995.
Cloth. $36.50. 322 + xx pp. .... Vendor G0259

Orleans County

Copeland, David Sturges. **History of Clarendon, from 1810 to 1888**. (1889) reprint 1993.
Cloth. $44.00. 382 pp. .... Vendor G0259

Pratt, J. Howard. **Memories of Life on the Ridge**. 1978. Indexed. Illus.
    Newspaper articles by the Town Historian of Gaines brought together into a book.
Paper. $8.00. 216 pp. .... Vendor G0093

Pratt, J. Howard. **Saga on the Ridge**. 1983. Indexed. Illus.
    Numerous stories about early settlers on the Ridge collected by the town historian.
Paper. $9.50. 213 pp. .... Vendor G0093

Sanford and Co.—Morrison's Reprint. **History of Orleans County 1824-1879**. (1879) reprint 1979. Illus.
Cloth. $56.00. 352 pp. .... Vendor G0112

Smith, Evelyn Rich. **Name Index to Arad Thomas' 1871 The Pioneer History of Orleans County**. 1982.
Paper. $5.00. 30 pp. .... Vendor G0093

Sumner, Samuel. **History of the Missisco Valley**. With Intro. Notice of Orleans Co. by Rev. S. R. Hall. (1860) reprint 1993.
Cloth. $17.50. 75 pp. .... Vendor G0259

Thomas, Arad. **Pioneer History of Orleans County,** Containing Some Account of the Civil Divisions of Western N.Y., with Brief Biogr. Notices of Early Settlers. (1871) reprint 1990.
Cloth. $49.00. 463 pp. .... Vendor G0259

Oswego County

Churchill, John C., et al. **Landmarks of Oswego County**. Part I, History; Part II, Biographical; Part III, Family Sketches. (1895) reprint 1994.
Cloth. $119.50. 843 + 72 + 348 pp. .... Vendor G0259

French, J. H., and Wayne E. Morrison, Sr. **Morrison's History of Oswego County, Towns, Villages, &c., 1860**. Illus.
Contact vendor for availability. .... Vendor G0112

History of Oswego County, with Illustrations & Biographical Sketches of Prominent Men & Pioneers. (1877) reprint 1991.
Cloth. $54.50. 450 pp. .... Vendor G0259

Otsego County

Everts and Fariss—Morrison's Reprint. **History of Otsego County 1740-1878**. (1878) reprint 1978. Illus.
Cloth. $56.00. 508 pp. .... Vendor G0112

Halsey, Francis W., with G. L. Halsey. **The Pioneers of Unadilla Village, 1784-1840,** with Reminiscences of Village Life, and of Panama & California from 1840 to 1850. (1902) reprint 1995.
Cloth. $39.00. 323 pp. .... Vendor G0259

History of Otsego County, with Illustrations & Biographical Sketches of Some of Its Prominent Men & Pioneers. (1878) reprint 1991.
Cloth. $47.50. 378 pp. .... Vendor G0259

Putnam County

Buck, Clifford M. **Dutchess County, NY Tax Lists, 1718-1787**. With Rombout Precinct by William Reese.
Cloth. $55.00. 305 pp. .... Vendor G0450

Greene, Marilyn Cole. **Town Minutes, Town of Carmel, Putnam County, New York, 1795-1839**. Indexed.
Minutes with names of pathmaster, fence viewer, pound master, and inspector of common schools.
Cloth. $26.90. 183 pp. .... Vendor G0450

Hand, Juliana Free. **The Andre Trail Book! Westchester County Treasure Hunt Tour: Treason in the American Revolution**. 1980. Illus.
Paper. $12.95. 93 pp. .... Vendor G0479

Queens County

Riker, James. **Annals of Newtown,** Queens County, Containing Its History from Its Settlement . . . with Many Interesting Facts Concerning the Adjacent Towns. With genealogies. (1852) reprint 1992.
Cloth. $47.00. 437 pp. .... Vendor G0259

Stoutenburgh, Henry A. **Documentary History of the Dutch Congregation of Oyster Bay, Queens Co.,** Island of Nassau (Long Island). 2 vols. (1902) reprint 1993.
A very rich source for early Long Island genealogy. Using the 1,000 baptisms in the

church records, the compiler traced the first Dutch settlers in Oyster Bay back to emigration & forward to 1902. Embraces some 3,000 families, including most well-known Dutch names & other non-Dutch names of area residents. Thoroughly indexed. Cloth. $97.50. 966 pp. .... Vendor G0259

Rensselaer County

Anderson, George Baker. **Landmarks of Rensselaer County**. (1898) reprint 1992. Cloth. $98.50. 570 + 460 pp. .... Vendor G0259

Gemmill, Eva H., and Marie E. Hoffman, eds. **Marcus Peck: Letters of a Civil War Soldier and His Family**. 1993. Illus. Paper. $15.50. 96 pp .... Vendor G0058

Gemmill, Eva H. **Remembering Three Churches**. 1984. Illus. Paper. $5.50. 52 pp. .... Vendor G0058

Hill, Florence. **Letters Home: Written by Poestenkill Servicemen 1941-45 and 1917-18**. 1991. Illus. Paper. $6.00. 62 pp. .... Vendor G0058

Hill, Florence M, comp. **Sketches of the 35 Supervisors of Poestenkill, NY 1848 to 1990**. 1991. Illus. Paper. $5.00. 56 pp. .... Vendor G0058

Hill, Florence M. **West of Perigo: Poestenkill Memories**. 1979. Illus. Paper. $10.25. 204 pp. .... Vendor G0058

Kelly, Arthur C. M. **Baptism Records of Gilead Lutheran Church, Brunswick, NY: 1777-1886**. Indexed. Cloth. $43.00. 242 pp. .... Vendor G0450

Kelly, Arthur C. M. **Vital Records of Evangelical Lutheran Church, Poestenkill, NY: 1833-1892**. Indexed. Paper. $7.00. 25 pp. .... Vendor G0450

Kelly, Arthur C. M. **Vital Records of Greenbush Reformed Church, East Greenbush, Rensselaer County, NY: 1788-1899**. Indexed. Cloth. $29.00. 145 pp. .... Vendor G0450

Kelly, Arthur C. M. **Vital Records of Trinity Lutheran Church, West Sand Lake, NY: 1784-1899**. Cloth. $32.00. .... Vendor G0450

Kelly, Arthur C. M. **Vital Records of Wynantskill Reformed Church, Wynantskill, NY: 1794-1889**. Cloth. $27.00. 136 pp. .... Vendor G0450

Mitchell, Marietta A., and C. Irene Kropp, Co-chairpersons. **From the Great Cooks Among Us**. 1983. Indexed. Illus.
    Includes histories of local organizations.
Paper. $7.50. 102 pp. .... Vendor G0058

Morrison, W. E., & Co. **Jones & Company (Troy Bell Foundry) Catalogue & History**. (1874) reprint 1984. Illus.
Paper. $14.00. 50 pp. .... Vendor G0112

Pockman, Rev. P. Theo., A.M. **Abstracts of Wills of Rensselaer County, New York**. 1891. Reprint on microfiche.
Order no. 623, $10.00. 312 pp. .... Vendor G0478

Ptak, Diane Snyder. **Cast in Stone, Selected Albany, Rensselaer and Saratoga County, NY, Cemetery Records**. Indexed.
  Burials, 18th and 19th century; 8,500 people.
Cloth. $35.00. 169 pp. .... Vendor G0450

Simm, Marie, and Eva Gemmill, eds. **The Dutch Settlement Church: West Berlin, New York**. 1981. Illus.
Paper. $5.25. 30 pp. .... Vendor G0058

Sylvester, Nathaniel Bartlett. **History of Rensselaer County,** with Illustrations & Biographical Sketches of Its Prominent Men & Pioneers. (1880) reprint 1992.
Cloth. $59.50. 564 pp. .... Vendor G0259

Weise, Arthur James. **Troy's One Hundred Years, 1789-1889**. (1891) reprint 1993.
Cloth. $48.50. 453 pp. .... Vendor G0259

Richmond County

Clute, J. J. **Annals of Staten Island, from Its Discovery to the Present Time**. (1877) reprint 1986. Indexed.
Cloth. $35.00. 464 pp. .... Vendor G0093

Clute, J. J. **Old Families of Staten Island**. (1877) reprint 1990.
Contact vendor for information. 103 pp. .... Vendor G0011

Morris, Ira K. **Morris's Memorial History of Staten Island**. 2 vols. (1900) reprint 1993.
Cloth. $49.50/vol., $95.00/set. 415 + 539 pp. .... Vendor G0259

Stillwell, John E., M.D. **Historical and Genealogical Miscellany:** Data Relating to the Settlement & Settlers of New Jersey, Volumes I-V. (1903-32) reprint 1993.
  Volumes I and II of this meticulously researched reference set consist of historical articles that will be of great interest to many who are researching early New Jersey and Staten Island, including transcripts of court records and church registers, quit rents, Friends' records, cemetery inscriptions, and more. Areas covered are Monmouth, Burlington, and Cape May counties, and Staten Island, N.Y.
  Volumes III-V contain hundreds of genealogical sketches of New Jersey families.
Contact vendor for information. 2,547 pp. in all .... Vendor G0010

Rockland County

Cole, David, ed. **History of Rockland County,** with Biographical Sketches of Its Prominent Men. (1884) reprint 1990.
Cloth. $49.50. 420 pp. .... Vendor G0259

Hand, Juliana Free. **The Andre Trail Book! Westchester County Treasure Hunt Tour: Treason in the American Revolution**. 1980. Illus.
Paper. $12.95. 93 pp. .... Vendor G0479

Kelly, Arthur C. M. **Index of the 1850 Federal Census of Rockland County, New York (surname only)**.
    Index of the *Rockland County, NY 1850 Federal Census*, transcribed by Lee Seth Wanamaker (see below).
Paper. $10.00. 33 pp. .... Vendor G0450

Wanamaker, Lee Seth, scr. **Rockland County, NY 1850 Federal Census**. Indexed by Arthur C. M. Kelly. 1996. Indexed.
Paper. $69.50. 561 pp. .... Vendor G0450

Saratoga County

Anderson, George Baker ("The Saratogian"). **Our County and Its People: A Descriptive & Biographical Record of Saratoga Co**. (1899) reprint 1994.
Cloth. $81.50. 584 + 203 pp. .... Vendor G0259

Cemeteries of the Town of Half Moon, Saratoga Co. (1963) reprint 1992.
Paper. $14.00. 74 pp. .... Vendor G0259

Grose, Edward F., with J. C. Booth. **Centennial History of the Village of Ballston Spa,** Including the Towns of Ballston and Milton. (1907) reprint 1995.
Cloth. $34.50. 258 pp. .... Vendor G0259

Ptak, Diane Snyder. **Cast in Stone, Selected Albany, Rensselaer and Saratoga County, NY, Cemetery Records**. Indexed.
    Burials, 18th and 19th century; 8,500 people.
Cloth. $35.00. 169 pp. .... Vendor G0450

Ritchie, Henry, and Cornelius Durkee. **Name Index to Sylvester's 1878 History of Saratoga County**. 1979.
    Included with Sylvester's "1878 History of . . ." (see below for vendor G0093 under "Sylvester, Nathaniel").
Cloth. $15.00. 75 pp. .... Vendor G0093

Saratoga County 1850 Federal Census, Town of Saratoga Transcript.
Cloth. $20.00. 76 pp. .... Vendor G0450

Saratoga County 1850 Federal Census: Town of Ballston Transcript.
Cloth. $15.00. 48 pp. .... Vendor G0450

Sylvester, Nathaniel. **History of Saratoga County**. (1878) reprint 1979. Indexed. Illus.
    Published by Everts & Ensign. Includes index listed above for vendor G0093 under "Ritchie, Henry."
Cloth. $50.00. 732 pp. .... Vendor G0093

Schenectady County

Davenport, David P. **1855 Census of Schenectady County, NY, Heads of Household**. Indexed.
Cloth. $41.00. 228 pp. .... Vendor G0450

Hanson, Jr., Willis T. **A History of Schenectady During the Revolution**. (1916) reprint 1988. Indexed.
This history encompasses the affairs of the whole Mohawk Valley and Border Wars during that period as well as Schenectady.
Cloth. $30.00. 304 pp. .... Vendor G0093

Kelly, Arthur C. M. **Baptism Records of Schenectady Reformed Church: 1694-1811**. Indexed.
Cloth. $55.00. 539 pp. .... Vendor G0450

Kelly, Arthur C. M. **Marriage Records of Schenectady Reformed Church, Schenectady, NY: 1694-1852**. Indexed.
Cloth. $30.00. 154 pp. .... Vendor G0450

Kelly, Arthur C. M. **Vital Records of Niskayuna Reformed Church, Schenectady, NY: 1783-1861**.
Cloth. $20.00. 85 pp. .... Vendor G0450

Kelly, Arthur C. M. **Vital Records of Princetown Reformed Church, Duanesburg, NY: 1824-1899**.
Cloth. $11.50. 30 pp. .... Vendor G0450

Kelly, Arthur C. M. **Vital Records of Scotia Reformed Church, Scotia, NY: 1818-1899**.
Cloth. $22.00. 102 pp. .... Vendor G0450

Kelly, Arthur C. M. **Vital Records of Woestina (Rotterdam) & Glenville Reformed Churches: 1800-1899**.
Cloth. $25.00. 119 pp. .... Vendor G0450

Morrison, W. E., & Co. **Westinghouse Threshing Machinery, &c**. 1970. Illus.
Paper. $10.00. 10 pp. .... Vendor G0112

Pearson, Jonathan. **Contributions for the Genealogy of the Descendants of the First Settlers of the Patent & City of Schenectady from 1662 to 1800**. (1873) reprint 1992.
Contact vendor for information. 324 pp. .... Vendor G0010

Van Santvoord, Cornelius W. **History of Schenectady County**. Indexed. Illus.
A reprint of the 1887 booklet with map and new index. Includes a brief history of each town and major industry, and an account of the French & Iroquois attack of Schenectady in 1690.
Paper. $6.95. 48 pp. .... Vendor G0160

Schoharie County

Brown, John. **Brief Sketch of 1st Settlement of Schoharie**.
  A reprint of the 1823 account of the German settlement of Schoharie County.
Stapled booklet. $5.00. 24 pp. .... Vendor G0160

Burton, A. **Schoharie County, NY Family Cemetery Inscriptions, Town of Wright**.
1961.
Paper. $7.00. 36 pp. .... Vendor G0450

Davenport, David P. **1855 Census of Schoharie County, NY, Heads of Household**.
Indexed.
Cloth. $47.00. 350 pp. .... Vendor G0450

Kelly, Arthur C. M. **Baptism Records of Schoharie Reformed Church, Schoharie,
NY: 1731-1894**. Indexed.
Cloth. $45.00. 256 pp. .... Vendor G0450

Kelly, Arthur C. M. **Baptism Records of St. Paul's Lutheran Church, Schoharie,
NY: 1728-1899**. Indexed.
Cloth. $49.00. 295 pp. .... Vendor G0450

Kelly, Arthur C. M. **Marriage Records of Lutheran and Reformed Churches of
Schoharie, NY: 1732-1899**. Indexed.
Cloth. $34.00. 185 pp. .... Vendor G0450

Kelly, Arthur C. M. **Vital Records of Lawyersville Reformed Church Lawyersville,
Schoharie Co., NY: 1790-1882**.
Cloth. $30.00. 139 pp. .... Vendor G0450

Kelly, Arthur C. M. **Vital Records of Middleburgh Reformed Church, Middleburg,
NY: 1797-1899**.
Cloth. $29.00. 146 pp. .... Vendor G0450

Partridge, Virginia P., with Susan F. Watkins. **Transcript of the 1800, 1810, and 1820
Federal Census of Schoharie County, New York**. 1992. Indexed. Illus.
Cloth. $49.95. 251 pp. .... Vendor G0450

Partridge, Virginia P., with Susan F. Watkins. **Transcript of the 1830 and 1840 Federal Census of Schoharie County, New York**. 1991. Indexed. Illus.
Cloth. $69.95. 350 pp. .... Vendor G0450

Sutch, G. E. **The Civil War: The Town of Prattsville**.
  Greene, Delaware, and Schoharie County enlistments and how the people left be-
hind were affected.
Paper. $7.50. 41 pp. .... Vendor G0160

Schuyler County

Cheney, T. Apoleon, and *The Havana Journal*. **Historical Sketch of the Chemung
Valley 1867**. 1986. Illus.
Cloth. $24.00. 66 pp. .... Vendor G0112

Cleaver, Mary Louise (Catlin). **History of the Town of Catharine, Schuyler County**. (1945) reprint 1988. Indexed. Illus.
Cloth. $80.00. 734 pp. .... Vendor G0112

Everts and Ensign—Morrison's Reprint. **History of Schuyler County 1854-1879**. Edited by Pierce and Hurd. (1879) reprint 1976. Illus.
Cloth. $56.00. 226 pp. .... Vendor G0112

History of Tioga, Chemung, Tompkins & Schuyler Counties, with Illustrations & Biographical Sketches of Some of Their Prominent Men & Pioneers. (1879) reprint 1991.
Cloth. $78.50. 687 pp. .... Vendor G0259

Morrison, Wayne E., Sr. **Catharine's Town, The Sullivan Expedition**. 1989. Illus.
Paper. $12.50. 24 pp. .... Vendor G0112

Morrison, Wayne E., Sr. **The Contiguous Towns, Schuyler and Chemung Counties**. 1989. Illus.
    Veteran, Catlin, Catharine, Hector, Dix, Montour.
Cloth. $25.00. 92 pp. .... Vendor G0112

Morrison, Wayne E., Sr. **History of Havana 1788-1895**. 1986. Indexed. Illus.
    It is the design of this work to narrate in a clear, simple, and intelligible manner the leading events connected with the illustrious history of Havana. Incidents were related more to illustrate the past than to amuse the reader, the objective being to show and trace the advancement of progress in a concise, unpretentious manner. Only the printed page can now bear testimony to the existence and endurance of those whose traditions perished with and in them so very long ago. The voluminous files of *The Havana Journal* were indispensable in the preparation of this work, as were other essential documents, maps, pictures, portraits, etc. The whole, as compiled, contains a copious source of alphabetical information appearing in the appended index, and is handsomely bound in cloth.
Cloth. $36.00. 406 pp. .... Vendor G0112

Pomeroy, Whitman & Co. **Atlas of Schuyler County 1874**. (1874) reprint 1976. Illus.
    County, town, village maps, 3 Havana illustrations.
Cloth. $60.00. 57 pp. .... Vendor G0112

Whitford and Morrison. **History of the Chemung Canal**. 1989. Illus.
Cloth. $28.00. 66 pp. .... Vendor G0112

Seneca County

Everts, Ensign, and Everts—Morrison's Reprint. **History of Seneca County 1786-1876**. (1876) reprint 1976. Indexed. Illus.
Cloth. $62.00. 280 pp. .... Vendor G0112

French, J. H., and W. E. Morrison & Co. **Plat Book of Ovid, Seneca County 1858**. 1976. Illus.
Paper. $22.00. 30 pp. .... Vendor G0112

French, J. H., and W. E. Morrison & Co. **Plat Book of Seneca Falls, Seneca County 1856**. 1976. Illus.
Paper. $22.00. 30 pp. .... Vendor G0112

French, J. H., and W. E. Morrison & Co. **Plat Book of Waterloo, Seneca County 1855**. 1976. Illus.
Paper. $22.00. 30 pp. .... Vendor G0112

Gibson, William T., John Delafield, and Wayne E. Morrison, Sr. **Plat Book of Seneca County Town & Village Maps 1850**. 1976. Illus.
Cloth. $30.00. 36 pp. .... Vendor G0112

Gravelding, Clarence. **Romulus Remembered**. 1990. Illus.
Recollections of the hamlet from 1915 to 1930.
Paper. $12.95. 130 pp. .... Vendor G0093

Knight, Anne R. **A Story of Townsendville, NY**. 1992. Indexed. Illus.
Living history of the Townsendville area, including Coan's Corners and Centreville, taken from the 1926 diary of Helen Colgate.
Paper. $12.00. 112 pp. .... Vendor G0093

Morrison, Wayne E., Sr. **Early History of Covert, Seneca County**. 1984. Indexed. Illus.
Cloth. $30.00. 172 pp. .... Vendor G0112

Morrison, Wayne E., Sr. **History of Lodi, Seneca County 1789-1894**. 1986. Indexed. Illus.
Cloth. $30.00. 141 pp. .... Vendor G0112

Morrison, Wayne E., Sr. **History of Ovid, Seneca County 1789-1889**. 1980. Indexed. Illus.
Cloth. $35.00. 338 pp. .... Vendor G0112

Morrison, Wayne E., Sr. **History of Romulus, Seneca County 1789-1876**. 1989. Indexed. Illus.
Cloth. $28.00. 160 pp. .... Vendor G0112

Morrison, Wayne E., Sr. **New York State Agricultural College at Ovid**. 1976. Indexed. Illus.
Cloth. $24.00. 160 pp. .... Vendor G0112

Morrison, Wayne E., Sr. **Postal History of Seneca County 1802-1984**. 1986. Indexed. Illus.
Cloth. $25.00. 135 pp. .... Vendor G0112

Morrison, Wayne E., Sr. **The Willard Asylum (Seneca County) 1869-1886**. 1976. Illus.
Cloth. $25.00. 72 pp. .... Vendor G0112

Seneca County Farm Register with Map 1938. Indexed. Illus.
Cloth. $30.00. 60 pp. .... Vendor G0112

Watrous, Hilda R. **The County Between the Lakes: Life and People to be Remembered Seneca County, New York, 1895**. 1988. Indexed. Illus.
Community, business and social history.
Cloth. $20.00. 221 pp. .... Vendor G0093

Watrous, Hilda R. **The County Between the Lakes: A Public History of Seneca County—1876-1982**. 1983. Indexed. Illus.

The book examines public works projects and public owned land within the county and their effect on the population. A full 12% of Seneca County is in public area, including the Seneca Army Depot (1939-93), Sampson Naval (1942-46) and Air Force (1950-56) bases, three State Parks, Hector Land Use Area, Montezuma Wildlife Refuge, the NYS Barge Canal, the NYS Thruway, and others.
Cloth. $20.00. 385 pp. .... Vendor G0093

Willers, Diedrich, Jr. **History of Fayette, Seneca County 1800-1900**. 1900. Indexed. Illus.
Cloth. $18.00. 160 pp. .... Vendor G0112

St. Lawrence County

Curtis, Gates, ed. **Our County & Its People: A Memorial Record of St. Lawrence County**. (1894) reprint 1994.
 Part I: History.
 Part II: Biographies and Personal Sketches.
Cloth. $72.00/Part I. $42.50/Part II. $109.50/Both parts in 1 vol. 720 +
420 pp. .... Vendor G0259

Durant, Samuel, and Henry B. Peirce. **History of Saint Lawrence County**. (1878) reprint 1982. Indexed. Illus.
 Published by L. H. Everts. Includes index listed below.
Cloth. $50.00. 914 pp. .... Vendor G0093

All Name Index to Durant's 1878 History of Saint Lawrence County. 1982.
 Included with Durant's "History of . . ." (see above listing).
Cloth. $15.00. 76 pp. .... Vendor G0093

Durant, Samuel W., and Henry B. Pierce. **History of Saint Lawrence County, 1749-1878,** with Illustrations & Biographical Sketches of Prominent Men & Pioneers. (1878) reprint 1994.
Cloth. $55.00. 521 pp. .... Vendor G0259

French, J. H., and Wayne E. Morrison, Sr. **Morrison's History of St. Lawrence County, Towns, Villages, &c., 1860**. Illus.
Contact vendor for availability. .... Vendor G0112

Sanford, C. E. **Early History of the Town of Hopkinton**. (1903) reprint 1991.
Cloth. $65.00. 604 pp. .... Vendor G0259

Steuben County

French, J. H., and Wayne E. Morrison, Sr. **Morrison's History of Steuben County, Towns, Villages, &c., 1860**. Illus.
Contact vendor for availability. .... Vendor G0112

Gordon, William Reed. **Keuka Lake Memories and the Champagne Railroad**. 1986. Illus.
 History of The Forked Lake, including aviation, the wine industry, water and rail transportation. Extensive illustrations.
Paper. $14.95. 256 pp. .... Vendor G0093

Morrison, Wayne E., Sr. **Morrison's Annals of Western New-York, 17 County History**. 1975. Illus.
Paper. $12.00. 72 pp. .... Vendor G0112

Roberts, Millard F., comp. **Historical Gazetteer of Steuben County,** with Memoirs & Illustrations. Part I: Historical & Biographical; Part II: Directory of Individuals & Businesses. (1891) reprint 1995.
Cloth. $62.50/Part I. $37.50/Part II. $94.50/Both parts in 1 vol. 592 + 354 pp. .... Vendor G0259

Suffolk County

Ferguson, Henry L. **Fishers Island, N.Y., 1614-1925**. (1925) reprint 1995.
Cloth, $29.50. Paper, $19.50. 103 pp. .... Vendor G0259

Griffin, Augustus. **Griffin's Journal: First Settlers of Southold**. 1857. Reprint on microfiche. Indexed.
Order no. 907, $14.00. 312 pp. .... Vendor G0478

Pelletreau, William S. **Early Long Island Wills of Suffolk County, 1691-1703,** with Genealogical and Historical Notes. (1897) reprint 1995.
Contact vendor for information. 289 pp. .... Vendor G0011

Sullivan County

Quinlan, J. E. **History of Sullivan County,** Embracing an Account of Its Geology, Settlement, Towns, with Biographical Sketches of Prominent Residents, Etc. (1873) reprint 1990.
Cloth. $72.00. 700 pp. .... Vendor G0259

Sivertsen, Barbara J., and Barbara L. Covey. **The Legend of Cushetunk:** The Nathan Skinner Manuscript and the Early History of Cochecton. 1993. Indexed. Illus.
    The Nathan Skinner Manuscript is a detailed source of genealogical, historical, and anecdotal information about the pioneer and Revolutionary War days from 1754 to 1783.
Paper. $17.00. 95 pp. .... Vendor G0160

Tioga County

Albertson, Capt. Charles L. **History of Waverly & Vicinity**. (1943) reprint 1994.
Cloth. $37.00. 319 pp. .... Vendor G0259

Everts and Ensign—Morrison's Reprint. **History of Tioga County 1791-1879.** Edited by Pierce and Hurd. (1879) reprint 1976. Illus.
Cloth. $56.00. 214 pp. .... Vendor G0112

History of Tioga, Chemung, Tompkins & Schuyler Counties, with Illustrations & Biographical Sketches of Some of Their Prominent Men & Pioneers. (1879) reprint 1991.
Cloth. $78.50. 687 pp. .... Vendor G0259

Morrison, Wayne E., Sr. **History of Havana 1788-1895**. 1986. Indexed. Illus.

It is the design of this work to narrate in a clear, simple, and intelligible manner the leading events connected with the illustrious history of Havana. Incidents were related more to illustrate the past than to amuse the reader, the objective being to show and trace the advancement of progress in a concise, unpretentious manner. Only the printed page can now bear testimony to the existence and endurance of those whose traditions perished with and in them so very long ago. The voluminous files of *The Havana Journal* were indispensable in the preparation of this work, as were other essential documents, maps, pictures, portraits, etc. The whole, as compiled, contains a copious source of alphabetical information appearing in the appended index, and is handsomely bound in cloth.

Cloth. $36.00. 406 pp. .... Vendor G0112

Tompkins County

Everts and Ensign—Morrison's Reprint. **History of Tompkins County 1817-1879**. Edited by Pierce and Hurd. (1879) reprint 1976. Illus.

Cloth. $56.00. 288 pp. .... Vendor G0112

Goodrich, George E., comp. & ed. **Centennial History of the Town of Dryden, 1797-1897**. (1898) reprint 1993.

Cloth. $35.00. 272 pp. .... Vendor G0259

History of Tioga, Chemung, Tompkins & Schuyler Counties, with Illustrations & Biographical Sketches of Some of Their Prominent Men & Pioneers. (1879) reprint 1991.

Cloth. $78.50. 687 pp. .... Vendor G0259

Kammen, Carol. **The Peopling of Tompkins County**. 1985. Indexed. Illus.

A social history of Tompkins County with stories of the people who settled the county.

Cloth. $19.95. 262 pp. .... Vendor G0093

Lewis, Helen F. **New York's Finger Lakes Pioneer Families, Especially Tompkins County**. 1991. Indexed.

Genealogical information on over seventy-five families, including Revolutionary soldiers in central New York.

Cloth. $69.95. 409 pp. .... Vendor G0450

Martin, Catherine Machan. **Records of Tompkins County, New York: Wills, Intestates, Bible, Church and Family Records**. Wills 1817 to Mid 1839, Liber A thru C with Added Wills and Notes Concerning Tompkins County, New York Early Families. 1995. Indexed.

Cloth. $45.00. 195 pp. .... Vendor G0756

Tryon County

Campbell, William W. **Annals of Tryon County,** or the Border Warfare of N.Y. During the Revolution. (1831, 1924) reprint 1993.

Cloth. $34.50. xx + 257 pp. .... Vendor G0259

Ulster County

Anjou, Gustave. **Ulster County, NY Probate Records from 1665**. (1906) reprint 1980. Indexed.
Seventeenth- and eighteenth-century wills and letters of administration on file at Kingston, NY.
Cloth. $40.00. 528 pp. .... Vendor G0450

Anjou, Gustave. **Ulster County, New York Probate Records** [from 1665] in the Office of the Surrogate, and in the County Clerk's Office in Kingston, N.Y. . . . with Genealogical and Historical Notes, and List of Dutch and Frisian Baptismal Names with Their English Equivalents. 2 vols. in 1. (1906) reprint 1996. Indexed.
Paper. $40.00. 528 pp. in all. .... Vendor G0011

Anjou, Gustave. **Ulster County, New York Probate Records, Volumes 1 & 2**. 1906. Reprint on microfiche. Indexed.
Order no. 737—Vol. 1, $16.00; order no. 738—Vol. 2, $14.00.
248 + 280 pp. .... Vendor G0478

Brink, Benjamin Myer. **The Early History of Saugerties**. Indexed.
The complete story of the settlement and development of the town of Saugerties. Stapled manuscript style, printed four pages to a page.
92 pp. (original was 365 pp.). .... Vendor G0160

Brink, Benjamin Myer. **Olde Ulster Volume I, 1905**.
Reprint of first year (of ten-year) magazine with a variety of competent historical and genealogical articles dealing with Ulster County and its people, including many transcripts of original documents.
Cloth. $29.95. 384 pp. .... Vendor G0160

Brink, Benjamin Myer. **Palatines of Olde Ulster**.
A reprint of ten articles from the genealogical and biographical magazine *Olde Ulster* (c. 1905-1914) on this early group of Hudson Valley settlers.
Paper. $9.95. 80 pp. .... Vendor G0160

Clearwater, Alphonso T., ed. **History of Ulster County**. (1907) reprint 1992.
Cloth. $75.00. 707 pp. .... Vendor G0259

Commemorative Biographical Record of Ulster County, Containing Biographical Sketches of Prominent and Representative Citizens, and of Many of the Early Settled Families. (1896) reprint 1996.
Cloth. $129.00. 1,330 pp. .... Vendor G0259

Elting, Irving. **Dutch Village Communities of the Hudson**.
A reprint of the 1886 study of Dutch influence on the social and political development of Hudson River communities. Focuses on New Paltz.
Paper. $8.95. 68 pp. .... Vendor G0160

Hoes, Roswell Randall. **Baptismal and Marriage Registers of the Old Dutch Church of Kingston, Ulster County, New York, 1660-1809**. (1891) reprint 1997. Indexed.
Cloth. $50.00. 797 pp. .... Vendor G0010

Kelly, Arthur C. M. **Baptism Records of Marbletown Reformed Church, Marbletown, NY: 1746-1871**. Indexed.
Cloth. $39.00. 218 pp. .... Vendor G0450

Kelly, Arthur C. M. **Marriage Records of Lutheran Churches of Athens, NY & West Camp, NY: 1705-1899**. Indexed.
Cloth. $22.00. 99 pp. .... Vendor G0450

Kelly, Arthur C. M. **Vital Records of Esopus Reformed Church, Ulster Park, NY: 1791-1899**.
Cloth. $29.00. 151 pp. .... Vendor G0450

Kelly, Arthur C. M. **Vital Records of Shokan Reformed Church, Shokan, Ulster County, NY: 1799-1899**.
Cloth. $21.00. 93 pp. .... Vendor G0450

LeFevre, Ralph. **History of New Paltz, New York, and Its Old Families** (from 1678 to 1820). 2nd ed. (1909) reprint 1996. Indexed. Illus.
This is the definitive history of New Paltz, one of the oldest Huguenot settlements in America and the cradle of surrounding settlements in Ulster and Orange counties, New York.
Paper. $55.00. 607 pp. .... Vendor G0011

Prehn, Florence, and Audrey M. Klinkenberg. **Ulster County Cemeteries, Ulster County, New York**. 1992. Indexed.
Cloth. $41.00. 325 pp. .... Vendor G0183

Sylvester, Nathaniel. **History of Ulster County**. (1880) reprint 1994. Indexed. Illus.
Cloth. $70.00. 900 pp. .... Vendor G0093

Sylvester, N. B. **History of Ulster County,** with Illustrations & Biographical Sketches of Its Prominent Men & Pioneers. (1880) reprint 1988.
Cloth. $74.50. 310 + 340 pp. .... Vendor G0259

Van Buren, Augustus H. **A History of Ulster Under the Dutch**.
Paper. $13.95. 146 pp. .... Vendor G0160

Versteeg, Dingman, trans. **Records of the Reformed Dutch Church of New Paltz, New York,** Containing . . . Registers of Consistories, Members, Marriages, and Baptisms. (1896) reprint 1992. Indexed.
Includes lists of church members and extensive records of marriages and baptisms, with references to several thousand early inhabitants, including those of Huguenot, Dutch, and English origins.
Paper. $22.50. 269 pp. .... Vendor G0011

Woolsey, C. M. **History of the Town of Marlborough, Ulster Co.,** from Its Earliest Discovery. (1908) reprint 1995.
Cloth. $51.00. 471 pp. .... Vendor G0259

Zimm. **The Concise History of Ulster County**. 1946. Reprinted. Illus.
Covers all the townships, major industries, and important people up to World War II. On a fully searchable, non-intrusive diskette (needs no hard disk space). DOS program for IBM-compatible computers.
IBM 3.5" diskette. $10.00 + shipping. .... Vendor G0160

Warren County

Holden, A. W. **History of the Town of Queensbury,** with Biographical Sketches of Many of Its Distinguished Men. (1874) reprint 1993.
Cloth. $55.00. 517 pp. .... Vendor G0259

McAlear, Robert. **Name Index to Smith's 1885 History of Warren County**. 1981.
Cloth. $15.00. 58 pp. .... Vendor G0093

Washington County

Jenks, Margaret R. **Granville Cemetery Inscriptions, Washington County, New York**. 1993. Indexed. Illus.
Paper. $33.00. xxvi + 282 pp. .... Vendor G0599

Johnson, Crisfield. **History of Washington County, New York**. (1878) reprint 1979. Illus.
    Does not include index. See next listing.
Cloth. $50.00. 704 pp. .... Vendor G0093

Name Index to Johnson's 1878 History of Washington County. 1983.
    Not included with Johnson's "1878 History . . ." from Vendor G0093 (see above listing).
Cloth. $15.00. 79 pp. .... Vendor G0093

Moore, Charles B. **Cemetery Records of the Township of Fort Ann, Washington County, NY**. 1995. Indexed.
Spiral bound. $24.00. 123 pp. .... Vendor G0698

Patten, Jennie M. **The Argyle Patent** and Accompanying Documents. (1928) reprint 1991.
    In 1764, a large number of Scottish Presbyterian colonists succeeded in securing the land grant known as the Argyle Patent, in Washington County, New York, upon which they took up residence. This work comprises a collection of the various documents produced in support of the Argyle claim and features genealogical notices of various Washington County families.
Paper. $9.00. 68 pp. .... Vendor G0011

Wayne County

Child, Hamilton, and Wayne E. Morrison, Sr. **History of Wayne County 1789-1869**. 1970. Illus.
Cloth. $28.00. 68 pp. .... Vendor G0112

McIntosh, W. H.—Morrison's Reprint. **History of Wayne County 1789-1877**. Everts, Ensign & Everts. (1877) reprint 1976. Illus.
Cloth. $81.00. 346 pp. .... Vendor G0112

Morgan, Janet, and Marlene Morgan. **Genealogical Abstracts from Palmyra, Wayne County, New York Newspapers 1810-1854**. 1995. Indexed.
Spiral bound. $49.00. 438 pp. .... Vendor G0697

Morrison, Wayne E., Sr. **History of Arcadia and Newark, Wayne County 1877**. 1989. Illus.
Cloth. $28.00. 68 pp. .... Vendor G0112

Morrison, Wayne E., Sr. **History of Clyde, Wayne County 1722-1969**. 1969. Indexed. Illus.
Cloth. $30.00. 116 pp. .... Vendor G0112

Morrison, Wayne E., Sr. **History of Galen, Wayne County 1812-1889**. 1980. Indexed. Illus.
Cloth. $30.00. 108 pp. .... Vendor G0112

Morrison, Wayne E., Sr. **History of Lyons, Wayne County 1877**. 1989. Illus.
Cloth. $28.00. 86 pp. .... Vendor G0112

Morrison, Wayne E., Sr. **History of Palmyra, Wayne County 1877**. 1989. Illus.
Cloth. $28.00. 98 pp. .... Vendor G0112

Wayne County Farm Register with Map 1938. 1938. Indexed. Illus.
Cloth. $30.00. 60 pp. .... Vendor G0112

West Camp

Kelly, Arthur C. M. **Baptism Records of St. Paul's Lutheran Church, West Camp, NY: 1708-1899**. Indexed.
Cloth. $22.00. 105 pp. .... Vendor G0450

Westchester County

Baird, C. W. **Rye. Chronicle of a Border Town:** History of Rye, Westchester Co., 1660-1870, Including Harrison & White Plains till 1788. (1871) reprint 1987.
Cloth. $59.50. 570 pp. .... Vendor G0259

Baird, Charles W. **History of Rye, Westchester County New York 1660-1870**. (1871) reprint 1994. Indexed. Illus.
  Book #1361.
Cloth. $49.50. 592 pp. .... Vendor G0082

Bolton, Robert. **History of the Several Towns, Manors & Patents of the County of Westchester from Its First Settlement to the Present Time**. Edited by C. W. Bolton. 2 vols. (1881) reprint 1995.
Cloth. $82.50/vol., $149.00/set. 782 + 826 pp. .... Vendor G0259

Caro, Edythe Quinn. **The Hills in the Mid-Nineteenth Century: The History of a Rural Afro-American Community in Westchester County, New York**. 1988. Illus.
Photocopy in report binder. $34.00. 184 pp. .... Vendor G0479

Cole, Rev. David. **Vital Records of Sleepy Hollow Reformed Church, Tarrytown, NY: 1697-1791**. Indexed.
Cloth. $25.00. 252 pp. .... Vendor G0450

Fox, Dixon Ryan. **Caleb Heathcote: Gentleman Colonist**. (1926) reprint 1971. Indexed. Illus.
  Book #1346.
Cloth. $15.00. 313 pp. .... Vendor G0082

Fuller, Elizabeth G., comp. **Index to the Westchester Historian, Vols. 1-65, 1925-1989**. 1990.
Paper. $29.00. 88 pp. .... Vendor G0479

Fuller, Elizabeth G., comp. **Index to the Westchester Historian, Vols. 66-70, 1990-1994**. 1995.
Paper. $5.75. 14 pp. .... Vendor G0479

Fuller, Elizabeth G, comp. **Personal Name Index to J. Thomas Scharf's History of Westchester County**. 1988.
Cloth. $29.00. 160 pp. .... Vendor G0479

Fuller, Elizabeth G., and Susan C. Swanson. **Westchester County: A Pictorial History**. (1982) reprint 1989. Indexed. Illus.
Cloth. $31.95. 200 pp. .... Vendor G0479

Hadaway, William S., ed. **The McDonald Papers**. 2 vols. 1926. Indexed.
  Papers read before the New-York Historical Society, prepared by John M. McDonald and based on his previous interviews with survivors of the American Revolution.
Cloth. $19.00. 236 pp. .... Vendor G0479

Hand, Juliana Free. **The Andre Trail Book! Westchester County Treasure Hunt Tour: Treason in the American Revolution**. 1980. Illus.
Paper. $12.95. 93 pp. .... Vendor G0479

Kelly, Arthur C. M. **Vital Records of Cortlandtown Reformed Church, Montrose, NY: 1741-1894**.
Cloth. $23.00. .... Vendor G0450

Madden, Joseph P. **A Documentary History of Yonkers, New York, Volume One: The Formative Years, 1820-1862**. 1992. Indexed. Illus.
  About half of this volume consists of narrative history while the balance presents transcriptions of records and a listing of residents with limited genealogical data.
Paper. $26.00. 303 pp. .... Vendor G0160

Madden, Joseph P. **A Documentary History of Yonkers, New York, Volume Two, Part One: The Unsettled Years, 1863-1860**. 1994. Indexed.
  Discusses the demographic, economic, and political influences of the specified time period, while providing information obtained from the Town Record Book and Associated Documents, newspaper microfilm, and other sources.
Paper. $30.50. 342 pp. .... Vendor G0160

Madden, Joseph P. **Documentary History of Yonkers, New York, Volume Two, Part Two: The Dutch, the English, and an Incorporated American Village, 1609-1860**. 1994. Indexed.

Contains detailed historical background from the earliest Dutch and English settlement to the pre-Civil War years.
Paper. $27.50. 286 pp. .... Vendor G0160

Old Dutch Burying Ground of Sleepy Hollow, in N. Tarrytown. A Record of the Early Gravestones & Inscriptions. (1953) reprint 1991.
Paper. $19.00. 192 pp. .... Vendor G0259

Pelletreau, William S. **Early Wills of Westchester County, New York from 1664-1784**. 1898. Reprint on microfiche. Indexed.
Order no. 729, $26.00. .... Vendor G0478

Roach, John. **Historic White Plains**. (1939) reprint 1993.
Cloth. $42.50. 395 pp. .... Vendor G0259

Sanchis, Frank E. **American Architecture, Westchester County, New York: Colonial to Contemporary**. 1977. Indexed. Illus.
Cloth. $24.95. 564 pp. .... Vendor G0479

Scharf, J. Thomas. **History of Westchester County, New York**. 3 vols. (1886) reprint 1992. Indexed. Illus.
  Book #1407.
Cloth. $159.50. 2,016 pp. .... Vendor G0082

Scharf, J. Thomas. **History of Westchester County,** Including Morrisania, Kings Bridge and West Farms, Which Have Been Added to New York City. 2 vols. (1886) reprint 1993.
Cloth. $89.50/Vol. I. $79.50/Vol. II. $159.50/set. 893 + 771 pp. .... Vendor G0259

Scharf, J. Thomas. **History of Westchester County, New York**. 2 vols. (1886) reprint 1992. Indexed. Illus.
  See page 436 under "Fuller, Elizabeth G." for a personal name index to this book.
Cloth. $149.50. 1,665 pp. .... Vendor G0479

Shonnard, Frederic, and W. W. Spooner. **History of Westchester County,** from Its Earliest Settlement to the Year 1900. (1900) reprint 1992.
Cloth. $67.00. 638 pp. .... Vendor G0259

Tombstone Records of Eighteen Cemeteries in Pound Ridge, New York. (1941) reprint 1983. Indexed. Illus.
  Book #1349.
Paper. $9.50. 96 pp. .... Vendor G0082

Weigold, Marilyn E., ed. **Westchester County: The Past 100 Years, 1883-1983**. 1984. Indexed. Illus.
Cloth. $29.95. 384 pp. .... Vendor G0479

The Westchester Historian. A journal, published quarterly, 1925-present.
Price of individual copies, $3.75; complete set, $760.00; microfilm (16mm) of v. 1-65, 1925-1989, $67.00. .... Vendor G0479

Wood, James. **History of the Town of Bedford, to 1917**. (1925) reprint 1993.
Paper. $9.00. 48 pp. .... Vendor G0259

Yonkers Board of Trade, comp. **Yonkers, Illustrated**. (1904?) reprint 1995.
    A photographic "album" of Yonkers at the turn of the century, with many hundreds of photos of homes, public buildings and parks, businesses and factories, etc.
Cloth. $32.50. 192 pp. .... Vendor G0259

Wyoming County

Beers, F. W.—Morrison's Reprint. **History of Wyoming County 1841-1880**. 1880.
Indexed. Illus.
Cloth. $56.00. 384 pp. .... Vendor G0112

Beers & Co., F. W. **History of Wyoming County 1841-1880**. (1880) reprint 1994.
Indexed. Illus.
    Includes index by French (see below) reset for clarity.
Cloth. $50.00. 424 pp. .... Vendor G0093

French, Robert. **Name Index to Beer's 1880 History of Wyoming County**. (1950) reprint 1983.
    Included with Beer's "1880 History of . . ." available from vendor G0093 (see above listing).
Cloth. $15.00. 40 pp. .... Vendor G0093

History of Wyoming County, with Illustrations, Biographical Sketches of Some Pioneers & Prominent Residents. (1880) reprint 1993.
Cloth. $37.50. 310 pp. .... Vendor G0259

Yates County

Cleveland, Stafford C. **History & Directory of Yates County,** Containing a Sketch of Its Original Settlement, with an Account of Individual Pioneers & Their Families. Vol. I (no more published). (1873) reprint 1993.
Cloth. $79.00. 766 pp. .... Vendor G0259

Cleveland, Stafford C.—Morrison's Reprint. **History of Yates County 1873**. 2 vols. (1873) reprint 1976. Indexed. Illus.
Cloth. $66.00. 1,200 pp. .... Vendor G0112

Author Index

Abbot, A., 266
Abbot, Herman, 226
Abbott, Susan Woodruff, 74
Abernethy, ___, 19
Adams, ___, 355
Adams, Gladys S., 69
Adams, James N., 109
Adams, James Truslow, 411
Adams, Nathaniel, 356
Adams, Richard, 375
Adams, Sherman W., 69
Adams, Silas, 225
Adams, William, 391
Addington, Robert M., 72
Addison, Norma, 41
Adelberg, Michael S., 370
Adjutant General State of Kentucky, 183
Alabama Historical Quarterly, 19
Albert, ___, 227
Albertson, Capt. Charles L., 430
Aldrich, George, 350
Aldrich, Lewis C., 419
Alexander, ___, 87
Alig, Leona Tobey, 135
Allardice, Bruck, 211
Allen, Desmond Walls, 27-30, 32, 34-51
Allen, Francis O., 69
Allen, M. O., 266
Allison, ___, 115, 117, 124, 126
Allison, Linda, 128
Allsop, Fred W., 30
Allyn, Charles, 76
Alvord, ___, 109
Andersen, Patricia Abelard, 246-247

Anderson, George Baker, 422, 424
Anderson, George W., 314
Anderson, Joseph Crook II, 227, 228
Anderson, Robert Charles, 1
Andreas, T., 306
Andrews, A., 69
Andrews, Charles M., 69
Andrews, L. F., 174
Angevine, Erma Miller, 82
Anjou, Gustave, 432
Annis, Daniel Gage, 356
Antrobus, Augustine M., 169
Appleton, William S., 292
Archives Committee of Gloucester, 267
Ardery, Mrs. William Breckenridge, 183
Ardoin, Robert Bruce L., 209, 213-214
Arellano, Fay Louise Smith, 79
Armitage, ___, 17
Armstrong, Barbra Kay, 375
Armstrong Company, J. M., 183
Armstrong, Ruth A., 176, 179
Armstrong, William C., 359
Armstrong, Zella, 11
Arnold, ___, 30
Arnold, H. B., Jr., 37
Arnold, H. Ross, 87
Arnold, J. N., 264
Arnold, John P., 306

Arnold, Norma S., 37
Arseneault, Judith A., 356
Arthur, Stanley Clisby, 209
Asbury, Henry, 114
Atkins, Leah Rawls, 20
Atkins, W. G., 273
Atkinson, Joseph, 366
Atwater, Edward E., 63, 74
Atwater, Francis, 69, 72
Atwater, Isaac, 311
Austin, Jeannette Holland, 87, 89
Austin, John Osborne, 1
Avery, Rev. J., 77

Babson, John J., 267
Bachar, Jacqueline Miller, 408
Bacon, Oliver N., 278
Baggs, M. M., 418
Bailey, Edwin C., 176
Bailey, Frederic W., 64, 255, 288
Bailey, Rosalie Fellows, 360, 376
Bailey, S. L., 267
Baird, Charles W., 435
Bakeman, Mary Hawker, 306-307, 312-313
Baker, ___, 274
Baker, Henry A., 77
Baker, Joseph E., 54
Baker, Ruthe, 367
Baldwin, Elmer, 124
Baldwin, Harrison C., 352
Ball, T. H., 135, 152
Ballard, Alta, 47
Ballard, James, 47
Ballou, ___, 388

Ballou, A., 294
Baltimore County Genea-
  logical Society, 240
Bancroft, Hubert H., 51
Banks, Charles Edward,
  1, 255
Banks County, Georgia
  Hebron Historical Soci-
  ety, 101
Banvard, Theodore James
  Fleming, 51, 84, 167,
  307, 376
Barber, Gertrude A., 413
Barber, John W., 255,
  360
Barbour, ___, 70
Barbour, Hugh, 376
Barbour, Lucius Barnes,
  69
Barekman, June, 151
Barker, William V. H.,
  407
Barnes, Robert W., 8,
  229-230, 239, 241
Barnes, Thomas G., 255
Barrington Public Li-
  brary, 358
Barrow, Healan, 250
Barrow, Lee G., 104
Barrows, J. S., 223
Barrus, H., 277
Barry, John S., 288
Barry, W., 278
Bartlett, Henrietta C.,
  385
Bassett, Frank G., 75
Bassett, William, 350
Batchelder, Pauline Man-
  ning, 252
Bateman, Newton, 110,
  115, 119, 133
Bates, Alfred C., 64
Bates, Betty Magoun,
  289
Bates, Edw. C., 295
Bates, Marlene Strawser,
  245
Bates, S. A., 285
Bathrick, M., 398
Battin, Judge William,
  172
Battle, J. H., 189-190,
  207

Baxter, Albert, 303
Baxter Co. Arkansas His-
  torical and Genealogical
  Society, 35-36
Bayley, Capt. W. H., 267
Bayor, Ronald H., 376
Beach, Joseph P., 74
Beal, Joyce Richmond,
  338
Beals, Kathleen C., 57
Beard, Alice L., 244
Beardsley, A., 76
Beatty, John D., 136
Beauchamp, Rev. W. M.,
  419
Beckwith, H. W., 132,
  147, 156
Bedford Historical Soci-
  ety, 352
Bedini, Sylvio A., 67
Beekman, George C., 371
Beers, ___, 114
Beers & Co., J. H., 140
Beers, F. W., 368, 390,
  405, 407, 414, 438
Beers, H. P., 211
Bell, Charles H., 356
Bell, Herbert C., 253
Bemis, Charles A., 350
Bendler, Bruce, 80
Benedict, W. A., 294
Benedict, William H.,
  370
Bennett, ___, 343
Bent, Allen H., 347
Bent, Charles, 134
Benton, Nathaniel S., 408
Bergen, Teunis G., 410
Bergeron, ___, 25
Bergeron, Arthur W., Jr.,
  211
Bicentennial Committee
  Members of Society,
  221
Bicentennial Gen.
  Comm., 277
Bickford, Christopher P.,
  64
Bigelow, Ella A., 278
Bigelow, W. Victor, 285
Bill, ___, 360
Bill, Ledyard, 294
Binford, J. H., 148

Bingham, W. H., 311
Birch, John Jesse
  Setlington, 140
Birdsall, B. P., 176
Bittinger, J. Q., 351
Black, Clifford, 19, 22-23
Black, Marcia McDonald,
  106
Black, Margaret K., 129
Blackman, Leah, 365
Blair, Ruth, 89
Blake, F. W., 294
Blake, Jonathan, 274
Blake, William P., 74
Blanchard, Charles, 141,
  143, 155-156, 157, 158,
  167
Bland, Doris Ellen
  (Witter), 134
Blassingame, John W.,
  211
Bleser, ___, 11
Blevins, Winfred, 17
Blodgett, George B., 267
Blois, John T., 300
Blood, Henry Ames, 352
Boddie, John Bennett, 11
Boddie, Mrs. John
  Bennett, 11
Bodge, George Madison,
  255
Boeckman, Laurel, 319
Bogardus, William
  Brower, 7
Bolles, J. R., 64
Bolton, Ethel Stanley,
  278
Bolton, Herbert E., 51,
  84, 209, 374
Bolton, Robert, 435
Boltwood, Edw., 262
Boltwood, Lucius M.,
  277
Bond, Henry, 279
Bond, Lydia K., 195
Booth, Andrew B., 209
Booth, J. C., 424
Borthwick, William, 405
Boswell, G. C., 72
Bouknecht, Carol Cox,
  84, 86-87
Bouton, N., 355
Bowen, C. W., 79

Bowen, Jessie Marsh, 310

Bowie, Effie Gwynn, 251

Bowman, Fred Q., 376, 405

Bowman, George Ernest, 2, 255

Boyd, J., 72

Boyd, Thomas H. S., 250

Boyd, William P., 411

Boyer, Carl, 3rd, 80, 360

Boyer, Dorothy Marvelle, 266

Bracy, Isabel, 397, 412

Bradbury, Charles, 227

Bradford, Laurence, 288

Bradsby, Henry C., 114, 164

Bragdon, Lester MacKenzie, 227

Bragg, ___, 89

Brain, John, 241

Brandenburg, John David, 89

Branson, Allegra, 381

Brasseaux, Carl A., 211

Breckenridge, Frances A., 74

Brentwood Hist. Society, 356

Brewer, George E., 22

Brewer, Mary Marshall, 81

Brewer, W., 19

Brewster, Charles W., 357

Bridges, Robert L., 390

Briggs, Erasmus, 403

Briggs, L. V., 288

Briggs, Mary S., 398

Brigham, Johnson, 174

Brink, Benjamin Myer, 376, 432

Brinkley, Douglas, 412

Britt, Albert S., Jr., 91

Broadfoot Publishing Company, 11, 255

Brockman, Paul, 138

Bronson, Henry, 75

Brookes, George S., 79

Brooks, C., 279

Brooks, R. R., 262

Brower, Philip P., 52

Brown, ___, 20, 94

Brown, A. J., 319

Brown, Abram English, 279

Brown, Albert, 21

Brown, Alonzo L., 307

Brown, Evelyn J., 178, 180-182

Brown, Francis H., 279

Brown, G. E., 261

Brown, George L., 404

Brown, George S, 1

Brown, Hal G., 350

Brown, Helen W., 251

Brown, John, 426

Brown, John Henry, 17

Brown, Oliver B., 261

Brown, Virginia Alleman, 365, 369-371, 373-374

Brown, Warren, 357

Bruce, Virginia M., 49

Brugger, Robert J., 230

Brumbaugh, Gaius Marcus, 230

Bryan, Charles, 310

Bryan, Mary G., 89

Bryan, William S., 320

Bryant, Charles S., 309, 313

Bryant, L. P., 277

Buck, Clifford, 398-399, 421

Buffalo Historical Society, 403

Bull, Sidney A., 279

Bunker, M., 411

Bunnell, A. O., 411

Burgert, Annette K., 9

Burgin, Edna Montgomery, 207

Burke, Jeanne M., 415

Burnham, Hank, 87

Burnisky, David L., 419

Burns, Loretta E., 209

Burr, Horace, 81

Burt, Henry M., 275

Burton, A., 426

Burton, Ann, 142, 300, 302, 305

Burton, Ann Mullin, 141

Burton, Cheryl, 142

Burton, Conrad, 142, 300, 302, 305

Bushman, ___, 255

Buss, Karen, 320

Butler, Caleb, 279

Butler, Francis Gould, 219

Butler, Mimi Jo, 98

Butruille, Susan G., 17

Byerley, Donna, 334

Bynum, ___, 12

Caffee, Barbara McDow, 38

Cain, Andrew W., 103

Cain, Cyril Edward, 318

Caldwell, ___, 210

Caldwell, J. R., 175

California Genealogical Society, 51

Callcott, ___, 230

Camp, David N., 67, 69-70

Campbell, ___, 225

Campbell, Hollis A., 75

Campbell, Jesse H., 89

Campbell, William W., 431

Cannon, Thomas H., 153, 159

Cape Cod Genealogical Society, 261

Carey, Dr. W. W., 145

Caro, Edythe Quinn, 435

Carothers, Bettie, 230, 241, 243-244, 248, 253

Carpenter, ___, 315, 277

Carr, ___, 230, 252

Carr, Daniel M., 346

Carr, Peter E., 51, 57

Carrier, Lois A., 110

Carter, W. C., 8

Casey, Marion R., 387

Cashin, ___, 12, 104

Cates, Joyce Hardy, 202

Caulkins, Frances M., 77

Cauthorn, Henry S., 151

Caverly, A. M., 350

Cemetery Committee, Lake County Genealogical Society, The, 121

Chamberlain, George Walter, 285

Chamberlain, M., 292

Chambers, Al, 414
Chambers, T. F., 360
Chandler, C. H., 352
Chandler, S., 279
Chapin, Alonzo B., 70
Chapin, Charles W., 275
Chapman, Chas. C., &
  Co., 121
Chase, F. S., 222
Chase, George Wingate,
  267
Chase, J. C., 357
Chase, Theodore, 1
Chenault, Anderson, 190
Cheney, T. Apoleon, 393,
  426
Cheney, T. C., 419
Chicago Genealogical
  Society, 116
Child, Frank Samuel, 67
Child, H., 351
Child, Hamilton, 392,
  434
Chipman, R. Manning,
  72
Chipman, Scott L., 1, 3
Chism, Stephen J., 30
Choate, D., 267
Christ, ___, 30
Christiansen, E. Joyce,
  324-325
Christoph, Florence, 388
Church, Madeline, 51, 54
Churchill, John C., 420
Churchman, Charles, 135
Cissna, Catherine A., 54
Claiborne, J. F. H., 315
Clark, ___, 128, 183
Clark, G. K., 286
Clark, J. J., 126
Clark, L. H., 420
Clark, Murtie June, 12
Clark, W. H., 221
Clark, W. L., 170, 174,
  176
Clary, Jeanne B., 56
Claybaugh, Joseph, 143
Clay County Historical
  Society, 178
Clayton, W. Woodford,
  364, 370, 372, 374
Clearwater, Alphonso T.,
  432

Cleaver, Mary Louise
  (Catlin), 427
Clements, S. Eugene, 230
Clements, William M., 34
Cleveland, Stafford C.,
  438
Clifford, Karen, 12
Clift, G. Glenn, 183-184
Cline, ___, 149
Clinton, ___, 12
Clute, J. J., 423
Coale, Joseph M., 241
Cobb, Mrs. Wilton Philip,
  100
Coburn, Louise Helen,
  225
Cochran, Dr., 125
Cochrane, Joseph, 126
Cochrane, Laura C., 243
Cochrane, W. R., 353
Coffin, J., 267
Coffman, Brenda
  Sutherland, 329
Coffman, David, 329
Cogswell, Elliott C., 353,
  356-357
Cogswell, L. W., 355
Colburn, Harvey C., 305
Colburn, W. P., 354
Coldham, Peter Wilson,
  230-231
Cole, A., 223
Cole, Adeline P., 267
Cole, Arthur Charles, 110
Cole, David, 423, 436
Cole, J. R., 79
Coleman, ___, 274
Coleman, Charles C., 419
Coleman, Ruby Roberts,
  345
Coles, David, 84
Colf, Mary Loeper, 419
Collier, Edward A., 394
Collin, John Francis, 394
Collins, Lewis, 184
Collins, Richard H., 184
Collons, G. K., 419
Colonial Dames of Dela-
  ware, 82
Colonial Society of Mas-
  sachusetts, The, 3, 255
Colorado Genealogical
  Society, Inc., 62-63

Colson, Lucy Wiggins,
  22, 25
Commission of the
  Dorchester Antiquarian
  & Historical Society,
  292
Concannon, Marie, 320
Conerly, Luke W., 319
Conklin, Emma B., 63
Connecticut Society
  Daughters of the Ameri-
  can Revolution, 64
Connelley, William E., 63
Conrad, ___, 209, 212
Conrad, John B., 199
Converse, Parker L., 279
Conway, Rosanne, 76,
  387
Cook, ___, 3
Cook, Mrs. Anna Maria
  Green, 96
Cook, Pat, 58
Cooley, Eli F., 369
Cooley, William S., 369
Coolidge, Lillian P., 292
Cooper, Marshall M., 120
Cooper, Martha L., 335
Cooper, Walter G., 102
Copeland, Alfred M., 275
Copeland, David Sturges,
  420
Coquillette, ___, 257
Corbit, R. M., 171
Cordley, R., 178
Corey, D. P., 279
Corning, Elwood, 419
Cothren, William, 2, 72
Cottage Grove Genea-
  logical Society, 156
Cotton, Jane Baldwin,
  231
Coulter, E. Merton, 89
Counts, Mrs. William H.,
  48
Covey, Barbara L., 430
Cowart, Cordell, 58
Cowart, Margaret
  Matthews, 22-25
Cowley, Charles, 279
Cox, ___, 296
Cox, Richard J., 231
Cox, Sam D., 344
Cox, W. W, 339

Crafts, J. M., 274
Craig, H. Stanley, 363, 365-367, 372
Craig, Marion S., 31, 44
Cranor, Henry Downes, 244
Crawford, L., 347
Crawford, Sybil F., 48
Crevecoeur, E. E., 180
Crissey, T. W., 72
Crosby, Anthony E., 238
Crosley, William George, 226
Cross, L. H. R., 355
Crowder, 110, 136, 184
Crowell, R., 267
Cunningham, H. H., 211
Cunningham, J. O., 115
Cunningham, Rosalie S. (Neall), 58
Currier, John J., 267
Curtis, Gates, 429
Curtiss-Wedge, Franklyn, 310-315
Cushman, D. Q., 222
Cutter, B., 279
Cutter, W., 279
Cutter, William Richard, 4, 64, 257, 279, 377

Daggett, John, 264-265
Dahlquist, Alfred J., 311
Dally, Joseph W., 370
Daily, W. N. P., 413
Daly, Marie E., 6
Danforth, Edward, 398
Daniels, G., 295
D.A.R., Thronateeska Chapter, Albany, Georgia, 100
Darby, Earl G., 177-183
Darlington, Jane E., 154
Darnell, Betty R., 196, 207, 334-335
Darnell, Ermina Jett, 102
Dassel Area Historical Society, 315
D'Autrechy, Phyllis B., 368
Davenport, David P., 388, 414, 425-426
Davenport, Elizabeth Osgood, 286

Davenport, George Lyman, 286
Davidson, Dianne Hatcher, 84
Davidson, Grace Gillam, 101, 104, 107
Davidson, Victor, 108
Davis, ___, 89
Davis, Charles Henry Stanley, 75
Davis, Helene, 249
Davis, John David, 364
Davis, Margaret P., 378
Davis, Robert Scott, Jr., 88-89, 92, 97-98, 102, 107
Davis, W. T., 288
Davis, Walter A., 295
Davis, Walter G., 215, 216, 348
Davis, William A., 134
Davis, William T., 2, 288
Dayton, Cornelia Hughes, 64
Deal, E. D., 352
Dean, Arnold L., 163, 165
Dean, John Ward, 347
Deane, Samuel, 288
Dearborn, ___, 355
Dearborn, Helen E., 353
DeArmond, Rebecca, 35, 40
Deats, Hiram E., 368-369
Deeter, Judy A., 51
DeForest, Heman P., 295
Deiler, J. Hanno, 210
Delafield, John, 428
De Lamar, Marie, 89, 106
Delaware County Historical Alliance, 145
Delaware State Archives, 81
Delorme, ___, 26
de Lue, Willard, 286
Demos, ___, 4, 257
Dennis, Pamela, 37
Densmore, Christopher, 376
Derby, P., 268
Derden, John K., 103
Dern, John P., 388
de Valinger, Leon, 80, 82
De Ville, Winston, 210

DeVries, Ellen, 344
Dewberry, Doris Evans, 43
Dewberry, Jimmie, 43
Dewey, ___, 70
Deyo, S. L., 221
Dickerman, J., 75
Diefendorf, Mary Riggs, 413
Dilts, Bryan Lee, 51, 64, 80, 82-84, 184, 210, 214, 232, 257, 300, 307, 316, 320, 346, 378
Din, Gilbert C., 211
Divine, Albert, 394
Divine, Gerta, 394
Dixon, Nancy Wagoner, 378
Dobson, David, 9
Dodd, Jordan R., 136
Dodd, Stephen, 75
Dodge, Nancy L., 347, 351
Doherty, Frank J., 399-400
Doherty, Thomas P., 80
Dole, Samuel Thomas, 218
Dollarhide, William, 21, 27, 35, 53, 63, 66, 81, 83, 85, 94, 108-109, 113, 139, 167, 177, 194, 212, 217, 237, 260, 301, 309, 317, 323, 341-342, 347-348, 363, 375, 387
Donahue, Marie, 228
Donahue, Mary E., 257
Dorgan, Maurice B., 268
Dorman, John Frederick, 190
Dorrel, Ruth, 136
Dorsey, James E., 89, 93, 103
Dougan, ___, 31
Douthat, James L., 19, 22-25, 197, 203-204, 207, 319
Dow, George F., 268
Dow, Joseph, 357
Downs, C. A., 351
Drake, F. S., 292
Drake, Samuel Adams, 347

Drake, Samuel G., 4, 257, 292
Draper, J., 295
Drew, Benjamin, 288
Drisko, G. W., 227
Dryden, Ruth T., 252
DuBose, Joel C., 19
DuBose, John W., 23
Dufour, Perret, 162
Dugan, Dorothy, 133
Dugan, Taylor, 117
Duis, E., 127
Dumont, William H., 89
Duncan, M. L., 305
Dunkle, Robert J., 293
Dunn, Jacob Platt, 139
Durant, Samuel, 429
Durkee, Cornelius, 424
Dutcher, Russell K., III, 370
Dutcher, Salem, 104
Dutchess County Genealogical Society, 400
Dutton, Bertha P., 17
Dwelley, ___, 289
Dyson, Byron H., 154

Eakle, Arlene H., 4
Eastman, J. R., 355
Easton, Augustus B., 307
Eaton, C., 222
Eaton, F. B., 357
Eaton, L., 280
Eberle, Scott, 403
Edwards, Lewis C., 345
Edwards, Maurice Dwight, 307
Edwards, Patricia N., 21, 317-318
Eisenberg, Gerson G., 232
Eldridge, J., 72
Ellis, C. H., 218
Ellis, Donna M., 232
Ellis, Franklin, 371
Ellis, L. B., 265
Ellis, Robert, 22, 25
Elting, Irving, 408, 432
Elwell, Edward H., 218
Ely, S., 120, 128
Ely, William, 184
Emerson, William A., 295

Emery, S. H., 265
England, Flora D., 19
Ensign, ___, 393, 427, 430-431
Epperson, Gwenn F., 378
Ernst, George, 228
Ernst, Robert, 415
Erwin, Mile, 135
Esarey, ___, 136
Essex Institute, The, 268
Etchieson, Meeks, 37-38
Evans, George C., 351
Evans, Tad, 89, 91, 96, 100, 104-106
Everett, Franklin, 303
Everts, ___, 393, 421, 427, 430-431
Evjen, John O., 378
Ewell, J. L., 268
Exley, Sheryl, 100

Fair, Patricia Stover, 239
Fairbanks, Jonathan, 330
Fairfield, Asa Merrill, 55
Family History Library, 4, 12, 16-17, 19, 26-27, 31, 51, 62, 64, 80, 83-84, 90, 108-110, 136, 167, 176, 184, 210, 214, 232, 257, 300, 307, 316, 320, 341-342, 346-347, 360, 374, 378
Farley, Alfred Earl, Jr., 100
Farley, Hilde Shuptrine, 100
Farley, William S., 12
Farmer, John, 4, 353
Farmer, Michal Martin, 90, 107
Farnham, Joseph E. C., 285
Farquhar, Roger B., 250
Fariss, ___, 421
Farrow, John Pendleton, 220, 226
Faulkinbury, Jim W., 52
Faust, Drew Gilpin, 12
Fay, Loren V., 378
Federal Writers Project of Works Projects Admin. (WPA), 265
Felldin, Jeanne Robey, 184

Felt, J. B., 269
Ferguson, Henry L., 430
Fernald, G., 219
Fernow, Berthold, 378
Field, Homer H., 175
Finley, Randy, 31
Finnell, Arthur Louis, 307, 310, 313
Fish, L. Douglas K., 350
Fish, Mrs. Edward A., 103
Fisher, Ernest B., 303
Fisher, Carleton E., 214, 221
Fisher, Sue G., 214
Fisher, William Scott, 415
Fiske, Arthur D., 262
Fitts, J. H., 357
Fitzgerald, A., 195
Flagg, C. A., 257, 300
Flagg, Ernest, 4
Fleishman, Thelma, 284
Fleming, W. P., 99
Flickinger, Robert E., 174
Florida Bureau of Historic Sites and Properties, Department of State, 84
Flower, G., 118
Floyd, Frank L., 269
Flynt, Wayne, 20
Foley, Helen S., 20-21
Folsom, George, 228
Folsom, Joseph Fulford, 366
Folsom, W. H. C., 307
Forbes, Harriette M., 295
Ford, Andrew E., 295
Ford, Don L., 169, 176-177
Ford, James E., 328
Ford, Stevens, 145, 152, 157, 162
Ford, Thomas, 110
Forkner, John L., 154
Fort William Bent Chapter NSDAR, 63
Foscue, ___, 20
Foster, Frances Smith, 12
Fowler, I. E., 184
Fowler, W. C., 74

Fox, Dianne, 144
Fox, Dixon Ryan, 436
Fox-Genovese, ___, 12
Franklin, Charles, 136, 137, 140-167, 195, 199-201, 203-207, 209
Franks, David, 415
Fraustein, Rebah M., 136
Frazier, ___, 80, 333
Freeland, Mary DeWitt, 295
Freeman, F., 261
Freeman, Leon Lewis, 204
Freeman, Melville C., 228
French, C. A., 315
French, J. H., 378, 391, 394, 397, 403, 405, 411-412, 418-419, 421, 427-429
French, Robert, 390, 438
Friedman, ___, 12
Friel, Florence, 367
Fries, Adelaide L., 90
Frost, John Eldridge, 214, 227-228
Frothingham, E., Jr., 293
Frothingham, Washington, 414
Fuller, Elizabeth G., 436
Fullonton, Joseph, 357
Furman, Gabriel, 410

Gabel, Laurel K., 1
Gable, John Allen, 412
Gage, T., 269
Gaines, W. Craig, 211
Gallagher, Gary, 13
Galloway, Patricia Kay, 211
Galpin, Henry J., 394
Galvin, Edward L., 6
Gammon, William J., 326
Gandrud, Pauline Jones, 20
Gannett, Henry, 80, 232, 257, 360
Garr, Margie, 36
Gaston, W. L., 343
Gates, Gilman C., 74
Gehrig, Pearl Sims, 327, 332

Gemmill, Eva, 422-423
Genealogical Council of Maryland, 232, 239, 244, 250-251
Genealogical Society of Allegany County, Maryland, 239
Genealogical Society of North Brevard, Inc., 85
Genealogical Society of North Orange County California, 52, 57
Genealogical Society of Yuma Arizona, 27
Genealogy Division, Indiana State Library, 136
General Society of Mayflower Descendants, 4
Gentges, Margaret H., 320, 329, 334, 336
Gentry, Lelia Thornton, 90
George, Nellie Palmer, 357
Georgia Historical Society, 90, 97-98
Gerrish, Henry, 225
Gerrish, Judson, 225
Gerwick, V., 127
Gibbs, ___, 137
Gibson, F., 367
Gibson, Florence, 371-372
Gibson, G., 367
Gibson, George, 371
Gibson, William T., 428
Giddings, Edward, 388
Gilbert, E., 357
Gilbert, Frank, 391
Gilbert, Frank T., 54
Gill, James, 110, 132, 350-351, 353, 357-358
Gill, Maryan, 110, 132, 350-351, 353, 357-358
Gilland, Steve, 247
Gillespie, C. B., 75
Gillespie, Samuel, 168
Gilman, E. S., 77
Gilmer, George R., 90
Gilmer County Heritage Book Committee, 102
Gilmore, Geo. C., 347
Gilroy, Frank, 132

Glossbrenner, A. J., 8
Gnann, Pearl Rahn, 90
Godcharles, Frederick A., 8
Godfrey, John E., 224
Godfrey, Marie H., 21
Goins, ___, 210
Gold, John L., 146
Gold, Theodore S., 72
Goodenough, G. F., 67
Goodrich, Albert M., 309, 311
Goodrich, George E., 431
Goodspeed, Weston A., 141, 150, 156-157, 159, 165-167
Goodspeed Publishing Company, 31, 316, 320, 323-330, 332-341
Goodwin, H. C., 397
Goodwin, Joseph O., 70
Goodwin, Nathaniel, 64, 257
Gooldy, Pat, 110, 137
Gooldy, Ray, 110, 137, 186
Gordon, ___, 145
Gordon, T. F., 379
Gordon, Thomas F., 360
Gordon, William Reed, 429
Goss, K. David, 257
Gott, L., 269
Gould, A. A., 353
Gould, Jay, 398
Gowdy, Catherine Lutes, 56
Gozzaldi, Mary Isabella, 280
Grafton Press, 72
Graham, John Simpson, 22
Grande, Joseph A., 403
Grant, Ellsworth S., 70
Grant, Marion Hepburn, 70
Gravelding, Clarence, 428
Gray, Ruth, 224
Green, Clement M., 221
Green, Karen M., 9, 186, 232
Green, Mason A., 276

Green, Samuel Abbot, 280
Green, Scott E., 348
Green, Stina B., 307, 310-315
Green, Thomas Marshall, 186
Greene, Francis Byron, 223
Greene, Marilyn Cole, 421
Greene, Nelson, 413
Greene County Historical & Genealogical Society, 41
Greenhalgh, Kathleen, 77
Greenlaw, Lucy Hall, 257
Gresham, John M., 186
Gridley, A. D., 418
Griffin, ___, 145
Griffin, Augustus, 430
Griffing, Stevenson & Co., 165
Griffis, Joan A., 110, 137
Griffith, Henry S., 289
Griggs, Susan Jewett, 79
Grimes, Janice L., 16
Grose, Edward F., 424
Gross, Elbridge H., 280
Gross, T. Johannes, 117
Groves, Marlene A., 217, 226
Guzik, Estelle M., 415

Hadaway, William S., 436
Haddock, John A., 409
Hadley, George Plummer, 353
Hadley, John V., 149
Hage, Anne A., 308
Hageman, J. F., 365, 370
Hager, L. C., 280
Hagerty, Gilbert, 379
Hagman, Harlan L., 411
Haimbaugh, Frank D., 145
Haines, G., 360
Hale, Albert, 153
Hale, G., 369
Hall, ___, 186
Hall, Charles, 379

Hall, Gwendolyn Midlo, 211
Hall, Mitchel, 202
Hallgren, Jeanne, 301
Halliburton, W. H., 35
Hallowell, Henry C., 280
Hallum, John, 31
Halsey, Edmund D., 371, 374
Halsey, Francis W., 421
Halsey, G. L., 421
Halsey, John J., 121
Hamilton, Oscar B., 120
Hamm, Thomas D., 136
Hammatt, Abraham, 269
Hammell, Jeanne M., 367
Hammond, Otis G., 348
Hampsten, Elizabeth, 17
Han, Lila, 304
Hancock, Mary, 98-99
Hand, H. Wells, 411
Hand, Juliana Free, 420-421, 424, 436
Hannah, Evelyn, 106
Hanson, ___, 32
Hanson, George A., 232
Hanson, J. W., 221, 269
Hanson, Robert B., 286
Hanson, Willis T., Jr., 425
Harden, Samuel, 141
Hardin, George A., 408
Harding, Lewis A., 144
Hardy, Anna Simpson, 222
Harmon, Ada Douglas, 117
Harmon, Wade F., 227
Harper, Lois, 144
Harrell, Mary Lee Barnes, 85
Harrelson, Helen, 304
Harriman, Walter, 355
Harrison, ___, 186
Hart, Matilda Spicer, 80
Hart, William A., 265
Hartman, David W., 84
Hartsook, Elisabeth, 232
Hartz, Emilie, 90-91
Hartz, Fred R., 90-91
Hartzler, Daniel D., 232
Harvey, Cornelium B., 364, 368

Harville, Ethel K., 129
Harwell, Richard Barksdale, 91
Harwood, ___, 149
Hasbrouck, Jacob L., 127
Hastings, H., 379
Hatch, William Collins, 219
Hatfield, Edwin F., 374
Hathaway, Warrine, 21
Havana Journal, The, 393, 426
Hawes, Lilla Mills, 91
Hawley, Emily C., 67
Hayes, A. B., 344
Hayes, Michael J., 58
Haynes, Williams, 77
Hays, Mrs. Louise Frederick, 103
Hayward, Elizabeth, 379
Hayward, S., 350
Hayward, W. W., 353
Hazeltin, G. W., 392
Hazen, H. A., 280
Hazlett, Charles A., 357
Hazzard, George, 149
Headley, Russel, 420
Hebert, ___, 210
Heideman, Marge, 311
Heinegg, Paul, 13
Heinemann, Charles Brunk, 186
Heise, David V., 252
Heisey, John, 233
Heiss, Betty L., 303
Heiss, Willard, 137
Hempstead, Fay, 32
Hempstead County Genealogical Society, 42, 45
Hennesey, W. B., 313
Henry, Carl D., 218
Herndon, Dallas T., 32
Herrick, Margaret, 379, 400
Heywood, W. S., 295
Hibbard, A. G., 72-73
Hichborn, Faustina, 226
Hicken, ___, 111
Hickenlooper, Frank, 173
Hickman, William Z., 332

Hicks, E. W, 121
Hiday, Nellie, 159, 200
Higginbotham, ___, 25
Higgins, Margaret Elliott, 83, 91
Higgins & Beldon & Co., 149
Hill, Everett G., 75
Hill, Florence M., 422
Hill, H. H., 135
Hill, John B., 353
Hill, S. B., 67
Hill, Sally, 222
Hillhouse, Albert M., 97
Hillman, Ralph E., 226
Hills, Leon Clark, 257
Hinchman, Lydia S., 285
Hine, C. G., 408
Hinman, Royal R., 2, 64
Hirsch, Arnold R., 211
Historic Oglethorpe County, Inc., 104
Hively, Emma A. Street, 59
Ho, Joseph Carval, III, 276
Hobart, B., 289
Hobart, Chauncey, 308
Hodges, Margaret R., 230
Hodgman, E. A., 280
Hoelle, Edith, 360, 363, 365-367, 372-373
Hoes, Roswell Randall, 432
Hoffer, Peter Charles, 269
Hoffman, Marie E., 422
Hoffman, Phil, 172
Hoffman, W. W., 202
Hogan, Roseann Reinemuth, 186
Hoggard, Lori, 37
Holbrook, Jay Mack, 65, 70, 258, 289, 293, 296, 348
Holcomb, Brent H., 13
Holcombe, R. I., 311
Holdcraft, Jacob Mehrling, 247
Holden, A. W., 434
Holland Society of New York, The, 379
Holloway, W. R., 154

Holmes, Clay W., 393
Holmes, Frank R., 4
Honeyman, A. Van Doren, 373
Hood & Co., S. L., 300
Hood, Margaret Scholl, 247
Hooper, Debbie, 233
Hoopes, Christina, 241
Hoopes, E. Erick, 241
Hornor, William S., 371
Horsman, Barbara Knott, 253
Horton, L. S., 352
Horton, W. H., 409
Horvath, George J., Jr., 241, 244
Hosley, William, 70
Hosmer, G. L., 220
Hough, Franklin B., 379, 409, 411
Houghton, William A., 296
House, Charles J., 214
Houston, Martha Lou, 91, 102
Howard, Timothy Edward, 161
Howe, Donald W., 292
Howe, Henry, 360
Howe, P. S., 366
Howell, George Rogers, 411
Howes, F. G., 274
Howland, Catherine, 300
Hoyt, David W., 2, 269
Hubbard, B. F., 5
Hubbard, F. A., 67
Hudson, Alfred S., 280-281
Hudson, C., 281
Hudson, Charles, 281
Hudson, Horace B., 311
Hughes, Buckner L., 186
Hughes, Nathaniel C., 186
Hughes, Sarah E., 75
Hume, Joan, 252-253
Humphrey, A. R., 343
Hunt, Charles W., 170
Hunt, T., 395
Hunt, Thomas, 395

Hunt, Thomas J. de la, 158
Huntington, E. B., 67-68
Huntting, Isaac, 400
Hurd, D. H., 68, 77, 269, 286, 349, 354-355, 357-358
Hyde, ___, 161
Hyde, Alexander, 262
Hyde, C. M., 262
Hynson, Jerry M., 239

Ibbotson, Patricia, 306
Idaho Genealogical Society, 109
Illiana Genealogical & Historical Society, 132-133
Illinois State Genealogical Society, 111-112
Imperial Publishing Co., 304
Indiana Historical Society, 142, 144, 152
Indian River Genealogical Society, Inc, 86
Ingmire, Frances T., 32, 148, 187, 210, 320, 324
Inman, Gloria Kay Vandiver, 184
Innes, J. H., 417
Inskeep, Carolee, 415-416
Institute of Science and Public Affairs, 84
Interstate Publishing Company, 175, 198, 302
Irish Genealogical Society, Intl., 310, 313-314
Irwin, W. B., 17

Jackson, Ernest, 132
Jackson, F., 281
Jackson, J. N., 306
Jackson, James R., 352
Jackson, Martha W., 194-195, 207
Jacobson, Judith, 258
Jacobson, Judy, 301, 411
Jacobus, Donald Lines, 65, 68, 75

James, D. Clayton, 211
James, Patricia R., 380, 409
Jameson, ___, 17
Jameson, E. O., 286
Jasper Co. Cemetery Survey, 120
Jenks, Margaret R., 434
Jenness, John Scribner, 355
Jennings, Herman A., 261
Jennings, R. Wayne, 176, 179
Jerome, Brenda Joyce, 197
Jillson, Willard Rouse, 187
Johnson, __, 91, 187
Johnson, A. W., 269
Johnson, Alfred, 227
Johnson, Amandus, 9
Johnson, Crisfield, 403-404, 434
Johnson, Edward F., 281
Johnson, Frances Ann, 352
Johnson, Jane Eliza, 68
Johnson, Murial Sampson, 220
Johnson, Oliver, 154
Johnson, William M., 373
Johnston, George, 244
Johnston, J., 223
Jones, Alfred E., 258
Jones, Caleb, 233
Jones, Charles Colcock, Jr., 104
Jones, Electa F., 262
Jones, Elias, 246
Jones, Frank S., 100
Jones, George F., 91, 100
Jones, Henry Z, Jr., 9, 380-381
Jones, Jack Moreland, 95, 106
Jones, Janice L., 338-339
Jones, Mary G., 99
Jones, Pomroy, 418
Jordan, John W., 8
Jordan, William B., Jr., 215
Jordan, Winthrop D., 211
Josephy, Alvin M., Jr., 17

Joslyn, Roger D., 293
Jourdan, Elise Greenup, 233, 245, 251
Judd, Sylvester, 277

Kaler, S. P., 167
Kammen, Carol, 381, 431
Kammen, Michael, 381
Kanely, Edna A., 233
Kardell, Caroline Lewis, 261
Karlsen, ___, 5
Keefer, Donald, 389, 414
Keene, Betsey D., 261
Keith, Charles P., 9
Kelby, William, 381
Keller, Roger, 253-254
Kellogg, Lucy Cutler, 274
Kellogg, Elijah, 219
Kelly, Arthur C. M., 5, 269, 372, 381, 389, 395-397, 400-402, 405-408, 414-416, 422, 424-426, 433, 435-436
Kelly, Nancy, 402
Kendall, Minnie Gray, 313
Kenny, Hamill, 233
Kentucky Adjutant-General's Office, 187
Kentucky Department for Libraries and Archives, 187-188
Kentucky Historical Society, 188
Kenway, Rita Johnson, 220
Kenyon Co., 166
Kernkamp, H. C. H., 306
Kershaw, W. L., 174
Kessner, ___, 416
Ketchum, William, 404
Kett & Co., H. F., 114
Kilbourne, Elizabeth Evans, 105
Kilbourne, Payne Kenyon, 73
Kilby, William Henry, 227
Kilmer, Lawrence W., 391
King, Junie Estelle Stewart, 188, 316

King, Marquis Fayette, 219, 223
Kingman, Bradford, 289
Kingsbury, F. B., 350
Kingsbury, H. D., 221
Kingsbury, J. D., 264
Kinney, James P., Jr., 101
Kinney, Shirley Foster, 101
Kirkham, E. Kay, 13
Kleback, Linda Pazics, 84
Klinkenberg, Audrey M., 433
Klos, Lloyd E., 381
Knab, Frederick, 277
Kneeland, F. N., 277
Kniffen, Fred B., 211
Kniffin, G. C., 189-190
Knight, Anne R., 428
Knight, Lucian L., 91
Knights, ___, 293
Knotts, Burton Ray, 44, 49
Knowles, William C., 74
Koehler, Albert F., 361
Koehler, Linda, 402
Kot, ___, 52, 321
Kozee, William C., 188
Kropp, C. Irene, 422
Krusell, Cynthia Hagar, 289
Kuhns, Maude Pinney, 293
Kulikoff, ___, 233
Kusek, Joan, 177, 183, 325, 332
Kushman, Howard Stewart, 307

Lacey, Ellen, 41
Lackey, Walter F., 46
Ladd, R. E., Jr., 269
LaFar, Mable Freeman, 98
Laine, J. Gary, 20
Lainhart, Ann Smith, 5, 293
Lake County (IL) Genealogical Society, 122-124
Lamb, Harold, 314
Lambdin, Mrs. Augusta, 103

Lambert, Rebecca T., 54-55
Lamson, D. F., 269
Lamson, F. B., 315
Lancaster, Daniel, 349
Landis, John T., 258
Lane, Helen H., 265
Lang, Herbert O., 60
Lang, S. D., 221
Lapham, Alice G., 269
Lapham, William Berry, 218, 224
Larned, Ellen D., 79
Larson, Constant, 310-311
Lathrop, Cornelia P., 68
Laurel County Historical Society, 202
Lawrence, Mary Melissa, 311
Lawrence, Ruth Keeler, 390
Lawson, Harvey M., 79
Lazell, T. S., 289
Leadbetter, C. F., 221
Leah, O. E., 140, 166
Leath, Mrs. Warren, 165
LeBey, Mrs. Charles, 90
Ledogar, Edwin Richard, 5, 65, 258
Lee, Eleanor Agnes, 13
Lee, S. F., 352
Lee, Wallace, 73
Lee, William, 142
Leeson, M. A., 131
LeFevre, Ralph, 433
Leffel, John C., 159
Leistner, Doris, 139
Lemont, Levi P., 225
Leonard, Cinda, 125
Leonard, Joseph A., 312
Lester, Eugenia Campbell, 381
Lester, Gary, 49-50
Lester, Memory Aldridge, 14
Lester, Tina, 49-50
LeVarn, Caspar L., 355
Levin, H., 188
Lewis, A., 270
Lewis, Helen, 301, 303, 381, 431
Lewis, I. N., 286

Lewis & Clark County Genealogical Society, 341-342
Lewis Publishing Co., 146-147, 163, 166, 371
Liahona Research, 20, 32, 83, 92, 112, 167, 188, 316, 321
Libby, Charles T., 215, 216, 348
Limeburner, Grace C., 220
Lincoln, George, 289
Lincoln, William, 296
Lindberg, Marcia Wiswall, 5
Lindsey, Benjamin J., 270
Lipscomb, ___, 316
Lister, Betty, 99
Litchfield Centennial, Inc., 127
Littell, John, 361
Little, Henry G., 70
Little, William, 352
Littlefield, Ada Douglas, 226
Livermore, A. A., 354
Livezey, Jon, 249
Livsey, Karen E., 382
Ljungstedt, Milnor, 10, 14
Locke, Arthur, 357
Locke, John Lymburner, 222, 226
Loepe, John I., 419
Long, Alice MacDonald, 220, 227
Long, E. Waldo, 289
Long, Helen R., 233, 239, 244, 247-248, 250, 254
Long, John H., 65, 189, 215, 259, 316, 348, 382
Long, Mary Beth, 254
Long, Vanessa, 254
Looney, Janice Soutee, 327, 334
Lord, C. C., 355
Lord, John King, 352
Lord, William G., 296
Loring, H. H., 153, 159
Los Banos Genealogical Society, 57

Losee, Clara, 402
Lossing, Benson J., 409
Louisiana Historical Association, 210
Love, Florene, 196, 199, 201, 203-206
Love, William DeLoss, 70
Lovell, Russell A., Jr., 261
Lovering, M., 276
Lowrie, Walter, 210, 316, 321
Lowry, James W., 402
Lowry, Robert, 316
Lucas, Silas Emmett, Jr., 92-93, 97, 101
Luckenback, Al, 239
Lumpkin County Heritage Book Commission, 103
Lunceford, A. Mell, Jr., 105
Lyford, James O., 356
Lyman, P. W., 277
Lynch, Thomas J., 376

MacGregor, Greg, 18
MacLeod, James, 14
MacWethy, Lou D., 382
Macy, Harry, Jr., 382
Macy, Obed, 285
Macy, William C., 285
Madden, Joseph P., 436
Madden, Lorraine L., 350
Maddus, Gerald, 80
Maddux, Dorris, 80
Madsen, Ken, 117
Maduell, Charles R., Jr., 210
Maine Genealogical Society, 216
Maine State Archives, 216
Mallary, R. DeWitt, 263
Mallick, Sallie, 247
Mallory, Rudena Kramer, 327
Malone, ___, 5, 212
Mann, Herman, 286
Manuel, Janet D., 250
Manwaring, Charles William, 65

Marchand, Sidney A., 212
Maresh, ___, 226
Marin County Genealogical Society, 56
Maring, R. H., 167
Marquand, Christina S., 263
Marshall, ___, 296
Martin, ___, 5
Martin, Catherine Machan, 431
Martin, Patricia Thomas, 23
Martin, William T., 23
Martinet, Tom C., 44, 48
Marvin, A. P., 296
Maryland Hall of Records, 8, 233
Maryland Historical Society, 234
Maryland State Archives, 234
Masley, Betty J., 185, 189
Mason, Elaine Hastings, 82
Massachusetts Secretary of the Commonwealth, 259
Masten, Arthur M., 389
Mather, Frederic Gregory, 382, 385
Mathews, ___, 14
Mathews, Barbara Stacy, 60, 62
Mathews, Kaydee, 93
Mathews, Nathan, 93
Matson, N., 114
Maxim, S. P., 224
Maydew, Randall C., 182
Mayhill, R. Thomas, 149
McAdams, Mrs. Harry Kennett, 189
McAlear, Robert, 434
McAllister, Rev. Donald, 224
McBee, May Wilson, 316
McBirney, Connie A., 139
McCall, Mrs. Howard H., 93
McCardle, William H., 316

McClure, Diane K., 116
McComish, Charles Davis, 54-55
McCormick, ___, 361
McCormick, Joseph N., 162
McCoy, W. H., 142
McDonough Co., Leo, 198
McDuffee, Franklin, 358-359
McEwen, ___, 145, 152, 157, 162
McFall, Pat, 39
McGinnis, William C., 370
McGregor, Malcolm G., 332
McHaffie, ___, 149
McIntosh, ___, 145, 152, 157, 162
McIntosh, W. H., 413, 419, 434
McKay, ___, 416
McKee, Lewis W., 195
McKenzie, Mary, 125
McKinsey, Folger, 248
McLane, Bobbie Jones, 28, 32, 34-51
McLean, Dolores (Vega), 58
McLellan, Hugh D., 219
McMann, Martha W., 129
McManus, Thelma S., 326, 337-338
McMillan, ___, 20
McNeil, W. K., 34
McNulty, J. Bard, 64
McQueen, Alex S., 97
Mead, Daniel M., 68
Mead, Spencer P., 68
Meagher, Timothy J., 376
Mean, Spencer P., 68
Meldrum, Charlotte, 364-365, 368, 373
Mellick, Andrew D., Jr., 361
Menard, ___, 252
Menefee, C. A., 55, 57, 59
Merrill, Arch, 382
Merrill, G. D., 217
Merrill, Georgia D., 349, 390

Merrill, J., 272
Merrill, J. L., 359
Merritt, J. F., 291
Merritt, W. W., Sr., 173
Merry, John F., 169
Mershart, Ronald V., 314
Messick, Mary Ann, 36
Metcalf, John G., 298
Meyer, Mary Keyser, 234, 392
Michaels, Brian E., 85
Middleton, ___, 234
Middleton, Wallace & Co., 154
Miller, Carolynne L., 138
Miller, E., 174
Miller, S. L., 223
Miller, Stephen B., 397
Miller, William J., 173
Mills, Gary B., 211
Milne, George M., 77
Milner, Clyde A., 18
Miner, Ed, 119
Mitchell, ___, 225
Mitchell, Marietta, 422
Mitchell, Nahum, 291
Mitchell, William Ansel, 172
Moger, Elizabeth, 376
Moneyhon, ___, 32
Monk, William, 412
Monroe, J. H., 392
Montzheimer, O. H., 173
Moody, Lillian, 41
Mooney, V. P., 177
Moore, Bernard, 130
Moore, Charles B., 434
Moore, Henry Miles, 179
Moore, Jacob B., 356, 358
Morebeck, Nancy Justus, 52
Morehouse, ___, 277
Morgan, James Logan, 34
Morgan, Janet, 435
Morgan, Marlene, 435
Morgan, Mary M., 138
Morgan, Ralph H., Jr., 249
Morrill, Dan L., 14
Morris, Ira K., 423
Morrison, ___, 388, 393, 427

Morrison, Betty Jean, 65
Morrison, L. A., 358
Morrison, Patricia J., 382
Morrison, W. E., & Co., 392, 423, 425, 427-428
Morrison, Wayne E., Sr., 382, 391-394, 397, 403-405, 411-413, 418-419, 421, 427-431, 434-435
Morrison's Reprint, 382, 384, 392
Morrow, Dale, 254
Morrow, Patricia, 406
Morse, Abner, 283
Morse, Charles A., 275
Morse, Howard, 402
Moscrip, F. A., 172
Mosher, Elizabeth M., 226
Moulton, A., 219
Mowbray, Calvin, 246
Mower, Walter L., 217
Moyes, Norman L., 136
Muckleroy, D. V., 22
Mullin, Michael, 14
Munro-Fraser, J. P., 54
Munsell, W. W., 398
Munson, G. C., 75
Murray, David, 398
Murray, Frederick G., 172
Murray, Janette S., 172
Murray, Joyce Martin, 203, 208
Myers, James T., 389
Myers, Margaret E., 247

Naas, Lucille, 224
Namaqua Chapter NSDAR, 62
Narrett, David E., 383
Nason, E., 283
Nation, Angela, 37
Naylor, Natalie A., 412
Neill, Edward D., 309-310, 312-313, 315
Nelson, W. R., 359
Nelson, William, 361, 364, 372
Nestler, Harold, 383
Newaygo City Bicentennial Commission, 304
Newberry, W. L., 38

Newby, Nancy, 201, 207
Newhall, J. R., 270
New Jersey Adjutant-General's Office, 361
New Jersey Historical Records Survey, 361
New Jersey State Archives, 361-362, 364-366, 369-371, 373
Newman, Harry Wright, 234, 239
Newman, John J., 138
Newson, T. M., 313
New York Adjutant-General's Office, 383
New York Historical Society, 383, 417
New York State Archives and Records Administration, 383-384
Nichols, L. A., 170
Nickell, Ella T., 205
Nickell, J. Wendell, 205
Nickell, Joe, 189, 205
Nicklas, Laurie, 52
Nightingale, Ruth, 419
Niles, J., 65
Noble, H. H., 379
Nodaway County Genealogical Society, 335-336
Noon, A., 276
Norris, J. E., 174, 176
North, C. M., 70
North, James M., 218
North Antelope County Genealogical Society, 342-344
Northeast Michigan Genealogical and Historical Society, 301
Northwest Missouri Genealogical Society, 324, 327-328, 330, 340-341
Norton, F. C., 71
Norton, John F., 350
Norton, Margaret Cross, 112
Norwood, Seth W., 226
Nottingham, Carolyn Walker, 106
Nourse, H. S., 298
Noyes, Harriette Eliza, 358

Noyes, J. O., 384
Noyes, Sybil, 215, 216, 348
Nulty, ___, 85
Nunnelly, Nona, 145-146

Oak, L., 224
O'Brien, M. J., 218
O'Byrne, Michael Cyprian, 124
O'Byrne, Mrs. Roscoe C., 138
O'Callaghan, Edmund B., 384-385
O'Connor, Carol A., 18
O'Connor, Thomas, 6
Odom, Dorothy Collins, 97
Oesterreicher, Michel, 85
Ogle, George, 166
Oglesbee, Rollo B., 153
Old Gaol Museum Committee, The, 228
Olds, Edward C., 204
Oldt, Frank T., 170
Old Woodbury Historical Society, 73, 75
Old York Historical and Improvement Society, 228
Oliver, Curtis John, 307
Olson, Michael R., 238
Olson, Roy F., Jr., 204-205
O'Neill, Francis P., 234, 241
Orcutt, S., 67-68, 73, 75-76
Ormesher, Susan, 321
O'Rourke, Timothy J., 253
Osborn, Donald Lewis, 326
Ostertag, Enid, 177
Ostertag, John, 177
Osvald, Karen E., 91
Oszakiewski, Robert A., 235
Otis, Amos, 261
Owen, David R., 235
Owen, Henry Wilson, 225
Owen, Thomas M., 20

Owre, James, 386
Ozarks Genealogical Society, Inc., 331-332

Packard, Jasper, 153
Paige, Lucius R., 259, 283, 299
Paine, Josiah, 261
Palmer, Lyman L., 55, 57
Pape, William J., 372
Paradise Genealogical Society, 53-54
Paris Cape Historical Society, 224
Parish, Charles Carlin, 418
Parker, Amasa J., 389
Parker, Benjamin Franklin, 349
Parker, Betty, 99
Parker, E. E., 354
Parker, E. L., 358
Parker, Edward, 321
Parker, J. Carlyle, 10, 53, 346, 362
Parker, Janet G., 346
Parkinson, Josiah, 320
Parks, Gary W., 83, 235
Parmenter, C. O., 278
Parran, Alice, 235
Parsegian, Valerie Phillips, 385
Parsons, L. B., 358
Partridge, Virginia P., 426
Passano, Eleanor Phillips, 235
Pate, John Ben, 106
Pattee, W. S., 287
Patten, Jennie M., 434
Patterson, William D., 223
Paul, Rodman, 18
Payne, Dorothy, 34
Pearson, Gardner W., 259
Pearson, Jonathan, 389, 425
Pease, ___, 112
Pease, J., 65
Pease, Theodore Calvin, 113
Peck, Chauncey E., 276
Peck, Epaphroditus, 71
Peck, J. L. E., 173

Peck, William F., 414
Peden, Henry C., Jr., 80, 189, 235, 239, 241-244, 247, 250, 252-253
Pedley, Avril J. M., 235
Peirce, Ebenezer Weaver, 6, 259
Peirce, Henry B., 429
Peirce, Mary F., 284
Pelletreau, William S., 430, 437
Penny, Morris M., 20
Penrose, Maryly B., 385
Perkins, D. A. W., 173
Perkins, M. E., 78
Perley, Sidney, 272
Perrin, William Henry, 114, 119, 129, 132, 135, 189-190, 195, 197, 199, 200, 206-208
Perry, Arthur Latham, 263
Perry, K. E., 68
Peter, Robert, 195, 200, 206-207
Peters, Joan W., 14
Peters, Marjorie Herlache, 117
Petitclerc, Emma L., 263
Phillips, Daniel L., 78
Phillips, James D., 272
Phillips, Marion G., 385
Phillips, Semira, 172
Piatt, Emma C., 128
Pierce, F. C., 299
Pierce, Henry B., 429
Pierce, Richard D., 272
Piet, Stanley, 242
Pilon, Robert L., 301
Pinckney, James, 406
Pinick, Merrie, 180
Pippenger, Wesley E., 83
Platt, Edmund, 402
Pleas, Edward, 150
Pleasant, Hazen H., 143
Plimton, Oakes, 284
Plummer, George F., 352
Pockman, Rev. P. Theo., A.M., 423
Polk, ___, 317
Pomeroy, Whitman & Co., 427
Pond Brothers, 309

Pope, Charles Henry, 216, 259, 348
Pope, William F., 34
Porter, Edward G., 293
Porter, Joseph W., 216
Porter, Will, 174
Potter, C. E., 354
Potter, Dorothy Williams, 15
Potter, Johnny L. T. N., 20
Powell, Jehun Z., 142
Powell, Lillian Lewis, 97
Power, Garrett, 242
Powers, J. H., 168
Prairie Farmer Publishing Co., 119-120
Pratt, H. H., 291
Pratt, J. Howard, 420
Pratt, William M., 293
Precision Indexing, 93, 339, 412, 416
Prehn, Florence, 433
Prentice, Edward, 78
Preston, Walter W., 249
Price, Clarence, 117
Price, Realto E., 169
Prichard, K. A., 76
Prince George's County Genealogical Society, 251-252
Provine, Dorothy S., 83
Prowell, George R., 365
Ptak, Diane Snyder, 389, 423-424
Pumroy, Eric, 138
Public Archives Commission of the State of Delaware, 82
Putnam, S., 354

Quaife, M. M., 130, 175
Queen, Carol, 42
Quigley, P. J., 170
Quinlan, J. E., 430
Quisenberry, ___, 190

Rafferty, ___, 321
Railey, William E., 209
Ramsdell, G. A., 354
Randall, O. E., 350
Randolph, H., 364
Ransom, Stanley A., 71

Raum, John O., 369
Raynor, Ellen M., 263
Read, Benjamin, 351
Reamy, Bill, 240, 242
Reamy, Martha, 240, 242
Redden, Robert, 81
Reed, Jonas, 299
Reed, Joseph R., 175
Reed, Parker McCobb, 225
Reener, Lynn (Boyd), 113, 127-128
Reeves, Lucy Marion, 34
Register, Alvaretta K., 93
Reid, Arthur, 385
Reid, W. Max, 413
Remich, Daniel, 228
Remick, Oliver Philbrick, 229
Rench, Dolores, 145-146
Rennick, ___, 190
Rerick Bros., 166
Researchers, The, 138
Retzer, Henry J., 235
Reynolds, Cuyler, 385
Reynolds, Lily, 99
Reynolds, Marion Lavender, 119
Rice, George Wharton, 223
Rice, J. C., 278
Rice, Shirley A., 385
Rich, S., 261
Richards, Lysander S., 291
Richardson, Hester Dorsey, 235
Richman, George J., 148
Richmond, C. W., 118
Richter, Gary, 310, 313
Richter, Wendy Bradley, 37-38
Ricord, Frederick W., 362, 374
Ridgely, David, 240
Ridlon, G. T., Sr., 225
Rietti, J. C., 316
Riggins, J. H., 34
Riker, Dorothy, 138-139
Riker, James, 416, 421
Riley, Benjamin Franklin, 22

Riley, Elihu S., 240
Riley County Genealogical Society, 177-183
Riley County Historical Society, 182
Rimg, Elizabeth, 216
Risley, T. G., 133
Ritchie, Henry, 424
Ritter, Priscilla, 284
Roach, John, 437
Roads, S., Jr., 272
Robb, C. J., 153, 159
Robb, Ruth Flesher, 118
Roberts, James A., 385
Roberts, Lewis E., 34
Roberts, Millard F., 430
Robertson, ___, 190
Robertson, Clara Hamlett, 177
Robertson, Donna J., 245
Robinson, ___, 138
Robinson, Reuel, 222
Robison, Jeannie F-J., 385
Rocker, Willard, 93
Rockwell, George L., 68
Rogers, Henry C., 418
Rogers, Justus H., 55
Rogers, N. K., 98
Rogers, William Warren, 20
Rohrbach, Lewis Bunker, 216, 294
Rolfe, ___, 355
Rood, James, 190
Root, Frank A., 63
Rose, Christine, 52, 58, 71, 76
Rose, Robert, 320
Rosenow, Diane, 312
Roser, Susan E., 6
Ross, Peter, 412
Ross, W. B., 144
Rothert, Otto A., 205
Rothstein, Elisabeth, 89, 106
Rounds, H. L. Peter, 266
Rouse, Parke, Jr., 15
"Roustabout," (Phil Hoffman), 172
Rowe, Ernest R., 219
Rowe, William Hutchinson, 219

Rowland, Arthur Ray, 93
Rowland, Dunbar, 15, 317
Rowland, Eron Opha, 317
Rowland, George, 41
Rowland, Oran W., 305
Royalty, James H., 150
Rudolph, ___, 138
Runnels, M. T., 349
Russell, D., 303
Russell, Donna Valley, 73, 236, 239, 247-248, 301
Russell, George Ely, 247, 254
Ruttenber, E. M., 386, 420

Salisbury Association, 73
Salter, Edwin, 371-372
Sampson, H. L., 219
Sanborn, Melinde Lutz, 6
Sanchis, Frank E., 437
Sanders, Eva, 158
Sanders, Faye Sea, 208
Sanders, Joanne McRee, 15
Sandweiss, Martha A., 18
Sanford, C. E., 429
Sanford, E., 266
Sanford, L., 386, 390
Sanford and Co., 420
Sarapin, ___, 362
Sargent, William M., 217
Saunders, James Edmonds, 20
Savage, James, 2, 6
Sawislak, ___, 116
Sawtelle, Ithamar B., 284
Saye, Albert B., 89
Schaefer, Christina K., 83
Schaeffer, Caspar, 373
Scharf, J. Thomas, 8, 236, 437
Schenk, Elizabeth H., 69
Scheuer, Cynthia, 164
Scheuer, Larry, 164
Schonert, Janet, 129
Schreiner-Yantis, Netti, 196, 199, 201, 203-206
Schulz, Peggy, 56

Schutz, John A., 6
Schwartz, Elsie, 118
Schweitzer, George K., 93, 113, 138, 190, 236, 259, 386
Scott, Kenneth, 76, 386-387, 389, 416-417
Scott, William W., 372
Sears, Ethel M., 179
Seaver, Frederick J., 404
Secomb, D. F., 354
Secretary of the Treasury, 85
Sedgwick, Sarah C., 263
Selby, Paul, 110, 115, 119, 133
Setterquist, Ruth, 58
Severance, C. S., 275
Seversmith, Herbert F., 412
Sewall, Samuel, 284
Seward, J. L., 351
Shallenberger, Mrs. E. H., 131
Shanklin, M., 156
Sharpe, William C., 75-76
Shattuck, L., 284
Shaw, Archibald, 144
Shaw, Aurora, 94
Shaw, H. K., 259
Shaw, William H., 367-368
Shea, Ann M., 387
Sheldon, G., 275
Sheldon, Hezekiah Spencer, 71
Shepard, E., 397
Sherman, Robert M., 262, 291
Sherman, Ruth Wilder, 262
Shinn, Josiah H., 35
Shirts, Augustus Finch, 148
Shofner, Jerrell H., 87
Shonnard, Frederic, 437
Shourds, Thomas, 362, 373
Shubert, Dwight, 40, 45
Shumway, Burgess McK., 53

Sickel, Marilyn Hambrick, 47-48
Sifakis, ___, 20, 35, 85, 94, 191, 212, 236, 321
Silliman, Sue Imogene, 301
Simm, Marie, 423
Simmons, ___, 289
Simmons, C. H., Jr., 259
Simmons Historical Publications, 200
Simms, Jeptha R., 387
Simonds, Thomas C., 294
Simons, Marc, 374
Sinclair, Donald A., 362
Singleton, Esther, 387
Sisco, Louis Dow, 242
Sistler, Barbara, 191-192, 201
Sistler, Byron, 191-192, 201
Sistler, Samuel, 191
Sittler, Melvin, 342
Sivertsen, Barbara J., 430
Skirven, Percy G., 236
Skordas, Gust, 232, 236
Skwiercz, Andrew L., 146
Slevin, Ruth, 140, 143, 146, 151, 157
Smith, ___, 113, 161, 407
Smith, Albert, 354
Smith, C. J., 354
Smith, Carroll E., 419
Smith, Clifford N., 15-16, 53, 138, 193
Smith, Daniel Blake, 236
Smith, Dora, 134, 193
Smith, E., 402
Smith, E. C., 278
Smith, E. Y., 264
Smith, Edward M., 402
Smith, Evelyn Rich, 420
Smith, F., 287
Smith, George Gillman, 94
Smith, Gloria, 58
Smith, H. Perry, 404
Smith, J. E. A., 264
Smith, J. M., 275
Smith, James F., 94

Smith, James H., 394, 402, 412
Smith, John H., 113
Smith, Leonard H., Jr., 262, 266, 291
Smith, Marjorie, 115, 119, 125
Smith, Mrs. Herschel W., 102, 104
Smith, Nelson F., 26
Smith, Norma H., 291
Smith, P. M., 278
Smith, Patricia D., 177
Smith, R. A., 169
Smith, R. D., 76
Smith, S. F., 284
Smith, Sarah Quinn, 107
Smith, T. Berry, 327, 332
Smith, W. T., 193
Smith, William C., 262
Snapp, William L., 133
Snell, James P., 369, 373
Society of Colonial Wars in the State of Connecticut, The, 78
Solano County Genealogical Society, Inc., 53, 58
Soldan, Dick, 183
Somers, A. N., 351
Sonoma County Genealogical Society, 59-60
Sorenson, Alfred, 343
South Bend Area Genealogical Society, 161-162
Southerland, ___, 20, 94
Southern California Genealogical Society, 6, 53, 65, 94, 109, 139, 177, 217, 236, 260, 321, 341-342, 348, 362, 374, 387
Spafford, Horatio Gates, 387
Spahr, D., 141
Sparling, Edmund L., 201
Spaulding, C. S., 354
Spear, Arthur, 222
Speer, William S., 17
Spencer, Richard Henry, 236
Spencer, W. D., 229

Spencer, Wilbur D., 217
Sperry, Kip, 65
Spooner, W. W., 437
Sprague, Stuart Seely, 193
Spurgeon, ___, 128
Spurr, W. S., 219
St. Clair Co. Genealogical Society, 126-127, 129, 131
St. Joseph Publishing Co., 326
Stachwin, Myron O., 260
Stackpole, E. S., 217, 229, 299, 359
Stacy, James, 103
Stanley, Dr. Josiah M., 299
Stanley, Lois, 321-323, 339
Starbuck, Alexander, 285
Stark, C., 356
Stark, J. H., 260
Starr, Edward Comfort, 73
State Historical Society of Missouri, 323
Stearns, E. S., 351-352
Stebbins, Rufus P., 276
Steele, ___, 15
Steele, Chris Ronald Poito, 260
Steele, James E., 168
Steelman, Georgene L., 368
Steelman, James F., 368
Steiner, B. C., 74, 76
Stenley, Virginia D., 244
Stephens, John H., 155
Stephens County Heritage Book Committee, 104
Stevens, Cj, 260
Stevens, John Austin, 417
Stevens, Kristine, 250
Stevens, Lewis Townsend, 366
Stevens, William B., 284
Stewart, J. R., 115
Stewart, James Hervey, 142

Stewart, William, 392
Stewart, William C., 94
Stiles, Henry R., 71, 410
Stillman, E. B., 170
Stillwell, John E., 362, 423
Stinchfield, J. C., 217
Stock, Walter D., 8
Stoddard, Francis R., 6
Stoddard, John H., 116, 118, 323
Stone, Charles, 127
Stone, Edwin M., 273
Stone, M. T., 351
Storrs, R. S., 276
Stoutenburgh, Henry A., 421
Stowe, J. M., 299
Strand, A. E., 309
Stratford, Dorothy Agans, 363
Stratton, Eugene Aubrey, 260
Strawn, C. C., 125
Strickland, Jean, 21, 317, 318
Stringer, Lawrence B., 125
Strobel, P. A., 94
Strong, Isabel L., 284
Stryker-Rodda, Kenn, 363, 386, 412
Stuart, Karen A., 232
Stuck, Charles A., Jr., 307
Sulgrove, Berry R., 155
Sullivan, Frank S., 179
Sullivan, Larry E., 231
Sullivan, Steven E., 222
Sumner, Samuel, 420
Sumner, William H., 294
Sutch, G. E., 398, 407, 426
Sutherland, James F., 193
Sutherland, Laine, 329
Swanson, Susan C., 436
Swart, Shirley, 193
Swartz, Ginny, 311
Swett, David Livingstone, 224-225
Swift, C. F., 262
Syler, Allen B., 38

Sylvester, Nathaniel Bartlett, 275-276, 278, 423, 424, 433
Symmes, Frank R., 371
Szucs, Loretto D., 116

Tadman, Michael, 15
Taker, A. E., 312
Talcott, Sebastian V., 6, 387
Tallahassee Genealogical Society, Inc., 85
Tanner, ___, 16
Tate, Bettie Bass, 205
Taylor, ___, 115, 124, 126, 217
Taylor, Anne Wood, 85
Taylor, Charles J., 264
Taylor, Harrison D., 206
Taylor, John M., 7
Taylor, Pete, 198, 208
Taylor, Philip Fall, 194
Taylor, Richard H., 7, 16, 18
Taylor, Robert M., Jr., 139
Taylor, Violet, 117, 129, 133
Teele, A. K., 287
Temple, J., 299
Temple, Josiah Howard, 275-276, 284
Tennessee Valley Authority, 16
Tennessee Valley Genealogical Society, 23-26
Tenney, Jonathan, 7, 390
Tepper, Michael, 7, 10, 243
Terry, Rose Caudle, 18, 323
Tessendorf, Kenneth R., 57
Thacher, James, 291
Thomas, Arad, 420
Thomas, James Walter, 237
Thompson, F. M., 275
Thompson, L., 359
Thompson, Robert I., 304
Thomson, ___, 52, 321

Thorndale, William, 21, 27, 35, 53, 63, 66, 81, 83, 85, 94, 108-109, 113, 139, 167, 177, 194, 212, 217, 237, 260, 301, 309, 317, 323, 341-342, 347-348, 363, 375, 387
Thornton, Mrs. S. S., 220
Thorp, L. Ashton, 354
Thorpe, Sheldon B., 76
Thresher, Mary G., 273
Thurston, Lois Ware, 227
Tilden, W. S., 287
Tilghman, Oswald, 253
Tilton, George H., 266
Timlow, Herman R., 71
T.L.C. Genealogy, 193, 195-200, 204-209, 240, 243, 245-246, 252-253, 317, 335, 364, 369
Todd, C. B., 69
Tolley, Michael C., 235
Tompkins, Flora, 407
Ton, C. Edward, 392
Torrence, Clayton, 237, 252
Torrey, Clarence A., 7
Torrey, R. C., 299
Tower, Henry M., 299
Tower, M., 403
Towner, Ausburn, 393
Townsend, Charles Delmar, 76, 273
Tracy, H. A., 294
Trask, John J., 78
Treynor Town & Country Club, 175
Trumbull, J. R., 278
Trumbuss, J. Hammond, 71
Tuck, Clyde E., 330
Turnbo, Silas Claborn, 35, 46-47
Turner, Hollis, 224
Turner, Priscilla, 103
Tuttle, William H., 412
Twitchell, Ralph Emerson, 375
Tyndall, John W., 140, 166
Tyne, John J., 391, 394, 413

Ulrich, ___, 7, 221
Underhill, E. H., 352
Union Hist. Co., 175
Union Publishing Co., 168
United States Bureau of the Census, 66, 217, 237, 260, 348-349, 388
Upper Snake River Valley Family History Center, 109
Usner, ___, 212
Utley, Robert M., 18

Valentine, David T., 417
Vallette, H. F., 118
VanAlstyne, L., 73, 403
Vanaman, Henryetta Walls, 40-41
vanAntwerp, Lee D., 291
Van Buren, Augustus H., 433
Van Loan, ___, 407
Van Santvoord, Cornelius W., 425
Van Valen, J. M., 364
Van Voorhis, John S., 10
Van Winkle, Daniel, 368
Van Wood, Ralph, 95
Varrell, W. M., 358
Vassar Bros. Institute, 403
Vaughan, Charles W., 349
Vedder, Jesse Van Vechten, 407
Venables, ___, 388
Vermilye, Thomas, Jr., 364
Versteeg, Dingman, 364, 433
Volkel, ___, 113, 237
Volkel, Lowell, 66, 113-114, 119, 139, 147, 164, 194
Volp, John H., 116
Voye, Nancy S., 260
Voyles, Edsel F., 40

Wadsworth, H. A., 273
Wager, Daniel, 418
Wagstaff, Ann T., 194
Waite, Otis F. R., 359
Walcott, Charles H., 285

Waldo, George C., Jr., 69
Walker, Harriet J., 113
Walker, L. J., 106
Wallace, W. A., 352
Walsh, ___, 252
Walters, David N., 146
Walters, H. Max, 146
Wanamaker, Lee Seth, 424
Ward, Andrew H., 299
Ward, Geoffrey C., 18
Ward, Robert David, 20
Ward, Warren P., 99
Warfield, J. D., 240, 250
Warner, ___, 114
Warner, Ezra J., 211
Warren, Emory F., 392
Warren, Henry P., 224
Warren, Mary Bondurant, 95, 106
Warren, Paula Stuart, 309
Washburn, Emory, 299
Washburne, E., 118
Washington County Historical Society, 26
Waters, Eleanor, 99
Waters, Henry F., 7
Waters, Margaret R., 139
Waters, T. F., 273
Watkins, Susan F., 426
Watring, Anna Miller, 243
Watrous, Hilda R., 428
Watson, ___, 149
Watson, Winslow C., 392, 404
Way, Julias, 366
Weaver, James B., 171
Webb, Franklin H., 397
Weber, Nancie Todd, 45, 329, 336, 340
Webster, H. S., 221-222
Webster, K., 354
Weeks, Eve B., 95
Weesner, Charles C., 164
Weigold, Marilyn E., 437
Weik, Jesse W., 160
Weinberg, ___, 81
Weiner, Pat B., 319
Weis, Frederick Lewis, 7, 10, 16
Weise, A. J., 390

Weise, Arthur James, 423
Weiser, Frederick S., 247
Welch, Samuel M., 404
Wellden, Eulalia Y., 25
Welles, Edwin Stanley, 72
Welles, R., 72
Wellman, Thomas B., 273
Wells, D. W., 278
Wells, Harry L., 54
Wells, J. W., 198
Wells, R. F., 278
Welsh, Willard, 181
Wentworth, William Edgar, 349, 359
West, William Sheperd, 10
Western NY Genealogical Society, Inc., 388
Westervelt, Frances A., 364
Weston, Thomas, 291
Weymouth Historical Society, 288
Wheeler, Edmund, 359
Wheeler, George Augustus, 220
Wheeler, Grace Denison, 78
Wheeler, Richard A., 78
Wheeler, William O., 371, 374
Whitcher, William F., 352
Whitcomb, F. H., 351
White, Alain C., 73
White, George, 95-99, 101, 106-107
White, John, 237
White, Lorraine Cook, 66
White, Richard, 19
White, Sarah Fleming, 95
White, Truman C., 404
Whitehead, John, 372
Whitehead, W. A., 370
Whitford, ___, 393, 427
Whitman, C. F., 223
Whitmore, William H., 294
Whitney, Mrs. L. M. Hammond, 413
Whitney, S. H., 222
Wickes, Stephen, 367
Wiek, Laura C., 73

Wiggin, Edward, 218
Wilcox, Alvin H., 309
Wilder, D., 299
Wiles, Richard C., 407
Wiley, Bell Irvin, 211
Wilkie, Franc B., 175
Willard, Frank H., 408
Willers, Diedrich, Jr., 429
Willey, Kenneth L., 227
Williams, ___, 95
Williams, Anna B., 64
Williams, Dorothy June, 149
Williams, E. Russ, 319
Williams, Harry Lee, 39
Williams, J. Fletcher, 313, 315
Williams, Thomas E. Q., 149
Williams, Thomas J. C., 248, 254
Williamson, Joseph, 217, 227
Willis, Geo. L., Sr., 207
Willis, Laura, 197, 201, 208
Wills, John, 229
Wilson, ___, 237
Wilson, Caroline Price, 98, 101
Wilson, Emily S., 349
Wilson, Fred A., 273
Wilson, George F., 321-323, 339
Wilson, George R., 139
Wilson, Maryhelen, 321-323, 339
Wilson, R. R., 179
Wilson, Samuel M., 194
Wilson, Theresa E., 16
Wilson, Thomas B., 363, 388
Winfield, C. H., 368
Wing, C. E., 221
Winship, J. P. C., 264
Winsor, Justin, 291
Wise, William E., 198, 199
Witmer, Tobias, 404
Witt, Elaine, 120
Wittemore, Edwin C., 222
Wittemore, Joel, 350

Wittmeyer, Alfred V., 417-418
Wittwer, Norman C., Jr., 369
Wolfe, Barbara, 139, 142, 160-161
Wolfe County Women's Club, 208
Wolfe, Janet Bingham, 85
Wolfe, William A., 85
Wood, Alley & Co., 59
Wood, Charles, 41-42
Wood, G. K., 353
Wood, Gregory A., 212, 237
Wood, Helen, 41-42
Wood, Henrietta Danforth, 226
Wood, James, 437
Wood, Robert F., 169
Wood, S. G., 277
Wood, Virginia Steele, 95
Woodruff, George C., 74
Woods, H. F., 288
Woodward, E. M., 365, 370
Woodworth, Olive Newell, 403
Woolen, William Wesley, 139
Wooley, Rose, 85
Woolsey, C. M., 433
Worcester, S. T., 354
Wormer, Maxine, 114-115, 126-129, 133
Worrel, S., 195, 197, 202
Worrell, Donald E., 303
Worthen, Mary F., 48
Worthen, Mrs. A. H., 356
Worthy, Rita Binkley, 89
WPA, 95, 114, 139, 194, 363
Wright, Barbara Epler, 364, 366
Wright, F. Edward, 81-82, 229-231, 237-238, 240, 243, 245, 247, 254
Wright, Henry Parks, 300
Wright, James A., 392
Wright, Lauren, 10
Wright, Mildred S., 26
Wright, Otis O., 266

458

Author Index

Wright, Pauline Williams, 38
Wyman, Thomas Bellows, 294

Yonkers Board of Trade, 438
Yoshpe, Harry B., 52
Young, Alexander, 260-261

Young, Andrew W., 166, 393
Young, E. Harold, 356
Young, Henry James, 248
Young, John Philip, 57
Young, Pauline, 107
Young, ___, 161
Yount, Beverly, 166

Zarowin, David, 257

Zimm, ___, 433
Zimmerman, Elaine Obbink, 243
Zimmerman, Kenneth Edwin, 243

Title Index

"100 Years of Progress." The History of Veterinary Medicine in Minnesota, 306

157th New York Volunteer (Infantry) Regiment - 1862-1865, 397

1300 "Missing" Missouri Marriage Records from Newspapers, 1812-1853, 323

1703 Masters of Families: New York City, New York, 416

1776 Census of Maryland, 230

1783 Tax List of Baltimore County, 241

1783 Tax List of Maryland, 243, 244, 248, 253

1787 Census of Bourbon County, 196

1787 Census of Fayette County, 199

1787 Census of Jefferson County, 201

1787 Census of Lincoln County, 203

1787 Census of Madison County, 204

1787 Census of Mercer County, 205

1787 Census of Nelson County, 206

1790 Census of Maine, 216

1795 Census of Kentucky, The, 193

1800 Census of Delaware, 80

1810-1840 Census, Bullitt Co. KY, 196

1810 Census with Index, Dutchess County, NY, 400

1820 Census of the Territory of Arkansas (Reconstructed), 34

1820 Federal Census for Indiana, 137

1821-1849 Land Entry Atlas, 149

1827 Land Lottery of Georgia, The, 92

1828 Tax List Prince George's County, Maryland, 251

1830 & 1840 Census, Spencer Co. KY, 207

1830 Private Land Claims in East Florida, 85

1832 Cherokee Gold Lottery, 95

1832 Cherokee Land Lottery of Georgia, The, 94

1832 Gold Lottery of Georgia, The, 92

1833 Land Lottery of Georgia and Other Missing Names of Winners in the Georgia Land Lotteries, The, 88

1833 State Census for Barbour County, Alabama, The, 21

1838 Michigan Gazetteer, 300

1840 DuPage County Federal Census, 118

1840 Limestone County Census, 24

1840 Louisiana State Wide Index to the Census, 210

1840 Taney County, Missouri Census: A Study of 565 Pioneer Households (Edited/Annotated), 340

1850 & 1865 Dutchess County Census Records: Amenia, 398

1850 & 1865 Dutchess County Census Records: Beekman, 398

1850 & 1865 Dutchess County Census Records: Clinton, 398

1850 & 1865 Dutchess County Census Records: Dover, 398

1850 & 1865 Dutchess County Census Records: E. Fishkill, 399

1850 & 1865 Dutchess County Census Records: Hyde Park, 399

1850 & 1865 Dutchess County Census Records: LaGrange, 399

1850 & 1865 Dutchess County Census Records: Milan, 399

1850 & 1865 Dutchess County Census Records: Northeast, 399

1850 & 1865 Dutchess County Census Records: Pawling, 399

1850 & 1865 Dutchess County Census Records: Pleasant Valley, 399

1850 & 1865 Dutchess County Census Records: Stanford, 399

1850 & 1865 Dutchess County Census Records: Washington, 399

1850 & 1880 Letcher County, Kentucky Census, 202

1850 Census of Central Arkansas: Hot Spring, Jefferson, Montgomery, Perry, Prairie, Pulaski, Saline, Scott, and Yell Counties, 34

1850 Census of Eastern Arkansas: Arkansas, Chicot, Crittenden, Desha, Greene, Mississippi, Monroe, Phillips, Poinsett, and St. Francis Counties, 34

1850 Census, Kentucky, 191

1850 Census, Mississippi Co. MO, 334

1850 Census of North Central Arkansas: Conway, Fulton, Independence, Izard, Jackson, Lawrence, Marion, Randolph, Searcy, Van Buren, and White Counties, 34

1850 Census of Northwest Arkansas: Benton, Carroll, Crawford, Franklin, Johnson, Madison, Newton, Pope, and Washington Counties, 34

1850 Census Prince George's County, Maryland, 251

1850 Census of Southern Arkansas: Ashley, Bradley, Clark, Dallas, Drew, Hempstead, Lafayette, Ouachita, Pike, Polk, Sevier, and Union Counties, 34

1850 Census, South West Kentucky: Counties of Christian, Logan, Simpson, Todd, Trigg, and Warren, 191

1850 Census, Spencer Co. KY, 207

1850 DuPage County Federal Census, 118

1850 Dutchess County Census Records: Fishkill, 399

1850 Dutchess County Census Records: Pine Plains, 399

1850 Dutchess County Census Records: Poughkeepsie, 399

1850 Dutchess County Census Records: Red Hook, 399

1850 Dutchess County Census Records: Rhinebeck, 402

1850 Dutchess County Census Records: Union Vale, 399

1850 Georgia Mortality Schedules or Census, 94

1850 Kentucky Census Series, 191-192, 201

1850 Ozark County, Missouri Census (Edited/Annotated), 336

1850 Taney County, Missouri Census (Edited/Annotated), 340

1855 Census of Montgomery County, NY, Heads of Household, 414

1855 Census of Schenectady County, NY, Heads of Household, 425

1855 Census of Schoharie County, NY, Heads of Household, 426

1855 Landowner Atlas Printed From Original Wall Map [Marion County, Indiana], 154

1855 Territory of Kansas Census—Vol. I, 176

1855 Territory of Kansas Census—Vol. II, 176

1857 Landowner Atlas Printed in Atlas Form From Original Wall Map [Henry County, Indiana], 149

1859 Deed Tables of Each Lot and Part of Lot as Sold by Holland Land Co., 404

1860 Albany County Mortality Schedule, 388

1860 California Census Index: Heads of Households and Other Surnames in Household Index, 51

1860 Cass Co. Michigan Census Index, 302

1860 Census of Chatham County, Georgia, The, 97

1860 Connecticut Census Index: Heads of Households and Other Surnames in Household Index, 64

1860 Delaware Census Index: Heads of Households and Other Surnames in Household Index, 80

1860 District of Columbia Census Index: Heads of Households and Other Surnames in Household Index, 82

1860 Douglas County, Missouri Census (Edited/Annotated), 329

1860 DuPage County Federal Census, 118

1860 Federal Census—Johnson Co., KS, 179

1860 Florida Census Index: Heads of Household and Other Surnames in Household Index, 84

1860 Indiana Census Index, 135

1860 Jackson County, Kentucky Census, 201

1860 Kankakee County Census, 121

1860 Letcher County, Kentucky Census, 203

1860 Madison County, Missouri Census, 334

1860 Van Buren County Michigan Census Index, 305

1865 Dutchess County Census Records: Red Hook, 402

1865 Dutchess County Census Records: Rhinebeck, 399

1867 Topographical Atlas Including Town, Township Landowner Maps, Business Directories [Chautauqua County, New York], 392

1870 Cass Co., Michigan Census Index, 302

1870 Census, Mississippi Co. MO, 335

1870 Census of Lafayette County Mississippi, 318

1870 Census, Pottawatomie County, Kansas, 180

1870 Census, Wabaunsee County Kansas, 182

1870 Davis County Kansas Census, 178

1870 Delaware Census Index: Heads of Households and Other Surnames in Household Index, 80

1870 District of Columbia Census Index: Heads of Households and Other Surnames in Household Index, 83

1870 Douglas County, Missouri Census + Wood-Richland Townships in Texas County (Edited/Annotated), 329

1870 DuPage County Federal Census, 118

1870 Federal Census, Riley County Kansas, 181

1870 Marion County, Arkansas Census (Edited/Annotated), 45

1872 History [Wayne County, Indiana], 166

1874 Landowner Atlas with Index [Wayne County, Indiana], 165

1874 People's Guide, a Business, Political, Religious Directory, 149

1875 Illustrated Historical Landowner Atlas, 149

1875 Kansas State Census, Riley County, 181

1876 Atlas of Illinois, 114

1876 Centennial History, 403

1876 Historical Atlas [Daviess County, Kentucky], 198

1879 Landowner Atlas with History and Biographies [Bartholomew County, Indiana], 140

1880-1887 Extracts, Bloomfield Vindicator, Stoddard Co. MO, 339

1880 Census, Bullitt Co. KY, 196

1880 Census Index: Clark County, Arkansas, 37

1880 Census of Allen Co., KY, The, 195

1880 Dekalb County, Alabama Census Index, 22

1880 Federal Census: Brown County Kansas, 177

1880 Federal Census: Clay County Kansas, 178

1880 Federal Census: Davis County Kansas, 178

1880 Federal Census, Dickinson County Kansas, 178

1880 Federal Census, Ellsworth County Kansas, 178

1880 Federal Census Greene County, Arkansas, 41

1880 Federal Census, Marion County Kansas, 179

1880 Federal Census, Marshall County Kansas, 179

1880 Federal Census, Mitchell County Kansas, 179

1880 Federal Census: Montgomery County Kansas, 180

1880 Federal Census, Morris County Kansas, 180

1880 Federal Census, Nemaha County Kansas, 180

1880 Federal Census, Pottawatomie County Kansas, 180

1880 Federal Census Republic County Kansas, 181

1880 Federal Census, Riley County Kansas, 181

1880 Federal Census, Wabaunsee County Kansas, 182

1880 Federal Census, Washington County Kansas, 182

1880 Jackson County, Alabama Census Index, 23

1881 History of Jackson Co., Michigan, 302

1883 History [Daviess County, Kentucky], 198

1883 Kankakee County Atlas, 121

1884 History (Originally Included in History of Morgan, Monroe, Brown Cos.), 155

1885 Kansas State Census, Riley County, 181

1887 Landowner Atlas, Township, Town Plats, Business Directories [Delaware County, Indiana], 145

1889 Biographical and Historical Souvenir of Clark Co., 142

1889 Honolulu Business Directory, 108

1890 "Census" of Clark County, Arkansas, 38

1890 Census of Randolph County, Arkansas, Reconstructed from the Personal Property Tax List, 48

1890 Census Sonoma County California Reconstructed, 59

1890 Census Substitute, St. Clair Co., IL, 131

1890 Kentucky Veterans Census Index, 184

1890 Louisiana Veterans Census Index, 210

1890 Maine Veterans Census Index, 214

1890 Maryland Veterans Census Index, 232

1890 Massachusetts Veterans Census Index, 257

1890 Michigan Veterans Census Index, 300

1890 Minnesota Veterans Census Index, 307

1890 Mississippi Veterans Census Index, 316

1890 Missouri Veterans Census Index, 320

1890 New York Veterans Census Index, 378

1890 Reconstructed Census of Greene County, Arkansas from Personal Property Taxlist, 41

1893 Landowner Atlas [Wayne County, Indiana], 166

1893 Portrait & Biographic Record of Kankakee County, 121

1895 Kansas State Census, Riley County, 181

1895 Map of Sonoma County, 59

1896 and 1920 Town and Township Atlases (Combined in One Book), 166

1897 History and Directory Including Portraits, Buildings, Township Directories, 304

1900 Census Index: Clark County, Arkansas, 37

1900 Federal Census Greene County, Arkansas, 42

1900 Kankakee County Atlas, 121

1900 Knott County, Kentucky Census, 202

1900 Letcher County, KY Census, 203

1900 Riley County Kansas Census Index, 181

1904 Georgia Community and Business Directory, 87

1904 Historical Encyclopedia of Illinois, 110

1905 Alabama Community and Business Directory, 19

1907 Confederate Census of Limestone, Madison, & Morgan Counties, 24, 25, 26

1910 Census Index: Clark County, Arkansas, 37

1910 Federal Census Greene County, Arkansas, 42

1910 Idaho Census Index, 109

1910 Knott County, Kentucky Census, 202

1910 Nevada Census Index: Heads of Households and Other Surnames in Households, 346

1910 Wayne Co., IN Census Index, 165

1911 Livingston County Atlas, 125

1915 Kankakee County Atlas, 121

1918 Camp Pike, Arkansas, Index to Soldiers' Naturalizations, 27

1920 Estill County Kentucky Census, 198, 199

1920 Federal Census Greene County, Arkansas, 42

1997 Pocket Guide to Genealogical Resource Centers of the Mid-Atlantic, 10

8,000 More Vital Records of Eastern New York State, 1804-1850, 376

10,000 Vital Records of Central New York, 1813-1850, 376

10,000 Vital Records of Eastern New York, 1777-1834, 376

10,000 Vital Records of Western New York, 1809-1850, 376

30,638 Burials in Georgia, 88

Abandoned and Semi-Active Cemeteries, 176

Abandoned Cemeteries of Jersey Co., 120

Abstract of Early Kentucky Wills and Inventories, 188

Abstracts of Bristol County, Massachusetts Probate Records, 1687-1745, 266

Abstracts of Bristol County, Massachusetts Probate Records, 1745-1762, 266

Abstracts of Chancery Court Records of Maryland, 1669-1782, 233

Abstracts of Charles County Court & Land Records, Vol. 1, 1658-1666, 245

Abstracts of Charles County Court & Land Records, Vol. 2: 1665-1695, 245

Abstracts of Charles County Court & Land Records, Vol. 3: 1694-1722, 245

Abstracts of Death Certificates from the Files of Herbert S. Bailey, Funeral Director, Darlington, MD, 1921-1961, Vol. I, A-L, 248

Abstracts of Early Virginia Rose Estates to 1850, 52

Abstracts of Georgia Land Plat Books A & B, 93

Abstracts of Obituaries in the Western Christian Advocate, 1834-1850, 139

Abstracts of Old Ninety-Six and Abbeville District Wills and Bonds, 107

Abstracts of Penobscot County, Maine Probate Records 1816-1883, 224

Abstracts of the Records of the Society of Friends in Indiana, 136

Abstracts of Wills, Chatham County, Georgia, 1773-1817, 98

Abstracts of Wills and Estates, O.C.R. Books, Barbour County, Alabama, 5-6, 1852-1856, 21

Abstracts of Wills of Monroe County, New York from 1821 to 1847, 413

Abstracts of Wills of Rensselaer County, New York, 423

Acadian-Cajun Genealogy: Step by Step, 210

Across the Years in Prince George's County [Maryland], 251

Adams Co. Index to Testators to 1880, 140

Addison Township Records, 117

Adoptions & Name Changes: Minnesota Territory & State, 1851-1881, 307

Africa in America: Slave Acculturation and Resistance in the American South and the British Caribbean, 1736-1831, 14

Africans in Colonial Louisiana: The Development of Afro-Creole Culture in the Eighteenth Century, 211

Agencies of State Government, 1820-1971, Parts I and II, 216

Alabama: Her History, Resources, War Record, and Public Men from 1540 to 1872, 19

Alabama: The History of a Deep South State, 20

Alabama Census Returns, 1820, 19

Alabama Marriages, Early to 1825, 20

Alabama Notes, 19

Alabama—S.A.R. Members & Ancestors 1903-1996, 19

Alaska Atlas and Gazetteer, 26

Albany, Georgia, Newspaper Clippings, Vol. I, 1845-1852, 96, 100

Albany Protocol, The, 1731-1750, 388

Albany to Tappan, 408

Alexander Co. 1850 Census Transcription, 114

All Name Index to Durant's 1878 History of Saint Lawrence County, 429

Allegany and Garrett Counties, Maryland Genealogical Research Guide, 239, 248

Allegany County & Its People, 390

Allegany County Index to Scharf's History of Western Maryland, 239

Allegany County, Maryland Rural Cemeteries, 239

Allen Co. Index to Testators to 1880, 140

Allen Co., KY Cemeteries Revisited, Vol. II, 194

Allen Co., KY Cemeteries & Graveyards Revisited, Vol. III, 194

Allen Co., KY Census for 1820, 194

Allen Co., KY Day Book 1826-1837, 194

Allen Co., KY Vital Statistics Revisited, 195

All-Name Index to MacIntosh's 1876 History of Ontario County, 419

All-Name Index to the 1860 Gazetteer of New York State, 375

An Alphabetical First and Last Name Index to Ellis' History of Columbia County, NY, 394

Ambiguous Lives: Free Women of Color in Rural Georgia, 1789-1879, 87

Amended Index Sonoma County Homestead Declarations 1860-1920, 59

American Architecture, Westchester

County, New York: Colonial to Contemporary, 437

American Indian Related Books in the SCGS Library, 53

American Indians of the Southwest, 17

American Vital Records from the Baptist Register, 1824-1832 and the New York Baptist Register, 1832-1834, 379

Ancestor Charts of Members—Volume 1, 111

Ancestor Charts of Members—Volume 3, 111

Ancestor Charts of Members—Volume 4, 111

Ancestor Charts of Members—Volume 5, 111

Ancestor Charts of Members—Volume 6, 111

Ancestor Charts of Members—Volume 7, 111

Ancestors of Western New York Genealogical Society Members, Vol. I, 388

Ancient Burying-Grounds of the Town of Waterbury, 76

"Ancient City, The": History of Annapolis, in Maryland, 1649-1887, 240

Ancient Historical Records of Norwalk, 67

Ancient North Yarmouth & Yarmouth, 1636-1936, 219

Anderson Cemetery in Decatur Township, Van Buren County, Michigan, 305

Andre Trail Book, The! Westchester County Treasure Hunt Tour: Treason in the American Revolution, 420-421, 424, 436

Ancestors of Cora Belle Adams 1881-1957, 10

Ancestors of Curtis Turner Davidson 1864-1924, 10

Ancestors of Sheperd Salisbury West 1876-1937, 10

Ancestors of Margie Willey 1877-1937, 10

Annals & Family Records of Winchester, 72

Annals & Recollections of Oneida County, 418

Annals of Annapolis, 240

Annals of Bangor, 1769-1882, 224

Annals of Brookfield, Fairfield County, 67

Annals of Newtown, 421

Annals of Oxford, 223, 394

Annals of Oxford Maine from 1829 to 1850, 223

Annals of Polk County & the City of Des Moines, 174

Annals of Portsmouth, 356

Annals of Salem, 269

Annals of San Francisco. . .with Biographical Memoirs of Some Prominent Citizens, 57

Annals of Staten Island, from Its Discovery to the Present Time, 423

Annals of Sudbury, Wayland & Maynard, Middlesex Co., 280

Annals of the Town of Concord, 356

Annals of the Town of Mendon, from 1659 to 1880, 298

Annals of Tryon County, 431

Annals of Witchcraft in New England & Elsewhere in the U.S., from Their First Settlement, The, 4

Anne Arundel Church Records of the 17th and 18th Centuries, 240

Anne Arundel County, Maryland, Land Records, 1700-1702, 240

Anne Arundel County, Maryland, Land Records, 1703-1709, 240

Anne Arundel County, Maryland, Land Records, 1708-1712, 240

Anne Arundel County, Maryland, Land Records, 1712-1718, 240

Anne Arundel County, Maryland, Land Records, 1719-1724, 240

Anne Arundel County, Maryland, Land Records, 1724-1728, 240

Anne Arundel Gentry, 239

Anne Arundel Gentry, Early Families of Anne Arundel County, Maryland, 239

Annual Report of the Land Agent of the State of Maine, 214

Antebellum Natchez, 211

Antelope County Cemetery Records, 342, 343, 344

Antioch Township Cemeteries, 122

Archives of Maryland (original series), 234

Archives of Maryland, New Series, Vol. I, 234

Argyle Patent, The, 434

Arizona Sentinel Newspaper Death Notices and Obituaries 1872-1899, The, 27

Arkansas 1850 Census Every-Name Index, 34

Arkansas Confederate Veterans & Widows Home Records, 32

Arkansas Confederate Veterans and Widows Pension Applications, 32

Arkansas' Damned Yankees: Index to Union Soldiers in Arkansas Regiments, 28

Arkansas Death Record Index, 1914-1923, 28

Arkansas Death Record Index, 1924-1933, 28

Arkansas Death Record Index, 1934-1940, 28

Arkansas Families: Glimpses of Yesterday Columns from the Arkansas Gazette, 34

Arkansas Folklore Sourcebook, An, 34

Arkansas Gazette Obituaries Index, 1819-1879, The, 30

Arkansas History Commission Bulletin of Information, Nos. 13, 14, 15, 16, The, 32

Arkansas Land Patents: Arkansas, Chicot, and Desha Counties (granted through 30 June 1908), 35, 37, 39

Arkansas Land Patents: Ashley County (granted through 30 June 1908), 35

Arkansas Land Patents: Baxter County (granted through 30 June 1908), 35

Arkansas Land Patents: Benton County (granted through 30 June 1908), 37

Arkansas Land Patents: Boone County (granted through 30 June 1908), 37

Arkansas Land Patents: Bradley County (granted through 30 June 1908), 37

Arkansas Land Patents: Calhoun County (granted through 30 June 1908), 37

Arkansas Land Patents: Carroll County (granted through 30 June 1908), 37

Arkansas Land Patents: Clark County (granted through 30 June 1908), 37

Arkansas Land Patents: Cleburne County (granted through 30 June 1908), 38

Arkansas Land Patents: Cleveland County (granted through 30 June 1908), 38

Arkansas Land Patents: Columbia County (granted through 30 June 1908), 39

Arkansas Land Patents: Conway, Faulkner, and Perry Counties (granted through 30 June 1908), 39, 47

Arkansas Land Patents: Crawford County (granted through 30 June 1908), 39

Arkansas Land Patents: Dallas County (granted through 30 June 1908), 39

Arkansas Land Patents: Drew County (granted through 30 June 1908), 40

Arkansas Land Patents: Eastern Arkansas Counties (Clay, Craighead, Crittenden, Cross, Greene, Lee, Mississippi, Monroe, Phillips, Poinsett, and St. Francis Counties, granted through 30 June 1908), 28

Arkansas Land Patents: Franklin County (granted through 30 June 1908), 40

Arkansas Land Patents: Fulton County (granted through 30 June 1908), 41

Arkansas Land Patents: Garland County (granted through 30 June 1908), 41

Arkansas Land Patents: Grant and Saline Counties (granted through 30 June 1908), 41, 49

Arkansas Land Patents: Hempstead County (granted through 30 June 1908), 42

Arkansas Land Patents: Hot Spring County (granted through 30 June 1908), 42

Arkansas Land Patents: Howard County (granted through 30 June 1908), 42

Arkansas Land Patents: Independence County (granted through 30 June 1908), 42

Arkansas Land Patents: Izard County (granted through 30 June 1908), 43

Arkansas Land Patents: Jackson, Lawrence, and Woodruff Counties (granted through 30 June 1908), 43, 50

Arkansas Land Patents: Jefferson County (granted through 30 June 1908), 43

Arkansas Land Patents: Johnson County (granted through 30 June 1908), 43

Arkansas Land Patents: Lafayette County (granted through 30 June 1908), 43

Arkansas Land Patents: Lincoln County (granted through 30 June 1908), 44

Arkansas Land Patents: Little River County (granted through 30 June 1908), 44

Arkansas Land Patents: Logan County (granted through 30 June 1908), 44

Arkansas Land Patents: Lonoke and Prairie Counties (granted through 30 June 1908), 44, 47

Arkansas Land Patents: Madison County (granted through 30 June 1908), 45

Arkansas Land Patents: Marion County (granted through 30 June 1908), 45

Arkansas Land Patents: Miller County (granted through 30 June 1908), 45

Arkansas Land Patents: Montgomery County (granted through 30 June 1908), 45

Arkansas Land Patents: Nevada County (granted through 30 June 1908), 45

Arkansas Land Patents: Newton County (granted through 30 June 1908), 46

Arkansas Land Patents: Ouachita County (granted through 30 June 1908), 46

Arkansas Land Patents: Pike County (granted through 30 June 1908), 47

Arkansas Land Patents: Polk County (granted through 30 June 1908), 47

Arkansas Land Patents: Pope County (granted through 30 June 1908), 47

Arkansas Land Patents: Pulaski County (granted through 30 June 1908), 48

Arkansas Land Patents: Randolph County (granted through 30 June 1908), 48

Arkansas Land Patents: Scott County (granted through 30 June 1908), 49

Arkansas Land Patents: Searcy County (granted through 30 June 1908), 49

Arkansas Land Patents: Sebastian County (granted through 30 June 1908), 49

Arkansas Land Patents: Sevier County (granted through 30 June 1908), 49

Arkansas Land Patents: Sharp County (granted through 30 June 1908), 49

Arkansas Land Patents: Stone County (granted through 30 June 1908), 50

Arkansas Land Patents: Union County (granted through 30 June 1908), 50

Arkansas Land Patents: Van Buren County (granted through 30 June 1908), 50

Arkansas Land Patents: Washington County (granted through 30 June 1908), 50

Arkansas Land Patents: White County (granted through 30 June 1908), 50

Arkansas Land Patents: Yell County (granted through 30 June 1908), 51

Arkansas Marriage Notices, 1819-1845, 34

Arkansas Marriage Records, 1808-1835, 34

Arkansas Marriages, Early to 1850, 32

Arkansas' Mexican War Soldiers, 28

Arkansas Newspaper Abstracts, 1819-1845, 34

Arkansas Pensioners, 1818-1900: Records of Some Arkansas Residents Who Applied to the Federal Government for Benefits Arising from Services in Federal Military Organizations, 34

Arkansas' Spanish American War Soldiers, 28

Arkansas Township Digest: Minor Civil Divisions, 1820-1990, 28

Arkansas Union Soldiers Pension Application Index, 28

Robert Armstrong—Plat Book of Those Indians Given Reservations After the 1817 Treaty, 19

Articles in *The New York Genealogical and Biographical Record* 1983-1995, Indexed by Principal Surname or Location, 382

Ashland Collegiate Institute and Musical Academy, 407

Atchison County, Missouri Atlas 1904, 324

Atchison County, Missouri Marriages 1863-1869, 324

Atlantic County, New Jersey Marriages, 363, 367

Atlas of Arkansas, 30

Atlas of Chautauqua County 1867, 392

Atlas of Florida, 84

Atlas of Great Lakes Indian History, 16

Atlas of Hunterdon County New Jersey from Recent and Actual Surveys, 368

Atlas of Illinois, 110

Atlas of Indiana, 135

Atlas of Kentucky, 183

Atlas of Maine, 214

Atlas of Maryland and Delaware, 79, 229

Atlas of Michigan, 300

Atlas of Minnesota, 306

Atlas of New Hampshire, 347

Atlas of New York State, 375

Atlas of Schuyler County 1874, 427

Atlases & Gazetteers: Florida, 84

Atlases & Gazetteers: Illinois, 110

Atlases & Gazetteers: Maryland/Delaware, 80, 229

Audrain County, Missouri—Grainger Furniture & Undertakers Company, 324

Authentic & Comprehensive History of Buffalo, 404

Authentic History of the Lawrence Calamity, 267

Avon Township Cemeteries, 122

Baca County, Colorado, Probate Index 1910-1992, 63

Baldwin County, Georgia, Newspaper Clippings (Union Recorder), Volume I, 1830-1833, 96

Baldwin County, Georgia, Newspaper Clippings (Union Recorder), Volume II, 1834-1836, 96

Baldwin County, Georgia, Newspaper Clippings (Union Recorder), Volume III, 1837-1839, 96

Baldwin County, Georgia, Newspaper Clippings (Union Recorder), Volume IV, 1840-1842, 96

Baldwin County, Georgia, Newspaper Clippings (Union Recorder), Volume V, 1843-1847, 96

Baldwin County, Georgia, Newspaper Clippings (Union Recorder), Volume VI, 1848-1853, 96

Balloting Book of the Military Tract 1825, The, 382

Baltimore County Families, 1659-1759, 8, 241

Baltimore County Land Records, 1665-1687, 242

Baltimore County, Maryland Deed Abstracts, 1659-1750, 241

Bangor Cemetery, Bangor, Butte County, California, 54

Baptism & Marriage Record, First Lutheran Chuch, Albany, NY: 1774-1842, 389

Baptism Record, Albany Reformed Church, 1683-1809, 389

Baptism Record, Poughkeepsie Reformed Church, 1716-1824, 401

Baptism Records of Caughnawaga Reformed Church, Fonda, NY: 1758-1899, 414

Baptism Records of Christ Lutheran Church, Germantown, NY: 1746-1899, 395

Baptism Records of Claverack Reformed Church, Claverack, NY: 1727-1899, 395

Baptism Records of Coxsackie Reformed Church, Coxsackie, NY: 1738-1899, 405

Baptism Records of 8 Episcopal Congregations of the Rhinebeck Area: 1816-1899, 400

Baptism Records of Gallatin Reformed Church, Gallatinville, NY: 1748-1899, 395

Baptism Records of German Flats Reformed Church, Herkimer, NY: 1763-1899, 408

Baptism Records of Germantown Reformed Church, Germantown, NY (East Camp): 1729-1898, 395

Baptism Records of Gilead Lutheran Church, Brunswick, NY: 1777-1886, 422

Baptism Records of Helderberg Reformed Church, Guilderland, NY: 1786-1860, 389

Baptism Records of Herkimer Reformed Church, Herkimer, NY: 1801-1899, 408

Baptism Records of Hillsdale Reformed Church, Hillsdale, NY (defunct): 1776-1849, 395

Baptism Records of Kinderhook Reformed Church, Kinderhook, NY: 1718-1899, 395

Baptism Records of Linlithgo Reformed Church, Livingston, NY: 1722-1899, 395

Baptism Records of Marbletown Reformed Church, Marbletown, NY: 1746-1871, 433

Baptism Records of Rhinebeck Reformed Church, Rhinebeck, NY: 1731-1899, 400

Baptism Records of Schenectady Reformed Church: 1694-1811, 425

Baptism Records of Schoharie Reformed Church, Schoharie, NY: 1731-1894, 426

Baptism Records of St. John's Lutheran Church, Manorton, NY: 1765-1872, 395

Baptism Records of St. Paul's (Zion's) Lutheran Church, Red Hook, NY: 1730-1899, 401

Baptism Records of St. Paul's Lutheran Church, Rhinebeck, NY (Wurtemburg): 1760-1899, 401

Baptism Records of St. Paul's Lutheran Church, Schoharie, NY: 1728-1899, 426

Baptism Records of St. Paul's Lutheran Church, West Camp, NY: 1708-1899, 435

Baptism Records of St. Peter's Lutheran Church, Rhinebeck, NY (StoneCh): 1733-1899, 401

Baptism Records of St. Thomas' Lutheran Church, Churchtown, NY: 1760-1899, 395

Baptism Records of Stone Arabia Reformed Church, Stone Arabia, NY: 1739-1899, 414

Baptism Records of Trinity Lutheran Church, Stone Arabia, NY: Pre-1751-1899, 414

Baptism Records of West Copake Reformed Church, Copake, NY: 1783-1899, 395

Baptism Records of Zion Lutheran Church, Athens, NY: 1704-1899, 405

Baptismal and Marriage Registers of the Old Dutch Church of Kingston, Ulster County, New York, 1660-1809, 432

Barbados Records: Marriages, 1643-1800, 15

Barbados Records: Wills, Vol. II: 1681-1700; Wills, Vol. III: 1701-1725, 15

Barbour Collection of Connecticut Town Vital Records, The, 66

Barbour County, Alabama Marriage Records, 1838-1859, 21

Barbour County, Alabama Obituaries from Newspapers, 1890-1905, 21

Barbour County Marriages 1838-1930, 21

(John Warner) Barber's Views of Connecticut Towns, 1834-36, 64

Barkhamsted & Its Centennial, 1879, to Which Is Added an Historical Appendix, 73

Barren County, Kentucky, Taxpayers, 1799, 195

Bartholomew Co. Index to Testators to 1880, 140

Bartholomew Co. Marriages 1821-1850, 140

Bates County, Missouri Births & Deaths 1883-1886, 325

Bates County, Missouri Cemeteries, 324

Bates County, Missouri Marriages Volume 1 1860-1877, 324

Bates County, Missouri Marriages Volume 2 1877-1883, 324

Bates County, Missouri Marriages Volume 3 1883-1895, 325

Battle of Groton Heights, The: A Collection of Narratives, Official Reports, Records, Etc., of the Storming of Ft. Griswold, 76

Baxter County Ancestors, Volume I, 35

Beech Grove Cemetery Records Muncie, Indiana from Office Records and Tombstone Inscriptions, 145

Belated Census of Earliest Settlers of Cape Girardeau County, Missouri, A, 326

Benton Co. Index to Testators to 1880, 140

Benton Co. Marriages 1840-1858, 140

Bent's Bibliography of the White Mountains, 347

Bergen County, New Jersey Deed Records, 1689-1801, 364

Bergen County, New Jersey Taxpayers, 1777-1797, 364

Bergen Records: Records of the Reformed Protestant Dutch Church of Bergen in New Jersey, 1666 to 1788, 364

Bethel Baptist Church Minutes 1806-1851, Excerpts from the Minutes 1851-1852, Membership Lists 1809-1909, 126-127, 129, 131

Beyond Bartholomew: The Portland [AR] Area History, 35

[Bibliographical] Reference List of Manuscripts Relating to the History of Maine, 216

Bibliography of Massachusetts Vital Records 1620-1905, 258

Bibliography of New York State Communities, A, 383

Bibliography of Published Genealogical Source Records, Prince George's County, Maryland, A, 251

Bibliography of the State of Maine, 217

Bibliography of the Writings on Georgia History 1900-1970, A, 93

Bicentennial Citizens and Their Ancestors, 117

Big Sandy Valley, The, 184, 187

Biographical and Genealogical History of Morris County, New Jersey, 371

Biographical & Genealogical History of the Counties of Cass, Miami, Howard & Tipton, 142, 150, 155, 163

Biographical and Historical Memoirs of Mississippi, 316

Biographical and Historical Record of Jay and Blackford Counties, 141, 151

Biographical & Historical Memoirs of Arkansas: General History of Arkansas, 31

Biographical and Pictorial History of Arkansas, 31

Biographical & Pictorial Memoirs of Elkhart & St. Joseph Counties, 146, 161

Biographical Cyclopedia of the Commonwealth of Kentucky, 186

Biographical Encyclopedia of Kentucky, of the Dead and Living Men of the Nineteenth Century, The, 183

Biographical History of Crawford, Ida & Sac Counties, 169, 171, 175

Biographical History of Tippecanoe, White, Jasper, Newton, Benton, Warren & Pulaski Counties, 140, 150, 156, 159, 163-164, 166

Biographical Memoirs of St. Clair County, 304

Biographical Record & Portrait Album of Tippecanoe County, 163

Biographical Record of Boone County, 168

Biographical Record of Jasper County, 332

Biographical Record of Whiteside County, 134

Biographical Review: Biographical Sketches of Leading Citizens of Oxford & Franklin Counties, 219, 223

Biographical Review: Life Sketches of Leading Citizens of Sagadahoc, Lincoln, Knox & Waldo Cos., 222, 225-226

Biographical Rosters of Florida's Confederate & Union Soldiers 1861-1865, 84

Biographical Sketches of Prominent Persons, 286

Biographical Sketches of the Leading Citizens of Hampshire County, 277

Biographies of the First Settlers of Rutland, 294

Births/Baptisms in Osage County, Missouri, 336

Births, Deaths and Marriages of the Nottingham Quakers, 1680-1889, 244

Births, Marriages, Deaths . . . "Eglise Francoise a la Nouvelle York," 1688-1806, 418

Black Families in Hampden County, Massachusetts 1650-1855, 276

Black House Papers—A Guide to Certain Microfilmed Land Records, 216

Black Rock, Seaport of Old Fairfield, 1644-1870, 68

Blackford Co. Index to Testators to 1880, 141

Blackford Co. Marriages 1839-1849, 141

Blount County, Alabama Marriages 1821-1844, 21

Bonne Terre Cemetery Index, Bonne Terre, MO, 338

Book of Names, The [New York], 382

Book of the General Lawes and Libertyes Concerning the Inhabitants of Massachusetts, The, 255

Boone & Clinton Counties, 141, 143

Boone Co. Index to Testators to 1880, 141

Boone County, Kentucky, Cemeteries, 195

Boone County, Kentucky, County Court Orders 1799-1815, 195

Boone County, Kentucky, Marriages, 1798-1850, 195

Born in Ohio and Living in Southwest Michigan in 1860, 300

Boston Beginnings 1630-1699, 293

Boston Births, Baptisms, Marriages, and Deaths, 1630-1699 and Boston Births, 1700-1800, 292

Boston Marriages, 292

Boston Records, 292

Boston Taxpayers in 1821, 294

Boundary Lines of Old Groton, 280

Bourbon Co. Will Abstracts 1788-1816. Vol. I, 195

Bourbon Co. Will Abstracts 1816-1824, Vol. II, 195

Bourbon Co. Will Abstracts 1825-1831, Vol. III, 195

Bourbon County, Kentucky, Court Orders, 1786-1793: An Every-Name Index, 196

Bourbon County, Kentucky Taxpayers, 1787-1799, 196

Boxboro, 280

Boyer Funeral Home Records, 1882-1926, Bonne Terre, MO, 338

Bradford & Foster Brook—The Peg Leg Railroad, 391

Breckinridge County 1870 Census, 196

Breckinridge County, Kentucky—Births 1852-1853, 1855-1859, 1861, 1874-1876, 1878, 1893-1894 and 1903-1904, 196

Breckinridge County, Kentucky—Deaths 1852-1859, 1861, 1874-1878, 1894, 1903-1904, 196

Breckinridge County, Kentucky—Marriages 1853-1859, 1861, 1875-1878, 1893-1894 and 1904, 196

Brentwood's 225 Years, 1742-1967, 356

Brief History of Logan County, A, 63

Brief Sketch of 1st Settlement of Schoharie, 426

Briefe Relation of the Voyage Unto Maryland, 237

Bristol, Connecticut ("In Olden Time New Cambridge"), Which Includes Forestville, 71

British Commission Land Claims, 1843 [Hawaii], 108

British Occupation of New York City 1781-1783, 417

Brooks County, Georgia, Newspaper Clippings, Vol. I, 1866-1889, 96

Brothers Rev. Robert Rose and Rev. Charles Rose of Colonial Virginia and Scotland, The, 52

Brown Co. Index to Testators to 1880, 141

Brown's Army, Joe: The Georgia State Line, 1862-1865, 88

Buckland, the North West Section of Manchester, 69

Bullitt County, Kentucky, Land Records, 1819-1825, 196

Burghers of New Amsterdam and the Freemen of New York 1675-1866, The, 417

Burial Hill, Plymouth, Massachusetts, 288

Burial Inscriptions of Berwick to 1922, 229

Burial Record, Baca County, Colorado, 63

Burlington County Marriages, 365

Burning of Chelsea, The, 293

Burying Grounds of Sharon, Conn., and Amenia & North East, NY, 73, 403

Butte County Cemetery 1862-1980 Oroville, Butte County, California, 54

By Their Markers Ye Shall Know Them: A Chronicle of the History and Restorations of Hartford's Ancient Burying Ground, 70

By-Gone Days in Ponsett-Haddam, Middlesex Co.: A Story, 74

By-Name Index to the Centennial History of Arkansas, The, 34

Caldwell County, Kentucky Vital Statistics—Births 1852-1910, 197

Calendar of Council Minutes 1668-1783, 378

Calendar of Delaware Wills, New Castle County, 1682-1800, A, 82

Calendar of Historical Manuscripts, 377

Calendar of Maryland State Papers, 8, 233

Calendar of New York Colonial Commissions 1770-1776, 386

Calendar of New York Colonial Manuscripts 1643-1803, 385

Calendar of Sussex County, Delaware Probate Records 1680-1800, 82

Calendar of the Warrants for Land in Kentucky, A, 194

California Cemetery Inscription Sources: Print and Microform, 52

California Locator, The. A Directory of

Public Records for Locating People Dead or Alive in California, 52

California Pioneer Register and Index, 1542-1848, 51

California Ranchos: Patented Private Land Grants Listed by County, 53

Calloway County, Kentucky Deed Books, Volume Three (Oct. 1834-June 1836), 197

Calloway County, Kentucky Tax Lists 1829-1831-1833, 197

Calloway County, Kentucky Tax Lists 1834-1835-1836, 197

Calloway County, Kentucky Wills & Administrations Volume Two, 197

Calvary Cemetery, St. Paul, & Its Predecessors Vol. 1, 1850-1878, 312

Calvary Cemetery, St. Paul, Vol. 2: 1879-1888, 313

Calvert County, Maryland, Rent Rolls, 1651-1776, 243

Calvert Papers, The: Calendar and Guide to the Microfilm Edition, 232

Camden County Marriages, 365

Campbell County, Kentucky, Marriages 1795-1850, 197

Canary Islanders of Louisiana, The, 211

Cape Cod Library of Local History and Genealogy, 262

Cape May County Marriages, 366

Cape May County Mayflower Pilgrim Descendants, 366

Captain John Mason, Founder of New Hampshire, 347

Carroll Co. 1850 Census Transcription & Mortality Schedule, 115

Carroll Co. Index to Testators to 1880, 142

Carroll County Index to Scharf's History of Western Maryland, 244

Cascades & Courage: The History of the Town of Vernon & the City of Rockville, 79

Casco Township—Bounty by the Lake. The History of Casco Township, Allegan County, Michigan 1844-1995, 301

Cass Co. 1855 State Census, 115

Cass Co. Index of Estates, 142

Cass Co. Index to Testators to 1880, 142

Cass Co. Marriage Book I, 1829-1851, 142

Cast in Stone, Selected Albany, Rensselaer and Saratoga County, NY, Cemetery Records, 389, 423, 424

Catalogue of the Names of the First Puritan Settlers of the Colony of Connecticut, A, 2, 64

Catharine's Town, The Sullivan Expedition, 427

Catholic Families of Southern Maryland, 253

Cedar County, Missouri 1870 Federal Census, 327

Celebration of the 150th Anniversary of the Organization of the Congregational Church & Society in Franklin, 1868, 77

Cemeteries of Greene County, Arkansas, 42

Cemeteries of Indian River County FL, 86

Cemeteries of Oglethorpe County, Georgia, 104

Cemeteries of Riley County Kansas Excluding Manhattan City Cemeteries, 181

Cemeteries of the Dwight Mission, London and Scotia Areas of Pope County, Arkansas, 47

Cemeteries of the NE Section of Dearborn Co., 144

Cemeteries of the Town of Half Moon, Saratoga Co., 424

Cemeteries of Toombs County, Georgia, 105

Cemeteries of Vermilion County, 132

Cemeteries of Vermilion County Volume I, Bount & Newell Twp, 132

Cemeteries of Vermilion County Volume II, Elwood & Love Twp, 132

Cemeteries of Vermilion County Volume III, Danville Twp. Part I, 132

Cemetery Books [Lancaster County, Nebraska]: Vol. I, 344

Cemetery Books [Lancaster County, Nebraska]: Vol. II, 344

Cemetery Books [Lancaster County, Nebraska]: Vols. III-IV, 344

Cemetery Books [Lincoln County, Nebraska]: Vol. V, 345

Cemetery Books [Lincoln County, Nebraska]: Vol. VI, 345

Cemetery Books [Lincoln County, Nebraska]: Vol. VII, 345

Cemetery Books [Lincoln County, Nebraska]: Vol. VIII, 345

Cemetery Index [Merced County, California]—1862-1989, 56

Cemetery Index [Merced County, California]—1990-1995, 56

Cemetery Inscriptions in Windsor, 70

Cemetery Inscriptions of York County, Maine, 228

Cemetery Records of the Township of Fort Ann, Washington County, NY, 434

Census of Indiana Territory for 1807, 136, 142, 144, 152

Census Tables for the French Colony of Louisiana from 1699 Through 1732, The, 210

Centennial Celebration of the Town of Longmeadow, 276

Centennial Celebration & Centennial History of the Town of Lee, The, 262

Centennial History of Chautauqua County, 392

Centennial History of Erie County, 404

Centennial History of Harrison, 219

Centennial History of Litchfield, 1853-1953, 127

Centennial History of Mason County, 126

Centennial History of Norway, Oxford County, Maine 1786-1886, 224

Centennial History of the Town of Dryden, 1797-1897, 431

Centennial History of the Town of Millbury, 294

Centennial History of the Town of Nunda, 1808-1908, 411

Centennial History of the Village of Ballston Spa, 424

Centennial History of the Villages of Iroquois & Montgomery, 120, 128

Centennial History of Waterville, Kennebec County, 1802-1902, 222

Center, The, 83

Central Arkansas Death Record Index, 1914-1923: Garland, Grant, Hot Spring, Lonoke, Perry, Prairie, Pulaski, and Saline Counties, 29

Central Arkansas Death Record Index, 1934-1940: Garland, Grant, Hot Spring, Lonoke, Perry, Prairie, Pulaski, and Saline Counties, 29

Century of Meriden, A: An Historic Record & Pictorial Description of the Town of Meriden, 75

Certificate Book of the Virginia Land Commission, 1779-1780, 188

Certificates and Receipts of Revolutionary New Jersey, 363

Chancery Books of Carroll County, 1837-1873, 244

Chancery Books of Carroll County, 1873-1889, 244

Charles County, Maryland, Court Records, 1774-1778: An Every-Name Index, 245

Charles County, Maryland, Land Records, 1722-1733, 245

Charles County, Maryland, Land Records, 1733-1743, 245

Charles County, Maryland, Land Records, 1743-1752, 245

Charles County, Maryland, Land Records, 1752-1756, 245

Charles County, Maryland, Land Records, 1756-1761, 245

Charles County, Maryland, Land Records, 1761-1765, 246

Charles County, Maryland, Land Records, 1765-1775, 246

Charles County, Maryland, Land Records, 1790-1796, 246

Charles County, Maryland, Orphans Court Proceedings, 1791-1803: An Every-Name Index, 246

Charles County, Maryland, Wills, 1780-1791, 246

Charles County, Maryland, Wills, Administration Accounts, Inventories, and Orphans Court Proceedings, 1777-1780, 246

Charleston Cemetery in Volinia Township, Cass County, Michigan, 302

Charlestown (MA) Vital Records, 293

Checklist of Eighteenth Century Manuscripts in the Georgia Historical Society, 91

Cherokee Cemetery 1863-1993, Butte County, California, 54

Cherokee Land Lottery [of Georgia, 1832], The, 94

Chicago and Cook County: A Guide to Research, 116

Chicago Area Death Notices from the Chicago Tribune, 116

Children's Aid Society of New York, The, 415

Chiles-Cooper Funeral Home Records, 1926-1982, Bloomfield, Stoddard Co., MO, 339

Christian County, Kentucky, Deed Book G (1816-1817), 197

Christian County, Kentucky Newspaper Abstracts, Volume Three (Kentucky New Era), 198

Christian County, Kentucky Newspaper Abstracts, Volume Four (Kentucky New Era), 198

Christian County, Kentucky, Wills and Estates, 1815-1823, 198

Chronicle of Claremont Township & Village, A, 310

Chronicles of Colonial Maryland, 237

Chronicles of the First Planters of the Colony of Massachusetts Bay, from 1623 to 1636, 260

Chronicles of the Pilgrim Fathers of the Colony of Plymouth from 1602 to 1625, 261

Chronology of Municipal History and Election Statistics, Waterville, 1771-1908, 221

Church Records in Minnesota: Guide to Parish Records of Congregational, Evangelical, Reformed & United Church of Christ Churches 1851-1981, 308

Church Records of Killingly, Connecticut, 79

Church Records of Rochester, New Hampshire, 358

Churches of Christ of the Congregational Way in New England, The, 7

Citizens of the Eastern Shore of Maryland, 1659-1750, 237

City of Hartford 1784-1984, The: An Illustrated History, 70

City of Hudson Burying Grounds, Interments 1829-73, Hudson, Columbia County, NY, 396

Civil War, The: The Town of Prattsville, 398, 407, 426

Civil War and New York City, The, 416

Civil War and Nodaway County, MO, The—Volume 1, 335

Civil War and Nodaway County, MO, The—Volume 2, 335

Civil War Burials in Baltimore's Loudon Park Cemetery, 243

Civil War in Kentucky, The, 186

Civil War in the American West, The, 17

Civil War in the Ozarks, 15

Civil War Records in the New York State Archives, 383

Civil War Soldier's Diary, Peter W. Funk, 150th NY Vol, 379

Clark Co. Index to Testators to 1880, 142

Clark Co. Marriages 1801-1849, 142

Clark County, Arkansas: A Genealogical Source Book, 38

Clark County, Arkansas: A Genealogical Source Book, v. II, 38

Clark County, Arkansas: Past and Present, 38

Clark County, Arkansas Obituaries and Death Notices 1914-1921, Volume 3, 38

Clark County, Kentucky Taxpayers, 1793 thru 1799, 198

Clark County Historical Journal, 37

Clarke County, Georgia Records, 1801-1892, 98

Claverick, Old and New, 397

Clay Co. 1850 Census Transcription, 115

Clay Co. Index to Testators to 1880, 143

Clay County, Missouri Marriages 1821-1881, 327

Clay Co. Will Abstracts 1848-1867, 143

Clinton Co. 1850 Census Transcription, 115

Clinton Co. Index to Testators to 1880, 143

Clinton Co. Marriage Book I, 1830-1849, 143

Clinton County, Missouri: Births 1883-1889 & Death Records 1883-1888, 327

Clinton County, Missouri: Deaths from Area Newspapers 1876-1894, 327

Clinton County, Missouri: Deaths from Area Newspapers 1895-1899, 327

Clinton County, Missouri: Deaths from Area Newspapers 1900-1904, 327

Clinton County, Missouri: Deaths from Area Newspapers 1905-1907, 328

Clinton County, Missouri: Deaths from Area Newspapers 1908-1910, 328

Clinton Vital Records, 221

Cobb Co. GA Marriage Book 1865-1937 Whites, 1865-1966 Colored, 99

Cobb County GA Cemeteries, Vol. II, 99

Cobb County GA Cemeteries, Vol. III, 98

Cobb County GA Family Tree Quarterly, 98

Cobb County Georgia 1840 Census, 99

Cobb County Georgia Deed Book A, Vol. I, 99

Coeymans and the Past, 388

Robert Cole's World: Agriculture & Society in Early Maryland, 230, 252

Colonial and Revolutionary Families of Pennsylvania, 8

Colonial Arkansas, 1686-1804, 30

Colonial Augusta: "Key of the Indian Country," 104

Colonial Chesapeake Society, 230

Colonial Clergy and the Colonial Churches of New England, The, 7

Colonial Clergy of Maryland, Delaware and Georgia, The, 10

Colonial Clergy of the Middle Colonies, The, 10

Colonial Clergy of Virginia, North Carolina and South Carolina, The, 16

Colonial Delaware Records: 1681-1713, 80

Colonial Delaware Soldiers and Sailors, 1638-1776, 80

Colonial Families of Anne Arundel County, 239

Colonial Families of the Eastern Shore of Maryland, Vol. 1, 229

Colonial Families of the Eastern Shore of Maryland, Vol. 2, 230

Colonial Georgia Genealogical Data 1748-1783, 89

Colonial History of Hartford, Gathered from the Original Records, 70

Colonial History of the Parish of Mount Carmel, 75

Colonial Marriage Bonds, 1711-1797, 361

Colonial New York: A History, 381

Colonial Soldiers of the South, 1732-1774, 12

Colorado Families, Vol. I-A, 62

Columbia County, NY Gravestone Inscriptions, 394

Colusa County, 55

Combined History of Randolph, Monroe & Perry Cos., 127, 128, 129

Commemorating Frostburg's Percy Cemetery: Restoration and Research, 238

Commemorative Biographical Record of Dutchess County, 399

Commemorative Biographical Record of Ulster County, 432

Community: Birthplace of Popular Consent, A Salute to New York's Bicentennial Towns, 385

Compendium of Arkansas Genealogy, A, 48

Compendium of Early Mohawk Valley Families, 385

Compendium of History & Biography of Central & Northern Minnesota, 307

Compendium of History & Biography of Minneapolis & Hennepin County, 311

Compendium of History & Biography of Northern Minnesota, 307

Compendium of the Confederate Armies: Alabama, 20

Compendium of the Confederate Armies: Florida and Arkansas, 35, 85

Compendium of the Confederate Armies: Kentucky, Maryland, Missouri, the Confederate Units and the Indian Units, 191, 236, 321

Compendium of the Confederate Armies: Louisiana, 212

Compendium of the Confederate Armies: South Carolina and Georgia, 94

Compiled Records of the Middlesex County, New Jersey Militia, 1791-1795, 370

Complete Index to the Names of Persons, Places and Subjects Mentioned in Littell's Laws of Kentucky, A, 193

Complete TVA Burial Removal Records, 16

Comprehensive Index to AT Andreas' Illustrated Historical Atlas of Minnesota—1874, 306

Concise History of Orange County, The, 419

Concise History of Ulster County, The, 433

Concord Births, Marriages & Deaths, 1635-1850, 279

Concord in the Colonial Period, 285

Condensed History of Wright County, 1851-1935, 315

Confederate Arkansas: The People and Policies of a Frontier State in Wartime, 31

Confederate Cherokees: John Drew's Regiment of Mounted Rifles, 211

Confederate Florida: The Road to Olustee, 85

Confederate Imprints at the Georgia Historical Society, 91

Confederate Mobile, 25

Congregational Churches of the West, The, 18

Connecticut 1670 Census, 65

Connecticut 1800 Census Index, 66

Connecticut Colonists: Windsor 1635-1703, 70

Connecticut Inscriptions New Haven County, Guilford—North Guilford, 76

Connecticut, Maine, Massachusetts, and Rhode Island Atlas of Historical County Boundaries, 65, 215, 259

Connecticut Revolutionary Pensioners, 64

Connecticut Sources for Family Historians and Genealogists, 65

Connecting to Connecticut, 65

Contiguous Towns, Schuyler and Chemung Counties, The, 393, 427

Contributions for the Genealogies of the First Settlers of the Ancient County of Albany, from 1630 to 1800, 389

Contributions for the Genealogy of the Descendants of the First Settlers of the Patent & City of Schenectady from 1662 to 1800, 425

Contributions to the Early History of Perth Amboy & Adjoining Country, 370

Copiah County, Mississippi Taxpayers, 1825-1841, 317

Cornstalk Militia of Kentucky, 1792-1811, The, 183

Coronado's Land: Daily Life in Colonial New Mexico, 374

Coroner's Inquest Book Number 1, Marin County, California 1857-1910, 56

Coroners' Reports, New York City, 1823-1842, 417

Coroners' Reports, New York City, 1843-1849, 417

Counties, Cities, Towns and Plantations of Maine, 216

Counties of Clay & Owen [Indiana], Historical & Biographical, 143, 158

Counties of Cumberland, Jasper & Richland [Illinois], Historical & Biographical, 116, 120, 129

Counties of LaGrange & Noble [Indiana], Historical & Biographical, 152, 157

Counties of Morgan, Monroe & Brown [Indiana], 141, 155-156

Counties of Warren, Benton, Jasper & Newton [Indiana]: Historical & Biographical, 141, 150, 156, 165

Counties of White & Pulaski [Indiana]: Historical & Biographical, 159, 166

Counties of Whitley & Noble [Indiana]: Historical & Biographical, 157, 167

County Archives in the State of Illinois, The, 113

County Between the Lakes, The: Life and People to be Remembered Seneca County, New York, 1895, 428

County Between the Lakes, The: A Public History of Seneca County—1876-1982, 428

County Boundary Map Guides to the U.S. Federal Censuses, 1790-1920: Alabama, 1800-1920, 21

County Boundary Map Guides to the U.S. Federal Censuses, 1790-1920: Alaska, 1880-1920, 27

County Boundary Map Guides to the U.S. Federal Censuses, 1790-1920: Arizona, 1860-1920, 27

County Boundary Map Guides to the U.S. Federal Censuses, 1790-1920: Arkansas, 1810-1920, 35

County Boundary Map Guides to the U.S. Federal Censuses, 1790-1920: California, 1850-1920, 53

County Boundary Map Guides to the U.S. Federal Censuses, 1790-1920: Colorado, 1860-1920, 63

County Boundary Map Guides to the U.S. Federal Censuses, 1790-1920: Connecticut, Massachusetts, Rhode Island, 1790-1920, 66, 260

County Boundary Map Guides to the U.S. Federal Censuses, 1790-1920: Florida, 1830-1920, 85

County Boundary Map Guides to the U.S. Federal Censuses, 1790-1920: Georgia, 1790-1920, 94

County Boundary Map Guides to the U.S. Federal Censuses, 1790-1920: Hawaii, 1900-1920, 108

County Boundary Map Guides to the U.S. Federal Censuses, 1790-1920: Idaho, 1870-1920, 109

County Boundary Map Guides to the U.S. Federal Censuses, 1790-1920: Illinois, 1800-1920, 113

County Boundary Map Guides to the U.S. Federal Censuses, 1790-1920: Indiana, 1800-1920, 139

County Boundary Map Guides to the U.S. Federal Censuses, 1790-1920: Iowa, 1840-1920, 167

County Boundary Map Guides to the U.S. Federal Censuses, 1790-1920: Kansas, 1860-1920, 177

County Boundary Map Guides to the U.S. Federal Censuses, 1790-1920: Kentucky, 1790-1920, 194

County Boundary Map Guides to the U.S. Federal Censuses, 1790-1920: Louisiana, 1810-1920, 212

County Boundary Map Guides to the U.S. Federal Censuses, 1790-1920: Maine, 1790-1920, 217

County Boundary Map Guides to the U.S. Federal Censuses, 1790-1920: Maryland, Delaware, District of Columbia 1790-1920, 81

County Boundary Map Guides to the U.S. Federal Censuses, 1790-1920: Maryland, Delaware, District of Columbia, 1790-1920, 83, 237

County Boundary Map Guides to the U.S. Federal Censuses, 1790-1920: Michigan, 1810-1920, 301

County Boundary Map Guides to the U.S. Federal Censuses, 1790-1920: Minnesota, 1830-1920, 309

County Boundary Map Guides to the U.S. Federal Censuses, 1790-1920: Mississippi, 1800-1920, 317

County Boundary Map Guides to the U.S. Federal Censuses, 1790-1920: Missouri, 1810-1920, 323

County Boundary Map Guides to the U.S. Federal Censuses, 1790-1920: Montana, 1860-1920, 341

County Boundary Map Guides to the U.S. Federal Censuses, 1790-1920: Nebraska, 1860-1920, 342

County Boundary Map Guides to the U.S. Federal Censuses, 1790-1920: Nevada, 1860-1920, 347

County Boundary Map Guides to the U.S. Federal Censuses, 1790-1920: New Hampshire, Vermont, 1790-1920, 348

County Boundary Map Guides to the U.S. Federal Censuses, 1790-1920: New Jersey, 1790-1920, 363

County Boundary Map Guides to the U.S. Federal Censuses, 1790-1920: New Mexico, 1850-1920, 375

County Boundary Map Guides to the U.S. Federal Censuses, 1790-1920: New York, 1790-1920, 387

County Clerks in New York State, 384

County Court Note-book and Ancestral Proofs and Probabilities, The, 10, 14

County of Christian, Historical & Biographical, 197

Courts of Admiralty in Colonial America: The Maryland Experience, 1634-1776, 235

Coweta County, Georgia Chronicles, 99

Coweta County Chronicles for One Hundred Years, 99

Crane Cemetery in Volinia Township, Cass County, Michigan, 302

Crawford Co. Index to Testators to 1880, 143

Crawford Co. Marriages 1818-1849, 143

Creole New Orleans: Race and Americanization, 211

Crisp County, Georgia: Historical Sketches, Volume I, 99

Crossing the Border, 377

Cuddeback Cemetery in Paw Paw Township, Van Buren County, Michigan, 305

Cumberland County Genealogical Data, 366

Cumberland County, N.J. Marriages, 366

Cumulative Index to Nassau County Historical Society Journal (1958-1988), 415

Daily News' History of Buchanan County & St. Joseph, 325

Dansville, 1789-1902, 410

Danvers, 267

[Danvers] Report of the Committee Appointed to Revise the Soldiers' Records, 272

Daughters of the American Revolution, Lineage of Namaqua Chapter Members, Loveland, Colorado, January 8, 1914 Through October 31, 1994, 62

Davenport Past & Present, 175

Daviess Co. Index to Testators to 1880, 143

Dearborn Co. Index to Testators to 1880, 144

Dearborn Co. Marriages 1803-1849, 144

Death and Obituary Notices from the Southern Christian Advocate 1867-1878, 13

Death Notices from the Bel Air Times, 1882-1899, 248

Death Notices in Limestone County Newspapers, 1829-1891, 24

Death Records from Missouri Newspapers, January 1854-December 1860, 321

Death Records from Missouri Newspapers, Jan. 1866-Dec. 1870, 322

Death Records from the Ancient Burial Ground at Kingston, 289

Death Records from the Missouri Newspapers: The Civil War Years, Jan. 1861- Dec. 1865, 322

Death Records of Missouri Men, 1808-1854, 322

Death Records of Pioneer Missouri Women, 1808-1853, 322

Deaths Recorded in Minneapolis City Directories 1887-1900, 311

Deaths Recorded in Minneapolis City Directories 1901-1910, 311

Deaths Recorded in St. Paul City Directories 1888-1910, 313

Decatur Co. Index to Testators to 1880, 144

Decatur Co. Marriages 1822-1849, 144

Declaration of Intention (First Papers) to Become a Citizen of the United States: Arapahoe (Denver) County Court, 63

Declarations of Intention of Santa Clara County, California 1850-1870, 52, 58

Dedham, 1635-1890, 286

Deed Abstracts of Warren County, Kentucky, 1797-1812, 208

Deed Abstracts of Warren County, Kentucky, 1812-1821, 208

DeKalb Co. 1855 State Census, 117

DeKalb Co. Index to Testators to 1880, 145

DeKalb Marriages 1837-1849, 145

Delaware Advertiser, 1827-1831: Genealogical Extracts, 80

Delaware Co. Index to Testators to 1880, 145

Delaware County: History of the Century, 1797-1897, 398

Delaware Genealogical Research Guide, 80

Delaware Genealogical Society Surname Index, 81

Delaware Historical and Genealogical Recall, The, 80

Delaware Indians: A Brief History, 375

Delaware Trails: Some Tribal Records, 1842-1907, 79

Delayed Birth Records at Dearborn County, Indiana, 144

Delegates to the Saint Joseph Constitutional Convention, 1838-1839. Final Report, 84

Denizations, Naturalizations, and Oaths of Allegiance in Colonial New York, 386

Dennis Vital Records, 1793-1900, 261

Des Moines, 174

Descendants of Noah and Margaret Crosby Mullin: A Scrapbook Family History, 141

Deserters and Disbanded Soldiers from British, German, and Loyalist Military Units in the South, 1782, 15

DeSoto Parish, Louisiana—Loose Marriages 1837-1860 & Marriage Book A 1843-1860, 213

Detroit River Connections, 301

Devil in the Shape of a Woman, The: Witchcraft in Colonial New England, 5

Devil's Disciples, The: Makers of the Salem Witchcraft Trials, 269

DeWitt Co. History Index, 117

Diaries of Samuel Mickle, Woodbury, Gloucester County, New Jersey 1792-1829, The, 367

Diary of Job Whitall, Gloucester

County, New Jersey 1775-1779, The, 367

Diary of Joshua Hempstead 1711-1758, 77

Diary of Matthew Patten of Bedford, New Hampshire 1754-1788, The, 353

Dictionary of the American West, 17

Digest of the Early Connecticut Probate Records, A, 65

Digging for Genealogical Treasure in New England Town Records, 5

Directory of Cayuga County Residents Who Supported Publication of the History of Cayuga County, New York, A, 392

Directory of Genealogical and Historical Articles Published in "de Halve Maen" from 1923 to 1991, 7

Directory of Local Historical, Museum and Genealogical Agencies in Missouri, 320, 323

Directory of Maryland Church Records, 233

Directory of Maryland's Burial Grounds, Vol. 1, 239, 244, 250, 251

Directory of Massachusetts Photographers 1831-1900, A, 260

Directory of Repositories of Family History in New Hampshire, 348

Directory of the Ancestral Heads of New England Families, 1620-1700, 4

Directory to Collections of New York Vital Records, 1726-1989, with Rare Gazetteer, 376

District of Columbia Marriage Licenses: 1811-1858, 83

District of Columbia Marriages, Early to 1825, 83

District of Columbia Probate Records, 1801-1852, 83

Divorces and Separations in Missouri, 1808-1853, 322

Doctors in Gray: The Confederate Medical Service, 211

Documentary History of Chelsea, A, 292

Documentary History of Rhinebeck, in Dutchess Co., 402

Documentary History of Rhinebeck, NY, 402

Documentary History of Suffield, in the Colony & Province of Massachusetts Bay in New England, 1660-1749, 71

Documentary History of the Dutch Congregation of Oyster Bay, Queens Co., 421

Documentary History of Yonkers, New York, Volume One: The Formative Years, 1820-1862, 436

Documentary History of Yonkers, New York, Volume Two, Part One: The Unsettled Years, 1863-1860, 436

Documentary History of Yonkers, New York, Volume Two, Part Two: The Dutch, the English, and an Incorporated American Village, 1609-1860, 436

Documents & Biography Pertaining to the Settlement & Progress of Stark Co., 131

Dodge County Newspaper Clippings, Vol. I, 1873-1892, 100

Dodge County Newspaper Clippings, Vol. II, 1893-1907, 100

Dodge County Newspaper Clippings, Vol. III, 1908-1919, 100

Dodge County Newspaper Clippings, Vol. IV, 1920-1928, 100

Doniphan County Cemeteries and Burial Sites, 169

Douglas Co. Cemetery Inscriptions, 117

Douglas County, Missouri 1880s Gazetteer, 329

Douglas County, Missouri Marriages 1840s-1900 (Reconstructed), 329

Dover, New Hampshire Vital Records, 359

Dover Farms, 287

Du Page County, Illinois Genealogical Records, 118

Dubois Co. Index to Testators to 1880, 146

Dubros Times: Depositions of Revolutionary War Veterans, 216

DuPage Landowners, 117

Dutch and the Iroquois, The, 379

Dutch New York, 387

Dutch Settlement Church, The: West Berlin, New York, 423

Dutch Systems in Family Naming, New York-New Jersey, 360, 376

Dutch Village Communities of the Hudson, 408, 432

(Dutchess Co.) History of "Little 9 Partners" of the N.E. Precinct & Pine Plains, 400

Dutchess County, NY, Churches and Their Records: Historical Directory, 402

Dutchess County, NY Tax Lists, 1718-1787, 399, 421

Dutchess County Probate Records: 1773-1865, 401

Earliest Tax Lists of Allen Co., KY 1815-1824, 195

Early and Modern History of Wolfe County, 208

Early Anglican Church Records of Cecil County, 244

Early Annals of Newington, 72

Early Arkansas Residents, 1814-1816, 31

Early Catholic Church Records in Baltimore, Maryland, 1782-1800, 242

Early Charles County, MD, Settlers, 1658-1745, 245

Early Church Records of Atlantic and Cape May Counties, New Jersey, 364, 366

Early Church Records of Bergen County, New Jersey, 1740-1800, 364

Early Church Records of Burlington County, 365

Early Church Records of Gloucester County, New Jersey, 368

Early Church Records of Groton, 1706-1830, 280

Early Church Records of New Castle County, DE, Vol. 1: 1701-1800, 82

Early Church Records of New Castle County, DE, Vol. 2: Old Swedes Church 1713-1799, 81

Early Church Records of Salem County, N.J., 373

Early Connecticut Marriages, 64

Early Court Records of Pulaski County, Georgia 1809-1825, 104

Early Days in Arkansas: Being for the Most Part the Personal Recollections of an Old Settler, 34

Early Days in Greenbush, 133

Early Days in Newington, 1833-1836, 70

Early Days of Norridgewock, 226

Early Days of Rock Island [IL] & Davenport [IA], 130, 175

Early Deaths in Savannah, GA 1763-1803: Obituaries and Legal Notices from Savannah Newspapers, 97

Early Families of Eastern and Southeastern Kentucky and Their Descendants, 188

Early Families of Gouldsboro Maine, 220

Early Families of Herkimer County, New York, 407

Early Families of Southern Maryland, 233

Early Families of Wallingford, Connecticut, 75

Early Georgia Wills and Settlements of Estates, Wilkes County, Georgia, 107

Early Germans of New Jersey, Their History, Churches, and Genealogy, 360

Early Histories of Belfast Maine, 226

Early History of Covert, Seneca County, 428

Early History of Leavenworth, City & County, 179

Early History of Lincoln County, 312

Early History of Saugerties, The, 432

Early History of Southampton, Long Island, with Genealogies, 411

Early History of the Town of Ellicott [Part of Johnstown], Chautauqua Co., 392

Early History of the Town of Hopkinton, 429

Early History of Upson County, Georgia, The, 106

Early History of Wilmot, The, 355

Early Indiana Trails and Surveys, 139

Early Kaskaskia, Illinois, Newspapers: 1814-1832, 110

Early Kentucky Householders, 1787-1811, 193

Early Kentucky Landholders, 1787-1811, 193

Early Kentucky Settlers, 184

Early Lawrence County, Arkansas, Records, 1817-1830, 44

Early Life & Times in Boone County, 141

Early Long Island Wills of Suffolk County, 1691-1703, 430

Early Louisville, Kentucky, Newspaper Abstracts, 1806-1828, 136, 184

Early Marriages of Baxter County, 36

Early Marriages Riley County, Kansas, 1855-1886, 181

Early Massachusetts Marriages Prior to 1800, 255, 288

Early Missouri Ancestors, Vol I, 322

Early Missouri Ancestors, Vol. II, 322

Early Missouri Marriages in the News, 1820-1853, 322

Early Naturalization Records—Wayne Co., IN, 165

Early Nineteenth-Century German Settlers in Ohio, Kentucky, and Other States, 193

Early Northampton, 277

Early Planters of Scituate, 291

Early Presbyterian Church Records from Minnesota 1835-1871, 309

Early Quaker Marriages from Various Records in N.J., 360

Early Records . . . of Albany . . . Rensselaerswych (Mortgages and Wills 1652-1660), 389

Early Records of Georgia: Wilkes County, 107

Early Records of the First Presbyterian Church at Goshen, New York, from 1767 to 1885, The, 419

Early Records of the LeSueur River Church of Waseca and Steele Counties, 314

Early Records of the Town of Lunenburg, 295

Early Settlements in Dutchess County, New York, A Compilation of the "Why. . .?" Stories, 400

Early Settlers of Alabama, 20

Early Settlers of Barbour County, Alabama, Vols. 1 and 2, 21

Early Settlers of Maryland, The, 236

Early Settlers of Nantucket, The, 285

Early Settlers of Rowley, 267

Early Wayne Co., IN Probate & Will Index, 165

Early Wills of Westchester County, New York from 1664-1784, 437

East Hartford: Its History and Traditions, 70

East Haven Register, in Three Parts (History & Vital Records), 75

East Kill Valley Genealogy, 403

Eastern Arkansas Death Record Index, 1914-1923: Clay, Craighead, Crittenden, Cross, Greene, Lee, Mississippi, Monroe, Phillips, Poinsett, and St. Francis Counties, 29

Eastern Arkansas Death Record Index, 1934-1940: Clay, Craighead,

Crittenden, Cross, Greene, Lee, Mississippi, Monroe, Phillips, Poinsett, and St. Francis Counties, 29

Eastport, Maine Vital Records, 227

Eastport & Passamaquoddy, 227

Ebenezer Record Book, 1754-1781, 100

Echoes of Yesteryears: Shiawassee County Schools, Antrim and Perry Townships, 1837-1987 Volume 8, 304

Echoes of Yesteryears: Shiawassee County Schools, Woodhull Township, Historical Records 1837-1962, County Rural School Teachers 1893-1934 Volume 9, 304

Edwards County 1825 State Census, 118

Edwards Co. 1850 Census Transcription, 119

Electronic Records [New York State], 384

Elegant Mistake, An, 407

Elkhart Co. Index to Testators to 1880, 146

Ellsworth. A Gossip About a Country Parish of the Hills, and Its People, a Century After Its Birth, 67

Elmira Prison Camp, The, 393

Elmore County, Alabama Marriage Records 1881-1893, 22

Enclosed Garden, The: Women & Community in the Evangelical South, 1830-1900, 12

Encyclopedia of Genealogy & Biography of Lake County, 152

Encyclopedia of New York State Ephemera & Americana, 383

Encyclopedia of the New West of Texas, Arkansas, Colorado, New Mexico and Indian Territory, 17

English Ancestry and Homes of the Pilgrim Fathers, The, 1

Entertaining Satan: Witchcraft and the Culture of Early New England, 4

Epitaphs from Burial Hill, Plymouth, Massachusetts, from 1657 to 1892, 289

Epitaphs in the Old Burying Ground of Deerfield, 274

Era of the Civil War, The [Illinois]: 1848-1870, 110

Ethnic Heritage in Mississippi, 315

Events of the Civil War in Washington County, Maryland, 253

Every Name Index to 1887 Atlas of Delaware County, 145

Every Name Index to the 1895 Plat Book of Freeborn County with Reprints of Selected Maps, 311

Every Name Index to the 1900 Standard Atlas of Grant County Minnesota, 311

Everyname Index to History of Allegany County Maryland, 239

Every-Name Index to Revolutionary Soldiers and Their Descendants, An: Missouri Edition, 320

Executive Journal of Indiana Territory, 139

(Fairfield) An Old New England Town: Sketches of Life, Scenery, Character, 67

Fairfield's Pioneer History of Lassen County, 55

Faithful and the Bold, The, 369

Families of Ancient New Haven, 65, 75

Families of Bergen County, New Jersey, 364

Families of Burke County, Georgia, 1755-1855, The, 97

Families of Early Hartford, Connecticut, 69

Families of Early Milford, Connecticut, 74

Families of the Pilgrims, 259

Families of Western New York, 377

Family Associations: Organization & Management, 52

Family Bible Records [Illinois]—Volume 1, 111

Family Bible Records [Illinois]—Volume 2, 111

Family History Centers: California, 51

Family History Centers: Mountain States, 17

Family History Centers: Nevada and Utah, 346

Family History Centers: North Central States, 16

Family History Centers: Northeastern States, 4

Family History Centers: Northwestern States and Hawaii, 17

Family History Centers: Southern States, 12

Family History Centers: Southwestern States, 17

Family of Rose of Kilravock [Scotland], 52

Family Records, or Genealogies of the First Settlers of Passaic Valley, 361

Family Register of the Inhabitants of Shrewsbury, 299

Family Venture, A: Men & Women on the Southern Frontier, 12

Farmingdale Vital Records to the Year 1892, 221

Fascinating Old Town on the Island in the Sea, 285

Fathers of the Ridge, 41

Fathers of the Towns, The: Leadership and Community Structure in 18th-Century New England, 3

Faulkner County Marriage Index 1873-1925, Volume I, 40

Fayette Co. Index to Testators to 1880, 146

Fayette Co. Will Records 1819-1895, 146

Fayette Co. Wills & Estates 1788-1822, 199

Fayetteville, Arkansas, National Cemetery, 50

Federal Naturalizations for the 1st District of Kansas Northeast 1856-1902, 177

Federal Road Through Georgia, the Creek Nation, and Alabama, 1806-1836, The, 20, 94

Ferguson-Jayne Papers, 398

Few of Our Friends in the Amador County Cemeteries, A, 54

Fifty Years in the Northwest, 307

Finding Aid for Naturalization Documents of San Mateo County, California, A, 57

Finding Aid (Index) for Scrapbook History of Decatur, Michigan 1829-1976, 300

First Alfred Seventh Day Baptist Church Membership Records, Alfred, NY, 390

First Arkansas Confederate Mounted Rifles, 29

First Boston City Directory (1789) Including Extensive Annotations by John Haven Dexter (1791-1876), 293

"First Census" of Kentucky, The: 1790, 186

First Century of the History of Springfield, The, 275

First Congregational Church of Preston, 1698-1898, 77

First Dorchester Families, 246

First Hundred Years, The, 1835-1936: Historical Review of Blue Island, 116

First Hundred Years, The, 1873-1973: White Cloud Area, 304

1st Land Entry Book of Union Co., IN, 163

1st Land Entry Book of Wayne Co., IN, 165

First Laws of the Commonwealth of Massachusetts, The, 257

First Laws of the State of Connecticut, The, 64

First Laws of the State of Delaware, The, 80

First Laws of the State of Georgia, The, 90

First Laws of the State of Maryland, The, 232

First Laws of the State of New Hampshire, The, 347

First Laws of the State of New Jersey, The, 360

First Laws of the State of New York, The, 378

First Parishes of the Province of Maryland, The, 236

First Presbyterian Church of Durham, 405

[First] Supplement to Torrey's New England Marriages Prior to 1700, 6

Fishers Island, N.Y., 1614-1925, 430

Fitchburg, Past & Present, 295

Fledgling Province, The: Social and Cultural Life in Colonial Georgia, 1733-1776, 88

Fleming County, Kentucky, Taxpayers, 1798 & 1799, 199

Fleming Co. Wills & Estates 1798-1822, Vol. I, 199

Fleming Co. Wills & Estates 1822-1834, Vol. II, 199

Flight of a Century (1800-1900) in Ascension Parish, The, 212

Florida Connections Through Bible Records. Volume I, 85

Florida County Atlas and Municipal Fact Book, 84

Florida Genealogist, The, Index, Volumes I-X, 1977-1987, 84

Florida Juror and Witness Certificates, Hillsborough Co. 1848-1860, 1862, 1885 and Holmes Co. 1848-1852, 1854-1855, 1857-1862, 1879, 1880, 1884, 86

Florida Juror and Witness Certificates, Jackson County 1848-64, 1866, 1870-77, 86

Florida Juror and Witness Certificates, Jefferson Co. 1849-1860, 1873, 1875, 1881 and Lafayette Co. 1859-1860, 1871, 1874-1875, 1877, 1879, 1881, 1884, 86

Florida Juror and Witness Certificates, Levy County 1852-1854, 1856-1857, 1861 and Liberty County 1859-1862, 1879-1881, 87

Florida Prison Records, 1875 through 1899, 84

Florida State Genealogical Society, Inc., Surname Directory 1995, 84

Florida Voter Registration Lists 1867-68, 85

Florida Voters in Their First Statewide Election, May 26, 1845, 85

Flowering of the Maryland Palatinate, The, 234

Floyd Co., Ga. 1890 - A Census Substitute - Vol. VII, 101

Floyd Co., Ga. Confederates - Vol. VIII, 101

Floyd Co., Ga. Marriages - Vol. I, The Early Years 1834-1884 2nd Ed., 101

Floyd Co., Ga. Marriages - Vol. II, 1883-1900, 101

Floyd Co., Ga. Marriages - Vol. IV, 3rd Ed., 101

Floyd Co., Ga. Miscellany - Vol. III, 2nd Ed., 101

Floyd Co., Ga. Vital Statistics - Vols. V & VI, 101

Floyd Co. Index to Testators to 1880, 147

Folklore and Firesides of Pomfret and Hampton, and Vicinity, 79

Footprints Through Idaho, 109

Foreign-Born Voters of California in 1872, The, 52

Forgotten People: Cane River's Creole of Color, 211

Forks of Elkhorn Church, 102

Formative Period in Alabama, 1815-1828, The, 19

Fort Smith, Arkansas, National Cemetery, 49

Forty-fifth Arkansas Confederate Cavalry, 29

Founders of Anne Arundel and Howard Counties, Maryland, The, 240, 250

Founding of New Acadia: The Beginning of Acadian Life in Louisiana, 1765-1803, 211

Fountain Co. Biographical Abstracts, 147

Fountain Co. Index to Testators to 1880, 147

Four Centuries on the Pascagoula, 318

Fourteenth Arkansas Confederate Infantry, The, 29

Fourth or 1821 Land Lotteries of Georgia, The, 92

Franklin, Jefferson, Washington, Crawford and Gasconade Counties (Missouri) (A History of), 328, 330, 332, 340

Franklin Co. Index to Testators to 1880, 147

Frederick County Backgrounds, 247

Frederick County Index to Scharf's History of Western Maryland, 247

Frederick County, Maryland, Genealogical Research Guide, 247

Frederick County Maryland Land Records, Liber B Abstracts, 1748-1752, 246

Frederick County Maryland Land Records, Liber E Abstracts, 1752-1756, 246

Frederick County Maryland Land Records, Liber F Abstracts, 1756-1761, 246

Frederick County Maryland Land Records, Liber G & H Abstracts, 1761-1763, 247

Frederick County Militia in the War of 1812, 247

Free African Americans of North Carolina and Virginia, 13

Freeman of Massachusetts, 1630-1691, 259

Fremont Township Cemeteries, 122

French and British Land Grants in the Post Vincennes (Indiana) District, 1750-1784, 138

French and Spanish Records of LA: A Bibliographical Guide to Archive and Manuscript Sources, 211

Friends of Illiana, 1826, 132

From Slavery to Uncertain Freedom: The Freedmen's Bureau in Arkansas, 1865-1869, 31

From the Great Cooks Among Us, 422

Frontier State (IL), 1818-1848, The, 112

Frontiers Aflame, 381

Frontiersmen of New York, 387

Fryeburg, Maine, 223

Fulton County, Arkansas, Folks, 1890-1893, 41

Fulton County, Arkansas, Tax Records 1849-1868, 41

Fulton Co. Index to Testators to 1880, 147

Fulton Co. Marriages 1835-1849, 147

Funeral Records in Greene County, MO: Alma Lohmeyer - Jewell E. Windle Funeral Home 1919-1932, 331

Funeral Records in Greene County, MO: Paxson Funeral Home Records 1900-1926, 331

Funeral Records in Greene County, MO: Register of Interment in Hazelwood Cemetery 1868-1915, 331

Funeral Records in Greene County, MO: Republic Funeral Home 1908-1978, 331

Funeral Records in Greene County, MO: Will & Alma Lohmeyer Funeral Home Records 1904-1918, 331

Gadsden Times, 1867-1871, The, 23

Garrard Co. Wills & Estates 1796-1819, Vol. I, 199

Garrard Co. Wills & Estates 1819-1833, Vol. II, 199

Garrett County Index for Scharf's History of Western Maryland, 248

Gazetteer of Grafton County, 1709-1886, 351

Gazetteer of Maryland and Delaware, A, 80, 232

Gazetteer of the State of Michigan, 300

Gazetteer of the State of New Jersey, A, 360

Gazetteer of the State of New York, 379

Gazetteer (1824) of the State of New York, 387

Gazetteer (1860) of the State of New York, 378

Gazetteer of the States of Connecticut & R.I., 65

Geary County Kansas Cemeteries Except Those in Junction City, 178

Genealogical Abstracts from Georgia Journal (Milledgeville), Newspaper 1809-1840: Vol. 1, 1809-1818, 90

Genealogical Abstracts from Georgia Journal (Milledgeville), Newspaper 1809-1840: Vol. 2, 1819-1823, 90

Genealogical Abstracts from Georgia Journal (Milledgeville), Newspaper 1809-1840: Vol. 3, 1824-1828, 91

Genealogical Abstracts from Georgia Journal (Milledgeville), Newspaper 1809-1840: Vol. 4, 1829-1835, 91

Genealogical Abstracts from Georgia Journal (Milledgeville), Newspaper 1809-1840: Vol. 5, 1836-1840, 89

Genealogical Abstracts from Palmyra, Wayne County, New York Newspapers 1810-1854, 435

Genealogical Advertiser, The [Massachusetts], 257

Genealogical and Family History of Central New York, 377

Genealogical and Family History of Southern New York and the Hudson River Valley, 385

Genealogical and Family History of the State of Connecticut, 64

Genealogical and Memorial Encyclopedia of the State of Maryland, 236

Genealogical and Personal Memoirs [Massachusetts], 257

Genealogical Atlas of Indiana, 136

Genealogical Data from Colonial New Haven Newspapers, 76

Genealogical Data from Colonial New York Newspapers, 386

Genealogical Data from Inventories of New York Estates 1666-1825, 386

Genealogical Data from New York Administration Bonds 1753-1799, 387

Genealogical Data from the New York Post Boy, 1743-1773, 387

Genealogical Dictionary of Maine and New Hampshire, 215, 216, 348

Genealogical Dictionary of the First Settlers of New England, A, 6

Genealogical Gleanings in England, 7

Genealogical History of Dover, The, 287

Genealogical History of Hudson & Bergen Counties, 364, 368

Genealogical History of the Town of Reading, 280

Genealogical Index to the Records of the Society of Colorado Pioneers, 62

Genealogical Journal of Jefferson Co., New York, 409

Genealogical Library Collection Shelf List, Paradise Genealogical Society, 53

Genealogical Material from Legal Notices in Early Georgia Newspapers, 90

Genealogical Notes [of the First Settlers of Connecticut and Massachusetts], 64, 257

Genealogical Notes of Barnstable Families, 261

Genealogical Notes of New York and New England Families, 6, 387

Genealogical Notes on the Founding of New England, 4

Genealogical Records [New York State], 386

Genealogical Register of Plymouth Families, 288

Genealogical Register of the First Settlers of New England, 1620-1675, A, 4

Genealogical Register of the Inhabitants & History of Sherborn & Holliston, 283

Genealogical Register of the Inhabitants of the Town of Litchfield, Conn., A, 74

Genealogical Research in Maryland: A Guide, 234

Genealogical Resources in Southern New Jersey, 360, 363, 365-367, 372-373

Genealogical Resources in the New York Metropolitan Area, 415

Genealogical Sources in the New York State Archives, 384

Genealogical Sources Reprinted from the Genealogical Section, Indiana Magazine of History, 138

Genealogical & Ecclesiastical History of New Britain, 69

Genealogies of Hadley [Massachusetts] Families, 277

Genealogies of Long Island Families, 411

Genealogies of New Jersey Families, 360

Genealogies of the Early Families of Weymouth, Massachusetts, 285

Genealogies of the Families of Cohasset Massachusetts, 286

Genealogies of the Families & Descendants of the Early Settlers of Watertown, 279

Genealogies & Estates of Charlestown, 1629-1818, 294

Genealogist's Handbook for New England Research, 5

Genealogy of Early Settlers in Trenton and Ewing, "Old Hunterdon County," New Jersey, 369

Genealogy of the French Families of the Detroit River Region 1701-1936, The, 301

Genealogy Success Stories: Personal Problem-solving Accounts That Encourage, Enlighten and Inspire You, 51

General History of Missouri from Earliest Times to the Present, 320

General History Section Index of Scharf's History of Western Maryland, 233

General Index to the Documents Relating to the Colonial History of the State of New Jersey, 362

Generals in Blue: Lives of the Union Commanders, 211

Generals in Gray: Lives of the Confederate Commanders, 211

Genesee Valley of Western New-York, 384

Gentry County, Missouri 1861 Tax Assessors Book, 330

Gentry County, Missouri Birth Records, 1868-1900, 330

Gentry County, Missouri Court Minute Records (Revised to One Vol.) 1845-1859, 330

Gentry County, Missouri Deaths, 1868-1910, 330

Gentry County, Missouri Marriage Index from Various Sources, 1885-1912 A-M, 330

Gentry County, Missouri Marriage Index from Various Sources, 1885-1912 N-Z, 330

Gentry County, Missouri Probate Index, 1885-1902, 330

Geographic Dictionary of Massachusetts, A, 257

Geographic Dictionary of New Jersey, 360

Geographical Gazetteer & Business Directory of Jefferson Co., 1684-1890, 409

Georgia 1870 Census Index, 93

Georgia Baptists: Historical and Biographical, 88

Georgia Black Book, The, Volume I: Morbid, Macabre, and Disgusting Records of Genealogical Value, 88

Georgia Black Book, The, Volume II: More Morbid, Macabre, and Sometimes Disgusting Records of Genealogical Value, 88

Georgia Citizens and Soldiers of the American Revolution, 89

Georgia County Biographical Series, Bryan County, 96

Georgia County Biographical Series, Burke County, 97

Georgia County Biographical Series, Chattooga County, 98

Georgia County Biographical Series, Dade County, 99

Georgia County Biographical Series, Effingham County, 101

Georgia County Biographical Series, Floyd County, 101

Georgia County Biographical Series, Walker County, 106

Georgia County Biographical Series, Wilkes County, 107

Georgia Genealogical Gems, 91

Georgia Genealogical Research, 93

Georgia Genealogy and Local History: A Bibliography, 89

Georgia Gold Rush, The: Twenty-Niners, Cherokees, and Gold Fever, 95

Georgia Governor and Council Journal, 1753-1760, 95

Georgia Governor and Council Journal, 1761-1767, 95

Georgia Intestate Records, 87

Georgia Land Lottery Papers, 1805-1914, The, 92

[Georgia] Marriages and Deaths, 1820 to 1830, Abstracted from Extant Georgia Newspapers, 95

Georgia Marriages, Early to 1800, 92

Georgia Marriages, 1801 to 1825, 92

Georgia Revolutionary War Soldiers' Graves, 87

Georgia Scenes, 90

Georgia: The WPA Guide to Its Towns & Countryside, 95

Georgians, The, 87

Georgians in the Revolution: At Kettle Creek (Wilkes Co.) and Burke County, 97, 107

Georgia's Roster of the Revolution, 91

German Regiment of Maryland and Pennsylvania, 235

Germans of Colonial Georgia, 1733-1783, The, 91

Gibson Co. Index to Testators to 1880, 147

Gillford, 314

Gilmer County, Georgia Heritage 1832-1996, 102

Gilmer's Georgians (Sketches of Early Settlers of Upper Georgia, the Cherokees and the Author), 90

Given Name Index to the Genealogical Magazine of New Jersey. Volume III, 363

Given Name Index to the Genealogical Magazine of New Jersey. Volume IV, 363

Glastonbury for Two Hundred Years: A Centennial Discourse, May 18th, 1853, 70

Glen Ellyn—The Story of an Old Town, 117

Glimpses of Old New England Life: Legends of Old Bedford, 279

Gloucester County Marriages, 367

Gloucester County Residents, 1850, 367

Gloucester Town and City Records Guide, 267

Gold! German Transcontinental Travelers to California, 1849-1851, 53

Golden Door: Italian and Jewish Immigrant Mobility in New York City, 1880-1915, 416

Gone But Not Forgotten: Cemetery Survey of the Eastern District, Douglas County, Missouri, 329

Gone to Georgia, 94

Good Old Times [Cumberland County, Maine], 219

Good Old Times in McLean County, 127

Good Wives: Image and Reality in the Lives of Women in Northern New England, 1650-1750, 7

Goodenows Who Originated in Sudbury, Massachusetts 1638 A.D., 51, 84, 167, 307, 376

Gorhamtown: A Pictorial History, 218

Gott's Island, Maine: Its People 1880-1992, 220

Govans, Village and Suburb, 241

Grand Army of the Republic—Missouri Division—Index to Death Rolls, 1882-1940, 320

Grand Jurors of Montgomery County, New York, 1816-1850, 405, 407-408, 414

Grand Rapids & Kent County, 303

Grandin (Carter County), MO Records: 1888-1912, 326

Grant Co. Index to Testators to 1880, 147

Grant Township Cemeteries, 122

Granville Cemetery Inscriptions, Washington County, New York, 434

Grave Importance, Of, 36

Grave Markers in Burke County, Georgia, with Thirty-nine Cemeteries in Four Adjoining Counties, 97

Grave Markers of Hennepin County Vol. 1, 311

Grave Markers of Hennepin County Vol. 2, 311

Graves County, Kentucky Tax Lists 1839 and 1840, 200

Graves of Montgomery, Treutlen, and Wheeler, 104-105, 107

Gravestone Chronicles: Some Eighteenth-Century New England Carvers and Their Work, 1

Gravestone Records in the Ancient Cemetery & the Woodside Cemetery in Yarmouth, 261

Gravestones of Guildhall, Vt. & Northumberland, N.H, 351

Graveyards of Boston, The, 294

Great Doctor Waddel (Pronounced Waddle), The, 14

Great Migration Begins, The: Immigrants to New England 1620-1633, 1

Great Register, The. 1880 Voter Registration of Yuba County, California, 60

Great Register of Marin County, California 1890, 56

Great Register of Voters Sonoma County 1890, 59

Great Wagon Road from Philadelphia to the South, The: How Scotch-Irish and Germanics Settled the Uplands, 15

Greene Co. Index to Testators to 1880, 148

Green County, Kentucky Births 1852-1879 and 1904, 200

Green County, Kentucky Deaths 1852-1879 and 1904, 200

Green County, Kentucky Marriages 1852-1903, 200

Green County, Kentucky, Taxpayers, 1795-1799, 200

Greene Co. Marriages Vol. I 1821-1844, 148

Greene Co. Marriages Vol. II 1845-1852, 148

Greene County, MO Cemeteries: Vol. 8 Pond Creek & Center Twps., Including White Chapel Cemetery in Campbell Twp, 331

Greene County, MO Cemeteries: Vol. 9 Campbell Twp. & Springfield (excluding large cemeteries), 331

Greene County, MO Cemeteries: Vol. 10 Maple Park Cemetery, 331

Greene County, MO Federal Census: 1840 Census & Map, 331

Greene County, MO Federal Census: 1900 Census & Map, Vol. 1 Boone & Walnut Grove Twp., 331

Greene County, MO Federal Census: 1900 Census & Map, Vol. 2 Cass, Murray, Robberson, Franklin, & Jackson Townships, 331

Greene County, MO Marriages: Book D-E 1874-1881, 331

Greene County, MO Marriages: Book F-G 1881-1885, 331

Greene County, MO Marriages: Book H-I 1885-1891, 332

Greene County, MO Marriages: Book J-K 1891-1895, 332

Greene Genes: A Genealogical Quarterly About Greene County, New York, 406

Griffin's Journal: First Settlers of Southold, 430

Griswold—A History, 78

Groton During the Indian Wars, 280

Groton During the Revolution, 280

Groton Historical Series, 280

Growing Up in the 1850's: The Journal of Agnes Lee, 13

Guide to 1910 Federal Census of Riley County Kansas, 181

Guide to 1841-1895 Indexes of Massachusetts Vital Records, 258

Guide to Cemetery Names & Locations in Lake County IL, 122

Guide to Family History Sources in the New Jersey State Archives, 361

Guide to Faulkner County, Arkansas, Loose Probate Packets, 1873-1917, 40

Guide to IL Researchers & Local Societies, 111

Guide to Kentucky Archival and Manuscript Collections, Vol. 1 (Albany-Burkesville), 187

Guide to Kentucky Archival and Manuscript Collections, Vol. 2 (Cadiz-Eminence), 187

Guide to Kentucky Archival and Manuscript Repositories, The, 186, 187

Guide to Kentucky Birth, Marriage, and Death Records (1852-1910), A, 186, 187

Guide to Louisiana Confederate Military Units, 1861-1865, 211

Guide to Manuscript Collections of the Indiana Historical Society and Indiana State Library, A, 138

Guide to Public Vital Statistics Records in Illinois, 114

Guide to Records in the New York State Archives, A, 384

Guide to Records Relating to Native Americans [in the New York State Archives], 384

Guide to Records Relating to the Revolutionary War [in the New York State Archives], 384

Guide to Research in Baltimore City and County, 241

Guide to State [Maryland] Agency Records—Histories and Series Descriptions, 234

Guide to the Acadians in Maryland in the 18th and 19th Centuries, A, 212, 237

Guide to the First Fifty Years of the Detroit Genealogical Magazine, The, 306

Guide to the Minnesota State Census Microfilm, 307

Guide to the Research Collections of the Maryland Historical Society, 231

Guide to Vital Statistics Record in Indiana, 139

Gulf Coast Colonials, 210

Guntersville Reservoir Cemeteries, 23, 25

Haddock's Centennial History of Jefferson County, 409

Half-Century of Minneapolis, A, 311

Nathan Hale and John Andre, Reluctant Heroes of the American Revolution, 411

Hames Collection: Pre-Statehood Land Records, 111

Hamilton Cemetery, Hamilton Township, Van Buren County, Michigan, 305

Hamilton Co. Index to Testators to 1880, 148

Hamilton Co. Marriage Records 1833-1843, 148

Hamilton Co. Naturalization Records 1855-1905, 148

Hamilton Co. Will Records 1823-1834, 148

Hamilton Co. Will Records 1835-1844, 148

Hammatt Papers, The, 269

Hancock Co. Index to Testators to 1880, 149

Hanover, 288

Hardin County, Illinois Deaths 1884-1919 and Notes from the Pleasant Hill Church Register, 119

Harford County, Maryland, Bible and Family Records, Vol. I, 248

Harford County, Maryland, Bible and Family Records, Vol. II, 248

Harford County Marriage Licenses, 1777-1865, 249

Harford County Wills, 1774-1800, 249

Harlan Co. 1850 Census, 200

Harrison Cemetery in Decatur Van Buren County, Michigan, 305

Harrison Co. Index to Testators to 1880, 149

Harrison Co. Marriage Register & Bonds 1794-1832, 200

Harrison Co. Marriages 1809-1849, 149

Harrison Co. Wills 1795-1818, Vol. I, 200

Harrison Co. Wills 1819-1832, Vol. II, 200

Harrison County, Kentucky Taxpayers, 1794 thru 1799, 200

Haskins Genealogy: The Descendants of Jonas Haskins (1788-1837) of Dutchess Co., New York, and Uhrichsville, Ohio, 402

Hatch, Match & Dispatch, Book 1. Index to The Baxter Bulletin, Mountain Home, Arkansas, 36

Hatch, Match & Dispatch, Book 2. Index to The Baxter Bulletin, Mountain Home, Arkansas, 36

Hazzard's History of Henry County, 1822-1906: Military Edition, 149

Heads of Families at the First Census of the United States Taken in the Year 1790: Connecticut, 66

Heads of Families at the First Census of the United States Taken in the Year 1790: Maine, 217

Heads of Families at the First Census of The United States Taken in The Year 1790: Maryland, 237

Heads of Families at the First Census of the United States Taken in the Year 1790: Massachusetts, 260

Heads of Families at the First Census of the United States Taken in the Year 1790: New Hampshire, 348-349

Heads of Families at the First Census of the United States Taken in the Year 1790: New York, 388

Heart of the White Mountains, The, 347

Heathcote, Caleb: Gentleman Colonist, 436

Hebron Presbyterian Church God's Pilgrim People 1796-1996, 101

Hempstead County, Arkansas Marriages January 1, 1900 Through December 31, 1912, 42

Hempstead County, Arkansas United States Census of 1830, 1840, 1850 and Tax Lists of 1828, 1829, 1830, 1831, 1832, 1839, 1841, 1842, 1847, 1848, 1849, 42

Hendricks Co. Index to Testators to 1880, 149

Henry Co. Index to Testators to 1880, 149

Heritage of Lumpkin County, Georgia 1832-1996, 103

Herrick, John, Ledger, Pine Plains, Dutchess County, NY, 1852-1889, 398

Hickman County, Kentucky Deeds Volume Three (1833-1834), 201

Hickman Enterprise Index, 1900 through 1902, 344

Hickory, Polk, Cedar, Dade and Barton Counties (Missouri), 324, 327-328, 332, 337

Highlights of Westbrook History, 219

Hills in the Mid-Nineteenth Century, The: The History of a Rural Afro-American Community in Westchester County, New York, 435

Hingham, Massachusetts History of the Town, 289

Historic Catskill, 407

Historic Duxbury in Plymouth County, 288

Historic Families of Kentucky, 186

Historic Homes, Places, Genealogical . . . Memoirs . . . Families of Middlesex County, Massachusetts, 279

Historic Indian Tribes of Louisiana: From 1542 to the Present, 211

Historic Maps of Kentucky, 183

Historic Missouri: A Pictorial Narrative, 323

Historic Mohawk, The, 413

Historic Montgomery County, 250

Historic Old Rhinebeck: History of Rhinebeck, NY with Genealogies of the Early Settlers, 402

Historic Rock Island County, 130

Historic Sketch and Biographical Album of Shelby County, 130

Historic White Plains, 437

Historical Address, Delivered at the Centennial Celebration of the Incorporation of the Town of Wilbraham, 276

Historical and Descriptive Sketchbook of Napa, Sonoma, Lake, and Mendocino, 55-57, 59

Historical and Genealogical Miscellany [N.J.], 362, 423

Historical Annals of Dedham, 286

Historical Atlas of Arkansas, 32

Historical Atlas of Louisiana, 210

Historical Atlas of Missouri, 321

Historical Brighton, 264

Historical Catalog of the First Church in Hartford, 1633-1885, 70

Historical Celebration of the Town of Brimfield, Hampden Co., 276

Historical Collections . . . Relating to the History and Antiquities of Every Town in Massachusetts, 255

Historical Collections of Georgia, 95

Historical Collections of New Jersey: Past and Present, 360

Historical Collections of the Georgia Chapters Daughters of the American Revolution. Vol. 1: Seventeen Georgia Counties, 91

Historical Collections of the Georgia Chapters Daughters of the American Revolution. Vol. 2: Records of Richmond County, Georgia (formerly Saint Paul's Parish), 104

Historical Collections of the Georgia Chapters Daughters of the American Revolution. Vol. 3: Records of Elbert County, Georgia, 101

Historical Collections of the Georgia Chapters Daughters of the American Revolution. Vol. 4: Old Bible Records and Land Lotteries, 90

Historical Collections of the Georgia Chapters Daughters of the American Revolution. Vol. 5: Marriages of Greene County, Georgia (1787-1875) and Oglethorpe County, Georgia (1795-1852), 102, 104

Historical Collections Relating to the Town of Salisbury, Litchfield County, 73

Historical Dates of the Town & City of Bath, 225

Historical Encyclopedia of Illinois, Cook Co. Edition, 115

Historical Encyclopedia of Illinois, Edited by Bateman & Selby, & History of St. Clair Co., 111, 130

Historical Gazetteer & Biographical Memorial of Cattaraugus Co., with Map and Illustrations, 391

Historical Gazetteer of Steuben County, 430

Historical Record of the Town of Cornwall, Litchfield Co., 72

Historical Records of a Hundred &
Twenty-Five Years: Auburn, 392
Historical Reminiscences of Early
Times in Marlborough, 278
Historical Review of Arkansas: Its
Commerce, Industry, and Modern
Affairs, 32
Historical Sketch and Roster of Com-
missioned Officers and Enlisted Men
[in the Aroostook War], 214
Historical Sketch of Amherst, 353
Historical Sketch of Clermont, NY, 395
Historical Sketch of Stockton Springs,
226
Historical Sketch of the Chemung Val-
ley 1867, 393, 426
Historical Sketch of the Town of
Clermont, 395
Historical Sketch of the Town of Deer
Isle, An, 220
Historical Sketch of the Town of Le-
icester, 299
Historical Sketch of the Town of Troy
& Her Inhabitants, 351
Historical Sketch of Troy and Her In-
habitants, 350
Historical Sketches of Andover, 267
Historical Sketches of Brookline, 288
Historical Sketches of Franklin County,
404
Historical Sketches of the Town of
Hanover, 288
Historical Sketches of the Town of
Moravia, 1791 to 1853, 392
Historical Sketches Relating to Spencer,
299
Historical Sketches & Reminiscences of
Madison County, 154
Historical Southern Families, 11
Historical & Biographical Records of
Kosciusko County, 152
Historical & Reminiscences of
Chickasaw County, 168
Historie of Ye Town of Greenwich,
Connecticut, 68
History & Antiquities of Boston, 292
History & Directory of Yates County,
438
History & Genealogy of Fenwick's
Colony, 373
History and Genealogies of Ancient
Windsor, 71
History and Genealogies of Ancient
Windsor 1635-1891, The, Vol. I, 71

History and Genealogies of Ancient
Windsor 1635-1891, The, Vol. II, 71
History and Genealogy of Fenwick's
Colony [N.J.], 362
History & Genealogy of the Families of
Chesterfield, 1762-1962, 277
History and Genealogy of the Families
of Old Fairfield, 68
History and Genealogy of the *May-
flower* Planters, 257
History and Published Records of the
Midway Congregational Church,
Liberty County, Georgia, 103
History and Reminiscences of
Dougherty County, Georgia, 100
History & Statistical Sketch of the Rail-
road City, A: A Chronicle of Its So-
cial, Municipal, Commercial &
Manufacturing Progress, 154
History & Traditions of Marblehead,
The, 272
History of Acworth, 359
History of Adair, Sullivan, Putman and
Schuyler Counties, The, 323, 337,
338, 339
History of Alameda County, 54
History of Alexander, Union& Pulaski
Counties, 114, 129, 132
History of Allegan & Barry Counties,
301, 302
History of Allegany County 1806-1879,
390
History of Altamonte Springs, Florida,
A, 87
History of Amesbury, 272
History of Ancient Sheepscot &
Newcastle, 222
History of Ancient Wethersfield, 69, 71
History of Ancient Woodbury, Connecti-
cut, 2, 72
History of Anderson County [Kentucky]
1780-1936, A, 195
History of Andover from Its Settlement
to 1829, 266
History of Andrew and DeKalb Coun-
ties, The, 323, 329
History of Androscoggin County, 217
History of Anoka County, 309, 311
History of Antrim, 353
History of Arcadia and Newark, Wayne
County 1877, 435
History of Arkansas County, Arkansas,
from 1541-1875, 35
History of Arlington, 1635-1879, 279

History of Aroostook, 218
History of Ashburnham, 299
History of Athol, 296
History of Audrain County, 324
History of Augusta, Maine, The, 218
History of Baldwin County, Georgia, 96
History of Bates County, 325
History of Bath & Environs, Sagadahoc Co., 1607-1895, 225
History of Baxter County, 1873-1973, 36
History of Bedford, 353
History of Bedford, New Hampshire 1737-1971, 352
History of Benton County, 167
History of Benton County & Historic Oxford, 140
History of Bergen County, 364
History of Bergen & Passaic Counties, 364, 372
History of Berkshire County, 262
History of Berlin, 70
History of Berrien & Van Buren Counties, 302, 305
History of Bethel Maine 1768-1890, 218
History of Beverly, 273
History of Billerica, 280
History of Boone County, 168, 325
History of Boothbay, Southport and Boothbay Harbor, Maine 1623-1905, 223
History of Bourbon, Scott, Harrison, and Nicholas Counties, with a Brief Synopsis of the Blue Grass Region, 195, 200, 207
History of Bourne, from 1622 to 1937, 261
History of Boxford, 272
History of Bridgeport & Vicinity, 69
History of Bristol, 71
History of Brookline, 354
History of Broome Co., 391
History of Brownville, 1824-1924, 225
History of Buchanan County, 325
History of Buckfield, Oxford Co., 223
History of Buffalo & Erie County, 404
History of Bureau County, 114
History of Burke County, Georgia, 1777-1950, A, 97
History of Burlington & Mercer Counties, 365, 370
History of Butler County, 177

History of Butler & Bremer Counties, Together with Biographies, 168
History of Butte County, 54
History of Callaway County, 325
History of Cambridge, 1630-1877, 283
History of Cambridge, 1630-1930, 280
History of Camden County, 365
History of Camden & Rockport, Maine, 222
History of Canaan, 352
History of Candia, 357
History of Cape Cod, The, 261
History of Cape May County, New Jersey, The, 366
History of Cape Porpoise, 228
History of Caroline County, Maryland, 243
History of Carroll County [Illinois], 115
History of Carroll County [Iowa], 168
History of Carroll County [Missouri], 326
History of Carroll County, New Hampshire, 349
History of Cass County [Indiana], 142
History of Cass County [Missouri], 326
History of Castine, Penobscot & Brooksville, 220
History of Cattaraugus Co., 391
History of Cayuga County, 391
History of Cecil County, Maryland, 244
History of Cedar County, 168
History of Central Arkansas, 31
History of Champaign County, The, 115
History of Chariton & Howard Counties, 327, 332
History of Charlestown, The, 293
History of Charlton County, 97
History of Chatham, 262
History of Chattahoochee County, Georgia, 98
History of Chautauqua, 393
History of Chautauqua County 1808-1874, 392
History of Chautauqua County 1846, 392
History of Chemung County 1836-1879, 393
History of Chenango & Madison Counties, 394, 412
History of Cheshire from 1694 to 1840, 74
History of Chester, 357
History of Chesterfield, Cheshire County, 1736 to 1881, 350

History of Christian County, Kentucky: Historical and Biographical, 197

History of Clarendon, from 1810 to 1888, 420

History of Clarke County, Alabama, 22

History of Clay County, 168

History of Clayton County, 169

History of Clinton, Maine, 221

History of Clinton County, 143

History of Clinton & Franklin Counties, 394, 404

History of Clyde, Wayne County 1722-1969, 435

History of Clymer, Chautauqua County 1821-1971, 392

History of Cohoes, 389

History of Cole, Moniteau, Morgan, Benton, Miller, Maries, and Osage Counties Missouri, 325, 328, 334-336

History of Columbia County, 395

History of Colusa & Glenn Counties, 54-55

History of Concord, 356

History of Concord, from 1725 to 1853, 355

History of Conecuh County, Alabama, 22

History of Contra Costa County, 55

History of Coos County, 351

History of Coosa County, Alabama, 22

History of Cornwall: A Typical New England Town, 73

History of Craighead County [Arkansas], 39

History of Crawford County, 143

History of Cumberland County [Kentucky], 198

History of Cumberland County [Maine], 219

History of Custer County, 343

History of Dakota County, 310

History of Dakota County & the City of Hastings, 310

History of Danbury, 1684-1896, 67

History of Daviess County, 198

History of Dearborn County, 144

History of Dearborn & Ohio Counties, 144, 157

History of Decatur County, 144

History of Decatur County, Georgia, 100

History of Deerfield, 1636-1886, A, 275

History of DeKalb County, 145

History of Delaware County [New York], 398

History of Delaware County [Indiana], 145

History of Delaware County [New York] 1797-1880, 398

History of Delaware County [Iowa] & Its People, 169

History of Des Moines County and Its People, 169

History of Dickinson County, A, 169

History of Dighton, the South Purchase, 1712, 265

History of Dodge County, 100

History of Douglas & Grant Counties, 310-311

History of Dublin, 350

History of Dubuque County, 170

History of Durham [Maine], 217

History of Durham [Connecticut], from Its First Grant of Land in 1662 to 1866, 74

History of Dutchess County, 402

History of East Boston, 294

History of East Haven, 75

History of Eastern Arkansas, 31

History of Easthampton, 277

History of Edgar County, 118

History of Effingham County, 119

History of Elizabeth, 374

History of Elkhart County, 146

History of Enfield, 69

History of Essex Co., 269

History of Essex & Hudson Counties, 367, 368

History of Fairfield, The, Volume I: 1639-1818, 69

History of Fairfield, The, Volume II: 1700-1800, 69

History of Fairfield County, with Illustrations & Biographical Sketches of Its Prominent Men & Pioneers, 68

History of Fairport, Monroe County 1877, 413

History of Farmington, Franklin County, Maine 1776-1885, A, 219

History of Fayette, Seneca County 1800-1900, 429

History of Fayette County, 170

History of Fayette County, Kentucky: With an Outline Sketch of the Bluegrass Region, 199

History of Fillmore County, 310
History of Fitzwilliam, 350
History of Fort Fairfield, 218
History of Fountain County (and Montgomery Co.), 147, 156
History of Framingham, A, 278
History of Framingham, Massachusetts, 284
History of Francestown, 353
History of Frederick County, Maryland, 248
History of Freeborn County, 310
History of Fulton County, 119
History of Galen, Wayne County 1812-1889, 435
History of Gardiner, Pittston & W. Gardiner, 221
History of Garland, 224
History of Gentry & Worth Counties, 330, 340
History of Gilmanton, 349
History of Gilsum, from 1752 to 1879, 350
History of Gloucester, Notes & Additions, 267
History of Goodhue County, 311
History of Gorham, Maine, The, 219
History of Goshen, 359
History of Grafton, Worcester Co., 299
History of Grant County, 179
History of Grant County Kentucky, 199
History of Great Barrington, 1676-1882, 264
History of Great Barrington, Berkshire County, 264
History of Greene County, 405, 407
History of Greene & Sullivan Counties, 148, 162
History of Greenfield, 1682-1900, 275
History of Greenfield, 1900-1929, 274
History of Greenfield, 1930-1953, 275
History of Greenwich, Fairfield Co., with Many Important Statistics, 68
History of Guilford, from Its First Settlement in 1639, 76
History of Hadley, 277
History of Hampden County, A, 275
History of . . . Hampton, New Hampshire from . . . 1638-1892, with Genealogies, 357
History of Hancock, 1764-1889, 353
History of Hancock Co. Indiana in the Twentieth Century, A, 149

History of Hancock County, 148, 149
History of Hardwick, Mass., The, 299
History of Harford County, Maryland, 249
History of Harrison County, 170
History of Hartland, the 69th Town in the Colony of Connecticut, 71
History of Harwich, Barnstable Co., 1620-1900, 261
History of Harwinton, 72
History of Hatfield in 3 Parts, 278
History of Havana 1788-1895, 393, 427, 431
History of Haverhill [New Hampshire], 351
History of Haverhill [Massachusetts], The, 267
History of Henderson County, 201
History of Hendricks County, 149
History of Hennepin County & the City of Minneapolis, 312
History of Henry County, 120, 150, 171
History of Herkimer County, 408
History of Herkimer County 1791-1879, 407
History of Hillsborough, 1921-1963, 352
History of Hillsborough County, 354
History of Hillsdale, Columbia Co., 394
History of Hope Maine, 222
History of Hudson (1673-1912), 354
History of Hudson County, 368
History of Hunterdon & Somerset Counties, 369, 373
History of Huntington County, 150
History of Illinois from Its Commencement as a State in 1818 to 1847, A, 110
History of Indianapolis & Marion County, 155
History of Iowa Falls, 1900-1950, 170
History of Ipswich, Essex & Hamilton, 269
History of Isleborough, 1764-1892, 220
History of Islesborough, Maine, 226
History of Jackson County, 171
History of Jackson County, Missouri, The, 332
History of Jefferson City, 328
History of Jefferson County [New York], 409
History of Jersey County, 120
History of Jerseyville, 1822 to 1901, 120

History of Jo Daviess County, 120
History of Johnson County, 333
History of Jones County, 171
History of Jones County, Past & Present, 171
History of Kalamazoo County, 302
History of Kendall County, 121
History of Kennebunk, 228
History of Kennebunkport, 227
History of Kent, 72
History of Kentucky, 184
History of Keokuk County, 171
History of Kipsbergen, Rhinebeck, NY, 402
History of Knox, Lewis, Scotland, and Clark Counties, The, 327, 333, 339
History of Knox County, 121
History of Knox & Daviess Counties, 143, 151
History of Laclede, Camden, Dallas, Webster, Wright, Texas, Pulaski, Phelps and Dent Counties, The, 326, 329, 333, 336-337, 340-341
History of Lake County, A, 121
History of Lamar County 1825-1932, The, 103
History of Lancaster, 351
History of LaPorte County, 153
History of LaPorte County & Its Townships, Towns & Cities, 153
History of LaSalle County, 124
History of Lawrence [Massachusetts], 273
History of Lawrence [Kansas], A, 178
History of Lawrence, Orange & Washington Counties, 153, 157, 165
History of Lebanon, 1761-1887, 351
History of Lee County [Illinois], 125
History of Lee County [Iowa], 172
History of Leitersburg District, Washington Co., 253
History of Leominster, The, 299
History of Lewis County, 410
History of Lincoln County, from Earliest Times to the Present, The, 333
History of Litchfield, 221
History of Litchfield County, 72
History of Little Egg Harbor Township, Burlington Co., 365
History of Littleton, in Three Volumes, 352
History of Livingston County [Illinois], 125

History of Livingston County [New York], 411
History of Lodi, Seneca County 1789-1894, 428
History of Logan County, 125
History of Londonderry, 358
History of Long Island, 412
History of Ludlow, The, 276
History of Lumpkin County for the First Hundred Years: 1832-1932, 103
History of Lynn, Essex Co., 270
History of Lynnfield, 1635-1785, 273
History of Lyons, Wayne County 1877, 435
History of Macon County, Georgia, 103
History of Macoupin County, 125
History of Madison County [Illinois], 126
History of Madison County [Indiana], 154
History of Madison County [New York], 413
History of Mahaska County, 172
History of Malden, Mass., 1633-1785, 279
History of Manchester, 354
History of Manistee County, 304
History of Marshall County, 173, 204
History of Marshfield, 291
History of Martha's Vineyard, Dukes Co., Mass., The, 266
History of McDonough County, 126
History of McLean County, 127
History of Meade County, A, 179
History of Melrose, 280
History of Merrimac & Belknap Counties, 349, 355
History of Methodism in Minnesota, 308
History of Miami County, 155
History of Michigan City, 153
History of Milford, with Family Registers, 354
History of Milton, 1640-1887, The, 287
History of Mississippi, A, 316
History of Mississippi, the Heart of the South, 317
History of Mitchell & Worth Counties, 173, 176
History of Monmouth County, 371
History of Monmouth & Ocean Counties, 371, 372
History of Monroe, 1761-1954, 352

History of Monroe County 1788-1877, 413
History of Montgomery County, Maryland, 250
History of Montgomery County [New York], 414
History of Montgomery & Fulton Counties 1772-1878, 405, 414
History of Montville, Formerly the North Parish of New London, 1640-1896 [with genealogies], 77
History of Morris County, 371
History of Mower County, 312
History of Muhlenberg County [Kentucky], A, 205
History of Nantucket, 285
History of Nantucket County, Island & Town, The, 285
History of Napa & Lake Counties, 55, 57
History of Natick, A, 278
History of Needham, Mass., 1711-1911, 286
History of Nevada, 346
History of New Bedford & Vicinity, 1602-1892, 265
History of New Boston, 353
History of New Britain, with Sketches of Farmington & Berlin, 67, 69, 70
History of New England, The, 2, 6
History of New Ipswich, 353
History of New Ipswich, 1735-1914, 352
History of New London, CT, 77
History of New London County, 77
History of New Paltz, New York, and Its Old Families, 433
History of Newark, 366
History of Newbury, 1635-1902, 267
History of Newfields, 1638-1911, 357
History of Newport, from 1766 to 1878, 359
History of Newton, 284
History of Newton, Lawrence, Barry and McDonald Counties, The, 324, 333, 334, 335
History of Newton County [Arkansas], 46
History of Newton County [Mississippi], from 1834 to 1894, 319
History of Norfolk, 1744-1900, Litchfield County, 72
History of Norfolk Co., The, 286

History of North Bridgewater, Plymouth Co., 289
History of North Brookfield, 299
History of Northampton, The, 278
History of Northeast Arkansas, 31
History of Northeast Indiana, 145, 152, 157, 162
History of Northfield, 1780-1905, 355
History of Northwestern Arkansas, 31
History of Norwich, from Its Possession by Indians to 1866, 77
History of Nottingham, Deerfield, Northwood, 356-357
History of O'Brien County, 173
History of Ogle County, 128
History of Old Braintree & Quincy, A, 287
History of Old Kinderhook, A, 394
History of Old Yarmouth, 262
History of Olmsted County, 312
History of Omaha, 343
History of Oneida County, 418
History of Ontario County, 419
History of Ontario County 1788-1876, 419
History of Orange County, 420
History of Orleans County 1824-1879, 420
History of Osceola County, 173
History of Oswego County, 421
History of Otisfield, Cumberland Co., 219
History of Otsego County, 421
History of Otsego County 1740-1878, 421
History of Ovid, Seneca County 1789-1889, 428
History of Page County, 174
History of Palmer, 276
History of Palmyra, Wayne County 1877, 435
History of Paris, 224
History of Parke & Vermillion Counties, 158, 164
History of Paxton, 294
History of Pelham, from 1738-1898, 278
History of Perinton, Monroe County 1812-1877, 413
History of Perth Amboy, 1651-1958, 370
History of Peru, in the County of Oxford, 224

History of Piatt County, 128
History of Pickens County, Alabama, from Its First Settlement in 1817-1856, 26
History of Pittsfield, 262
History of Pittsfield, Berkshire Co., 264
History of Pittsfield, New Hampshire, 356
History of Plymouth, New Hampshire, 352
History of Plymouth County, 289
History of Posey County, 159
History of Pottawattamie County, 175
History of Poughkeepsie, 402
History of Poweshiek County, 175
History of Prescott, 292
History of Ramsey County & the City of St. Paul, 313
History of Randolph & Macon Counties, 334, 337
History of Raymond, 357
History of Redding, The, 69
History of Rehoboth, A, 266
History of Rensselaer County, 423
History of Renville County, 313
History of Rice County, 313
History of Richardson County, 345
History of Ridgefield Connecticut, The, 68
History of Rochester, from 1722 to 1890, 359
History of Rochester, & Monroe County, 414
History of Rockingham County & Representative Citizens, 357
History of Rockingham & Strafford County, 357, 358
History of Rockland County, 423
History of Romulus, Seneca County 1789-1876, 428
History of Rowley, The, 269
History of Rutland, Worcester County, A, 299
History of Rye, Westchester County New York 1660-1870, 435
History of Saco and Biddeford, 228
History of Saint Joseph County [Indiana], 161
History of Saint Lawrence County [New York], 429
History of Saint Lawrence County [New York], 1749-1878, 429
History of Salem [MA], 272

History of Salem [NH], 357
History of Saline County, 338
History of Salisbury, 355
History of Sanbornton, 349
History of Sangamon County, 130
History of Santa Barbara & Ventura Counties, 57, 60
History of Saratoga County, 424
History of Schenectady County, 425
History of Schenectady During the Revolution, A, 425
History of Schuyler County 1854-1879, 427
History of Scituate [Massachusetts], 288
History of Scott County, The, 175
History of Seneca County 1786-1876, 427
History of Seward County, 339
History of Seymour, with Biographies and Genealogies, 76
History of Shelby County, Kentucky, 207
History of Sidney, Maine, 221
History of Solano County, 59
History of Solano & Napa County, 56, 58
History of South Arkansas, 31
History of South Boston, 294
History of Southington, 69
History of Spencer, 295
History of Spencerville, 145
History of Stamford Connecticut, 67
History of Stamford from Its Settlement in 1641 to 1868, Including Darien, 68
History of Stanislaus County, 60
History of Stanstead County, Province of Quebec, The, 5
History of Stephenson County, 131
History of Stoneham, Massachusetts, 284
History of Sudbury, 1638-1889, 281
History of Sullivan County, 430
History of Sussex & Warren Counties, 373, 374
History of Sutton, 356
History of Swansea, 1667-1917, 266
History of Swanzey, from 1734-1890, 351
History of Talbot County, 1661-1861, 253
History of Tama County, 175
History of Taunton, 265

History of Tazewell County, 131

History of Temple, 352

History of the Arkansas Press for a Hundred Years and More, 30

History of the Chemung Canal, 393, 427

History of the City of Albany, 390

History of the City of Belfast, The, Volume II, 227

History of the City of Brooklyn, 410

History of the City of Grand Rapids, 303

History of the City of Lincoln, 344

History of the City of Minneapolis, 311

History of the City of New York, 417

History of the City of Paterson, 372

History of the City of St. Paul, & of the County of Ramsey, 313

History of the City of Trenton, 369

History of the City of Vincennes, from 1702 to 1901, 151

History of the City of Watervliet, 1630 to 1910, 389

History of the Colony of New Haven to Its Absorption into Connecticut, with Supplementary History & Personnel of the Towns of Branford, Guilford, Milford, Stratford, Norwalk, Southold, Etc., 63, 74

History of the Community of Treynor, 175

History of the Connecticut Valley in Massachusetts, 275-276, 278

History of the Counties of Woodbury & Plymouth, 174, 176

History of the County of Du Page, 118

History of the County of Montgomery, 173

History of the Early Settlement of Bridgewater, 291

History of the Early Settlement of Newton from 1629-1800, with a Genealogical Register, 281

History of the English Settlement of Edwards Co., 118

History of The Farm, Mendon, Monroe County 1828-1958, 413

History of the First Century of Parsonsfield, 228

History of the First Congregational Church of Stonington, 1674-1874, 78

History of the Formation, Settlement & Development of Hamilton County, 148

History of the Fourth Regiment of Minnesota Infantry Volunteers During the Great Rebellion, 307

History of the German Churches in Louisiana (1823-1893), A, 210

History of the Lake & Calumet Region of Indiana, 152-153, 159

History of the Marine Society of Newburyport, 267

History of the Minnesota Valley, 308

History of the Missisco Valley, 420

History of the Mississippi, the Heart of the South, 15

History of the Montgomery Classis, 413

History of the Municipalities of Hudson County, 1630-1923, 368

History of the Old Presbyterian Congregation of the People of Maidenhead & Hopewell, at Pennington NJ, 369

History of the Old Tennent Church, 371

History of the Old Town of Derby, 1642-1880, with Biographies & Genealogies, 76

History of the Old Town of Stratford & the City of Bridgeport, 68

History of the Oranges, in Essex Co., 367

History of the Origin of the Town of Clinton, 1653-1865, 295

History of the Original Town of Concord, 403

History of the Pioneer Families of Missouri, A, 320

History of the Plantation of Menunkatuck, and the Original Town of Guilford (including Madison), 74, 76

History of the Several Towns, Manors & Patents of the County of Westchester from Its First Settlement to the Present Time, 435

History of the St. Croix Valley, 307

History of the State of Kentucky, A: The General History, 189

History of the State of Kentucky, A: The First Edition, 189

History of the State of Kentucky, A: The Second Edition, 189

History of the State of Kentucky, A: The Third Edition, 189

History of the State of Kentucky, A: The Fourth Edition, 189

History of the State of Kentucky, A: The Fifth Edition, 189

History of the State of Kentucky, A: The Sixth Edition, 190

History of the State of Kentucky, A: The Seventh Edition, 190

History of the State of Kentucky, A: The Eighth Edition, 190

History of the Swedish-Americans of Minnesota, 309

History of the Synod of Minnesota— Presbyterian Church USA, 307

History of the Town Hanover, The, 289

History of the Town Medford, Middlesex Co., 279

History of the Town Milford, 294

History of the Town of Abington, Plymouth Co., from Its First Settlement, 289

History of the Town of Amherst, 277

History of the Town of Amherst, Hillsborough Co., from 1728 to 1882, with Genealogies, 354

History of the Town of Andover, 1751-1906, 355

History of the Town of Ashfield, Franklin County, 274

History of the Town of Bedford, 279

History of the Town of Bedford, to 1917, 437

History of the Town of Berkley, 266

History of the Town of Berlin, Worcester Co., 296

History of the Town of Bernardston, Franklin Co., 274

History of the Town Of Bowdoinham, Maine, The, 225

History of the Town of Candia, Rockingham Co., 358

History of the Town of Canterbury, 1727-1912, 356

History of the Town of Carlisle, 1754-1929, 279

History of the Town of Carver, 289

History of the Town of Catharine, Schuyler County, 427

History of the Town of Cheshire, Berkshire County, 263

History of the Town of Claremont, 359

History of the Town of Concord, Middlesex Co., 284

History of the Town of Conesus, Livingston Co., 410

History of the Town of Danvers, 269

History of the Town of Dorchester, 292

History of the Town of Douglas, 295

History of the Town of Dunbarton, Merrimack Co., 356

History of the Town of Dunstable, A, 283

History of the Town of Durham (Oyster River Plantation) with Genealogical Notes, 359

History of the Town of Duxbury, Massachusetts with Genealogical Registers, 291

History of the Town of Essex from 1634-1868, 267

History of the Town of Exeter, 356

History of the Town of Fitchburg, 299

History of the Town of Franklin, 286

History of the Town of Freetown, 265

History of the Town of Gloucester, 267

History of the Town of Goffstown, 1733-1920, 353

History of the Town of Goshen, Hampshire Co., 277

History of the Town of Goshen, with Genealogies & Biographies, 72

History of the Town of Groton, 279

History of the Town of Hamden, with an Account of the Centennial Celebration, 74

History of the Town of Hampton, 357

History of the Town of Hampton Falls, 357

History of the Town of Hanover, 352

History of the Town of Haverhill, 352

History of the Town of Hawley, Franklin Co., 273

History of the Town of Henniker, Merrimac Co., 355

History of the Town of Hingham, 289

History of the Town of Holland, 276

History of the Town of Hollis, 354

History of the Town of Hubbardston, 299

History of the Town of Industry Maine, 1787-1893, 219

History of the Town of Jefferson, 1773-1927, 351

History of the Town of Keene, from 1732 to 1874, 351

History of the Town of Kirkland, 418

History of the Town of Lancaster, Mass., 296

History of the Town of Ledyard, 1650-1900, 77

History of the Town of Leeds, Androscoggin Co., 217

History of the Town of Lexington, Middlesex Co., 281

History of the Town of Litchfield, 1720-1920, 73

History of the Town of Manchester, 1645-1895, 269

History of the Town of Marlborough, Cheshire County, NH, 350

History of the Town of Marlborough, Middlesex Co., 281

History of the Town of Marlborough, Ulster Co., 433

History of the Town of Mason, 353

History of the Town of Medfield, 1650-1886, 287

History of the Town of Middleboro, 291

History of the Town of Middlefield, 278

History of the Town of Mont Vernon, 354

History of the Town of New London, Merrimac Co., 1779-1899, 355

History of the Town of Newburgh, 420

History of the Town of Northfield for 150 Years, 275

History of the Town of Oxford, 295

History of the Town of Paris & the Valley of the Sauquoit: Anecdotes & Reminiscences, 418

History of the Town of Peterborough, Hillsborough Co., 354

History of the Town of Plymouth [Connecticut], 72

History of the Town of Plymouth [Massachusetts], 291

History of the Town of Princeton, The, 294

History of the Town of Queensbury, 434

History of the Town of Remington & Vicinity, Jasper County, 150

History of the Town of Richmond, 350

History of the Town of Rindge, 351

History of the Town of Rochester, New Hampshire 1722-1890, 359

History of the Town of Rockport, 269

History of the Town of Rye, 1623-1903, 358

History of the Town of Shirley, 279

History of the Town of Somerset, Shawomet Purchase, 1677, Incorporated 1790, 265

History of the Town of Southampton, 411

History of the Town of Stonington, Connecticut, 78

History of the Town of Stonington, County of New London, 1649-1900, 78

History of the Town of Sullivan, 1777-1917, 351

History of the Town of Sunderland, 275

History of the Town of Surry, Cheshire Co., 350

History of the Town of Sutton, 1704-1876, 294

History of the Town of Sutton, Vol. II, 1876-1950, 295

History of the Town of Waldoboro, 223

History of the Town of Warwick, 274

History of the Town of Wayne, Kennebec Co., 221

History of the Town of Wentworth, 352

History of the Town of Westford in the County of Middlesex, 1659-1883, 280

History of the Town of Whately, 274-275

History of the Town of Wilton, Hillsborough Co., 354

History of the Town of Winchedon, Worcester Co., 296

History of the Town of Wolcott, from 1731 to 1874, 75

History of the Town of Worthington, The, 278

History of the Towns of Bristol & Bremen in the State of Maine, 223

History of the Towns of New Milford & Bridgewater, 1703-1882, 67, 73

History of the Twenty-seventh Arkansas Confederate Infantry, 35

History of the Upper Mississippi Valley, 309

History of the White Mountains, 347

History of Thomaston, Rockland & So. Thomaston, 222

History of Tioga, Chemung, Tompkins & Schuyler Counties, 393, 427, 430, 431

History of Tioga County 1791-1879, 430

History of Todd County, Kentucky, 207

History of Tolland County, 79

History of Tompkins County 1817-1879, 431

History of Topsfield, 268

History of Torrington, 73

History of Townsend, 284
History of Trigg County, Kentucky: Historical and Biographical, 208
History of Tuolumne County, 60
History of Turner County, 106
History of Ulster County, 432, 433
History of Ulster Under the Dutch, A, 433
History of Union, 79
History of Union County, 374
History of Union & Middlesex Counties, 370, 374
History of Van Buren County, 305
History of Vermilion County, 132
History of Vigo County, with Biographical Selections, 164
History of Wabash County, 164
History of Wabasha County, 314
History of Walpole, from Its Earliest Times, A, 286
History of Ware County, Georgia (revised), The, 106
History of Warner New Hampshire from 1735 to 1879, The, 355
History of Warren, 352
History of Warren County, 175
History of Warrick, Spencer & Perry Counties, 158, 161, 165
History of Washington, 359
History of Washington County, Alabama, The, Vol. II, 26
History of Washington County, Maryland, A, 254
History of Washington County, New York, 434
History of Washington County & the St. Croix Valley, 315
History of Waterbury, 75
History of Waterford, Oxford County, 224
History of Waverly & Vicinity, 430
History of Wayne, Fayette, Union & Franklin Counties, 146-147, 163, 166
History of Wayne County, 165, 166
History of Wayne County 1789-1869, 434
History of Wayne County 1789-1877, 434
History of Weare, 1735-1888, 354
History of Wenham, The, 266
History of West Mystic, 1600-1985, A, 77
History of Westborough, 295

History of Westchester County, 437
History of Westchester County, New York, 437
History of Western Arkansas, 31
History of Western Maryland, 8, 236
History of Westminster, 295
History of Weymouth, 288
History of Whiteside County, 134
History of Whitley County, 167
History of Wilbraham, 276
History of Wilkinson County [Georgia], 108
History of Will County, 134
History of Williamson County, 135
History of Windham, 1719-1883, 358
History of Windham County, 79
History of Winona County, 315
History of Winthrop, 1630-1952, 221
[History of] Wiscasset in Pownalborough, 222
History of Woburn, Middlesex Co., 284
History of Wolfeborough [New Hampshire], 349
History of Woodford County, Kentucky, 209
History of Woodstock, 79
History of Woodstock, Maine, 224
History of Worcester, 296
History of Worcester County, 295
History of Wright County [Minnesota], 315
History of Wright County [Iowa], 176
History of Wyoming County, 438
History of Wyoming County 1841-1880, 438
History of Yates County 1873, 438
History of York County [Maine], 228
History of York County, PA, 8
Home History, 404
Home in the Woods, A: Pioneer Life in Indiana, 154
Homes of Old Woodbury, 73, 75
Honey Out of the Rafters, 378
Hood, Margaret Scholl, Diary 1851-1861, 247
Hoosier Faiths: A History of Indiana's Churches and Religious Groups, 138
How to Research a Family with Illinois Roots, 113
Howard Co. Index to Testators to 1880, 150
Howard County Maryland Records Volume I: Cemeteries, 249

Howard County Maryland Records Volume II: More Cemeteries, 249

Howard County Maryland Records Volume III: Even More Cemeteries, 249

Howard County Maryland Records Volume IV: Additional Cemeteries Plus Manumission Records, 249

Howard County Maryland Records Volume V: More Cemetery Inscriptions Plus Family Bible Data, 249

Howard County Maryland Records Volume VI: A Continuation of Howard County Cemetery Records, 249

Howard County Maryland Records Volume VII: St. John's Cemetery and Inscriptions from the St. John's Episcopal Church Columbarium, 249

Howard County Maryland Records Volume VIII: Additional Cemetery and Interment Information for Ten Howard County Grave Sites, 249

Hudson, The: From the Wilderness to the Sea, 409

Hudson-Mohawk Genealogical and Family Memoir, 385

Hudson, NY Newspapers, Vol. 1, Deaths, 1802-1851, 396

Hudson, NY Newspapers, Vol. 2, Marriages, 1802-1851, 396

Huguenots or Early French in New Jersey, The, 361

Hundredth Town, The: Glimpses of Life in Westborough, 1717-1817, 295

Hunterdon County Court of Common Pleas, Minutes, 1714-1908, 369

Hunterdon County, New Jersey Fisheries 1819-1820, 368

Hunterdon County New Jersey Militia 1792, The, 368

Hunterdon County, New Jersey Taxpayers, 1778-1797, 369

Huntington Co. Index to Testators to 1880, 150

Hutchinson, A Prairie City in Kansas, 181

IL Libraries with Genealogical Collections, 112

IL Marriage Records Index (Pre-Statehood to at least 1900), Third Edition, 112

Illiana Ancestors Volume 5, 1993, 1994, 1995, Genealogy Column in the Commercial News, Danville, Illinois, 110, 137

Illinois 1820 Census Index, 113

Illinois 1830 Census Index, 110

Illinois 1840 Census Index, 114

Illinois 1850 Mortality Schedule with Index, 113

Illinois 1860 Mortality with Index, 113

Illinois 1870 Mortality Schedule with Index, 113

Illinois & Effingham County, 110, 119

Illinois Census Returns, 1810 [and] 1818, 112

Illinois Census Returns, 1820, 112

Illinois Country, 1673-1818, The, 109

Illinois: Crossroads of a Continent, 110

Illinois Genealogical Research, 113

Illinois Historical, Wabash County Biographical, 133

Illinois in the Civil War, 111

Illinois Marriages, Early to 1825, 112

Illinois Place Names, 109

Illinois Regiment, 113

Illinois Soldiers & Sailors Home at Quincy, 114

Illustrated Album of Biography of the Famous Valley of the Red River of the North and the Park Regions, 308

Illustrated Historical Atlas of the State of Minnesota, 306

Illustrated History of Kennebec County, 1625-1892, 221

Illustrated History of Lowell, 279

Illustrated History of Lowell & Vicinity, 281

Illustrated History of Monroe County, 173

Illustrated Laconian, The, 349

Immigrant Life in New York City, 1825-1863, 415

Immigrants in Madison County, New York 1815-1860, 412

Immigrants to Osage County Missouri and Their Immigrant Ships, 336

Immigrants to the Middle Colonies, 10

In and About Hartford: Its People and Places, 70

In Joy and Sorrow: Women, Family, and Marriage in the Victorian South, 11

In Pursuit of Justice—A History of the Keene Police Department, 350

Index, 1830 Federal Population Census for Indiana, 135

Index 1840 Federal Population Census, Indiana, 136

Index for 1921 Atlas of Lancaster County, Nebraska, 344

Index for Biographical and Genealogical History of Southwestern Nebraska 1904, 342

Index for the 1903 Plat Book of Lancaster County, Nebraska, 344

Index of "Kentucky Ancestors" Vol. 1-15 (1965-1980), 193

Index of Land Documents in the Possession of the Gloucester County Historical Society, 368

Index of Marriage Licenses, Prince George's County, Maryland 1777-1886, 251

Index of Names Appearing in Smith's 1885 History of Broom County, 391

Index of Obituaries and Marriages of the (Baltimore) Sun, 1861-1865, 241

Index of Obituaries and Marriages in the [Baltimore] Sun, 1866-1870, 234

Index of Obituaries and Marriages of the (Baltimore) Sun, 1871-1875, 241

Index of Pioneers from Massachusetts to the West, An, 257, 300

Index of the 1850 Federal Census of Rockland County, New York (surname only), 424

Index of the Source Records of Maryland, An, 235

Index to 1759 Warrants and Surveys of Province of Pennsylvania Including Three Lower Counties (Delaware), 81

Index to 1880 Federal Population Census of Macomb County, Michigan, 303

Index to Arkansas Confederate Pension Applications, 29

Index to Arkansas Confederate Soldiers, 29

Index to Bates County, Missouri Probate Papers 1850-1923, 325

Index to Clark County, Arkansas Court Records: 1834-1839, 37

Index to Clark County, Arkansas Court Records: 1840-1844, 38

Index to Clark County, Arkansas Court Records: 1845-1858, 38

Index to Colonial New York Wills, Volumes 1-8, 416

Index to Confederate Pension Applications, Commonwealth of Kentucky, 187

Index to Conway County, Arkansas, Deed Books A & B, 1825-1843, 39

Index to Deaths in the Mankato City and Blue Earth County Minnesota Directories from 1892-1930, 309

Index to Deaths in the Winona City and County Directories from 1906-1930, 315

Index to District of Columbia Wills, 1801-1920, 83

Index to Georgia Wills, 88

Index to Georgia's 1867-1868 Returns of Qualified Voters and Registration Oath Books (White), 88

Index to Herrick's 1858 Map of Harford County, Maryland, 248

Index to Hough's 1854 *History of Jefferson County, NY*, 409

Index to Kent County Probates 1680-1925, An, 81

Index to Morse's Historic Old Rhinebeck, 401

Index to Mortuary Records Koon's Funeral Home North Brevard County Titusville, Florida Nov. 1924-Jun. 1946, 85

Index to Mortuary Records of North Brevard County Florida 1946-1980, 85

Index to Naturalization Records of Harford County, Maryland, A-L, 248

Index to Naturalization Records of Harford County, Maryland, M-Z, 248

Index to New York State Wills, Volumes 9-15, 1981 Index to the New York Historical Society Collection, 1900-1906, 416

Index to New York Wills, Volumes 9-15, 381

Index to Probate Book B (1847-1851): Clark County, Arkansas, 38

Index to Revolutionary Soldiers in Indiana, 139

Index to Revolutionary War Manuscripts, 361

Index to San Franciso Marriage Returns 1850-1858, 57

Index to Smith's Documentary History of Rhinebeck, 401

Index to Some of the Family Records of the Southern States, 13

Index to St. Clair Co., IL Probated and Non-Probated Wills 1772-1964, 131

Index to Stryker's Register of New Jersey in the Revolution, 361

Index to the 1800 Census of New York, 375

Index to the 1810 Census of Kentucky, 194

Index to the 1820 Census of Kentucky, 184

Index to the 1820 Census of Maryland and Washington, D.C., 83, 235

Index to the 1830 Census of Georgia, 93

Index to the 1862 Military Census of Lake County IL, 122

Index to the Biographies in 19th Century California County Histories, An, 53

Index to the "Black River and Northern New York Conference Memorial" Series, 380

Index to *The Cotter Courier*, Cotter, Arkansas: Dec. 11, 1903 thru May 30, 1918, 36

Index to *The Cotter Record*, Cotter, Arkansas: Jan. 15, 1909 thru Dec. 30, 1937, 36

Index to the DAR Bible Records of Jefferson County, NY, 409

Index to the DAR "Records of the Families of the California Pioneers," Volumes 1-27, 53

Index to the Early Marriage Records of Lancaster County Nebraska 1866-1912, 344

Index to the Encyclopedia of Pennsylvania Biography, 8

Index to the Great Register of Solano County, California, 1890, 58

Index to the Headright and Bounty Grants in Georgia from 1756-1909, Revised Edition, 92

Index to the Past & Present of Lake County IL, 122

Index to the Portrait & Biog. Album of Lake County IL, 122

Index to the Probate Records of Prince George's County, Maryland 1696-1900, 251

Index to the Public Domain Computer Conversion Project, 122

Index to the Records of the Wally-Mills-Zimmerman Funeral Home, Elkhart, Indiana, April 1912-October 1988, 146

Index to the Sharp County Record Newspaper, Evening Shade, Arkansas 1877-1883, 50

Index to the Sonoma Searcher V 1, #1-V 15, #4 (1973-1988), 59

Index to the Westchester Historian, Vols. 1-65, 1925-1989, 436

Index to the Westchester Historian, Vols. 66-70, 1990-1994, 436

Index to United States Census of Georgia for 1820, 90

Index to Wyandotte County, Kansas Final Naturalizations 1859-1947, 183

Index to Wyandotte County, Kansas Petitions for Naturalization 1867-1906, 183

Indexes of Hope Farm Press Publications, 379

Indexes to Los Angeles County Marriages, Book 1: August 1851-March 1870, 56

Indian Frontier of the American West, 1846-1890, The, 18

Indian Place Names in Alabama, 20

Indian Tribes of Hudson's River Vol. I (to 1700), 386

Indian Tribes of Hudson's River Vol. II (1700 to 1850), 386

Indiana 1820 Enumeration of Males, 138

Indiana 1850 Mortality Schedule, 139

Indiana Gazetteer, 137

Indiana Genealogical Research, 138

Indiana, Her Counties, Her Townships, and Her Towns, 138

Indiana Home, The, 136

Indiana Land Entries—Vincennes District, 1807-1877, 139

Indiana Marriages, Early to 1825, 136

Indiana Source Book I; Genealogical Material from the Hoosier Genealogist, 1961-1966, 137

Indiana Source Book II; Genealogical Material from the Hoosier Genealogist, 1967-72, 137

Indiana Source Book III; Genealogical Material from the Hoosier Genealogist, 1973-1979, 137

Indiana Source Book IV; Genealogical Material from the Hoosier Genealogist, 1979-1981, 137

Indiana Source Book V; Genealogical Material from the Hoosier Genealogist, 1982-1984, 137

Indiana Source Book VI; Genealogical Material from the Hoosier Genealogist, 1985-1988, 137

Indiana Source Book VII; Genealogical Material from the Hoosier Genealogist, 1989-1990, 138

Indiana Source Books Index, Vols. 1-3, 137

Indiana Sources for Genealogical Research in the Indiana State Library, 138

Indiana Territorial Pioneer Records, Vol. I, 136

Indiana Territorial Pioneer Records, Vol. II, 136

Indiana Territorial Pioneer Records, Vol. III, 136

Indiana War of 1812 Soldiers, 136

Indiana Wills Phase I (to 1850) and Phase II (1851-1898), 137

Indiana's African American Heritage, 137

Indians, Settlers & Slaves in a Frontier Exchange Economy: The Lower Mississippi Valley Before 1783, 212

Inhabitants of Baltimore County, 1692-1763, 243

Inhabitants of Baltimore County, 1763-1774, 241

Inhabitants of Cecil County, 1649-1774, 244

Inhabitants of Kent County, Maryland, 250

Inhabitants of New Hampshire, 1776, 349

Inhabitants of New York, 1774-1776, 388

Inheritance and Family Life in Colonial New York City, 383

Inscriptions from Gravestones in Glastonbury, 70

Inscriptions from the Burial Grounds of Lunenburg, 296

Inscriptions from the Gravestones of Derby, with Additions & Corrections, 75

Inscriptions on the Tombstones and Monuments in the Graveyards at Whippany and Hanover, Morris County, New Jersey, 371

Inscriptions on Tombstones & Monuments, 374

Inside the Great House: Planter Family Life in Eighteenth-Century Chesapeake Society, 236

Interment Records 1883-1929 Lorraine Cemetery & Mausoleum, 243

Inventory of Confederate Pension Applications, Commonwealth of Kentucky, 187

Inventory of Maryland Bible Records, Vol. 1, 232

Inventory of the County Archives of Delaware: #1—New Castle County, 82

Inventory of the Early Records of the Kentucky Insurance Bureau and Department (1870-1936), 188

Inventory of the Louisiana Historical Association Collection on Deposit in the Howard-Tilton Memorial Library, Tulane University, 210

Inventory of the Records of the Bank of Kentucky (1806-1835), 188

Inventory of the Records of the Bank of the Commonwealth of Kentucky (1820-1830), 188

Inventory of the Records of the Frankfort Bank (1818-1820), 188

Iowa Marriages, Early to 1850, 167

Ipswich in the Mass. Bay Colony, 273

Ipswich in the Mass. Bay Colony, Volume II, 273

[Ipswich] Jeffrey's Neck & the Way Leading Thereto, 273

Irish Experience in New York City, The: A Select Bibliography, 387

Irish in New England, 6

ISGS Celebrates 25 Years (1968-1993), 112

ISGS Quarterly—25-Year Index, 112

ISGS Quarterly, Volumes I-XXV & 25 Year Index, 112

Isle of Shoals, The: An Historical Sketch, 355

It's Your Misfortune and None of My Own: A New History of the American West, 19

Izard County, Arkansas, Tax Records 1829-1866, 43

Jackson and Brooks, Maine Church Records, 226

Jackson Co. Index to Testators to 1880, 150

Jackson Co. Marriages 1817-1850, 150

Jackson, Maine Vital Records Prior to 1892, 226

Jasper Cemeteries, Crooked Creek, and Fox Townships, 120

Jasper Co. Index to Testators to 1880, 150

Jay Co. Index to Testators to 1880, 151

Jefferson Co. Index to Testators to 1880, 151

Jefferson Co. Marriages 1811-1849, 151

Jefferson Co. Wills 1780-1814, 201

Jefferson Co. Wills 1814-1822, 201

Jefferson Co. Wills 1823-1837, 201

Jefferson Co. Wills 1838-1846, 201

Jefferson County & Birmingham: Historical & Biographical, 23

Jennings Co. Index to Testators to 1880, 151

Jennings Co. Marriages 1818-1849, 151

Jessenland Burial & St. Thomas Cemetery, Sibley County, MN, 314

Jessenland Civil Records: Birth & Death, Sibley Co., MN, 314

Jessenland Marriage Records, Sibley County, Minnesota, 314

Johnson County, 202

Johnson County, Arkansas, 1880 Federal Census, 43

Johnson Co. Index to Testators to 1880, 151

Johnson Mortuary Death Records 1904-1937, The, 27

Johnston, Rev. William Henry—His Ministry in Northeastern Missouri, 323

Jones & Company (Troy Bell Foundry) Catalogue & History, 423

Journal of the Reverend John Guaiacum Zubley, A.M., D.D., March 5, 1770 through June 22, 1781, The, 91

Jubilee: Mount Holly Cemetery, Little Rock, Arkansas, Its First 150 Years, 48

Kankakee County Civil War Veterans, 121

Kansas Biographical Index: State-wide & Regional Histories, 177

Kansas Chief, The Weekly, Volume 8, January 1892 thru December 31, 1893, 177

Kansas Farm Family, A, 182

Kansas Territorial Settlers of 1860, 177

Kenilworth—The First Fifty Years, 116

Kennebec Valley, The, 222

Kent County, Delaware, Land Records, 1680-1701, 81

Kent County, Delaware, Land Records, Volume 2, 1702-1722, 81

Kent County, Delaware, Land Records, Volume 3, 1723-1734, 81

Kenton County, Kentucky Index #1, 202

Kenton County, Kentucky, Marriages, 1840-50, 202

Kentuckians in Illinois, 193

Kentuckians in Missouri, 193

Kentuckians in Ohio and Indiana, 193

Kentucky 1810 Census Index, 194

Kentucky 1820 Census Index, 194

Kentucky 1830 Census Index, 193

Kentucky: A Brief Genealogical Guide, 186

Kentucky Ancestry, 186

Kentucky Atlas of Historical County Boundaries, 189

Kentucky Books in Print, 1996 Edition, 185, 189

Kentucky [Court and Other] Records [Vol. I], 183

Kentucky Gazette, 1787-1800 & 1801-1820, The: Genealogical & Historical Abstracts, 186

Kentucky Genealogical Research, 190

Kentucky Genealogical Research: An Investigative Approach, 189

Kentucky Guide to Vital Statistics, 194

Kentucky in the War of 1812, 190

Kentucky Lake Reservoir Cemeteries. Volume 1, 197, 203, 204, 207

Kentucky Land Grants, The, 187

Kentucky Land Warrants, for the French and Indian Revolutionary Wars, 194

Kentucky Marriage Records, 188

Kentucky Marriages, 1797-1865, 184

Kentucky Marriages, Early to 1800, 188

Kentucky Memories of Uncle Sam Williams, 187

Kentucky Obituaries, 1787-1854, 184

Kentucky Pension Roll for 1835, 188

Kentucky Pioneer and Court Records, 189

Kentucky Pioneers and Their Descendants, 184

Kentucky Place Names, 190

Kentucky Soldiers of the War of 1812, 183, 187
Kern Cemetery in Porter Township, Van Buren County, Michigan, 305
Keuka Lake Memories and the Champagne Railroad, 429
King and People in Provincial Massachusetts, 255
Reuben King Journal, 1800-1806, The, 95
Kings County, 410
Knox Co. Index to Testators to 1880, 151
Knox Co. Land and Court Records, 151
Kosciusko Co. Index to Testators to 1880, 152

Lafayette County Legacy, 319
LaGrange Co. Index to Testators to 1880, 152
Lake Co. IL Fed. Census, 1870: Vol. 1 Antioch-Avon-Grant-Newport-Warren, 122
Lake Co. IL Fed. Census, 1870: Vol. 2 Benton-Waukegan, 123
Lake Co. IL Fed. Census, 1870: Vol. 3 Cuba-Ela-Fremont-Wauconda, 123
Lake Co. IL Fed. Census, 1870: Vol. 4 Deerfield-Libertyville-Shields-Vernon, 123
Lake Co. IL Fed. Census, 1880: Vol. 1 Deerfield, 123
Lake Co. IL Fed. Census, 1880: Vol. 2 Vernon-Ela, 123
Lake Co. IL Fed. Census, 1880: Vol. 3 Cuba-Wauconda-Fremont, 123
Lake Co. IL Fed. Census, 1880: Vol. 4 Libertyville-Shields, 123
Lake Co. IL Fed. Census, 1880: Vol. 5 Waukegan, 123
Lake Co. IL Fed. Census, 1880: Vol. 6 Warren-Avon-Grant, 123
Lake Co. IL Fed. Census, 1880: Vol. 7 Antioch-Newport-Benton, 123
Lake Co. IL Fed. Census, 1900: Vol. 8 Waukegan, 123
Lake Co. IL Fed. Census, 1900: Vol. 1 Fremont-Wauconda-Grant, 123
Lake Co. IL Fed. Census, 1900: Vol. 2 Libertyville-Vernon, 123
Lake Co. IL Fed. Census, 1900: Vol. 3 Antioch-Avon, 123
Lake Co. IL Fed. Census, 1900: Vol. 4 Cuba-Ela, 123

Lake Co. IL Fed. Census, 1900: Vol. 5 Benton-Newport-Warren, 123
Lake Co. IL Fed. Census, 1900: Vol. 6 Shields, 123
Lake Co. IL Fed. Census, 1900: Vol. 7 Deerfield, 123
Lake County IL Landowners Map 1873 Index, 124
Lake County IL Marriages Vol. 1 (1839-1859), 124
Lake County IL Marriages Vol. 2 (1860-1880), 124
Lake County IL Marriages Vol. 3 (1881-1901), 124
Lake Co. Index to Testators to 1880, 152
Lake Co. Marriages 1837-1850, 153
Lake Villa Township Cemeteries, 124
Lakeside Cemetery in the Village of Decatur, Michigan, 305
Lakes & Legends of Central New-York, 384
Lancaster County Nebraska District Court Records, Intention to Naturalize: 1867-1944, 344
Land Claims, Vincennes District, House Document No. 198. Claims, 1783-1812, 152
Land Claims in the Eastern District of the Orleans Territory, 210
Land Claims in the Mississippi Territory, 316
Land Claims in the Missouri Territory, 321
Land! Georgia Land Lotteries; Oregon Donation Land; Oklahoma Land Rushes, 94
Land Office and Prerogative Court Records of Colonial Maryland, 232
Land Records of Prince George's County, Maryland, 1710-1717, The, 251
Land Records of Prince George's County, Maryland, 1717-1726, The, 251
Land Records of Prince George's County, Maryland, 1726-1733, The, 251
Land Records of Prince George's County, Maryland, 1733-1739, The, 251
Land Records of Prince George's County, Maryland, 1739-1743, The, 251

Land Records of Somerset County, Maryland, 252

Land Records of Sussex County, Delaware, 1769-1782, 82

Land Records of Sussex County, Delaware, 1782-1789, 82

Land Records of the Attakapas District, Vol. II, Part I: Conveyance Records of Attakapas County, 1804-1818, 212

Land Records of the Attakapas District, Vol. II, Part 2: Attakapas-St. Martin Estates, 1804-1818, 212

Landholders of Northeastern New York, 1739-1802, 376

Landmarks of Albany County, 389

Landmarks of Oswego County, 420

Landmarks of Rensselaer County, 422

Landowners on the 1897 (Wall) Map of Carroll County, Indiana, 142

LaPorte Co. Index to Testators to 1880, 153

Laurel Grove Cemetery, Savannah, Georgia, 97

Law in Colonial Massachusetts, 1630-1800, 257

Lawrence, Yesterday & Today (1845-1918), 268

Lawrence County, Alabama, 1820 State Census, 24

Lawrence County, Arkansas, Loose Probate Papers, 1815-1890, 44

Lawrence County, Arkansas, Tax Records, 1829-1838, 44

Lawrence Co. Atlas 1870, 153

Lawrence Co. Marriages Vol. I 1818-1834, 153

Lawrence Co. Marriages Vol. II 1835-1843, 153

Lawrence Co. Marriages Vol. III 1844-1851, 153

Lawrence Co. Will Abstracts 1819-1850, 153

Law's Alabama Brigade in the War Between the Union and the Confederacy, 20

Laws of the Royal Colony of New Jersey 1703-1775, Volumes II-V, 362

Lawyers and Lawmakers of Kentucky, 188

Leading Facts of New Mexican History, 375

Lebanon: Three Centuries in a Conn. Hilltop Town, 77

LeDoux, Emma, and the Trunk Murder, 51

Lee Co. 1850 Census Transcription, 125

Legend of Cushetunk, The, 430

Legends of Woburn, 1642-1892, 279

Legends of Woburn, 1642-1892. Second Series, 279

Lenox and the Berkshire Highlands, 263

Leominster Traditions, 295

Leslie County, Kentucky Marriage Index, 1878-1982, 202

Lest We Forget, or Character Gems Gleaned from South Arkansas, 34

Letters About the Hudson River 1835-1837, 408

Letters Home: Written by Poestenkill Servicemen 1941-45 and 1917-18, 422

Lewis & Clark County, Montana Cemetery Records: Church of Sacred Heart, 1866-1908, 342

Lewis & Clark County, Montana Cemetery Records: Forestvale Cemetery, 1890-1984, 342

Lewis & Clark County, Montana Cemetery Records: Resurrection Cemetery, 1907-1990, 342

Lewis & Clark County, Montana Cemetery Records: Rural County-wide Cemetery and Others, 342

Lewis & Clark County, Montana Cemetery Records: Sunset Memorial Gardens, 1954-1986, 342

Lewis & Clark County, Montana: Marriage Index, 1866-1985, 341

Lewis & Clark County, Montana: Surname Directory, Volume 1, 1994, 341

Lexington. Record of Births, Marriages & Deaths to Jan. 1, 1898, 281

Lexington Epitaphs, 279

Liberty Men and Great Proprietors: The Revolutionary Settlement on the Maine Frontier, 1760-1820, 217

Life & Times in Hopkinton, 355

Life of Billy Yank: The Common Soldier of the Union, 211

Life of Johnny Reb: The Common Soldier of the Confederacy, 211

Life on the Ohio Frontier: A Collection of Letters from Mary Lott to Deacon John Phillips, 408

Lincoln Co. Wills & Estates 1781-1807, 203

Lincoln Co. Wills & Estates 1808-1822, 203

Linn County, A History, 172

Lisbon, Maine Vital Records Prior to 1892, 217

List of British Subjects at Honolulu, 1856, 108

List of Foreigners Residing in Honolulu, 1847, 108

List of Persons Whose Names Have Been Changed in Massachusetts, 1780-1892, 259

List of Revolutionary Soldiers of Berwick, 229

List of the Early Settlers of Georgia, A, 88

Lists of Inhabitants of Colonial New York, 385

Lists of Officials . . . of Connecticut Colony . . . 1636 through . . . 1677 and of New Haven Colony . . . [with] Soldiers in the Pequot War . . ., 65, 75

Litchfield Book of Days, The, 72

Little Commonwealth, A: Family Life in Plymouth Colony, 257

Little Nine Partners: A History of Pine Plains, NY with Genealogies of the Early Settlers, 400

Littleton, 281

Lives Passed: Biographical Sketches from Central New York, 381

Livingston Genealogical Register, 397

Local Sources for African-American Family Historians: Using County Court Records and Census Returns, 14

Location and Driving Directions to All Known Cemeteries, 48

Logan County, Kentucky Deed Abstracts, 1792-1813, 203

Logan County, Kentucky Deed Abstracts, 1813-1819, 203

Long Island Genealogical Source Material, 412

Long Island Genealogies, 411

Long Island, New York 1870 Census Index, 412

Long Island Source Records, 411

Lonoke County Arkansas Cemetery Inscriptions, 44

Lonoke County [Arkansas] Marriage Index 1921-1951, Volume 2, 45

Los Angeles County Cemeteries to 1940, 56

Los Angeles County Marriages, Book 2: March 1870-December 1872, 56

Los Angeles County Marriages, Book 3: January 1873-July 1875, 56

Los Angeles County Marriages, Book 4: July 1875-May 1877, 56

Lost and Found: Albany (New York) Area Church and Synagogue Records 1654-1925 and Supplement, 389

Lost Town of Cork, The, 218

Louisiana 1911 Census Confederate Veterans or Widows, 209

Louisiana Census Records. Volume I: Avoyelles and St. Landry Parishes, 1810 and 1820, 209, 213, 214

Louisiana Census Records. Volume II: Iberville, Natchitoches, Pointe Coupee, and Rapides Parishes, 1810 and 1820, 209, 213

Louisiana Colonials, 210

Louisiana History: The Journal of the Louisiana Historical Association, 210

Louisiana Purchase Bicentennial Series in Louisiana History, The, Volume I: The French Experience in Louisiana, 209

Louisiana Troops 1720-1770, 210

Loyalists of Massachusetts, The, 258, 260

Lubec, Maine Vital Records, 227

Lynn in the Revolution, 270

Lyon County Minnesota Atlas 1926, 312

Machias: Index of Surnames to George W. Drisko's "Narrative of the Town of Machias," 227

Macon [Georgia] Telegraph, The, (v.1 #1-v.7 #13; Nov. 1, 1826-Dec. 26, 1832) Abstracts of Marriage, Divorce, Death, and Legal Notices, 90

Madison Co. 1850 Census Transcription, 126

Madison Co. Index to Testators to 1880, 154

Madison County, Kentucky Taxpayers, 1787-1799, 204

Madison Co. Wills & Estates 1785-1813, 204

Maine Families in 1790, Volume I, 215

Maine Families in 1790, Volume 2, 215

Maine Families in 1790, Volume 3, 215

Maine Families in 1790, Volume 4, 215

Maine Families in 1790, Volume 5, 216

Maine Historical Magazine, The (Formerly The Bangor Historical Magazine, 4 Volumes), 216

Maine Marriages 1892-1966, 216

Maine Probate Abstracts, 214

Maine Probate Abstracts: 1687-1800, 214

Maine Town Microfilm List: Town and Vital Records, and Census Reports, 216

Maine Wills, 1640-1760, 217

Making of Connersville and Fayette County, The, Vol. 2, 146

Manchester, Indiana, 144

Manchester of Yesterday, 354

Manchester-by-the-Sea, 269

Manhattan Nationalist, Dec. 23, 1870-Dec. 30, 1871, 181

Manual for Illinois Genealogical Research, 110

Manual for Indiana Genealogical Research, 137

Manuscript Collections of the Maryland Historical Society, The, 235

Map of Delaware County, Indiana, 1874 (Atlas), 146

Maps of Indiana Counties in 1876, 138

Marion County, Arkansas, Tax Records 1841-1866, 45

Marion Co. [Illinois] 1850 Census Transcription, 126

Marion Co., IN Birth Records 1882-1907, 154

Marion Co., IN Complete Probate Records Jan. 1830-August 1852, 154

Marion Co., IN, Indianapolis, Mortality Records 1872-1882, 154

Marion Co. Index to Testators to 1880, 154

Marion County, Mississippi, Miscellaneous Records, 319

Marlborough Burial Ground Inscriptions, 281

Marriage, Death, and Legal Notices from Early Alabama Newspapers, 1818-1880, 20

Marriage and Death Notices from Alabama Newspapers and Family Records, 1819-1890, 20

Marriage and Death Notices from Southern Christian Advocate, Vol. 1 (1837-1860), 13

Marriage and Death Notices from Southern Christian Advocate, Vol. 2 (1861-1867), 13

Marriage and Death Notices from The Southern Patriot 1815-1848, Vol. 1 (1815-1830), 16

Marriage and Death Notices from The Southern Patriot 1815-1848, Vol. 2 (1831-1848), 16

Marriage Applications, Vermilion County, Illinois 1826-1852, 132

Marriage Applications, Vermilion County, Illinois 1853-1874, 132

Marriage Applications, Vermilion County, Illinois 1875-1877, 133

Marriage Applications, Vermilion County, Illinois 1878-1881, 133

Marriage Applications, Vermilion County, Illinois 1882-1891, 133

Marriage Bonds of Lafayette County, MS, Vol. I, 319

Marriage Licenses in the Howard District of Anne Arundel County 1840-1851, 249

Marriage Licenses of Caroline County, Maryland, 1774-1815, 244

Marriage Licenses of Clark County, Arkansas (Unclaimed), 38

Marriage Licenses of Frederick County, 1778-1810, 247

Marriage Licenses of Frederick County, 1811-1840, 247

Marriage Notices from the Southern Christian Advocate1867-1878, 13

Marriage Record, Albany Reformed Church, 1683-1804, 389

Marriage Record, Poughkeepsie Reformed Church, 1746-1824, 401

Marriage Record of German Flats and Herkimer Reformed Churches, Herkimer, NY: 1781-1899, 408

Marriage Records: Greene County, Arkansas 1876-1881, 41

Marriage Records of Caughnawaga Reformed Church, Fonda, NY: 1772-1899, 415

Marriage Records of Claverack Reformed Church, Claverack, NY: 1727-1899, 396

Marriage Records of 1st and 2nd Reformed Churches of Coxsackie, NY: 1797-1899, 405

Marriage Records of Four Reformed Congregations of Old Rhinebeck, NY: 1731-1899, 401

Marriage Records of Germantown, Gallatin, Copake, & Hillsdale Reformed Church: 1736-1899, 396

Marriage Records of Hancock County, Maine Prior to 1892, 220

Marriage Records of Hunterdon County, New Jersey, 1795-1875, 369

Marriage Records of Kinderhook Reformed Church, Kinderhook, NY: 1717-1899, 396

Marriage Records of Linlithgo Reformed Church, Livingston NY: 1723-1899, 396

Marriage Records of Lutheran and Reformed Churches of Schoharie, NY: 1732-1899, 426

Marriage Records of Lutheran Churches of Athens, NY & West Camp, NY: 1705-1899, 406, 433

Marriage Records of Lutheran & Reformed Churches, Stone Arabia, NY: 1739-1899, 415

Marriage Records of Manorton, Churchtown, Germantown, & Barrytown Lutheran Churches: 1794-1899, 396

Marriage Records of New Lebanon, NY: 1795-1852, 397

Marriage Records of Schenectady Reformed Church, Schenectady, NY: 1694-1852, 425

Marriage Records of St. Charles County, Missouri, 1805-1844, 339

Marriage Records of Three Lutheran Congregations of Rhinebeck, NY: 1746-1899, 401

Marriage Records of Townsend, Massachusetts 1737-1830, 284

Marriage Returns of Oxford County Maine, Prior to 1892, 224

Marriage Returns of Washington County, Maine Prior to 1892, 227

Marriage Returns of York County, Maine Prior to 1892, 228

Marriages, Monroe & Conecuh Counties, Alabama, 1833-1880, 22, 25

Marriages and Burials from the Frederick, Maryland Evangelical Lutheran Church, 247

Marriages and Deaths from the Maryland Gazette, 1727-1839, 230

Marriages and Deaths from the National Intelligencer (Washington, D.C.) 1800-1850 (Microfilm), 83

Marriages and Deaths from the New Yorker (Double Quarto Edition) 1836-1841, 387

Marriages and Obituaries from Early Georgia Newspapers, 93

Marriages and Obituaries from the Macon Messenger, 1818-1865, 93

Marriages in Chatham County, Georgia: Volume I, 1748-1852, 97

Marriages in Chatham County, Georgia: Volume II, 1852-1877, 98

Marriages in Goshen, Connecticut, 73

Marriages in Lincoln County, Nebraska, Volume 4 1886-1889, 345

Marriages of Arapahoe County, Colorado 1859-1901, 63

Marriages of Hancock County, Georgia, 1806 to 1850, 102

Marriages of Monmouth County, New Jersey, 1795-1843, 371

Marriages of Morgan County, Alabama, 1818-1896, 26

Marriages of Rev. Harmanus Van Huysen, 1794-1825, 389

Marriages of Solano County, California, 1853-1893 (Marriage License Applications), 58

Marshall Co. Index to Testators to 1880, 155

Marshfield: A Town of Villages 1640-1990, 289

Marshfield, Massachusetts Vital Records, 291

Martin Co. Index to Testators to 1880, 155

Martin Co. Marriages 1820-1850, 155

"Mary & John," The: A Story of the Founding of Dorchester, MA, 1630, 293

Maryland 1800 Census, 237

Maryland: A Middle Temperament, 1634-1980, 230

Maryland Calendar of Wills, Vols. 1-8, 231

Maryland Calendar of Wills, Vols. 1-16 (complete set), 231

Maryland Calendar of Wills, Vol. 2: 1685-1702, 231

Maryland Calendar of Wills, Vol. 3: 1703-1713, 231

Maryland Calendar of Wills, Vol. 4: 1713-1720, 231
Maryland Calendar of Wills, Vol. 5: 1720-1726, 231
Maryland Calendar of Wills, Vol. 6: 1726-1732, 231
Maryland Calendar of Wills, Vol. 7: 1732-1738, 231
Maryland Calendar of Wills, Vol. 8: 1738-1743, 231
Maryland Calendar of Wills, Vol. 9: 1744-1749, 237
Maryland Calendar of Wills, Vol. 10: 1748-1753, 237
Maryland Calendar of Wills, Vol. 11: 1753-1760, 237
Maryland Calendar of Wills, Vol. 12: 1759-1764, 238
Maryland Calendar of Wills, Vol. 13: 1764-1767, 238
Maryland Calendar of Wills, Vol. 14: 1767-1772, 238
Maryland Calendar of Wills, Vol. 15: 1772-1774, 238
Maryland Calendar of Wills, Vol. 16: 1774-1777, 238
Maryland Deponents, 1634-1799, 235
Maryland Eastern Shore Vital Records, Book 1: 1648-1725, 238
Maryland Eastern Shore Vital Records, Book 2: 1726-1750, 238
Maryland Eastern Shore Vital Records, Book 3: 1751-1775, 238
Maryland Eastern Shore Vital Records, Book 4: 1776-1800, 238
Maryland Eastern Shore Vital Records, Book 5: 1801-1825, 238
Maryland Freedom Papers: Volume I, Anne Arundel County, 239
Maryland from Overseas, To, 234
Maryland Gazette, The, 1727-1761: Genealogical and Historical Abstracts, 9, 232
Maryland Genealogical Research, 236
Maryland Genealogies, 233
Maryland. Index to the Wills of St. Mary's County, 1662-1960 and Somerset County, 1664-1955, 252-253
Maryland Marriages, 1634-1777, 229
Maryland Marriages, 1778-1800, 229
Maryland Marriages, 1801-1820, 229
Maryland Militia in the Revolutionary War, 230

Maryland Naturalization Abstracts, Volume 2, 235
Maryland Oaths of Fidelity, 230
Maryland Records, 230
Maryland Rent Rolls, 239, 241
Maryland Research Guide, 233
Maryland Revolutionary Records, 234
Marylanders in the Confederacy, 232
Marylanders to Carolina, 235
Marylanders to Kentucky, 1775-1825, 189, 235
Marylanders Who Served the Nation, 232
Mason County, Kentucky, County Clerk Court Orders, 1789-1800: An Every-Name Index, 204
Mason County, Kentucky, Court Orders, 1803-1816: An Every-Name Index, 204
Mason County, Kentucky, Taxpayers, 1790-1799, 204
Massachusetts and Maine Families, 216, 259
Massachusetts Bay Connections, 258
Massachusetts Birth, Marriage, & Death Indexes 1841-1895, 258
Massachusetts Cemetery Records: Quabbin Park 1741-1984, 258
Massachusetts Church Records: Scituate 1695-1871, 289
Massachusetts Church Records: Sutton, Warren, 296
Massachusetts Genealogical Research, 259
Massachusetts Magazine, The: Marriage and Death Notices, 1789-1796, 260
Massachusetts Officers and Soldiers 1702-1722, Queen Anne's War to Dummer's War, 257
Massachusetts Officers and Soldiers 1723-1743, Dummer's War to War of Jenkin's Ear, 260
Massachusetts Officers and Soldiers in the French and Indian Wars, 1755-56, 257
Massachusetts Soldiers in the French and Indian Wars 1748-1763, 260
Massachusetts Vital Record Transcripts 1620-1849, 258
Massachusetts Vital Records 1620-1905 (originals), 258
Massachusetts Vital Records to 1850 (old printed series), 258

Massachusetts Vital Records to the Year 1850: Abington, 290

Massachusetts Vital Records to the Year 1850: Acton, 281

Massachusetts Vital Records to the Year 1850: Alford, 263

Massachusetts Vital Records to the Year 1850: Amesbury, 270

Massachusetts Vital Records to the Year 1850: Andover, 270

Massachusetts Vital Records to the Year 1850: Arlington, 281

Massachusetts Vital Records to the Year 1850: Ashburnham, 296

Massachusetts Vital Records to the Year 1850: Ashfield, 274

Massachusetts Vital Records to the Year 1850: Athol, 296

Massachusetts Vital Records to the Year 1850: Becket, 263

Massachusetts Vital Records to the Year 1850: Bedford, 281

Massachusetts Vital Records to the Year 1850: Beverly, 270

Massachusetts Vital Records to the Year 1850: Billerica, 282

Massachusetts Vital Records to the Year 1850: Bolton, 296

Massachusetts Vital Records to the Year 1850: Boxboro, 282

Massachusetts Vital Records to the Year 1850: Boxford, 270

Massachusetts Vital Records to the Year 1850: Boylston, 296

Massachusetts Vital Records to the Year 1850: Bradford, 264

Massachusetts Vital Records to the Year 1850: Brewster, 261

Massachusetts Vital Records to the Year 1850: Bridgewater, 290

Massachusetts Vital Records to the Year 1850: Brimfield, 276

Massachusetts Vital Records to the Year 1850: Brockton, 290

Massachusetts Vital Records to the Year 1850: Brookfield, 296

Massachusetts Vital Records to the Year 1850: Brookline, 286

Massachusetts Vital Records to the Year 1850: Buckland, 274

Massachusetts Vital Records to the Year 1850: Burlington, 282

Massachusetts Vital Records to the Year 1850: Cambridge, 282

Massachusetts Vital Records to the Year 1850: Carlisle, 282

Massachusetts Vital Records to the Year 1850: Carver, 290

Massachusetts Vital Records to the Year 1850: Charlemont, 274

Massachusetts Vital Records to the Year 1850: Charlton, 297

Massachusetts Vital Records to the Year 1850: Chelmsford, 282

Massachusetts Vital Records to the Year 1850: Chelsea, 293

Massachusetts Vital Records to the Year 1850: Chester, 276

Massachusetts Vital Records to the Year 1850: Chilmark, 266

Massachusetts Vital Records to the Year 1850: Cohasset, 286

Massachusetts Vital Records to the Year 1850: Conway, 274

Massachusetts Vital Records to the Year 1850: Dalton, 263

Massachusetts Vital Records to the Year 1850: Dana, 266

Massachusetts Vital Records to the Year 1850: Danvers, 270

Massachusetts Vital Records to the Year 1850: Dartmouth, 265

Massachusetts Vital Records to the Year 1850: Dedham Town Records, 287

Massachusetts Vital Records to the Year 1850: Deerfield, 274

Massachusetts Vital Records to the Year 1850: Douglas, 297

Massachusetts Vital Records to the Year 1850: Dover, 287

Massachusetts Vital Records to the Year 1850: Dracut, 282

Massachusetts Vital Records to the Year 1850: Dudley, 297

Massachusetts Vital Records to the Year 1850: Dunstable, 282

Massachusetts Vital Records to the Year 1850: Duxbury, 290

Massachusetts Vital Records to the Year 1850: E. Bridgewater, 290

Massachusetts Vital Records to the Year 1850: Edgartown, 266

Massachusetts Vital Records to the Year 1850: Essex, 270

Massachusetts Vital Records to the Year 1850: Foxborough, 287

Massachusetts Vital Records to the Year 1850: Framingham, 282

Massachusetts Vital Records to the Year 1850: Georgetown, 270

Massachusetts Vital Records to the Year 1850: Gill, 274

Massachusetts Vital Records to the Year 1850: Gloucester, 270

Massachusetts Vital Records to the Year 1850: Grafton, 297

Massachusetts Vital Records to the Year 1850: Granville, 276

Massachusetts Vital Records to the Year 1850: Great Barrington, 263

Massachusetts Vital Records to the Year 1850: Greenfield, 274

Massachusetts Vital Records to the Year 1850: Groton, 282

Massachusetts Vital Records to the Year 1850: Halifax, 290

Massachusetts Vital Records to the Year 1850: Hamilton, 270

Massachusetts Vital Records to the Year 1850: Hanover Records, 1727-1857, 290

Massachusetts Vital Records to the Year 1850: Hanson, 290

Massachusetts Vital Records to the Year 1850: Hardwick, 297

Massachusetts Vital Records to the Year 1850: Harvard, 297

Massachusetts Vital Records to the Year 1850: Haverhill, 270

Massachusetts Vital Records to the Year 1850: Heath, 274

Massachusetts Vital Records to the Year 1850: Holliston, 282

Massachusetts Vital Records to the Year 1850: Hopkinton, 282

Massachusetts Vital Records to the Year 1850: Hubbardston, 297

Massachusetts Vital Records to the Year 1850: Hull, 290

Massachusetts Vital Records to the Year 1850: Ipswich, 271

Massachusetts Vital Records to the Year 1850: Kingston, 290

Massachusetts Vital Records to the Year 1850: Lawrence, 271

Massachusetts Vital Records to the Year 1850: Lee, 263

Massachusetts Vital Records to the Year 1850: Leominster, 297

Massachusetts Vital Records to the Year 1850: Lincoln, 282

Massachusetts Vital Records to the Year 1850: Lowell, 282

Massachusetts Vital Records to the Year 1850: Lynn, 271

Massachusetts Vital Records to the Year 1850: Malden, 282

Massachusetts Vital Records to the Year 1850: Manchester, 271

Massachusetts Vital Records to the Year 1850: Marblehead, 271

Massachusetts Vital Records to the Year 1850: Marlborough, 282

Massachusetts Vital Records to the Year 1850: Medfield, 287

Massachusetts Vital Records to the Year 1850: Medford, 283

Massachusetts Vital Records to the Year 1850: Medway, 287

Massachusetts Vital Records to the Year 1850: Mendon, 297

Massachusetts Vital Records to the Year 1850: Methuen, 271

Massachusetts Vital Records to the Year 1850: Middlefield, 277

Massachusetts Vital Records to the Year 1850: Middleton, 271

Massachusetts Vital Records to the Year 1850: Milford, 297

Massachusetts Vital Records to the Year 1850: Millbury, 297

Massachusetts Vital Records to the Year 1850: Montague, 274

Massachusetts Vital Records to the Year 1850: Montgomery, 276

Massachusetts Vital Records to the Year 1850: Nantucket, 285

Massachusetts Vital Records to the Year 1850: Natick, 283

Massachusetts Vital Records to the Year 1850: New Ashford, 263

Massachusetts Vital Records to the Year 1850: New Bedford, 265

Massachusetts Vital Records to the Year 1850: New Braintree, 297

Massachusetts Vital Records to the Year 1850: New Salem, 274

Massachusetts Vital Records to the Year 1850: Newbury, 271

Massachusetts Vital Records to the Year 1850: Newburyport, 271

Massachusetts Vital Records to the Year 1850: Newton, 283

Massachusetts Vital Records to the Year 1850: Northbridge, 297

Massachusetts Vital Records to the Year 1850: Oakham, 297

Massachusetts Vital Records to the Year 1850: Otis, 263

Massachusetts Vital Records to the Year 1850: Oxford, 297

Massachusetts Vital Records to the Year 1850: Pelham, 278

Massachusetts Vital Records to the Year 1850: Pembroke, 290

Massachusetts Vital Records to the Year 1850: Peru, 263

Massachusetts Vital Records to the Year 1850: Petersham, 297

Massachusetts Vital Records to the Year 1850: Phillipston, 297

Massachusetts Vital Records to the Year 1850: Plympton, 290

Massachusetts Vital Records to the Year 1850: Princeton, 297

Massachusetts Vital Records to the Year 1850: Reading, 283

Massachusetts Vital Records to the Year 1850: Rehoboth, 1642-1896, 264

Massachusetts Vital Records to the Year 1850: Richmond, 263

Massachusetts Vital Records to the Year 1850: Rochester, 290

Massachusetts Vital Records to the Year 1850: Rockport, 271

Massachusetts Vital Records to the Year 1850: Rowley, 271

Massachusetts Vital Records to the Year 1850: Roxbury, 293

Massachusetts Vital Records to the Year 1850: Royalston, 297

Massachusetts Vital Records to the Year 1850: Rutland, 298

Massachusetts Vital Records to the Year 1850: Salem, 271

Massachusetts Vital Records to the Year 1850: Salisbury, 271

Massachusetts Vital Records to the Year 1850: Sandisfield, 264

Massachusetts Vital Records to the Year 1850: Saugus, 272

Massachusetts Vital Records to the Year 1850: Scituate, 290

Massachusetts Vital Records to the Year 1850: Sharon, 287

Massachusetts Vital Records to the Year 1850: Shelburne, 274

Massachusetts Vital Records to the Year 1850: Sherborn, 283

Massachusetts Vital Records to the Year 1850: Shirley, 283

Massachusetts Vital Records to the Year 1850: Shrewsbury, 298

Massachusetts Vital Records to the Year 1850: Southborough, 298

Massachusetts Vital Records to [the Year] 1850: Southbridge, 296

Massachusetts Vital Records to the Year 1850: Spencer, 298

Massachusetts Vital Records to the Year 1850: Stoneham, 283

Massachusetts Vital Records to the Year 1850: Stow, 283

Massachusetts Vital Records to the Year 1850: Sturbridge, 298

Massachusetts Vital Records to the Year 1850: Sudbury, 283

Massachusetts Vital Records to the Year 1850: Sutton, 298

Massachusetts Vital Records to the Year 1850: Taunton, 265

Massachusetts Vital Records to the Year 1850: Templeton, 298

Massachusetts Vital Records to the Year 1850: Tewksbury, 283

Massachusetts Vital Records to the Year 1850: Tisbury, 266

Massachusetts Vital Records to the Year 1850: Topsfield, 272

Massachusetts Vital Records to the Year 1850: Truro, 261

Massachusetts Vital Records to the Year 1850: Tyngsboro, 283

Massachusetts Vital Records to the Year 1850: Tyringham, 263

Massachusetts Vital Records to the Year 1850: Upton, 298

Massachusetts Vital Records to the Year 1850: Uxbridge, 298

Massachusetts Vital Records to the Year 1850: W. Boylston, 298

Massachusetts Vital Records to the Year 1850: W. Bridgewater, 290

Massachusetts Vital Records to the Year 1850: W. Newbury, 272

Massachusetts Vital Records to the Year 1850: W. Stockbridge, 263

Massachusetts Vital Records to the Year 1850: Wakefield, 283

Massachusetts Vital Records to the Year 1850: Walpole, 287

Massachusetts Vital Records to the Year 1850: Waltham, 283

Massachusetts Vital Records to the Year 1850: Warren, 298
Massachusetts Vital Records to the Year 1850: Washington, 263
Massachusetts Vital Records to [the Year] 1850: Webster, 296
Massachusetts Vital Records to the Year 1850: Wenham, 272
Massachusetts Vital Records to the Year 1850: Westborough, 298
Massachusetts Vital Records to the Year 1850: Westford, 283
Massachusetts Vital Records to the Year 1850: Westminster, 298
Massachusetts Vital Records to the Year 1850: Westport, 265
Massachusetts Vital Records to the Year 1850: Weymouth, 287
Massachusetts Vital Records to the Year 1850: Winchendon, 298
Massachusetts Vital Records to the Year 1850: Windsor, 263
Massachusetts Vital Records to the Year 1850: Worthington, 278
Massachusetts Vital Records to the Year 1850: Wrentham, 287
Master Index of Known Burials, Vermilion County, Illinois, Part I, 133
Master Index of Known Burials, Vermilion County, Illinois, Part II, 133
Master Index to Lonoke County Arkansas Cemetery Inscriptions, 44
Mattapoisett & Old Rochester, 291
Mayflower Births and Deaths, 6
Mayflower Deeds & Probates, 6
Mayflower Descendant 1620-1937, The, 258
Mayflower Descendants and Their Marriages for Two Generations After the Landing, 258
Mayflower Families Through Five Generations, 4
Mayflower Increasings, 6
Mayflower Marriages, 6
Mayflower Reader, The, 2, 255
McCracken County Cemeteries, Vol. III, Expanded Version, 204
McCracken County Cemeteries, Vol. IV (Mount Kenton), 204
McCracken Co., KY Newsletters, Vol. 1, 1984-88, 205
McCracken County School Records, for 1915-1916, 204

McDonald County, Missouri 1870 Federal Census, 334
McDonald Papers, The, 436
McLean Co., Burials in Lexington Cemetery, 127
McLean Co., Pleasant Hill Cemetery Records, 127
Medicine in Colonial Massachusetts, 1620-1820, 255
Meeker County Cemeteries, 312
Membership Records of Seventh Baptists of Central New York State 1797-1940s, 386
Memoirs & Reminscences, 373
Memorial History of Augusta, Georgia, 104
Memorial History of Bradford, 264
Memorial History of Hartford County, 1633-1884, 71
Memorial of the Town of Hampstead, 358
Memorial of the Town of Hampstead, Additions & Corrections, 358
Memorial Record of Southwestern Minnesota, 308
Memorial & Biographical History of the Counties of Fresno, Tulare & Kern, 55, 60
Memorial & Biographical Records & Illustrated Compendium of Biography, 343, 345, 346
Memorials of the Grand River Valley, 303
Memories of Life on the Ridge, 420
Meneely Bell Foundry of West Troy, Albany Co., N.Y, 388
Men & Women of Nebraska, 346
Mercer Co. Wills & Estates 1786-1808, 205
Mercer Co. Wills & Estates 1808-1821, 205
(Meriden) Recollections of a New England Town, 74
Meriwether County, Georgia, Cemeteries, 103
Merrill's New York, Arch, 382
Methodist Records of Baltimore City, Vol. 1: 1799-1829, 241
Methodist Records of Baltimore City, Vol. 2: 1830-1839, 242
Miami Co. Index to Testators to 1880, 155
Miami Co. Marriages 1843-1855, 155

Michigan Censuses 1710-1830 Under the French, British, and Americans, 301

Michigan Military Records, 301

Michigan Quakers: Abstracts of All Known Extant Records of Friends Meetings in Michigan (1831-1960), 300

Michigan Voyageurs: Notary Book of S. Abbot, Mackinac Island, 1807-1817, 303

(Middleboro) Descriptive Catalog of Members of the 1st Congregational Church, 288

Middling Planters of Ruxton Maryland, 1694-1850, 241

Midwife's Tale, A, 221

Milford, 1880-1930, 298

Military & Civil History of the County of Essex, 404

Military Annals of Lancaster, 1740-1865, 298

Military Annals of Mississippi, 316

Military Bounty Lands: The Balloting Book & Other Documents Relating to Them in N.Y, 382

Military History of Mississippi, 1803-1898, 317

Military Minutes of the Council of Appointment of the State of N.Y., 1783-1821, 379

Militia: New York State Provincial & Revolutionary War Organizations, 376

Militiamen, Rangers, and Redcoats: The Military in Georgia, 1754-1776, 91

Milledgeville, Georgia, Newspaper Clippings (Southern Recorder), Vol. I, 1820-1827, 89

Milledgeville, Georgia, Newspaper Clippings (Southern Recorder), Vol II, 1828-1832, 89

Milledgeville, Georgia, Newspaper Clippings (Southern Recorder), Vol III, 1833-1835, 89

Milledgeville, Georgia, Newspaper Clippings (Southern Recorder), Vol IV, 1836-1838, 89

Minnesota Genealogical Journal, 308

Minnesota in the Civil & Indian Wars, 1861-1865, 308

Minnesota Land Owner Maps & Directories, 307

Minnesota Society of the Sons of the American Revolution Centennial Registry, 307

Minnesotans in the Civil & Indian Wars, 308

Minnesota's Mining Accidents 1900-1920 and Mining Deaths 1889-1990, 310, 312, 314

Minnesota's World War II Army Dead, 308

Minnesota's World War II Navy Casualties, 308

Minutes of the Baptist Church on Paint Rock River & Larkin Fork in Jackson County, Alabama, 23

Miscellaneous History of New London, from the Records & Papers of the New London Historical Society, 77

Miscellaneous Record Book, Yuba County, California. Book I, 62

Mississippi, 317

Mississippi as a Province, Territory, and State, 315

Mississippi Atlas of Historical County Boundaries, 316

Mississippi County Court Records, 316

Mississippi Court Records, 1799-1835, 316

Mississippi Marriages, Early to 1825, 316

Mississippi Provincial Archives: French Dominion, 1729-1748, Volume IV, 211

Mississippi Provincial Archives: French Dominion, 1749-1763, Volume V, 211

Mississippi Territory in the War of 1812, 317

Missouri Cemetery Inscription Sources: Print & Microform, 321

Missouri Confederate Pensions and Confederate Home Applications Index, 321

Missouri Marriages, Early to 1825, 321

Missouri Marriages, 1826 to 1850, 321

Missouri Marriages Before 1840, 321

Missouri Marriages in the News, 1851-1865, 322

Missouri Marriages in the News, Vol. II, 1866-1870, 323

Missouri Newspapers on Microfilm at the State Historical Society, 321, 323

Missouri Ordeal, 1862-1864: Diaries of Willard Hall Mendenhall, 333

Missouri Plat Books in the State Historical Society of Missouri, 319, 321

Missouri Sources, Queries & Reviews Volume 1, 323

Missouri Taxpayers, 1819-1826, 322

Missouri Union Burials—Missouri Units, 321

Mistress of Riversdale: The Plantation Letters of Rosalie Stier Calvert, 1795-1821, 230

Modern History of New Haven & Eastern New Haven County, 75

Mohawk Valley: Its Legends & History, 413

Momento Mori, 269

Monroe Co. 1850 Census Transcription, 127

Monroe Co. Index to Testators to 1880, 155

Monroe Township Cemeteries, Nodaway County, Missouri 1960, 335

Montgomery County, Georgia: A Source Book of Genealogy and History, 103

Montgomery County, Georgia, Newspaper Clippings, Vol. I, 1886-1905, 104

Montgomery County, Georgia, Newspaper Clippings, Vol. II, 1906-1919, 104

Montgomery Co. IL Cemeteries—Volume 1, 113, 127

Montgomery Co. IL—Hart Cemetery, 128

Montgomery Co. [Indiana] Index to Testators to 1880, 156

Montgomery Co. [Indiana] Marriages 1823-1849, 156

Montgomery Co. [Indiana] Wills 1852-1869 and Marriages 1837-1847, 156

Montgomery Co. [Indiana] Wills 1868-1883, 156

Montgomery County, Kentucky Taxpayers, 1797 & 1799, 205

Montgomery County, Maryland, Marriage Licenses, 1798-1898, 250

Montgomery County Index to Scharf's History of Western Maryland, 250

Moravian Families of Carroll's Manor, Frederick County, Maryland, 247

Moravian Families of Graceham, Maryland, 248

Moravians in Georgia, 1735-1740, The, 90

More Death Records from Missouri Newspapers, 1810-1857, 322

More Maryland Deponents, 1716-1799, 235

More Palatine Families, 9, 380-381

Morgan Co. Index to Testators to 1880, 156

Morgan County, Kentucky, Cemetery Records, 205

Morgan County, Kentucky, First Court Order Book 1823-30, 205

Morgan County, Kentucky, Genealogical Sourcebook with the 1830-40 Censuses, 205

Mormons at the Missouri, 1846-1852, 343

Morris's Memorial History of Staten Island, 423

Morrison's Annals of Western New-York, 17 County History, 382, 391, 404, 405, 411, 418, 430

Morrison's History of Broome County, Towns, Villages, &c., 1860, 391

Morrison's History of Cattaraugus County, Towns, Villages, &c., 1860, 391

Morrison's History of Cayuga County, Towns, Villages, &c., 1860, 391

Morrison's History of Chenango County, Towns, Villages, &c., 1860, 394

Morrison's History of Cortland County, Towns, Villages, &c., 1860, 397

Morrison's History of Erie County, Towns, Villages, &c., 1860, 403

Morrison's History of Genesee County, Towns, Villages, &c., 1860, 405

Morrison's History of Lewis County, Towns, Villages, &c., 1860, 410

Morrison's History of Livingston County, Towns, Villages, &c., 1860, 411

Morrison's History of Madison County, Towns, Villages, &c., 1860, 412

Morrison's History of Niagara County, Towns, Villages, &c., 1860, 418

Morrison's History of Oneida County, Towns, Villages, &c., 1860, 418

Morrison's History of Onondaga County, Towns, Villages, &c., 1860, 419

Morrison's History of Oswego County, Towns, Villages, &c., 1860, 421

Morrison's History of St. Lawrence County, Towns, Villages, &c., 1860, 429

Morrison's History of Steuben County, Towns, Villages, &c., 1860, 429

Morrison's A. B. C. Reader, Mrs., 382

Mortuary Records, with Genealogical Notes of the Town of Spafford, Onondaga Co., 419

Mothers of Invention: Women of the Slaveholding South in the American Civil War, 12

Mount Holly Cemetery, Little Rock, Arkansas, Burial Index, 1843-1993, 48

Mt. Elliott Cemetery Burial Records, Detroit, 1845-1861, 305

Municipalities of Essex County, 1666-1924., 366

Muster Rolls and Other Records of Service of Maryland Troops in the American Revolution, 1775-1783, 234

Muster Rolls of N.Y. Provincial Troops, 1755-1764, 383

Myersville, Maryland, Lutheran Baptisms, 1832-1849, 1861-1897, 247

Name Index to Arad Thomas' 1871 The Pioneer History of Orleans County, 420

Name Index to Beer's 1878 History of Montgomery & Fulton Counties, 414

Name Index to Beer's 1879 History of Allegany County, 390

Name Index to Beer's 1880 History of Wyoming County, 438

Name Index to Johnson's 1878 History of Washington County, 434

Name Index to Smith's 1880 History of Chenango & Madison Counties, 394, 413

Name Index to Smith's 1885 History of Warren County, 434

Name Index to Sylvester's 1878 History of Saratoga County, 424

Names and Abstracts from the Acts of the Legislative Council of the Territory of Florida, 1822-1845, 85

Names and Sketches of the Pioneer Settlers of Madison County, 412

Names in Stone, 247

Names of Soldiers of the American Revolution [from Maine], 214

Narrative History of Dover, A, 287

Narrative History of South Scituate/ Norwell, A, 291

Narrative History of the Town of Cohasset, A, 285

Narrative of the Town of Machias, 227

Natchez Before 1830, 317

Natchez Court Records, 1767-1805, The, 316

National Road—1828, 14

Naturalization & Related Records, 384

Naturalizations in the Marine Court, New York City, 1827-1835, 417

Naturalizations in the Marine Court, New York City, 1834-1840, 417

(Needham) Epitaphs from Graveyards, 286

Nelson Co. [Kentucky] Marriages 1785-1810, 206

Nelson Co. [Kentucky] Marriages 1811-1830, 206

Nelson Co. [Kentucky] Marriages 1831-1850, 206

Nelson Co. [Kentucky] Wills & Estates 1785-1807, 206

Nelson County, Kentucky Taxpayers, 1793-1799, 206

Nevada Biographical and Genealogical Sketch Index, 346

Nevada County, Arkansas United States Census of 1880, 45

New Amsterdam and Its People, 1626-1902, 417

(New Bedford) Whaling Masters, 265

New Brunswick in History, 370

New England Families, Genealogical and Memorial, 4

New England Genealogy, 4

NEHG [New England Historical and Genealogical] Register, The, 1847-1994 (CD-ROM), 5

New England Historical and Genealogical Register, The, Index, Vol. 1, 5

New England in Albany, 7, 390

New England Marriages Prior to 1700, 7

New England Miniature: A History of York, Maine, 228

New England Vital Records, 1831-1840, 1

New England Vital Records, 1841-1846, 3

New England Vital Records, 1847-1852, 3

New England Vital Records, 1853-1858, 3

New England Vital Records, 1859-1865, 3

New England Vital Records, Volume 5, 3

New England Vital Records from the Exeter News-Letter 1831-1840, Volume 1, 3

New England Vital Records from the Exeter News-Letter 1841-1846, Volume 2, 3

New England Vital Records from the Exeter News-Letter 1847-1852, Volume 3, 3

New England Vital Records from the Exeter News-Letter, 1853-1858, 3

New Hampshire 1732 Census, 348

New Hampshire 1776 Census, 348

New Hampshire 1800 Census Index, 350-351, 353, 357, 358

New Hampshire and Vermont Atlas of Historical Boundaries, 348

New Hampshire Residents 1633-1699, 348

New Haven Vital Records, 1649-1850, 75

New Jersey and the Revolutionary War, 360

New Jersey Biographical and Genealogical Notes, 361

New Jersey Biographical Index, A, 362

New Jersey Calendar of Wills, 1670-1780, 361

New Jersey from Colony to State, 1609-1789, 361

New Jersey Heirs to Estates from Partitions and Divisions: Middlesex County, 1780-1870, 370

New Jersey Heirs to Estates from Partitions and Divisions: Monmouth, Mercer & Burlington Counties, 365, 369, 371

New Jersey Heirs to Estates from Partitions and Divisions: Morris County, 1785-1900, 371

New Jersey Heirs to Estates from Partitions and Divisions: Warren & Sussex Counties, 1789-1918, 373-374

New Jersey Index of Wills, Inventories, Etc., 363

New Jersey Marriages, 361

New Jersey State Census, 1855-1915, 362

New Madrid County, Missouri Court Orders, 1816-1825, 335

New Netherland Roots, 378

New North Church, Boston [1714-1799], The, 293

New Orleans French, 1720-1733, The, 210

New York Alien Residents, 1825-1848, 387

New York Atlas of Historical County Boundaries, 382

[New York] Calendar of Wills, 378

New York City Court Records, 1684-1760, 416

New York City Court Records, 1760-1797, 417

New York City Court Records, 1797-1801, 417

New York City Court Records, 1801-1804, 417

New York [City] Directory from 1786, 415

New York City Methodist Marriages 1785-1893, 415

New York Foundling Hospital, The, 416

New York Genealogical Research, 386

New York in the Revolution as Colony and State, 385

[New York]: Index of Awards On Claims of the Soldiers of the War of 1812, 383

New York Irish, The, 376

New York Revolutionary War Pensioners, 1840, 381

New York State Agricultural College at Ovid, 428

New York: State Census of Albany County Towns in 1790, 389

New York State County Atlases—Post Civil War, 384

New York's Detailed Census of 1855, Greene County, 405

New York's Finger Lakes Pioneer Families, Especially Tompkins County, 381, 431

Newaygo White Pine Heritage, 304

News' History of Passaic, The, 372

Newspaper Abstracts of Western Maryland, Vol. I: 1786-1798, 238

Newspaper Abstracts of Western Maryland, Vol. 2: 1799-1805, 238

Newspaper Abstracts of Western Maryland, Vol. 3: 1806-1810, 238

Newton Co. Index to Testators to 1880, 156

Newton, Massachusetts, 1679-1779: A Biographical Directory, 284

Newtown's History, and Historical Ezra Kevan Johnson, 68

Nicknames: Past & Present, 52

Nineteenth Century Apprentices in New York City, 417

Ninth U.S. Census—1870 Index of Solano County, California, 58

Noble Co. Index to Testators to 1880, 157

Noble Pursuit, A: The Sesquicentennial History of the New England Historic Genealogical Society 1845-1995, 6

Nodaway County Pension Records—Volume 1, 335

Norridgewock Register, 1903, 225

North Haven Annals: History of the Town from Its Settlement, 1680, to Its First Centennial, 1886, 76

Northampton, the Meadow City, 277

Northampton of Today, Depicted by Pen and Camera, 277

Northborough History, 299

Northern California Marriage Index 1850-1860, 52

Northern New Hampshire Graveyards & Cemeteries, 347

Northwestern Arkansas Death Record Index, 1914-1923: Benton, Boone, Carroll, Madison, Marion, Newton, Searcy, and Washington Counties, 29

Northwestern Arkansas Death Record Index, 1934-1940: Benton, Boone, Carroll, Madison, Marion, Newton, Searcy, and Washington Counties, 29

Northwestern Indiana, from 1800 to 1900, 135

Norwalk After Two Hundred Fifty Years, 68

Notable Men of Alabama: Personal & Genealogical, 19

Notable Southern Families, 11

Note-Book Kept by Thomas Lechford, Lawyer in Boston, 293

Notes Geographical and Historical, 410

Notes on Wenham History, 1643-1943, 267

Notices from New Jersey Newspapers, 1781-1790, 363

Notices from the New Hampshire Gazette, 348

Notices from the New Hampshire Gazette, 1765-1800, 348

Obituary Dates and Family Ties, 156

Obituary Dates from the Denni Hlasatel 1891-1899, 116

Obituary Dates from the Denni Hlasatel 1930-1939, 116

Obituary Dates from the Denni Hlasatel 1940-1949, 116

Obituary Records, Records from the Ministry, Family Histories, 132

Official & Statistical Register of the State of Mississippi, Military History Only, 317

Official History of Fulton County, 102

Official History of Greene County, 407

Ohio Books in Print, 185

Ohio Co. [Indiana] Index to Testators to 1880, 157

Ohio Co. [Indiana] Marriages 1844-1849, 157

Ohio Co. [Indiana] Marriages 1844-1882, 157

Ohio County, Kentucky, in the Olden Days, 207

Old Academy on the Hill, The: A Bicentennial History 1791-1991, 228

Old and New Monongahela, The, 10

Old Bergen History & Reminiscences, 368

Old Burial Grounds of New Jersey: A Guide, 362

Old Burying Ground of Fairfield: Memorial of Many Early Settlers & Transcript of the Inscriptions & Epitaphs on the Tombstones Found in the Oldest Burying Ground in Fairfield, 68

Old Dutch Burying Ground of Sleepy Hollow, in N. Tarrytown, 437

Old Eliot, 229

Old Families of Louisiana, 1608-1929, Volume 1, 209

Old Families of Salisbury and Amesbury, Massachusetts, The, 2, 269

Old Families of Staten Island, 423

Old Gravestones of Columbia County, NY, 396

Old Homes in Stonington, with Additional Chapters & Graveyard Inscriptions, 78

Old Houses of the Ancient Town of Norwich, 1660-1800, 78

Old Indian Chronicle, The, 257

Old Kent: The Eastern Shore of Maryland, 232

Old Kittery and Her Families, 229

Old Land Records of Colbert County, Alabama, 22

Old Land Records of Franklin County, Alabama, 23

Old Land Records of Jackson County, Alabama, 23

Old Land Records of Lauderdale County, Alabama, 23

Old Land Records of Lawrence County, Alabama, 24

Old Land Records of Limestone County, Alabama, 24

Old Land Records of Madison County, Alabama, 24

Old Land Records of Marshall County, Alabama, 25

Old Land Records of Morgan County, Alabama, 25

Old Marblehead Sea Captains & the Ships in Which They Sailed, 270

Old Miscellaneous Records [of the Supervisors and Assessors, through 1742], (Dutchess Co.), 403

Old Mobile: Fort Louis de la Louisiane, 1702-1711, 25

Old Monmouth of Ours, This, 371

Old Newmarket: Historical Sketches, 357

Old Planters of Beverly in Massachusetts, 269

Old River Town, An, 226

Old Settlers' Stories, Volume 2, 125

Old Settlers' Tales, Pottawatomie & Nemaha Counties, 180

Old Somerset on the Eastern Shore of Maryland, 252, 237

Old Southern Bible Records, 14

Old Times in Old Monmouth, 371

Old Times Not Forgotten: A History of Drew County Arkansas Land Patents: Conway, Faulkner, and Perry Counties (granted through 30 June 1908), 40

Old Tombstones & Unusual Cemeteries in Columbia County, NY, 394

Olde Ulster Volume I, 1905, 432

Olney: Echoes of the Past, 250

One Hundred and Sixty Allied Families, 1

"One Hundred Years": History of Morris, 1859-1959, 73

One Room Schools of the Town of Chenango, 390

Only More So: The History of East Hartford 1783-1976, 71

Orange Co. Index to Testators to 1880, 157

Orange Co. Marriages 1816-1850, 157

Orderly Book of the "Maryland Loyalists Regiment," June 18, 1778, to October 12, 1778, 233

Orderly Book of the Three Battalions of Loyalists, 381

Oregon Trail Sources, Queries & Reviews Volume 1, 18

Oregon Trail Sources, Queries & Reviews Volume 2, 18

Oregon Trail Sources, Queries & Reviews Volume 3, 18

Oregon Trail Sources, Queries & Reviews Volume 4, 18

Original Land Entries Saline County Arkansas, 49

Origins of Williamstown, 263

Orrington, Maine Cemetery Inscriptions, 224

Orrington, Maine Vital Records Prior to 1892, 225

Other Days in Greenwich, or Tales & Reminiscences of an Old New England Town, 67

Other Generals in Gray, 211

Our County [Bristol County, MA] and Its People, 265

Our County and Its People: A Descriptive & Biographical Record of Saratoga Co., 424

Our County & Its People: A Memorial Record of St. Lawrence County, 429

Our County & Its People [Chemung County, NY], 393

Our County & Its People [Erie County, NY], 404

Our County & Its People [Oneida County, NY], 418

Our Heritage [Berne, Albany Co., NY], 389

Overland Stage to California, 63

Overland: The California Emigrant Trail of 1841-1870, 18

Owen Co. Index to Testators to 1880, 158

Owen Co. Marriages Vol. I 1819-1844, 158

Owen Co. Marriages Vol. II 1845-1853, 158

Owen Co. Misc. Tax Lists 1819-1829 and Declarations of Intent, 158

Owen Co. Misc. Vol. II, 158

Owen Co. Tax Lists 1843, 158

Owen Co. Will Abstracts 1819-1861, 158

Owosso Michigan A to Z, 304

Oxford History of the American West, The, 18

Palatine Families of New York, The, 380

Palatine Roots, 378

Palatines of Olde Ulster, 432

Papers of the Military Historical Society of Massachusetts, 255

Parceling Out Land in Baltimore, 1621-1796, 242

Paris, Maine: The Second Hundred Years 1893-1993, 224

Parish Registers St. Paul's Episcopal Church, Indianapolis, IN, Vol. 1 1870-1910, 154

Parish Registers St. Paul's Episcopal Church, Indianapolis, IN, Vol. 2 1911-1954, 154

Parke Co. Index to Testators to 1880, 158

Parke Co. Marriages 1833-1844, 158

Particular Assessment Lists for Baltimore and Carroll Counties, 1798, The, 241, 244

Passaic Valley in Three Centuries, Past & Present, The, 372

Passenger Arrivals at the Port of Baltimore, 1820-1834, 243

Passenger Ships Arriving in New York Harbor: Vol. 1, 1820-1850, 416

Passengers to America, 7

Passports Issued by Governors of Georgia, 1785 to 1809, 88

Passports Issued by Governors of Georgia, 1810 to 1829, 88

Passports of Southeastern Pioneers, 1770-1823, 15

Past & Present of Alameda County, 54

Past and Present of Boone County, 114

Past and Present of City of Rockford and Winnebago Co., 135

Past & Present of Dallas County, 169

Past & Present of Greene County [Illinois], 119

Past & Present of Greene County [Iowa], 170

Past & Present of Greene County [Missouri], 330

Past & Present of Jasper County, 171

Past & Present of La Salle County, The, 124

Past & Present of Marshall County, 172

Past & Present of O'Brien & Osceola Counties, 173

Past & Present of Rock Island County, 130

Past & Present of St. Paul, 313

Past & Present of the City of Decatur and Macon County, History & Biographical, 125

Past & Present of Warren County, 133

Past & Present of Winneshiek County, 176

Past & Present of Woodford County, The, 135

Patents and Deeds and Other Early Records of New Jersey 1664-1703, 361

Patriarch of the Valley, The—Isaac W. Sullivan, 59

Patriotic Roster of LaSalle County, 124

Patriotic Roster of Livingston County, 125

Peck, Marcus: Letters of a Civil War Soldier and His Family, 422

Peirce's Colonial Lists, 6, 259

Pen Pictures of St. Paul, 313

Pence Funeral Home, Conway, Arkansas, Volume I, 1881-1904, 40

Pence Funeral Home, Conway, Arkansas, Volume II, 40

Pence Funeral Home, Conway, Arkansas, Volume III, 1926-1945, 40

Pennsylvania and Middle Atlantic States Genealogical Manuscripts, 10, 362

Penobscot County, Maine Marriage Returns Prior to 1892, 224

Pensioners on the Rolls as of 1 January 1883 (Living in Minnesota) with Every Name Index, 309

Peopling Indiana: The Ethnic Experience, 139

Peopling of Tompkins County, The, 431

Perry Co. 1850 Census Transcription, 128

Perry County, A History, 158

Perry Co. Index to Testators to 1880, 158

Perry Co. Marriages, 1827-1850, 128

Personal Name Index to J. Thomas Scharf's History of Westchester County, 436

Personal Name Index to Orton's "Records of California Men in the War of the Rebellion, 1861 to 1867," A, 53

Personalities of Melvin Hill Cemetery, Phelps, Ontario County, New York, The, 419

Peterson Funeral Home, Waukegan IL Index to Burials (1865-1945), 124

Petitions for Name Changes in New York City, 1848-1899, 417

Petitions of the Early Inhabitants of Kentucky to the General Assembly of Virginia, 1769 to 1792, 190

Phillip's Elite Directory of Private Families, 1881-1882, 416

Pickwick Landing Reservoir Cemeteries, 22, 24, 319

Pictorial History of Arkansas from Earliest Times to 1890, A, 32

Pictorial History of World War II Veterans from Laurel County, Kentucky, A, 202

Picture Book of Earlier Buffalo, 403

Picturesque New London and Its Environs—Groton—Mystic—Montville—Waterford, 78

Piermont, New Hampshire, 1764-1947, 352

Pike Co. Index to Testators to 1880, 159

Pioneer Ancestors of Members of The Society of Indiana Pioneers, 136

Pioneer Families of Clark County, 142

Pioneer Families of Eastern and Southeastern Kentucky, 188

Pioneer Families of Lancaster County, 345

Pioneer Families of Northwestern New Jersey, 359

Pioneer Family: Life on Florida's Twentieth-Century Frontier, 85

Pioneer History of Becker County, A, 309

Pioneer History of Camden, Oneida County, 418

Pioneer History of Cortland County, 397

Pioneer History of Orleans County, 420

Pioneer History of Pocahontas County, 174

Pioneer History of the Champlain Valley, 392

Pioneer Kentuckians with Missouri Cousins, 187, 320

Pioneer Settlers of Osage Co., Gasconade Co., and Maries Co., Missouri, 320, 330, 334, 336

Pioneer Settlers of Utica, 418

Pioneer Times in the Onondaga Country, 419

Pioneers and Makers of Arkansas, 35

Pioneers of Maine and New Hampshire, 1623-1660, The, 216, 348

Pioneers of Massachusetts (1620-1650), 259

Pioneers of Polk County & Reminiscences of Early Days, 174

Pioneers of Superior Wisconsin, 314

Pioneers of the Bluestem Prairie, 177-183

Pioneers of Unadilla Village, 1784-1840, The, 421

Pioneers on Maine Rivers, 217

Place Names in Alabama, 20

Placenames of Maryland, The: Their Origin and Meaning, 233

Plano: Birthplace of the Harvester, 1854-1954, 121

Plantation Mistress, The: Woman's World in the Old South, 12

Planters of The Commonwealth in Massachusetts, 1620-1640, The, 1, 255

Plat Book of Ovid, Seneca County 1858, 427

Plat Book of Seneca County Town & Village Maps 1850, 428

Plat Book of Seneca Falls, Seneca County 1856, 427

Plat Book of Waterloo, Seneca County 1855, 428

Pleasant Valley: A History of Elizabethtown, Essex Co., 404

Plummer, Edward Clarence, History of Bath, The, 225

Plymouth Colony: Its History and People, 1620-1691, 260

Plymouth Colony Wills and Inventories, Vol 1, 1633-1669, 259

Plymouth County Marriages, 1692-1746, 291

Pope Co. Marriages 1816-1839, 129

Port Arrivals and Immigrants to the City of Boston, 1715-1716 and 1762-1769, 294

Porter Co. 1850 Census Transcription, 159

Porter Co. Index to Testators to 1880, 159

Porter Co. Marriages 1836-1849, 159

Portland & Vicinity, 218

Portrait & Biographical Album of Henry County, 120

Portrait & Biographical Album of Johnson & Pawnee Counties, 344, 345

Portrait & Biographical Album of Louisa County, 172

Portrait & Biographical Album of Mahaska County, 172

Portrait & Biographical Album of McLean County, 127

Portrait & Biographical Album of Newaygo County, 304

Portrait and Biographical Album of Peoria County, 128

Portrait & Biographical Album of Polk County, 174

Portrait & Biographical Album of Rock Island County, 130

Portrait and Biographical Album of Whiteside County, 134

Portrait & Biographical Record of Macoupin County, 126

Portrait & Biographical Records of Delaware & Randolph Counties, 145, 160

Portrait & Biographical Records of Jasper, Marshall & Grundy Counties, 170-171, 173

Portsmouth & Newcastle Cemetery Inscriptions, 357

Posey Co. Index to Testators to 1880, 159

Postal History of Seneca County 1802-1984, 428

Pottawatomie County Kansas 1900 Federal Census Abstract, 180

Pottawatomie County Kansas Marriages, 1856-1886, 180

Poughkeepsie, Dutchess County, NY Newspapers: Marriages, 1826-1851, 401

Prairie County Arkansas Cemetery Inscriptions, 47

Prairie County, Arkansas Pioneer Family Interviews, 47

Prairie Farmer's Directory of Champaign County, 115

Prairie Farmer's Directory of Ford County, 119

Prairie Farmer's Directory of Shelby County, 130

Prairie Farmer's Reliable Directory of Farmers and Breeders in Greene and Jersey Cos., 119-120

Prairie Pioneers, Volume 1, 112

Prairie Pioneers, Volume 2, 112

Prairie Pioneers—Index to 2,830 Ancestors, 112

Preliminary Inventory of the Land Entry Papers of the General Land Office, 52

Presbyterian Records of Baltimore City, Maryland, 1765-1840, 242

Price Funeral Home Records, Maryville, Nodaway County, Missouri 1960, 336

Prince George's County Land Records, Volume A, 1696-1702, 251

Prince George's County, Maryland, Land Records, 1739-1743, 252

Probate Court Records, Cook County, Illinois, Docket Book A, 1871-1872, 116

Probate Court Records, Yuba County, California, June 3, 1850-March 29, 1852, 62

Probate Records [New York State], 384

Probate Records of Essex County, 1635-1681, The, 268

Probate Records of Essex County, Massachusetts, The, 268

Probate Records of Lincoln County Maine 1760 to 1800, The, 223

Proceedings at the Celebration of the 250th Anniversary of the Settlement of Guilford, 1639-1889, 76

Profits in the Wilderness: Entrepreneurship and the Founding of New England Towns in the Seventeenth Century, 5

Proprietors Records, Newbury, Massachusetts 1720-1768, 273

Proprietors' Records of the Town of Waterbury, 1677-1761, 76

Proud Mahaska, 1843-1900, 172

Providence-1649: The History & Archeology of Anne Arundel County, Maryland's 1st European Settlement, 239

Provincetown, or Odds & Ends from the Tip End, 261

Provincial Councillors of Pennsylvania Who Held Office Between 1733 and 1776, The, 9

Public Record Repositories in Maine, 216

Publishments, Marriages, Births, Deaths of Gorham, Maine, 219

Pulaski Co. 1850 Census Transcription, 129

Pulaski Co. Index to Testators to 1880, 159

Putnam Co. 1850 Census Transcription, 129

Putnam Co. Index to Testators to 1880, 160

Putnam Co. Marriages Vol. I 1822-1837, 160

Putnam Co. Marriages Vol. II 1838-1847, 160

Quabbin: The Lost Valley, 292

Quaker Census of 1828, 378

Quaker Crosscurrents: Three Hundred Years of New York Yearly Meetings, 376

Quaker Records of Southern Maryland, 1658-1800, 235

Queen of the Mist, 418

Rambles About Portsmouth, 357

Rambles in Old Boston, 293

Randolph County, Arkansas, Marriages, 1821-1893, 48

Randolph County, Arkansas, Marriages, 1893-1923, 48

Randolph Co. [Illinois]1825 State Census, 129

Randolph Co. [Indiana] Index to Testators to 1880, 160

Randolph Co. [Indiana] Marriages 1819-1852, 160

Randolph [Maine] Vital Records to the Year 1892, 222

Reading Backwards On My Knott Heritage, 253

Recollections of the Early Settlement of Carroll County, 142

Reconstructed 1790 Census of Delaware, 80

Reconstructed 1790 Census of Georgia, The, 89

Record of Deaths in the First Church in Rowley, Massachusetts 1696-1777, 267

Record of Interments at the Friends Burial Ground, Baltimore, Maryland, A, 241

Record of Service of Connecticut Men in the Army and Navy of the United States, During the War of the Rebellion, 65

Record of Services of Officers and Enlisted Men, Kittery & Eliot, 229

Record of the Juvenile Inmates of the Home for the Friendless 1862-1868, Detroit, MI, 306

Records and Files of the Quarterly Courts of Essex County, 268

Records and Files of the Quarterly Courts of Essex County, Massachusetts; Vol. 9: September 25, 1683-April 20, 1686, 273

Records of Effingham County, Georgia, 101

Records of Hampstead, New Hampshire, 358

Records of Jasper County, Georgia, 1801-1922, 102

Records of Jasper County, Mississippi. WPA Source Materials, Will Abstracts 1855-1914, 318

Records of LaSalle Co., 124

Records of Lee Co., 124

Records of Louisiana Confederate Soldiers and Louisiana Confederate Commands, 209

Records of McHenry Co., 126

Records of Officers and Men of New Jersey in Wars 1791-1815, 361

Records of Old Otterbein Church, Baltimore, Maryland, 1785-1881, 242

Records of Oxford, 295

Records of Peoria Co., 128

Records of Randolph Co., 129

Records of Rev. Edward F. Cutter of Maine 1833-1856, 226

Records of Revolutionary War Veterans Who Lived in Madison County, 412

Records of St. Paul's Cemetery 1855-1946, Located at Druid Hill Park, 243

Records of St. Paul's Parish, Vol. 1, 240, 242

Records of the Church of Christ in Buxton, Maine 1763-1817, 228

Records of the First Church in Salem, Massachusetts, 1629-1736, 272

Records of the First Church of Wareham, Massachusetts, 1739-1891, 291

Records of the First Reformed Church of Baltimore, 1768-1899, 242

Records of the Holy Trinity (Old Swedes) Church from 1697 to 1773, 81

Records of the Holy Trinity (Old Swedes) Church from 1697 to 1773—Index & Errata, 81

Records of the Massachusetts Volunteer Militia, 259

Records of the Reformed Dutch Church of New Paltz, New York, 433

Records of the Town of Braintree, 1640-1793, 285

Records of the Town of Cambridge, 1630-1703, 284

Records of the Town of Plymouth [1636-1705, 1705-1743, 1743-1783], 2, 288

Records of Tompkins County, New York: Wills, Intestates, Bible, Church and Family Records, 431

Records of Warren Co., 133

Records of Washington County, Georgia, 106

Red Diamond Regiment: The 17th Maine Infantry, 1862-1865, 215

Red Hook, Dutchess County, NY Newspapers, Deaths, 1859-1918, 400

Red Hook, Dutchess County, NY Newspapers, Deaths, 1919-1936, 400

Red Hook, Dutchess County, NY Newspapers, Marriages, 1859-1936, 400

Refugees of 1776 from Long Island to Connecticut, The, 382

Register . . . Early Settlers of Kings County, New York from . . . First Settlement, 410

Register . . . of the Early Settlers of Kings County, Long Island, N.Y., 410

Register of Deaths in Savannah, GA, 98

Register of Maryland's Heraldic Families 1634-1935, 235

Register of New Netherland, 1626-1674, The, 384

Register of Vietnam War Casualties from Kentucky, 188

Registers of the Births, Marriages, and Deaths of the "Eglise Francoise a la Nouvelle York" [French Church of New York], from 1688 to 1804, 417

Registration of Axis Aliens in Kansas January 1918 thru June 1918, 177

Religion in the Old South, 14

Remarks of My Life Pr Me Hezekiah Prince 1786-1792, 222

Remember the Raisin!, 184

Remembering IL Veterans, 112

Remembering Three Churches, 422

Reminiscences of Bureau County, 114

Reminiscences of Quincy, 114

Reminiscences of Syracuse [Onondaga County, NY], 419

Reminiscences of the Revolution, 385

Reminiscent History of the Ozark Region of Arkansas and Missouri, A, 31, 320

Rent Rolls of Somerset County, 1663-1723, 252

Reports of City Physicians 1860-1869: Detroit, Wayne County, Michigan, 306

Reprint of Official Register of Land Lottery of Georgia 1827, 91

Research in Georgia: With a Special Emphasis Upon the Georgia Department of Archives and History, 89

Research in Indiana, 136

Research in Indiana Courthouses: Judicial and Other Records, 138

Research in Minnesota, 309

Research in the District of Columbia, 82

Research Outline: Alabama, 19

Research Outline: Alaska, 26

Research Outline: Arizona, 27

Research Outline: Arkansas, 31

Research Outline: California, 51

Research Outline: Colorado, 62

Research Outline: Connecticut, 64

Research Outline: Delaware, 80

Research Outline: District of Columbia, 83

Research Outline: Florida, 84
Research Outline: Georgia, 90
Research Outline: Hawaii, 108
Research Outline: Idaho, 109
Research Outline: Illinois, 110
Research Outline: Indiana, 136
Research Outline: Iowa, 167
Research Outline: Kansas, 176
Research Outline: Kentucky, 184
Research Outline: Louisiana, 210
Research Outline: Maine, 214
Research Outline: Maryland, 232
Research Outline: Massachusetts, 257
Research Outline: Michigan, 300
Research Outline: Minnesota, 307
Research Outline: Mississippi, 316
Research Outline: Missouri, 320
Research Outline: Montana, 341
Research Outline: Nebraska, 342
Research Outline: Nevada, 346
Research Outline: New Hampshire, 347
Research Outline: New Jersey, 360
Research Outline: New Mexico, 374
Research Outline: New York, 378
Researcher's Library of Georgia History, Genealogy, and Records Sources, A, Vol. I, 89
Researcher's Library of Georgia History, Genealogy, and Records Sources, A, Vol. II, 89
Residents of the Mississippi Territory, 21, 317
Resident's Recollections, A, 381
Resources at the Library of the Solano County Genealogical Society, Inc.—December 1992, 58
Revised History of Dorchester County, 246
Revolutionary Census of New Jersey: An Index Based on Rateables, of the Inhabitants of New Jersey During the Period of the American Revolution, 363
Revolutionary Patriots of Anne Arundel County, 239
Revolutionary Patriots of Calvert and St. Mary's Counties, Maryland, 1775-1783, 243, 253
Revolutionary Patriots of Cecil County, 244
Revolutionary Patriots of Delaware, 1775-1783, 80
Revolutionary Patriots of Frederick County, MD, 1775-1783, 247

Revolutionary Patriots of Kent & Queen Anne's Counties, 250, 252
Revolutionary Patriots of Montgomery County, Maryland, 1776-1783, 250
Revolutionary Records of Maryland, 230
Revolutionary Soldiers Buried in Illinois, 113
Revolutionary Soldiers Buried in Indiana [Bound with:] Supplement, 139
Revolutionary Soldiers in Alabama, 20
Revolutionary Soldiers in Kentucky: Also a Roster of the Virginia Navy, 190
Revolutionary Soldiers Resident or Dying in Onondaga Co., 419
Revolutionary War Damages, 364, 365, 366, 369, 370, 371, 373
Rhinebeck, NY, 18th and 19th Century Death Records, 401
Rhinebeck, NY Newspapers, Vol. 1, Deaths, 1846-1899, 401
Rhinebeck, NY Newspapers, Vol. 2, Marriages, 1846-1899, 402
Richard and Rhoda, Letters from the Civil War, 385
Ridgefield in Review, 67
Riley County Kansas 1915 State Census Abstract, 182
Riley County Kansas Marriage License Index 1887-1897, 182
Riley County Kansas Marriage License Index 1898-1906, 182
Riley County Kansas Marriage License Index 1906-1914, 182
Riley County Kansas Marriage License Index 1914-1918, 182
Ripley Co. [Indiana] Index to Testators to 1880, 160
Ripley County (MO) Records: Cemeteries, Part I, 337
Ripley County (MO) Records: Cemeteries, Part II, 337
Ripley County (MO) Records: Cemeteries, Part III, 337
Ripley County (MO) Records: Macedonia Cemetery, 337
Ripley County (MO) Records: Marriages, 1860-1881, and Mortality Schedules, 1850-1880, 337
Ripley County (MO) Records: Marriages, 1881-1887, 338
Ripley County (MO) Records: Naylor (Masonic) Cemetery, 338

Ripley County (MO) Records: Obituaries, 1874-1910, 338
Ripley County (MO) Records: Personal Tax Lists, 1873 and 1877, 338
Ripley County (MO) Records: Stephens-Richmond Cemetery, 338
River Towns of Connecticut, The: A Study of Wethersfield, Hartford & Windsor, 69
Rockland County, NY 1850 Federal Census, 424
Rogerenes, The: Some Hitherto Unpublished Annals Belonging to the Colonial History of Connecticut, 64
Roll of New Hampshire Soldiers at the Battle of Bennington, August 16, 1777, 347
Rolls of Connecticut Men in the French and Indian War, 1755-1762, 64
Romulus Remembered, 428
Theodore [Roosevelt] and Alice: A Love Story, 412
Theodore Roosevelt, Many-Sided American, 412
Rose, Frederick, Family of Wayne and Hardin Cos., Tennessee, North Carolina, and Virginia, 52
Rose Hill Cemetery in Volinia Township, Cass County, Michigan, 302
Rose, Robert, of Wethersfield and Branford, Connecticut Who Came on the Ship Francis in 1634, 52, 71, 76
Rose War Files: Land Bounty Records, 52
Roster of Civil War Soldiers from Washington County, Maryland, 254
Roster of Revolutionary Soldiers in Georgia, 93
Roster of Soldiers and Patriots of the American Revolution Buried in Indiana, 138
Roster of the People of Revolutionary Monmouth County [New Jersey], 370
Roustabout's History of Mahaska County, 172
Rowley, Records of the First Church, 272
Rowley Town Records, 1639-1672, 272
Rugged and Sublime: The Civil War in Arkansas, 30
Rural Cemeteries, Clay County Kansas, 178

Rural Landowners of Barbour County, Alabama, 21
Rush Co. Index to Testators to 1880, 160
Rush Co. Marriages 1822-1849, 160
Rye. Chronicle of a Border Town, 435
Rye on the Rocks, 358

Saco Valley Settlements & Families, 225
Saga on the Ridge, 420
Salem County, New Jersey Census 1860, 372
Salem County [New Jersey] Marriage Records, 372
Salem County [New Jersey] Wills, 372
Salem in the Eighteenth Century, 272
Salem Inscriptions from the Charter Street Cemetery, 268
Saline Co. Marriages 1847-1880, 130
Salisbury, Connecticut, Records: Vital, Gravestones, Deeds, Taxpayers, 73
Salzburgers and Allied Families, Georgia, 90
Salzburgers and Their Descendants, Being the History of a Colony of German, Lutheran, Protestants Who Emigrated to Georgia in 1734, 94
San Francisco: A History of the Pacific Coast Metropolis, 57
San Francisco Passenger Departure Lists—Vols. I-IV, 51, 57
San Francisco Probate Index 1880-1906: A Partial Reconstruction, 57
Sanborn, Minnesota 1881-1981 Centennial History, Including the Townships of Charlestown and Germantown, 309, 313
Saratoga County 1850 Federal Census: Town of Ballston Transcript, 424
Saratoga County 1850 Federal Census, Town of Saratoga Transcript, 424
Saybrook at the Mouth of the Connecticut River: The First One Hundred Years, 74
Scandinavian Immigrants in New York, 1630-1674, 378
Schoharie County, NY Family Cemetery Inscriptions, Town of Wright, 426
Schubdrein-Schibendrein Family in Germany, 1668-1751, The, 100
Scots on the Chesapeake, 1607-1830, 9
Scott Co. [Indiana] Index to Testators to 1880, 160

Scott Co. [Kentucky] Marriages 1793-1850, 207

Scott County, Kentucky Taxpayers, 1794 thru 1799, 207

Scott Co. [Kentucky] Wills & Estates 1795-1822, 207

Scrapbook History of Decatur, Michigan 1829-1976, 300

Seafaring in Colonial Massachusetts, 255

Search for Georgia's Colonial Records, The, 91

"Second Census" of Kentucky 1800, 184

Second Looks: A Pictorial History of Buffalo and Erie County, 403

Second or 1807 Land Lottery of Georgia, The, 92

Second Supplement to Torrey's New England Marriages Prior to 1700, 6

Selected Union Burials—Missouri Units, 321

Seneca County Farm Register with Map 1938, 428

Service Men from North Reading in the Revolution, 284

Sesquicentennial History of the Town of Greene, Androscoggin Co., 1775 to 1900, 217

Settlers and Residents, Town of Germantown, Columbia County, NY, Volume 1, Part 1: 1710-1899, 396

Settlers and Residents, Town of Germantown, Columbia County, NY, Volume 1, Part 2: 1790-1875, 396

Settlers and Residents, Town of Clermont, Columbia County, NY, Volume 2, Part 1: 1756-1899, 396

Settlers and Residents, Town of Clermont, Columbia County, NY, Volume 2, Part 2, State-Federal Census, 396

Settlers and Residents, Town of Livingston, Columbia County, NY, Volume 3, Part 1: 1710-1899, 397

Settlers and Residents, Town of Livingston, Columbia County, NY, Volume 3, Part 2, State-Federal Census: 1790-1875, 397

Settlers and Residents, Town of Livingston, Columbia County, NY, Volume 3, Part 3, Road Lists of Landowners: 1803-1850, 397

Settlers' Children: Growing up on the Great Plains, 17

Settlers of Maryland, 1679-1700, 230

Settlers of Maryland, 1701-1730, 231

Settlers of Maryland, 1731-1750, 231

Settlers of Maryland, 1751-1765, 231

Settlers of Maryland, 1766-1783, 231

Settlers of the Beekman Patent, The: Volume I, Historical Records, 399

Settlers of the Beekman Patent, The: Volume II, Families Abbot - Burtch, 400

Settlers of the Beekman Patent, The: Volume III, Families Burtis - Dakin, 400

Settling the West, 17

Seventeenth-Century New England, 3

Seventh Arkansas Confederate Infantry, The, 30

Seymour, Past & Present, 75

Shane Manuscript Collection, The: A Genealogical Guide to the Kentucky and Ohio Papers, 186

Sharon [District], Connecticut, Probate Records, 1757-1783, 73

Shawneetown Land District Records 1814-1820, 119

Shelby Co. Index to Testators to 1880, 161

Shelby Co. Marriages 1822-1849, 161

Shelby Co. Wills & Estates 1792-1817, 207

Shelby Co. Wills & Estates 1817-1824, 207

Ship Passenger Lists: New York and New Jersey (1600-1825), 360

Ship Passenger Lists: Pennsylvania and Delaware (1641-1825), 80

Shipping Days of Old Boothbay, The, 223

Shirley Uplands & Intervales, 278

Side-lights on Maryland History, 235

Simpson Co., KY Census for 1820, 207

Sittler Index of Surnames from the Nebraska State Journal, 342

Six Nations of New York, Mohawks, Oneidas, Onondagas, Senecas, Tuscaroras, The: The 1892 United States Extra Census Bulletin, 388

Sketch of the History of Attleboro, 264-265

Sketch of the History of Newbury, Newburyport & West Newbury, from 1635-1845, A, 267

Sketches & Chronicles of the Town of Litchfield, 73

Sketches & Records of South Britain, 76

Sketches of Brooks History, 226

Sketches of Catskill, NY, 406

Sketches of Hudson, 397

Sketches of Maryland Eastern Shoremen, 236

Sketches of Some of the First Settlers of Upper Georgia, of the Cherokees, and the Author, 90

Sketches of Southington: Ecclesiastical & Others, 71

Sketches of the History of the Town of Camden, 222

Sketches of the Old Inhabitants & Other Citizens of Old Springfield of the Present Century, 275

Sketches of the 35 Supervisors of Poestenkill, NY 1848 to 1990, 422

Skowhegan on the Kennebec, 225

Skulking Way of War, The: Technology and Tactics Among the New England Indians, 5

Slave Testimony: Two Centuries of Letters, Speeches, Interviews, and Autobiographies, 211

Slavery Days in Old Kentucky, 187

Smoldering City: Chicagoans and the Great Fire, 1871-1874, 116

Solano County, California—1852 State Census Index, 58

Solano County, California—1993 Pioneer File Index, 58

Solano County Cemeteries Volume I—Rockville Cemetery, 58

Solano County Cemeteries Volume II—Vacaville, Elmira & Surrounding Areas, 58

Solano County Cemeteries Volume III—Benicia City Cemetery Burials, 58

Solano County, California Will Book I, 1856-1876, 58

Soldiers in King Philip's War, 255

Soldiers of Oakham, 300

Soldiers, Sailors, & Patriots of the Revolutionary War—Maine, 214

Solon Township: Out of the Wilderness, 303

Some Annals of Nahant, 273

Some Cemeteries of Brown County, 177

Some Cemeteries of Jasper Co., 120

Some Cemetery Records from North and South Egremont, Berkshire County, Massachusetts, 262

Some Early Records & Documents of and Relating to Windsor, 1639-1703, 72

Some Early Tax Digests of Georgia, 88

Some Georgia County Records, Vol. 1, 92

Some Georgia County Records, Vol. 2, 92

Some Georgia County Records, Vol. 3, 92

Some Georgia County Records, Vol. 4, 93

Some Georgia County Records, Vol. 5, 93

Some Georgia County Records, Vol. 6, 93

Some Georgia County Records, Vol. 7, 93

Some Sullivan Co. Early Marriages 1815 to 1857, 162

Some Things about Coventry-Benton, 352

Somerset County Historical Quarterly, 373

Somerset County, Maryland Orphans Court Proceedings, 1777-1792 and 1811-1823, 252

Somerset Sampler, A: Families of Old Somerset County, Maryland, 1700-1776, 252

Sonoma County Coroner's Inquests 1852-1896, 59

Sonoma County Death Records 1873-1905, 59

Sonoma County Delayed Birth Certificates 1855-1971, 60

Sonoma County Marriages 1847-1902, 60

Source Records from Pike County, Mississippi, 1798-1910, 319

Sources of Genealogical Help in California Libraries, 53

Sources of Genealogical Help in Connecticut, 65

Sources of Genealogical Help in Idaho, 109

Sources of Genealogical Help in Indiana, 139

Sources of Genealogical Help in Kansas, 177

Sources of Genealogical Help in Maine, 217

Sources of Genealogical Help in Maryland, 236

Sources of Genealogical Help in Massachusetts, 260

Sources of Genealogical Help in Missouri, 321

Sources of Genealogical Help in Montana, 341

Sources of Genealogical Help in Nebraska, 342

Sources of Genealogical Help in New England, 6

Sources of Genealogical Help in New Hampshire, 348

Sources of Genealogical Help in New Jersey, N.J., 362

Sources of Genealogical Help in New Mexico, 374

Sources of Genealogical Help in New York, 387

South Jersey Church Records, Baptisms, Marriages, Deaths 1750-1900, Vol. 1, 367

South Jersey Church Records, Baptisms, Marriages, Deaths 1750-1900, Vol. 2, 367

Southeastern Arkansas Death Record Index, 1914-1923: Arkansas, Ashley, Bradley, Chicot, Cleveland, Desha, Drew, Jefferson, and Lincoln Counties, 30

Southeastern Arkansas Death Record Index, 1934-1940: Arkansas, Ashley, Bradley, Chicot, Cleveland, Desha, Drew, Jefferson, and Lincoln Counties, 30

Southeastern Michigan Pioneer Families, 301, 303, 381

Southern Bivouac, The, 12

Southern Campaigns of the American Revolution, 14

Southern Christian Advocate Death and Obituary Notices, 1867-1878, 13

Southern Columbia County, New York Families, 396

Southern Congregational Churches, 16

Southern Historical Society Papers, The, 11

Southold Connections, 411

Southwestern Arkansas Death Record Index, 1914-1923: Calhoun, Clark, Columbia, Dallas, Hempstead, Howard, Lafayette, Little River, Miller, Nevada, Ouachita, Pike, Sevier, and Union Counties, 30

Southwestern Arkansas Death Record Index, 1934-1940: Calhoun, Clark, Columbia, Dallas, Hempstead, Howard, Lafayette, Little River, Miller, Nevada, Ouachita, Pike, Sevier, and Union Counties, 30

Spanish and British Land Grants in Mississippi Territory, 1750-1784, 16

Spanish Borderlands, The: A Chronicle of Old Florida and the Southwest, 51, 84, 209, 374

Speculators and Slaves: Masters, Traders, and Slaves in the Old South, 15

Spencer Co. [Indiana] Cemetery Inscriptions, 161

Spencer Co. [Indiana] Index to Testators to 1880, 161

Spencer Co. [Indiana] Marriages 1818-1855, 161

Spencer Co. [Indiana] Marriages 1855-1863, 161

Spencer Co. [Indiana] Wills 1818-1839, 161

Spencer County, Kentucky Cemeteries Then and Now Volume 2, 207

Springfield, 1636-1886, 276

St. Anne Catholic Church Marriage Records, 121

St. Bernard Church Records, Alpena, Michigan, 1864-1925: Baptisms 1864-1894, Marriages 1870-1894, Funerals 1870-1925, 301

St. Catherines Cemetery Transcription, Scott County, Minnesota (Spring Lake Twp.), 313

St. Clair County, Alabama Genealogical Notes, 26

St. Clair County, Alabama Genealogical Notes No. 2, 26

St. George's Parish Records, 1689-1793, 242

St. John the Baptist Cemetery, Burnsville, Dakota Co., MN, 310

St. John's & St. George's Parish Registers, 1696-1851, 242

St. Joseph Co. Index to Testators to 1880, 161

St. Joseph County, Indiana Cemetery Inscriptions Volume 1: Greene, Liberty, Lincoln Townships, 161

St. Joseph County, Indiana Cemetery Inscriptions Volume 2: Penn Township, Part 1 (Mishawaka City, St. Joseph, St. Francis, Laing, Smith, First Mishawaka Cemeteries), 162

St. Joseph County, Indiana Cemetery Inscriptions Volume 3: Penn Township, Part 2, Fairview (Partial), Pleasant Valley, Hebrew Orthodox, Eutzier-Hollingshead, Byrkit, Ferrisville Cemeteries, 162

St. Louis, Missouri 1870 Census Index, 339

St. Mary's County, Maryland, Administrative Accounts, 1674-1720, 253

St. Mary's County, Maryland, Rent Rolls, 1639-1771, 253

St. Patricks Cemetery, Cedar Lake Twp., Scott Co. MN, 313

St. Paul United Church of Christ Records, 1839-1939, 131

St. Peters Cemetery Transcription, Credit River Twp., Scott County, Minnesota, 314

St. Thomas Parish Baptisms, Owings Mills, Maryland, 1732-1995, 243

St. Thomas Parish Deaths and Burials, Owings Mills, Maryland, 1728-1995, 243

St. Thomas Parish Marriage Records, Owings Mills, Maryland, 1738-1995, 243

St. Thomas' Parish Register, 1732-1850, 242

Standard History of Adams & Wells Counties, 140, 166

Standard History of Champaign County, A, 115

Standard History of Starke County, Indiana 1915, A, 162

Stark County & Its Pioneers, 131

Stark Co. Marriages 1839-1866, 131

Starke Co. Index to Testators to 1880, 162

Stephens County, Georgia and Its People, Vol. 1, 104

Steuben Co. Index to Testators to 1880, 162

Stockbridge, 1739-1939: A Chronicle, 263

Stockbridge, Past & Present, 262

Stockholm Cemeteries, Wright County Minnesota, 315

Stoddard Co., MO 1883-1887 Birth Records, 339

Stoddard Co., MO 1883-1887 Death Records, 339

Stone Records of Groton, The, 77

Stones and Bones: Cemetery Records of Prince George's County, Maryland, 252

Stones from the Walls of Jericho, 398

Stonington Chronology, 1649-1949, Being a Year-By-Year Record of the American Way of Life in a Connecticut Town, 77

Stonington Houses: A Panorama of New England Architecture, 1750-1900, 78

Stories of Brooksville, 220

Stories of Early 20th Century Life, 284

Story of an Old Farm, The, 361

Story of Ascension Parish, The, 212

Story of Berwick, The, 227

Story of Byfield, The, 268

Story of Cedar Rapids, The, 172

Story of Duxbury, 1637-1937, The, 289

Story of Georgia and the Georgia People, 1732 to 1860, The, 94

Story of Old Fort Plain & the Middle Mohawk Valley, The, 413

Story of Townsendville, NY, A, 428

Story of Walpole, 1724-1924, The, 286

Story of Ypsilanti, The, 305

Subject Guide to Records in the Massachusetts Archives, 260

Subject Index to the Colorado Genealogist, Vols. 1-42 (1939-1981), Parts I and II, 62

Sullivan Co. Index to Testators to 1880, 162

Sullivan Co. Will Abstracts 1844-1864, 162

Sunset Cemetery, Manhattan, Kansas Including Inscriptions and Sexton's Records, 182

Surname Directory of Sonoma County Genealogical Society 1991-1992, 60

Surname Index to the Colorado Genealogist, Vols. 1-10 (1939-1949), Parts I and II, 62

Surname Index to the Colorado Genealogist, Vols. 11-20 (1950-1959), Parts I and II, 62

Surname Index to the Colorado Genealogist, Vols. 21-41 (1960-1980), 62

Swedish Settlements on the Delaware, 1638-1664, The, 9

Sweet Chariot: Slave Family and Household Structure in Nineteenth Century Louisiana, 212

Swiss Settlement of Switzerland County, 162

Switzerland Co. Index to Testators to 1880, 163

Switzerland Co. Marriages 1814-1849, 163

Tales of the Amarugia Highlands of Cass County, Missouri, 326

Taliaferro County, Georgia, Records and Notes, 105

Taverns & Turnpikes of Blandford, 1733-1833, The, 277

Terrell County, Georgia, Newspaper Clippings, Volume I, 1866-1872, 105

Texas Bend Journal, Mississippi Co. MO, 335

Third or 1820 Land Lotteries of Georgia, The, 92

Thirty-eighth Arkansas Confederate Infantry, The, 27

Thomas County, Georgia, Newspaper Clippings, Vol. I, 1857-1875, 105

Thomas County, Georgia, Newspaper Clippings, Vol. II, 1876-1881, 105

Thomas County, Georgia, Newspaper Clippings, Vol. III, 1882-1888, 105

Thomaston, Maine Vital Records from the Thomaston Recorder 1837-1846, 222

Thousands of Idaho Surnames, 109

Tidewater Families of the New World and Their Westward Migrations, 12

Tippecanoe Co. Index to Testators to 1880, 163

Tipton Co. Index to Testators to 1880, 163

Tobacco and Slaves: The Development of Southern Cultures in the Chesapeake, 1680-1800, 233

Tobacco Coast: A Maritime History of Chesapeake Bay in the Colonial Era, 234

Tombstone Inscriptions from a Few Cemeteries in Howard County Maryland, 249

Tombstone Inscriptions of Cecil County, Maryland, 245

Tombstone Inscriptions of Govans Presbyterian Church Cemetery, 240

Tombstone Inscriptions of Hopewell United Methodist Church Cemetery, Cecil County, Maryland, 245

Tombstone Inscriptions of West Nottingham Cemetery, Cecil County, Maryland, 245

Tombstone Records of Eighteen Cemeteries in Pound Ridge, New York, 437

Topographical Dictionary of 2885 English Emigrants to New England, 1620-1650, 1

Town History of Weare, from 1888, 353

Town Minutes, Town of Carmel, Putnam County, New York, 1795-1839, 421

Town of Genesee Sesquicentennial 1830-1980, 390

Town of Roxbury, The, 292

Town of Weston, 284

Township Maps of Brown County, Kansas 1887, 177

Tracing Your Mississippi Ancestors, 316

Traditions & Records of Brooksville, 220

Traditions & Records of Southwest Harbor & Somesville, Mt. Desert Island, 220

Traditions and Transitions: Every Person is a Book, 358

Transcript of the 1800, 1810, and 1820 Federal Census of Schoharie County, New York, 426

Transcript of the 1830 and 1840 Federal Census of Schoharie County, New York, 426

Trigg County 1880 Families, 208

Trigg County, Kentucky Deeds, Volume One (1820-1824), 208

Trigg County, Kentucky Newspaper Abstracts, Volume Twenty-eight, 208

Troy, Maine Vital Records Prior to 1892, 226

Troy's One Hundred Years, 1789-1889, 423

Truro, Cape Cod: Landmarks & Seamarks, 261

Truth About the Pilgrims, The, 6

Tumult and Silence at Second Creek: An Inquiry into a Civil War Slave Conspiracy, 211

Turnbo's Tales of the Ozarks: Bear Stories, 46

Turnbo's Tales of the Ozarks: Biographical Stories, 46

Turnbo's Tales of the Ozarks: Deer Hunting Stories, 46

Turnbo's Tales of the Ozarks: Incidents, Mean Tricks and Fictitious Stories, 46

534					*Title Index*

Turnbo's Tales of the Ozarks: Panther Stories, 46
Turnbo's Tales of the Ozarks: Schools, Indians, Hard Times and More Stories, 46
Turnbo's Tales of the Ozarks: Snakes, Birds and Insect Stories, 46
Turnbo's Tales of the Ozarks: War and Guerrilla Stories, 46
Turnbo's Tales of the Ozarks: Wolf Stories, 47
Twenty-seventh Arkansas Confederate Infantry, The, 27
Two Centuries of New Milford, 72

UCLA Library: Sources of Genealogical Help, 53
Ulster County Cemeteries, Ulster County, New York, 433
Ulster County, New York Probate Records, 432
Ulster County, NY Probate Records from 1665, 432
Union Burials—Missouri Units, 321
Union Co. Index to Testators to 1880, 163
Union Co. Marriages 1818-1880, 132
Unruly Women: The Politics of Social and Sexual Control in the Old South, 12
Upham Cemetery 1858-June 1993, Butte County, California, 54
Upstate New York in the 1760s, 388
Useful Guide to Researching San Francisco Ancestry, A, 57

Valley of the Upper Maumee River, with Historical Account of Allen County and the City of Ft. Wayne, 140
Vanderburgh Co. Index to Testators to 1880, 163
Vanocaten: A Farley-Reid Genealogy, 12
Vermilion Co. Pioneers, 132
Vermillion Co. Index to Testators to 1880, 164
Vermillion Co. Land & Marriage Records 1838-1844, 164
Vermillion Co. Marriages 1844-1861, 164
Veterans Discharge Extractions: Greene County, 41

Veterans Who Applied for Land in Southern California 1851-1911, 51
Victorian Gentlewoman in the Far West, A: The Reminiscences of Mary Hallock Foote, 18
Vidette Cavalry, 20
Vigo Co. Index to Testators to 1880, 164
Vigo Co. Will Abstracts 1818-1860, 164
Vital Records 1790-1829 from Dover, New Hampshire's First Newspaper, 349
Vital Records [New York State], 384
Vital Records of Acquackanonk Reformed Church, Passaic, NJ, 372
Vital Records of Amsterdam Reformed Church at Manny's Corners: 1799-1828, 414
Vital Records of Berwick, South Berwick and North Berwick Maine, 228
Vital Records of Christ Lutheran Church, Ghent, Columbia Co., NY: 1801-1901, 397
Vital Records of Cortlandtown Reformed Church, Montrose, NY: 1741-1894, 436
Vital Records of Emmanuel Evangelical Lutheran Church, Chatham Village, NY: 1874-1899, 397
Vital Records of Esopus Reformed Church, Ulster Park, NY: 1791-1899, 433
Vital Records of Evangelical Lutheran Church, Poestenkill, NY: 1833-1892, 422
Vital Records of Falmouth, Massachusetts, 261
Vital Records of Ghent, W. Ghent, Mt. Pleasant, & Stuyvesant Falls, NY, Reformed Church: 1775-1899, 397
Vital Records of Glen Reformed Chuch, Glen, NY: 1805-1882, 414
Vital Records of Greenbush Reformed Church, East Greenbush, Rensselaer County, NY: 1788-1899, 422
Vital Records of Hamilton, Massachusetts, to 1849, 269
Vital Records of Hamilton Union Presbyterian Chuch, Guilderland, Albany Co., NY: 1824-1899, 390
Vital Records of Hyde Park Reformed Church, Hyde Park, NY: 1810-1899, 403

Vital Records of Jerusalem Reformed Church, Feura Bush, Albany County, NY: 1792-1890, 390

Vital Records of Kent and Sussex Counties, Delaware, 1686-1800, 81, 82

Vital Records of Kingston, New Hampshire 1694-1994, The, 356

Vital Records of Kittery, Maine Prior to 1892, 227

Vital Records of Lawyersville Reformed Church Lawyersville, Schoharie Co., NY: 1790-1882, 426

Vital Records of Lincolnville, Maine Prior to 1892, 226

Vital Records of Londonderry, New Hampshire, 1719-1910, 356

Vital Records of Lynnfield, Massachusetts, to 1849, 273

Vital Records of Manchester, Massachusetts, to the End of the Year 1849, 273

Vital Records of Mapletown Reformed Church (Middletown) Canajoharie, NY: 1803-1901, 414

Vital Records of Middleburgh Reformed Chuch, Middleburg, NY: 1797-1899, 426

Vital Records of Mount Desert Island and Nearby Islands 1776-1820, 220

Vital Records of New Hackensack, Dutchess County, NY Reformed Church, 403

Vital Records of Niskayuna Reformed Church, Schenectady, NY: 1783-1861, 425

Vital Records of North Yarmouth, Maine, Second Edition, 218

Vital Records of Norwich, 1649-1848, Parts I & II, 78

Vital Records of Norwich 1659-1848, 78

Vital Records of Paramus, Bergen County, NJ, Reformed Church, 364

Vital Records of Plymouth, Massachusetts to the Year 1850, 291

Vital Records of Prattsville Reformed Church, Prattsville, NY: 1798-1899, 406

Vital Records of Princetown Reformed Church, Duanesburg, NY: 1824-1899, 425

Vital Records of Remarkable Records of Rev. Gideon Bostwick: 1770-92, St. James Episcopal Church, Great Barrington, MA, 5

Vital Records of Salem, 268

Vital Records of Sandwich, Massachusetts to 1885, 261

Vital Records of Saugus, Massachusetts, to 1849, 273

Vital Records of Scotia Reformed Church, Scotia, NY: 1818-1899, 425

Vital Records of Shokan Reformed Church, Shokan, Ulster County, NY: 1799-1899, 433

Vital Records of Sleepy Hollow Reformed Church, Tarrytown, NY: 1697-1791, 436

Vital Records of St. James Episcopal Church, Great Barrington, MA: 1827-1899, 264

Vital Records of St. John's Episcopal Church, Johnstown, NY: 1815-1899, 405

Vital Records of the Town of Barnstable and Sandwich, 262

Vital Records of the Town of Fairhaven, Massachusetts to 1850, 266

Vital Records of the Town of Middleborough, 291

Vital Records of the Towns of Eastham and Orleans [Massachusetts], 262

Vital Records of Townsend, Massachusetts, 280

Vital Records of Trinity Lutheran Church, West Sand Lake, NY: 1784-1899, 422

Vital Records of Up Red Hook, Tivoli, Mellenville, & Linlithgo NY Reformed Church: 1766-1899, 402

Vital Records of Wenham, Massachusetts, to the End of the Year 1849, 273

Vital Records of Westford to the End of the Year 1849, 285

Vital Records of Woestina (Rotterdam) & Glenville Reformed Churches: 1800-1899, 425

Vital Records of Wynantskill Reformed Church, Wynantskill, NY: 1794-1889, 422

Vital Records of Yarmouth, Massachusetts, 262

Vital Records of York Maine Prior to 1892, 227

Vital Statistics of Eastern Connecticut, Western Rhode Island, South Central Massachusetts, 5, 65, 258

Volunteer Soldiers in the Cherokee War—1836-1839, 21, 95

Waban: Early Days, 1781-1918, 284

Wabash Co. Index to Testators to 1880, 164

Wabash County, Indiana Marriages 1835-1899, 164

Wabaunsee Cemetery, Wabaunsee Kansas, 182

Walpole As It Was and As It Is, 350

Wampum, War and Trade Goods West of the Hudson, 379

War of 1812 Bounty Lands in Illinois, 113

War Service Records & Searches, 384

Ward's History of Coffee County, 99

Warren Cemetery Tombstone Inscriptions and Burial Records, Warren Township, Lake County, Illinois, 121

Warren Co. [Illinois] 1850 Census Transcription, 133

Warren Co. [Indiana] Index to Testators to 1880, 164

Warren Co. [Indiana] Will Abstracts 1830-1858, 165

Warren County, Kentucky, Deed Books, 1821-1825, 208

Warren Township Cemeteries, 124

Warrick Co. Index to Testators to 1880, 165

Warwick, Biography of a Town, 1763-1963, 275

Washington County, GA Land Warrants, 1784-1787, 106

Washington County, Georgia, Newspaper Clippings, Vol. I, 1852-1866, 106

Washington County, Georgia, Newspaper Clippings, Vol. II, 1867-1880, 106

Washington County, Georgia, Newspaper Clippings, Vol. III, 1881-1889, 106

Washington Co. [Illinois] 1850 Census Transcription, 133

Washington Co. [Indiana] Index to Testators to 1880, 165

Washington County, Kentucky Court Order Book 1792-1800, 208

Washington County, Kentucky Taxpayers, 1792-1799, 208

Washington County [Maryland] Cemetery Records, 254

Washington County [Maryland] Church Records of the 18th Century, 1768-1800, 254

Washington County, Maryland, Genealogical Research Guide, 254

Washington County [Maryland] Index of Scharf's History of Western Maryland, 254

Washington County [Minnesota] Miscellaneous Death Listings 1871-1930, 315

Wayne County, Illinois Cemetery Inscriptions, Volumes I-IV, VI-XI, 134

Wayne County, Illinois Cemetery Inscriptions, Volume V, 134

Wayne County, Illinois Newspaper Gleanings, 1855-75, 134

Wayne County, Illinois Newspaper Gleanings, 1876-1879, 134

Wayne Co. [Indiana] Index to Testators to 1880, 165

Wayne Co. [Indiana] Marriages 1811-1860, 166

Wayne County [New York] Farm Register with Map 1938, 435

We Were There, Clark Countians in World War II, 37

Weik's History of Putnam County, 160

Wells Co. Index to Testators to 1880, 166

West, The: An Illustrated History, 18

West Dunstable, Monson & Hollis, 354

West of Perigo: Poestenkill Memories, 422

Westchester County: A Pictorial History, 436

Westchester County: The Past 100 Years, 1883-1983, 437

Westchester Historian, The, 437

Western Arkansas Death Record Index, 1914-1923: Crawford, Franklin, Johnson, Logan, Montgomery, Polk, Pope, Scott, Sebastian, and Yell Counties, 30

Western Arkansas Death Record Index, 1934-1940: Crawford, Franklin, Johnson, Logan, Montgomery, Polk, Pope, Scott, Sebastian, and Yell Counties, 30

Western Maryland Genealogy—a Quarterly Journal, 236
Western New York Land Transactions, 1804-1824, 382
Western New York Land Transactions, 1825-1835, 382
Westerwald to America, 9
Westinghouse Threshing Machinery, &c., 425
Westport Cumberland Presbyterian Church Records Volume I 1865-1896, 332
Westport Cumberland Presbyterian Church Records Volume II 1897-1908, 332
Wheeler Reservoir Cemeteries, 24-25
"Where They Sleep," Cemetery Inscriptions of Pulaski County, Illinois Book V, 129
White Co. Index to Testators to 1880, 166
White Co. Marriages 1834-1849, 166
White River Journal—Des Arc, Arkansas, Abstracts of Death Notices, 48
Whites Among the Cherokees, 95
Whiteside Co. 1850 Census Transcription, 134
Whitley Co. Index to Testators to 1880, 167
Who Was Who in Bullitt Co. (in 1850), 196
Who's Your Hoosier Ancestor?, 138
Wilkes Co., GA Deed Books A-VV 1784-1806, 107
Wilkes County Papers, 1777-1833, The, 107
Willard Asylum (Seneca County) 1869-1886, The, 428
Williamstown & Williams College, 263
Williamstown: The First Two Hundred Years, 1753-1953, 262
Windham, 407
Windham in the Past, 218
Winslow Vital Records, to the Year 1892, 221
Winslows of Careswell in Marshfield, 289
Winthrop Fleet of 1630, The, 1
Witchcraft Delusion, The: The Story of the Witchcraft Persecutions in Seventeenth-Century New England, Including Original Trial Transcripts, 7

Within the Plantation Household: Black and White Women of the Old South, 12
Witnessing Slavery: The Development of Ante-Bellum Slave Narratives, 12
Woburn Marriages, from 1640 to 1873, 281
Woburn Records of Births, Deaths, and Marriages from 1640-1873, 281
Women Before the Bar: Gender, Law, & Society in Connecticut: 1639-1789, 64
Women's Voices from the Oregon Trail, 17
Women's West, The, 17
Wood, Jethro, Inventor of the Modern Plow, 391
Woodbridge and Vicinity: The Story of a New Jersey Township, 370
Woodford County, Kentucky Taxpayers, 1790 thru 1799, 209
Woodford Co. Wills & Estates 1789-1815, 209
Woodford Co. Wills & Estates 1815-1826, 209
Worcester County, Maryland Marriage Licenses, 1795-1865, 254
Worcester County Warnings 1737-1788, 299
Worth County, Missouri: Death Notices from Area Newspapers 1874-1893, 340
Worth County, Missouri: Death Notices from Area Newspapers 1894-1899, 340
Worth County, Missouri: Death Notices from Area Newspapers 1900-1903, 341
Worth County, Missouri: Death Notices from Area Newspapers 1904-1906, 341
Worth County, Missouri: Death Notices from Area Newspapers 1907-1910, 341
WPA Guide to 1930's New Jersey, The, 363
Wyandotte County, Kansas Cemetery Records Volume I, 183

Yankee Destinies: The Lives of Ordinary Nineteenth-Century Bostonians, 293
Yarmouth, Nova Scotia, Genealogies, 1

Yates City Community Centennial, 1957, 135

Ye Ancient Burial Place of New London, 78

Ye Historie of Ye Town of Greenwich, Co. of Fairfield and State of Conn., with Genealogcal Notes on [many] Families, 68

Yearbook of the Holland Society of New York, 379

Yonkers, Illustrated, 438

Yorba Linda Star, The: Death Notices & Obituaries, Volume I, 1920-1929, 52, 57

York Maine Then and Now: A Pictorial Documentation, 228

York Township Records, 117

Zion Evangelical Lutheran Church Cemetery and Burial Records 1837-1988 and Souls Register 1888, 117

Index to Advertisers

Arkansas Research, 28
Bergen Historic Books, 360
Clearfield Company, 2, 8
Edgar County Genealogical Society, 118
Gateway Press, Inc., 61
Genealogical Publishing Company, Inc., 215
General Society of Mayflower Descendants, 256
Greene Genes, 406
Heart of the Lakes Publishing, 380
IDL Research, 185
Illinois State Genealogical Society, 109
International Forum, 408
J E H Research, 82, 242
Jackson, Frances, 108
Kaufman, Dr. Frank L. & Odette, 53

Kinship, 386
Komives, Ralph, 83
Louisiana State University Press, 211
Masley, Betty, 185
McManus, Thelma S., 322
Morrison & Co., W. E., 377
Morrow, Patricia, 406
Nestler, Harold R., 383
New York Genealogical and Biographical Society, The, 375
Park Genealogical Books, 306
Rose Family Association, 52
Tate County, Mississippi, Genealogical & Historical Society, Inc., 318
UMI, 33
Villier, Caroline R., 167
West, William Sheperd, 10
Wise, William E., 198